'72   52519   6.00

CALIFORNIA

CALIFORNIA

A History of the Golden State

WARREN A. BECK
and
DAVID A. WILLIAMS

Garden City, New York
DOUBLEDAY & COMPANY, INC.

Grateful acknowledgment is made for use of "Hands," copyright 1929 and renewed
1957 by Robinson Jeffers. Reprinted from *Selected Poetry of Robinson Jeffers*,
by Robinson Jeffers, by permission of Random House, Inc.

We also acknowledge the following for granting use of the photographs herein:
The Henry E. Huntington Library, San Marino, California (2)
Metropolitan Water District (28)
Historical Collections, Security Pacific Bank, Los Angeles (9, 13, 22b & c, 23, 25a)
Wine Institute (1, 3, 6, 31)
Worden Collection, Wells Fargo Bank History Room, San Francisco (22a)
Title Insurance and Trust Company (8, 11, 18, 21)
Southern Pacific (4, 14, 15, 16, 20)
Southern California Edison Company (26, 27)
Los Angeles County Museum of Natural History (7)
Bancroft Library, University of California (10, 30)
San Francisco Convention and Visitors Bureau (25b)
Lockheed California Company (24)
Soil Conservation Service, U. S. Department of Agriculture (29)
Los Angeles Department of Water and Power (19)
California Historical Society (5)
San Francisco Public Utilities Commission (17)

Dedicated to:

PHYLLIS M. BECK

RUTH B. WILLIAMS

CONTENTS

ILLUSTRATIONS

MAPS

Introduction

This book, like so many others, is the result of the contributions of
a number of people. Scores of scholars have contributed to the un-
veiling of California's past and we owe them a considerable debt.
We deeply appreciate the contribution of Ynez Haase of Santa
Barbara, whose cartographical skills are manifested in the maps
herein. Our colleagues and friends, Professors Nicholas P. Hardeman,
Jackson K. Putnam, and Mrs. Anna Marie Hager, gave us the
benefit of a careful reading while the manuscript was in preparation.
Their suggestions, sometimes pointed, but always valuable and appreciated, enabled us to sidestep some of the pitfalls inherent in the
writing of a survey of the history of California. They are, of course,
absolved of any responsibility for errors of fact or interpretation
found in these pages. We have profited from the use of the magnificent resources of the Henry E. Huntington Library in San Marino
and enjoyed the co-operation and assistance of the staffs of the libraries of California State University, Fullerton, and California State
University, Long Beach. The staffs of such other places as the Bancroft Library in Berkeley, the California Historical Society in San
Francisco, the California State Library and State Archives in Sacramento have also been very helpful.

We also owe a debt to a number of individuals who helped. Miss
Diane Nassir of Santa Barbara did a considerable amount of work
on the bibliographies. Mrs. Sara Allen and Mrs. Evelyn Vogen of
Long Beach found time at awkward and difficult moments to assist
with the essential clerical tasks. Our professional colleagues, the late
John Hawgood of the University of Birmingham, England, William
Brandon of Monterey, Irving Ahlquist of Long Beach, Edwin Carpenter of the Huntington Library, John Barr Tomkins of the Bancroft Library, Wilbur and Beth Jacobs of the University of Califor-

nia, Santa Barbara, Manuel Servin of Arizona State University, helped in a variety of ways that are deeply appreciated.

Our students contributed as well. Through the years they have subjected our presentation of California history to their own kind of scrutiny. Their challenging skepticism has made it necessary for us to re-examine our interpretation of California history on a continuing basis. We hope this book will evidence our commitment to the separation of myth and reality in California's past; we hope as well that it may encourage them to demonstrate their concern for the present and future by an involvement with California's past.

Among the individuals who contributed in a very special way were the late Dr. Allan Nevins of the Huntington Library and the late Dr. Stuart L. Bernath of California State University, Long Beach. Their examples of productive scholarship in the midst of great personal adversity were inspiring.

WARREN A. BECK, *California State University, Fullerton*
DAVID A. WILLIAMS, *California State University, Long Beach*

April 1972

CALIFORNIA

CHAPTER I

The Stage

The Judaic-Christian heritage of the Western world stressed that somewhere was to be found a terrestrial paradise. From its initial discovery the New World was looked upon by Europeans as fulfilling the prophecies of a Garden of Eden contained in the books of Genesis and Daniel. This is what Christopher Columbus had in mind when he reported to the Spanish sovereigns that "there are great indications of this being the terrestrial paradise, for its site coincides with the opinion of the holy and wise theologians whom I have mentioned." The stories of Prester John, the tales of the seven cities of Cibola whose golden pavements glistened in the sun, the fable of El Dorado where gold had been accumulated for centuries, and even the belief of Ponce de León and others that there existed a fountain capable of restoring the ephemeral joys of youth are all examples of the dream of Europeans that America was truly the promised land. And when one considers the great wealth found in Mexico and Peru and the bountiful supply of fish and game in parts of the New World, men of that day cannot be blamed for believing as they did.

The origin of the name "California" was a result of the belief in the existence of a terrestrial paradise. A romantic Spanish novelist, Garci Ordóñez de Montalvo, in an effort to capitalize on the stories circulating after Columbus' voyages, inadvertently named the Golden State in a passage in his novel *Las Sergas de Esplandian:*

Now I wish you to learn of one of the strangest matters that has ever been found in writing or in the memory of mankind . . . Know ye that on the right hand of the Indies there is an island called California, very close to the Earthly Paradise, and inhabited by black women without a single man among them, for they live almost in the manner of Amazons. They are robust in body with stout, passionate hearts and great strength. The island itself is the most rugged with craggy rocks in the world. Their weapons are all of gold as well as the trappings of the wild beasts which they ride after taming, for there is no other metal on the whole island.

Initially it was the Spanish who took the wealth of the New World as their own but by the seventeenth century the English had effectively challenged their hegemony in North America. The British success inspired one British cleric to point out that Almighty God had reserved North America for the English, His chosen people, and that it was part of the prophecy that they were called to develop this veritable Garden of Eden.

This belief that there was a promised land where the soil was richer, the grass greener, and the air purer caused American frontiersmen to move ever westward in pursuit of it in the nineteenth century. And California was the land which most fulfilled their expectations.

THE PHYSICAL SCENE

A salient feature of California is the fact that it is a large state, being third in size among the fifty states, Alaska and Texas only being larger. Its area of 158,693 square miles is approximately equal to the size of New England, New York, and Pennsylvania. This tremendous area extends 650 miles in length between 32°42" to 42° north latitude. In fact, its longest distance north and south from Crescent City to Yuma, Arizona, is 825 miles. Its longitude is from 114° to 124°29" west with its width varying from 150 to 250 miles. The eastward curve of the state is so pronounced that San Diego lies farther to the east than does Reno, Nevada, although Eureka, a northern port city, is the most westward city in the United States. It has a coastline nearly 1200 miles in length, which is approximately equal to the distance between Boston, Massachusetts, and Charleston, South Carolina.

Its vastness has been a prime factor in the historical development of the state. The difficulty of getting northern and southern Californians to work together has been caused mainly by diverse interests largely molded by geography. The problems of distance have been compounded by the lack of navigable rivers and the presence of rugged mountain ranges which have complicated transportation from one part of the state to another. The more than 400 miles between the two main population centers of San Francisco and Los Angeles may not seem significant in the middle of the twentieth century but a century ago it effectively isolated the one area from the other.

Not only were Californians separated from each other in their vastness, they were also remote from the remainder of civilization. Located on the very periphery of Spain's holdings in the New World, Spanish occupation of California was late, coming exactly 250 years after the first settlement on the Pacific coast, in 1519. Since California was separated from the population centers of Mexico by the inhospitable Pacific Ocean and miles of arid wasteland it was difficult for prospective migrants to make their way there. Hence, Spanish domination of California was, at best, a tenuous thing. Even under the more dynamic Americans the problem of isolation posed by the stormy ocean on the west, adverse winds and currents, and 1500 miles of sparsely settled and predominantly arid land on the east was to have a profound influence upon the historical development of California.

The most striking quality about the land of California is its diversity. In fact, the state contains within its borders a geographic variety that is comparable to that found in the other forty-nine states of the Union. In no other state are there so many variations in topography. In some parts of the state snow-capped peaks abound, one of which, Mount Whitney, is the second highest peak in the nation. Only 60 miles from Mount Whitney lies Death Valley, the lowest area on the continent. In other parts, there are vast areas of desert wasteland. In fact, so much of California is inhospitable to man that only about 10 per cent of the state's land area supports 90 per cent of the state's population.

It is the land forms which influence the use man makes of California; for they determine the weather, drainage conditions, soils, and natural vegetation. More importantly, the land forms influence where man lives, and what kinds of communication and transportation he has.

The general pattern of California land forms is rather simple. The state has two important mountain chains, the coastal range and the Sierra Nevada, which traverses most of its length. Lying between them is the Central Valley, which is some 450 miles in length and 50 in width. The mountains covering more than one half of the state's surface include the Cascades in the northeastern corner of the state. Mount Lassen, in this range, was an active volcano as late as 1921. In fact, those who climb this peak will find steam vents at the top which signal the slumbering volcano which lies beneath the snow. The people in this area are concerned mainly with lumbering, grazing, and tourism.

The coast range is of non-volcanic origin and roughly parallels the coast in a northwest-southeast direction. However, it has many spurs which extend inland in an east-west direction. One such spur, the Tehachapi Mountains, connects the coast ranges with the Sierra Nevada, and forms something of a natural boundary between the northern and southern regions of the state. The Sierra Nevada is the most impressive mountain range in California, containing many peaks over 13,000 feet. Created by the raising and tilting of a great block of the earth's crust, the Sierra Nevada gradually slopes on its western side but drops off abruptly on the east. Besides its significant role as a recreational area and its past importance in mining, the Sierra Nevada is of immense value as a source of water for the parched Central Valley.

The mountains have made possible man's use of much of California. These barriers reach up high enough to snatch moisture from the prevailing westerly winds. Water is the chief resource of the Sierra Nevada range today. The aridity of the eastern or leeward slope is testimony to the effectiveness of the mountains as a means of wringing moisture from the winds. The coastal range, being lower, does not extract as much moisture as the Sierra Nevada, but exerts a similar influence. Both contribute to the alluvial mantle which covers the valley floor.

It is the valleys where most Californians reside and which produce the bulk of the state's agricultural yield. Most important of these is the Central Valley, the largest agricultural area west of the Rockies.

There are numerous valleys, of all sizes, nestling in the coastal range. Each has its distinctive climate, and, frequently, its distinctive agricultural complex. Most of these valleys are longitudinal, none extend for any distance; some open to the sea. The most important valleys are: the Napa-Livermore; the Santa Clara-Santa Rosa, which fronts on San Francisco Bay; the Salinas; the San Luis; the Santa Maria; the Santa Ynez; and the Santa Clara of the south. The Los Angeles lowland, the largest lowland area in California which directly fronts on the sea, actually contains several valleys. They include the San Fernando, the San Gabriel, and the San Bernardino. Inland are found the Imperial and Coachella valleys. The southeastern portion of the state is largely desert, except for man-made oases.

Among the more impressive achievements of man's adaptation to the arid desert of southeastern California is the Imperial Valley, a half-million-acre greenhouse which is the largest irrigation district of its type in the Western Hemisphere. Once a part of the Colorado Desert, whose parched land received less than three inches of rain in a year, it was apparently destined to remain forever beyond the reach of man. However, around the turn of the century the first steps were taken to transform it into a vast farmland of boundless productivity.

An essential first step was the construction of a canal system, essentially gravity-operated, which tapped the water of the nearby Colorado River. In the years that followed the farmers came, broke the soil, planted and harvested, and supplemented the initial canal system until some 1700 miles of aqueduct brought life-giving water to the rich blanket of alluvial soil that covered the valley. As cultivation grew, however, a new problem appeared which threatened the tentative victory won over the desert.

This new threat was the increasing salinization of the soil, an inevitable consequence of extensive irrigation in a desert region. As the salt in the earth was leached to the surface, and the deposits were supplemented by the mineral content of the water, the soil became poisoned. By the 1920s a crisis was reached as thousands of acres of land had to be abandoned. The solution came out of a crash program of research by federal and state agencies and the construction of a vast network of tile drainage pipes and ditches which drain away the used water with its accumulated salts and deposit it into the Salton Sea. The capital costs were tremendous and the continuing water costs for this "flushing" operation are considerable. The half-million-acre greenhouse has been saved, however, and remains today as a striking example of the manner in which man can conquer the desert. However, the problem of salinization remains, temporarily checked, but still threatening.

GEOGRAPHIC INFLUENCES

Geographic influences have played a major role in the historical development of California. In most instances, especially in terms of climate, they have been a positive force. Yet the geography of California has severely handicapped man's utilization of the state. Perhaps the most significant restrictive factor has been the peripheral location in relation to other parts of the world. At one time, the state was a remote outpost of the Spanish empire, and until the air age, has been outside the mainstream in the United States. Before the advent of the railroad, just reaching California was a formidable task. The early Spaniards who came by sea had to sail in small boats in an age when nautical science was in its infancy. They found the sea voyage from the settled areas of Mexico to California extraordinarily long and hazardous. En route they discovered that the Pacific Ocean was anything but peaceful along the California coast. Their fragile craft battled treacherous currents as well as adverse and constantly shifting winds. Sometimes it took nine months to make the journey from Acapulco to California. Because there were no intermediate ports of call, travelers had to live on what their boats could carry; consequently malnutrition and scurvy were common. The mortality rate on these early voyages averaged nearly 50 per cent. Frequently, California-bound ships did not have enough able-bodied seamen to bring their craft to anchor when they reached port. Is it any wonder that seamen had to be rounded up at the point of a bayonet or from the prisons for ships destined for California?

The approaches to California by land were even more formidable. The routes from the Spanish settlements in Mexico or New Mexico were over waterless deserts. Even if the natural elements could be surmounted, the Indians still had to be contended with, and some trails were closed by the natives. Expeditions that were able to reach the present boundaries of California often met disaster in such trackless wastes as the Colorado Desert. Those who came in the American period by the southern route had to cross large areas of sand through which wagons could not readily travel; in addition, the shifting of the sand made it impossible to create trails. Those who came the northern route had to cross the Sierra Nevada range. John Bidwell, the leader of the first overland American immigrant train to reach California, spoke for many when he said, "If California lies beyond those mountains we shall never be able to reach it." And many did not. The Donner party is a classic example of the disaster that could overtake an overland party.

When the Spanish reached California, they still faced the problem of how to live in a barren and inhospitable land; there was nothing available that could provide a regular source of food. In the midst of the green richness of the irrigated fields of today, it is difficult to understand the despair of Gaspar de Portolá, who, when first viewing the region, commented that Spain's Russian rivals were welcome to such a desert. The fact that the Indians used acorns as one of their staples is testimony to the initial food problems of the early European settlers. Not until a regular food supply was established were the early settlers on a secure footing.

Another initial barrier to early settlement by the Spaniards was the apparent paucity of mineral wealth. In spite of their constant quest for gold and silver the Spanish failed to uncover California's treasure in precious metals. Several factors caused such an oversight. The Spanish and their Mexican legatees usually explored and lived close to the relative security of the coast. They were concerned with ranching and bringing the true gospel to the Indians. All of this tended to keep them out of the gold regions and their preoccupation with other matters left little time for mining. Then too, the Indians inhabiting California had never discovered the gold themselves, or, if they had, they made no use of it, unlike the natives of Mexico and South America. Had the Spanish discovered the state's gold, how different the history of California might have been! Although this initial lack of minerals has been more than offset by recent exploitation, especially of petroleum, California still lacks substantial

struck a few hours later during the morning rush hour the loss of
lives would have been very great. If this much damage could result
from a "lesser" quake, what will happen when the long-feared
"major" quake hits? A national magazine predicted in 1971: "The
same thing will happen again—only worse."

THE CLIMATIC SCENE

The diversity of the state's physical scene is also true of California's
climatic scene. Strictly speaking, there is no such thing as "California
climate." The state has not one but many climates, in fact every
climate but the true tropical. Some areas along the northern coast
have recorded as much as 100 inches of rainfall the same year an
area in the southeast corner was receiving a mere 2 inches. While
deep snow and bitter cold are plaguing one part of the state, another
has flowers blooming. The advantage to man of such great variation
in climate is that, contrary to Mark Twain's dictum, California
residents can do something about the weather. By the simple expedient of driving a few miles, they can be in an entirely different
climatic area.

The great variation in climate can be partially explained by the
size of the state. After all, the northern tip of California is at the
same latitude as Chicago or New York, while the southern edge
is at the same latitude as Savannah, Georgia. Latitude does not, however, tell the whole story. Equally important as determinants of
climatic conditions are distance from the ocean, the situation in
reference to the mountains, and the altitude. In fact, there can be a
variety of climates within a relatively small area. It is possible to go
skiing within sight of orchards in bloom, or to see snow-capped peaks
while surfing in the Pacific.

Mount San Jacinto, for example, which overlooks the famed resort
of Palm Springs, reaches upward some 11,000 feet. The precipitous
rise from its base to its peak represents the sharpest ascension in the
United States, and the traveler passes through a gamut of life zones
ranging from the Sonoran to the Hudsonian on the route from the
Palm Springs Racquet Club to the peak, although the lateral distance
traveled is less than 15 miles. A tramway takes full advantage of this

unique geographic feature as it carries its riders from a typical Southern California desert scene to a lush pine forest.

A NOTE ON CLIMATE

Helping to make much of California's climate attractive to man is a pleasant sensible temperature (that temperature which people feel or which is reported to the senses). One of the prime determinants of the sensible temperature is the amount of moisture in the air. Evaporation involves a transfer of moisture and heat, and it takes place more readily when the air is hot and dry. In the case of the human body, evaporation involves taking much sensible heat from the body surface, and cooling results. The more evaporation, the more the body will cool. When the air is hot and damp, there can be little evaporation, and thus little cooling of the body. Consequently, the air becomes oppressive to human beings. Conversely, there is little moisture in cold, dry air because air at low temperature cannot hold much water vapor. In addition, because cold, dry air is not a good conductor, the body does not lose as much heat by conduction as it does when the air is cold and damp, damp air being a good conductor. Thus, severe cold in winter is much less chilling when the air is dry than when it is damp. So "dry" heat and "dry" cold can be tolerated with much less discomfort than when the air is moist. Hence, in those areas of the state with arid conditions, Californians find the weather most pleasant regardless of what the thermometer might record. By avoiding the direct rays of the sun in even the desert areas of the state, man suffers but slight discomfort and incurs little risk of heat prostration.

A distinguishing characteristic of California's climates is the presence of only two seasons (wet and dry) instead of the usual four found in other parts of the United States. They are caused by the seasonal shifting of prevailing winds. During the winter months the westerly winds blow in from the ocean, bringing precipitation. The rainfall is received from September to April, with most of it falling in December, January, and February. Rain during the summer is virtually unknown. During the late spring, the summer, and the early months of the fall, hot, drying winds frequently blow toward the ocean from the inland desert regions, causing summer drought-like conditions.

Another feature of California's climatic scene is the prevalence of coastal fogs during the summer and fall months, caused when warm, moisture-laden breezes are cooled and partially condensed by passing over the cold coastal waters. This fog drifts in during the night and forms an insulating blanket which helps to keep the temperature low until it is dissipated by the sun in the early forenoon. These coastal fogs also account for a significant amount of precipitation.

The climate normally thought of as "Californian" is that which prevails in the coastal areas of the southern part of the state. The year-round weather has made this region a refuge for "health seekers" from the rest of the nation. The annual temperature range seldom exceeds fifteen degrees, and though the summers are warm, they are seldom hot. Frosts may occur but they are usually light, thus permitting a year-round growing season.

A PERFECT CLIMATE?

The climate of Southern California is equable: a commodity that can be labeled, priced, and marketed. It is not something that you talk about, complain about, or guess about. On the contrary, it is the most consistent, the least paradoxical factor in the environment. Unlike climates the world over, it is predictable to the point of monotony. In its air-conditioned equability, it might well be called artificial. The climate is the region. It has attracted unlimited resources of manpower and wealth, made possible intensive agricultural development, and located specialized industries, such as motion pictures. It has given the region its rare beauty.

Carey McWilliams, *Southern
California Country*, pp. 6–7.

Although the climate of California has been justly credited for much of the influx of population into the state, it must also be listed as a restrictive natural influence: for one of the characteristics of California has been the struggle of man to adjust to the water situation. For generations cycles of drought have parched pastures, dried up normal water supplies, ruined farmers who have invested in irrigation projects or tried to raise crops with the natural moisture, and brought extensive areas of the state to the verge of disaster. Since geological evidence exists that California's southeastern desert country once supported luxuriant vegetation, it is obvious that cycles of drought are nothing new to the state.

A by-product of the lack of moisture has been fire. With its summer-dry shrublands, its large forests, and roads which take people into even the remote areas of the state, California has one of the worst fire problems of any area in the world. Not only have precious stands of timber been reduced to ashes, but in recent years valuable urban centers have been destroyed. For example, the Bel Air fire of November 6, 1961, in some respects a forest fire, was the fifth costliest fire in United States history.

All too frequently, the drought cycles are succeeded by heavy rainfall which produces floods. In fact, past devastation from too much water has far exceeded the damage from earthquakes. Most susceptible to flooding are the valley areas where most Californians reside. Moreover, the high cost of land in rapidly growing urban regions has prompted builders to erect homes on hillsides where the danger of destruction from mudslides is very great. In addition to building water reservoirs, flood control channels, and levees and dams, Californians have even been forced to relocate towns as a result of frequent floods. The erection of numerous dams and other key water-controlling structures has substantially reduced flood damage in the state, but the massive devastation caused by the floods in northern California in December 1964 is ample proof that much remains to be done. It is ironical that Californians must keep themselves busy with the construction of irrigation facilities on the one hand and flood control projects on the other.

Even the weather, so ideal in much of the state, has shortcomings. Unseasonal frosts have always plagued California fruit growers and large expenditures have been made in order to protect the tender orchards. High winds, frequently up to 100 miles per hour, have also damaged agriculture as well as doing extensive damage to coastal shipping and to other property. The modern motorist who finds it difficult to drive in a heavy fog should appreciate the hazard it presented to sailing ships seeking to find port in the pre-electronic era. Last, but by no means least, the state's weather is made less pleasant by the presence of smog.

FLORA AND FAUNA

The plant and animal life of California is as diverse as its climate. In the approximately 150,000-square-mile area of California is found the largest number of species of fauna of any similar area in the United States. In the rich tapestry of flora, there is considerable endemism, that is, there are many plants that are found in California and nowhere else in the world. The presence of such diversification in plant life is a reflection of the enormous range of climate and topography of the region. Since California's climate varies from the subtropical to the arctic, its topography from the desert in the southeast to the moist forested areas of the northwest, it follows that a wide variety of flora and fauna would be present. Of the life zones of North America, all are found in California except the tropical. Just as is true of climate, their distribution depends on elevation as well as latitude. The isolation of the state from the rest of the continent has contributed to the uniqueness of the state's plant and animal life. Undoubtedly, some species have entered the state from Mexico or Oregon but few have survived the long passage from the east across arid lands and the mountains.

Biologists have divided California into six life zones, in each of which the altitude and climatic conditions are approximately similar throughout the zone. The lower Sonoran is the lowest in altitude and the warmest. It includes the greater part of the Central Valley from Red Bluff to Bakersfield, the arid and desert regions south and east of the Sierra to the Nevada and Arizona lines, as well as several valleys from the Salinas Valley south. Unique among the flora are the California fan palm found in the Colorado Desert section and the Joshua tree of the Mohave Desert. Various species of sagebrush and desert brush abound, the latter being restricted to areas of 10 inches of rainfall or less. Mammals, mainly nocturnal, several species of birds, and reptiles unique to the state are found in this zone. The tule elk, once plentiful in the marshlands of the Tulare Basin, is today found only in a state park near Bakersfield.

The upper Sonoran zone includes the foothill country of the

Sierra Nevada, the lava plateaus of the northeastern corner of the state, the western slopes of the Sacramento Valley, the inner chains of the coast range and valleys from Mendocino County to San Francisco Bay, and the coastal region immediately to the south of that bay. Here is found a variety of heavy brush vegetation called chaparral as well as scrub oaks and several species of pine which grow in areas of limited precipitation. Such plant life provides excellent cover for wildlife and this zone has many birds, rabbits, antelope, and even the ring-tailed cat (a relative of the raccoon). This was the natural habitat of the once feared grizzly and the California condor, largest flying bird of the Northern Hemisphere. It is also a region rich in flowers.

The Transition zone includes all of the coast country north of San Francisco, the Santa Cruz Mountains, the well-watered northeastern counties, and a long belt between 2500 and 5000 feet in the Sierra. This zone includes most of the state's forests, and thus supplies the greater part of the commercially valuable timber. The redwood is especially valuable since it does not rot and is almost impervious to insects. It is one of the tallest trees in the world. Beneath the tall trees there is generally a luxuriant growth of underbrush. Flanking the redwoods to the east are Douglas firs, as well as many other coniferous and deciduous trees. South of Lake Tahoe is found one of the oldest trees known, the Sequoia gigantea (a type of redwood), which may be four thousand years old. This forest area abounds in animal life of all kinds.

The Canadian, Hudsonian, and Arctic-Alpine zones lie in the higher elevations of the mountain ranges. The Canadian has extensive stands of pine but much brush also. The Hudsonian zone is a belt of forest immediately below the timber line. Certain types of stunted and twisted pines are found here. The Arctic-Alpine zone is a treeless area above 10,500 feet. Its economic significance lies in the amount of its snow cover, which provides much-needed water for the more settled areas below.

Some animals range through several zones, especially the mule deer, the coyote, and the mountain lion—still found in California. The tremendous expanse of land that man has been unable to utilize has remained the habitat of countless forms of wildlife. Deer, mountain sheep, weasels, badgers, raccoons, muskrats, beavers, and even mountain lions are found on the very fringes of civilization.

In view of these influential natural restrictions and the difficulty of the early Europeans to adjust to the geography and climate of California, the fact that the state today is the most populous in the nation is evidence of man's ability to adjust to nature. The introduction of air transportation has materially reduced the onetime significance of the state's isolation. The rise to importance of the Orient in world affairs has placed California in a strategic location instead of its previously peripheral position. Man's technology has made once scarce water available for farming, for industrial uses, and for domestic purposes. The potential water supply available through the desalinization of ocean water may, in the not too distant future, completely eliminate any water problem in the state. Air conditioning has made possible extensive human habitation of the desert. In fact, after considering man's success in his continual conflict with nature for control of California in the past, the state's citizens assume that they can continue to solve the problems arising from man's efforts to utilize the resources of the Golden State to their maximum extent.

CHAPTER II

The First Californians

When the Spaniards arrived in California they found a relatively large number of Indians already in residence. Authorities differ; the anthropologist Alfred L. Kroeber estimated 133,000, while others claim that there were as many as 275,000 natives within the present boundaries of California when the white man first arrived. The first Californians were not warlike, had little in the way of government or religion, did not use pottery, and, with some exceptions, did not practice agriculture. The Spanish Franciscans, used to the more advanced Indians of Mexico, labeled the indigenous Californians as backward and primitive. The Anglo frontiersmen, who compared them to the Plains Indians or to the tribes of the Northwest, were equally contemptuous. Dubbed "Diggers" because of the mistaken belief that they lived only by grubbing for roots, many writers reported that California's Indians were the most primitive in North America.

Today a more realistic appraisal is possible, as some of the prejudices of earlier years have been dimmed by the passage of time, and a more scientific approach to ethnic topics has developed. Many of the myths about them have been disproven. First of all, the imputation of lethargy and indolence has been revised. The Indians appeared lazy because they only did that work which was necessary for them to survive and prosper. No Puritan ethic drove them. Then too, successive occupiers of California (Spaniards, Mexicans, and Americans) virtually dispossessed and enslaved the Indians when they could. The natives understandably were unable to develop any enthusiasm for work under such conditions. Conquerors usually develop a self-serving rationale to explain and justify their subjugation and exploitation of the conquered. The stereotype of the indolent Californian comes from such a milieu.

California Indians were also accused of being dirty. The truth is that there were far more deaths from unsanitary conditions after the white man arrived than before. In their native state, the Indians used the temescals (sweathouses) to bathe; but in the missions bathing was a rarity. They also burned their old dwellings and built fresh ones, and they simply moved when their camping grounds became unsanitary. These aboriginal "public health" measures had considerable merit; and they were definitely superior to the mission practices which replaced them.

The first residents of California were also accused of having lax morals. This judgment was made by observers who used a non-Indian moral frame of reference. They did not understand that the Indians' moral standards were appropriate to their society. In some respects these standards were lowered with the arrival of the Spanish soldier, who introduced hard liquor and prostitution to the natives. Finally, the natives were treated with contempt because they were not as warlike as other Indians of North America. But when is it proper to describe a group of people as "inferior" because they shunned conflict whenever possible?

THE SOCIETY

Generalizing about the state's Indians is as difficult as generalizing about much else in California. For there were 7 basic linguistic groups within the state but these were in turn subdivided into 21 or 22 linguistic families. Furthermore, these, in turn, have been subdivided into 135 different idioms. With only two exceptions, the diversified Indians of California were all hunters and gatherers rather than producers of food. Although they were concentrated along the coast and in the river valleys, the aboriginal population tended to reflect the capacity of a given area to sustain the optimum population. It was the most densely inhabited area north of Mexico in pre-Columbian times. (See accompanying table.)

In this land of tongues and diverse cultures, the Indians of a particular village had to travel but a short distance to encounter an unintelligible language. The inability of the natives to communicate with many of their brethren doubtless retarded the intermingling of

FAMILIES		1770	1910
Penutian:			
Pen group: Maidu, Wintun, Yokuts	39,000		
Uti group: Miwok, Costanoan	18,000		
Total		57,000	3,500
Hokan:			
Northern group: Shastan, Chimariko, Karok, Yana	9,000		
Pomo	8,000		
Washo in California	500		
Southwestern group: Esselen, Salinan, Chumash	13,500		
Yuman (9,500, less 3,000 in Arizona)	6,500		
Total		37,500	6,000
Shoshonean:			
Plateau branch	6,000		
Kern River branch	1,000		
Southern California branch	16,500		
Total		23,500	4,050
Athabascan		7,000	1,000
Yukian		4,000	200
Algonkin (Yurok, Wiyot)		3,500	800
Lutuami in California		500	300
Total		133,000	15,850

tribes at an early period, and proved a handicap when the missionary fathers tried to convert them to Christianity. The great diversity of the natives can be attributed to the fact that California was a stopping place for many groups of aborigines as they made their way from Asia through Alaska and then down the Pacific coast. Then too, the great diversity of the state's topography and climate facilitated the development of numerous Indian entities.

Similar varieties existed in their physical appearance. Heizer and Whipple declared: "California has among its living tribes examples of the shortest and tallest peoples of the whole American continent."

R. F. Heizer and M. A. Whipple, eds., *The California Indians, A Source Book,* Berkeley and Los Angeles, 1951, p. 74.

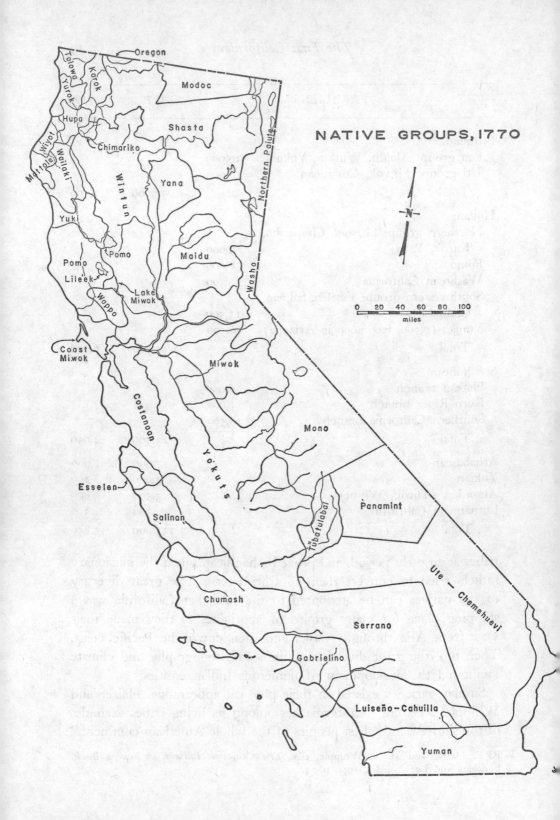

NATIVE GROUPS, 1770

Oregon

Tolowa
Yurok
Karok
Hupa
Wiyot
Mattole
Wailaki
Chimariko
Yuki
Wintun
Yana
Shasta
Modoc
Northern Paiute
Washo
Pomo
Lileek
Maidu
Lake Miwok
Wappo
Coast Miwok
Costanoan
Yokuts
Miwok
Mono
Esselen
Salinan
Tübatulabal
Panamint
Chumash
Serrano
Gabrielino
Ute — Chemehuevi
Luiseño — Cahuilla
Yuman

N

0 20 40 60 80 100
miles

In general, the tallest and most handsome were found in the northern part of the state with both the height and appearance being changed as one progressed southward. There were, however, many exceptions. Bancroft, no friend of the first Californians, described the women of the northern tribes as "quite handsome." Though most of the Indians were short, by Caucasian standards, Chief Solano, of the Suisunes, was described as being 6 feet, 7 inches in height, and well proportioned. There were also many other tall, fine-looking men, especially among the mountain tribes. Despite the fact that their culture was less developed, as contrasted with that of other North American tribes, the first Californians displayed much ability to master the Spanish language, to read music, and to acquire considerable knowledge of the mechanical arts.

THE ECONOMIC BASIS

The economy of the first Californians indicated tremendous talent in adapting to the wide variety of resources found in the natural environment of the state. From the north to the extreme south, food, clothing, and houses revealed the ability of the natives to adjust to the gifts of Mother Nature. Along the northern coasts, some tribes built an economy around salmon, which were abundant in the streams. Indians of central California and Southern California utilized the acorn, which was found in abundance, while those of the extreme south, the Yumans of the Colorado River, built an economy around corn that was similar to that of the "corn culture" Indians of the Southwest.

In general the Indians lived in harmony with the ecology of the region they inhabited. Their hunting and gathering economy produced little in the form of surplus. Small tribes were the rule and diversified exploitation of the natural resources of the environment was characteristic. There was some nomadic and seasonal movement within the relatively small area in which they subsisted and its residents came to know it well.

The collection, preservation and utilization of food was of basic importance to the California Indians. Here too, they displayed versatility and diversity. Unlike some other tribes, they stored food and the large population partially is explained by their adaptation to the existing food supply. The main staple of large numbers of Indians was the acorn, which occupied a status similar to that of corn among the Pueblo tribes.

The process by which the acorn was made into human food was more complex than the transforming of wheat into bread. Acorns were gathered in season and stored. They were then hulled in preparation for the more complex processing. The kernels were pounded with stone mortars and sifted until a fine yellow meal was produced. In fact, a common sound heard on approaching an Indian village was the pounding of the pestles in the mortars, as the Indian women prepared the acorn flour. The presence of toxic tannic acid made it necessary to leach the yellow meal by pouring warm water over it. The Indians heated their water by dropping hot stones into watertight baskets. The whole system of gathering the acorns, hulling them, pounding them, leaching the tannic acid out, and then subsequent storage required some six to eight baskets, all made especially for the purpose. The acorn was so important to the natives that there were conflicts over the control of oak groves.

Next to the acorns, the Indians ate many kinds of grasses, herbs, roots, and berries. Many seeds and nuts were pressed into flour and then cooked into a mush which was combined with berries, fresh wild onions, or bits of meat. Buckeyes, pine nuts, horse chestnuts, and piñon nuts could be processed. The Modoc burned away tule tops to obtain small seeds for such use. The first Californians ate little meat because they lacked domestic animals and were not accomplished hunters. Without adequate weapons for the chase, they usually built pits and traps to catch larger game. They shunned the grizzly bear, believing him to be possessed of a demon, and prudently avoided pitting their primitive weapons against him. One way of hunting deer was simply to run the animal with relays until he fell from exhaustion. Fish and shellfish, among the coastal Indians, were important food items. They were usually caught by means of nets and traps, although the Santa Barbara Islands Indians also used spears. The Yumans and Mohaves dropped seeds into the mud of the flood plain, thereby producing the basics of their diet: corn, beans, pumpkins, squash, and similar items.

When it came to clothing, the first Californians were children of nature who dressed in a manner appropriate to the mild climate and were usually attired as scantily as a modern California bather. The women wore a short skirt or petticoat of two pieces. It was made of either buckskin or, more commonly, plant fibers. The men usually went naked, although sometimes they wore a breechcloth of bark or skin wrapped around the waist. During periods of inclement weather both sexes were attired in robes made of either rabbit or deerskin, depending on availability. Most tribes went barefoot except in bad weather. During the winter, the northern California tribes usually wore moccasins. The Southern California tribes normally wore sandals. The men usually went bareheaded but the women had an interesting basketry cap, which kept the tumpline of a burden basket from rubbing their foreheads. It was a round, bowllike cap of basketry which was frequently made quite beautifully and decorated in a tribal style. Tattooing was a common form of decoration among both men and women. Some men used paint, especially the Modocs. The northern tribes pierced the cartilage of the nose in order to wear ornaments. Some also wore strings of beads or shells, in addition to earrings.

Houses of the first Californians were extremely simple. In fact, it was not uncommon for the southern tribes to sleep out in the open during much of the year. The typical shelter, made in a conical shape of poles and banked with earth with the usual opening for smoke, was a principal type of dwelling. Some tribes had semi-underground houses with the upper portion earth-covered. The usual house of the Southern California Indian was 9 feet high and about 16 feet in diameter. It was made by setting poles in the ground and lashing them together at the top. The house was then covered or thatched by tying bunches or even whole clusters of plants to the cross poles.

Among some tribes a large communal building was of greater significance than the family dwelling. It was called the temescal and had a wide variety of uses. In some respects, this building played a role similar to that of the kiva among the Pueblo tribes. Here most of the important tribal decisions were made; it was sometimes used as a place of refuge for the men when they wanted to escape the female members of the tribe, or as a sweathouse. In the latter function, a fire was built until the temescal was oppressively hot.

Once perspiring profusely, the brave rushed from the heated interior and jumped into cold water. In some respects the practice was similar to the Finnish sauna and was socializing, hygienic, and medicinal.

The native arts were not highly developed. Pottery was almost non-existent, except for that found among the Yumans, who probably learned pottery making from Arizona Indians. It was in basketry that the first Californians excelled. They made many kinds of beautiful and useful baskets. Basket making was developed to a fine art, a principal outlet for aesthetic creative impulses. The women of the Pomo tribe produced baskets so fine that a magnifying glass is needed in order to count the stitches. Some of the baskets were decorated with woven-in feathers and adorned with pendants and beads. Others were so finely made that they were used to carry water. In addition to the baskets, the typical household utensils were stone mortars for grinding seeds, horn and shell knives and spoons, nets of vegetable fiber, and rush mats that were used for beds.

Indian boats used were of three types: the dugout canoe, the tule balsa, and the plank canoe. The dugout canoe was fashioned from logs by the northern and northwestern tribes and showed considerable talent in light of their primitive tools. The tule balsa fashioned of bundles of tules was common, being found in much of the state. The Chumash plank canoe, fashioned of planks and waterproofed with brea, was used by the tribes along the Santa Barbara Channel. Boats of a similar design were found along the Oregon coast and in the South Pacific, perhaps another evidence of a common Asiatic heritage. The Chumash made not only plank canoes but also nets and effective fishing tools and spears. They were, in fact, among the most proficient fishermen in North America. They also tapped the marine produce of shellfish and seals, and enjoyed generally a relatively high standard of living.

In no area were the native arts as poorly developed as in the field of weapons. They were few and inferior in quality, primarily consisting of small-sized bows and arrows and flint-tipped lances. In fact, only the Yumans had a weapon in the form of a war club which had been designed solely for human combat. In their fights with each other the natives used stones with telling effect. The net, the snare, and the pit were basic tools used to hunt game. The first Californians made up in subtlety for what they lacked in weapons when on the hunt. They used decoys in hunting birds and animals. Occasionally they would stalk game in a disguise made of the head and skin of the animal they were seeking or they would use stuffed specimens of the birds they were hunting.

The simple economy of the Indians probably changed very little from the time the first immigrants settled the area thousands of years ago. The fact that they usually had enough to eat and little concern over inclement weather may have inhibited change. Then too, geographic isolation limited contact with other tribes, and thus lessened acculturation.

CULTURAL ENVIRONMENT

The California Indians had little, if anything, in the way of political institutions. Among them tribes did not exist in the normal sense of the word. Many of the arrangements were so vague as hardly to be called political. The basic structure was a patrilocal band, which might consist of a dozen families related through the father's line. They were not nomadic, but usually remained for generations within a specific area, exploiting the combination of resources. They might be friendly with other groups with the same language and might even have arrangements to co-operate for war, ceremonial purposes, or even intermarriage. The vague political structure provided the chiefs with little authority. Among some tribes the chieftaincy was hereditary, while in others the chief may simply have been an older man of ability or experience.

Though the natives were normally peacefully inclined, fighting was not unknown. It occurred for the usual reasons: a quarrel over women or the possession of acorn groves or other valuables. They were not as disposed to battle as were the other tribes of North America. However, they were capable of fierce fighting if they were challenged. Instead of conflicts being tribal warfares, they were more often in the nature of local feuds which might be settled by a single battle. Frequently, little blood was shed and both sides held a big celebration at the end of the conflict.

A chief had little authority; it was nearly impossible for him to lead a band in battle. Each family was a group unto itself: transgressions against the group or its members were expiated with token payments of goods. The crime of adultery was far more serious, however, for the wife was considered an economic asset. The man could escape punishment for this offense through payment, but the woman might be put to death.

The California Indians did not have an elaborate and complex religious life. However, they were much concerned with their relationship to nature and the supernatural. Contact with the supernatural world was made through the shaman or medicine man, who was as much a witch doctor as a priest. One of the more effective techniques of the shaman was sucking the evil spirit from the body of a patient through a special tube or stick. In spite of the fact that they practiced medicine not entirely in keeping with the texts of today's practitioners, they did possess some knowledge of the curative effects of herbs and did accomplish some good. One of the favorite remedies for the most illnesses was the temescal treatment.

In addition to the control of disease there were three types of specialists among the shamans. These were rain doctors, rattlesnake doctors, and bear doctors. Naturally, rain or weather doctors were most common in the southern or drier portions of California. Such shamans used their particular talents like the prophet Samuel, to make impressions by demonstrations. The rattlesnake doctor was known in most of the region except for the northwestern corner. His difficult task was to prevent snakebite, or if unsuccessful, to cure the unfortunate victim. Among some tribes, such as the Yokuts and northern Maidu, there were elaborate public ceremonies in which the shamans handled rattlesnakes. The bear shamans were found throughout the area, except for the northwestern and southeastern corner. It was believed that the bear doctor could turn himself into the feared grizzly bear and in this form destroy enemies. They usually operated by encasing themselves in bearskins. Though greatly feared, they were popular, as it was believed their destructive faculties were used only against foes.

In the absence of public ceremonies it was inevitable that ceremonial activity of the Californians would be concentrated around the family. Hence, birth, puberty, marriage, and death became occasions for religious observances, as is true of most societies. In many tribes, the husband kept to his house for several days after the birth of a child, abstaining with his wife from meat and salt. In some, the husband incuriously shared and simulated the wife's labor pains. Boys were initiated into the life of the tribe in some areas by simple ceremonies which involved fasting, whipping, piercing of the ears, and indoctrination into the existing traditions. However, the girls went through a far more elaborate ritual. A girl reaching maidenhood often fasted and had to refrain from touching her head with her hands. A special stick was provided with which she could touch her hair. It was believed that the girl's behavior at this period in her life was very critical for her future. Consequently, there were many prescriptions covering her future duties; such as gathering firewood, being industrious, always being modest in deportment, and similar admonitions.

Marriage was an extremely informal ceremony, and was usually accompanied by purchase although the price was nominal. Among some tribes the amount that was paid for a bride determined a man's status in the community. Polygamy was common everywhere, but in the southern part of the state only the chief was permitted more than one wife. The reason for its absence there was apparently more economic than social. Slavery was little practiced.

There were many unusual social habits. It was necessary for the widow to crop or singe off her hair and cover the stubble as well as her face with pitch, usually for a year after the death of her husband. A mourning necklace was worn by women in some tribes, while in others the widow wore a belt made of the hair cut from her head. There was much fear of twins.

It was after a death that the most imposing ceremonies were held. They never touched their dead, usually turning over this task to a tribe with which they were in kinship. They avoided all mention of the departed's name but did hold an elaborate funeral ceremony. Sometimes the official ceremony was held a year later. About half of the tribes cremated their dead, while the remainder buried them.

These ceremonies were an occasion for much celebration. There were dances for every occasion: one celebrated the salmon catch, another commemorated the birth of a child, one welcomed a visiting tribe, and there were peace as well as war dances. They even had a dance in the autumn in appreciation of their harvest, which bears a striking resemblance to the Puritan Thanksgiving feast. Although the natives had some musical instruments which included flutes, rattles, whistles, and drums of various kinds, the dances were principally based upon song.

The natives had a large number of games which were played with great vigor, generally by the men. The women were too busy working to take time out for such things. Some of these were similar to lacrosse or football today. A more significant diversion was, however, gambling. All contests were heavily backed by bets of shell money or skins. In addition, a guessing game was played by means of concealing articles in the hand or in obvious places. It was similar to the "shell game" of the carnival circuit although it was probably more honest.

Another form of diversion was provided by the organized religious cults. They were the Kuksu (big head) Cult, found in central California, and the Toloache (Jimson weed) Cult, found in Southern California. These cults included most of the male members of the tribes and were intended to initiate the young people into the affairs of the tribe. The Kuksu rites were practiced usually in the wintertime by a group of dancers who represented gods. Their faces were painted and they were disguised by curtains of feathers, grass, or rushes. The Toloache Cult centered its activities about the taking of the narcotic Jimson weed plant, which induced hallucinations. The narcotic was fed to novitiates, under the supervision of an older member of the cult. The interpretation of the hallucinations induced were considered portents of the boy's future. The initiates were also instructed by means of ground paintings. Since the rituals of these cults included a large number of dances and songs they became a significant part of the diversion of the natives.

These, then, were the first Californians. Large in numbers when compared to the rest of the aborigines of North America, they made a remarkable adaptation to the multiple environments of California and every student of the state's history is obligated to consider them.

HANDS

Inside a cave in a narrow canyon near Tassajara
The vault of rock is painted with hands,
A multitude of hands in the twilight, a cloud of
    men's palms, no more,
No other picture. There's no one to say
Whether the brown shy quiet people who are dead intended
Religion or magic, or made their tracings
In the idleness of art; but over the division of years
    these careful
Signs-manual are now like a sealed message
Saying: "Look: we also were human; we had hands, not
    paws. All hail
You people with the cleverer hands, our supplanters
In the beautiful country; enjoy her a season, her beauty,
    and come down
And be supplanted; for you also are human."

—ROBINSON JEFFERS

CHAPTER III

The Age of Exploration

In 1542, only a half century after Columbus landed in the New World, the Spanish discovered Alta California. However, it was to be more than two centuries before effective settlements were made. The delay between arrival and initial settlement resulted from several factors: the remoteness of Alta California from existing spheres of Spanish influence, the difficulty of the passage, the absorption of Spanish interest and energy elsewhere, and the general unattractiveness of the land itself.

Throughout the long period between 1542 and the beginning of settlement in 1769, the Spanish had a continuing interest in the settlement of California. This urge to colonize the area stemmed from the lingering hope that gold might someday be found there, that profit could be made from pearl fishing, or that riches in some other form might be discovered. Of more importance was the perpetual fear that foreigners might settle the area, especially the French, the Russians, or the English, and use California as a base of operations against Mexico. There was also the legend of the Straits of Anián, the Northwest Passage that was reputed to be the short route to the wealth of Cathay. California, lying adjacent to the mythical straits, would play a role of great strategic importance in the event of foreign control of the straits. Finally, continuing Spanish interest in the settling of the area stemmed from the need for a base of operations to facilitate the trade between Mexico and the Philippines.

THE SPANISH BACKGROUND

That the Spanish were the first Europeans to settle in California was partially determined by the early sixteenth-century history of

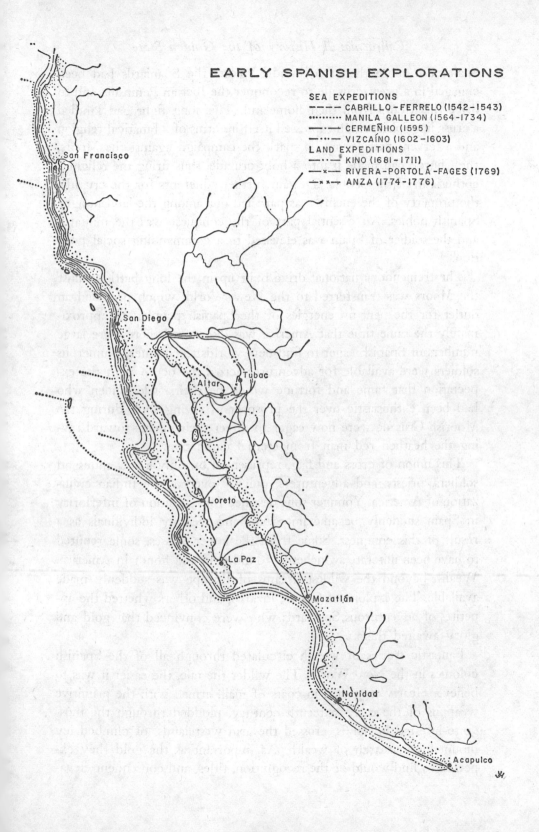

EARLY SPANISH EXPLORATIONS

SEA EXPEDITIONS
- – – – CABRILLO–FERRELO (1542–1543)
- •••••• MANILA GALLEON (1564–1734)
- —·—· CERMEÑHO (1595)
- —··— VIZCAÍNO (1602–1603)

LAND EXPEDITIONS
- —··•· KINO (1681–1711)
- —×— RIVERA–PORTOLÁ–FAGES (1769)
- —×—×— ANZA (1774–1776)

San Francisco

San Diego

Tubac

Altar

Loreto

La Paz

Mazatlán

Navidad

Acapulco

Spain. For more than two hundred years the Spaniards had been engaged in a great crusade to reconquer the Iberian Peninsula and to drive the Moors from their homeland. This long fight had kindled a crusading spirit which expressed itself in terms of a fanatical religion and a fervent patriotism. To spark the campaign against the Moors, the Church had made it into a holy crusade, thus firing the religious enthusiasm of the people. To gain further adherents for the crusade, the property of the enemy was parceled out among the land-hungry Spanish nobles. An essential part of the conquest was the military, and the soldier of Spain was elevated to a commanding social position.

The tremendous national drive built up in the long battle against the Moors was transferred to the New World, which provided an outlet for the pent-up energies of the Spanish people. At approximately the same time that America was discovered there were large numbers of Spanish eager to find new worlds to conquer. Numerous soldiers were available for adventures across the ocean with the expectation that fame and fortune would be theirs. Clergymen who had been enthusiastic over the prospect of saving souls during the Moorish Crusade were now eager to direct their talents toward saving the heathen red man from eternal damnation.

This union of cross and flag, represented by only a few thousand soldiers, priests, and adventurers, quickly overran the Indian civilization of America. Younger sons destined for a position of inferiority in Spain suddenly became important and wealthy individuals as a result of this conquest. Some from the lower classes, some reputed to have been illiterate swineherds, found gold and honor in America. Wealth beyond the wildest dreams of Europe was suddenly made available. The exploits of Cortés, Pizarro, and others whetted the appetites of adventurous Spaniards who were convinced that gold and glory awaited them.

Fantastic stories of wealth circulated through all of the Spanish colonies in the New World. The wilder the tale, the easier it was to believe. Hearty men clad in coats of mail, armed with the primitive weapons of the early sixteenth century, plodded through the mosquito-infested lowlands, crossed the arid wastelands, or climbed icy mountains in search of wealth. As important as the gold they expected to find would be the recognition, titles, and consequent elevation in social stature at home in Madrid. They were usually accompanied by religious zealots who believed their rewards would be in the hereafter, for having "saved" the souls of the Indians.

Out of this perpetual quest for "glory, God, and gold" came the initial exploration and final settlement of California. White men first came to California as a result of the search for the mythical cities of Cibola. The legend of the seven cities of Cibola originated about 1150. In that year the Moors captured the city of Mérida, Spain, and among the Christians fleeing from the Moslem conquerors were seven bishops and their congregations. They were reputed to have sailed away westward, finally landing on some beautiful island. There, they burned their ships and founded seven cities that ultimately became great and wealthy. In fact, they were reputed to be so rich that the sun glistened upon pavements of gold. When the Spanish, seeking these lost cities, first asked the natives about them, the Indians hastened to oblige. For the red man rather quickly sensed that the white man had an insatiable taste for precious metals, and by concocting stories about where such wealth could be found, the Spaniards would continue their search elsewhere and leave the Indian alone. Hence, already existing fantastic legends of great wealth grew with the telling. And who could blame men who had been present at the conquest of the great treasures of the Aztecs and the Incas for believing such tales?

EARLY EXPLORATIONS

The initial impetus toward the discovery of California was supplied by Hernando Cortés, the conqueror of Mexico. Although Cortés conquered the Aztec empire and acquired riches beyond the wildest dreams of most men, he also acquired an insatiable appetite for more. Word reached him of the great wealth to be found in cities far to the northwest. In addition to the allure of gold, Cortés was interested in the "California islands," which he believed were near the Straits of Anián, the long-sought passage through North America. This belief that the elusive straits from sea to sea had at last been found was stressed by Cortés in a dispatch to the king in 1524 and was consistently used by him to justify further conquest.

After many problems were overcome, Cortés in 1532 dispatched a fleet from Acapulco to explore California; but little of importance was accomplished by this effort. Another fleet was sent out which ultimately fell under the leadership of Fortún Jiménez. It was under the latter's leadership in 1533 that Baja California was discovered. Reports of wealth in pearls prompted Cortés to establish a colony at the site of the modern city of La Paz in 1535. However, it did not flourish and the effort was abandoned in 1537. According to Bernal Díaz del Castillo, the barren area was heartily cursed by the unhappy Spaniards, who were generally disappointed.

Interest in California was further stimulated by the wanderings of the famous pedestrian Cabeza de Vaca. A member of the Narváez expedition to Florida in 1528, Cabeza de Vaca and his colleagues escaped Florida by building horsehide boats but were shipwrecked near the present site of Galveston, Texas. Most of the unfortunate Spaniards were either drowned or killed by the local Indians. Escaping with three of his friends, Cabeza de Vaca wandered through much of the Southwest. In 1534 he and his fellow castaways made their way back to the Spanish settlements in northern Mexico. They brought stories of large settlements of people who lived in permanent dwellings and, of more importance, gave evidence of considerable wealth. Cabeza de Vaca reported "many fine signs of gold, antimony, iron, copper, and other metals." Stories such as these were most welcome to the ears of those who yearned for more Indian plunder, and who had visions of finding another rich Aztec kingdom. The viceroy of New Spain, Antonio de Mendoza, sent Friar Marcos de Niza to make an exploratory trip into the present states of New Mexico and Arizona.

The reports of Cabeza de Vaca which were substantiated by Friar Marcos led directly to the Coronado expedition. Viceroy Mendoza, a jealous rival, blocked Cortés' attempts to send a land expedition to the seven golden cities which Friar Marcos described in such vivid detail. Though unable to send out a land expedition, the conqueror of Mexico was able to dispatch one of his captains from La Paz by sea. His commander, Francisco de Ulloa, explored the Gulf of California to the mouth of the Colorado River. The major significance of the Ulloa expedition lay in that he disproved the belief that the Californias were islands. He also revealed some of the geographical reality of the area, establishing the fact that Lower California was a peninsula and revealing the relationship of the Colorado River to the Gulf of California.

Meanwhile, Viceroy Mendoza had dispatched the ill-fated Francisco Vásquez de Coronado on his fruitless search for the seven cities of Cibola. This expedition was confined to New Mexico but it had a bearing upon the early exploration of California. Partly as a result of a mistake by Friar Marcos in computing his geomatical position, it was believed that the pueblos of New Mexico were much closer to the head of the Gulf of California than they actually were. Therefore, the expedition under the leadership of Hernando de Alarcón was planned to bring supplies to Coronado. Alarcón sailed up the Colorado River some distance in an effort to contact his chief. Coronado's lieutenant, Melchor Díaz, was sent to pick up the supplies coming by sea. He failed to meet Alarcón but found a message and letters. It is probable that members of both the Alarcón and the Díaz groups crossed the Colorado and explored a short distance into what is today the state of California, thus perhaps being the first white men to set foot in the state.

The most significant of the early explorations of California was made by Juan Rodríguez Cabrillo, a Portuguese in the service of the Spanish crown. An experienced and competent navigator, Cabrillo explored most of the shoreline of the present state of California before his death. In command of two small ships which were barely seaworthy, the Cabrillo expedition left La Navidad in Mexico on June 27, 1542, a dangerously late start when adverse winds and currents were prevalent. After three arduous months the expedition entered what is now San Diego Harbor on September 28, 1542. After resting for six days, the fleet again sailed northward, reaching Catalina Island on October 7. They also visited the sites of the present cities of San Pedro, Santa Monica, and Ventura. Continuing their journey northward, the fleet passed Point Conception on October 18. Heavy storms slowed their northward passage and made it hazardous to examine the coastline closely and locate the large rivers or bays which had been reported by the Indians. Their main objective was the Straits of Anián. The expedition probably reached as far north as Fort Ross, but unfortunately adverse sailing conditions prevented them from discovering the Bay of Monterey, the Golden Gate, and the Bay of San Francisco. In fact, some authorities believe that the expedition may have gone as far as latitude 42°30″ where the Rogue River enters the Pacific. The expedition explored some 800 miles of coastline, located and named scores of places (many of which were subsequently renamed), and laid claim to a vast territory for Spain but it failed to discover either the legendary straits or wealthy Indian kingdoms to be exploited. Consequently, the Spanish were reserved in their approval of the expedition's accomplishments and its significance was overlooked. Bartolomé Ferrelo succeeded Cabrillo, who died from an injury.

The failure of the Coronado expedition and the reports of Cabrillo cooled the faith of the Spaniards that the wealthy cities of Cibola and the Straits of Anián existed. Their interest in further expansion northward was also lessened as a result of the bloody Mixton War which began in 1542. This Indian uprising of northwestern Mexico started a general conflict that lasted for many years and made further expansion into the frontier areas so hazardous that it was discouraged by the government. In fact, Spain may never have extended its influence out of the central plateau of Mexico if silver had not been discovered at Zacatecas in 1546.

These valuable deposits initiated a mining rush which extended westward and northward as new deposits were discovered. The wealth of these silver mines demanded the subjugation of the Indian tribes at great cost in money and in lives. Silver mining required a heavy outlay in capital investment as well as a sizable population and gave to the mining frontier an air of permanence. As the mining frontier expanded, Spanish control of Mexico accompanied it. The necessity of a continual supply of labor also extended Spanish control in Mexico. This was met by the forceful recruiting of Indian slave labor to work in the mines. Hunting expeditions roamed far and wide scouring the country for their unwilling slaves. The nefarious traffic gave thrust to Spanish frontiering impulses. The extension of the mining frontier in Mexico, therefore, provided a basis from which the ultimate settlement of California was to be made. However, much time was to pass before any direct effort was made to establish colonies in California.

THE MANILA GALLEONS

Interest in possible settlement of California existed in the last half of the sixteenth century and the first part of the seventeenth as a by-product of the trade with the Philippines which began in 1565 and lasted until 1815. Although it was never large, it had a definite influence as an incentive to the settlement of California. Sailing from Acapulco, carrying bullion, the ships made the westward journey in some two or three months. On the return voyage the products of the Orient were carried to be sold in the mining centers of Mexico, Peru, or even shipped all the way to Spain itself. The basic staples were silks and spices, but almost every luxury item known to the Far East was included. The lengthy homeward passage was extremely hazardous. Because the profit to be made on luxury goods was so great, space aboard ship was at a premium. Consequently, few ships took on adequate supplies of water and food so that the crew suffered accordingly. The ships usually reached America along the California coast. Their crews, decimated by scurvy, were often hard pressed to man and operate their ship.

The great profits of this trade made it imperative to reduce the incredibly high death rate. For that reason there was a constant interest in a port of call where inbound ships could stop, where the men could recover their health, where the ship's stores could be replenished, and where necessary repairs on the ship could be made. Another need was a port of call for the Manila galleons and a base where protection could be provided against pirates and foreign enemies. Thus, the Philippine trade provided one of the encouragements to the settlement of California, and prevented it from being ignored by Spanish policy makers.

Sir Francis Drake's visit to California in 1579 was another incentive to settlement by the Spanish. They were constantly interested in keeping foreign intruders out of their "Pacific lake," and they also feared that California might provide a base from which the wealthy mining districts of Mexico might be attacked.

In the second half of the sixteenth century Protestant England and Catholic Spain were in a "cold war" that did not develop into a full shooting fray until 1588. This conflict was partially religious in origin, but it was also a struggle for hegemony in the New World. Numerous English sea captains kept the rivalry going by preying upon the Spanish ships hauling the riches of America to Spain. Drake was a renowned member of this large group which combined patriotism with plunder.

Drake's visit to California was an indirect result of his audacious attack on Spanish treasure ships. The English sea captain realized that the ports of the Atlantic side would be protected against English freebooters, and he correctly predicted that they would not be expected on the Pacific coast. He therefore sailed around the Cape, plundered Spanish treasure ships on the west coast of South America, and raided all the way to Panama, until his *Golden Hind* was stuffed with plunder. Knowing that the Spanish would be lying in wait for him if he returned by the route he had come, Drake sought a different homeward route. He failed to find one in the fog-shrouded waters of the North Pacific, turned southward, and landed in Drake's Bay in June 1579. There he rested his men, refurbished his ship, and then struck boldly westward across the Pacific. His extraordinarily rapid return to London stimulated reports that he had discovered the illusive Straits of Anián.

Drake was followed by other intruders, such as the Englishman Thomas Cavendish, who captured the Manila galleon of 1587. Each new intrusion alarmed the Spanish and convinced them that counteraction was necessary. The counterstroke envisioned the establishment of Spanish bases and settlements in Alta California.

For these reasons, several commanders of the Manila galleons were instructed to find a suitable port which could be used as a way station. In 1584 Francisco de Gali, who commanded the galleon that year, was instructed to inspect the California coast on his homeward journey and reported "a very fair land, wholly without snow, and with many rivers, bays, and havens." In the summer of 1587 another galleon commander, Pedro de Unamuno, entered Morro Bay near San Luis Obispo and took possession of the area in the name of the king of Spain.

Sebastián Rodríguez Cermeño, a Portuguese, was selected to make the necessary surveys of the California coast. In command of the Manila galleon of 1595, Cermeño reached the coast near Eureka, then sailed southward, surveying the coast. He took soundings, and searched for a suitable port before anchoring at Drake's Bay, which he renamed San Francisco Bay (to the later confusion of historians). Although considerable time was spent refurbishing their ship, it was wasted, as the vessel was wrecked with the consequent loss of its valuable cargo. Fortunately, a launch had been built to be used for further inshore explorations and it was pressed into service for the return voyage to Mexico. The epic trip home was punctuated with adventure, hardship, and suffering and the hardy band which survived were given a cool welcome. Cermeño was disciplined, for he had lost the Manila galleon and its cargo.

Of more lasting significance in the history of California was the exploration of Sebastián Vizcaíno. A moderately successful merchant, Vizcaíno lost heavily when Cavendish captured the Spanish galleon in 1587, but apparently was able to recoup his fortune in other areas. In company with others, he obtained royal permission to exploit the pearl fisheries in Baja California in return for which he was to explore the Alta California coast. More than likely, the hope that riches were still to be found in this area provided the primary motivation for the effort but these promoters advised the crown that they were acting from altruistic motives and only desired to explore California so as to secure it against potential enemies, find the elusive Straits of Anián, and bring the gospel to the poor savages. Juan de Oñate used a similar rationale to justify the conquest of New Mexico in 1598. The crown, hesitant to explore the frontiers of New Spain in the face of general Indian unrest, gave permission reluctantly.

After preliminary explorations in Baja California, Vizcaíno left Acapulco on May 5, 1602. He proceeded up the coast, visiting the same points charted earlier by Cabrillo and renaming them in spite of orders to the contrary. The presence of a competent cartographer and the wide circulation of the accounts of Vizcaíno's exploration resulted in the new names becoming permanent—names such as San Diego, Santa Catalina, Santa Barbara, Point Conception, Monterey, Buena Ventura, and others. The most northerly point reached by the expedition was probably the 41° latitude though some claim it went as far as the 43° parallel.

Vizcaíno may justly be designated as the first Chamber of Commerce booster for the state of California. For example, the explorer was so effusive in his praise of Monterey Bay that those who followed had difficulty in recognizing it. Named after the current viceroy of Mexico, it was described as being "secure against all winds" and "well equipped with water, wood, and good timber." In addition, the expedition reported that the Indians told stories about the presence of much gold in the interior. (How different the history of the state might have been if these reports had been taken seriously!)

In spite of the fact that fully one half of the crew died, mostly of scurvy, Vizcaíno's expedition was considered a success. Unfortunately, a change of officials in Mexico City prevented a follow-up. The new viceroy, Juan de Mendoza y Luna, Marqués de Montesclaros, apparently jealous of the exploits of his predecessor, decided that California would not serve as a port of call for the Manila galleons. Instead, a search was instituted for non-existent North Pacific islands which would serve this purpose better. Then too, it was stressed that a Spanish settlement at Monterey might be captured by an enemy and used as a base of operations against Spain. Such arguments delayed action toward the colonization of California and it was to be another 150 years before such work would be carried through to completion.

Another factor which undoubtedly worked against a decision to colonize California was the problem the Spanish encountered in New Mexico. For the latter province turned out to be a white elephant and the crown could ill afford another such colony which would act as a steady drain upon the royal treasury. Not only was there no gold to be found, but the Indians proved troublesome and finally drove the Spanish from the area in 1680. Although the province was reconquered, the lessons of New Mexico dampened the enthusiasm of the Madrid authorities in financially backing the settlement of California. While interest in California lagged from 1600 to 1650, the Spanish frontier in Mexico continued to expand. Obviously, there were natural limits to the expansion of the mining frontier but about the time the mining frontier was losing its thrust, a new element for the North Mexico frontier was introduced. The mission, from rude beginnings, evolved into a complex institution which enabled the Spanish to deal effectively with Indian populations.

The mission was intended to accomplish many objectives. First of all, it grew out of the effort of the Spanish crown to Christianize the native. Early in the conquest of the New World the Spanish displayed solicitude for the soul of the Indian. At times the Spanish brutally exploited the natives in the mines or in the fields; nevertheless, interest in the Christianization of the Indian was always a goal of the crown. There was frequently a harsh contrast between concern for the Indian's soul and the Indian's physical well-being in Spanish America.

The first and most enduring objective of the missionaries was to bring the "true faith" to the Indian. There was another objective, however: Spanish civilization could be brought to the natives by stripping them of their native culture and Hispanizing them. In the process they could learn the Spanish language, learn to build European-style homes, learn agriculture, learn the Spaniard's mode of dress, and above all, learn handicrafts or other work that would make them useful citizens of the crown. It was first thought that the missions should last ten years, but this was soon found to be too short a period of time to accomplish their objective. Most lasted much longer than a decade, some missions lasted for more than a century.

The most able developers of this important institution for the Hispanization of the natives were the Jesuits. Although their missions were never as extensive in North America as they were in South America, they were nevertheless of considerable importance. The Jesuits laid the basis for the ultimate settlement of California by "reducing" the Indians of northwestern Mexico and Baja California to Christianity in the nearly two centuries which separate 1591 and 1767.

The success of the Jesuits was primarily the work of Fathers Eusebio Francisco Kino and Juan María Salvatierra. Father Kino was enthused over the challenges of this area and inspired his successor Salvatierra. Kino was described by Herbert E. Bolton as "the most picturesque missionary pioneer of all North America—explorer, astronomer, cartographer, mission builder, ranchman, cattle king, and defender of the frontier." He was a scholarly man who grasped the practical basis on which the missions must rest if they were to succeed. He was responsible for the first wheat brought to California. In his remarkable career Kino founded twenty-nine missions, baptized more than four thousand neophytes, and made more than fifty overland expeditions. Of only slightly less importance was Salvatierra, who carried on Kino's work and established at Loreto the first permanent European settlement in Baja California.

Not only did these men brave the blazing desert heat of the Southwest on their missionary expeditions, they also arranged for the financing of their work, as the royal treasury of Spain had little funds. Father Salvatierra and Father Juan de Ugarte organized the Pious Fund in 1697, which came to be the principal source of support for the missions of both Baja and Alta California. Initially, funds were solicited from private donors who turned over money, the interest of which went to support the mission. In some instances estates were bequeathed to the Pious Fund. Ultimately, it controlled large areas of land, much livestock, and other resources.

After the Jesuits were expelled in 1767 from the Spanish-speaking world, revenue from the Fund continued to support the work of Franciscan and Dominican missionaries in Alta and Baja California until 1808. In that year the beginnings of the Mexican War for Independence brought financial chaos and the end of revenues from the Fund. Spain and later Mexico recognized their obligation but lacked the ability to pay the monies due. In 1842 President Antonio López de Santa Anna incorporated the fund into the national treasury. In 1875 a mixed claims commission decided Mexico should pay the bishops of the state of California the sum of $400,000 to settle the Pious Fund. In 1902 a similar decision was made by the Hague Tribunal but fiscal instability prevented Mexico from paying the obligation. It was not until 1967 that final payment was made by the Mexican government to the archdiocese of San Francisco and the diocese of Monterey in settlement of the long-standing claim.

As far as California settlement was concerned, Spain was immobilized for almost 150 years by domestic troubles, problems with her international rivals, England and France, and the difficulties faced in administering her far-flung empire. A basic reality prompted Spanish settlement in Alta California. The Manila galleons still needed a port of call and European intruders still ventured into the Pacific lake of Spain. Franciscans, who succeeded the Jesuits in 1767, saw in the north missionary opportunities, while entrepreneurs of various kinds envisioned in this land which fronted on the Pacific opportunities of an economic nature.

But the initiation of the settlement of California awaited the congruence of a number of these factors. "Bourbon reforms" brought administrative changes to a hidebound and debilitated Spanish bureaucracy; the Seven Years' War, which ended in 1763, brought about a realignment of European spheres in the New World, and the Dominican and Franciscan orders which succeeded the Jesuit order brought a new outburst of missionary zeal. When these forces coincided and an energetic, dynamic, new *visitador-general*, José de Gálvez, entered the picture in 1765, the lethargy of a century and a half was shrugged off and New Spain's policy makers embarked on an expansion of the frontier which set a new northern border for New Spain at Monterey, California.

Although much of his time was spent on other duties, Gálvez never lost sight of his orders, "to send an expedition to rediscover and people the bays of San Diego and Monterey," and furthermore he understood that Spain's inactivity in Alta California might well result in the establishment of a foreign base there. Baja California and San Blas were bases for this colonizing expedition. Though none too prosperous, they were tapped for the essential supplies. To ensure success, four separate units were dispatched, two by land and two by sea. Careful planning marked every step of the effort; ultimate success was due as much to the careful planning which preceded the initial effort as it was to the ability of those charged with carrying the plans to fruition.

José de Gálvez never saw Alta California but he played a major role in the initiative of Spanish settlement. He combined zeal with careful planning, and effectively dealt with the miles of red tape which enmeshed Spanish bureaucracy of the eighteenth century. An astute politician, he obtained the support of the viceroy, the Marquis Francisco de Croix, for the venture. And realizing the essential fiscal needs of the expedition, he assembled the necessary financial resources. Gálvez contributed much, although his contributions are frequently overlooked.

THE PORTOLÁ-SERRA EXPEDITION

Gaspar de Portolá, governor of Baja California, who led a military land party, was a soldier whose earlier devotion to duty kept the embryo colony at San Diego from being abandoned at a crucial moment. The most prominent member of the expedition was Father Junípero Serra. In fact, a Serra legend has been created which makes it difficult to evaluate realistically his accomplishments. Charles E. Chapman described him as "an enthusiastic, battling, almost quarrelsome, fearless, keen-witted, fervidly devout, unselfish, single-minded missionary." Much of the fame of Father Serra is more the result of the beatification by his colleague, Father Francisco Palou, who in a biography credited most of the early successes in the founding of California to him. However, even allowing for exaggeration, Father Serra remains an outstanding figure. Father Fermín Francisco de Lasúen may have been equal to Serra in ability but lacked a Boswell to establish his fame.

The first of the two small ships to sail from Baja California was the *San Carlos*, which left La Paz on January 9, 1769. Though the *San Antonio* did not sail until February 15 it was the first to reach San Diego, on April 11, taking 55 days to make the voyage. All aboard except the two friars were sick with scurvy; however, no lives were lost. It was not until April 29 that the *San Carlos* reached port having taken 110 days for the voyage. All on board were ill and twenty-four had died of scurvy.

Those who made the journey by land fared poorly as well. Captain Fernando de Rivera y Moncada, later a governor of California, led the first detachment. He was accompanied by Father Juan Crespi, destined to become one of the more notable clerics of the province. The entourage included twenty-five soldiers, three muleteers, and forty-two Christian Indians. Their march was made more difficult because of the lack of feed and water for the four hundred head of cattle that were brought with them. It was May 14 before Rivera arrived, taking fifty-one days to cover some 400 miles.

The second party was led by Portolá, accompanied by Serra, who made the journey with an ulcer in his leg. This group traveled from May 15 to July 1, taking forty-eight days to reach San Diego. The journey was easier than that of Rivera's party as they were not driving livestock. From the approximately three hundred men who left for California in the two land expeditions, approximately one half reached their destination. Most of the remainder died en route, though some of the missing doubtless deserted.

In spite of the fact that most of those at San Diego were ill when Portolá arrived, the governor made arrangements to leave at once on the remainder of the journey, the trek to Monterey. The *San Antonio* was sent to its home base at San Blas for needed supplies. The *San Carlos* was to sail northward and meet the land expedition at Monterey so as to help them with provisions. Portolá headed this group accompanied by Father Crespi. Fortunately, the latter kept a diary of the trip which has proven invaluable to historians. As they made their way northward, the party gave permanent names to many of the points they visited. They reached the site of Monterey on October 2 but failed to recognize it. Unfortunately, Vizcaíno had extravagantly described it as "a fine harbor sheltered from all winds," and the Portolá party did not recognize the area.

Early in November the expedition stumbled upon "a great arm of the seas, extending to the southeast further than the eye could reach." This discovery of San Francisco Bay was far more important than the failure to locate Monterey. Of more immediate significance was the failure to contact the supply vessel with needed provisions. Apparently the Spaniards had little talent for foraging for food, nor were they able to barter for supplies with the natives. In order to stave off starvation they were reduced to eating their mules.

Portolá and his band returned to San Diego on January 24 "smelling horribly of mules" and found conditions there very discouraging. Many at San Diego had died of scurvy, and constant trouble with the Indians had been experienced. The lack of provisions made matters so serious that Governor Portolá decided to send Rivera to Baja California for supplies so that the party would be able to hold on at San Diego. Legend has it that Portolá determined to abandon the expedition unless a relief ship arrived at a stated time. Father Serra and his fellow clerics protested vigorously but when they could not alter the governor's decision they prayed for a relief ship to appear. According to this legend, a sail appeared over the horizon at the last minute and thus saved the colonization of California! This arrival of the *San Antonio* on March 23 with provisions removed any immediate possibility of an abandonment of the colony. It also made it possible for Portolá to return north again in search of the elusive Monterey. This time they were successful in their quest for the port, and on June 3, 1770, the presidio and mission were formally inaugurated at Monterey. With this act, the work of Portolá was ended in Alta California and he returned to other duties in New Spain, leaving Pedro Fages in command. Thus, the settlement of California was accomplished, after having been projected for ·only 250 years!

CHAPTER IV

The Spanish Era

Although a promising beginning had been made in Spain's effort to settle California, the fledgling colony was to continue a precarious existence for many years. Few in numbers, the Spaniards had to be constantly on their guard against an Indian uprising, for if the "first Californians" had so desired their numbers alone would have enabled them to overwhelm the intruders. The abortive uprising in San Diego of 1769 was an ominous portent of potential disaster which the Spanish never forgot. Starvation was an even greater threat. As Professor Chapman suggests, "the Spaniards in Alta California occupied a position resembling that of the Robinson Crusoe of literature. They were set down in a land that was rich in potentialities, but lacking in the immediate requirements of civilized life."

When one considers the agricultural richness of the state at a later day, the obvious question is why didn't the Spaniards raise their own food so as to ward off starvation? They did not initially because few of them had any more than a rudimentary knowledge of farming; some had tilled the soil in Mexico but there was little understanding of this new agricultural environment. Some planted what little seed they had available, usually with discouraging results. It was not until 1773 that the mission at San Gabriel showed any agricultural promise at all. Bountiful crops awaited the missionaries who brought seeds, plants, and—more important—the technical know-how to make this potential Eden bloom.

Almost three centuries before, the Spaniards learned that in the settlement of the Caribbean they had to establish a base of operations on the island of Hispaniola where European flora and fauna could be raised. Only when a sufficient supply of food was available could the continental conquest begin. For example, efforts to conquer the Argentine failed initially but were later successful when the Spaniards returned to discover herds of cattle in the pampas, descendants of a small number left earlier. To make settlements secure in California domestic animals and food crops had to be developed to sustain the local population. The few animals which survived the hazardous trip were too precious to be killed for food initially and were retained for breeding purposes. By the beginning of 1774 there were only 616 head of livestock at the five missions. It was obvious that if the new colony was to survive and prosper, it would be necessary to bring immigrants and supplies in large quantities from Mexico. Most shipments had to come by water via a long and difficult sea voyage from San Blas. The supply ships were few and followed an erratic schedule.

The sea route was inadequate as a means of sending settlers and livestock to the new colony, and as a communications route it left much to be desired. The viceroy of New Spain, Antonio Mariá de Bucareli y Ursúa, evolved a general project to remedy this and other problems of the far-flung northern frontier of Spain's empire. A basic objective of his project was the establishment of a land connection between Sonora and California. A strong colony to be used as a base in the Gila-Colorado country was projected. In addition, Bucareli planned to send the surplus livestock of New Mexico overland to sustain the early settlers of California. The explorations in 1776 of Fathers Domínguez and Escalante from New Mexico were a part of this over-all program that ultimately led to the establishment of the old California trail from the Rio Grande to the Pacific coast.

The opening of an overland trail from northern Mexico to Alta California was primarily due to the work of Father Francisco Garcés, a young Franciscan priest of San Xavier del Bac, and Juan Bautista de Anza. The former, stirred by missionary zeal, traveled alone and in company in search of souls and a better understanding of the geographical reality which lay obscured in the early 1770s. Father Garcés made several trips into the watershed of the lower Colorado alone and acted as a guide for the Bucareli-inspired expedition led by de Anza in 1774. Setting out from Tubac with a government-sponsored and -financed party, de Anza made his way to the Colorado crossing near Yuma in 1774. There he laid the basis for the future security of the trail by establishing friendly relations with the Yumans and their reigning chief, Salvador Palma. A generous gift giving convinced the Yumans that their relationship with these strangers from the south was to be one of considerable advantage.

With the co-operation of the natives assured, de Anza made a trip via the difficult desert crossing of Southern California and was able to return and make a second trip with 240 persons. Unfortunately, the trail blazed by de Anza and Garcés was open only a few years. In Mexico City a chain of blunders and fortuitous chances spelled disaster for the project that had begun so auspiciously.

The officer in charge of defense of the northern frontier was Teodoro de Croix, who believed that the best interests of Spain lay in eliminating the Apache Indians on the northern frontier, especially in Texas, New Mexico, and Chihuahua. To accomplish this with the limited resources available, it was necessary to neglect the neophyte colony in Alta California. The promised Yuman mission was delayed until 1780 and undoubtedly disappointed the Indians, who expected a more prompt coming of the missionaries and the gift giving their arrival entailed. The Indians were generally disappointed with the scarcity of gifts which accompanied the formal ceremony.

Disappointment was laced with anger as they saw and sensed Spanish interest in their land, corn, and women. Almost before the more sensitive of the Spanish understood their predicament, the Yumans fell on them and killed more than thirty soldiers and four priests of the party. The incident which triggered the clash in 1781 is unknown, for no formal investigation produced a complete examination of witnesses and evidence. The few survivors fled across the Southern California desert to sanctuary at Mission San Gabriel. There they reflected on the incident which brought martyrdom to Father Garcés and the four Franciscans and prosaic death to so many. Subsequently a number of the captives of the Yuman massacre were ransomed.

The closing of this land communication and supply route had lasting significance for the development of California. From this time on, practically no new settlers came to the area, nor did much in the way of supplies and livestock arrive. Consequently, Alta California developed slowly and never became a flourishing part of New Spain. In fact, during the Spanish period the area settled was only a small strip of land hugging the coastline and by 1821, when Spain's tenure ended, the Spanish population was small, just a little more than three thousand. If Spain had been able to populate this northernmost outpost of the Hispanic world, it would have been much more difficult for the United States to seize control.

SPANISH INSTITUTIONS

Spain used in the colonization of California the mission, the presidio, and the pueblo, all of which evolved in other parts of the Spanish world. Of these institutions, the mission was easily the most important. In all, twenty-one were established in Alta California stretching from San Diego in the south to Sonoma in the north. Of these, nine were founded by Father Serra, the others by his successors. Approximately thirty miles apart, they were scattered along El Camino Real. The King's Highway was usually little more than a bridle path and in many places followed the ocean beaches and was all but impassable in rainy weather.

The basic prerequisites for a mission site were good soil, a convenient water supply, and Indians. Usually, a location was found in a river valley where there was a water supply. Missionaries used such good judgment in their selection of locations that they controlled the most valuable lands in the province early in the colonial period. The jealousy resulting from this would ultimately be a factor in their undoing. Partially because of their location, partially because of an ample labor supply, and partially because of the able leadership provided by the Franciscan friars, the missions flourished far more than did the secular institutions. Within a few years of the initial founding of Spanish settlements in California, the missions were producing an abundance of crops and their livestock soon became so plentiful that a surplus was available to others.

In actuality, the Franciscans conquered and settled California. The mission as an institution had been effectively used elsewhere to expand the frontiers of Spain in the New World but nowhere with more success than in California. Given the lack of Spanish settlers, and without the ability of the Franciscans to exploit Indian labor, it is

A MISSION CHRONOLOGY

The missions and the dates of their founding were:

July 16, 1769   San Diego de Alcalá
June 3, 1770   San Carlos Borromeo de Monterey
July 14, 1771   San Antonio de Padua
Sept. 8, 1771   San Gabriel Arcángel
Sept. 1, 1772   San Luis Obispo de Tolosa
Oct. 9, 1776   San Francisco de Asís (or Dolores)
Nov. 1, 1776   San Juan Capistrano
Jan. 12, 1777   Santa Clara
Mar. 31, 1782   San Buenaventura
Dec. 4, 1786   Santa Barbara
Dec. 8, 1787   La Purísima Concepción
Aug. 28, 1791   Santa Cruz
Oct. 9, 1791   Nuestra Señora de la Soledad
June 11, 1797   San Jose
June 24, 1797   San Juan Bautista
July 25, 1797   San Miguel Arcángel
Sept. 8, 1797   San Fernando Rey de España
June 13, 1798   San Luis Rey de Francia
Sept. 17, 1804   Santa Ynéz
Dec. 14, 1817   San Rafael Arcángel
July 4, 1823   San Francisco Solano

highly questionable whether the Spanish outpost could have remained in California.

The missions and their tireless administrators the Franciscans were primarily responsible for the establishment of an enduring Spanish settlement in Alta California. Their contributions were indispensable in this land where Spanish settlers were few and the support of the government limited. The missionaries exploited Indian labor, learned the secrets of climate and soil to produce food and herds, and most importantly (to them) brought the true gospel to the "benighted Indian."

Not only did the missions supply much of the foodstuff for the Spanish population, but they also sparked a desire to open up the interior of California. Numerous explorations were made in an effort to find new mission sites, to capture runaway neophytes (new converts or Christian mission Indians) from the missions, and to impress upon non-mission Indians the dangers of raiding livestock from the settled areas or harboring runaways. Typical of these expeditions was that of Father Garcés, who played such a significant role in the opening of the overland route via the Colorado River with de Anza. In 1776 he traveled extensively through the interior of California to learn something of the country between California and Moqui, in present-day northern Arizona. The wandering friar first went up the Colorado region to the Mohave villages where he set out westward to San Gabriel. From this point he proceeded north into the Kern River country where he then turned eastward to the Moqui villages. No recommendations for mission sites resulted from his activities nor did an overland route to New Mexico result immediately.

Between 1805 and 1821 hardly a year went by without an exploratory foray being made by the Franciscans, usually accompanied by a small contingent of soldiers. They moved out from the missions established on the coast, ultimately traversing most of the great valley of California. They also made their way along the coast north of San Francisco into the area claimed by the Russians. Many runaway Indians and horses were recovered, non-mission Indians captured, and numerous clashes with the Indians occurred. Many suitable sites for mission installations were found. More often than not limited resources precluded the implementation of a recommendation. One of the more favorable sites was that near Lake Tulare around which numerous Indian tribes were found. Conditions here were almost ideal but the potential was never exploited. Although these expeditions had limited accomplishments, Spain's knowledge of the region was greatly expanded.

Of less importance than the missions were the presidios, or military fortresses, which were intended to protect the missions from Indians or foreign intruders. The English captain Vancouver described the presidio at San Francisco in 1792 as "a square area, whose sides were about 200 yards in length, enclosed by a mud wall, . . . above this wall the thatched roofs of the low small houses just made their appearance . . . the only entry into it, is by a large gateway." Some of the walls were 2 feet thick and 12 feet high enclosing an area of approximately 750 square feet. At the corners were towers pierced with loopholes for defensive purposes. In addition, inside the walls were firing platforms built about 8 feet from the ground thereby giving the soldiers some protection when under attack but which also served as roofs over barracks, stables, shops, and storerooms. Some of the presidios were well constructed and were quite formidable when first built. But according to most descriptions by foreign travelers, they were poorly maintained and with the passage of years fell into decay. Had they been subject to attack, according to Vancouver, they could easily have been taken by an invader.

The weakness of the presidios reflected Spain's lack of interest in and thus her lack of attention to California. The military received limited supplies from New Spain, but these virtually stopped after 1810 because of the unsettled political conditions in Mexico following the Hidalgo uprising. As a general rule, the soldiers were poorly equipped, poorly paid, poorly trained, and so few in numbers that the Indians could have been a real menace if they had been so inclined. There were only 372 soldiers in the entire province in 1812. On one occasion, the fort at San Francisco, the most important in the province, had to borrow gunpowder from the visiting Russians in order to return a proper salute. By necessity, most of the soldiers were compelled to supplement their meager pay by raising crops or plying a trade. Many of the troops were of a very low moral caliber. If one is to believe the Franciscan fathers, who were not totally unbiased in their judgments, the soldiers spent most of their time in a not-too-gentle wooing of the Indian women. The image of the leather-jacketed soldier which emerges from clerical accounts is that of a military figure who preferred seduction and debauchery to soldiering.

California was divided into four military districts with presidios in each. One was established at San Diego on July 16, 1769; at Monterey on June 3, 1770; at San Francisco on September 17, 1776; and at Santa Barbara on April 21, 1782. Monterey, as the center of provisional government, was ostensibly the most important. However, Fort San Joaquin, adjacent to the entrance to San Francisco Bay, was actually most significant. The presidios intimidated the Indians and curtailed uprisings. More importantly, however small and weak the Spanish military establishment, its presence helped to bar foreign intruders. An assault on these outlying presidios of the Spanish borderlands would demand a response which, however uncertain, could not be disregarded. Besides "protection" the presidios provided a nucleus around which towns slowly developed. The soldiers had small houses or barracks within the walls of the presidio initially but later were forced to build outside. Retired soldiers, traders, and others also built their homes near the military fortresses for the protection and trading opportunities they offered. Thus, the presidios became the economic, political, and social centers of the infant colony.

A striking element of Spanish civilization was its urban character. When the Spaniards came to the New World, they brought with them their urban proclivities and founded cities almost as soon as they landed. The Spaniards of the eighteenth century, like the Americans of the twentieth century, preferred the city to farm and field. Consequently, the pueblo or town figured prominently in Spanish plans for the settlement of California. And in providing for towns, the Spaniards engaged in city public planning long before the concept became popular. The towns of California were planned with the expectation that their residents would raise enough food so that dependence upon supplies from San Blas could be reduced and ultimately eliminated. More importantly, the towns were intended to provide militias which would help in the defense of this outpost of empire. Such a citizen army could be provided at a substantially lower cost than a like number of regular troops and thus help the depleted royal treasury.

As was true in the rest of Spanish America, the pueblos of California were planned down to the most minute detail in accordance with the Laws of the Indies. Before a town was located, it was first determined whether there was an adequate water supply available, wood for both building purposes and fires, sufficient arable land for the populace, and sufficient pasture as well as soil for the construction of adobe structures. Once the site had been selected, the location of the plaza was determined, as this was to be the center of the town. Around the plaza were grouped the church, the town hall, and other important buildings. Once land had been set aside for these purposes, amounts were allocated for residences, farm land, and pasturage.

To induce colonists to come to the province, the Spanish authorities provided many incentives. Each settler received a house lot, a parcel for farming, and use of the common pastureland. A loan of livestock and some implements was also initially made. Settlers received a small subsidy amounting to about $10 a month for the first two years and $5 a month for the next three years. Finally, settlers were to be exempt from taxes during this first five-year period.

For these considerations, the settlers were required to sell their surplus produce to the presidio and to serve in the town militia. They were also obligated to perform certain community tasks such as digging irrigation canals, erecting roads and public buildings, and such other work of a similar nature that might be deemed necessary. After a five-year period, they could obtain permanent title to their land. A town registry recorded such allocation and served proof of title. In theory, prospective settlers were carefully screened to ensure that only the finest came to California. Viceroy de Croix described the ideal colonist as an experienced farmer who was "without any known defect or vice which would make him undesirable in a town to be established in the midst of the heathen." Hopefully the Indians would emulate these model Spanish citizens, thus furthering the task of bestowing the blessings of Spanish civilization upon the Indians.

Unfortunately, these objectives were not realized and California towns frequently attracted the dregs of humanity from New Spain. The low caliber of settlers was partially caused by California's unattractive image. As a potential home to most Mexicans the province "was like mentioning the end of the world." To supply even the few settlers that did make their way northward, the jails of Sinaloa and Sonora had to be emptied. While these recruits were sometimes deep-dyed criminals, they included responsible citizens who were victims of the harsh and unreasoning penal code of the day.

The province became a kind of Australian penal colony where questionable individuals of both sexes made their way. Needless to say, such people did not always make the best citizens and second-generation Californians greeted their arrival with overt hostility. Dedicated and able colonists were frequently treated in the same manner as outright felons, thereby further discouraging settlement from Mexico.

In spite of generous government support and elaborate planning, the pueblos of Alta California never really prospered. A combination of reasons was responsible. In the first place, California was intended to serve as a buffer to repel possible intruders. But both the will and the monetary reources which were essential were lacking. The settlers who came were also a problem, for they were poorly trained for frontiering and more inclined to find ways to exploit the Indians than labor themselves. Additional problems in the form of a hidebound and restrictive mercantilistic system and the weight of a monumental bureaucracy restrained the growth of the province. As serious as any other factor was the lack of a market for the agricultural produce of the colony. Restrictions kept foreign trade and commerce to a minimum. When the potential market consisted of sales to the local population at fixed prices, there was little reason for men to extend themselves in farming and ranching. The consequences of all these circumstances were mirrored in the lethargic economic growth of Alta California during the Spanish period.

The first pueblo was founded at San Jose on November 29, 1777. Fourteen families totaling sixty-six persons formed the nucleus of this settlement. On September 4, 1781, while Washington's army besieged Cornwallis a continent away, Nuestra Señora la Reina de los Angeles de Porciúncula was established. For obvious reasons, the settlement of twelve families was soon known as Los Angeles. In the founding party of forty-six persons there were represented four continents, for the group included Spanish, Negro, Indian, and Asian backgrounds. Los Angeles was truly a cosmopolitan city in its beginning.

One of the more interesting of the pueblos was Villa de Branciforte, established near the present site of Santa Cruz in 1797. It was founded shortly after a confrontation in the Pacific Northwest at Nootka Sound demonstrated the relative weakness of Spain and the growing strength of England in the Pacific. Viceroy Branciforte believed that a settlement of retired soldiers would provide an additional safeguard against English encroachments. Most of the prospective inhabitants would consist of men who had retired from the Spanish forces in the Philippines and come to the province via the Manila galleon. The project would result in a general strengthening of the Spanish military establishment in Alta California.

Unfortunately for the planners, a number of problems beset the pueblo. The opposition of the Franciscans of the mission of Santa Cruz was vigorous and vehement. They maintained (and possibly with good reason) that the settlers were not only intruders but also diseased and debauched colonists who had little experience with farming and little inclination to learn. Far from contributing to the well-being of the vicinity, they would corrupt and debauch the Indians. That there were reasons for the missionaries to complain is to be seen in several events which involved some of the colonists of Branciforte. An assassination attempt on the commander of the presidio of Monterey as well as the governor of California gave graphic evidence of the violent and disorderly proclivities of some of the new settlers. Their general inability to survive and prosper was also evidence of their unsuitability to frontiering in Alta California.

Private ranchos were not originally intended as an institution to settle California. Scattered ranchos were hard to defend and control, and the authorities discouraged them. However, forces were at work which resulted in the emergence of a number of ranchos in spite of official disapproval. The granting of the use of private tracts of land as remuneration for services, or in some instances for money and supplies furnished to the government, though limited, was significant. Officials who had little gold and much land utilized the latter to fulfill obligations. Some grants were also made for political reasons or personal friendship and sometimes a combination of such things was involved. The result was some twenty-five ranchos and the creation of a small landed elite. It was a pattern familiar in colonial Spanish America. Authority for making such grants originated in a regulation sent from the viceroy to Governor Rivera in 1773. Two provisional grants were made by Governor Fages in 1784 and were the first to become large permanent grants.

On these ranchos a small but self-sufficient community developed. While gardens and orchards produced food, it was livestock that furnished the economic base. However, it was not until the advent of the hide and tallow trade that private ranchos became significantly involved in commerce. These early grants formed the basis of the extensive rancho system that dominated society during the Mexican period. It was the casual manner in which grants were made and tracts measured and located which produced monumental problems for the Anglo-American legal system after 1848.

SPANISH ADMINISTRATION

Under Spain, Alta California had limited importance. Removed from the centers of population, and contributing little to the empire, it was all but ignored. Only when foreign intruders threatened was the administration at Mexico City concerned. Sparsely populated, it had perhaps 3270 non-Indian residents in 1820, just before the rule of Spain ended. After the beginning of the wars for independence in Mexico in 1810, what little support that had earlier been forthcoming came virtually to an end.

In this area so remote and so insignificant within the framework of the Spanish empire, few men of stature were appointed. Proven administrators were sent to more important positions; California generally received those of lesser reputation. Occasionally, a governor emerged as a man of talent, but he was the exception rather than the rule. Government in California tended to be absolutist, as much authority was given to the governor. The framework of government was based upon the Echeveste *reglamento* of 1773, the instructions to Governor Rivera of the same year, those to Governor de Neve in 1776, and the de Neve *reglamento* of 1779. The governor was a veritable dictator, being the military and political chief of state and exercising executive, legislative, and judicial functions. Actually, there was little need for much political administration with so few people scattered throughout the province. About the only political conflict of note was a chronic dispute between the missionaries and the governor as to who had the supreme authority. Such a conflict was common in most of the Spanish colonies.

The basic official on the local level was the alcalde. The pueblos of San Jose, Los Angeles, and the Villa de Branciforte were granted alcaldes as their civil magistrates. Usually elected by his own community, the authority of this official was not confined to the immediate boundaries of a small pueblo but more often extended far

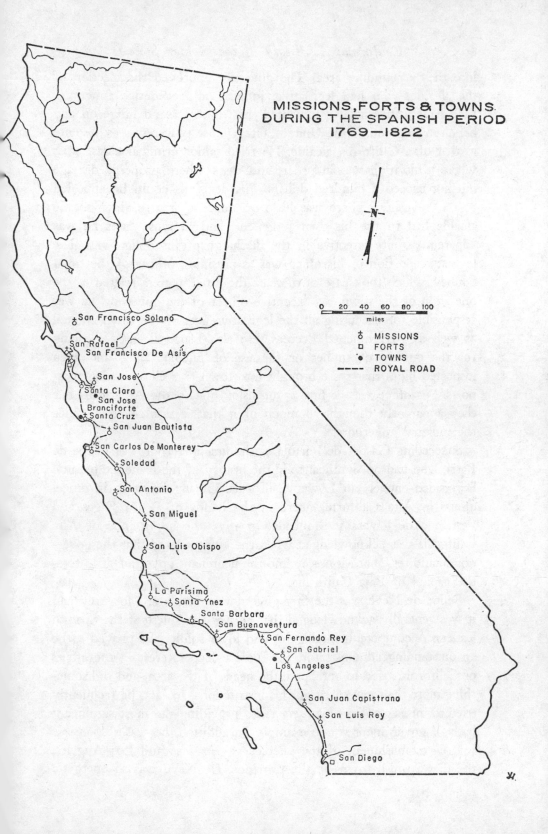

MISSIONS, FORTS & TOWNS.
DURING THE SPANISH PERIOD
1769—1822

N

0 20 40 60 80 100
miles

⚲ MISSIONS
☐ FORTS
● TOWNS
----- ROYAL ROAD

San Francisco Solano
San Rafael
San Francisco De Asis
San Jose
Santa Clara
San Jose
Branciforte
Santa Cruz
San Juan Bautista
San Carlos De Monterey
Soledad
San Antonio
San Miguel
San Luis Obispo
La Purisima
Santa Ynez
Santa Barbara
San Buenaventura
San Fernando Rey
San Gabriel
Los Angeles
San Juan Capistrano
San Luis Rey
San Diego

into the surrounding area. The governor approved the election of the alcalde, who had legislative, judicial, and executive functions. One American official commented that there was no judge on any bench in England or the United States whose power was as absolute as that of a California alcalde. He tried minor criminal cases, cases where arbitration was in order, and cases where property damage did not exceed a hundred dollars. His decisions could be appealed to the governor. There was little organized system of law, so the alcalde had to use his own judgment, and in most cases he was apparently quite effective in the discharge of his obligations. The legislative portion of his office was as presiding officer of the town council, which took care of most of the usual matters related to the operation of the town. As executive officer of the governor, he was responsible for executing all the legislative acts of the town council as well as governmental decrees. He also issued licenses allowing for the cutting of timber or the use of pueblo lands, and even inspected hides that were brought into town as well as issuing passports. His office was at first a confusing one to the Americans but they apparently thought so much of it that it was retained under the military governors.

Succeeding Gaspar de Portolá as the first governor was Felipe de Barri, who had no significance in the history of the province because he resided entirely in Lower California. During his term in office, affairs in Alta California were in the hands of Pedro Fages and Fernando de Rivera y Moncada. In 1775 the importance of Alta California was acknowledged when the king ordered that the governor should reside at Monterey and the lieutenant governor at Loreto, the capital of Baja California.

Felipe de Neve was the first governor to reside at Monterey and it was generally acknowledged that he was the ablest of the Spanish leaders. A competent, intelligent, and loyal soldier, he proved to be an outstanding administrator. He took a deep interest in the affairs of California, tried to anticipate the needs of the area, and did something more than just carry out his instructions. In fact, he frequently tried to initiate policy; his *reglamento* providing the most significant basis of government is one example. In addition, he was responsible for the establishment of the pueblos at San Jose and Los Angeles, the first Spanish towns in the province. De Neve was so energetic

in defending the prerogatives of the civilian branch of the government from what he considered encroachments by the missionary
leaders that he incurred the wrath of the good friars, and as a result, has been labeled by some clerical historians as "a meddlesome
theorist."

GOVERNOR DON FELIPE DE NEVE

*Felipe de Neve arrived in Mexico in 1764 or 1765. A military engineer,
he was engaged in such duties until appointed by Viceroy Bucareli,
acting governor of the Californians in December 1774. He came to
Monterey in 1776 instructed by Bucareli to examine the prospects of
establishing pueblos in Alta California. De Neve came, traveled, considered, and wrote reports which commended a number of sites including
that which later became Los Angeles.*

*In the years which followed de Neve spurred developmental work in
the province, looking toward self-sufficiency, reported to his superiors,
called upon them for aid, and published on June 1, 1779, the reglamento
which was to be the governing instrument during the remaining period
of Spanish rule. He also became embroiled in a controversy with Father
Junípero Serra which distracted both men from their more serious work.
He pursued his ambitious plans for the extension of the missions, the
reinforcement of the presidios, and the establishment of pueblos. His
contributions were considerable—when everything is considered he was
the most able of the Spanish governors of California.*

*While on an expedition to revenge the Yuma massacre of 1781 he was
informed of his promotion to Inspector General of the Frontier Provinces. Only two years later, after further decorations and promotion to
Brigadier General and Commander General of the Frontier Provinces, he
died.*

Unfortunately for California, de Neve was elevated to a more
important position in New Spain in 1782 and was succeeded by Pedro
Fages. However, in many respects the latter was a worthy successor
to Felipe de Neve. He was responsible for the granting of large
tracts of land which became the basis of the late rancho system. He
continued the disputes of de Neve with the missionaries over questions
of policy and jurisdiction. His administration was seriously marred by
the conduct of his wife, Doña Eulalia, a tempestuous Catalan lady of

rank and social standing. She was at first reluctant to come into the northern wilderness but when she reached her destination, she was appalled by life in Monterey and longed for the social world of Mexico City. When she was unable to convince her husband to give up his post, the good lady barred him from her boudoir and then when this did not humble him, tried to obtain a divorce. After some six years of domestic turmoil, Pedro Fages asked to be and was relieved of his post on the grounds of ill health. In his ten years as governor, Fages had introduced a number of fruit trees, shrubs, and grapevines which were a lasting contribution to the province.

After brief tenure by two insignificant individuals, Diego de Borica became governor in 1794, and he deserves to be remembered as the kind of enthusiastic booster of California who, after only a brief residence, could write to friends that if they wanted to "live much and without care, come to Monterey." He described the province in words that would warm the heart of any modern promoter: "this is a great country; climate healthful, between cold and temperate; good bread, excellent meat, tolerable fish; . . . plenty to eat, but the most astounding is the general fecundity . . . The climate is so good and all are getting to look like Englishmen [in other words, fair in features]. This is the most peaceful and quiet country in the world. One lives better here than in the most cultured court in Europe."

José Joaquín de Arrillaga, who served a brief tenure as acting governor in 1794, became governor in 1800 and remained in the office until his death in 1814. His administration was marked by a reconciliation between the civil and religious authorities. This new and unique state of affairs was created by Arrillaga's realization that the province would have to depend upon the missions for much of its food supply, at least until the laity could be convinced to spend more time in the fields. He forced the missions to turn over their surplus production in return for drafts on the Spanish government. The missionaries objected strenuously, but there was little they could do about it. By the end of the Spanish regime, they held over $400,000 in promissory notes that were worthless. After 1810, the series of disorders in New Spain isolated California to a point where it no longer received supplies from San Blas. In addition, Arrillaga's term was marked by the continued intrusion of fur traders, whalers, the seekers of hides and tallow, as well as foreign merchants. He was succeeded by Pablo Vincente de Solá, one of the weakest of the governors. This martinet of limited ability was to have the unpleasant task of presiding at the liquidation of Spain's rule in California in 1821.

ECONOMIC ACTIVITIES

In this land isolated from the outside world, it was inevitable that the primary economic activity would be based upon self-sufficient agriculture. The mission became the principal organization and leading economic institution. The economic success and achievement of the missions were the result of several factors. The effective utilization of Indian labor, the development and exploitation of fertile well-watered land, the use of seed and stock which readily adapted itself to the California scene: all contributed. Under Franciscan direction the combination produced flourishing autarchic agricultural communities.

The prosperity of the missions was eyed covetously by the laity. Their tremendous herds of horses, cattle, sheep, and swine were drawn upon to stock many private ranchos. The crops consisted of maize, wheat, barley, beans, and grapes for wine, all of which flourished in spite of the primitive nature of agriculture as practiced in early California. Rudimentary farming tools were the rule. The plow was made of two pieces, one formed out of a crooked branch of timber cut from a tree, fastened to a pole, and simply used to make a rut in the ground. A harrow was unknown but sometimes a half of a log was used to level the fields. Fortunately, the richness of the soil when irrigated ensured bountiful crops, in spite of such practices. Most produce was transported by oxcarts, or carretas, clumsily constructed with bottom frames on which were raised a few bars standing upright and connected at the top with other bars. Their wheels were hand-hewn out of a large tree. In the absence of grease they made a frightful noise. Sometimes mule trains were used to haul goods for short distances.

The primary item of diet was beef, as one might expect. Coffee or chocolate was drunk when they could be obtained; but since trade and commerce were limited by stifling official restrictions, such items were scarce. As early as the 1780s trade in otter skins, much in demand in China, began. Lumber from the redwood forests, cut by Indians under the supervision of the clerics, was also shipped to ports as far away as Peru. By 1800 California had a surplus of crops and livestock, but it lacked consumer goods. The colony needed cloth, articles of furniture, agricultural tools, candles, as well as luxury items. The weakness of the defenses of California, the disruption in the affairs of the Spanish empire, and the need for these products led to an expanding trade at the beginning of the nineteenth century. English and Yankee merchantmen made their way to this out-of-the-way land to exchange diversified merchandise for sea otter skins, hides and tallow, lumber, wheat, or such other products as the Californians might have.

THE SOCIAL SETTING

With an abundance of food and with few wants the Californians under Spanish rule lived in what many have described as an Arcadian period. As Bancroft puts it: "life here was almost like a returning of the world to its infancy; a returning of mankind to artless, thoughtless boyhood, when science held little sway, and men led simple lives, . . . it is almost as in the early days of Greece, when religion was but a love of the beautiful." The Anglos who visited the Hispanic world have always been impressed at the ability of the Spanish to enjoy life. With little thought for the future they were not afraid to take time to live in the here and now. To them, pleasure came before business. Fiestas were numerous and there was a wide variety of amusements. The people loved to dance, and had a dance for every occasion. The violin and the guitar furnished most of the music for such occasions, but the clarinet and harp were also played. There were some dramatic presentations but much recreation was associated with horseback riding. All learned to ride at an early age and a man's home was the back of a horse. In their horsemanship, the Californians rivaled the fabled Gauchos of the Argentine. Afoot, the Californian was an equal; on horseback he was superior to most adversaries. Naturally, horse racing was one of the leading forms of amusement, along with cockfighting and bear and bull fighting.

There was no question that there was a great deal of happiness in Spanish California, but to describe this land as "more free from care, anxiety, and trouble than any others in the world" is more than just an exaggeration. It ignores the fact that this was not the happiest existence for mission Indians, who frequently sought to flee from their bondage. Nor was it existence in a paradise for most of the lower classes. The myth of Arcadian California of the Spanish era is plausible only by overlooking some of the harsh reality of life at that time. Beginning with Helen Hunt Jackson in the 1880s, a large number of Anglo writers, disenchanted with their own society, overlooked flaws and bestowed virtues upon Spanish California in defiance of the facts. In twentieth-century America about all that remains of the picturesque Spanish heritage is the place names, which few Anglos can properly pronounce. Spain's brief tenure in California ended with the independence of Mexico in 1821 and left little permanent imprint on the land.

CHAPTER V

The Mexican Era

Charles E. Chapman flatly declared, "Strictly speaking, there was no Mexican period of California history." In some respects this is a valid observation which properly focuses attention on the lack of change which accompanied the change of flags. The basic Hispanic institutions remained; Spanish sovereignty ended in Alta California in 1821, but the sovereignty of Spanish institutions remained. The province, always removed and isolated from the center of the stage, was little influenced by the revolutionary turmoil which followed Father Hidalgo's Grito de Dolores in 1810. The supply ships from San Blas no longer arrived, communication with Mexico City was cut off, but in general life went on as before in this now self-sufficient colony. The most significant change was the breach in mercantilistic barriers through which poured foreign traders. Ships bulging with diversified merchandise brought ideas, practices, and things which were to have a profound influence on the society. And they were also to bring this attractive land which fronted on the Pacific to the attention of others who prided themselves on their ability to make the most of nature's bounty.

The Mexican revolt against Spanish rule was led by reactionary forces who feared the liberal regime which had seized control in Spain in 1820. When news of the successful Mexican revolt reached them in 1822, the officials and people of California swore formal allegiance to the new government. However, the ties remained tenuous, the Californians accepting the enduring political instability of Mexico which was reflected in frequent governmental changes. The news which lay behind these changes seldom arrived before Californians were faced with a *fait accompli*. Acceptance then was partially based on ignorance. Mexico was kept so busy with her own problems that she slighted the administration of the province.

Neglect was manifested in several ways: governors of modest talents who had little comprehension of the problems of California were appointed; and inadequate support was given the poorly trained and inept army. The poorly and infrequently paid military forces were pushed by necessity toward brigandage. The character of Mexican administration bred contempt for it among the California populace. Resistance to Mexican authority grew out of such contempt, but it was also spawned by the quarrel between those who favored a strong central government in Mexico City and those who championed a political system of autonomous states. This conflict between the centralists and the federalists absorbed Mexico's energies and produced a state of near anarchy for much of the nineteenth century.

In addition to California's resistance to administration from Mexico City, the province was wracked by a bitter struggle between north and south, a conflict between Church and state, and numerous personality clashes: all combined to produce disorder. Despite the political instability, the province went through extensive economic changes, expansion from the coastal area inland, and the development of a substantial export trade.

THE AGE OF CAUDILLOS

In some respects the struggle for power in California was similar to that which went on in the rest of Latin America immediately following independence from Spain. There were basic differences in political ideology, but often the root of the conflict remained the desire for personal prestige. Unlike conflicts elsewhere in Spanish America, those in California were largely bloodless. Leaders indulged in bombastic pronouncements, dire threats, and much pageantry and maneuvering on the field of battle, but seldom was anyone seriously injured, let alone killed. Some have suggested that the reason for the mildness of military action stemmed from the cowardliness of the native Californians. The manner in which they stood up to the United States army of General Kearny at the Battle of San Pascual disproves such a thesis, however. Others have contended that the easy life in California created a mild disposition among the soldiers so that they really were not ready to fight with the vigor found elsewhere. Perhaps the most logical explanation for the relative lack of bloodshed was the fact that much of the Spanish population was related either by blood or marital ties and few desired to shed the blood of their family.

Pablo Vicente de Solá (1815–22) was the last of the Spanish governors. A representative of the new Mexican government supervised an election by the governor's commissioners which saw Luis Argüello, a California-born Spaniard, chosen as the new governor. His administration was marked by the establishment of San Francisco Solano, the last of the missions. In addition, he had to face Indian revolts at the missions of Santa Ynez, Santa Barbara, and Purísima Concepción in 1824. Such revolts reflected the growing unrest among the mission Indians, but only the uprising at Purísima was of major significance. In the initial outbreak, seven Indians and four white men were killed and the Indians remained in control of the mission for nearly a month. It took an army of one hundred men to subdue the Indians.

Don José María Echeandía arrived from Mexico as the new governor in 1825. He has been described as a "tall, thin, juiceless man, possessing but little force of character or enterprise, and much concerned about the effect of the California climate upon his none too robust health." A lieutenant colonel of engineers, an engineer by vocation, he was said to be somewhat inflexible. The antagonism against him resulted in a series of revolts that spread throughout Mexican California. Echeandía was probably little worse than other governors, but his pronounced hostility toward the missions and his steps toward secularization earned him the undying enmity of the mission fathers. He had the usual difficulties of assembling sufficient resources to support the government. And he had problems with the missionaries as he continued the practice of obtaining supplies from the missions in exchange for government drafts of dubious value.

Among Echeandía's more constructive measures was a concerted effort to improve education, by establishing the first school for the Spanish in the province. He used mission funds for the purpose, a rather unique reversal of Church aid to public schools. His difficulties began when he decided that the sunshine of San Diego was more conducive to health than the fog-enshrouded, cool, windy

THE MEXICAN GOVERNORS OF CALIFORNIA

Pablo Vicente de Solá, holdover from the Spanish administration to
November 1822

Luis Argüello, governor ad interim from
November 22, 1822 to November 1825

José María Echeandía, governor from
November 22, 1825 to January 1831

Manuel Victoria, governor from
January 1831 to December 9, 1831

José María Echeandía, governor from
December 1831 to January 1833

(Pío Pico has been inaccurately regarded by some writers as governor
during this period.)

José Figueroa, governor from
January 1833 to September 29, 1835

José Castro, acting governor from
September 1835 to January 1836

Nicolás Gutierrez, acting governor from
January 1836 to May 3, 1836

Mariano Chico, governor from
May 3, 1836 to July 31, 1836

Nicolás Gutierrez, acting governor from
September 6, 1836 to November 4, 1836

Juan Bautista Alvarado, revolutionary governor from
December 1836 to July 1837
constitutional governor from
July 1837 to December 31, 1842

Manuel Micheltorena, governor from
December 31, 1842 to February 22, 1845

Pío Pico, governor from
February 22, 1845 to July 1846

area of Monterey. There is a suspicion that his interest in San Diego was induced more by the charms of one Señorita Josefa Carrillo than the sunshine of the area. Regardless of his motives, the citizens of Monterey looked askance at this arbitrary decision to move the capital south. This was one of the first evidences of the enduring antagonism between northern and southern California which remains to this day.

In 1828 a failure to pay the army led to a short-lived mutiny. However, the following year a more serious revolt broke out under the leadership of Joaquín Solís, who was both a former soldier and a former convict. Solis received funds from the alien traders in Monterey and also had the backing of the mission fathers who were most unhappy over the governor's efforts to effect secularization. The Solís forces from the north met the governor's army at Santa Barbara, where a "battle" of several days' duration ensued. The only casualty was a horse who strayed into the path of a cannon ball. Echeandía pursued the disintegrating rebel force back to Monterey, captured them, and sent Solís and the other ringleaders into exile in Mexico. The most important aspect of Echeandía's administration was the development of plans to secularize the missions. Although the governor has frequently been described by critics as an enthusiastic advocate of secularization, there is considerable evidence to indicate that he was responsive to pressures from the Mexican government and the non-religious community of California. Before retiring from office in 1831, Echeandía discovered that the climate of Monterey was not as rigorous as he had originally assumed and returned to spend a year there.

His successor, Lieutenant Colonel Manuel Victoria, was a military disciplinarian who was aghast at the relaxed way of life in California and determined to whip the predominantly ex-convict army into a proper fighting force. Just as Echeandía incurred opposition when he made San Diego his seat of government so Victoria's act of taking up residence at Monterey made him unpopular in the south. Victoria was a champion of military authority who, in determination to bring "law and order," instituted the death penalty for even minor offenses. The easygoing Californians were shocked at such extreme measures, and they were antagonized by Victoria's comments about their laziness and their unwillingness to engage in manufacturing. Of most importance, however, was the fact that he suspended Echeandía's decree of secularization. That step made him extremely unpopular with those who coveted mission lands and ultimately he had only the support of the Franciscan fathers and the foreign traders. The latter applauded his emphasis on "law and order."

Revolt broke out in the south in 1831 under the leadership of former governor Echeandía, who was currently living in San Diego.

Governor Victoria, with some thirty soldiers, met the insurgents at the "battle" of Cahuenga Pass on December 4, 1831. Somehow or other, the usual script was violated and blood was shed. Two men were killed, one of them Romualdo Pacheco, whose infant son and namesake's political career led to the governor's chair at Sacramento at a later date. More importantly, Governor Victoria was wounded and took refuge in the mission at San Gabriel. Disenchanted with governing California, he soon resigned to return to Mexico. A political compromise between north and south was evolved with Echeandía ruling in the south and one Augustín Zamorano, the first important printer, wielding the scepter of authority in the north.

The most competent of the Mexican governors was General José Figueroa, who took office in January 1833. Formerly a governor of Sonora and Sinaloa, he had also a distinguished service record in the campaigns against the fierce Yaqui Indians. His first act was to grant amnesty for all of those engaged in earlier rebellions. He sent an exploration party under Mariano Guadalupe Vallejo to Bodega Bay and Fort Ross. The move indicated the continued concern of Mexican officialdom over the Russian presence. As a result of Figueroa's encouragement several towns were established, including Petaluma and Santa Rosa. Such measures strengthened Mexican control of the area, and advanced the frontier of Mexican California.

Governor Figueroa's administration was marred by the chaos resulting from the secularization of the missions. He came to California with orders from the Mexican government to proceed with this program. Figueroa pursued secularization at a measured tempo, but events were making policy. For years the pressure to secularize the missions of California had been growing. General anti-clericalism gave thrust to the movement, but there were other circumstances involved. The landed elite of California covetously eyed mission lands, herds, and Indian labor. As they speculated on their own future as well as the future of the missions, they saw them intertwined. To make that future more acceptable, a particular kind of secularization was necessary. When Figueroa appeared on the scene, the time for secularization was at hand. The most important unanswered question had to do with how it should be implemented.

The governor's hand was forced as the result of the intrigues of one José María Padrés. A former resident of California whom Governor Victoria had exiled for his opposition to the governor's plans for the missions, Padrés had developed an elaborate colonization scheme which united state objectives as well as personal advantage. Essentially Padrés envisioned the colonization of mission lands. Thereby the population of the province would be increased and its security against Russian encroachments would be improved. About a decade before, the Mexican government had opened the door to such enterprises and under this measure the Austin family had begun the American settlement and development of Texas. With the backing of a wealthy Mexican, José María Hijar, Padrés initiated the project in 1834 when the first party of 120 settlers were brought to the province. The Californians looked askance at these intruders for they envisioned themselves as future owners of the mission lands. The possibility of open conflict was ended when the Hijar-Padrés contract to settle in California was canceled in Mexico City as a result of a political change. They fled California amid a spate of charges that they had conspired against the governor. The colonists, generally of superior stock, ultimately settled in Sonoma Valley. The Hijar-Padrés episode convinced Californians that secularization had to take place at once. Unrest among the Indians caused by the nebulous promise of immediate freedom was an additional factor which convinced the governor that he should proceed with the long-delayed program.

After the death of Figueroa in 1835 the political make-up of California became, if anything, even less stable than it had been in the past. José Castro succeeded Figueroa in 1835, only to resign in favor of Lieutenant Colonel Gutíerrez on January 2, 1836. In April of the same year Colonel Mariano Chico arrived from Mexico as the new governor and lasted only three months. During this brief period, Chico managed to make himself thoroughly hated. His unpopularity stemmed from his identification with a new centralist constitution which replaced the old federalist document of 1824 and eliminated much of the independence enjoyed by the Californians. His troubles were compounded when he tried to pass off his mistress as his niece at a social function. As was usually the story with unpopular Mexican governors, he was put aboard ship rather than being eliminated in a harsher fashion. He was briefly succeeded by Gutíerrez, who in turn was deposed by Juan Bautista Alvarado in a popular uprising in 1836.

The independence of the sovereign state of Alta California was declared on November 7, 1836, by Alvarado until such time as Mexico returned to the federalist constitution of 1824. The citizenry of Los Angeles and San Diego objected and "armies" again took the field. With battle imminent, Alvarado agreed to accept a new constitution in 1836 in spite of the fact that it was centralist in character. His action probably was dictated by the shaky hold he had upon the province. He accepted appointment as acting governor under this constitution which he had once found so objectionable. Armed conflict was renewed with a battle at San Buenaventura in March 1837. Somehow, one of the soldiers happened to get in the way of a bullet and was killed. A later battle was fought south of San Juan Capistrano which Bancroft has described as "for the most part one of tongue and pen, though a cannon was fired once or twice doing no harm." Alvarado continued as governor until 1842, preoccupied with Indian problems and the dissidents of Los Angeles and San Diego.

He was succeeded by General Manuel Micheltorena, described as "a genial gentleman who was in many ways deserving of better fortune than fate accorded him as ruler of the Californios." Authorities in the south initially welcomed him since this meant an end to northern domination. Unfortunately, Micheltorena's army was composed of poorly paid and ill-fed cholos who were not above taking anything they could get their hands on to satisfy their needs. With only twenty-five cents in the treasury, the governor would have been hard put to pay them even if he had been so inclined. The thievery of Micheltorena's army soon made him unpopular in the south, and once the citizens of Monterey became familiar with it, they likewise vigorously objected to being governed by such a military force. When he failed to act within the three-month time limit, the revolution flared again, with a battle being fought near Los Angeles on January 20, 1845. On February 20 and 21, another battle at Cahuenga Pass was fought. Both sides had a large number of Americans in their contingents, but fortunately the foreigners did not enter the conflict. The Americans organized a poker game on a hill above the battleground, where they watched. There was a great deal of cannonading, but only one horse was killed. As a result of the "battle" the governor left for Mexico, thus ending what little authority that nation had over California. Pío Pico was installed as civil governor and José Castro as the military commandant. Pico moved the capital to Los Angeles, while Castro and the provincial traders and customhouse officials remained at Monterey. Thus, the north had control of the funds and the south had the prestige of being the capital.

While the comic opera conflict for political leadership was in progress, Americans in increasing numbers arrived on the scene. Whaling, the fur trade, the hide and tallow trade, all helped to make the United States aware of this land and its potential. And when these outsiders arrived, they quickly found acceptance. Before long Mexican families had an infusion of Yankee blood and native businesses were Yankeeized. The authorities looked on warily. The bitter lesson of Texas was a constant reminder of how this trickle might become a flood and eventuate in a transformation of the province into a state. But the ability of the Mexican authorities to meet the threat was limited. In Alta California of the early 1840s, Mexican officials were handicapped by limited resources and a resistance to their authority expressed by the Californians. They represented a society and government which was convulsed with internal problems, and which could provide them with little more than vague advice to withstand the tide of American immigration. The writ of Mexican authority, never strong, eroded. As the erosion proceeded, the transplanted group of Americans became increasingly numerous and important in the life of the province. Californians accepted this development.

SECULARIZATION OF THE MISSIONS

The secularization of the missions was the most important event of the Mexican period. From the first, the missions had played an important role in California. Perhaps the most significant of the institutions utilized by Spain in the conquest of California, they were the means whereby Hispanic civilization was introduced. They provided the essentials in food without which the colony would have floundered in its early days. Strung along the coast, they served as a chain of communication which linked the separate parts of the province. They gathered the Indians, organized and trained them, disarmed them, and in general provided indispensable services to this distant outpost of empire.

There is a stereotype of the mission and the mission period which is as pervasive and essentially false as the stereotype of the southern slave plantation. The happy, singing, cheerful slave who labored in the fields under the supervision of a kindly old master has a counterpart in Alta California of the mission time—the docile Indian who gratefully served benign, black-robed, gentle friars. The Indian lot was, thanks to the missionaries, an easy one in which in exchange for small amounts of labor he shared in the life and society of the mission community. According to this version of events, the Indians welcomed the gentle Franciscan friars and willingly participated in the Hispanic version of Thomas More's Utopia.

An objective evaluation of the Franciscan missionary effort in Alta California properly stresses the dedication and sacrifices of the friars. Isolated often for prolonged periods from other Europeans, improvising in many areas, forced to depend upon their own meager resources, they came upon a land which showed little trace of the work of a man and in the course of several decades made a permanent mark. It is startling but revealing to learn that thirty friars administered a complex mission system of more than ten thousand Indians. The severest critics of the Franciscans cannot question their integrity and dedication, but realistic and scholarly appraisal of their work must be concerned with something more than motives. There is a body of evidence which indicates that the missions and the missionaries had flaws. First of all, the objective of Hispanizing the Indians in a period of ten years was never realized. Far from transforming the Indian in a decade into a self-sufficient member of Spanish society, the mission experience apparently tended to build dependence upon the missionaries by their wards. This was manifested graphically in the years that immediately followed secularization. Then the wardship was terminated and thereafter a common sight was a wandering mission Indian who found it most difficult to function without the direction of the friar and impossible to return to the Indian society he had once known.

The ongoing failure of the missions was reflected in a falling birth rate and a tremendous disparity between births and deaths among the Indians of the missions. Between 1769 and 1833 there were 62,000 deaths and only 29,000 births in the missions. Of those born, approximately three quarters died in infancy. The fearful mortality rate and the general lack of enthusiasm of California Indians for the missions threatened their very existence and forced the friars to use the military to round up recruits in much the same way the impressment gangs once assembled sailors for British warships.

The mortality rate of the mission Indians was caused by several factors. First of all, no one of that time understood that most diseases were caused by germs, for the work of Lister and Pasteur and Semmelweis was still decades away. Consequently, the most elementary of hygienic measures were unknown and an outbreak of disease tended to spread widely and rapidly in a mission community. Secondly, the Europeans brought to California diseases to which they were relatively immune, but when such things came among a population devoid of natural immunity, the consequences were tragic. The loss of life from such things as measles, chicken pox, and smallpox was frightful and this was compounded by the incidence of debilitating venereal diseases, arthritis, and the like. The life-style of the Indian not only provided him with a nutritious diet but with practices which safeguarded his health. Moving when a village site became filthy, burning a shelter upon the death of an inhabitant, bathing in the temescal—all were health guards which were denied the mission Indian. He lived in a permanent abode whose rooms were like cells. Public health measures were few. His diet was changed markedly and by no means for the better.

The change in his life-style was not confined to physical conditions of life. The Indian was stripped of his culture. The old certainties which had guided him in his aboriginal life were gone in this strange new world dominated by Europeans and European values. They were punished for indulging in natural human behavior by these sturdy practitioners of celibacy. The cultural shock was immediate and severe. It produced lethargy and resistance and flight. The latter was a common reaction.

The missionaries trained the Indians in the multiple tasks involved in building and operating the missions. They were trained in weaving, brickmaking, pottery, tanning, smithing, cooking, herding, and the diversified tasks of farming. While some of those trained rose to the rank of minor foreman, leadership was centralized in the friar. He was not only the fountain of authority but the chief administrator. The dependence of the Indian upon his friar became an enduring aspect of the relationship which survived secularization. The subordination of the Indian was complete. If necessary, coercion was used, but more often than not, more subtle techniques were employed to ensure dominance and control by the missionaries. Their control was so complete that they "loaned" Indians to the ranchos to work when necessary or profitable.

The religious zeal of the missionaries led to an emphasis on the work of bringing the true faith to the neophytes, but even here the Franciscans were partially defeated. More often than not, the Indian accepted the forms and the rituals without concerning himself with the substance of belief. In much the same way that other primitive people have reacted to the religious views of a sophisticated and powerful people, the Indians of California gave token acceptance of the religion of the intruder and received tokens and gifts of various kinds which made the process agreeable.

Secularization was, to an extent, inevitable. In a land where an indispensable economic resource was Indian labor, the continued monopolization of that resource by the Church was intolerable. The Jesuit order had incurred a great deal of enmity as it built virtually independent economic empires upon Indian labor. While the general populace took measured pride in the religious achievements of the missionaries, they became increasingly envious of the material prosperity of the mission establishments. Located on the most favorable sites, the missions reflected the zeal of the Franciscans and the investment of great quantities of Indian labor in great herds of livestock, sprawling fields of grain, and productive vineyards and orchards. The prosperous missions stood as a bulwark against the encroachments of newcomers. In effect, a pre-emption excluded new settlers and thwarted plans to develop the province with new colonists. Some contemporary critics declared flatly that the missionaries' failure to prepare the Indians for Spanish citizenship was simply a subtle way to perpetuate their position of power.

Governor Diego de Borica voiced this suspicion in 1796 when he stated, "Under the laws of the Indies the mission Indians should be free from the guardianship in ten years, with the missions becoming Indian parishes; but those of New California, at the rate they are progressing, will not become so in ten centuries; the reason, God knows, and men also know something about it." The reluctance of the Franciscans to permit a further peopling of Alta California was evidenced in a number of things. They opposed the granting of lands; they opposed the coming of new Spanish settlers, and their opposition created hostility toward them. Conflict between the Franciscans and the citizenry spilled over into the religious sphere. On several occasions, the friars refused to celebrate mass at the pueblos and presidios.

As early as 1813 the Spanish Cortes passed a law calling for immediate secularization of all missions that had been in existence for more than ten years, but the law had no effect in California, for it was never implemented. But Mexico's independence from Spain sealed the Franciscan fate. Throughout the colonial era the Creoles, or those born in the colonies, had always been distrustful of gachupins, or the spurned ones who were of the Spanish-born elite. The newly independent republican government was equally distrustful of all royalist-minded gachupins. The reluctance of much of the clergy to pledge allegiance to the new republican governments, their covert and sometimes overt sympathy for the royalists led to suspicion and sometimes open hostility after independence. In some parts of Spanish America they were expelled and a Mexican law of 1827 called for the expulsion of all Spanish-born friars. Although not enforced, this step and other signs of hostility tended to cut off the supply of new clergy. The Franciscans, largely Spanish-born, were involved and as California-stationed missionaries died, retired, or were incapacitated, there were no replacements. The missionary establishment, never large, became increasingly handicapped. And the growing enthusiasm for representative government, the separation of Church and state, and a curbing of Church influence were additional problems for the clerics. Increasing numbers of Mexicans felt that the mission system was incompatible with republican ideals.

When Governor Figueroa appeared on the scene, circumstances

were combining to force secularization. Interested in an orderly conversion of the system, he sought to follow a gradual program, but he soon found that events would wait on no man or governor. The Padrés-Hijar contract, which would have converted some of the coveted mission property into a project which would primarily benefit its promoters and a passel of newcomers, forced the governor's hand. On August 9, 1834, ten of the missions were secularized. The following year six more were placed under secular control and another five were placed under the stewardship of secular administrators in 1836.

The process of secularization, supervised by a secular administrator appointed by the governor, involved the distribution of about half of the mission properties among the Indians. Each mission Indian family was to receive a share in land as well as livestock. The balance of the property was to be conserved for the support of the religious establishment. A number of regulations were promulgated in the hope that the transition of the Indian from the mission community to life as a citizen of the secular community would be facilitated. They were forbidden to sell their land or kill or otherwise dispose of their share of the livestock. The hope, of course, was that the Indians would be able to be self-sufficient.

In practice things did not work out very well. Some administrators carried out their responsibilities with judgment and care; others, however, enriched themselves or their families or relatives with mission property and livestock. This was one problem. Another was the propensity of rancheros who resided near a mission to help themselves to the livestock or property of the Franciscans.

The Indians, as some observers anticipated, found themselves in a most difficult position. Ostensibly possessed of property, they had little notion of what they should do with it. Without the guidance of the friars they were left rudderless. Some sold their property for a pittance; others abandoned it and returned to live with non-mission Indians; others were cheated of their shares and reduced to a state of near peonage on the ranchos. Secularization for them meant a change of servitude.

THE ERA OF THE RANCHEROS

Ranching was the dominant economic activity of Mexican California. Its sway was so complete that it touched every aspect of life and society. The economy of the province became a one-commodity economy in which the chief produce was derived from the vast herds of cattle which roamed over an open range. The dominant exports were hides and tallow. The latter was produced by rendering from the carcasses of the steer. The hides were sun-dried, partially cured, and were shipped by the thousands to the rapidly growing leather industry of New England. Once the leather industry of Massachusetts and vicinity had obtained a supply of leather from Mexico, Venezuela, and the Argentine, but rapid growth and the decimation of the herds during the wars of independence forced a search for an alternate supply, which was found in California where land and climate had created a stockman's paradise. Begun in the early 1820s, the trade mushroomed. It had tremendous implication for the future of California.

The ranchos replaced the missions as the leading institutions of California in the 1830s. Spanish authorities had not envisioned such a development. On the contrary, the ranchos did not figure large in official plans for California's development. When the Mexican flag replaced the Spanish ensign, there were about two dozen functioning ranchos in the province, but by the end of the Mexican era, there were hundreds. Expansion of ranching was the result of several factors. The land and climate were involved, for such was the abundance of forage and the advantage of climate that the few hundred head of livestock brought north from Baja California multiplied rapidly. Growth also reflected the appearance of a market which could be readily tapped; it was also one of the by-products of the secularization of the missions. When the division of mission land and herds was completed and the chief rivals to land, grass, and Indian labor eliminated, the spread of ranching was accelerated.

Ranching traditions in California followed the customs and laws originally evolved in Spain and later transferred to Mexico. Cattle ranching was on an open range basis, that is, cattle roamed about an area foraging on the natural grass. In the course of time, herds were often mixed. Separation took place at the annual roundup, where cattlemen branded their livestock with brands duly registered. The roundup or rodeo itself was in accord with established procedures and presided over by a judge of the plains. In addition to being a necessary part of ranch life, it was also an opportunity for the relatively isolated ranchero family to enjoy a great festive occasion.

Hides were cured by the simple process of staking them out in the hot sun. After being scraped clean, they were then salted and were ready for shipping. Tallow was rendered in large iron kettles, the latter sometimes purchased from whaling vessels, and then poured into rawhide bags, or *botas*, the latter sometimes holding as much as a 1000 pounds each.

The importance of hides to California's economy is illustrated by the fact that they became known as "California bank notes." During the Mexican era some fifty to eighty thousand hides were shipped annually with the average price from $1.50 to $2.50 each. Purchase of hides and tallow was arranged with the ranchers by a shipowner's agent who had been sent in advance. Foreign merchants accepted the hides in payment for goods. They usually extended long-term credit to the rancheros. As one observer put it, "The merchants sold to the rancheros and other Californians whatever goods they wanted, to any reasonable amount, and gave them credit from one killing season to another. I have never known of a single incident in which a note or other written obligation was required of them. At the time of purchasing they were furnished with bills of the goods, which were charged in the account books, and in all my intercourse and experience in trade with them, extending over many years, I never knew a case of dishonesty on their part." Rancheros were invited aboard ship to pick out the goods they desired from the diversified merchandise of the cargo. Some traders established local offices on shore, where hides and tallow were gathered in shipload quantities. Both the rancheros and the traders had an interest in evading customs duties and were adept smugglers. The fact that Monterey had the only customs house encouraged smuggling, and no duty was paid on perhaps one third of all goods.

While the Americans figured large in this trade with California, a significant portion of it arose internally and involved Mexicans. In 1834 a caravan arrived overland from New Mexico with 1645 serapes, 341 blankets, and other woolen goods. The vessels which operated under the Mexican flag were quite numerous, eleven making an appearance in Alta California ports in 1842, almost equaling the United States fleet.

THE CALIFORNIA TRADE

Serapes, fancy suits, embroidered with gold and silver thread, with silver or copper buttons, and with silver and gold braid on the breeches; shoes for men and women of satin, deerskin and cotton; country and beaver hats; rebozos of silk and cotton, some of which brought in California the price of $150, costing in Mexico $15 or $16, and for which there was a large trade, for the women used no other cloak; cowhide boots; riding saddles, some very cheap, and others costly. Some of them were sold in California for as much as $300 each, and many of these were sold, for all the rich rancheros wanted them.

Other commodities were wool protectors, that is, goat skins made to cover the legs while riding horseback in the rain, and many other manufactured articles of minor importance.

Among the principal articles for consumption in California which came from Mexico in large quantities were sugar, panocha, and brandy made of sugar cane. The foreign goods were French and English calicos, white muslin, percale, etc.

How lucrative the trade was then will be seen. The merchandise on the bark Clarita *was valued at $10,000, and after having been converted into money by me on the California coast, it produced $64,000 in one year.*

José Arnaz, *Memoirs of a Merchant.*

Manufacturing undoubtedly declined after the secularization of the missions, but it is incorrect to say that it disappeared. Some ships were built, with the assistance of foreign craftsmen. There was some weaving of woolen fabrics at the missions, hides were tanned for shoes, and there were apparently many shoemakers in the colony, some of whom had the charming custom of making satin shoes for their brides. The processing of tallow, or soap, and candles was another home industry. A few craftsmen made articles

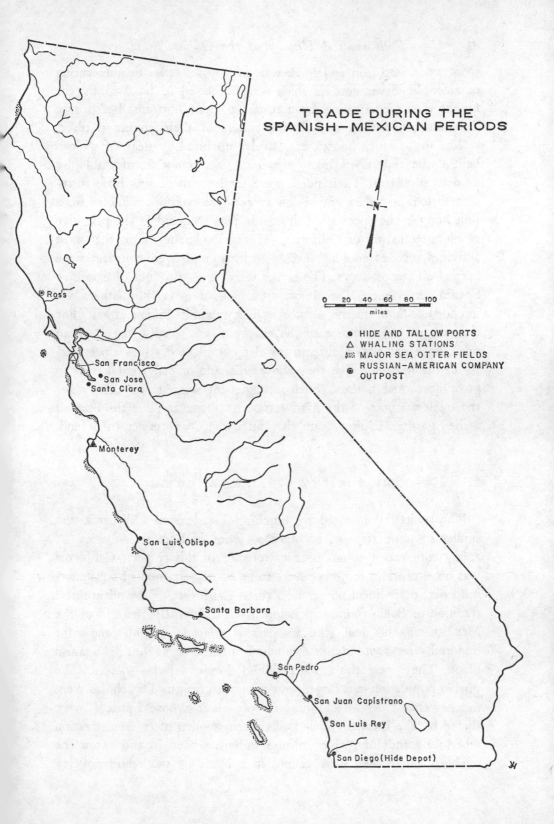

TRADE DURING THE
SPANISH–MEXICAN PERIODS

N

0 20 40 60 80 100
        miles

● HIDE AND TALLOW PORTS
△ WHALING STATIONS
▒ MAJOR SEA OTTER FIELDS
◉ RUSSIAN–AMERICAN COMPANY
   OUTPOST

◉ Ross

San Francisco
● San Jose
Santa Clara

▲ Monterey

● San Luis Obispo

● Santa Barbara

San Pedro ●

● San Juan Capistrano

● San Luis Rey

● San Diego (Hide Depot)

from wood and iron and there was, of course, some manufacturing of alcoholic beverages. Rawhide was processed to be used by the rancheros for everything from reatas to chair bottoms, bedsprings, floor mats, and even to hold the rafters of their homes in place.

The adobe ranch houses, extensively inhabited by fleas (if we can believe the reports of many travelers), were not comfortable by modern standards. Their floors were earthen, there was little furniture, little if any glass, and seldom were there even doors except for a hide hung in the opening. Such homes, however, did fit the primitive ranching economy of California. The mild climate meant that most activities such as cooking, eating, visiting, and even courting were carried on out of doors. The homes were also a product of extensive Spanish experience. The almost total lack of exterior openings was intended as a protective device against possible Indian attack. For this reason also the house of the ranchero was usually placed on an open, unshaded site. A foreign traveler commented, "It is a peculiarity of the Mexicans that they allow no shade or ornamental trees to grow near their houses." Such arrangement suggests an affinity for the treeless aspect of the Mediterranean village and for the Spanish walled garden. It also meant that such a site was easier to defend.

THE SOCIETY OF THE RANCHEROS

The society dominated by ranching in Mexican California was similar in some respects to other societies of Spanish America. A ruling elite was a common characteristic. In this respect, California was no exception, for there were some "forty-six men of substance, influence, or political power who ruled California." The oligarchical tradition of Spain found expression in California. By the end of the Mexican era, this small elite was part of a larger elite of some eight hundred, the *gente de razón*, which prided itself on its Spanish blood. They were the rancheros who dominated this society. The pueblo population was largely lower class in origin. The cholos were the hewers of wood and drawers of water whose burdens were shared by the Indians. Their ranks were swollen after secularization when thousands of former mission Indians settled in and about the pueblos. There they were caught in a cycle of work and poverty which closely resembled peonage. The cholos were largely mixed blood, mestizos, whose ancestry included Indian forebears. The landowning elite, stressing its Spanish lineage, drew careful lines which set them apart from their cholo countrymen.

The society was frontier in character. Most of the rancheros were recent arrivals to the lofty heights of the landed gentry. While they were not of the blooded families of other parts of Spanish America, where lineage, land, and status could be traced over several centuries, they were brimful of pride, even arrogance. They looked down on the cholos and new settlers, frequently confusing the two and rejecting both groups.

The social system provided the rancheros with a relatively pleasant and secure life. They lived simply but well. Surrounded by inferiors who did the bulk of the labor, the ruling elite had good reason to look upon their life and times as a sort of golden age. It was not that they lived well by modern standards, but the rough, rude pleasures and comforts of the time were available in ample amounts. Little wonder that they were to hearken back to this time when their life-style changed drastically in the years which followed acquisition by the United States.

Foreign observers, especially from the United States, made much of the lack of formal education and the indolence of the native Californians. One observer estimates that of the California population in 1845, perhaps only one hundred were literate. This should come as no great surprise to those familiar with that society. The work of ranching on the open range requires little knowledge that comes from books. One could live and one did live well without formal education. The indolence of the Californian is also a reflection of his society in his times. When ample supplies of cheap Indian labor were available there was little reason for the *gente de razón* to do much. When the American observers, stern Calvinists out of New England, looked at the society of California, they observed much but perceived little. Had they been less blinded by the dominant values of their own society, they would have realized that the Californians lived in a style befitting their way of life.

Most foreign observers agreed that the Californians lived in the pleasant present and were little concerned with the future, as were the Yankees, who thus marched to a different drummer. The Californians enjoyed life, made much of family ties, shared in the joys of parenthood, and reveled in the simple joys of food, drink, and friendship. When the Yankees came among them with their obsessive concern for work, achievement, and property, the clash of cultural values was immediate and profound. In the long run, Yankee values were to overwhelm them and the life of the Californians vanished.

CHAPTER VI

The Intruders

As the decades of the nineteenth century passed in measured sequence, the nation born as a result of the American Revolution grew in stature. Giant steps westward were taken until the outlying fringes of the country touched the limits of a debilitated Spanish empire beyond the Mississippi. Given hindsight, Americans of today perceive an air of inevitability in the expansion of the United States. A sense of mission—ofttimes denoted by the phrase "manifest destiny" —gave western thrust to the movement. As Americans looked at the West they perceived national greatness and individual opportunity. As they came to understand the limited grasp that the Spanish and their legatees, the Mexicans, had on the trans-Mississippi West, they became increasingly impatient of the failures of Spain and Mexico. Intolerance was accompanied by a growing interest. The stage was being set for another giant step to the West by the United States—a step that picked up the American flag in Missouri and set it down in the surf of the Pacific.

American interest in the land beyond the Sierras developed early in the nineteenth century, became intense in the early forties, and culminated in the acquisition of Alta California by the United States in 1848. A half century separated the stirring of U.S. interest and the negotiations which terminated the Mexican War. A detailed account of the period would include the names of a number of Yankees of diverse background who contributed in a large or small way to the planting of the United States flag on this land fronting on the Pacific. The ground would include buckskin-clad mountain men, hardy seamen out of New Bedford, a Harvard dropout who put aside his books on a physician's advice and took ship on a California-bound hide and tallow trading vessel, and an intrepid explorer of obscure antecedents. It would also include the names of a great many other individuals and groups whose roles are unsung or unknown.

Peripatetic Yankees who pursued opportunity to the borderland on the Pacific contributed to the awakening of American interest. They sometimes found the fulfillment of their aspirations in California, but sometimes too encountered disaster and emerged with little to show for their efforts. Their experiences were varied, but almost all of them found multiple attractions in this land of much potential. Hard-bitten men, sternly Calvinistic in background, they appraised the land and the society in graphic phrases which extolled the natural beauty and wealth of the land and sharply criticized its inhabitants and their institutions. The criticism stressed the ineptness of the citizenry and their failure to capitalize on the opportunities which were so abundant. To New Englanders, descendent from generations which grappled with, and conquered, a hostile environment, the limited achievements of Spain and Mexico in California were evidence of inferiority. Americans, they thought, would do better with this land. Such criticism shaped the thinking of those who linked the destinies of the United States and Mexico.

Many of the early visitors to this outlying province of Spain were impressed with the potential of the country and the deficiencies of the Spanish regime. Jean Françoise de Galaup de la Pérouse in 1786 headed a round-the-world French expedition which found haven in the harbor of Monterey. The visiting Frenchmen peered dispassionately at the society and found little to praise and much to criticize. A major theme was the inept manner in which the Spanish colonial establishment was directed. "A few soldiers married to Indian women living in the forts or scattered out as squads of guards at the different missions are the only representatives of Spain in this part of America." Implied was the conclusion that the Spanish presence was not only limited but likely to be transitory.

A number of other visitors came to similar conclusions. Four years after la Pérouse, George Vancouver sailed into the Bay of San Francisco en route to Nootka Sound, where British and Spanish imperial objectives had clashed in 1789. He reported to his superiors in the British Navy that this most strategic port was unprotected and poorly developed. Instead of a barrier "to their more southern and valuable settlements on the border of the North Pacific," defenseless San

THE CLASH IN FRONTIER VALUES

The conquest of America's Far West during the three decades that followed Andrew Jackson's elevation to the Presidency was only accomplished by the expulsion of well-established European peoples: the English, whose Hudson's Bay Company ruled supreme in the vast empire of the Columbia River basin; and the Spanish-Mexicans, whose ranchos and presidios stretched in a giant arc from the fog-shrouded harbor at San Francisco to the fertile fields of eastern Texas. Their uprooting was a victory for the Anglo-American frontier technique. Developed over the course of centuries by cocksure pioneers, this emphasized the role of the individual in the subjugation of nature, giving him free rein to exploit the new land for his own benefit. The frontier philosophy of Spain, on the other hand, subordinated the individual to the state; the pioneer's principal function was not to enrich himself but to help create a strong nation and a powerful church. In the clash between these two techniques—these two differing ways of life—the outcome was never in doubt. The conflict ended with the triumphant American frontiersmen planting their flag—and their crops—on the blue Pacific's shores, the conquered continent behind them.

Ray Allen Billington, *Far Western Frontier*, p. 1.

Francisco was an open invitation to attack. This part of the Spanish borderland, begun with high hopes of a defensive bulwark against the encroachments of other nations, was after years of existence a languishing settlement which showed little evidence of a connection with any "European or civilized nation."

William Shaler, a resourceful American sailor and trader, came to the California coast in the opening years of the nineteenth century. Engaged in the sea otter trade, he traveled extensively along the coast, crossed the Pacific to China before returning to the Atlantic coast, and reporting his findings in the *American Register*. His comments were succinct. California was a land of considerable attraction and potential, an outlying, neglected province of Spain. Thinly populated and poorly equipped for defense, it would fall before the first determined effort to wrest it from the Spanish. In essence, Shaler confirmed what others had reported—the Spanish presence in California was limited, and the province could readily be transformed into a U.S., a British, or a Russian possession.

Such comments on the absence of a European, that is a Spanish, presence in California went to the heart of a problem which Spain's colonial authorities never solved. Their hold on the province could never be secured by military means alone. The most certain bulwark against foreign encroachment was settlement by Spanish colonists; but a generation of effort following the founding of the first pueblo produced little concrete achievement. Not only was the population limited but it was neither industrious nor thrifty. The presence of an Indian labor force, the debilitating influence of bureaucratic regulations, the absence of a market for agricultural produce, the general feudal cast of the Spanish colonial effort, all contributed to the lack of progress. A generation of effort produced great missionary monuments but not the stable Spanish society which might have endured.

The activities of the Americans did not go by the Spanish authorities and their interest in the province gave rise to some apprehension. Misgivings as to the intentions of these Yankees were expressed in reports that found their way to viceregal desks: "The Anglo-Americans within the past few years have not only begun to frequent the waters surrounding our possessions in quest of fish, pearls, and furs, but, confident that there is nobody to restrain them, they come with arrogant boldness to anchor in our very harbors, and to act with the same liberty as if they were Spanish," reported an official to his superiors. He closed with a blunt warning that "this proud nation, constantly increasing its strength, may one day venture to measure it with Spain, and acquiring such knowledge of our seas and coasts may make California the object of its attack."

Apparently there was little the Spanish authorities could do about these Americans who came in "quest of fish, pearls, and furs," for they appeared in increasing numbers on the land which fronted on the Pacific to engage in a variety of enterprises. Whalers out of New England ports wandered across the oceans of the world in protracted voyages that lasted as long as three years. They searched for the elusive sperm, right, grayback, and blue whale, wandering through the vast reaches of the Pacific as the chase and their hunter's lore directed. The coastal waters were a broad highway which was used by the gray whale to get to spawning grounds in the warm coastal waters off Baja California, and the whalers came to intercept their quarry. When bottoms fouled and lack of fresh food menaced the health of crews, the captains sought sanctuary in a suitable cove. There, in quiet water ships were careened, bottoms scraped and calked, fresh water procured, running gear repaired, and fresh produce secured to thwart the menace of scurvy.

The whalers who came to the coast to hunt, as well as succor crews and refurbish ships, had sporadic contacts with the local populace. They bartered and traded to mutual advantage, ignoring customs and trading regulations. They learned something about the land and its people and carried away a mixed set of impressions which contributed to the growing awareness by the United States of the province. They came in increasing numbers in the third decade of the nineteenth century, as many as two dozen ships crowding into San Francisco Bay. When they landed in New England ports after interminable voyages, the information which they had assembled was disseminated. American awareness of the rich golden land which lay on the greatest of oceans became more pronounced.

THE MARINE FRONTIERSMEN

Throughout the opening decades of the century, the whalers were outnumbered by the maritime traders who "doubled the Horn" and anchored in California harbors with holds bulging with a broad miscellany of trade goods. One of the lures which brought them to the coast was the California sea otter, one of the most attractive and beautiful of the native mammals. Relatively large animals which varied from 5 to 11 feet in length, otters once lived in profusion in the coastal waters of the North Pacific. They lived almost their entire life in the water, subsisting on a diet of crabs, clams, mussels, abalones, and other shellfish. An intelligent, curious, and friendly creature, it was prized for its pelt, which ranged from reddish brown to black with silvery hairs that gave it sheen. It was an alluring and durable fur, especially prized in the Orient, where a single pelt of exceptional quality might be sold for hundreds of dollars. A fortune awaited men who acquired such skins from Indians along the North American Pacific coast for such trifles as knives, hatchets, and mirrors.

U.S. interest in the trade began shortly after the close of the American Revolution, as maritime entrepreneurs of New England cast about for new markets and trading areas to replace those closed to them by the British. A young American, John Ledyard, who accompanied Captain James Cook in 1778 in his search through the North Pacific for a Northwest Passage while other Americans were involved in revolution, contributed to the awakening of American interest.

JOHN LEDYARD'S REPORT ON THE FUR TRADE
OF THE NORTH PACIFIC COAST

The country round this sound is generally high and mountainous though further to the northward and eastward it appears more open and level. It is entirely covered with woods, such as maple, ash, birch, oak, hemlock, but mostly with tall well grown pine . . . The light in which this country will appear most to advantage respects the variety of its animals, and the richness of their fur . . . We purchased while here about 1500 beaver, besides other skins, but took none but the best, having no thoughts at that time of using them to any other advantage than converting them to the purposes of cloathing, but it afterwards happened that skins which did not cost the purchaser six-pence sterling sold in China for 100 dollars. Neither did we purchase a quarter part of the beaver and other fur skins we might have done, and most certainly should have done had we known of meeting the opportunity of disposing of them at such an astonishing profit.

John Ledyard, *A Journal of Captain
Cook's Last Voyage to the Pacific
Ocean . . .* , p. 70.

Along the northwest coast some of Cook's men acquired sea otter pelts from unsophisticated Indians for mere trinkets. Subsequently, when the expedition touched China they found that ordinarily canny Chinese traders would pay handsome prices for sea otter pelts.

Ledyard subsequently returned to the United States, his head filled with fur trading schemes and a fund of information about the North American Pacific coast and its adjacent waters. He had survived not only the voyage but a period of incarceration in "barracks" as a British subject of doubtful loyalty. In 1783, several years before the official report of Cook appeared, Ledyard published his journal. It stirred considerable interest, but Ledyard failed to obtain the venture capital for a trading expedition. He returned to Europe, where he secured the support of Thomas Jefferson and John Paul Jones for a daring plan to publicize the trade possibilities of the Northwest. Ledyard set out on an overland trek across Siberia to the Pacific. From that point he was to ship to the Nootka Sound and then walk eastward across the continent to the Atlantic coast. Thereby he would demonstrate, among other things, that the United States lay astride a great potential trading land of the world. However, he was arrested as an illegal visitor to Russia, and deported before his trek had gotten him to the Pacific. Some years later, on January 10, 1789, he died in Cairo, a member of an exploring expedition into Africa. His dream of launching an American fur trade along the Pacific coast, however, did not die with him.

Within a decade there were dozens of ships scouring the coastal waters of California and the Northwest coast, trapping and trading for the pelts which found a ready market in the trading centers of the Far East. Profits spurred the hunters and broadened competition as Yankee, Russian, British, and Spanish parties came to compete with the traditional hunters of the coast—the Indians. California Indians hunted the sea otter for years without making an appreciable dent in its numbers, but when the Europeans arrived with new techniques and weapons, the picture changed. Once the sea otters gathered in great herds beyond the surf line or assembled on the beaches so that the land appeared to be "covered with black sheets." All this changed with the arrival of Yankees and Russians, who sometimes joined hands in a single enterprise—the Russian-American Fur Company, for example—and began the harvesting of the fur crop.

In 1803 a single ship procured 1800 pelts. On the following voyage one hundred Aleuts were part of the party and the catch rose to nearly 5000 skins. Other ships were equally successful. In a single season as many as 17,000 pelts were taken. Spanish authorities attempted to regulate the trade in the interest of protecting their own stake in the fur trade, but Spain's power and will were distinctly limited. In the last decade of the eighteenth and in the first two decades of the nineteenth century, more than a hundred American ships visited the coast north of Baja California. Many concentrated in the waters north of Cape Mendocino but sizable numbers busied themselves in the coastal waters south. The generally small and fast ships were commanded by bold and resourceful young Yankees who ignored or circumvented Spanish authority. Overtrapping finally brought a change. When a crew's catch dropped from seven hundred skins to several dozen, it was time to look to other fields. The heyday of the sea otter trade ended about 1820 but its impact lingered on, for it helped to focus American attention on the Pacific province of Spain. Driven almost to extinction, the sea otter has been making a comeback in recent years. According to the most recent census taken by the Department of Fish and Game, there are approximately eight hundred sea otters in the coastal waters of California.

Years before the traffic in sea otter pelts came to a halt, another kind of peltry was coming to the fore. Like the otters for which they were often mistaken, fur-bearing seals abounded in the waters off the coast of Alta California. Sometimes they covered an island with a mantle of fur and presented the sealer with another opportunity to tap nature's bounty. From the closing years of the eighteenth century until the decline of the trade, largely because of the decimation of the herds through overtrapping, Americans were prominent in it. Traveling from such distant ports as Philadelphia and New York, Yankee sealers scoured the waters off California. When an island blanketed with seals was discovered, landing parties went forth to slaughter methodically the animals, which were nearly helpless on land. Physical exhaustion of the sealers or extermination of the herd would bring a halt to the killing. Despite the protests of Spanish authorities, the Anglo-Americans systematically gathered the pelts, which became one of the principal items in the commerce that linked New England ports and maritime crossroads like Canton, China. The heyday of the sealers and the ottermen lasted for roughly three decades, but in that short period, modest American concerns like Bryant Sturgis & Company realized considerable profit.

THE RUSSIANS ARRIVE

The intruders were not always from the United States, for the British, the Russians, the French, and even the Prussians exhibited interest in Alta California.

The Russians came on the scene early, came in force, and remained long after an uncertain Spanish welcome had become frosty. They came soon after the Nootka Sound confrontation demonstrated the impotence of Spain and compelled withdrawal and the concentration of Spanish forces and efforts below the 42nd parallel. The Russian presence on the coast was slight. Fort Ross, north of San Francisco Bay, was the principal center of Russian activities. In limited areas nearby, foodstuffs, grain, cabbage, potatoes, and beets, were grown to supply Russian establishments in the northern Pacific as well as the far-ranging fur-gatherers who served the Russian-American Company in much the same way that the employees of Hudson's Bay served their corporate employer.

For a time the Russians sought the foodstuffs they needed through irregular and ad hoc arrangements made with American sea captains. When such arrangements proved to be unsatisfactory, emissaries of the company in 1806 headed south from Alaska to search for a site where foodstuffs could be produced. In early April they landed in San Francisco where Count Nikolai Petrovich Rezanov was greeted with reserve by the authorities. A beautiful young señorita, Concepción Argüello, daughter of the commandant, was taken with the Russian nobleman. Their romance, perhaps the most renowned in the history of California, began with a formal engagement and a commitment to seek the necessary papal permission to join the communicants of the Roman Catholic and Russian Orthodox churches.

While the lovers were doing what young lovers do, negotiations aimed at establishing trade relations between Alta California and the Russian settlements in the north continued. Eventually they terminated on an indecisive note, with Governor Arrillaga promising only that he would refer the matter to the viceregal level. Rezanov left his bride-to-be in quest of the emperor's permission to marry. En route to the Russian capital, he was stricken while crossing Siberia and died.

His intended bride awaited word of his fate for years, buoying up hope with remembrances of her beloved. Many years later, at the age of sixty, she entered a convent and a half-dozen years later she died.

If the Russians could not open trade with the Spanish province, they could and did establish a fort and settlement, Fort Ross, from which they might secure the necessities they sought. The way was paved by a party which headquartered on Bodega Bay during the summer of 1809. A party of Aleutian hunters busied themselves with the sea otter while another part of the group erected some buildings. A few years later, in 1812, another party came to Bodega Bay and in the vicinity continued the search for the elusive otter. Once again buildings were constructed, some twenty miles north of the earlier site, the whole comprising a substantial fort. The area round the fort produced grains—wheat and barley—and fresh produce in the form of potatoes, cabbage, and beets. Fruit trees were planted and cattle, horses, sheep, and hogs were raised. To a degree the Russians in Sitka and other northern settlements had a new and more dependable source of food.

However, the diminishing fur catch, the development of other sources of food for the northern settlements, and the declining profits of their California activities led policy makers of the Russian-American Company to consider disposing of their establishment. In 1841 John Sutter purchased the livestock, farming tools, cannon and ammunition for a small down payment and a large piece of paper. The Russians had maintained a foothold in California for a generation, unwelcome intruders who were tolerated by the Spanish and Mexicans because their stay was of mutual advantage. Far from being dangerous enemies they had proved to be tolerably good neighbors and their departure was peaceful and the cause of some regret.

THE RECKLESS BREED OF MEN

Another group of American intruders contributed to breaking down the isolation of the coast from the active and growing Yankee nation east of the Mississippi. The mountain men, aptly termed a "reckless breed," came overland rather than by sea. In the late 1820s, these tough, durable, resourceful men came out of the east and

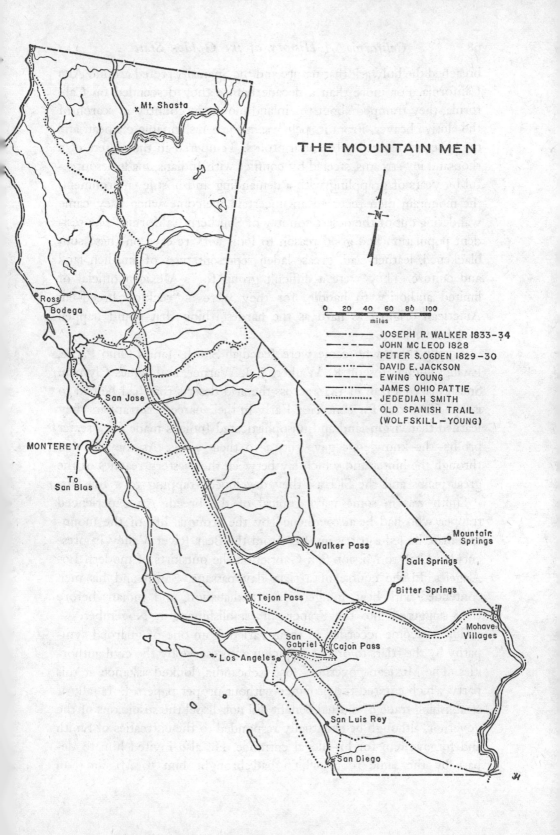

THE MOUNTAIN MEN

x Mt. Shasta

N

Ross
Bodega

0   20 40 60 80 100
         miles

JOSEPH R. WALKER 1833-34
JOHN MC LEOD 1828
PETER S. OGDEN 1829-30
DAVID E. JACKSON
EWING YOUNG
JAMES OHIO PATTIE
JEDEDIAH SMITH
OLD SPANISH TRAIL
(WOLFSKILL-YOUNG)

San Jose

MONTEREY

To
San Blas

Walker Pass

Mountain
Springs

Salt Springs

Tejon Pass

Bitter Springs

Mohave
Villages

San
Gabriel   Cajon Pass

Los Angeles

San Luis Rey

San Diego

JH

breached the bulwark that nature and the Spanish erected around Alta California. For more than a decade before they descended on California, they tramped about the inland mountain country in search of the elusive beaver. From its pelt was made a fashionable chapeau and the process involved substantial profits. Tempered in the waters of a thousand icy streams, steeled by conflict with Indians, made resourceful by years of grappling with a demanding and hostile environment, the mountain men received an uncertain welcome when they came wandering out of the desert country of Southern California. The resident population had good reason to look with reserve on these sun-blackened, leather-clad, grease-laden representatives of an alien land and culture. They were a difficult group for a Mexican official of limited authority to handle, for they were a "reckless breed—an American original as hard as the hardest thing that could happen to [them]."

Among those who came were Jedediah Smith, James Ohio Pattie, Ewing Young, Joseph R. Walker, J. J. Warner, and James Clyman. Smith blazed a trail in 1826 across the arid deserts that had helped to isolate California for centuries. Early in their careers as trappers they learned that virgin land and unsophisticated Indians made for greater profits—the knowledge gave thrust to their work. As they hunted through the hinterland which lay between the western reaches of the great plains and the Sierras, they developed trapping to a fine art.

Smith was in some ways typical of the breed. An experienced trapper who had been toughened by the arduous life of the mountain man, he led a party in 1826 from the Bear River Valley in present-day Utah to Mission San Gabriel on the outskirts of modern Los Angeles. In the course of a sixty-day passage, Smith and his men contended with heat, hunger, thirst, exhaustion, and Indians before they staggered into the Franciscan establishment in November.

The welcome accorded to them varied from one of guarded sympathy by the friars to one of suspicion and reserve by the civil authorities. The Mexican governor, José Echeandía, looked askance at this party which entered the province without proper papers. Soft talk of establishing trade of mutual benefit did not dispel the suspicions of the governor, although he eventually responded to the entreaties of Smith and forgave him for his illegal entrance. He also invited him to depart by the same route which had brought him to Mission San

Gabriel and turned aside all suggestions that the time was ripe for mutual trade. Had he known that Smith was to submit written reports to the United States Secretary of War, Echeandía might have been even more suspicious of this party of overland interlopers.

CALIFORNIA'S SACRAMENTO VALLEY IN 1828

If Missionaries could be useful in Civilizing and Christianizing any Indians in the World their efforts should be turned toward this valley. The Indians are numerous honest and peaceable in their dispositions. They live in a country where the soil is good and the climate pleasant with the exception of 2 or 3 months in the winter when there is too much rain. There is seldom any frost and I have seen snow but once in the valley of the Buenaventura. (Sacramento) [. . . the Indians] are placed in a country one would think rather calculated to expand than restrain the energies of man a country where the Creator has scattered a more than ordinary Share of his bounties . . .

> Jedediah Smith Journal in Maurice S.
> Sullivan, ed., *The Travels of Jedediah
> Smith* (Santa Ana, Calif., 1934), pp.
> 72–73.

Smith left the mission in January 1827, his stock of horses and supplies augmented, his men rested and well prepared for the trip back to Bear River Valley. His route, apparently intended to be the same by which he had come to California, changed sharply after he passed through Cajon Pass. Turning north into the San Joaquin Valley, the party sought a breach through the walls of the Sierras. The first attempt to cross the snow-covered ramparts of the mountains resulted in the loss of several horses and a forced return to the warmth and security of the valley. Leaving the bulk of the party encamped on the Stanislaus River, Smith and two companions challenged the icy Sierras a second time. The reduced party made the first recorded crossing of the Sierra rampart—a prodigious feat which was surpassed when the three men made their way across the trackless Great Salt Lake Desert. The trek was described as "one of the greatest single exploits in the whole history of western exploration."

When he came out of the West to rejoin his party at Bear Lake after an absence of almost a year, Smith was twenty-nine and deserving of an extended rest from the hardships of the trail. However, in less than a fortnight he was wending his way southwest again toward Mission San Gabriel.

Retracing the route of the previous year, the party made good time until the crossing of the Colorado River. There a band of Mohave Indians fell upon the group in the midst of the crossing. The toll was ten men dead. The balance of the party, including three walking wounded, experienced ten days of incredible hardship as they traveled across the bleak desert wastes which lay between the Colorado and sanctuary at Rancho San Bernardino. The reception was less cordial than it had been the year before and even worse treatment was to come.

Succored by the friendly friars, Smith led the party northward to the group left on the Stanislaus in the previous spring. After rejoining them, Smith went forth to make his peace with Governor Echeandía. He found the governor in Monterey, smoldering with resentment at the highhanded manner in which his instructions had been flouted. With little ado, Smith was thrown into jail to languish for a month before American sea captains and American residents interceded and obtained the necessary permission for him to leave the province. Smith reassembled his men, and in late December the party headed northward for an exit from Mexican territory via the Oregon country. Their route led through the Sacramento Valley, a trapper's paradise. Beaver were plentiful, the Indians harmless, and bear and other game abundant. They traveled leisurely, gathering pelts and feasting as they went. It was June when they reached the Pacific. For the next month they traveled northward through some of the most rugged and beautiful country along the Pacific coast. Never far from the prevailing Pacific sea breezes, surrounded by virgin forest of fern and redwood which teemed with game, the men grew fat and apparently somewhat complacent.

In mid-July, near the mouth of the Umpqua River in southern Oregon, disaster struck when a band of Indians attacked the party. Only Smith and three men survived. They made their way to safety in the Hudson's Bay Company establishment of Vancouver. The following spring the "Knight in Buckskin" returned to Pierre's Hole in present-day Idaho. A few years later, in 1831, Smith made a sudden rendezvous with death at a water hole on the Cimarron River when a band of Comanche warriors surprised him.

Smith's brief stay in California was laced with significance. Perhaps his greatest contribution lay in pioneering the trails which were to be used by a multitude of restless Americans who came after him. As Dale Morgan, his chief biographer, pointed out: "In the exploration of the American West, Jedediah Smith is overshadowed only by Meriwether Lewis and William Clark. During his eight years in the West Jedediah Smith made the effective discovery of the South Pass; he was the first man to reach California overland from the American frontier, the first to cross the Sierra Nevada, the first to travel the length and breadth of the Great Basin, the first to reach Oregon by a journey up the California coast."

Smith's journal did not reach the public until it was published in modern times but what he had seen and done in the West became known to ever widening circles and reached such places as Washington and London. Mountain men became conscious of the opportunities that awaited them in the Far West, corporate representatives of the Hudson's Bay Company saw similar visions in the streams of California, and the implications of the tenuous hold of the Mexican government on the trans-Mississippi West were not lost on Americans who were imbibing the heady draught of "manifest destiny." Smith described California in glowing terms as "a country where the creator has scattered a more than ordinary Share of his bounties." Although he had not succeeded in prying open provincial doors to American trade and commerce he had demonstrated that the doors had locks and American keys might fit.

Soon after Smith made a final exit from California, another American intruder made his appearance. James Ohio Pattie, miner, trapper, fur trader, explorer, Indian fighter, rescuer of damsels in distress, and the first American to practice medicine in California, came in response to the lure of fur. Interest in mining brought him into New Mexico via the Santa Fe trail, but returns were limited. When more promising opportunities in the form of the fur trade appeared, James and his father Sylvester Pattie responded. Their initial venture in 1825 began in promise and ended in disappointment with a substantial loss of pelts taken in the Gila River Valley to Indians.

In the following year, a second expedition into the Gila River Valley took them on a broad sweep of western America. They returned eventually to Santa Fe where, declared Pattie, "disaster awaited us," for the governor, on the pretext that they had not been licensed, confiscated their catch.

Despite this disappointing end to the venture, Pattie was soon traveling across the trackless reaches of New Mexico and Arizona to California. Once again the search for beaver led the party onward into a bleak land which promised much hazard and limited rewards to those who challenged it. The party of thirty, headed by the elder Pattie, left Santa Fe in the fall of 1827.

The experiences of the Pattie party are the stuff from which great adventure yarns are fashioned. After some initial successes, they lost the bulk of their livestock to Indian horse thieves while camped on the Colorado. Afoot in hostile country, they constructed rude rafts and attempted to float down the Colorado to a Spanish settlement. At the mouth of the Colorado, convinced there was no Spanish settlement to which they could turn, they decided to cache their furs and make their way westward to the coast.

In mid-February after burying their peltry in a well-concealed spot on the western bank of the river they set out. For the next three weeks the group stumbled uncertainly across the desert country. They were finally reduced to the desperate expedient of drinking urine to slake flesh-destroying thirst before they staggered into Mission Santa Catalina in Baja California, sun-blackened specters of men. A band of Dominican fathers tended to their immediate needs and then sent them off to San Diego to face Governor Echeandía, still irritated from his last encounter with a Yankee mountain man —Jedediah Smith.

They were promptly thrown into a vermin-ridden *calabozo* while Mexican bureaucrats considered their fate. In spite of their passports signed by the governor of New Mexico, they were regarded with considerable suspicion. Sylvester Pattie died in the jail allegedly from the effects of the ordeal of the desert passage. Occasionally the lot of the prisoners was improved thanks to the entreaties of American sea captains, although the authorities apparently were not inclined to set them free.

However, as a result of a number of unusual circumstances, Pattie and his men were released. A smallpox epidemic was raging, and when it was learned that Pattie had vaccine with him, he was pressed into service. In exchange for his services as a plague fighter, Pattie was to have his freedom. After inoculating the garrison and populace of San Diego, Pattie set off on a grand tour of Alta California, from San Luis Rey to San Juan Capistrano to San Gabriel and thence to "a small town, inhabited by Spaniards, called the town of the Angels." Eventually he reached San Francisco Bay, having allegedly vaccinated some 22,000 people. While the authorities considered a suitable reward, Pattie traveled to Fort Ross, where he vaccinated its population. The Russians paid him $100.

The reward which the Mexican authorities thought suitable was a stretch of land on the coast and a thousand head of cattle, the gift to become effective "after he became a Catholic and a subject of their government." Unlike a number of other Yankees who were presented with similar options, Pattie was outraged by the offer. Although he took his case to higher authorities in Mexico City, the offer was not modified and it was not accepted. Upon his return to Tennessee, Pattie published the *Personal Narrative of James Ohio Pattie*. To the present time it has entertained, intrigued, and informed Americans interested in California and the Southwest of the 1820s and 1830s.

Other Anglos came in the footsteps of Jedediah Smith and James Ohio Pattie. Ewing Young led a group of about forty men out of Santa Fe and ultimately into San Gabriel in 1832. The Young brigade tarried but a few days in the mission, which was becoming a crossroads for the Yankee intruders, before heading north into the San Joaquin Valley via the Tejon Pass. There in the valley they encountered a Hudson's Bay Company brigade and for a time they joined forces, although competition and company policy forbade any long-term collaboration.

The Hudson's Bay Company had been operating in California for some time, and through superior organization skimmed the cream of the beaver supply in Alta California. In part prompted by the reports of the peltry resources that Smith had described when he wandered into Fort Vancouver after the Umpqua River massacre, the company came into the area early, organized well, capitalized on its experience and superior resources, and eventually dominated the field. The returns from California were commensurate with its dominant position, but its presence in California was to be temporary, for company officials began to lose interest as the supply of beaver declined.

Young discovered a resource of the region which might be as profitable to the mountain men as the beaver—the herds of horses and mules which ran wild in the stockman's paradise of Southern California. Everywhere in the Rocky Mountain West, the inevitable decline of the beaver trade was seen in falling prices and the decreasing beaver population. Beaver trappers were forced to investigate other lines. The trade in horses, which multiplied rabbitlike in the benevolent environment of sun, grass, and water in Alta California, was a promising if untried business. Essentially it involved the acquisition of stock by purchase, trade, or theft in California for the market in Santa Fe.

While the trade promised much, Young and other mountain men who became horse traders discovered that it also had a number of hazards. Indians along the trail were alert to any herd that passed. Horse thievery had been honed to a fine art by the Indians of western America, and any herd represented a challenge. On one occasion, a party which left Los Angeles with seven hundred animals arrived in Santa Fe with about a third of that number. Young, who made a number of such trips, eventually settled in Oregon and became a permanent and respected resident, although he arrived on the scene accompanied by reports that he had acquired the herd he brought with him under peculiar circumstances. In his horse-trading days, Young made a substantial contribution toward making the trail between Santa Fe and Los Angeles a permanent route.

Travelers who came across the continent to California by way of the central route that stretched across the great basin along the Humboldt River Valley and thence west across the Sierras and down into the central valley of California had good reason to thank another mountain man, Joseph R. Walker. In the summer of 1833, his military superior, Captain Benjamin Bonneville, dispatched Walker on a reconnaissance into what is now western Utah and Nevada. Inclined to interpret his orders broadly, Walker set forth on an epic journey of exploration and discovery that made him a major figure in the exploration of western America.

1. California's contrasts in climate and altitude produce striking vistas—here snow-capped mountains present a backdrop for a vineyard in winter.

2. In this twentieth-century photograph, a modern representative of the first Californians is depicted with specimens.

3. Father Junípero Serra, Franciscan founder of nine of the twenty-one missions in the days of Spanish occupation of California. His biographer, Father Francisco Palou, credits him with the early successes in the founding of California, and describes him as a "fervidly devout, unselfish, single-minded missionary."

4. Mission San Diego. This was the first mission to be established in California. Founded by Father Serra, it suffered in 1769 from disease and a critical lack of provisions and was saved by the last-minute approach of a relief ship.

5. Helvita, established by Captain John Sutter in 1840, was a large, self-sustaining agricultural development which accommodated the overland parties of the Mexican period.

6. The Spanish influence in dress can be seen vividly in the costumes of these men, shown in a painting by James Walker. The *vaqueros* lassoed bears for spectacles such as bull and bear fights, popular in the secular spirit of California of the mid-1800s.

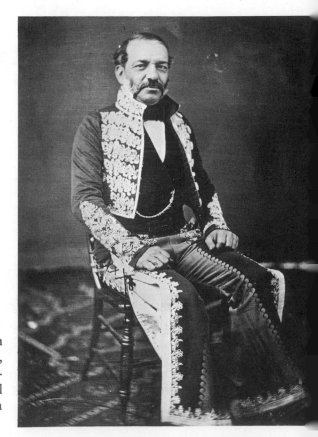

7. Andrés Pico, shown in Spanish-period outfit here, led a large force of Californians against General Stephen W. Kearny at San Pascual in 1846.

Blazing a trail down through the Humboldt River Valley, Walker's party emerged out of the desert on the eastern reaches of the Sierras.

In late fall, they cast about for a passageway through the ramparts of the Sierras before one of the scouts found a promising trail. Five days of incredible effort brought them to one of the great wonderlands of nature in California, the Yosemite Valley. The fantastic vistas which lay before them were not diverting, for by then, each member of the group was being overwhelmed by exhaustion, cold, and hunger. A scout discovered an Indian trail by which they made their way down the western slopes of the mountains toward the great valley below. En route they found a second wonder of nature, the Sequoia gigantea, awe-inspiring trees that reached toward the heavens and "some of which would measure from 16 to 18 fathoms round the trunk at the height of a man's head above the ground." When they reached the floor of the San Joaquin Valley, they paused for a well-deserved rest in this veritable Eden. They were the first party of white Americans to make an east-west crossing of the Sierras.

Walker's reconnaissance of western America was not complete. On the contrary, soon he and his men drifted south and then headed eastward again for a second crossing of the Sierras by way of the pass which today bears his name. On the eastern slopes they found the well-watered Owens Valley, which they followed northward into Nevada. Retracing their steps along the Humboldt River, the party eventually rejoined Captain Bonneville, encamped on the Green River.

A few years later, Walker returned to California by way of Walker Pass as the leader of a wagon train. The change in occupation marked the passing of the mountain men and the dawn of a new day in western America. The fur trade was dying from overcompetition, overtrapping, and the substitution of silk for beaver in fashionable male headgear. Walker's trek, in some respects, was an attempt to prolong the heyday of the beaver trade by uncovering new and untrapped streams. He made a number of discoveries in the course of his journey, but he failed to discover the virgin streams which might have given a new lease on life to the mountain men. Their day was almost done.

There are any number of mountain men who might be treated at length in a history of California. Some came with Smith, Pattie, Young, and Walker and others came on their own. Some of the mountain men were so taken by Alta California that they remained as permanent residents. J. J. Warner, who described his adopted land as "A lovely, beautiful land as the sun ever kissed or the dews of heaven watered, a delightful climate where the Junes ever linger; . . . one long siesta of delight," was typical of this group of the "reckless breed of men" who figured in the history of the Golden State. In their search for beaver pelts in California and the West, they explored at first hand the country, developed the means to cope with the countryside, discovered the trails, fords, and passes that facilitated travel and communication, reported on the potential of the country, and in a variety of ways contributed to the coming of the Americans. Their reports stimulated interest and created awareness of the land beyond the Sierras. It is difficult to measure exactly the manner in which they hastened the day when Americans would come and change the flag, but they made a marked contribution.

THE HIDE AND TALLOW TRADE

The most important contact between Alta California and the United States came as a result of the hide and tallow trade. Developing early in the nineteenth century, the trade was an attempt to exploit one of Alta California's most abundant resources—the vast herds of cattle which roamed the landscape. Their numbers reflected the operation of biological laws and an environment which was literally a cattleman's paradise. A fertile land covered with abundant forage, a hardy breed of cattle, a moderate climate, vast stretches of pasturage—all these combined to make a substantial part of settled Spanish and Mexican California a vast ranch. The principal mission herds numbered in the thousands: San Luis Rey, 27,500; San Gabriel, 25,725; San Fernando, 10,240. There were also substantial private herds. The great lack was an available market for the beef; in its absence, the trade in the hides and the tallow rendered from the carcasses developed.

The traffic in hides and tallow began at the turn of the nineteenth century as Spanish ships carried these products to other ports of the empire. The trade picked up volume and participants in the 1820s, gathered increasing momentum during the following twenty years, but eventually went into decline in the 1850s as the population of California grew and presented cattle producers with a market for their beef.

A British concern, Begg and Company, pried open the door to trade by foreigners when they negotiated an agreement with the padres under which they were permitted to purchase and deal in hides, tallow, and manufactured products. Hugh McCulloch and William E. P. Hartnell came to California in 1822 to represent the concern. Known to their Spanish-speaking contemporaries as "Macala y Arnel," the two men became prominent in the life of the province and established some enduring trade ties and practices.

American entrepreneurs came on the scene in the 1820s. Soon ships from New England, principally out of Boston, frequented the coastal waters of the province, calling at widely scattered ports and exchanging their cargoes of trade goods for "California bank notes" or hides and arrobas of tallow. Richard Henry Dana's student days at Harvard were interrupted for an extended period when he came to California on the *Pilgrim* in 1835. For months he sailed as a common sailor, observing, working, and making detailed notes. Upon his return to Boston he completed his education and wrote a classic account of life in California and the hide and tallow trade called *Two Years Before the Mast*. Like Pattie's *Narrative*, Dana's book whetted interest and made Americans more aware of Alta California.

PARADE OF INTRUDERS

Official American interest in the province developed early and grew apace with the interest and activity of whalers, traders, trappers, and hide and tallow men from the United States. Almost from the outset, the possibility of acquiring this land was a prominent feature of United States interest. And the growing official interest was matched by an increasing interest on the part of restless Americans who faced west in the Mississippi Valley and savored the reports of land on the Pacific coast.

RICHARD HENRY DANA

Richard Henry Dana was born on August 1, 1815, in Cambridge, Massachusetts, into a distinguished New England family. His student days at Harvard were marked at the beginning of his junior year with an attack of measles which impaired his vision. Unable to deal with the strain his studies placed on his eyes, he shipped aboard the brig Pilgrim *shortly after his nineteenth birthday. His ship shortly thereafter left Boston for a hide and tallow voyage to the coast of Alta California. His adventures and observations of that two-year saga comprise the material for* Two Years Before the Mast.

Dana returned to Cambridge in 1836 and studied law upon graduation. His accomplishments in letters as well as law were impressive. Although he received a great deal of praise as an author after the publication of Two Years Before the Mast *and* The Seaman's Friend, *he eventually decided to make a career of the bar. In the twenty years which preceded the Civil War he was involved in anti-slavery politics both as a member of the Free-Soil party and as a crusading lawyer who defended fugitive slaves.*

A second bout of ill health brought Dana back to San Francisco in the summer of 1859. His observations of California twenty-four years after he had written about the hide and tallow trade form a unique epilogue found in many of the later editions of Two Years Before the Mast. *In the course of both visits, Dana traveled widely, saw many things, reported accurately in prose that was clear and readable. A great many of his readers were dependent upon Dana for impressions of California and he served them well.*

While working on a legal monograph on international law he abruptly died in 1882 in Rome. He was buried in a cemetery near the burial plots of Keats and Shelley. It seemed a fitting resting place for the boy who went voyaging to the California coast a half century earlier and returned a man.

The reports stressed the positive—the climate, the boundless fertility of the land, the vast stretches of unoccupied land, and the tenuous ties that bound this province to Mexico. All of these features promised opportunity to those who would brave the hazards of the overland route to the Pacific. The depression years of the late 1830s stimulated a wave of migration which swelled in the early forties.

The people who came fled from stagnant and unpromising conditions. They came in great measure because California was a land of a second chance in much the same way that America represented a land of second chance to European immigrants in the eighteenth and nineteenth centuries. And just as Europeans had responded to exaggerated reports of American opportunity and enterprise, so the settlers who left the Mississippi Valley behind them were enticed by reports of matchless climate, unbounded fertility, and opportunity without dimension.

The first of the great overland parties that came trail-blazing out of Platte County, Missouri, in May 1841, the Bidwell-Bartleson party, consisted of some sixty persons of varied background and experience. John Bidwell, historian of this expedition and future candidate for the presidency, produced one of the best of the overland narratives. The party left Sapling Grove, a few miles from modern Kansas City, in mid-May 1841, traveling in the wagon train style that was an enduring part of the American legend. The group proceeded west and north along the Platte River, thence to Independence Rock, from which the route led along the Sweetwater to its source before they came to a way station in the Bear Lake Valley. A short time later the party divided, half opting for Oregon, the balance continuing by way of Salt Lake, the Humboldt, and the Walker River to the eastern slopes of the Sierras. It was late fall, and the winter snows which would completely block the mountain passes were in the offing. The odds were against a successful crossing, but the party defied the odds and emerged out of a rough and rain-soaked passage along a tributary of the Stanislaus to the San Joaquin River. There they were welcomed at the ranch of "Dr." John Marsh at the foot of Mount Diablo.

Only a few weeks later a second overland party made its way into Los Angeles. The Workman-Rowland party was led by William Workman and John Rowland, merchants and traders of considerable experience in the Southwest. Their passage west had been comparatively easy, as they traversed the route which connected Santa Fe and Southern California. Benjamin D. Wilson was a member of the group headed for China. His stop in Los Angeles was intended to be a temporary pause in his trek across the Pacific, but it became a permanent one, for "Don Benito" Wilson remained

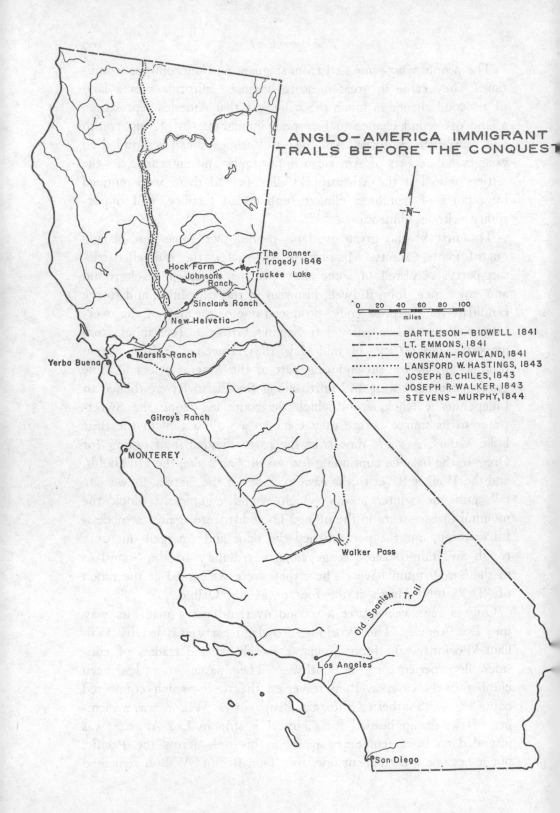

ANGLO-AMERICA IMMIGRANT
TRAILS BEFORE THE CONQUEST

N

The Donner
Tragedy 1846

Hock Farm
Johnson's
Ranch
Truckee Lake

Sinclair's Ranch

New Helvetia

Yerba Buena   Marsh's Ranch

Gilroy's Ranch

MONTEREY

Walker Pass

Old Spanish Trail

Los Angeles

San Diego

0 20 40 60 80 100
miles

--------••••• BARTLESON—BIDWELL 1841
-- -- -- --   LT. EMMONS, 1841
----------   WORKMAN—ROWLAND, 1841
•••••••••••• LANSFORD W. HASTINGS, 1843
----------- JOSEPH B. CHILES, 1843
-- -- -- -- JOSEPH R. WALKER, 1843
-·-·-·-·-·   STEVENS—MURPHY, 1844

in Southern California for the rest of his life, a prominent land-owner and rancher.

The following year was a slack time in migration to California, but in 1843 a number of overland parties made their way into the province. Lansford W. Hastings led a party of forty settlers down from Oregon. Joseph B. Chiles, who had returned to Missouri after making the trek to California with the Bidwell-Bartleson party, brought a smaller group to California by way of the Oregon trail and Oregon. Joseph R. Walker brought another wagon train into California via the Owens Valley and Walker Pass. A year later the Andrew Kelsey party and the Stevens-Murphy party made the trek. By the spring of 1845 there were all sorts of rumors afloat as to the magnitude of the upcoming migration. Reports of thousands of people making preparations in the Mississippi Valley for the journey to the Pacific began to circulate. In fact, however, a little more than 250 migrants arrived.

The following year saw the outbreak of the Mexican War and the onset of a completely different kind of migration as units of the military forces of the United States came. In that same "year of decision," the greatest single tragedy of the overland migration unfolded. The Donner party was a well-equipped group that started from Independence, Missouri, in May 1846 in sturdy wagons laden with the necessities as well as a substantial amount of coin. They were detained en route so that the season was well advanced when they came to the eastern slopes of the Sierras.

By this time the months of arduous travel, frustrating delays, backbreaking obstacles, and subtle psychological processes had demoralized and divided the caravan. On the trail through the Sierras, a near panic-stricken group which had lost all sense of discipline and order had the full weight of a winter storm break upon them. Almost before they could make the most rudimentary arrangements to cope with the cold and the snow, they were trapped in bottomless drifts that covered the landscape. As the cold grew more intense and their plight more real, they resorted to a variety of expedients to ward off the wintry blasts and the pangs of hunger. Famine could not be forestalled long by strips of boiled leather or the bark from trees. Eventually the starving immigrants turned to cannibalism. A little more than half of those who went into the Sierras

with the Donner party survived. While the accounts of the party
and its rendezvous with destiny in the Sierras in the winter of 1846
stress the courage and fortitude of the people who made up the
caravan, it might well be described as an object lesson of what
can happen to a group which becomes demoralized when faced
with great dangers.

By 1846 there was a sizable number of transplanted Americans
resident in California—nearly seven hundred. Undoubtedly their
numbers would have increased in the years that followed, and
perhaps a replay of the Texas game would have ensued whereby
a change of flags would have taken place when the resident population decided to throw off the yoke of Mexico. There was no chance
for this to happen, however, for in "1846, the year of decision,"
war broke out between Mexico and the United States. One consequence of that war was the acquisition of California by the United
States.

AMERICAN ACQUISITION

American interest in the acquisition of California was a natural
outgrowth of the many visits to the area by its citizens. Seekers of
sea otter pelts, sealers, whalers, beaver trappers, hide and tallow
traders, and even merchants reported on the many attractions of
the province. Permanent residents, first as traders and then as farmers
in the 1840s, reinforced popular American interest in acquisition.
Washington officials were aware of the growing interest of its citizenry in the territory and were concerned lest this thinly populated
outpost of Mexico fall into the hands of a European power.

Russia removed herself from the competition for California by
leaving Fort Ross and selling its movable property to John A. Sutter
in 1839. Citizens of Prussia who developed interest about the time
the Russians were leaving cast covetous eyes in the direction of the
Pacific coast prize. Recognizing that "the sovereignty of Mexico
over California may hardly at present [1842] be said to be more
than a paper one" an ambitious scheme to plant a German colony
was proposed. Nothing came of it, however, and to most Americans
the French were considered more a threat than the Prussians. French

interest originated with the visit of La Pérouse in 1786. It was strengthened in the 1820s and 1830s when French merchant vessels visited California frequently. A book written by Eugène Duflot de Mofras in 1844, based upon a two-year survey of the North Pacific coast, sought to interest France in the acquisition of California, but to no avail.

It was the British who were most feared as competitors in the American quest for California. In 1839 a Scotch merchant, Alexander Forbes, residing in Mexico published *California: A History of Upper and Lower California*. Based in part on material furnished by Abel Stearns, a United States resident in Los Angeles, this book presented an ingenious scheme whereby British investors holding Mexican bonds could exchange them for California land. When Britain appointed a vice-consul to Monterey in 1842 many Americans were convinced that London was planning to implement the project. Further evidence of British scheming was seen in the proposal of an Irish priest in 1846, Eugene McNamara, to settle his countrymen in California. Actually, American fears were groundless as the archives reveal that British officials discouraged all efforts to push them into a California venture. The New York *Courier*, however, measured American apprehension in 1843 when it declared, "This idea that England is desirous to possess herself of the Californias seems as great a bugbear with the American people as the designs of Russia on India are with the English."

First efforts to obtain California came during the Jackson administration. The President's envoy to Mexico, Anthony Butler, "who was as fit for a diplomatic mission as a crowbar is for a cambric needle," tried to purchase the area by bribing Mexican officials. Across one of his proposals Jackson wrote, "A. Butler. What a scamp." But Washington officials did not recall the "scamp" and Mexico had to dismiss him. When Butler failed in his bungling bribery attempt and tried to implicate the President, Jackson labeled him a rogue and a liar in whom there was "neither truth, justice, or gratitude." The administration of Old Hickory, however, made two other attempts to obtain the San Francisco Bay area and the President even recommended that Texas claim the region as a prelude to her annexation to the United States.

Official American interest in California remained quiescent under

Van Buren but was renewed during the Tyler administration. Waddy Thompson, Washington's representative to Mexico City, convinced the President and Secretary of State Daniel Webster that the acquisition of California was an absolute necessity. One of his extravagant descriptions read: "As to Texas, I regard it as of but little value compared with California—the richest, the most beautiful, the healthiest country in the world . . . The harbor of St. [San] Francisco is capacious enough to receive the navies of all the world, and the neighborhood furnishes live oak enough to build all the ships of those navies!" During the Webster-Ashburton Treaty negotiations with Britain in 1842, President Tyler proposed settling the Oregon dispute on the line of the Columbia River if Britain would pressure Mexico into selling northern California to the United States, but nothing came of the proposal.

Just how interested the Tyler administration was in acquiring California was revealed on October 20, 1842. On that day, Commodore Thomas ap Catesby Jones, commander of United States naval forces in the Pacific, seized Monterey. While in Peru, Jones became convinced that war was imminent and that a British fleet was en route to seize California. He decided to act first. After seizing the virtually defenseless Mexican post Jones was embarrassed to discover that there was no war. He made the proper apologies to Governor Micheltorena and departed, but Mexican authorities were deeply disturbed by this concrete evidence of Yankee design.

James K. Polk was elected President in 1844 on an expansionist platform and the acquisition of California was one of the chief aims of his administration. In carrying out his objective, Polk was ready to go to war, providing, of course, that Mexico would appear to be the aggressor. But he preferred to purchase California, or, unable to do so, to foment a Texas-style revolt against Mexico followed by annexation. To accomplish the latter, Secretary of State James Buchanan instructed Thomas O. Larkin, resident pioneer and United States consul in Monterey, "to arouse in their [the Californians] bosoms that love of liberty and independence so natural to the American continent." It was stressed that although Washington officials had no desire "to interfere between Mexico and California, they would vigorously interpose to prevent the latter from becoming a British or French colony." Larkin was appointed a Confidential Agent of the President and virtually instructed to foment a revolt among native Californians who were so exasperated with Mexican misrule that they had only recently driven out Governor Micheltorena and his troops. Naturally, this had to be accomplished with the utmost discretion. The instructions continued: "Whilst the President will make no effort and use no influence to induce California to become one of the free and independent States of this Union, yet if the People should desire to unite their destiny with ours, they could be received as brethren, whenever this can be done, without affording Mexico just cause for complaint."

THE FRÉMONT EPISODE

Polk could possibly have been successful in letting "events take their course," had it not been for the impetuosity of John Charles Frémont and men of like mind. A son-in-law of the influential and expansionist Missouri senator Thomas Hart Benton, and an officer of the elite Army Corps of Topographical Engineers, Frémont had attained a national reputation by the time of his California adventure. He had led a series of exploring and scientific trips through the West authorized by Congress. The first of these in 1842 was only to the South Pass in the Rockies via the Oregon trail, but his wife's enchanting literary style made the report of the trip into a best seller. The second expedition, 1843–44, was to Oregon and then south along the eastern side of the Cascades and the Sierras. Frémont crossed the mountains in midwinter to Sutter's Fort, went south through the San Joaquin Valley, over the Tehachapi Pass, and then eastward by the old Spanish trail. The expedition had been unreported for months and was presumed "lost," resulting in widespread publicity. Again, Jessie Benton Frémont made the challenge of the elements and the Indians into a narrative of stark adventure which became another best seller and made Frémont a household word.

The winter of 1845 found Frémont again in California with sixty-two men on his third expedition. Mexican authorities, worried over the exact nature of this "scientific" expedition, which was equipped with a cannon, had previously ordered the "Pathfinder" to leave

California and on this occasion only granted permission to winter in the area if they remained some distance from the coast. When the entire party arrived in Salinas, General José Castro was convinced of their bad faith and ordered them to leave immediately. Frémont then built fortifications atop Hawk's Peak (or Gavilan Peak but now called Frémont Peak) and apparently was prepared to battle for the mastery of California. After three days he thought better of it and made his way "slowly and growlingly" northward.

Near the Oregon border Frémont was overtaken by Lieutenant Archibald H. Gillespie. The Marine Corps officer had traveled across Mexico to California posing as a merchant but carrying special messages from Secretary of State Buchanan to Consul Larkin at Monterey. He showed Frémont a copy of the dispatch to Larkin, as well as a packet of letters from Senator Benton, but historians have speculated that he may have carried special orders from President Polk. Gillespie has only acknowledged "That I was directed by Mr. Buchanan to confer with Col. Frémont and make known to him my own instructions which were . . . to watch over the interests of the United States and to counteract the influence of any foreign agents who might be in the country with objects prejudicial to the United States . . ."

Frémont's version of the messages he received was vague: "The letter of Senator Benton . . . was a trumpet giving no uncertain note. Read by the light of many conversations and discussions with himself and other governing men in Washington, it clearly made me know that I was required by the Government to find out any foreign schemes in relation to California, and to counteract them so far as was in my power. His letters made me know distinctly that at last the time had come when England must not get a foothold; that we *must be first*. I was to *act*, discreetly but positively." In other words, he interpreted his father-in-law's letter as an imperative to act in the interests of the United States. In terms of his personal ambitions Frémont's actions were correct. Bancroft points out that: "His decision made him subsequently a popular hero, a senator of the United States, a candidate for the presidency, a millionaire ad interim, a major-general; in fact, it gave them greater prominence than has perhaps ever been attained in the United States by any other man of no greater ability. He was essentially a lucky fellow."

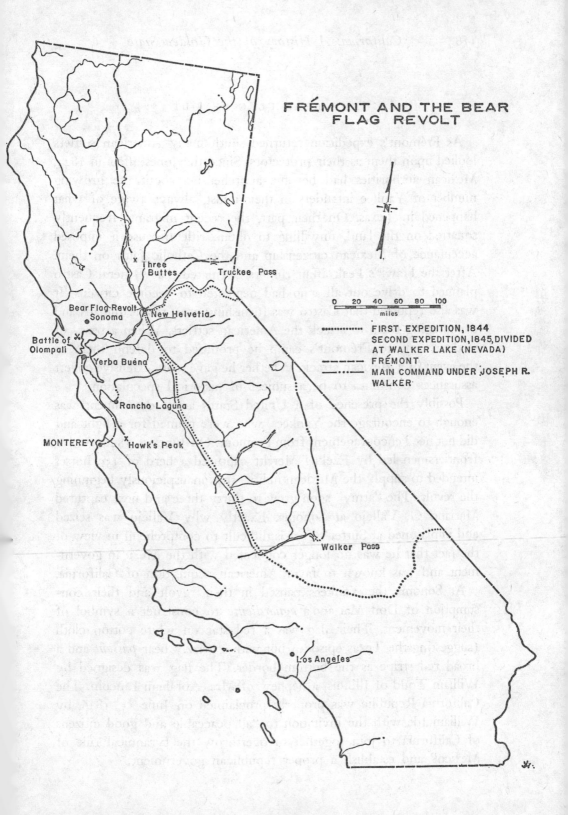

FRÉMONT AND THE BEAR
FLAG REVOLT

x Three
Buttes   Truckee Pass

Bear Flag Revolt
• Sonoma   x New Helvetia

Battle of x
Olompali

• Yerba Buéna

• Rancho Laguna

MONTEREY •   x Hawk's Peak

Walker Pass

• Los Angeles

0   20 40 60 80 100
miles

••••••••• FIRST EXPEDITION, 1844
━━━━━━ SECOND EXPEDITION, 1845, DIVIDED
          AT WALKER LAKE (NEVADA)
━ ━ ━ ━ FRÉMONT
━ • ━ • ━ MAIN COMMAND UNDER JOSEPH R.
          WALKER

N

THE BEAR FLAG REVOLT

As Frémont's expedition returned south many American settlers looked upon them as their protectors. Since the Jones affair in 1842, Mexican authorities had become apprehensive about the growing number of Yankee intruders in their midst, always aware of what happened in Texas. On their part, the recent migrants frequently squatted on the land, unwilling to obtain title because it imposed acceptance of Mexican citizenship and the Catholic faith on them. After the Hawk's Peak affair rumors circulated that General Castro planned to drive out all who had neglected to become citizens. It was also reported that Castro was furnishing arms to the Indians and encouraging them to attack the American settlers. When a party of settlers came to Frémont's camp he promised to defend them in the event of a Mexican attack. Whether he gave more extensive covert assurances continues to be a subject of historical speculation.

Possibly the presence of a United States army detachment was enough to encourage the Yankees, who were primed for a fight and did not need encouragement from Frémont. On June 10, 1846, twelve frontiersmen led by Ezekiel Merritt captured a herd of 150 horses intended to supply the Mexican militia, thus inauspiciously beginning the revolt. The "army" soon grew to thirty-three and next captured Mariano G. Vallejo at Sonoma. Exactly why Vallejo was seized and imprisoned at Sutter's Fort is difficult to comprehend in view of the fact that he was no longer connected with the Mexican government and was known to favor American acquisition of California.

At Sonoma the Yankees paused in their revolt and their consumption of Don Mariano's *aguardiente* to construct a symbol of their movement. Their flag was a red star on white cotton cloth (suggesting the Texas episode) but with a grizzly bear *passant* and a broad red stripe as the bottom border. The flag was designed by William Todd of Illinois, a nephew of Mrs. Abraham Lincoln. The California Republic was properly proclaimed on June 15, 1846, by William Ide with the invitation to "all peaceable and good citizens of California to join together to overthrow the tyrannical rule of Mexico" and establish a proper republican government.

The provincial authorities sent a force to Sonoma to subdue the revolutionaries but were repulsed at the "battle" of Olompali, in which there may have been a casualty. Frémont overtly cast his lot with the Bear Flaggers, marching his men into Sonoma on June 25, and thereby seized the mantle of leadership from William Ide. On July 7 the Stars and Stripes were raised over Monterey, thus ending the Bear Flag Republic, which since has endured more in legend than it ever did in fact.

THE MEXICAN WAR

The Mexican War was caused by the expansionist plans of President Polk and Mexico's unwillingness to accept United States annexation of Texas. Most of the hostilities which decided the fate of California took place south of the Rio Grande. When finally convinced that war had actually begun Commodore John Drake Sloat, commander of the United States fleet in the Pacific, sailed to Monterey. He reached that port on July 2, and then, possibly remembering the embarrassment of Commodore Jones in 1842, he waited five days before going ashore and formally claiming California. His proclamation to the people was conciliatory and friendly in tone, promising to respect the rights of individuals, especially their freedom of worship. Unfortunately, Sloat was in ill health and shortly turned his command over to Commodore Robert F. Stockton.

Stockton, from New Jersey and a grandson of one of the signers of the Declaration of Independence, was a superpatriot very intolerant of the Mexican citizenry and was determined to rule the conquered people with an iron hand. Although a career Navy man who saw service in the War of 1812, he frequently took long furloughs from the service to manage the family business. He designed and built the first propeller-driven warship, the U.S.S. *Princeton*, and made other innovations in the Navy. An exponent of "narrow, chauvinist, aggressive nationalism," according to a biographer, Stockton had been a special agent of President Polk in Texas in 1845, and, it is claimed, helped arouse the Texans to fight Mexico. Always more of a politician than a career Navy man (he was later a United States senator and sought the presidential nomination of the Know-Nothings), he saw the conquest of California as an opportunity to further his ambitions.

Stockton issued a proclamation on July 23, which threatened the native populace with dire punishment if they failed to co-operate with their conquerors. He also enlisted the Bear Flaggers into the United States Army, promoting Frémont to major and Gillespie to captain. Initially, there was no opposition and the American forces marched through the province taking possession as they went. On August 13, 1846, they took control of Los Angeles, virtually completing the conquest.

If the American leaders had used tact and friendliness the bloodless character of the occupation probably would have continued. But Gillespie attempted to carry out the harsh and unrealistic restrictions decreed by the doctrinaire Stockton. Within a month the Angelenos were alienated and antagonized. On September 23 a small group filled "with patriotism and perhaps wine" attacked the American garrison of only fifty men. Gillespie was able to send a courier, Juan Flaco (Lean John) Brown, to Stockton at San Francisco for help. Brown eluded his pursuers by jumping his horse across a 13-foot ravine and traveled the distance between Los Angeles and San Francisco in less than five days. But Gillespie and his men could not hold out. The Angelenos were magnanimous in victory. The Americans were permitted to leave Los Angeles after promising they would sail from San Pedro immediately. A group of American settlers at Chino Rancho near Pomona were also forced to flee.

At San Pedro Gillespie's force met the relief party from San Francisco and the two groups joined in an effort to regain Los Angeles. Marching inland in intense heat the United States force met the Californios at Domínquez Rancho in the "Battle of the Old Woman's Gun." The conflict was named for a cannon which had been used at the plaza on festive occasions in peacetime. Hidden away from the invaders, it was revealed by an old woman of the pueblo. Mounted on the front axle of a wagon, it, along with mounted horsemen equipped with lances, forced the Americans to retreat again to San Pedro. At Santa Barbara and San Diego the Yankees were also forced to flee.

Meanwhile, the army of Stephen Watts Kearny was marching on California. Leaving Fort Leavenworth in June with a force of more than 1600 men, General Kearny was instructed to capture Santa Fe and California. After the bloodless conquest of New Mexico, Kearny sent most of his troops to assist General Taylor in Mexico and started for California with only 300 men. Meeting Kit Carson carrying messages from Stockton to Washington officials relating that the conquest of California had been completed, he sent all but some 100 of his troops back to Sante Fe. With Carson to guide him, Kearny made the harsh desert crossing, which taxed both men and their mounts.

Near the Indian village of San Pascual, Kearny's weary force encountered a detachment of Californios under Andrés Pico. Using exceptionally poor judgment the American attacked early on the morning of December 6, despite a cold mist and a fog-shrouded unfamiliar battlefield. Kearny was urged to immediate battle by Carson and Captain Gillespie. Wet gunpowder silenced their guns, and mounted on either worn-out mules or undisciplined horses, recently seized from the Mexicans, the Americans were no match for the lance-equipped and superbly mounted Californios. Kearny's force lost twenty-one killed and eighteen wounded in the most significant battle on California soil while Pico's force had but one fatality and eighteen wounded. Kit Carson and Lieutenant Edward F. Beale slipped through hostile country, reached San Diego, and summoned help to the battered American force.

But San Pascual was to be the last victory for the Californios. Dissension within their ranks made it impossible to put a unified command in the field. Their gunpowder was of such poor quality that their artillery was largely ineffective. On January 10 Kearny and Stockton's forces recaptured Los Angeles after a minor skirmish at the San Gabriel River. On January 13, 1847, Andrés Pico surrendered to Frémont, who had marched southward with some three hundred men. The Cahuenga Capitulation ended the conflict and the Americans were in full control of California.

Later in the same year Nicholas Trist negotiated the Treaty of Guadalupe Hidalgo, which brought the war to an end. The treaty was signed in February of 1848. By its terms, Mexico ceded California and a huge expanse of territory in the trans-Mississippi West to the United States. American acquisition of California was a reality.

CHAPTER VII

The Golden Fleece

It is one of the great ironies of California's history that Spain, whose conquistadores early developed an insatiable thirst for gold and silver, whose national coffers were swollen with bullion torn from Incas and Aztecs, and whose national power rested in large measure on a golden base, should fail to find the golden placers of the Sierras. Almost from the beginning of her stay in America, her representatives found, developed, and exploited the mineral resources of her imperial domains, but neither Spain nor her successor, Mexico, discovered the gold deposits which were to be the cornerstone of California—as influential in her history as any other factor.

The explanation for the Spanish failure is compounded of a number of factors. Confined to the seacoast, and concerned with missionary activities among Indians who had not—like their kindred in Mexico —discovered gold, the friars, rancheros, and the soldiers who represented Spain and subsequently Mexico in Alta California found no gold in large measure because they were not looking for it. They found souls to save, they found a stockman's paradise, they found a rich golden land of endless summers, but they did not find the placer deposits of California. How different the destiny of California, Spain, Mexico, and the United States might have been had the discovery been made by representatives of Spain.

There were indications of the presence of gold prior to 1848. A half a dozen years before, a young man named Francisco López discovered bits of gold clinging to the roots of some wild onions plucked from the ground near what is today Newhall. A number of men came to exploit these placer deposits, and as these were exhausted, they fanned out over the countryside in search of similar finds. There were promising indications but nothing as rich as the López discovery, and interest waned. However, from these deposits came substantial amounts of gold, some of which found its way into the United States mint in Philadelphia. It also produced a report to the Mexican government of mineral wealth in California. There were other indications that gold was present in the province. Indians and friars occasionally turned up with small amounts of raw gold, but little change resulted. It remained for a transplanted Yankee, James Wilson Marshall, to uncover the gold which was to transform California.

Marshall, an associate of John Sutter, was at work in January 1848 on the construction of a sawmill at Coloma on the American River. He was foreman of a party of several carpenters and a number of Indians which had done some of the preliminary work. At night they allowed the river to run through the tailrace so that it might be deepened and broadened. One morning, said Marshall later, "I went down as usual, and after shutting off the water from the race I stepped into it near the lower end, and there upon the rock, about six inches beneath the surface of the water, I DISCOVERED THE GOLD." In these simple words, the skilled wheelwright and sometime Bear Flagger described the event which was to transform his world.

Marshall reported his find to his companions. To quiet their skepticism as well as his own, Marshall subjected his flakes of yellow to some elementary tests. To his relief, the pieces of metal were malleable—fool's gold or iron pyrites would have been brittle. Four days after the discovery he rode to the Sutter fort to report the find and weigh its implications with Sutter. The two men subjected the pieces of gold to further testing before they were satisfied. Then they began to plan. Evidently they realized that secrecy was important, but the cat was already out of the bag. Not only was the news known to the other members of the party working on the mill, but it gradually began to percolate through the population, reaching ever widening circles, traveling across the Pacific, eastward along the lines of trade and commerce to New Orleans, Baltimore, New York, and Boston, and finally it made its way at the close of the year into President James K. Polk's annual message.

Meanwhile, Sutter considered the implications of the discovery. He had built a feudal barony in the valley, a vast landed enterprise which stretched out over the countryside. It was nearly self-sufficient, a combination fort, farm, trading post, and ranch on which roamed thousands of head of cattle, horses, sheep, and hogs. All of what it was and what it would be in the future hinged on an adequate supply of labor. What now would happen to his Hawaiian Kanakas and Indians when they learned that in the nearby hills they could pick gold from the ground? While he made attempts to keep the discovery secret, Sutter also set out to acquire rights to the area around the discovery site from the Indians. To strengthen his hand he dispatched an employee, Charles Bennett, to Monterey to induce the military governor, Colonel Richard B. Mason, to make him a special grant of the land in the way that Mexican governors made grants. Sutter was successful in his negotiations with the Indians. In exchange for a few pieces of used clothing and other trinkets, he obtained the exclusive use of a tract of land, some ten or twelve miles square, for three years. Colonel Mason, however, refused to accommodate Sutter, and Bennett, although enjoined to secrecy, told a number of people.

The inevitable result was a growing influx of people into the area. At first they came from the immediate vicinity, to Sutter's loss, then from the major settlements in northern California. Gradually the news made its way to all the far-flung ports of the world, hitting first such maritime crossroads as the Hawaiian Islands. In the beginning, the tale was embroidered in each telling, but on its heels came proof in the form of bags and bottles of dust. Skeptical men listened and looked and lost their skepticism. Before long the hills and valleys around Coloma were filled with men who industriously dug in the dirt and sand or earth and streams. March, April, and May were months in which the human tide was building. By the beginning of June the madness had caught on, San Francisco was being drained of its population, the ships in the harbor were losing their crews, the *Californian* and the *Star* suspended for lack of printers, and Elder Sam Brannan was having the last laugh on the doubters of the city who accorded his shouting mid-May performance of "Gold! Gold! Gold! from the American River," with unbelieving good humor. The lawyer abandoned his client, the farmer his field, the mate his vessel, the sergeant his squad—all caught up in the excitement—all anxious to see for themselves. And the reality, especially in the beginning, was everything that tale and wild imagination promised. A servant returned from the fields in a few weeks with over $2000. Four men who employed Indians at the Feather River diggings collected in a number of weeks more than $75,000. A boy of fourteen cleared more than $3400 in less than two months. Two men working as partners took about $1000 from their claim in a day. A little girl found a stone of almost pure gold which weighed between 6 and 7 pounds.

Sutter went into the mining country with a hundred Indians and about fifty Kanakas. The party met with some success, but he was not to enjoy a spectacular career as a miner. Others did far better. Antonio Francisco Coronel and some of his associates were led to rich deposits by Indians. One of his party found a 12-ounce nugget, another took away as much gold as he could carry in a towel and sold his claim to a man who took out 52 pounds of coarse gold from it in the following week. Thomas Larkin reported to his superior in Washington that about $20,000 in dust had been exchanged by June 1 for merchandise in San Francisco. Military Governor Richard B. Mason reported to his superiors in mid-August 1848 that he had visited much of the mining country and learned at first hand that the placers were producing from $30,000 to $50,000 a day. He enclosed 228 ounces of metallic proof.

As these results became known, the flow of migration accelerated. Deserters from the ships in the bay and the Army, Indians from the gold country, Sonorans who came flocking from the northern Mexican mining frontier were among the first to arrive. They also came from the Pacific ports, from Mexico and Hawaii, from Oregon, even from China, in the first year of the gold rush. By May there were hundreds in the fields, but their numbers increased rapidly until by the close of the year there were close to 10,000. A year later there were approximately 40,000. Thereafter the number rose toward 100,000 where it remained until the 1860 census revealed that there were 82,537 men who claimed mining as their occupation out of a total population of 300,015.

In the beginning they worked placer deposits with elementary techniques and rudimentary tools. Much of the gold had been created when hot liquids of mineral constituents were forced into fissures and cracks in the earth's mantle. The pattern was usually highly irregular and much money has been made or lost in part because of the unpredictable irregularity of gold and silver veins. The California gold rush of 1848 was not aimed at such deposits but was concerned with gold which had been washed or eroded out of such veins and deposited by alluvial processes. Ofttimes such materials were deposited in stream beds, existing or prehistoric, on the bottoms of the streams or on their banks. There it lay until the miners located it. The job of separating it from gravel, rock, and sand was relatively simple, for natural processes had already done much of the work. The simplest of equipment was necessary, a pick and shovel, a pan, perhaps a wheelbarrow. With these a miner worked over the gravel or sand deposited in or near a stream and ferreted out the gold flakes or particles. The operation required energy, limited anounts of capital, and motivation. In the beginning year, the gold rush was a treasure hunt in which the hunters needed but elementary tools. However, as the months passed, the treasure hunt evolved in the direction of a modern industry.

MINING

In the beginning, mining for gold was an uncomplicated process which involved simple tools. The gold-bearing sand and gravel was gathered in a pan with sloping sides. Water was wafted through the material in a circular fashion, carrying away the sand and gravel and leaving the heavier gold in the bottom. Soon after an experienced miner, Isaac Humphrey, arrived on the scene, the rocker was introduced, a major improvement. The rocker was shaped like an old-fashioned cradle. The material was shoveled into the top and then water was run through while the device was rocked. The agitation and the water coursing through the material carried away the dross and left the gold resting behind in the cleats on the layers of the device.

The long tom worked on similar principles. It was a long trough whose bottom was lined with cleats. Material shoveled into one end of the tom was washed down through the trough. The gold was deposited against the bottom cleats. Periodically the tom would be cleaned, the gold taken out. Its introduction was another innovation, one of a never ending line of improvements in technology which changed the character of mining.

Innovations were frequently forced on the miners by circumstances. Thus where there was inadequate water to work the claim the miner was obligated to bring either water to the claim or the ore to water. In either case, his work was somewhat more arduous and perhaps too difficult for a single man to undertake. Perhaps a dam had to be constructed, and one or more canals or ditches to bring the water to the site. This entailed planning, some capital expenditures

---

THE CALIFORNIA DIGGINGS

A turn of the road presented a scene of mining life, as perfect in its details as it was novel in its features. Immediately beneath us the swift river glided tranquilly, though foaming still from the great battle which, a few yards higher up, it had fought with a mass of black obstructing rocks. On the banks was a village of canvas that the winter rains had leached to perfection and round it the miners were at work at every point. Many were waist-deep in the water, toiling in bands to construct a race and dam to turn the river's course; others were intrenched in holes, like grave-diggers, working down to the "bed rock." Some were on the brink of the stream washing out "prospects" from tin pans or wooden "batteas," and others worked in company with the long tom, by means of water-sluices artfully conveyed from the river. Many were coyote-ing in subterranean holes, from which from time to time their heads popped out, like those of squirrels, to take a look at the world, and a few with drills, dissatisfied with nature's work, were preparing to remove large rocks with gunpowder. All was life, merriment, vigor, and determinations, as this part of the earth was being turned inside out to see what it was made of.

Frank Marryat, *Mountains and Molehills,*
or Recollections of a Burnt Journal
(New York, 1855), pp. 213ff.

---

before a return could be realized, and often the co-operation of a number of men working together. In the early 1850s river mining developed in California. It also involved considerable planning, the expenditure of sizable amounts of capital before a return could be realized, and the participation, either on shares or as an owner and employees, of a number of men. Essentially it involved the building of a dam which would divert a river or stream so as to expose the bottom. Once the bottom was uncovered, the usual tools of the miner could be utilized to process the sand and gravel at the bottom of the river. The operation required the investment of substantial

THE DEVELOPMENT OF HYDRAULIC MINING

Early in the following year, in March of 1853, Edward E. Matteson began mining on American Hill, just north of Nevada City. He had once narrowly escaped being killed while digging under a gravel bank with a pick, a common occurrence, and he suggested to his partners that they try breaking down the bank of a cut they had made into the hillside not by pick, but by a stream of water. At first his partners opposed the idea, on the ground that it was not worth the trouble and expense, but Matteson had his way. Chabot, a sail-maker by trade, constructed a hose for them, and Eli Miller, Matteson's partner and a tinsmith, made a tapered nozzle of sheet iron. Hose and nozzle were attached to a barrel on top of the bank to regulate the head of water which was carried to it by Chabot's wooden penstocks. Matteson sent round to the Rock Creek Water Company on the 7th of March to double their water order to sixteen inches, and the experiment was made. To their delight, the jet of water turned the bank into sliding mud and washed it into and through their sluice. The gold, being much heavier than gravel and dirt, settled behind riffle boards in the bottom of the sluice. Given water, ground, drainage, and the proper equipment, one man could do in a day what dozens could hardly do in weeks. They had revolutionized gold mining and invented a process which was eventually to spread all over the world.

Robert L. Kelley, *Gold vs. Grain,*
The Hydraulic Mining Controversy
in California's Sacramento Valley
(Arthur Clark, 1959), pp. 27–28.

ber of such sites, but in much of the southern fields, they were few and far between. Hydraulic mining was really a large-scale industrial enterprise. It was usually conducted by a company, perhaps a joint-stock company, which had the necessary capital to secure the equipment and the site, meet a payroll, and figure costs and returns over a period of time. Hydraulic mining required the construction of facilities to gather the needed water and bring it to the site. Dams, ditches, and flumes were built. One company alone, in 1853, spent more than $600,000 on such preliminary work, and within four years millions of dollars were invested in such installations, and hundreds of miles of ditches, some as long as fifty miles, had been dug. Some of them are still to be seen today ferrying water from one site to another, although the day of the hydraulic miner is long past. The independent miner who had little to contribute but his labor could participate in this venture but only as a hired employee of the company. Hydraulic mining's appearance was a major step in the direction of changing the nature of mining in California from a treasure hunt in which all comers could participate to a modern industrial operation. It also often transformed verdant vistas into something resembling a moonscape.

The third important type of mining, "quartz" or "lode" mining, made an abortive start in the early fifties when a number of promoters and companies made efforts to tap the quartz-rich gold resources of California. The techniques were much different than those which prevailed in the exploitation of placer deposits, and a number of companies and investors lost heavily as they stumbled along in the hope of organizing and operating a quartz mine. It took more than a half-dozen years of trial and error and experimentation before the techniques were mastered.

Quartz mining is directed at recovering gold in rock. Sometimes veins in the quartz are on or near the surface, but more often than not they lie beneath the earth and require a complex set of operations. The miner must locate a vein, trace it, sink a shaft, drift tunnels to follow the vein, dig the ore, bring the ore to the surface, crush it, and then separate the gold from the dross material. Each step must be planned, financed, and co-ordinated. Experience and expert judgment is essential. The whole process requires considerable capital, usually beyond the resources of a single individual, and accordingly the joint-stock company was often the typical corporate form for quartz mining.

Although the bulk of the gold received before the Civil War was from placers, California played a leading role in the development of quartz mining. In the early fifties, miners experimented with various methods as they tackled the problems that quartz mining presented. Among the more essential steps in the processing of quartz ore was its crushing. In Latin America, the arrastra had been used for generations for this purpose. This was a circular area hard-surfaced and encased with low stone walls. Heavy stones were attached to an arm and then dragged through the ore by a mule, around and around, crushing the ore as they moved. Sometimes a water wheel was the motive force. It was a crude device, but it served when there was nothing more efficient available. It crushed the ore and the pulverized material was then processed with water or mercury to separate the gold.

An improvement over the arrastra was the stamping mill. As the name suggests, this device was a series of stamps or hammers attached to a shaft which alternately rose and fell on ore in a container. The ore was stamped, then the crushed material was treated with water and mercury and run through settling devices which separated the gold or amalgam (gold and mercury) from the dross materials. The improvements made in the stamping mill by Californians made it a much more efficient device than it had been and eventually it became generally known as the "California stamp mill."

Other improvements were to come in the wake of the California stamp mill. In general terms the evolution of mining in the Sierras in the fifteen years after 1849 followed a pattern. In the early years, the abundant placer deposits were worked with simple and rudimentary tools and methods. However, as they were exhausted it became necessary to develop more sophisticated equipment. As the technology became more complex, law, finance, corporate organizations, etc. became more complex.

The more sophisticated mining technology changed the nature of the industry. No longer was it possible for a miner outfitted with simple tools of pick and shovel to compete. Now it was necessary to think in terms of long-term development, substantial amounts of capital, managerial know-how, and the like. The miner of yesterday became the hired workers of the mining entrepreneur of today. In the flush early years a miner averaged something like $16 to $20 per day, but year by year that total fell until $3 became a standard daily wage. Of course as the miner's take fell so fell the cost of living. Eggs which had once sold for a dollar apiece sold for five cents apiece in the 1860s, and other prices dropped accordingly. The significant point was that gold mining in the Sierras had changed fundamentally, and most facets of society were to reflect that change. Once miners' courts had settled claim disputes in a roughhewn democratic fashion. A group of working miners would hear the respective claims and render instant justice by deciding the case then and there on its merits. This was typical of the early days, but when technology became sophisticated there also came sophistication to the law. When mining enterprises involved thousands or hundreds of thousands or even millions of dollars it was intolerable to any claimant that a group of miners should put aside their tools for a moment and organize a court which would decide title to such property.

As the search for gold continued, and as the most promising deposits were worked, it became increasingly important to develop the tools and techniques which would allow the less promising deposits to be exploited. And as these techniques appeared, it became more possible to work deposits which had been disregarded in the past. This sometimes resulted in several rushes into a given area. The first featured the miners who were interested in the placers. When these deposits were exhausted, the settlement might languish as miners left for more promising areas. Subsequently a technological improvement would make it possible for miners to work once again with profit in what had been regarded as an exhausted area. A striking modern example was the gold rush sparked by the development of scuba-diving equipment. A few years ago, young men who were experienced with such equipment found that they could pluck gold from the stream beds of rivers which drained out of the western Sierras. The rush lasted only a short time, but it graphically illustrated the general principle that mining is very much affected by technological change and improvement.

It is difficult to do much more than estimate the amount of gold which was produced by the California fields. A modern estimate puts the output for 1852 at more than $80,000,000, a total which dropped to $69,000,000 in the two years which followed this peak. The average output in the period from 1850 to 1865 was $50,000,000. From 1865 to the close of the century, gold production was relatively stable. It ranged from $10,000,000 to $20,000,000 per year. The grand total for the entire period was $1,300,000,000. Not all of this found its way into the American economy, for substantial amounts made the journey to England or some other country. However, there can be little doubt that it had a powerful impact on the American economy, for it made available tremendous amounts of capital which could be used to underwrite general economic development. In California the impact of placer gold, and later quartz gold, was seen in the farms, factories, homes, banks, buildings, transportation facilities, and industries which appeared. A sizable amount of the gold flowed outward from the state in payment for goods and services consumed or rendered in California, and this too served as a stimulant to American maritime and commercial circles.

ROUTES TO EL DORADO

The miners who came to the rich golden land of California usually chose what they thought was the least expensive and the most direct, certain, and convenient route. There were three major routes which American Argonauts followed; the first led overland, a second was a seaward passage to the Isthmus of Panama and then up the West Coast to California, the third led round Cape Horn, a voyage which took from four to eight months.

For the inhabitants of the Atlantic coast ports and states, the sea routes were preferable to the overland trek. Exact figures are difficult to come by, but there can be little doubt that thousands of transplanted Easterners came to California by way of Panama or Cape Horn. When news of the gold discovery reached the East Coast it stirred considerable interest. Experienced sailors, veterans of the otter trade, whaling expeditions, and hide and tallow ventures, were available. A number of them had doubled the Horn and sailed along the coast of Alta California. Ships were mustered, some drawn from other lines, hastily outfitted with the crudest of accommodations, and chartered to enterprising companies who were anxious to capitalize on the demand for passenger space to El Dorado. Thousands came as passengers on the vessels of the Pacific Mail Steamship line, which advertised a thirty-day passage.

Sometimes individuals would join together to travel over the 6000-mile route. The Republic Company of New York, which left New York for Panama in April 1849, was typical of the joint venture. A difficult crossing of the Isthmus in which they encountered voracious mosquitoes, yellow fever, bad water and worse food, and heat left a number of them as invalids on the west coast. On the trip northward they recovered, and when they arrived in San Francisco in June, they took off for the gold fields and the strike which would change them into men of affluence. By the time of their arrival, the Bay of San Francisco was crowded with vessels which swung untended at anchor, the crews having deserted the sea for the Sierras.

The Isthmian route had a number of variations. Some crossed to the Pacific via Nicaragua. Some came to a Gulf of Mexico landing at Veracruz then crossed overland to Mazatlán for a voyage northward which terminated in San Francisco. How many found permanent resting places en route is unknown, but that many did is beyond question. The fact that they arrived by the thousands in California is eloquent testimony of the durability of the Argonaut.

The much maligned Cape Horn route was the longest but in many respects the easiest way to California. Ships which loaded in eastern ports with passengers and freight faced a sea voyage of four to eight months which covered a distance of some 9000 miles. The most difficult passage was through the Strait of Magellan, where fog, treacherous currents, and gale-force winds tested ship and seamen. More than one vessel failed the test and came to grief on the coast of Tierra del Fuego, but a great many ships made it through. The interminable sea voyages eventually ended, but not until passengers had been subjected to weeks of confinement in foul-smelling quarters, subsistence on bad water and worse food, and shipboard epidemics of cholera, scurvy, dysentery, and influenza. When they landed in San Francisco after such a trek, they were likely to be in need of rehabilitation before the balance of the trip to the gold-mining country. But thousands came this way. Exactly how many came via the Isthmus or the Horn is unknown although customhouse records indicate that 549 ships arrived in San Francisco between April and December 1849. They carried a total of slightly more than thirty thousand passengers. Undoubtedly some of them came from foreign rather than American ports.

More thousands came via the overland trails to California. Many Argonauts turned to these trails because they were closer at hand for residents of the Mississippi Valley, they involved a minimum of cash, and they entailed a kind of travel which was familiar to most

Americans. The vehicle that many used was the covered wagon—the "prairie schooner" as it is better known. An American original which was designed in Conestoga, Pennsylvania, and further improved as a result of experiences on such overland travel routes as the Santa Fe trail, this most durable and useful of vehicles brought thousands of forty-niners to the gold country beyond the Sierras.

The covered wagon which many of the forty-niners used on the overland trails was not the heavy, lumbering Conestoga, but a much lighter vehicle. The body or bed of stout timber often had sides which sloped. It frequently had a false floor beneath which were stored reserve supplies. The top was of canvas, waterproofed with paint or oil and supported by bows of hickory. Flaps at the front and back allowed the canvas to close around a room which was some 4 by 10 feet. The top was a protection against the weather and the stout body was additional protection against such hazards as arrows. The most vulnerable portion of the vehicle was the running gear. However stoutly made, wheels which were subjected to the stresses encountered in hundreds of jolting miles of cross-country travel invariably paid a toll of spokes, hubs, and axles. Other parts of the running gear, such as tongues, doubletrees, and the like were equally liable to damage. The overlanders who survived ofttimes were accompanied by skilled wheelwrights, or they became skilled themselves as a result of their many experiences improvising repairs on the road.

The roads which they followed were not roads but trails marked out by pioneering parties like the Rowland-Workman party before the gold discovery. The most popular route led west from St. Louis, Independence, or St. Joseph, through the South Pass in the Rocky Mountains. The trail led north and west along the Platte River through the South Pass and west, skirting the Great Salt Lake on the north. In present-day Nevada, the trail ran southwest toward the Sierras along the Humboldt River. The Sierra crossing via the Truckee Pass or Donner Pass brought the party to the end of the trek at Sacramento.

While this was the most popular of the overland trails, accommodating some twenty-five to thirty thousand travelers, there were other routes. Southern trails gathered travelers from eastern towns and cities, led them across the Southwest through Texas, New

THE OVERLAND TRAIL TO EL DORADO

Fatigue and heat causes the train to move slowly. We continued on, I directed the teamsters not to urge the mules; and entered a very extraordinary looking country. Road N. W. through several hundred yards of high clay bluffs and hills, of the most delicate and beautiful warm tints, in horizontal strata. Road-powder blinding and choking one. Afternoon the road branched around a low bluff to the right; where, in 200 yards I found, near an orange colored clay spur, a well or tank of water, and a crowd of thirsty men and animals surrounding it. A few yards to left of this another, similar hole filled up with a dead ox, his hind-quarters and legs only sticking out, above ground. Dead oxen thick about here, and stench suffocating. The road here sweeps round westerly, a few hundred yards, then S. W., descending very gradually, to a level white clay hill, beat perfectly bare of everything but dust, carcasses, and relics of used up wagons, &c by innumerable travellers and camps. Passed in afternoon, including those at the wells (3/4 mile in rear) 30 dead oxen. Several lame and abandoned oxen here, and the wreck of a wagon. My train came up slowly, from 4 p.m. till dusk. One mule exhausted and we consigned him to this depot of carcasses. The high rugged mountains opposite, appeared perfectly sterile; and no other growth below, but sage and greasewood. Sun set clear, light airs N. E., Temp. 66°.

September 21. Commences clear, with a moderate breeze from the N. E., Temp. 34°. Course N. of W. and very crooked; but generally level white earth, and small dusty sage bushes scattered over it. Thus far, counted on either side of the trail and some on it, 40 dead oxen, and 1 dead horse. 3 miles further we reached a plain slightly elevated above the last, over which we travelled, still N. of W. a couple of miles, and noon'd on right of trail, surrounded by carcasses, and wrecks of wagons, and every kind of property. Gave mules a bit of grass and quart water each. Passed, and about the spot where we halted to rest 66 dead oxen, and 1 dead mule, 3 abandoned wagons and 3 carts. Burnt remains of several wagons; and innumerable ox yokes, chains, bows, &c. Dead oxen often in groups, particularly around an abandoned or burnt vehicle.

Georgia Willis Read and Ruth Gaines, eds.,
*Gold Rush, The Journals, Drawings, and
Other Papers of J. Goldsborough Bruff,
Captain, Washington City and California Mining
Association, April 2, 1849–July 20, 1851*
New York, Columbia U. Press, 1949),
pp. 147–49.

Mexico, and Arizona and then northward to the gold fields. En route the parties traveled in the footsteps of Spanish missionaries, fur traders like the Patties, and horse traders who had journeyed along the old Spanish trail or the Gila trail. Such routes had a number of advantages. Not only was the climate milder but they passed through a number of settlements where provisions might be secured. A party which set out from Westport, now modern Kansas City, Missouri, along the Santa Fe trail, then paralleling the Gila River to the Colorado, thence across the desert of Southern California could expect to arrive in the mining country one hundred days after departure. En route the party would grapple with the trail obstacles that brought grief to many, but if they were organized well, and adequately led and provisioned, a series of 18-mile days would eventually bring them to the placers of the Sierras.

The problems of the overlanders of 1849 were many. The Indian menace receives a full measure of attention in popular literature and in movie and television scripts, but the hazards of Indian attack were far overshadowed by other dangers. One of the biggest problems was disease. Deadly cholera was epidemic in the western world on several occasions in the period from 1847 to 1853. An especially virulent disease which could reduce a robust man to a helpless invalid in hours, it often struck without warning. If the victim was a head of a family on their way to the diggings the whole family was placed in jeopardy.

Scurvy also took a dreadful toll. Although its cause as well as its cure was known to medical men in 1849, the overlanders blithely ignored the problem when provisioning themselves with salt meat, beans, and flour and setting off on the trip to the Pacific coast. En route they lived on a diet devoid of fruits and vegetables and before long the lack of ascorbic acid manifested itself. At first the victim was fatigued, then he broke out in skin sores and eruptions, soon legs became swollen and teeth loosened in their sockets. Death was not far off when these latter stages were reached and thousands of the overlanders reached a permanent destination in the form of a trailside grave long before they could get to the Sierras.

Starvation was also a problem and sometimes joined both scurvy and cholera in a diabolical trio. Perhaps cholera would do its evil work first, weakening men and making them more susceptible to scurvy. In the convalescent stage animals were frequently neglected, repairs to the running gear of wagons overlooked, and the basis for a general disaster laid. Scurvy weakened and debilitated and finally the effect of accumulated neglect appeared in the form of wagons that could not proceed, animals that were dying, and a food supply that was inadequate. Soon the overland trail was frequented by walkers, men, women, and children who were no longer part of an organized emigrant train but simply pedestrians who were bent on walking to the promised land. Such people were in desperate straits, reduced to eating the putrefied flesh of dead animals and subsisting like animals on whatever the country had to offer.

But disease was not the only hazard. A traveling party was also very much dependent on the supply of forage for their stock. Those who were first on the overland trails in the spring of the year had first chance at the forage, and those who came in their wake found the grass cropped and the supply inadequate. A company was frequently forced to turn aside from the main trail to search for grass, as indispensable to the overlander as gas is to the modern motorist. An adequate supply of water was also a major concern. There were stretches along the overland trails where there was more than enough, but there were also places where there was no water for miles. Along Sublette's Cutoff, for example, some 35 miles of hard, arid land lay between watering places. Another 40 miles of desert lay between the end of the Humboldt River to the Carson or Truckee River. To men and animals who had already been stretched almost beyond endurance by the trail, a 40-mile desert passage was a cruel running of the gauntlet which sapped at life and sometimes reason.

The overland trails were marked by the forty-niners and those who came in their wake in an enduring fashion. In the beginning, wagons were generally loaded and packed with essential provisions and treasured belongings which men and women could not bear to leave. As the miles of trail passed beneath the wheels, however, treasured items became burdens. A trail of abandoned furniture, stoves, dishes, barrels, and cooking utensils marked the passage of the overlanders. More than one hundred years after the great migrations across the land to California, one can trace the trails by the abandoned goods which still lie in the sands leached by a century of sun and rain. On the Lassen trail in northern California, one can

still find the signs that emigrant parties passed that way, and in
various places on the trails wagon rims wore still-visible ruts into
stone.

The great migration of 1849 and 1850 brought thousands of people
to California via the overland trails. Sometimes the fires of the wagon
trains would stretch out into the night as far as the eye could see.
Apparently a large part of the population of the East was headed for
California. A substantial number of those who came did not stay.
They were attracted by the golden fleece. Even after they arrived
and found the new land abundantly blessed, they continued to think
in terms of a return to the land of their youth when they found the
strike which would transform them into people of means. Thus, the
population of California, although it reached more than 380,000 in
1860, was limited by the great numbers of people who came, "saw
the elephant," and returned to tell their family and their friends of
the fabulous land beyond the Sierras. They had been part of a great
migration, an odyssey of a people comprised of thousands of individual odysseys. A contemporary writer used simple words for his
appraisal of the overlanders' trek: "The experience of any single
man, which a few years ago would have made him a hero for life,
becomes more commonplace when it is but one of many thousands."

LIFE IN THE MINES

In some respects the California gold rush developed along patterns
which were familiar to those who had observed at first hand the
westward movement of the American people. That great expansionist drive, which had begun for the people of the United States at
the close of the American Revolution and continued unabated
through the first half of the nineteenth century, had taken American
people and American institutions into the land beyond the Alle-
ghenies and then beyond the Mississippi. As it proceeded, as men
marched into the virgin wilderness in search of adventure or economic betterment, they took with them the matrix of social, political,
and economic customs appropriate to the society they left behind.
There on the frontier they retained that which was useful, modified
a great deal, and improvised ways of doing things. For a time the

frontier society reverted to an earlier and more primitive society. Sophisticated civilization reappeared in time, but it was different, a blend of the new and the old with a leavening dash of something entirely unique and different.

This was the California experience in the gold rush period, although here it was different in that the process was accelerated. Here, for example, men confronted mining problems and questions. To be sure there had been mining rushes in the westward movement before Marshall's discovery. The rush into the gold country of Georgia and the lead-mining country around Galena, Illinois, are cases in point. Silver and copper mining in the Southwest attracted the attention of the first Americans to come into the trans-Mississippi West, but these episodes furnished few precedents for the forty-niners. They were forced to devise codes of mining laws and regulations. In the absence of an acceptable code, they drew up laws which were steeped in pragmatism and eminently suited to their situation. Thus, they provided that claims should be limited in size to that which was appropriate to the richness of the strike and the nature of the labor and tools which were available. No man might claim a greater portion of a placer deposit than he might work. The use of slaves was prohibited. The presence of tools on a claim was an essential mark of possession, and a claim which was not worked for a specified period of time was considered abandoned. Questions of right and possession which were not easily settled by appliciation of the rules were submitted to a "miners' court," an ad hoc group of miners who would hear the merits of the case and render instant justice. Often a dispute over a claim was referred to the recorder or register of claims who was charged with the responsibility of recording claims, or perhaps an alcalde was given the responsibility of making a Solomon-like decision. The mining codes of the forty-niners illustrated the general tendency of frontiersmen to adapt and improvise a workable system to deal with problems which arose from their environment.

There were other ways in which the frontiering experience shaped the life of men in the California mines during the gold rush. For example, in the absence of a formal police force and an organized system of courts, men turned to innovations in this field as well. The individual who harvested the yield of another's sluice or stole another

A CRITIC OF JUDGE LYNCH

A scene occurred about this time [January, 1849] that exhibits in a striking light, the summary manner in which "justice" is dispensed in a community where there are no legal tribunals. We received a report on the afternoon of January 20th, that five men had been arrested at the dry diggings, and were under trial for a robbery. The circumstances were these: A Mexican gambler, named Lopez, having in his possession a large amount of money, retired to his room at night, and was surprised about midnight by five men rushing in his apartment, one of whom applied a pistol to his head, while the others barred the door and proceeded to rifle his trunk. An alarm was given, some of the citizens rushed in, and arrested the whole party. Next day they were tried by a jury chosen from among the citizens, and sentenced to receive thirty-nine lashes each, on the following morning.

Never having witnessed a punishment inflicted by Lynch-law, I went over to the dry diggings on a clear Sunday morning, and on my arrival, found a large crowd collected around an oak tree, to which was lashed a man with a bared back, while another was applying a raw cowhide to his already gored flesh. A guard of a dozen men, with loaded rifles pointed at the prisoner, stood ready to fire in case of an attempt being made to escape. After the whole had been flogged, some fresh charges were preferred against three of the men, two Frenchmen, named Garcia and Bissi, and a Chileno, named Manuel. These were charged with a robbery and attempt to murder on the Stanislaus River, during the previous fall. The unhappy men were removed to a neighboring house, and being so weak from their punishment as to be unable to stand, were laid stretched upon the floor. As it was not possible for them to attend, they were tried in the open in their absence, by a crowd of some two hundred men, who had organized themselves into a jury, and appointed a pro tempore judge. The charges against them were well substantiated, but amounted to nothing more than an attempt at robbery and murder; no overt act being even alleged. They were known to be bad men however, and a general sentiment seemed to prevail in the crowd that they ought to be got rid of.

At the close of the trial, which lasted some thirty minutes, the Judge put to vote the question whether they had been proved guilty. A universal affirmative was the response; and then the question, "What punishment shall be inflicted?" was asked. A brutal-looking fellow in the crowd cried out, "Hang them." The proposition was seconded, and met with almost universal approbation. I mounted a stump, and in the name of God, humanity, and law protested against such a course of proceeding, but the crowd, by this time excited by frequent and deep potations of liquor from a neighboring groggery, would listen to nothing contrary to their brutal desires, and even threatened to hang me, if I did not immediately desist from any further remarks. Somewhat fearful that such might be my fate, and seeing the utter uselessness of further argument with them, I ceased, and prepared to witness the horrible tragedy.

Thirty minutes only were allowed the unhappy victims to prepare themselves to enter on the scenes of eternity. Three ropes were procured, and attached to the limb of a tree. The prisoners were marched out, placed upon a wagon, and the ropes put around their necks. No time was given them for explanation. They vainly tried to speak, but none of them understanding English, they were obliged to employ their native tongues, which but few of those assembled understood. Vainly they called for an interpreter, for their cries were drowned by the yells of a now infuriated mob. A black handkerchief was bound around the eyes of each; their arms were pinioned, and at a given signal, without priest or prayer-book, the wagon was drawn from under them, and they were launched into eternity. Their graves were dug ready to receive them, and when life was entirely extinct, they were cut down and buried in their blankets. This was the first execution I ever witnessed. God grant that it may be the last!

E. Gould Buffum, *Six Months in the Gold Mines* (Philadelphia, 1850), pp. 83–85.

---

man's poke was likely to encounter another form of instant justice, in the form of a vigilance committee. These episodes have frequently furnished the novelist with story material and in the light of modern standards, this improvised court of law repels rather than attracts, but to the honest miner of the gold rush, the vigilance committee filled a vacuum. Some way of dealing with the lawless and the violent had to be devised. In the absence of a police and court system, the miners simply took the law into their own hands. A culprit who found himself before a committee of vigilance was usually in a most difficult situation, for the traditional safeguards of Anglo-Saxon jurisprudence were conspicuous in their absence. The accused was likely to be faced with the evidence. He was usually given some sort of a chance to explain or defend. The jury, sometimes the entire group of miners which heard the evidence, was likely to render a verdict without delay. Sentence was immediately pronounced and immediately carried out. If the defendant were to be whipped and banished, that chore was performed at once and the culprit drummed out of camp. If hanging or ear cropping were in order that too would be done forthwith. There was no room in this system for protracted procedures or appeals and often the most elementary rights of a defendant were sacrificed.

Life in the mines in the flush days of the early fifties reflected many of the characteristics of the boom town of America that has been spawned by an oil strike or a mineral find. In the course of a short time, perhaps months, a town or city was built. In the beginning, those first on the ground improvised solutions to the problems which arise when men assemble in numbers and live together. Problems of shelter, food, clothing, security, and order all must be dealt with. Each presented special problems to the forty-niners.

The problem of shelter was not pressing in the summer, for most of the placers were to be found below the 2500-foot level. At that elevation, California's climate in the spring and summer months is quite tolerable. Nights are usually cool, but not cold, and one needs but a minimum of protection against the elements. Canvas was an appropriate building material. In more than one mining settlement, "substantial" homes were built of canvas, the balance of muslin. In the winter, however, conditions changed markedly, for the coming of the winter rains and snow made shelter a necessity. Men built log cabins and, when lumber became available, rude frame buildings. Stone was usually plentiful but more often than not labor costs precluded its use, except in limited amounts for foundations. Sometimes the inadequate shelter in the mining country, coupled with the difficulty men had in working the placers of rain-swollen streams, sent large numbers of men off to winter in San Francisco, Sacramento, or San Jose. In the spring they returned to their work in the gold counties.

The very nature of placer mining discouraged the building of permanent settlements, for as the deposits of a particular region were exhausted, the miners were likely to pick up their tools and head for new diggings. They were a restless lot who were prone to look upon a field more distant as one more promising than their own. When the take from a claim declined, their inclination to wander was intensified. One day, perhaps with little notice to his neighbors, a miner would pick up and pack out. They were prey to every rumor of a rich strike. When such news hit a camp, men often threw caution to the winds and set out forthwith, determined to be first on the scene, and first to reap the rich harvest of gold. Sometimes promoters and merchants in an area, anxious to attract customers, would spread such rumors in a neighboring settlement. When the miners arrived, thirsting for knowledge of the latest news from the rich strike, and perhaps thirsting for other things as well, their wants would be met—at a profit of course. Business would boom for a time and then the disappointed miners would slowly disperse to other fields: another humbug, another disappointment, another flash in the pan.

The miners who worked in the placers had difficult working conditions. As long as they were on their own they kept whatever hours they pleased but usually the span from early morning to dark represented a workday. The work was hard physical labor, digging, shoveling, pulling or pushing a wheelbarrow. Often the miners worked in water, cold running streams that arose in the Sierra snow pack, sometimes for the entire day. Cold feet, swollen joints, sniffles were the least of the problems which came out of this. More serious consequences in the form of pneumonia or influenza often came to the miner in the placers. Dormant conditions flared up. Poor diet and even worse medicine complicated matters. Miners whose ailments rendered them incapacitated often suffered without either doctor or medicine, perhaps getting well or perhaps succumbing to their ailment.

The uncertainty of his life was reflected in the behavior of the forty-niner. As far as the gold itself was concerned, he had seen and heard of examples of lodes uncovered by happenstance that turned a hard-working but poor miner into a man of wealth. The unlikely prospect of such a thing happening buoyed and sustained miners and brought to their behavior an erratic element. Miners who could be content with a small but regular return were as exceptional as the gold seeker who could withstand the temptations rumor proffered him. And the miner who could manage his money prudently after he accumulated a pile was also unusual.

Uncertainty and hard work was very much a part of his life. Accordingly, the miner sought diversion on Sunday from the previous six days of unremitting toil. He found it in a variety of ways, many of them unacceptable in the community from which he came. Removed from the restraints of his family and home, he drank, he gambled, he consorted with loose women, and he broke the Sabbath with vengeance. In the smaller mining settlements, vice was poorly organized and men improvised accordingly. A tent, a few boards placed over carpenter's horses, a cask of rotgut, and a few barrels for seats were the essentials for a drinking establishment. A pack of well-worn cards, some dice, or other rudimentary gambling devices made the drinking establishment a gambling casino. There took place the operation which produced many a pile. "Mining the miners" was every bit as profitable as grubbing around on a wet and backbreaking claim. The men with soft hands, alert eyes, elegant dress, and the shrewd knowledge of human nature that comes from professional gambling wound up with a great deal of the gold which had been taken from the placers.

Merchants also obtained a share. They often took advantage of circumstances and miners and did their part in relieving the gold seekers of a share of their poke. It is significant that many of the great fortunes which had their genesis in the gold rush period of California came out of gold rush merchandising. Leland Stanford, Collis P. Huntington, Mark Hopkins, and Charles Crocker are examples of men who took their first giant step toward affluence as merchants and storekeepers.

They performed an essential service by supplying the miners with necessities. It was the merchant who provided the food, clothing, tools, and the like which enabled miners to survive and perhaps prosper. Sometimes the local merchant became a partner of the prospector. All that was required was a persuasive miner, a grocer stocked with goods, and an informal understanding that the merchant would obtain a share of any gold found in exchange for credit extended. Commodities were extremely expensive in the boom days of the early fifties, but as the decade progressed, the cost of living declined. In the earlier days when the miner's purse was heavy he usually found that he paid dearly for whatever goods and services he required.

The abundant supply of gold in the flush times was manifested in a variety of ways. In addition to driving the prices of commodities to lofty heights, the substantial output of gold accelerated the development of a diversified economy in California. In this land, the man of daring and competence in the field of commerce found opportunity pounding on his door. A man who came ashore in San Francisco carrying a bundle of eastern newspapers discovered he could sell them for a dollar apiece. A young lady who learned to improvise baked $11,000 worth of pies in a small iron skillet. Laundresses were in such short supply that dirty clothes were sent to Hawaii to be washed. A doctor cleared $75 to $100 per day in the early fifties; other men of medicine received $15 to $20 for office calls and $50 to $100 for a house call at night. But it was the entrepreneur rather than the professional who made great sums of money and in the process shaped the economy of California. In this land, bustling with newcomers who had many unmet wants and needs, the man who could furnish some of those necessities and luxuries was in a position to prosper. The merchants were prime examples of the restless entrepreneurs who struck out at the main chance, measuring the market of California and ordering goods from their suppliers.

Unfortunately for many of these men of commerce, storage facilities were limited and credit was hard to come by. To complicate their problems, their supply lines were long and uncertain, and a merchant in San Francisco who ordered supplies which he would not receive for four to six months operated in the dark. By the time the ship arrived in the bay carrying his order, the market might be glutted and he might be forced to dispose of his merchandise at a loss. But while this was a problem, the production of large amounts of gold, and the existence of a substantial population which produced little and had many needs, lured people into lines of enterprise, chiefly commercial, which would have taken years to develop in the ordinary run of events. Lumbering became an important industry early in the fifties, agricultural enterprises of various kinds appeared in the first year of statehood, and the demand for mining equipment of various kinds stimulated the growth of foundries and iron-fabrication plants. Steamship companies which ran well-equipped, substantially built, and well-operated steamboats on the rivers which led into the interior were part of the accelerated development of the California economy. Hotels and amusement resorts of various kinds were prosperous.

Impressive growth statistics revealed the development and maturation of the economy which had taken place in the first years of the gold rush. In 1856 San Francisco was the fourth port in the Union in total tonnage, outranked only by New York, New Orleans, and Philadelphia. By that year, substantial amounts of exports other than gold were passing through California's chief port. Quicksilver, lumber, flour, and hides were prominent and the accumulated gold exported from 1849 through 1856 amounted to $322,383,856.

The fantastic growth that had transformed the outlying province of Mexico into a bustling American community was to be seen in other things. Ninety-one newspapers and periodicals were published in California in the mid-fifties, including two in French, two in German, two in Spanish, and one in Chinese. There were 2 telegraphic lines in operation, 131 gristmills, 373 sawmills, a sugar refinery, a paper mill, numerous foundries and machine shops, 18 tanneries, and 4 large distilleries. Steamships and sailing vessels were being constructed on California waterways, whalers and salmon fishermen were active along the coast and in the inland waters.

Agricultural growth had also produced spectacular results. Almost ten million bushels of wheat, barley, and oats were produced in California fields by the middle of the fifties, and farm stock in horses, cattle, mules, sheep, and swine increased by quantum jumps. And this was but a prologue to the fantastic growth in California farming that was to come in the next generation. The magic touch of gold was to be seen everywhere. Its most significant impact was the production of a society and economy of diversity, complexity, and maturity which belied its age.

SAGA OF THE COMSTOCK

The Comstock lode, though located in Nevada, is an integral part of California history. It was discovered when California miners were meeting decreasing success and the flush days of the gold rush were becoming a memory. Thousands of miners, expert in the diverse skills involved in placer, quartz, and hydraulic mining, were looking for a new El Dorado. Its existence was announced in June 1859 in an assay report in Grass Valley which appraised several specimens of a bluish-black ore from Nevada's Mount Davidson at an almost unbelievable $1595 in gold and $4791 in silver per ton. Within hours the rush was on as thousands of Californians made haste to the discovery site, eager to be in on the ground floor of what promised to be a new bonanza.

Mining on and about Mount Davidson had been carried on since the early fifties but it was not until the end of the decade that two experienced prospectors, Peter O'Riley and Patrick McLaughlin, turned up a sizable deposit in Gold Canyon. Their success attracted the attention of a vocal Virginian, Henry Comstock, who talked his way into a partnership and gave his name to the lode. From the beginning they thought themselves handicapped by the presence of an apparently worthless heavy, bluish-black material. Cursed, shoveled aside, and discarded, it was this "worthless" debris which California assayers pronounced incredibly rich.

The deposits of the Comstock were much different than those previously worked by Californians. The initial discovery was comprised of outcroppings of ledges which extended deep into the earth. Ranging downward thousands of feet, they presented miners with tremendous problems in bringing them to the surface. And once they were brought to the mills, unlocking the gold and silver presented another complex of problems. The nature of the deposits and the complexity of recovery operations were powerful influences which shaped the history of the Comstock.

The nature of the deposits brought into being some seventy-five joint stock companies which blanketed the discovery site with claims. The result was not only conflict, but near-chaos, as thousands of rival claimants jockeyed for place and position. Fists, knives, and guns were brought into play before the courts addressed themselves to the problems and brought a measure of order and structure. One result was a new set of legal principles and precedents which thereafter undergirded American mining law. Shares of the dozens of corporations involved were soon bought and sold, at first in a haphazard manner.

The San Francisco Mining Exchange was established in 1862 as the West's first stock exchange. Operating without supervision in an atmosphere of feverish speculation, stocks fluctuated wildly in price. From time to time, insiders manipulated the market, artificially raising and depressing prices, and taking full advantage of their manipulations to enrich themselves at the expense of the trading public. (In 1966 the watchdog Securities Exchange Commission ordered the Mining Exchange closed on the grounds that it was manipulated by those who directed it for their "personal and unconscionable gain.")

In the Comstock mines, miners grappled with problems which were without precedent in mining history. As they followed leads into the earth, they discovered deposits broadening into soft and crumbly material. As the ore was removed and traditional timbering constructed to support the overhead, the work became ever more hazardous, for the tried and true methods of the past failed to support the massive burdens. A brilliant solution was devised by a German-born quartz-mining engineer, Philip Deidesheimer, in the form of cubes fabricated of massive timbers which were joined together in columns or "honeycomb" fashion. When filled with rock debris, square-set timbering provided the strength essential if the work was to continue.

Heat, water, and ventilation were a troublesome trio which the miners had to confront. At the 50-foot level flooding necessitated the installation of massive steam pumps. Ventilation became a problem which was met by the construction and installation of the most advanced blowing system ever built. Despite this equipment, the supply of air was never more than adequate. Heat became so oppressive (at 3000 feet, water of 170 degrees was encountered) that miners could work only a half hour before they had to seek relief beneath a blower, consuming copious amounts of ice water. But the work went on, miners wrestling with problems as they appeared, modifying work schedules, and adopting new tools and techniques as needed.

One of the most imaginative proposals attempting to deal with the multiple problems of the Comstock was the work of San Francisco tobacco merchant Adolph Sutro. Sutro proposed digging a 3- to 4-mile tunnel leading upward from the Carson Valley to the lowest reaches of the mines. It would serve as a means to remove excess water and improve ventilation as well as provide for a more efficient means of removing the ore. Despite tremendous problems, which included the opposition of existing mill owners whose works would be supplanted by new mills in the Carson Valley, the work was completed, but not until 1878. By then, the glorious days of the Big Bonanza were over and the full value of the Sutro tunnel was never realized.

The mill operators also encountered unprecedented problems. In one instance, a lack of facilities and expertise led to the shipment of ore to England for processing! Step by step, the mill operators produced the techniques involved in extracting the gold and silver. A young self-taught metallurgist, Almarin B. Paul, made a major contribution by constructing the first stamping mill and adapting some of the procedures developed in California quartz mining. From his work, supplemented by others, the Washoe pan process emerged. It involved pulverizing the ore, mercury, heat, salt, and copper sulphate with settling devices and traps. The consequence was a technology for mining which was superior to any known in the world.

California was involved in every aspect of the Comstock. It trained and furnished the labor and management force. Capital assembled by San Francisco banks and investors financed most of the mills and mines. The Bay City's foundries and shops fabricated the machinery for mine and mill. Its mercantile and commercial community provided Virginia City with the broad range of goods and services essential to the more than thirty thousand people who took up residence there. California furnished many of the lawyers who came and did battle in the courts, David S. Terry, former Justice of the California Supreme Court, for example, and the "soiled doves" of San Francisco found new opportunities in Virginia City.

As was often the case in mining, the rewards of the Big Bonanza were distributed unevenly. Most of the miners worked for a daily wage which averaged $4. Tradesmen and professionals who serviced the miners enjoyed a measure of prosperity during the early days and some California concerns grew rich on the Comstock trade. But it was a small handful of bankers and financiers who acquired the lion's share of the wealth produced by the mines. William C. Ralston, founder of the Bank of California, William Sharon, his chief representative in Virginia City, John W. MacKay, James G. Fair, James C. Flood, and William S. O'Brien were the major figures in a saga of frenzied finance. Separately and in various combinations, they invested in mines and mills, speculated in securities, and generally grasped opportunity. The saga of the Comstock is a dramatic tale which a modern historian, Rodman Paul, recounts in a scholarly fashion in *Mining Frontiers of the Far West.*

The total output of the Comstock, approximately 57 per cent silver and 43 per cent gold, amounted to almost $300,000,000 in the twenty-two years of its heyday following 1859. In a little more than two decades of varying prosperity, fortunes were made and lost, vast amounts of bullion torn from the earth and tremendous amounts of capital injected into the California economy. The flush times of the sixties gradually gave way. About the time the golden spike was being driven at Promontory Point marking the union of the Central Pacific and Union Pacific track, predictions were being made that the lode was played out. In fact, its greatest day coincided with the beginning of the depression of 1873 when the heart of the lode was discovered. In the ensuing ten years, the mines produced more than $100,000,000 before they began to fade. The Comstock died in the early 1880s, when the total output dropped to a little more than $1,000,000.

That there may be life yet in the Comstock was revealed in a U. S. Geological Survey released in 1968 which reported that two areas north of Virginia City were possible extensions of the Comstock and warranted further investigation by modern geophysical and geochemical methods. Modern bonanza king Howard Hughes began buying thousands of mining claims in Nevada about this time. No public announcement of his objectives has been made as yet but there remains speculations about the possibility of a revival of the Comstock. If this happens, a new and dramatic page in California history can be envisioned.

CHAPTER VIII

The Americanization of California

Nominal American sovereignty over California was established by proclamation on July 7, 1847, de facto American sovereignty in the course of the fighting of the Mexican War, and de jure sovereignty with the signing of the Treaty of Guadalupe Hidalgo in February 1848. On the heels of the establishment of American sovereignty came the gold rush and the triggering of accelerated growth of California which transformed the Mexican province into a bustling American state. The metamorphosis took less than a decade. When it was completed, California was for better or worse an American society, inhabited by Americans and dominated by American institutions.

CREATING A CONSTITUTIONAL BASE

California had an economic, political, and social system when the Yankees succeeded in wresting the province from Mexico in 1848. The economy had changed little in the decades which followed the establishment of Mexican sovereignty. It remained essentially a pastoral economy in which the principal effort was directed at producing livestock and limited amounts of foodstuffs for the resident population. Trade and commerce was limited to sporadic exchanges, often by barter, between residents and the owners of the supercargoes of hide and tallow ships. Great feudal estates or ranchos were scattered along the coast south from what is Marin County today; small settlements near the pueblos of Los Angeles, San Jose, and Monterey and the decaying remains of a number of the missions contained the bulk of the population of the *gente de razón*.

The Mexican political system had a number of defects but it worked fairly well considering the problems which it faced and the limited resources which it commanded. The governors, appointed by the central government in Mexico, and removed from direct supervision of superiors, exercised considerable authority. That they did not always exercise it well is evidenced in the frequent clashes between them and the local populace that took place and the fact that in a fifteen-year period California had nine governors.

The governor appointed prefects, regional administrative officers, and subprefects or local administrative officers. A legislative body elected to four-year terms made policy and laws for the province. Alcaldes were local officials who ruled over towns or cities with the assistance of a legislative council called an *ayuntamiento*. The alcalde combined in his office the powers of a mayor, a justice of the peace, and a police chief. He was, in short, one of the most important officials in the Mexican scheme of government.

American military representatives who were first on the scene assumed the powers and responsibilities of government in 1847. The governor was supplanted, but other elements of the Mexican system were preserved and adopted for a time. Alcaldes, with the authorization of the American military, continued to exercise authority, and an *ayuntamiento* in San Francisco continued to operate. These attempts to use elements of the Mexican political system were a response to a need for effective government and the lack of an American system. Military government then was a mixture of American military and Mexican political forms.

Had California gone through the usual leisurely growth that characterized other territorial possessions of the United States, the new system might have worked satisfactorily during the period of transition. However, the discovery of gold on the American River and the flood of immigration which was unleashed accelerated the development of California and made it imperative that an effective political framework be established. These local conditions demanded the creation of an American system, but there were other factors of a national nature which also pressed for action.

On the national scene, the decade of the forties had seen the building of great tension and conflict between the representatives of the societies which were incorporated into the American political union. The onset of the Mexican War escalated the conflict, for Northerners in great numbers viewed the war as a part of a conspiracy of the "slave power" to acquire more land for slavery. Southerners and Westerners had mixed feelings about the war, but they generally supported it. In the North volunteers were limited, but they flocked to the colors in the South. In the course of the war a Pennsylvania congressman, David Wilmot, introduced an amendment to an appropriations bill which would have prohibited slavery from any of the territories which might be acquired as a result of the war. Although the Wilmot Proviso did not become law it focused national attention on the conflict between the two societies as they competed for place and advantage in the West. To the pro-slavery Southerner, the proviso was a tricky attempt to deprive the South of the fruits of victory won by its sons on the field of battle; to the anti-slavery Northerner, it represented a legitimate attempt to stay the spread of slavery into the West.

The conflict between the sections reared its head again shortly after the ratification of the Treaty of Guadalupe Hidalgo when the Congress of the United States hammered out a bill organizing a territorial government in Oregon. Despite adamant southern opposition, slavery was excluded from Oregon. Significantly, it required the defection of two southern senators, Sam Houston of Texas and Thomas Hart Benton of Missouri, to pass the measure. The debate between pro-slavery and anti-slavery representatives created much heat and shed little light on the controversy. Its termination as an anti-slavery victory made pro-slavery representatives more vigilant and determined that they would win the next battle. That next battle entailed the entrance of California into the Union. Benton speeded its coming by suggesting to the citizenry of California that they follow the example set by Oregon settlers and simply establish a government of their own choosing.

General Zachary Taylor, who like several other military heroes won the presidency on the field of battle, anticipated a crisis if the question of California's admission should be prolonged. Accordingly, he attempted to forestall it by instructing his military governor in California, General Bennett Riley, to expedite the formation of a state government. Riley promptly authorized the holding of an election to select delegates to a constitutional convention in August 1849. A month later the group assembled in Monterey, where they tackled the problems of writing a constitution. The impatience of a rapidly growing population put pressure on the delegates, who came together at the initiative of President Taylor.

The convention assembled in Monterey in a stone school building which Reverend Walter Colton had erected some years before and which is still standing. In a 30-by-60-foot hall on the second floor, the forty-eight delegates set to work on a framework of government. The group was relatively young although rich in experience; the youngest delegate was only twenty-five, the oldest fifty-three. A half dozen were native Californians, and three, although born elsewhere, had lived in the province for years and wedded señoritas. Their preferred language was Spanish. Most of the group had come to California before Marshall uncovered the gold in the millrace on the American. By occupation they were mixed, twelve were lawyers, ten were farmers or rancheros, seven were merchants, and several were military officers. John Sutter was present—his California dream was still a reality. Thomas O. Larkin, who had served the United States well as its first California consul, was also present. Among the men who were later to have brilliant careers was William M. Gwin, intimate friend of Andrew Jackson, and Henry W. Halleck. Gwin was to reach a pinnacle of political power as a senator from California, while Halleck became a prominent member of the law firm of Halleck, Peachy, and Billings before he served the Union Army as its commander in chief during the Civil War. Elisha Oscar Crosby, transplanted New Yorker who had served in a similar convention in New York in 1846, was also present. He was equipped by experience and he also had a copy of the New York constitution. This partially explains the similarities between the two constitutions.

William Gwin preened for the chairmanship but the convention selected Dr. Robert Semple, a dentist, printer, and a Bear Flagger. Gwin took this rebuff in stride and went on to impress a great many people. Experienced in political gatherings, he was a tall and distinguished man who looked as if he should wear a toga.

The convention was faced with many problems, but it dealt with them systematically and consequently accomplished a great deal.

The convention worked through committees. In general a committee of two members from each election district reported each draft article to the convention, which, as a committee of the whole, took appropriate action. To guide them the delegates had copies of the constitution of Iowa as well as that of New York. The latter had been revised in 1846 and most constitution writers of the next decade freely drew upon it. The United States Constitution also influenced the document which was drawn up in Colton Hall.

There were few major controversies in the convention. The resolution which might have sparked the greatest differences was surprisingly passed unanimously: neither slavery nor involuntary servitude was to be tolerated in California. That decision ensured controversy when the question of California's admission came before the Congress. Having been bested in Oregon, pro-slavery spokesmen were determined to have a different outcome in California, but even before they were confronted with the issue, Californians had taken a stand.

The boundary question also provoked considerable discussion before the matter was put to rest by fixing the boundaries along the present lines. Some delegates advocated a much larger state, stretching eastward and encompassing much of present-day Nevada and Utah. One objective, though not spelled out, was the avoidance of divisive debate in the Congress when other states were created in the region. If the whole should be included within California, then the question would not arise. The question of suffrage also produced a sharp disagreement. The majority of delegates wished voting restricted to white males over twenty-one, but as José de la Guerra pointed out, this would have disqualified a number of Californians who were of mixed background. As a matter of fact, one of the delegates, Manuel Domínguez, was of Indian background and thus the restriction would have barred him from voting. This absurdity was eliminated by a half absurdity: the legislature was empowered to admit Indians or their descendants to the voting rolls. To guard against the "abuse" of this procedure it was specified that a two-thirds vote of the legislature was necessary.

The constitution incorporated the traditional rights of citizens of the United States Constitution but it went beyond the Bill of Rights. A declaration of rights affirmed the inalienable rights of the people, "among which are those of enjoying and defending life and liberty; acquiring, possessing, and protecting property; and pursuing and obtaining safety and happiness." Calfornians were assured not only of the pursuit but the achievement of "safety and happiness." They were also assured of such fundamental rights as freedom of speech, assembly, petition, religion, press, habeas corpus, and trial by jury.

The constitution provided for the usual government of three branches: executive, judicial, and legislative. The legislature was to be comprised of members elected to a two-house body. Apportionment of seats was according to population. Executive power was vested in six elected officials: governor, lieutenant governor, controller, attorney general, superintendent of public instruction, and surveyor general. The governor was to appoint a number of lesser officials, had a veto over legislative acts, and was empowered to call the legislature into special session. The judicial branch consisted of a supreme court of three elected justices and three branches of lower courts: district, county, and justice courts. All judges were to be elected.

A system of public schools was created, the public debt limited to $300,000, and the legislature forbidden to create any corporation except for municipal purposes. The latter restriction reflected the Jacksonian animus against corporations, particularly those which issued paper money. Taxes were to be uniform throughout the state and county assessors were to be elected. The constitution which emerged was quite democratic in form and substance and it served California for a generation.

When the convention met for the final session, John Sutter presided, replacing Robert Semple, who was ill. In the harbor of Monterey, a number of ships displayed their colors and a salute of thirty-one guns was fired, one for each of the states as the delegates signed the document. The thirty-first round was for the new state of California. The celebration was premature, for it was almost a year before the doors of the Union were opened to receive the new state.

A month later the voters of California went to the polls in limited numbers to ratify the constitution and to select the state and legislative officers who initiated state government in California. They also elected two congressmen. Without so much as a by-your-leave from the Congress, which usually authorized such proceedings, the citizenry of California formed a state. The constitution was ratified by a vote of some 12,000 to 800. Edward Gilbert and George W. Wright were elected congressmen and Peter H. Burnett, lawyer, newspaperman, agent for John A. Sutter, Oregon pioneer, gold miner, and former judge of the Oregon supreme court, was elected governor. The legislature which was chosen met in December and thereupon began the work of creating a legislative framework for the state.

BUILDING AN AMERICAN SYSTEM

A short time after the legislature met, the intrepid pathfinder John C. Frémont was elected senator. His colleague was William M. Gwin, who turned from his labors in the constitutional convention to representing California in the Senate. Whether they or their colleagues to the House of Representatives, Edward Gilbert and George W. Wright, would be admitted to the Congress was a moot question. The president, the military governor, the convention delegates, the electorate, and the officials selected had all acted without the permission of Congress. The response to all this by official Washington was likely to be mixed. The fact that this new political entity sought admission as a free state placed further hazards in her path, for the representatives of the slave South, still smarting from the defeat inflicted on them in the Oregon bill, were determined to prevent the unbalancing of the Union which the entry of a free state entailed.

The question of California's admission came before a Congress which was divided into implacably hostile camps of pro-slavery and anti-slavery representatives. So antagonistic were the representatives that there was talk of secession and disunion before any real business had been transacted. On the eve of the greatest crisis which had ever confronted the nation, men talked in terms of destroying the confederacy which joined them. Before the Congress had ended its term, the nation had walked through the shadows, its lawmakers had battered one another with words as well as fists and guns, and it required the combined statesmanship of leading congressional figures to avert the final disaster. In the eye of the hurricane were the hopes of Californians for admission.

The struggle over California began soon after President Taylor, in his annual message to Congress, recommended the speedy admission of the state, asserting that since New Mexico would soon take similar action, Congress should leave the settlement of territorial questions to these spontaneous movements. Southerners were adamant that this should not happen. If California should enter the Union of fifteen slave and fifteen free states, the delicate balance in the Senate would be destroyed. Having lost a majority position in the House some years before, the South was determined that she would preserve equality in the Senate at all costs.

The conflict between the sections escalated as the session unfolded. Southern representatives pushed a fugitive slave bill and in bellicose speeches denounced northern attempts to pass the Wilmot Proviso, northern attacks on slavery, and northern assaults on southern interests. In one impassioned moment a southern senator declared, "We do not intend to stand still and have our throats cut."

While such threatening rhetoric echoed in the chamber and reverberated throughout the country, two major figures of the political arena, Stephen A. Douglas and Henry Clay, were putting together a legislative package which would stay the forces for disunion. Clay was especially effective when he posed the alternatives which faced the nation in this crisis. If fire-breathing Southerners would indeed secede, they would provoke war and not an ordinary war but "furious, bloody, implacable, exterminating" civil war, for disunion and war were synonymous. To avert that calamity, to build a phalanx of groups and interests which would unite in defense of national unity, Clay proposed a program which would admit California; organize New Mexico and Utah as territories without action on the status of slavery; adjust the western boundary of Texas; prohibit the slave trade in Washington, D.C., but not slavery; pass a strict fugitive slave law; have the federal government assume the Texas public debt incurred prior to annexation; and put the Congress on record in a formal declaration that it had no power to interfere with the interstate slave trade.

These proposals sparked the greatest debate which the Congress had ever witnessed. They brought into the debate the great senatorial triumvirate of John C. Calhoun, Henry Clay, and Daniel Webster.

None of them was to live long after this episode. Calhoun was so ill that one of his final speeches to the Senate was read by a fellow southern senator. Generally, the moderate voices in the House and Senate rallied to the compromise which was emerging, and with Clay and Douglas rallying their supporters and the defenders of the Union in the House and Senate, the Compromise of 1850 was passed. It provided for the admission of California; an adjustment of the Texas-New Mexico boundary and the payment of $10,000,000 to Texas in exchange for relinquishing her claims to the territory involved; the organization of New Mexico and Utah as territories, the status of slavery to be determined by "popular sovereignty"; a more stringent fugitive slave act; and the abolishment of the slave trade in Washington, D.C. The nation had stood for a time at the chasm of disunion, but then took a giant step backward from the gulf. Webster, who played a major role in rallying unionist sentiments to the compromise, wrote a friend, "I can now sleep of nights."

The news of California's admission on September 9, 1850, reached the Pacific coast some weeks later. A giant celebration was staged in San Francisco with a parade and speeches commemorating the event. Thereafter it became a state holiday. However, long before the news arrived, California was behaving as though it were a state. The legislature, which had been elected at the same time the constitution was ratified, had been sitting in San Jose and passing laws to implement the fundamental framework of government. Subsequently dubbed the "Legislature of a Thousand Drinks," because a member frequently interrupted the course of debate with a proposal to adjourn for "liquid refreshments," the body of lawmakers accomplished a great deal. A court system was established, judges and justices selected, and a civil and criminal practice act was passed. The latter was so advanced that it was adopted by other states which came into the Union after California. A liberal divorce law was passed, lotteries were forbidden, and a homestead law passed by which a man's home was exempted from seizure and forced sale by his creditors.

In some respects, the legislature shared the unenlightment of Governor Peter H. Burnett. Although he disclaimed any prejudice against Negroes, he recommended that they be barred from California in a message to the legislature. In the same message he pointed out "That a war to the extermination will continue to be waged between the races, until the Indian race becomes extinguished . . ." To the surprise of a great many people, Burnett resigned about a week after he put these sentiments in his annual message, but the point of view that he manifested did not disappear from the capitol. A law to prohibit Negro immigration failed to clear the legislature because of the adamant opposition of a number of more enlightened lawmakers, but Burnett's recommendation that grand larceny be made a capital offense received the approval of a majority of the legislature and was written into law.

The legislature took other more constructive steps by dividing the state into counties and arranging for county government to be established as well as providing city charters for a number of the more important settlements. San Francisco, for example, was provided with a framework of municipal government which was as advanced as that of any city in the Union. A tax system was established, including one ill-advised revenue measure which apparently was intended to tax foreign miners by requiring them to purchase monthly licenses for twenty dollars. Heralded as a means of raising substantial sums of money, the miners' tax produced, in fact, modest revenue but much disorder, for miners were little inclined to submit to this discriminatory tax.

The legislature also had problems in settling on a site for the capital. During the Mexican period it had been shifted repeatedly by the governors from Monterey to San Diego, Santa Barbara, and Los Angeles. The first American legislature met at San Jose. Speculators and city boosters of various kinds, however, kept the question open by pushing one site or another as it suited their interests. The capital was moved to Vallejo when Mariano G. Vallejo and his associates promised a substantial tract of land and a number of buildings to the state. However, when the lawmakers assembled, the accommodations promised were still largely in the drawing stage. Sacramento boosters succeeded in luring the legislature to that city; a year later it tried Benicia only to return permanently to Sacramento in 1854.

THE POLITICAL WORLD OF CALIFORNIA
DURING THE FIFTIES

The Americans brought political as well as social and economic institutions to California. This aspect of the Americanization of the state has not always received the attention it merits, and writers and historians frequently have allowed their political prejudices to color their interpretation of this subject.

The men who came to California during the gold rush came with political philosophies, affiliations, and often ambitions. These helped to mold the political arena of California during its formative decade. The dominant national political parties of the 1840s were the Whig and Democratic. The former, headed by Henry Clay and Daniel Webster, was slowly dying although its presidential candidate, Zachary Taylor, was elected in 1848. The Democratic party, on the other hand, was a vigorous organization, and it readily became the dominant party in California. The Whigs competed in an organized way until 1854, when they gave up the ghost. For a short time, California was a single-party state, but with the demise of the Whigs there appeared new parties, the Know-Nothings or American party and the Republican party. The Know-Nothings won spectacular victories in 1855, but shortly thereafter they too went into eclipse. Toward the close of the decade the two dominant parties were the Republican and the Democratic, and these remained fixtures of California's political arena.

A great many of the men who came in the first years that followed the discovery of gold were Democrats, but then, as now, this party included men of various views. Many of them were pro-slavery in their outlook. Young, active, and intelligent representatives of the South, they thought the society that had produced them was worthy of emulation. Another large group of the Democrats of this period was from northern and western states and they were inclined to view their free societies as fitting models for California to follow. Few of them were abolitionists, but most were objectively anti-slavery. These were the major groupings of the California Democracy, as the party was popularly known, although there was a third group—apparently always a part of every American political party—which had few principles other than a thirst for the rewards of political life. They thirsted or "hunkered" for office, and they cared little for program or policy so long as they were successful.

The slavery question then was to play a major role in politics. There was little likelihood that slavery could be transplanted to California, but the Chivalry, as the pro-slavery Democrats were called, were always sensitive to the political interests of the South and were ever ready to advance those interests. One way was to divide the state and create a slave state in the southern half. This objective was pursued vigorously but was never realized. However, the Chivalry attained other political objectives. They succeeded in passing a fugitive slave law, for example, and because they controlled federal patronage throughout the decade, they were very influential in the party. In the 1860 Charleston Democratic Convention, which split and nominated two presidential candidates, the California delegates sided with the ultras of the South. Only one other free-state delegation joined them. A final measure of pro-slavery strength in the Democratic party was seen in the election of 1860 when twenty-six of the thirty-six-man state committee of the party resigned to campaign for John C. Breckinridge, the pro-slavery candidate.

California's political arena reflected not only a number of national trends but also the aspirations of a number of state leaders. Two of these men, William M. Gwin and David C. Broderick, were among the most outstanding and colorful political figures that California has ever produced. Gwin was a member of the California constitutional convention of 1849. On the eve of his departure, he informed Stephen A. Douglas that he intended to return to Washington as a senator. That ambition was realized when he was elected by California's first legislature. Thereafter he remained one of the most prominent figures of state politics, a leader of the Chivalry, a tall, distinguished veteran of politics, protégé of Andrew Jackson and a friend of other figures of American politics.

David C. Broderick, Gwin's chief rival for Democratic leadership, was the product of a much different background. Born of Irish immigrant parents in the shadow of the national Capitol in 1820, Broderick was a resident of New York City's Greenwich Village section for many years. Apprenticed in the stonecutter's trade of his father, Broderick's formal education was limited to a single year in a public school. Broderick when fourteen was also confronted with the burden of providing for himself and his family when his father died.

He was a man of considerable intelligence and ambition. Early in life Broderick developed an insatiable interest in books. He read widely in history, economics, and literature, and eventually became a remarkably well-educated man. In 1846 he ran for Congress in New York City but was defeated by a combination of Whigs and disaffected Democrats who opposed his egalitarian views, and nativists who believed that political offices should not go to people of Irish Catholic immigrant background. He never ran for office in New York again, but he remained active in politics. Although he was never a member of the Tammany Society, he observed this effective political machine at first hand; he also observed the changing urban political arena of New York City. Like Gwin, he informed a friend upon his departure for San Francisco in 1849 that he intended to return as a senator.

These two men and their respective followings in the Democratic party battled throughout the decade. From the beginning Broderick voiced his anti-slavery convictions. As a senator from San Francisco County, he fought Governor Burnett's bill to forbid Negro immigration to California, as well as the fugitive slave law. Gradually he built an organization which was based in San Francisco but which reached into all parts of the state. In program he was an anti-slavery Democrat. His chief opponents, Gwin and the Chivalry, were numerous in California but had strength beyond their numbers because the two national Democratic administrations, of Pierce and Buchanan, channeled patronage to them. At this time when parties furnished voters with ballots at the polls and polling places were widely scattered and frequently isolated, the patronage appointees of the Chivalry represented a legion which blanketed the state.

The battle between the two groups was waged fiercely throughout the decade. In 1854 Broderick and the Chivalry directed independent campaigns in the course of which Broderick's group was outpolled three to one. In that same year Broderick unsuccessfully attempted to stage a premature election for the Senate seat of

Gwin. In 1855 the breach between the two branches of the Democratic party enabled a new party, the American or Know-Nothings, to sweep the field, electing a governor, J. Neely Johnson, and the rest of the slate.

The Know-Nothings had no political program and had they not had the secret support of Chivalry-minded Democrats in the 1855 elections, they probably would not have been successful. When they won, however, the factions of the Democratic party began to take a second look at the fruits of their disunity. In the presidential campaign of 1856 they united behind the candidacy of James Buchanan and won substantial victories. Even though John C. Frémont headed the rival Republican ticket, the Democrats carried California. Broderick was a principal figure in the election, working behind the scenes and assisting a number of assemblymen and state senators. When the legislature convened in 1857 and turned to the selection of two senators, Broderick's work in the campaign paid off in his election to the United States Senate.

Once he was elected, Broderick became the object of the attention of the aspirants to the other seat. Eventually the negotiations for his support produced an agreement whereby Gwin relinquished control of patronage in exchange for Broderick's support. In effect, Broderick struck a body blow at the Chivalry, for he deprived them of that which gave them life and muscle—control over federal appointments in California. However, when the two senators reached Washington, James Buchanan, intimate friend of Gwin, refused to honor the agreement they had made. On the contrary, the President deliberately used the patronage to cripple Broderick's wing and strengthen the Chivalry.

Relations between Broderick and Buchanan went from bad to worse as the President's policy in Kansas unfolded. Here it became apparent that the pro-slavery forces enjoyed the covert support of federal appointees, and when the President openly endorsed the admission of Kansas under the odious pro-slavery Lecompton Constitution, the die was cast. Broderick denounced the President's decision as an incitement to civil war. Thereafter, Broderick, the adamant Free-Soiler and the chief opponent of the spread of slavery into the trans-Mississippi West, became a major target for the Buchanan administration and the Chivalry in California. When the latter successfully resumed its dominance of the party and began the purging of Broderick's followers, he turned to the organization of an independent Democratic party.

In 1859 his Anti-Lecompton Democratic party, the Lecompton Democratic party, and the Republican party competed for votes. The division of anti-slavery sentiment and the patronage monopoly of the Chivalry brought victory to the Lecompton Democrats, in spite of a major effort by Broderick. He stumped the state, speaking to the issues wherever an audience could be assembled. While he had been defeated, he demonstrated anew his ability, and politicos who looked ahead to 1860 realized that he was a force with which to reckon. Broderick did not play a direct role in that election, however, for a short time after the balloting of 1859 he was killed in a duel. Indirectly, however, he played a major role, for his death made him a symbol of the anti-slavery cause. Broderick Democrats flocked to the Republican standard in 1860 and Lincoln carried California. A major result was the eclipse of the Chivalry faction of the Democratic party. Deprived of federal patronage by the Republican victory, the Chivalry languished for a time, remained a threat to the stability of California during the Civil War years but went into permanent decline by the end of the war.

THE CIVIL WAR IN CALIFORNIA

The great distance from the scene of most fighting determined that California would not be involved in the actual warfare. However, the state did figure prominently in the initial plans of the Confederacy, and if these designs had been brought to fruition, the whole story of California in the Civil War would have been different. A small group decided at the onset of the war that the capture of California would be invaluable to the Confederate cause. They thought General Albert Sidney Johnston, commander of the U. S. Army on the Pacific slope, would assist in the plot. Johnston, however, declined to become involved although when he was relieved of his command, he made his way to the South by stagecoach, recruiting officers for his Confederate command en route. The superb port facilities at San Francisco would have made it possible for Confederate commerce destroyers to operate in the Pacific, and, ignoring the realities of American geography, they thought the port would provide a place of entry for supplies from Europe. The gold of California would also make it possible for them to buy necessary military supplies in Europe. Most important, an easy conquest of such a vast territory would enhance the prestige of the Confederacy in Europe to a point where recognition for the government in Richmond would be forthcoming. Recognition may have brought England and France into the war against the North. The Confederates believed that such a development would be a giant step toward victory.

The first step in this grandiose scheme was an invasion of New Mexico in the summer of 1861, the capture of Tucson followed by the organization of the Arizona Territory within the Confederacy. The threat to California of this initial invasion so alarmed the Union that a division was prepared to march from Fort Leavenworth, Kansas, to meet the Confederate challenge. In addition, a detachment of Colorado volunteers was sent into New Mexico, and in California the famed California Column under the leadership of General James Henry Carleton was prepared to meet the threat. Fortunately for the Union, Colonel E. R. S. Canby, the departmental commander in New Mexico, with the help of the Colorado volunteers, forced the invading Confederates to leave New Mexico. Deprived of their base the Confederates no longer threatened the Pacific coast. The California Column spent its time fighting Indians in New Mexico instead of Confederates. Judge David S. Terry joined the Confederate Army and attempted to organize another southern expedition to conquer California but it never got off the ground.

When the Civil War began Californians had the choice of remaining loyal to the Union, joining the Confederacy, or forming an independent republic. There was much sentiment in favor of a Pacific Republic, especially during the indecisive months between Lincoln's election and the firing on Fort Sumter. Proponents of the Pacific Republic, drawn principally from the Chivalry wing of the Democratic party, included Senator Gwin, Congressmen Burch and Scott, and Governor John B. Weller. The proposed western confederacy included California, New Mexico, Utah, Oregon, and Washington. Several resolutions favoring such a new nation were introduced in the legislature in 1861 and found some newspaper support. However, a resolution supporting the Lincoln administration passed 49 to 12, indicating the strength of Union sentiment.

Pro-Union sentiment was marshaled by Edward D. Baker, who

EDWARD DICKINSON BAKER

The most authentic California Civil War hero was Edward Dickinson Baker, soldier and senator who was in the course of a brilliant career, the close personal friend of Abraham Lincoln and David C. Broderick. Born in London in 1811, he came to Belleville, Illinois, after a prolonged stay in Philadelphia. Admitted to the bar, he moved to Springfield in 1835, where he joined the brilliant group of young lawyers which included Stephen A. Douglas, Abraham Lincoln, and Lyman Trumbull.

Baker bested Lincoln for a Whig congressional nomination and was subsequently elected in 1844. When the Mexican War began he resigned his seat and raised a regiment of volunteers. He served with distinction during the war, at its conclusion returned to the practice of law, and was soon re-elected to Congress. In 1852 he joined the trek to California where he found almost instant prominence in law and politics. By this time his native talents in oratory had been developed considerably and he was widely regarded as the most able orator on the West Coast.

His skill as a trial lawyer was demonstrated when he defended Charles Cora, who was being tried for the murder of U. S. Marshal William Richardson. Despite long odds he secured a hung jury. His achievement, however, brought him a full measure of public disapproval. In politics he was first a Whig but he became a prime mover in the establishment of the Republican party. Thereafter, while he was a Republican, he found frequent occasion to co-operate with anti-slavery Democrats led by Broderick.

After Broderick was struck down by David S. Terry, Baker delivered the funeral oration. Baker subsequently moved to Oregon, where he was elected senator in 1860 by a combination of Republicans and anti-slavery Democrats. His service in the Senate was interrupted by the outbreak of the Civil War when he was appointed a colonel of volunteers. He was killed in one of the first battles of the war, Ball's Bluff, October 21, 1861. Lincoln, who named one of his sons Edward Baker Lincoln, was moved to tears by the news of his death. Baker's body was brought back to San Francisco, where he was given a hero's funeral. He was buried in Lone Mountain Cemetery, not far from the grave of Broderick.

---

was elected senator from Oregon shortly before the war. On his way to Washington he stopped in San Francisco, where he made an impassioned oration in behalf of the Union. Months later he resigned his seat and became a general. At the Battle of Ball's Bluff in October 1861, he was killed. Abraham Lincoln was profoundly moved by the death of his friend and California was moved as well by an impressive funeral held in San Francisco. Thomas Starr King, a prominent Unitarian minister in San Francisco, and Methodist cleric Myron C. Briggs also played a role in marshaling support for the Union.

In the election of September 1861 the Unionist party, comprised of Democrats and Republicans, polled over two thirds of the vote. However, there was continued apprehension of the plans and projects of Confederate sympathizers. It is not possible to gauge accurately the extent of southern support in California but one contemporary estimate was three eighths of the total population. Included were several newspapers, some of the leaders of the Chivalry branch of the Democratic party, and scattered communities such as Visalia, El Monte, Ventura, and San Bernardino. A judge of outspoken sympathy for the Confederacy, James C. Hardy, was removed from the bench by impeachment. Secret secessionist societies emerged such as the Knights of the Golden Circle and Knights of the Columbian Star but it is futile to try to estimate their membership. Southern sympathizers did make an abortive attempt to outfit a vessel as a privateer in San Francisco but were thwarted by authorities. Throughout the war an attack on California cities by Confederate commerce destroyers was feared, especially when the *Shenandoah* entered Pacific waters toward the end of the war. A number of California-based whalers were victims of the *Shenandoah* but no attacks on coastal cities were made.

During the Civil War California furnished 15,725 volunteers for the Union Army. Most of these troops saw service in the West, as the War Department did not transport such volunteers to fight in the East. However, an arrangement was made allowing some 500 Californians to enlist under the quota of Massachusetts. In addition to manpower, the state contributed $1,200,000 to the Sanitary Commission (the Red Cross equivalent), much of it from mining communities. California's contribution amounted to one fourth of the total raised in the United States. Finally, the mines continued to produce. Shipments of bullion from California sustained the financial system of the nation through the trying years of the Civil War.

CHAPTER IX

Vigilantes, Filibusters, and Duelists

Hubert Howe Bancroft wrote two massive volumes on *Popular Tribunals* or vigilantism. As the title suggests and as his dedication to William T. Coleman confirms, this examination of vigilante committees generally approves of these ad hoc organizations which seized power and dispensed "justice." One is tempted to conclude that this is an overemphasis and not in line with the canons of objective scholarship, although most historians generally agree with Bancroft.

That there were vigilantes in profusion in the gold country of California during the eighteen fifties is well known and most knowledgeable students of California history are also aware of the two episodes in the history of San Francisco when vigilance committees seized control of the city. What is not as well understood is the genesis of these committees of vigilance. And there are other questions that arise when an inquiring mind turns to the subject. For example, what they accomplished is not clearly understood nor has the justification for vigilante activity always been made apparent.

An examination of the sources indicates that vigilante groups were organized in many towns and camps of gold rush California. They apparently appeared more frequently in areas where there was no police or court system. It was a time of much violence and little security for person or property. In the absence of police and courts miners improvised in this area as they did in many others. Culprits were haled before an improvised bar of justice. The entire group or a jury would hear the evidence, weigh it, and pronounce judgment. A sentence would be carried out immediately and then the miners would return to their usual routine. The system had a number of desirable features. Justice was rendered by one's peers; sentences were carried out immediately and were generally appropriate to the offense; and since there were no regular officials or facilities available, the convicted offender was punished and usually banished.

The lawyer and jurist of today would look askance at these ad hoc groups which donned judicial robes and in the name of justice whipped, hanged, banished, or tarred and feathered. One can plead necessity—the imperative to keep men from sliding back into the jungle—which a complete absence of law and order represents. However, it must never be overlooked that expediency and justice are often antithetical and vigilante groups tread a narrow line beyond which they become mobs.

That some of the vigilante groups of the gold rush period performed a valuable service to the communities which spawned them is beyond doubt. That others, however, became mobs of inflamed men which cast aside the constraints of civilization and became bloodthirsty savages is also the case. Why one group proceeded to handle their business with care and dispatch while another botched things from beginning to end is difficult to explain. In Dry Diggings a group in 1849 conducted a lynching in the guise of a vigilante trial and execution. As a result of the episode the town became known as Hangtown. Today it is known as Placerville.

On the other hand, there were vigilance committees which performed in a different fashion. Stephen J. Field, who was appointed to the Supreme Court by Abraham Lincoln in 1863, was part of a trial of an alleged thief. The man was arrested on a warrant, the booty was found on him in open court, and he was convicted after a trial which lasted half a day. Upon conviction, there was a further problem since there was no jail and if he should be fined and set free, the crowd would probably lynch him. Field solved this problem by sentencing the man to fifty lashes and banishment. The sentence was promptly carried out, the crowd appeased, and the ends of justice served. Field obviously understood how justice might best be served when no formal court was available.

The most famous of the vigilance committees were the San Francisco committees of 1851 and 1856. In some respects these were two distinct operations but in others the two committees were episodes in the life of the same organization. The first committee of vigilance in San Francisco was preceded by other attempts to control the lawless who crowded into the city in the first year of the gold rush. The incident which brought the 1851 committee into being began with the apprehension of a burglar. This bold thief made off with a safe in broad daylight and when he saw that he was to be overtaken in a rowboat as he made his escape, he threw the evidence—the safe—into the bay. His captors brought him back to the scene of his crime and there exchanged stories of how unsafe San Francisco was for decent people because of the likes of this desperado. Soon a committee of vigilance was organized and the prisoner, John Jenkins, was haled before it, given a summary trial, and sentenced to immediate execution. The prisoner, who was as brainless as he was bold, cursed his captors and a minister who was given an opportunity to do what he could to ease the passage of the condemned from this world to the next. The vigilantes eventually tired of his abusive tongue and dragged him out into the night where an immense throng had gathered to witness the execution. A small group of objectors led by David C. Broderick were brushed aside and the culprit was hanged.

At the coroner's inquest, only Broderick named names of the men who had played leading roles, while other witnesses pleaded poor vision, faulty light, or uncertain memory. However, the committee countered the damaging revelations of Broderick by publishing a list of their membership and a statement that they were all equally responsible. Thereafter, the committee set out to clean up the town. A number of men were hanged, some banished, and an unknown number fled the wrath of the committee. Having accomplished their objectives, the committee suspended operations. Throughout their effort they had apparently enjoyed the support of the respectable men of property of San Francisco, although a small minority resisted the usurpation of power.

It is difficult to measure the impact of the committee of 1851 on the city, although the fact that it was resurrected a few years later implies that the work was imperfectly done. In any case, in 1856 the city of San Francisco was seized by a second committee of vigilance. The events which precipitated the second committee began in 1855 with the establishment of the *Bulletin* with James King of William as publisher and editor and with the murder of William Richardson, United States marshal for the Northern District, by Charles Cora. King was a well-known member of the banking community whose firm, Adams and Company, went to the wall in a panic in 1855. King switched from banking to newspaper publishing and from the beginning displayed a unique touch. A Puritan set down in a raw, sinful community, he lashed about him with his pen, attacking corruption and immorality wherever he found them. The circulation of the *Bulletin* increased and King acquired the reputation of a moral gadfly as well as a long list of enemies.

The second major figure in the drama, Charles Cora, was a gambler who supplemented his income from the gaming tables with gifts from a notorious madam, Arabella Ryan. On one occasion when Cora took his mistress into polite society, Marshal Richardson provoked a quarrel which cost him his life. Cora was remanded to jail and was probably headed for disaster when his lady love procured for him the services of Edward D. Baker. Baker, a masterful orator who had learned his craft of trial lawyer at the side of Abraham Lincoln when both were young lawyers in Illinois, prepared his case carefully, exploited the facts, which showed Richardson was the aggressor, and secured a hung jury. Baker handled his case so well that on one occasion, a plurality of the jury favored acquittal.

Arabella Ryan and Charles Cora rejoiced as King predicted they would in an editorial entitled "The Heavens Be Hung with Black," which declared "thieves and harlots would rejoice" at the verdict. In succeeding issues of the *Bulletin* King flailed at his growing list of enemies and finally he came to James Casey, a member of the Board of Supervisors and a rival newspaper editor. King, in spite of a warning from Casey, publicized Casey's New York police record. That night en route home he met Casey. Exactly what happened next is difficult to determine, for most of the witnesses were anything but objective. According to Casey he warned the editor to defend himself and when King went for his gun, Casey drew his own and shot him. According to the version of King partisans, the ex-convict Casey ambushed an unarmed newspaper editor.

While King fought for his life and Casey languished in the city jail, the members of the committee of vigilance of 1851 reassembled. Casey and Cora were taken from jail to the headquarters of the committee, given a trial, and sentenced to execution. Conviction was assured when King died in the midst of deliberation. As James King of William's funeral cortege made its way through the streets, the two men were hanged from beams thrust out from the vigilance committee headquarters. At the last moment, Cora was wedded to his mistress and Casey was permitted to address the crowd of witnesses. He denied that he had murdered, but merely used the means typical of his time to avenge a grievous wrong that had been done him.

The committee did not stop with the execution of Cora and Casey. On the contrary, this was the beginning of its work. Ostensibly, the objective was the cleansing of the city of the hoodlums and shoulder-strikers or strong-arm men, and corrupt politicians who had tyrannized it so long. The 1851 committee had been concerned with crimes against property but this group concentrated on the political figures who allegedly packed ballot boxes, manipulated honest men, intimidated voters, and in general corrupted the political life of the city. Such people were to be eliminated, the body politic purged so that it might once again become a vibrant democratic system. A principal target of the committee was Broderick, allegedly the mastermind behind the gang.

After enrolling thousands of men beneath their banner, the committee organized itself as a paramilitary organization. An executive committee or general staff was a policy-making group which functioned under the direction of the principal leader, William T. Coleman. An intelligence system was organized to gather information about the corrupters of the political system, and a system of police was also established as well as a court system. Incumbent officers of city and county government were invited to resign and the incumbent jurists requested to leave their courts. The governor, J. Neely Johnson, elected on the Know-Nothing ticket in 1855, vacillated, at one time appearing determined to suppress the insurrection but on other occasions temporizing. The appointment of a San Francisco banker and graduate of West Point, William T. Sherman, as commander of the state forces gave some people confidence that the committee would soon be suppressed. However, when Sherman found that he could not muster sufficient manpower or arms he resigned.

The drive against the dissolute who allegedly corrupted the political life of the city proceeded. A major effort was made to assemble evidence against Broderick and his associates. Judge James McGowan, who had been his political ally, escaped arrest and incarceration, but dozens of Broderick's associates were seized and imprisoned. The political hostility of the committee to the Democratic party was obvious, for almost all of the men arrested, tried, and punished were Democrats. The opposition to the committee, dubbed the "Law and Order" party, included many incumbent officeholders of the city, county, and state governments, as well as large numbers of lawyers and judges. They bitterly denounced the charges that the courts were ineffective or corrupt but in a contest between the two groups it was obvious that the vigilance committee was better led, better organized, and more united.

On one occasion a member of the committee attempted to arrest one of the opposition in the presence of David S. Terry, Justice of the Supreme Court. A general melee broke out. In the course of it, the Justice used his favorite weapon, the bowie knife, to inflict a savage wound on the arresting officer. He was promptly seized and while the wounded man fought for his life, the vigilance committee considered its next step. Their prisoner, David S. Terry, was a former Texas Ranger, a product of the culture of the plantation South and the wild frontier of the Rio Grande country, who had been elected to the Supreme Court in 1855 as a Know-Nothing. The committee had begun with the intention of driving the wirepullers and ballot-box stuffers from the California scene, but now they had one of the highest officers in the state in custody. To deal with him as they had dealt with Casey or Cora would undermine the very fabric of government. As they pondered their dilemma and pressured Terry to solve their problem by resigning, the wounded man recovered. That improved the situation considerably. Terry was released with the suggestion that he resign, but a short time later he was back on the bench in Sacramento, where he awaited his next rendezvous with destiny, on the field of honor with Broderick.

The vigilance committee, meanwhile, was running out of steam. At its height they had thousands of men on the rolls, several facilities to maintain, and substantial expenses. At the outset, emotion spurred them but as week after week passed, the activity became much less exciting. It was all well and good to take up arms and defend the city and its society against the general assaults of the hoodlum elements, but as they were rounded up or went into hiding or were banished the committee had fewer and fewer dragons to slay. Spokesmen later said that since the work of the committee was done, it decided to disband. There is good reason to believe that costs and boredom had something to do with the dissolution. A final parade of six thousand men organized in military fashion and a reception at Fort Gunnybags, their headquarters, brought the episode to a close.

From that time to this, historians have generally been approving of the committee. They describe it as a necessity brought into being by the breakdown of the courts, the venality of the police, and the presence in the city of political organizations which ran municipal government in a corrupt manner. At such times, say such spokesmen, it is entirely proper for the respectable elements to take power, cleanse the body politic, and restore the citizenry to power. A minority challenges this view. Essentially spokesmen for this position assert that it was not simply a confrontation between good and evil, but a matrix of conflict which pitted men of various ethical views and political persuasions against one another. That the committee was motivated by political considerations in part is to be seen in the statistics which show that: "four men were hanged, twenty-eight banished, and two hundred and sixty arrested. All were Democrats." That Broderick was a chief target of the committee is also apparent although it appears that he was too big a figure for them to deal with summarily. They made a massive effort to find evidence which would convict him of any one of a number of offenses—ballot-box stuffing, corruption, bribery, etc.—but not a single solid piece of evidence was uncovered. The failure of the vigilance committee to produce anything to support the allegations against Broderick is strongly suggestive that none existed.

According to the pro-vigilance interpretations the city of San Francisco was improved immensely as a result of the "purifying work" of the committee, but a recent examination of the incidence of crime in the pre-vigilance and the post-vigilance periods exhibits little significant difference. Perhaps the most important change that came to the city was in the field of politics. Before the onset of the committee, the Chivalry Democrats, the Broderick-led Democrats, the Whigs, and the Know-Nothings competed for control of the city government. After the committee had done its work, which physically smashed the Broderick organization and discredited the Chivalry, a new political organization, the People's party, reigned supreme. It was essentially the political arm of the vigilance committee. During its period of dominance, city and county expenditures were curbed. Municipal improvements and services were also reduced. In part these changes reflected the changing situation of the city. In the early fifties when San Francisco was a settlement struggling to become a town and later a city it was necessary to build in great part from scratch. Naturally in those years of pioneering when the price level was inflated, public expenditures tended to be quite high. In summary, while a case may be assembled for the establishment of the vigilance committee, it is possible to balance that case. In view of the damage that is done to the democratic tradition by resort to vigilance committees, it would seem that the pro-committee spokesmen have their work cut out for them.

VIGILANTES OF THE HINTERLAND

San Francisco's committees of vigilance were preceded as well as followed by similar groups which operated in the mining camps, the towns, and the settlements in the hinterland. They were a mixed assortment: some were efficient and well organized, others were mobs pure and simple. In 1855, according to Bancroft, there were forty-seven vigilante executions—twenty-four for theft, nineteen for murder, and four "for minor offenses." Unfortunately he did not indicate the specific minor offenses which led to execution.

The San Francisco committee of 1851 was the prototype which was followed by other groups. A Sacramento committee was organized about a fortnight after the San Francisco committee and followed the same plan of operation. It distinguished itself by executing a highway man who had been granted a pardon by the governor. Not content with the execution, they burned the governor in effigy; had he been present they might have resorted to stronger measures. Other committees were organized in such places as Marysville, Stockton, Chico, Nevada City, Grass Valley, Sonora, Visalia, and elsewhere. Generally they came to power when there was considerable dissatisfaction with the police and courts or when there were no such facilities. In the name of preserving a degree of civilization they destroyed one of its most basic institutions—the right to a fair trial;

in the interest of upholding the law they took the law into their own hands and broke it. While they may sometimes be excused in view of the extreme provocation that sometimes preceded them, these substitutes for Anglo-Saxon legal procedures were productive of many evils and few lasting benefits. If men of good will had devoted a portion of the time and energy which was consumed by vigilance committees to supporting the police and courts, they and their society would have been better off.

The vigilance committees functioned in a variety of ways. One had a blacksmith produce a branding iron of HT for horse thief and culprits were branded on the hip or cheek according to the gravity of their offense. They were also whipped, the number of lashes reflecting not the crime but the endurance of the offender. Heads were frequently shaved, ears cropped, and cheeks branded. In one instance a man who had defrauded a member of his family was taken from jail and swung several times from a tree limb to persuade him to return the property. He was persuaded. A committee in Santa Clara bailed an offender from jail, administered a lashing, and then returned him to the custody of the authorities. In San Jose in 1851 two Mexicans, father and son, were convicted by a vigilante court of cattle stealing and sentenced to twenty-six lashes each. The son arose and requested that he take his father's punishment as well as his own. Upon further consideration, the court took the plea into consideration and released the father with a fine of five dollars.

Some of the committees were simply mobs bent on vengeance. Consider, for example, the group in Downieville which brought a Mexican woman to their improvised bar of justice. The night before, a drunken miner celebrating the Fourth of July broke down the door to her cabin. The woman grabbed a knife and defended herself and her home. The next moment the man lay dying in the dust of a knife thrust to the heart. A mob seized the woman, took her into the plaza, and organized a kangaroo court which convicted her forthwith and sentenced her to be hanged. She was given a half hour to prepare to meet her maker and then taken to a bridge where a rope with a noose was prepared. She mounted the ladder, adjusted the noose around her neck, pulling a braid of hair free, and with the "hungriest, craziest, wildest mob standing around" was hanged. During the trial it had been difficult to keep the mob from tearing her limb from limb, but after it was over there was no further need for restraint. The "hanging of the woman was murder," said a witness and there seems no reason to argue with that judgment.

Los Angeles was eclipsed by San Francisco in many ways during the first generation of American rule, but not in vigilante activities. Although her committees were not as large as those of the metropolis beside the bay, they were quite active. A meeting of prominent citizens in the mayor's office in 1851 laid the groundwork for a unique committee of vigilance which was organized under the auspices of the law. However, it did not operate long as a lawful organization. In midsummer two men who had allegedly robbed and murdered two cattle buyers on the San Diego to Los Angeles trail were hanged on a gallows atop Fort Hill. A few years later another multiple execution by a committee took place in the late afternoon sun. One of the victims was a shoemaker, Cipriano Sandoval. Several years later his innocence was established when the actual killer made a deathbed confession.

In January 1855, when a Supreme Court stay of execution reached Los Angeles postponing a day of judgment for David Brown, a convicted murderer, the incumbent mayor, Stephen C. Foster, resigned and led a mob which broke into the city jail and seized the prisoner. Brown was dragged to a gateway opposite the courthouse and mounted on a chair with a noose around his neck; he gently chided the assemblage for their lack of expertise before he kicked over the chair and died. Brown's comment came upon the heels of another botched hanging which preceded his execution. On that occasion the knot came untied and it was necessary to pick the prisoner up and repeat the operation. The lack of know-how is somewhat incongruous in view of the frequent use of the gallows in Los Angeles. The mayor who led the mob was re-elected a short time after he had participated in the execution of Brown.

The heyday of the vigilance committees was the twenty years that followed the discovery of gold, although periodically California has witnessed a renewal of vigilante activities. Even in the twentieth century men have turned from the regular system of administering justice to ad hoc groups which have taken the law into their own hands. Almost always, the step appears to be justified to those in attendance although sober second thoughts frequently lead to other conclusions.

GRAY-EYED MEN OF DESTINY

During the 1850s California was a staging area for a number of filibustering expeditions against Mexico, Hawaii, or Central America. Baja California and the state of Sonora were the chief objectives of a number of the filibusters. Both areas were thought to be rich in resources, but were poor in sovereignty. The absence of a stable political, social, and economic system provided a power vacuum into which moved the filibuster. In some respects a conquistador of the nineteenth century, such men sensed opportunity in these unstable regions and attempted to seize power and control over them by means of their weapons. It is tempting to overgeneralize beyond this point, but the careful observer will note that filibustering expeditions differed in leadership, objectives, personnel, and results. The differences reflect the mosaic of causes which brought them into being.

Some of the expeditions were in an American tradition which began early in the nineteenth century. Aaron Burr and William Walker, for example, walked similar paths toward their personal destinies. Burr had grandiose visions of a private kingdom which would be carved out of a debilitated Spanish empire in America. Walker came a half century later, but his objective was similar to that of Burr. Andrew Jackson in Florida in 1818, although a commissioned general in the United States Army, postured in the classic filibustering manner. His protégé in Texas, Sam Houston, followed the lead of Old Hickory in destroying the sovereignty of the existing power in anticipation of American acquisition. John C. Frémont and his Bear Flaggers had some of the characteristics of filibusters. In sum, such expeditions were a part of the American past.

For a number of reasons California was aptly fitted as a staging ground for filibustering expeditions during the gold rush period. After the early flush years of forty-nine and fifty, there was assembled in California an assortment of restless adventurers whose taste for hard work in the mines had been satisfied. Most of them had learned that placer mining was a far cry from the romantic visions they once had. They had also learned that placer mining was frequently unrewarding and many were open to other propositions. When organizers of filibustering expeditions sought recruits, they found them in the backwash of the placer mining country, temporary residents of San Francisco. These men were, if not professional soldiers or veterans of the Mexican War, at least proficient enough with firearms to serve in a private army. Most were tempered by frontier living, many had contempt for Latins generally, few had an abiding respect for law, especially the law of foreigners, many were willing to follow a leader who promised them gold, land, and adventure.

The romantic notions which led the Argonauts to the field of honor also led them to the banners of filibusters. The fascination of the uniform and the military enabled the vigilance committee of San Francisco of 1856 to muster more than six thousand men who were happy to demonstrate their concern for public peace and safety and march in dress parade. Filibusters and vigilantes were often cut from similar cloth.

Not all of the expeditions were directed and staffed by Americans. On the contrary, several were of foreign composition and even anti-American in inspiration and outlook. There were several French expeditions, for example, which were organized in California, but directed by French aristocrat-adventurers and composed of French citizens. The France which spawned them was the Second Empire, created by Louis Napoleon out of the ruins of the abortive revolution of 1848 and the Second Republic. He revived old imperial dreams and merged them with visions of a new empire. His regime was permeated with the trappings, pomp, parades, and pretense of the France of yesteryear—of *The* Napoleon. A number of the citizens of France imbibed of the heady brew of empire and militarism and when they came to California in the 1850s they brought with them a taste for such things. When they came as members of mining companies their energies were fully absorbed by the demands of placer mining, but when the reality of the placer mines left them frustrated and disappointed their energies sought other outlets. A number turned to filibustering.

The first expedition against Sonora was organized in 1851 in San Francisco by a young French nobleman, the Marquis Charles de

Pindray. When it landed in Guaymas it differed from other filibustering expeditions in that it apparently came to Mexico in good faith in response to an invitation from the Mexican government, which sought colonists and miners to populate its northern frontier province of Sonora. These transplanted Europeans would secure the area against the Yaquis and develop it for themselves and for Mexico. Almost from the time they arrived, however, the French filibusters had problems with the resident Mexican population. As they marched into the interior of Sonora toward a tract of land which had been set aside for them, friction increased. Pindray, as the leader of the aliens, was caught in the middle of the conflict between his own group and the Sonorans. Internal discord wracked the filibusters. When Pindray fell ill, the problems of the group mounted and when he was found dead of a pistol shot in the head, the expedition neared final collapse. The survivors, pondering the fate which had dogged them and speculating on the nature of their leader's death, made their way to the coast and quit the country.

In a matter of months, a second filibustering expedition, also led by a French nobleman, Count de Raousset-Boulbon, was organizing for a similar descent on Mexico. To avoid conflict with the government, Raousset traveled to Mexico City, where he secured an agreement with the government. Under it, Raousset and a company he had organized were to have a concession for the development and exploitation of the mineral resources of northern Sonora in exchange for bringing a group of colonists and armed men into the area and defending the region against the onslaughts of Indians. A British banking house, Jecker and Company, furnished much of the essential capital in exchange for half of the company's grant.

With the financial support of Jecker and Company, the co-operation of the authorities of the central government of Mexico, and the assistance of Dillon, French consul in San Francisco, Raousset apparently headed a going concern. He had little trouble recruiting a force in San Francisco and in June 1852 the group landed in Guaymas. However, behind the scenes trouble was brewing in the form of a rival group which was also interested in the mineral resources of northern Sonora. With the support of a British banking group, Baron, Forbes and Company, Raousset's rivals secured the support of the military governor of Sonora, General Blanco.

Blanco, by various pretexts, delayed the advance of Raousset's group into the interior. Finally he posed conditions on their entry into the concession area which brought him into a confrontation with Raousset. The latter decided that his authority from the central government justified his defiance of this subordinate state official and he attempted to rally some of the residents of Sonora to his banner. With his forces augmented with local recruits he marched against Blanco's headquarters at Hermosillo, where he won a smashing victory over a superior force at a small loss of lives.

The victory of Hermosillo was not to be duplicated. On the contrary, things began to go bad from this time forward. Seriously weakened by illness, Raousset was unable to carry on as a conqueror. When the new governor of Sonora promised unmolested passage to the seacoast if the force would withdraw, Raousset and his men returned to San Francisco.

This should have been the end of the filibustering dreams of Raousset, but after consultation with his backers and a renewed promise of support, he went off to Mexico City. There he once again received the preliminary blessings of the central government headed by Santa Anna only later to lose that support. Undaunted by Santa Anna's recalcitrance, Raousset proceeded to organize for a new descent on Sonora. This time he was harassed by the American authorities in San Francisco, but a fellow filibuster, William Walker, inadvertently aided him when his expedition mounted an attack on Baja California. Alarmed at the activities of Walker, Santa Anna directed the Mexican consul in San Francisco to enlist French citizens for a colonizing venture in Sonora. The objective was to secure the area against the encroachments of Americans.

Raousset eventually succeeded in recruiting a force of several hundred men, but when he and his men landed in Guaymas he found them reluctant to pursue an attack against Mexican authority. When he persisted in an assault with a fraction of his force, the filibusters were badly defeated. Many were killed and wounded and those who survived, including Raousset himself, took refuge in the French consulate. Subsequently, when promised amnesty, they surrendered their arms. One exception was made, however. Raousset was sentenced to death by a military court. Taken from his cell in the early morning after the last rites of the Church, Raousset faced a firing squad. The bullets brought an end to this Napoleon-Don Quixote and with his death there came an end to French filibustering expeditions in Mexico for some time.

Even before Raousset reached the end of the string before a Mexican firing squad, another small, intense man of consuming ambitions and grandiose plans was preparing to take a hand in the game of filibustering. William Walker, born in Tennessee, the son of a Scotch banker, was raised in Nashville, where his father was a prominent businessman. Early in life, Walker developed a number of traits which were to characterize him until death. He was small, intelligent, avid for learning but impatient of discipline, quiet—even taciturn—proud, and stubborn. "From the very beginning his chief weapon in life must have been his fighting spirit," asserts a recent biographer.

A youth of capacious intellect and driving ambition, Walker graduated *summa cum laude* from the University of Nashville at fourteen and five years later graduated from the University of Pennsylvania Medical College. He was one of the youngest qualified physicians in the country. Two years of European studies at the Sorbonne and the University of Heidelberg followed. When he returned to Nashville he was to his contemporaries "the most accomplished surgeon that ever visited the city." The profession of medicine repelled him and he soon turned to the study of law. For a short time he practiced in New Orleans as a partner of Edmund Randolph, brilliant scion of the distinguished Randolph family of Virginia.

His legal career was as brief as his career in medicine. In 1848 he turned to journalism. As the foreign editor of the New Orleans *Crescent,* he reported the turbulent news from a Europe caught up in the revolutions of 1848. Like a fellow member of the *Crescent*'s staff, Walt Whitman, Walker's sympathies for the revolutionaries were undisguised. In the course of a single year the *Crescent* made a mark in the world of journalism but it also acquired a long list of enemies. Perhaps the final straw that alienated it from its subscribers and advertisers was its opposition to a filibustering expedition against Cuba. Supported by John C. Calhoun, who hoped to transform Cuba from a Spanish colonial possession into another bastion of slavery, the Lopez expedition met with the instant and complete disapproval of the *Crescent.* To make its opposition effective, the *Crescent* in

August 1849 printed an exposé of the Lopez expedition which revealed the location of the ship assembly points and encampments and thereby brought the glare of publicity to the project. The intervention of the federal government followed. Close on the heels of the federal government came bankruptcy to the *Crescent* and the end of Walker's career as a foreign editor.

In June of 1850 a dusty, weather-beaten Walker turned up in San Francisco for a reunion with Edmund Randolph and a new start as a journalist. His new employer was John Nugent, publisher of the *Herald*, a lively Democratic sheet destined to play a major role in California in the fifties. Walker's vehemently expressed opinions soon brought him to the attention of much of the city's population. When he attacked the clarity and legality of a local jurist's ruling one step followed another to a meeting on the field of honor with a friend of the judge. The result was a serious wound to Walker. On four other occasions Walker dueled but he never inflicted a wound on an opponent, although he was wounded twice.

Among the many friends Walker made in San Francisco was Raousset. In many ways they were peas from the same pod, incurable romantics who envisioned themselves as men of destiny. Both were courageous to the point of being foolhardy, each had an indomitable will. Although he weighed about 120 pounds with his weapons girded about him, Walker was an impressive man. His piercing gray eyes peered out of a small, befreckled face. Slow of speech, and slow to anger, he was a veritable lion when aroused. When he learned of Raousset's Napoleonic schemes for Sonora, he envied him and then decided to emulate him.

Like Raousset, Walker put a colonizing front on his expedition. His San Francisco backers, who were primarily interested in the mineral resources of Mexico, were quite willing to tolerate his rhetoric of liberation and freedom but they had very material objectives in mind. Walker landed in La Paz, Baja California, in November 1853, where a great conqueror of the sixteenth century, Cortés, had established a short-lived colony. The small group of mercenaries landed without opposition, captured the town and some of its officials, and proclaimed the Republic of Lower California. William Walker was, of course, its president. The arrival of a hundred reinforcements from San Francisco signaled the beginning of the second phase of the plan—the invasion of Sonora by way of the land bridge at the head of the Gulf of California.

It also marked the transformation of the expedition from one which might have secured the co-operation of the local population into an alien force which commandeered supplies and antagonized the local citizenry. The ships which brought reinforcements also carried arms and ammunition but little food. The consequences were inevitable. The men were put on short rations and their morale eroded. Foraging parties antagonized the local populace. The expedition was changed into a band of freebooters so far as the residents of Baja California were concerned and it required all of Walker's gifts of leadership to maintain discipline. To aggravate his problems further he learned that James Gadsden, the American minister to Mexico, had purchased a piece of northern Mexico for $10,000,000 on the final day of 1853. At the same time in a separate letter he branded Walker as a violator of federal law who would be dealt with by American authorities.

Unwilling to accept defeat, Walker persisted in his attempts to set up a puppet Republic of Lower California and Sonora. Imposing iron discipline on his men, Walker led them to the Colorado River, but by then the regiment had lost a sizable part of its numbers through desertion and sickness. At the Colorado, they lost their cattle in the crossing of the river. Their situation was desperate. The response of half the regiment was desertion and the quickest possible trip to Fort Yuma, an American sanctuary some 70 miles away. The remainder recrossed the river to rejoin a group of invalids left behind; then, harassed by Mexican irregulars, they headed north for the border. Although footsore and practically in tatters, at the crossing Walker mustered the dignity of a colonel and formally surrendered his force of thirty-four men to the American authorities.

An ordinary man would have had his fill of filibustering after these experiences, but Walker was no ordinary man. A "gray-eyed man of destiny," he had a self-image in which was blended diverse elements. He was possessed by the "spirit of manifest destiny," and ready, willing, and able to do his bit in the "liberation of oppressed peoples and nations." He was a self-proclaimed heroic conqueror who would "liberate" and bring enlightenment. He trod the thin line which separates the comic-opera figure from the man of destiny. A small deviation would lead to disgrace and disaster, but for some time Walker successfully avoided the misstep. When he returned to San Francisco he was lionized. The man who had come close to being a modern Don Quixote in his expedition against Sonora was indicted by federal authorities for the transparent violations of the laws of neutrality. But a jury of his peers acquitted him after eight minutes of deliberation, an outcome which was not surprising in view of public sentiment. Walker returned to journalism and a fling at politics in California, but his mind was still crowded with heady dreams of the self-appointed liberator. Rumors circulated in San Francisco that Walker's filibustering days were not over and restless adventurers awaited his call to arms.

The call eventually came. The new venture would use old leadership, tactics, and some veterans of the expedition against Sonora and Baja California, but focused on a new theater of operations. Hundreds of recruits came forward when Walker fastened a filibustering eye on Nicaragua. Like Sonora and Baja California, this Central American state was cursed by political instability. A promising land but accursed by chaos, civil war, poverty, disease, and rule by political generals. Presidents came and went, parties rose and fell from power, and an enduring contest between political factions aligned with British or American interests set the stage for the entry of a man like Walker.

For the next five years Walker stood at the juncture of great political and economic forces and struggled to mold them. Central America was the site of a prospective short ocean route to California for the United States. It was as well the place where British and American interests and objectives clashed. It was also the scene where actors who had imbibed the heady draught of "manifest destiny" accompanied by the representatives of New York transportation magnates mingled with the hard-bitten men of Walker's legion.

There can be little doubt that Walker was at times a tool of other men and interests—a device which rivals used to belabor Commodore Vanderbilt—but at other times this knight-errant was in full command of his fortunes and used other men. He attempted to use Nicaraguan Democrats against legitimists, Vanderbilt against his rivals and his rivals against Vanderbilt, Britons against Americans and vice versa, and the pro-slavery South against the representatives of the North. In the end he was abandoned and a final attempt in 1860 to seize Honduras ended abortively. Walker was besieged and he surrendered to a British naval officer who turned him over to the local authorities. On September 12, 1860, at Trujillo, Honduras, he was taken from an improvised cell to the remnants of a ruined stone wall. Calm and resolute, he was given the last rites of the Church. The priests stepped from his side, and a firing squad fired a volley into his diminutive figure.

As the exploits of Walker monopolized the attention of newspaper editors in the 1850s, yet another California filibuster broke into print. Henry A. Crabb, like Walker, was born and raised in Tennessee. He came to California early in the gold rush, settled in Stockton, and for a time pursued a career in law and politics. He was elected to the legislature as a Whig, although in outlook he was pro-slavery and closely aligned to the Chivalry faction of the Democratic party. As the Whigs declined in numbers and influence, Crabb turned, like many other politicians, to the rising American or Know-Nothing party. When that party triumphed in 1855, he was a leading candidate for the United States Senate, but his well-known affinity for slavery barred his election. For a time he may have considered the filibustering field which Walker was to exploit in Nicaragua, but he turned his attention from Central America to Sonora. Conditions in Sonora in 1856 had changed very little from what they had been earlier in the decade. Still rich in potential but poor in stable government and menaced by Indians, Sonora was apparently a prize which a strong man of vision might acquire. Crabb was such a man. Of chivalric background, he was a self-anointed aristocrat who would bring peace, order, and stability to this troubled land. A Mexican wife of distinguished lineage and numerous relatives in Sonora were the means whereby an invitation was extended to Crabb to bring an armed band of colonists to Sonora.

Crabb needed little encouragement. In January 1857 a force of about one hundred heavily armed and well-supplied men left San Francisco for San Pedro. On the first day of spring 1857, their overland march by way of Fort Yuma had brought them to a small Mexican town just below the border, Sonoita. From there Crabb issued a letter proclaiming his peaceful intentions to settle as colonists but warned that he would defend himself if he were attacked. Meanwhile, the Mexican authorities were preparing a hot reception. The call to arms addressed to the Mexican people of Sonora by the governor ended with "death to the filibusters."

When Crabb led about two thirds of his party out of Sonoita toward Hermosillo they were attacked on the trail. This was probably the last clear chance the group had of reaching safety but they disregarded it and pushed farther into Sonora. On April 1 they fought their way into a small town, Caborca. There in a number of small abobe houses they found a temporary refuge, but the net drew tighter. Besieged, they were finally put into a desperate plight when the roofs of the buildings were set afire. An emissary was sent forth with a flag of truce to arrange surrender. When the men came out, their guns were taken away and their arms pinioned. A few hours later, as the sun announced the arrival of a new day, executions began. When they ended, fifty-eight men lay dead. The only survivor was a fourteen-year-old. Soon after this episode the small group which had been left behind by Crabb at Sonoita was also massacred. Thus the fourteen-year-old was the only survivor of the ill-fated expedition. This brutal ending to the Crabb expedition made a considerable stir in the press and the United States government protested vehemently. However, the cold facts of the case left the United States in a difficult position. While Crabb and his men clutched the guise of peaceful colonists, they were in fact filibusters, who were acting outside the law and were entitled to all the protection extended to pirates. Sonora was never faced with the problem of dealing with another Walker or Crabb. They had walked in the footsteps of Houston, but the path had terminated in disaster rather than honor.

THE FIELD OF HONOR

Article XI, Section 2 of the California constitution of 1849 reads: "Any citizen who shall fight a duel, send or accept a challenge, or act as a second or knowingly assist any who should do this shall not be allowed to hold any office of profit or to enjoy the right of suffrage." Perhaps no other single section of the constitution was violated more completely and frequently during the next ten years. It was violated by men from all walks of society. In view of the widespread violation of other provisions of the constitution regarding right to counsel and trial by jury by vigilantes, perhaps it is not surprising that this article should be violated.

Dueling was apparently one of the more popular pastimes of Californians during the 1850s, so widespread that it is difficult to determine the number of encounters on the field of honor. An examination of the newspapers of the time indicated that several hundred such engagements broke into public print. Probably two or three times that many took place but were not reported. Duels were not only numerous, but they varied considerably. Sometimes they were conducted in strict accord with a ritualized code of honor which governed all things from the mode of dress of the seconds to the number of doctors who were to attend. In other instances only the form was utilized and the encounter was nothing more than a fight with guns.

The individuals who engaged in dueling represented a large part of the population. Men of southern background, among whom the defense of personal honor through individual combat was accepted, were frequently involved, but men from the states of the Middle West as well as the East were also represented. The concept of personal honor was most important to the men of southern plantation society. They left many things behind them, but they brought the code to California and they lived and sometimes died by it.

The code of honor was a collection of practices and rules which had emerged over a period of centuries before the chivalry of the plantation South applied it in an American setting. The code was based on the notion that each individual had personal honor which must not be impugned by another individual. A personal insult, a social slight, or a reflection cast on Church, hearth, or kin must elicit from the man who observed the code a particular response. The first measure and the last were all determined by the ritual of the code. So involved was it that expert knowledge in the code was needed and men such as Charles Fairfax, of the Virginia and British Fairfaxes, were frequently consulted. He was the last word, the final arbiter who could determine what the next step should be or what meaning should be attached to a particular phrase.

One of the first duels fought in San Francisco pitted two serape-clad Mexicans in a knife fight to the death. Another encounter in 1848 pitted an officer of Stevenson's regiment against a clerk in a hide and tallow house. It was fought with rifles and ended with one of the principals—the officers—so badly wounded that an arm had to be amputated. Newspaper editors frequently figured in affairs of honor, usually because they published something disparaging about another individual. Congressman Edward Gilbert, editor of the *Alta California*, was killed in a duel with James W. Denver, who was, in the course of a busy political life, Secretary of State of California, a congressman, a territorial governor, a Union general, and the man for whom the principal city of Colorado is named. In 1854 two newspaper editors, Frank Washington of the San Francisco *Times and Transcript* and Charles A. Washburn of the city's *Alta California*, fought with rifles at forty paces. Washburn was badly wounded. William Walker, who was to gain a measure of lasting fame as a filibuster, while editing a newspaper in San Francisco in 1850 met a fellow editor, William H. Carter, on the field of honor. Walker was wounded but survived to fight another day. One of the most renowned of the many encounters pitted Joseph McCorkle, a congressman, against Senator William M. Gwin. The men had disagreed over a lady, say some accounts, but more likely over federal patronage. In any case they agreed to meet on the field of honor with rifles. Witnesses came to the scene with picnic baskets and the like, prepared for an interesting outing. The two men blazed away at one another and when the smoke had settled an innocent jackass was found mortally wounded. Gwin and McCorkle, doubtless relieved by the narrow escape each had experienced, declared themselves satisfied and the affair was ended. A newspaper editor commented that the wrong jackass had been killed!

While some of these encounters had a comic-opera air, others were deadly serious matters. They frequently grew out of political antagonisms. At such times a Whig was pitted against a Democrat or a Chivalry Democrat was pitted against an anti-slavery Democrat. In 1855 Charles Lippincott affronted a prominent Know-Nothing.

The duel which followed featured double-barreled shotguns loaded with ball. The inevitable death of one of the combatants followed.

Another of the more notable encounters was fought on Angel Island in San Francisco Bay between George Pen Johnson and William I. Ferguson. The former was a political aide to William Gwin, a stalwart member of the Chivalry faction, and author of a law which made dueling a criminal offense. His opponent, William I. Ferguson, was a genial young man from Illinois, a friend of Abraham Lincoln, and as a state senator from Sacramento a staunch ally of Broderick. At the duel, the men used pistols to assail one another. Three times they exchanged shots without injury. Each time the seconds of each party parleyed and each time Johnson was unappeased. On the fourth exchange, Ferguson fell with a severe wound in his right thigh. Physicians advised amputation, but Ferguson steadfastly declined until his condition forced an operation which he did not survive. His opponent was tried but was acquitted when doctors testified that the wound would not have been fatal had Ferguson submitted to the amputation earlier. Ironically, the author of the law which made dueling a criminal offense escaped punishment.

A further touch of irony was the fate which brought David S. Terry and David C. Broderick together as pallbearers for Ferguson. A year later the two men faced one another on the field of honor in the second most famous duel in American history. The encounter took place a few days after the close of the election of 1859. Shortly after the balloting, incensed at the slurs, insults, and epithets of his opponents, Broderick accepted a challenge. His opponent was not his principal political antagonist Gwin, but a tall, truculent former Texan and stalwart figure of the Chivalry, David S. Terry. Terry had been elected to the Supreme Court and was completing his term when he challenged Broderick. They met on September 13, 1859, on the field of "honor" near Laguna Merced, just across the San Francisco-San Mateo line. The pistols, brought to the site by the Terry party, had been used in practice by the judge. When the word to fire was given, Broderick's pistol misfired, the bullet striking the ground about 6 feet in front of him. A second later, Terry, from twenty paces away, shot him in the chest. Broderick lingered for three days before he died. His funeral was the largest ever held in

California. A close friend and Abraham Lincoln's closest friend, Edward D. Baker, delivered a funeral oration which remains a classic.

The Chivalry realized no advantage from the death of Broderick. Gwin had predicted in the campaign that "if we kill him it will make him a martyr," and this was exactly what happened. At the Republican national convention in 1860 a giant portrait of Broderick looked down at the gathering and Broderick Democrats helped Lincoln carry California in 1860. During the Civil War years Broderick's name was prominent in the rhetoric of patriotic speakers.

Public opinion turned sharply against Terry and his allies in the Chivalry. When it was learned that the gunsmith at the duel warned that Broderick's pistol had a hair trigger, suspicion that Broderick had been assassinated became widespread. After some delay Terry was haled before a court presided over by a fellow member of the Chivalry. In a legal proceeding which was permeated with fraud and farce, the charges were quashed. Terry went free to fight again as an officer of the army of the Confederate States of America. His benefactor-judge James C. Hardy was impeached and removed from the bench for disloyalty during the Civil War, but Terry survived the war and returned to California and the practice of law. His death in a lurid encounter with the bodyguard of Supreme Court Justice Stephen J. Field brought a fitting end to the career of California's "Dueling Judge."

For all practical purposes the Terry-Broderick encounter brought an end to California's dueling period. There were several affairs of honor in the years that followed but the most famous duel in California's history produced a popular revulsion which led to the disappearance of dueling and duelists. The decline of personal combat in defense of honor reflected several changes in society as well. As society became more stable, as the civilizing influences of family and home and Church appeared, as the Chivalry declined in numbers and influence, there was less need for this remnant of the Age of Chivalry. In some respects dueling, vigilantism, and filibustering were spawned by the society of the 1850s; when that society disappeared, duelists, vigilantes, and filibusters disappeared.

CHAPTER X

Transportation

Wherever men assemble, they build transportation facilities to carry themselves and their goods where necessity or fancy dictates. These facilities reflect the needs, desires, and capabilities of the society of which they are a part. In Indian times in California, for example, foodstuffs were carried by Miwok Indians in large cone-shaped baskets; Chumash fishermen navigated the Channel Island waters in craft built of wood cast up by the sea, and ingenious rafts made of tules ferried Indians of the interior valleys across lakes and marshes. In Spanish times the sailing ship, mule train, and ox-drawn *carreta* appeared. The entry of the Americans brought steam vessels as well as the clipper ship. Oxcarts gave way to the Concord stage and huge freighting wagons. Soon the Pony Express began its now legendary rides across country. On the first trip, the Pony Express made the final leg into San Francisco on a great paddle-wheel steamboat. A historical instant later, the railroad locomotive was introduced. The railroad transformed the state, touching and shaping every aspect of society, but before its work was done, another innovation, the automobile, appeared.

The history of transportation in California followed familiar lines. Transportation facilities evolved from the rudimentary and primitive to the complex and sophisticated. They reflected the society which spawned them, but at the same time they shaped and molded the society of which they were a part. They made it possible for men to do things which were previously impossible. However, in some respects, California's situation gave a unique cast to her transportation history. In this land, removed from much of the western world and isolated from even its immediate neighbors by geographic barriers, the development of transportation had far-reaching ramifications. The lack of adquate facilities to carry produce to market limited the exploitation of California's agricultural potential for a time. In this productive land, a substantial part of its agricultural potential lay fallow. When means appeared to carry its produce to markets, the consequences were immediate and widespread. In summary, the existence, distribution, and availability of transportation facilities had far-reaching social, economic, and political consequences which were not always immediately apparent.

THE CLIPPER SHIPS

American mariners became interested in California early in the nineteenth century. During the Spanish and Mexican periods, American vessels engaged in the fur trade, whaling, or the hide and tallow trade became so numerous on the coast that "Boston ship" became a generic term which was part of the vocabulary of the general Spanish-speaking citizenry. Interest and experience derived from hundreds of voyages and contacts gave American mariners advantage at the outset of the gold rush. They had the know-how, the personnel, and the ships. When the gold rush created unprecedented demands for transportation to Alta California, they stepped in and met the need. Hundreds of ships made their way under the American ensign to San Francisco, the chief port of entry. A half thousand passed through the Golden Gate before July 1850. A great many of them, long past their prime but pressed into service for a last voyage, made their way round the Horn to a final resting place in the waters of San Francisco Bay. Deserted by crews as well as by owners, the abandoned hulks swung on rust-covered anchor chains for months and even years—forgotten derelicts which eventually disintegrated and sank, fell victim to fires, or were broken up for scrap. Some found a final period of service as floating warehouses, hotels, stores, lodging houses, brothels, and one even served for a time as an improvised jail for the lawless and disorderly of San Francisco.

These ugly ducklings of the sea were soon followed by an armada of the most beautiful ships ever constructed—the clipper ships. From keel to topmast, they were built for speed, their hulls streamlined and their running gear designed to carry a "cloud of canvas." They were ruggedly constructed of stout oak and spruce, so that even when seas were rough and wind conditions adverse, they could be driven. They were commanded and crewed by men who had been steeled by sailing in all the oceans of the world. When such men were given such ships, they set records which no one since has bettered.

The clipper ship boom years were in the decade which preceded the Civil War. The boom was launched by a number of peculiar circumstances which pushed the price of freight to California to $60 a ton and provided maritime investors with the opportunity to recoup the cost of construction of a clipper in a single voyage to San Francisco. That matrix of circumstances lured a number of men and their ships into the trade. In a single year more than twenty vessels designed for the California trade were to be seen on the ways of the shipyards of New England. Some of them, finished before the close of 1850, made the run to San Francisco before freight rates dropped drastically. They began to decline as more ships were attracted, although the commerce remained profitable throughout the decade.

The most celebrated clipper ship voyage was that of the *Flying Cloud*, a stately greyhound of the sea, designed expressly for the California trade. Its maiden run in 1851 took it out of New York on June 2, round the Horn for the northward run on July 17, and off North Beach in San Francisco on August 31. The passage of 13,610 nautical miles had taken just eighty-nine days and twenty-one hours. At times, the *Flying Cloud* made eighteen knots and in one day she sailed 374 miles. Less than a month later, another clipper made the return voyage in seventy-six days. Her captain was so impressed with this feat that he requested it be engraved with his name on his tombstone.

The heyday of the clipper ship, when as many as five ships arrived in San Francisco within forty-eight hours, lasted a brief few years in the 1850s. A sharp decline of freight rates and the inexorable march of steam power soon relegated the clipper to the misty memories of old mariners. For a time, they had played an important role in bringing freight to a far-off California market which was the preserve of men who had gold and much need for the assorted output of eastern America. The demise of the clipper was hastened by the coming of steam, but it was also speeded by men who saw that geography dictated a full use of the Isthmus of Panama in the transporting of goods and people to and from California. When a railroad was completed across the Isthmus, clipper ship speed was offset and the clipper ship era in California was doomed.

EXPRESS COMPANIES—GENESIS OF
WELLS, FARGO AND COMPANY

Express companies operated in eastern states long before the gold rush, but it was in this period that they flourished and developed along a number of new lines which characterize their operations to the present time. One of the first express companies began as a private postal service when an enterprising young man, Alexander Todd, proposed to a group of miners that they each pay him a dollar to act as their agent in claiming their mail in San Francisco. Upon delivery of the mail to the miners in the field, in this instance in Jacksonville, Todd was to receive an ounce of gold dust per letter. Such rates would horrify a modern patron of the post office, but to the lonely miner of the Sierras who had been for months without a word from home, an ounce per letter was cheap enough.

Within weeks, Todd had a lucrative business in operation as thousands of miners subscribed to his service. Soon the operations of the company expanded to include dozens of gold rush towns and camps. Additional service was also provided to include the mailing of letters and the delivery of gold dust to banks in San Francisco for a fee of 5 per cent of its value. The profits rose accordingly, to as much as $1000 a day by Todd's figuring. Operating out of a permanent headquarters in Stockton, Todd organized daily service to San Francisco from dozens of towns in the interior. The company utilized its own facilities supplemented with those of staging companies which served adjacent areas.

The success of Todd and other pioneer express companies, notably Weld and Company, operating as early as 1849 out of Marysville and San Francisco, attracted the attention of other enterprising businessmen. In the decade which preceded the Civil War as many as three hundred express companies operated in California. Some were "one-man, one-mule" outfits, but others were substantial concerns which employed dozens of men and much equipment. A restless and mobile population drifting wherever gold or rumors of gold dictated, and scattered throughout the state, provided opportunity to young men of enterprise and limited capital.

Success brought mixed blessings. Not only were competitors attracted to this profitable business, but the valuables attracted the attention of holdup men. As serious as the bandits who waylaid expressmen on lonely passages of the roads were the quiet thieves in the night—trusted employees of the companies who embezzled—sometimes absconding with huge sums of gold dust which had been entrusted to the company. Todd reported losses of more than $150,-000 in a few years. Fire was another hazard which struck often and sometimes with disastrous results. Todd was "burned" nine times in several years.

In the early years of the fifties, the express business attracted hundreds of enterprising young men who had little capital but much ambition and initiative. In the field from the beginning was Adams and Company, destined to rise to a prominent place in California commerce and make its name a household word. An announcement in the *Alta California* in November 1849 heralded the arrival of Adams and Company Express, a well-known concern in New England. In three short years the company built a statewide organization. It absorbed rival concerns—Todd's Express for instance —and affiliated with others and eventually established itself as the largest as well as the most efficient express concern in the state. Its operations extended beyond California, for it delivered mail as well as gold and cash to an area which stretched from the Sierras to New England via such transit points as Sacramento, San Francisco, the Isthmus of Panama, New York, and Boston.

As it grew to the largest business establishment in California, Adams and Company diversified. Soon its express operation was rivaled in size with a banking service. Through thousands of loans, it underwrote enterprises of every size and description and its fortunes became tied to companies and individuals scattered throughout the state. It was, in fact, the giant of the business world of California; it handled more dust and cash, dealt with more people,

and gave financial services to more enterprises than any other concern.

The only serious rival of Adams and Company was another express concern, born in New York in 1845 as a partnership of Henry Wells and William George Fargo. In 1849 these men were attracted to California as a promising new field of operations, but it was not until 1852 that they organized a new concern, Wells, Fargo and Company. From the beginning the enterprise showed great promise, for it had skilled and experienced management as well as sizable amounts of capital, much of it eastern money. Like its rival, Adams and Company, it not only operated an express and freighting business but also engaged in banking.

In July 1852 its California operations began. From the start, fortune smiled on Wells, Fargo. The pioneering work had already been done in California, and in some respects, Wells, Fargo simply followed in the footsteps of earlier concerns. It affiliated with other express companies, purchased some, and drove still others out of business through competition. Its working arrangements with the Pacific Mail Steamship Company expedited its traffic to the Atlantic states via the Isthmus, and its network of lines established or acquired in California in the first two years of operations covered every part of the state. By 1854 the infant born but two years before was ready to challenge the leadership of Adams and Company.

The two firms became involved in a competition which delighted their customers as express rates fell and each concern strove to outdo the other. The competitive spur drove management and employees alike toward improved schedules and service. Both concerns apparently prospered, but they became immersed in their operations and oblivious of an impending crisis which subjected both to the greatest stress either had experienced.

The crisis which affected every concern in California (197 businesses in San Francisco alone failed) began in February 1855 when the latest dispatches from the East announced the failure of Page, Bacon and Company, a St. Louis, Missouri, bank which had a branch in San Francisco. The failure of Page, Bacon in St. Louis placed the San Francisco branch under heavy pressure as nervous depositors withdrew their funds. To complicate the problem, the local bank had recently shipped almost a million dollars in gold to its hard-

pressed parent concern in Missouri. The run on Page, Bacon and Company gathered momentum and soon depositors of other banks began withdrawing their money. Every bank in California felt the pressure, and when the major banks in Sacramento suspended operations, hysteria seized San Francisco's affluent citizenry.

Banks which had sizable reserves were able to meet the withdrawals, but concerns which were extended were vulnerable. Adams and Company had long skirted with such peril—a month prior to its failure on February 23, 1855, its assets exceeded its liabilities by a small margin of little more than 10 per cent. That margin would have been sufficient in prosperous times, but it vanished quickly in the panic which followed "Black Friday," February 22, 1855. For a time, the management of Adams and Company hoped that the concern could continue its express operations even if its banking department was forced to suspend, but the close relationship of the two operations in the company made this impossible. To complicate the concern's problems was a loss of public confidence. A great many people believed that Adams and Company had defrauded some of its depositors by closing its doors before its gold reserve was exhausted and by mingling the bullion of shippers and depositors. Investigations following the closing indicated that the company had conducted its operations in an imprudent fashion which contributed to its downfall. They also revealed details which intrigued and incensed former depositors. An illegal, unrecorded transfer of substantial amounts of bullion on the eve of its closing and the discovery of some of the books of Adams and Company floating in the bay were two graphic pieces of evidence. Among other complaints was one aired against its San Francisco personnel which indicated that bank officers had reassured depositors of the bank's soundness until the eve of its suspension. People who lost their savings were incensed. So widepread was the antagonism to Adams and Company that all hopes of resurrecting the concern were doomed. It required ten years of litigation to sort out the affairs of the bankrupt concern. In that decade the company was paralyzed and its assets consumed by the expenses of litigation.

Wells, Fargo was also shaken by the panic which drove Page, Bacon and Adams and Company to the wall, but it survived. In part its survival was due to superior management and more prudent finan-

cial practices than those of its competitors. It had always maintained a sizable cash reserve as well as a substantial excess of assets over liabilities. In advance of the crisis, its management was strengthened in San Francisco and given considerable authority. Although it was forced to suspend operations for a short time—from February 23 to February 27 in San Francisco—when it reopened its doors, it met all demands. As a matter of fact, the panic strengthened Wells, Fargo and Company, for the general public concluded its survival was evidence of inherent strength.

The disappearance of Adams and Company from express as well as banking in San Francisco left Wells, Fargo as the major concern in the field. Soon it was expanding operations not only in California but into the Pacific Northwest. The day when Adams and Company was a household word was no more. For ensuing generations, Wells, Fargo, banking and express, was part of the lexicon of the business and commercial world.

FREIGHTING, STAGING, AND THE PONY EXPRESS

The same decade witnessed the building of the Isthmian railroad, the establishment of regular steamship service linking the Atlantic and the Pacific coasts, and the formation of regular stage and freighting routes across the expanse which separated the Mississippi Valley and California. Such developments coming within a single ten-year period reflected a similar complex of circumstances. As the gold rush unfolded on the West Coast, bringing accelerated growth in the population and creating unprecedented demand for transportation facilities, entrepreneurs came forward to fill such needs. In the Great Basin region, military needs coupled with those posed by the great overland migration placed opportunity before the men who could deliver the goods. And the frontier communities which lay in isolated enclaves in the Southwest, as well as the tiers of settlements which led the advance into the trans-Mississippi West, all awaited the coming of the transportation facilities which would end their isolation.

Among the first on the scene were the freighting outfits, who began the mastery of their business meeting military supply needs during the Mexican War. One of the first to operate under a military contract system was James Brown, who delivered goods to Santa Fe in 1848 for the War Department. He prospered, and pleased the Army. In 1850 he acquired a partner, William H. Russell, and a renewal of his freighting contract with the Army, but before he fully understood the capability of his new partner, James Brown contracted typhus and died. Russell acquired an associate, William B. Waddell, and several years later the two men acquired a third partner, Alexander Majors. The three partners, Russell, Majors, and Waddell, became leading figures in the movement of men and freight in the trans-Mississippi West until the Civil War.

Russell, Majors, and Waddell became the largest of the freighting concerns, acquiring thousands of head of livestock, hundreds of wagons, and nearly two thousand men. They planned well, organized carefully, and by the middle of the 1850s the concern was not only the largest but the most efficient freighting outfit in the West. Unexpected fortune came their way when the Mormon War of 1857 piled unexpected new demands upon them. The Army required further supplies for the Utah Expedition, and Russell, Majors, and Waddell were forced to deal with this contingency. About this time there occurred the first of a series of disasters that drove the company toward bankruptcy. Mormon guerrillas captured and burned several of the caravans, and others were entrapped in winter drifts on their way to sanctuary at Fort Bridger. To complicate matters, the concern was unable to obtain payments for past services because War Department appropriations were exhausted.

Russell, doubtless discouraged by the setbacks, was not prepared to throw in the sponge. Still thinking in grandiose terms and anticipating a mining rush into the Pikes Peak country, he formed a new concern, the Leavenworth and Pikes Peak Express Company, which started staging operations between Denver and Leavenworth in the spring of 1859. Limited traffic, heavy expenses amounting to $1000 a day, and an inadequate income—no government subsidy was available—soon brought the company to a crisis. Russell's response was the acquisition of a concern that ran a monthly mail between Independence and Salt Lake City under a $130,000 annual subsidy. The cost of the purchase and new expenses incurred in the building of new way stations brought Russell's firm to the brink of bankruptcy. His associates, Waddell and Majors, observed from the sidelines for a time before they decided to take a hand. The Russell enterprise was reorganized as the Central Overland, California and Pikes Peak Express. Profits from freighting were to nurture the staging operation and hopefully restore prosperity to the whole business. Success hinged on the hope that the staging and mail-carrying operation across the Central route would enable the embattled concern to wrest the lucrative subsidy for carrying mail to California away from the Butterfield Overland Mail. To focus attention on the Central route and create an image of efficiency and rapid service, Russell persuaded his partners to join him in the organization of the famed Pony Express.

The Pony Express, the most renowned transportation system ever developed in the West, was conceived as a means of publicizing the facilities and capabilities of the Central Overland, California and Pikes Peak Express Company. It was to be an overwhelming success in focusing the nation's attention as Russell desired, but it was also a financial disaster for COC and PP, which in the course of sixteen months suffered a deficit of nearly a half-million dollars. Russell lured his two partners, Majors and Waddell, into supporting his project. The three giants of western freighting had coped with many problems, but the $500,000 loss they incurred with the Pony Express eventually drove their major corporate enterprise into bankruptcy. Russell wound up in a jail cell when he and an obliging government clerk in the Department of the Interior dipped into Indian trust funds to aid the near bankrupt company whose initials cynics said stood for: "Clean Out of Cash and Poor Pay."

The Express was intended to focus attention on the COC and PP, which was then at a considerable disadvantage in its competition with the Butterfield Overland Mail. The latter, which followed an "oxbow" route across the Southwest to California, enjoyed the support of a number of Democratic politicians in Washington and a fat government subsidy. Russell hoped that his dramatic demonstration of the advantages of the Central route would produce publicity as well as business, private and government, for the COC and PP.

It was a daring undertaking, for not only would the costs be considerable, but a number of other problems would beset the company. The line ran just short of 2000 miles from St. Joseph, Missouri, to Sacramento, California. En route scores of stations serviced the eighty riders and their five hundred mounts. Each man rode from 30 to 50 miles in the beginning, although later 75 to 100 miles became common, and in an emergency a rider once rode 280 miles. Securing stock, building stations, procuring equipment, and employing riders, roustabouts, blacksmiths—all were major problems.

The service began on April 3, 1860, when the first mail left St. Joseph for California and its counterpart left San Francisco for St. Joseph. Ten days later they reached their destinations and received tumultuous welcomes. Mail was carried at $10 an ounce, later reduced to $2. The partners subsequently declared that it cost them as much as $38 to deliver a piece of mail. For sixteen months the riders, forty headed east and forty west, rode the trail. Before the operation came to a close they traveled some 650,000 miles and lost but one shipment, while successfully handling almost thirty-five thousand pieces of mail.

The telegraph, which linked East and West on October 24, 1861, brought an abrupt end to the Pony Express some forty-eight hours later. The end should have come much sooner for Majors, Russell, and Waddell, for the Pony Express cost them not only a half-million dollars but their place as transportation titans in the West. It brought financial disaster to their company, but it created a saga of adventure which has intrigued young men of every generation since the hoofbeats of the last pony stopped echoing across the land in October 1861.

The completion of the transcontinental line came as no surprise to the riders of the Pony Express, for they repeatedly passed the construction crews who placed the poles and strung the singing wires of the telegraph. Its arrival in California was preceded by the construction of a number of local lines which connected some of the major towns with San Francisco. The first had been completed in 1851 to convey news of ship arrivals. It joined Point Lobos to the Merchants Exchange in San Francisco and provided almost immediate notice of the arrival of incoming ships to the commercial world of the city. Two years later a line joined San Jose and another led to Marysville. At the close of the decade San Francisco and Los

Angeles were linked and within a year the transcontinental line was completed. Its completion was timely, for the ties which joined California to a dissolving Union needed strengthening.

THE PACIFIC MAIL AND ITS RIVALS

The first steamship to complete the voyage from the Atlantic coast to San Francisco was the *California*, built especially for the California traffic (and ready military conversion) by the Pacific Mail Steamship line in 1848. A little more than 1000 tons burden, constructed to carry freight, mail, and a small number of passengers, she left New York on October 6, 1848. Her route led southward around the Horn and then up the west coast of South America to the Golden Gate. She was the third steamship to travel through the Strait of Magellan: two English ships preceded her. En route she picked up additional passengers, more than four hundred in total, who crowded the cabins, holds, and decks and obstructed the crews in the working of the ship. On the last day of February 1849 the *California* sailed through the Golden Gate, picked a way through the crowded waters of the bay to a salute of the guns of five warships, and dropped her anchor to mark an end to a memorable voyage of almost 150 days. There she stayed for the next four and a half months, tended only by a single engineer—the only member of the crew who did not desert the ship for the golden placers of the Sierras.

The Pacific Mail line was organized in early 1848 to develop steamship facilities from Panama to California. Subsidized heavily by the federal government for carrying a monthly mail, and directed by William H. Aspinwall, Pacific Mail soon had a dominant position in the marine traffic which linked the East Coast and California via the Isthmus of Panama. It survived in spite of cutthroat competition which would have driven other enterprises to early bankruptcy.

Pacific Mail's prosperity was based in part on a lucrative annual subsidy from the United States Post Office of some $900,000. Aspinwall and his associates were forced to share this with Cornelius Vanderbilt, who demanded $40,000 and later $60,000 a month in exchange for a promise to stay out of the carrying trade to California. In spite of such extraordinary expenses, Pacific Mail prospered. Obviously the maritime trade to California via the Isthmus of Panama was a promising field. A congressional investigating committee subsequently pointed out that its lucrative nature reflected the generosity or naïveté of the federal government.

Pacific Mail had a full share of critics who were intolerant of her service and schedules, her fares, and her monopoly. In the opinion of the general public, Pacific Mail was overly concerned with her corporate fortunes and too little interested in fast, cheap, and convenient service to the Pacific coast. While her critics fumed, the company prospered. Incorporated in 1848 with a capital stock of a half-million dollars, its stock was successively raised until it reached $20,000,000 in 1866. The increase reflected the general growth of the company as its ships multiplied, its dock and general port facilities improved, and its labor force grew.

One of the great bottlenecks in the Isthmus route to California was the miasmic crossing from the Caribbean to the Pacific. Here the rudest of facilities, primitive trails, and mahogany log canoes propelled at the rate of a mile an hour by pole, combined with such hazards as clouds of mosquitoes, bad water, and endemic disease, hampered the movement of men and goods in either direction. The obvious necessity of a railroad to link the Atlantic and Pacific coasts soon brought an American company into the picture. Construction began in the early summer of 1850 but the work of surveying a route, cutting through the jungle, building a roadbed, and laying track was incredibly difficult. Nearly five years after the work had begun, in January 1855, the first train made the trip from the Atlantic to the Pacific. In a sense, it was the first transcontinental railroad in the Western Hemisphere.

The completion of the railroad was a tremendous boon to those interested in travel to and from California as well as those interested in the movement of freight in either direction. The once arduous journey across the Isthmus could now be completed in hours, and hundreds of thousands of passengers made the trip in the coaches of the Isthmian railroad. The movement of bullion was also facilitated. The co-ordination of ship arrivals and departures with train movements provided the traveler to or from California with a quick, convenient, and moderately comfortable transit, a vast improvement over the route which the Argonauts traveled. The railroad's completion brought a further decline in traffic around the Horn and popularized the Isthmian route to California until the completion of the transcontinental railroad in 1869 opened new options to travelers and shippers to and from California.

While Russell, Majors, and Waddell were traveling their road of high adventure, grandiose plans, and near bankruptcy, other staging and freighting enterprises were contributing to the development of transportation lines linking California with the Mississippi Valley. Some of the entrepreneurs involved were tempered in the uncertainties of freighting and staging in the gold rush years in California. James Birch, for example, began operations in New Helvetia in 1849, running passengers in and about Sutter's famed establishment in fair weather and foul. Birch was a tough and resourceful man who developed a reputation for being efficient and reliable. His firm prospered and in 1854 he played a principal role in the creation of a near monopoly of staging in northern California in the form of the California Stage Company. In spite of great efforts, the company never controlled more than half of the approximately 3000 miles of stage lines in the state in the fifties although it was the most important single concern in the field, far overshadowing any one of dozens of independent concerns.

The California Stage Company, absolutely dependent upon good roads, lobbied for state and local action in this area but also built and improved roads along its stage lines. It was not alone in this field, for all of the concerns involved in transporting men, goods, and mail contributed. In Southern California, for instance, the freighting firm of Alexander and Banning contributed to the upkeep of roads in and about Los Angeles, as well as those leading to such points in the interior as Salt Lake City, the mining districts on the Kern River, and Fort Yuma. Private individuals also contributed by building and maintaining turnpikes, and the state legislature appropriated substantial sums of money for the building and improvement of roads in California. They were a far cry from the interstate highways and freeways that provide Californians of today with the finest system of highways in the world, but even before the Civil War, the roads of California linked most of the towns and settlements in the state with passable roads.

The roads were used by hundreds of vehicles of express, freight, and staging companies. The California Stage Company alone, in the late fifties, operated twenty-eight daily stage lines. It employed hundreds of agents, drivers, and hostlers, about a thousand horses, and more than a hundred Concord coaches and wagons. In the course of a single year, the company's vehicles traveled more than a million miles. Awarded various contracts to carry the mail (approximately 1200 miles of mail routes in 1858), the company served an area which stretched from Portland, Oregon, to Sacramento in 1860. It deliberately concentrated on northern California, but despite this voluntary curtailment of its activities, it was the giant of the staging business in California through the Civil War.

While roads, staging, express, and freighting services were being established within California, her links with the lands beyond the Sierras remained relatively undeveloped. California's organized lines of communication came through the Golden Gate, and she remained dependent upon the Pacific Mail for postal connections with the outside world.

The federal government took the first of a series of halting steps to establish an overland postal service to and from California in 1851, when a contract was awarded to a concern to carry the mail monthly between Salt Lake City and Sacramento, California. Such were the uncertainties that a letter from California could take as long as sixty days to cover the ground to Missouri. It was a beginning, but little more than that. About the same time, a regular monthly service was inaugurated along the Santa Fe trail which ultimately linked Santa Fe to Missouri was well as El Paso and San Antonio. From this complex came, in 1857, a line stretching westward to San Diego. The contract awarded by the Post Office went to James Birch, veteran of the staging business in California and recently resigned president of the California Stage Company. Birch was to provide semi-monthly service on the San Antonio and San Diego Mail line for $150,000 per year. Although the route ran through an area which was inhabited principally by Apaches and horned toads and terminated in an insignificant town in the south, Californians hoped that it was the beginning of something far better.

Birch had his eye on an even bigger plum in the form of a contract to establish a monthly mail which would link the Mississippi

Valley and California. Shortly after the inauguration of the San
Antonio and San Diego service, dubbed by some observers who
noted the widespread use of mules the "Jackass Mail," Birch died.
Ironically this titan of the staging business was traveling as a passenger
on the *Central America* when the ship went down in a storm off
the coast of Florida. The irony of Birch's "indiscretion" in choosing
to travel by ship rather than by carriage was noted by many
observers. However, his San Antonio and San Diego Mail line
survived and even prospered under new leadership. The nearly 1500-
mile route across Apache-infested desert land was still being traveled
by the coaches in the first year of the Civil War, although when the
Butterfield Overland Mail began operations in September of 1858,
it handled the bulk of mail and passengers of the Jackass line for the
600 miles which separated San Diego and El Paso.

The Butterfield Overland Mail received the lucrative contract to
organize a regular overland mail service to California within a week
of Birch's death. The chief figure of the new enterprise was John
Butterfield, founder of the American Express Company, intimate
friend of James Buchanan, pillar of the Democratic party, and
beneficiary of a decision made by Aaron Brown, postmaster general
of Buchanan's Cabinet. The competition was intense as prospective
carriers of the mail to California sought the contract, which promised
handsome returns to the company chosen. Butterfield had mastered
the staging and express business in New England, and he and his
associates, who included W. G. Fargo of Wells, Fargo and Company, demonstrated a similar grasp of lobbying when they obtained
the coveted contract in the face of intense competition by other
hopefuls. Butterfield's concern would carry the mail as well as
passengers by way of a route that joined St. Louis and Memphis with
San Francisco. Sturdy Concord coaches wandered south and west
by way of an oxbow route which began in St. Louis and Memphis,
then down through Fort Smith, Arkansas, on through El Paso and
Fort Yuma to Los Angeles. At the City of the Angels the lumbering
coaches swung north for the last stretch of the 2750-mile journey
which ended in San Francisco. The company promised semi-weekly
service in twenty-five days or less for an annual subsidy of $600,000.

Californians were always somewhat critical of the Butterfield
line. It was not so much that the food was bad at its way stations,

its service uncertain and an ordeal for its passengers so much as the widespread conviction that the line was the result of "politics." Most observers believed the South dictated the route with the view of realizing a sectional advantage. Most Californians also believed that a faster schedule was possible along the Central route. But Butterfield continued to be favored by the federal government in spite of all attacks by Apaches and critical citizens of California. The oxbow route was followed until the opening of the Civil War. With the election of Lincoln, secession, and the initiation of hostilities, including Confederate attacks on Butterfield facilities, the line was moved to the Central route. There Russell, Majors, and Waddell received a handsome government subsidy for maintaining a daily stage run.

The financial problems of Russell, Majors, and Waddell were becoming unmanageable, however, by the spring of 1862, and they sold their interest in western staging to a new titan of the freighting and staging business in the West, Ben Holladay. He promptly began the building of a network of lines which covered a large part of the West to California. At its height his empire included 345 miles of lines, he employed hundreds of men, and his equipment rivaled the rolling stock of an army. For a time, Holladay and Wells, Fargo competed on a "no holds barred" basis, but on November 1, 1866, Ben Holladay sold his business to his chief rival for $1,800,000. On the eve of the joining of rails at Promontory Point, the "Napoleon of the West" demonstrated once more in this timely sale that he was a man of considerable vision.

COASTAL VESSELS AND THE INLAND WATER CARRIERS

Geographic factors played a major role in shaping the transportation systems of California. The Pacific ocean front from the beginning was involved in the carrying of men and their goods to and away from the area. The two great river systems, the Sacramento and the San Joaquin, which penetrated the hinterland and provided two great networks of water highways, were heavily used by shippers and travelers. The Sacramento, which emerged from the high country around Redding, flowed southward in the middle of a broad valley before it merged 320 miles later with the waters of the San Joaquin in the delta. There the waters of the two streams blended with the waters of the Pacific as they found their way inland through the Bay of San Francisco. There also mingled the craft of the Pacific and the craft of the inland waters, each hurrying to and fro, each using the facilities which nature provided. What they carried and how well they carried it varied according to the period and the craft, cargo, and motive power available.

The coastal waters were utilized by the first Europeans on the scene and all those who came after them. Not only did the first explorers come via the ocean but the colonizers who came in the late eighteenth century to establish an outpost of the Spanish empire were dependent upon the men and supplies brought by the sea. Throughout the Spanish and Mexican periods, the ocean was a major facility used to come to California or to leave it. During the gold rush period dozens of ships, sailing as well as steamers, were involved in the coast traffic. The coasters carried passengers, mail, and freight between California and a number of ports in Mexico and Central America. They provided essential services and dividends for investors until the completion of the transcontinental railroad sharply changed the picture.

The coasters had their counterpart in a fleet of offshore vessels which operated out of San Francisco and touched such far-flung ports as Hong Kong, Yokohama, Sydney, and Honolulu. The Pacific Mail flag became familiar in such harbors and in the 1870s the subsidiary of the Central Pacific Railroad, the Occidental and Oriental Steamship line, became a formidable competitor.

While the coastal waters were used from the beginning by the Spanish and those who came after them, the inland river systems were neglected. The *gente de razón* who were confined to the fringe of land along the coast had little need for these rivers which drained the interior. Spanish explorers like Gabriel Moraga in 1808 and Luis Argüello in 1817 and 1821 led small parties which charted the lower reaches of the San Joaquin and the Sacramento, but for the most part they remained unknown and unused river highways. When John Sutter appeared on the scene in 1839, things began to change. As he built a great feudallike duchy, Sutter had need for means to carry passengers and freight to him as well as the varied produce downriver. When the Russians liquidated their holdings in and about Fort Ross, Sutter acquired among other things a river craft. He promptly named it the *Sacramento* and it became a familiar sight in its travels between the fort and San Francisco Bay. In 1847 she was joined by the *Sitka*, a 37-foot craft which had a teapot of a steam engine, the first appearance of steam craft on the river.

With the advent of the gold rush there arrived dozens and eventually hundreds of craft which crowded the riverbanks in Sacramento. It was the beginning of a new era when the great paddle-wheel steamers would provide regular, comfortable, and even luxurious accommodations to travelers between San Francisco and Sacramento. A craft named for the river, prefabricated in New York, and assembled in San Francisco in the summer of 1849 led the way. Close in its wake came the *McKim*. The *Mint*, the *Senator*, and the *Miner* all arrived before the close of the year. Light-draught steamers also came in the first year to operate on the upper Sacramento and its tributaries, the Yuba and Feather. In the spring of 1850, California-built steamers like the *Tehama* were launched to join in a cutthroat competition for the passenger trade which reduced the fare from $30 to as little as $10. By the spring of the following year, the fare fell to as little as $1 as additional steamers and facilities entered the picture.

Competition brought ruin to a number of the smaller operators and consolidation to others. In 1854 the California Steam Navigation Company was organized out of a merger of the vessels of some of the more prominent operators. It set out to obtain a lion's share of the traffic and in a remarkably short time it was the biggest mover of passengers and freight on the river. The independents remained to vex the "gargantuan monopoly," but from the time it was organized until it was purchased by the Central Pacific Railroad Company in April 1869, the California Steam Navigation Company dominated river traffic. Once the resources of the railroad were put in the scales, the independents were lost.

The paddle-wheel days on the Sacramento and the San Joaquin persisted as long as the great side-wheelers and stern-wheelers could compete on an economic basis with other forms of freight and passenger moving. The steamers suffered setbacks from time to time in the form of bursting boilers which sometimes took a heavy toll of life and snags which ripped through bottom timbers and sent craft to watery graves. Luxurious accommodations and the grace of steamboat travel made them competitive even after the arrival of the railroads. Even today the riverboats move great cargoes of grain and freight, although now diesel-driven tugs have replaced the sternwheelers of yesteryear. The boats were driven from the river by the locomotive and still later by the diesel truck and tug. Their passing was hastened by the debris of hydraulic mining which clogged the inland passages of the great valley. However, thanks to modern dredging and engineering, Sacramento and Stockton remain great inland ports whose facilities accommodate ocean-going steamers which bring diversified cargoes and carry away the rice, wheat, wine, cement, and canned goods of the Sacramento and San Joaquin valleys.

By the final year of the Civil War, California had a transportation system which satisfied many of its immediate needs. Coastal vessels carried passengers and freight between such points as San Francisco and San Diego, and touched many Central American and Mexican ports on the Pacific. Offshore vessels still made their way around the Horn in either direction and linked far-flung ports of the western Pacific with California. Paddle-wheel steamers plied the inland waters of the Sacramento and the San Joaquin as well as some of their tributaries. The Pony Express was no more, but there was overland service via the facilities of Wells, Fargo and Ben Holladay, and the tracks of the Central Pacific were thrusting eastward for their junction with the Union Pacific. Within the state, staging and express lines linked most of the population centers, and the humming wires of the telegraph provided nearly instantaneous communication between the major cities and towns as well as telegraphic communication with the eastern states. Local railroads were portents of the future. A great deal had been done during the gold rush period, and the state was on the eve of the greatest transportation development of the age. Those who were aware of the manner in which transportation facilities open up an area and its resources had good reason to be optimistic as they contemplated the California scene in 1865.

THE BIG FOUR

While Californians welcomed each improvement in their transportation system, all looked forward with special anticipation to the building of a railroad which would link the Mississippi Valley with the Pacific coast. This cherished project was discussed whenever Californians gathered. Some questioned whether it could ever be built and operated on a paying basis but the vast majority of the citizenry thought the need imperative, the benefits to the state numerous and beyond dispute, and they were determined to see the Pacific Railroad built.

The proposal to link the Pacific coast with the Mississippi Valley with transportation facilities had a long history. A decade before the first railroad was built in 1826 in the United States, young Thomas Hart Benton proposed the building of facilities which would supplement the Missouri and Columbia rivers with canals and roads and tie St. Louis with a port on the Pacific in the Northwest. That transportation artery would channel the commerce of Asia across America and the United States would benefit accordingly. Asa Whitney, a veteran of the China trade, proposed in 1846 the construction of a railroad across western America to the Pacific for similar reasons. George Wilkes in the same year envisioned a railroad which would be subsidized with a huge grant of public land stretching on either side of the right of way all the way to the Pacific in Oregon. Both men exhibited considerable vision, for the railroad subsequently followed the broad outline which they sketched some sixteen years before the first major step in the project was taken.

The project was almost breathtaking in scope. Its construction entailed the marshaling of vast amounts of capital, a labor force which amounted to a small army, quantities of tools, materials, and equipment beyond precedent, and planning, surveying, and engineering on an enormous scale. It would also be an undertaking which might never return dividends to investors. Glowing projections of traffic originating in Asia might never be realized. Pending the appearance of the exotic freight of the Orient the railroad would be dependent on traffic which originated in the region through which it passed. The prospects of such traffic appearing in the untenanted West which the railroad traversed on its way to the Pacific were minimal. As every railroad man knows, traffic in the form of passengers or freight is essential to the survival and prosperity of a railroad.

There were, in short, tremendous problems which lay astride the path of the railroad to the Pacific. Prospective investors were wary, politicians and government officials looked cynically—perhaps realistically—at the problems, and even proponents of the railroad became discouraged as they saw that problems were both larger and more numerous than prospective solutions. Moreover, during the 1850s the Pacific Railroad proposal became a part of the sectional conflict which wracked the Union. Southerners became increasingly concerned with the possibility that the building of the railroad would hasten the coming of an anti-slavery society to the west. They were also interested in the location of the eastern terminus and the route which the road would follow to the Pacific. Representatives of the free states were equally interested in such matters. A route which meandered through the Southwest on its way to San Francisco was in the southern interest but a track that ran along more northern parallels would strengthen the enemies of the South. Accordingly during the fifties, division over route, financing, and terminus made it difficult to commit the federal government to the project. The Pacific Railroad Survey Act of March 1853 authorized the United States Corps of Topographical Engineers to make surveys. Government expeditions examined the various routes—dispassionately and objectively reporting on five—but it was not possible to pass a Pacific Railroad Act until secession. When the southern interest was no longer represented in Congress, a Pacific Railroad Act was passed.

This essential first step could not have been taken without the assistance of a young railroad builder, Theodore Judah. Judah, the secretary of the House as well as the Senate committee which considered the Pacific Railroad Act, was one of the chief promoters of the railroad. A graduate in civil engineering who mastered railroad construction in New York, Judah came to California in 1854 to survey and supervise the construction of the first railroad on the Pacific coast. A year later, having completed a 20-mile short line which led out of Sacramento toward the placer country in the Sierras,

Judah became interested in the greatest project of the age. Interest was transformed into obsession, said some observers. Whatever it should be called, Judah's commitment to the building of the railroad was the central concern of his life from this time forward.

Judah's success in the form of the Pacific Railroad Act of 1862 had been preceded by years of effort which had been sprinkled with failures. There was little doubt in his mind of the feasibility of the railroad from the engineering point of view, but it was not engineering problems and obstacles but other barriers that prevented the enterprise from getting under way. One such problem was assembling the necessary capital and support. Californians, however interested in the railroad, were inclined to look askance at him when he approached them with the proposal that they invest in the enterprise. Any number of proposals to build railroads in California had ended in failure. Investors had learned prudence and when this was coupled with the public preference for profitable mining investments it became most difficult to raise sufficient capital.

In 1859 the discovery of the mineral deposits on the Comstock brought a new factor into the picture—a factor which played a major role in the initiation of the railroad. As the Comstock boom gathered momentum it became increasingly apparent that transportation companies which served the mines and miners would share in the treasure wrested from its bonanzas. Judah's proposal to build the first stretch of the overland railroad out of Sacramento up through Dutch Flat across the Sierras and down the eastern slopes in the vicinity of rapidly growing Virginia City became more feasible and attractive. The incorporation of the Central Railroad Company of California was the necessary first step in the direction of giving corporate structure and direction to the enterprise. It also provided investors with the opportunity of getting in on the ground floor of the greatest enterprise of the age. Appropriately, the step was taken in the little Sierra town of Dutch Flat and its local citizenry invested the first significant sums.

Having acquired organization and a limited amount of money, Judah then set out to raise the rest of the necessary capital. Gimlet-eyed investors in San Francisco heard his proposals and then sent him on his way empty-handed. Everywhere investors greeted him with skepticism until one quiet autumn night in 1860 he gathered a small group above the hardware store of Huntington, Hopkins and Company in Sacramento. Men of moderate wealth formed a majority of the dozen men present. None was distinguished, although Leland Stanford was known beyond the city of Sacramento as a founder of the Republican party of California and an aspiring politician. No one saw the historic importance of the gathering and none of the men could possibly have known that four of the group would found dynasties of wealth as a result of a chain of events which was initiated that evening.

Judah's emphasis in this gathering was on the value of the railroad as a supply facility for the Comstock and the profits which awaited those who built and controlled it. That approach was most persuasive to Leland Stanford, wholesale grocer, Charles Crocker, dry goods dealer, and Mark Hopkins and Collis P. Huntington, partners in a wholesale hardware establishment. As these men of substance and foresight looked at Judah's plans they became increasingly excited and interested. Before the evening was over they had committed themselves to the purchase of stock and assumed some of the major positions in the corporation: Stanford as president, Huntington, vice-president, and Hopkins, treasurer. In June 1861 the Central Pacific Railroad Company was formally incorporated.

The question of federal support was not settled until the following year. In the interim, Theodore Judah, with the assistance of the California congressional delegation, persuaded the assembled law-makers that the road was a military necessity, and that the Central route was not only practical but a means of strengthening the bonds that tied California to the Union. This persuasive rhetoric had impact. Congressmen who had heard their fill of speeches of disunion and secession marshaled behind the Pacific Railroad Act of 1862. The absence of southern opponents facilitated its passage.

The bill was all that Judah and his associates could have wanted. It named the Central Pacific and the Union Pacific as the concerns which would build the road. The route was to proceed out of Omaha westward or eastward out of Sacramento. Each concern was to be subsidized with loans and land grants. The loan was in the form of United States bonds to be issued at the rate of $16,000 per mile of track laid on level ground, $32,000 in the semi-mountainous land, and $48,000 per mile in the mountains. The loan was to be a thirty-year mortgage although this was changed in 1864 to a second mortgage, providing a first mortgage lien to private investors. The Central Pacific received a total of $25,800,000 in federal bonds. The two concerns were also subsidized by extensive tracts of land. Not only did they receive a right of way, but also twenty alternate sections of land on each side of the line. In more concrete terms this amounted to half the land in a strip 40 miles wide. While not of great immediate value, the land had considerable potential value. Without it, as well as the financial aid provided, the Pacific Railroad would not have been built in the Civil War period. These are the salient features of the Pacific Railroad Act of 1862 as modified in 1864.

The first work began in January 1863 in Sacramento amid a flurry of speeches and brassy music from a band which gave color and sound to the occasion. The railroad began its slow passage across the terrain which lay before Sacramento and the crests of the Sierras. The physical obstacles which lay before them were enormous but other problems were as numerous and as threatening as anything to be found in the elevations of the mountains. Monetary problems vexed the operation from the beginning. Launched in the midst of a national war, both companies found that investors had a singular lack of enthusiasm for their project. Supply problems were enormous, for the war consumed the steel and men and tools which the railroad construction needed in prodigious amounts.

Labor was a major problem in California, for the Comstock was booming and absorbing the surplus of labor that had existed in the final years of the gold rush decade. What was not going into the galleries of the mines of Virginia City was being absorbed by its supporting industries of supply and transportation. The mines of Nevada gave employment not only to the men who went down into its shafts but also to a host of artisans who carried supplies to the mines and processed the ores which were produced.

Without labor, nothing could be done. Crocker and his associates tried various expedients before they settled on the prime labor supply which was to build the road. Mexicans from the south were envisioned but these premature *braceros* were not used. The use of Confederate prisoners was also contemplated but the necessary permission could not be obtained. Out of the need came an experiment with Chinese labor and when this proved successful Orientals were gathered up from a hundred towns and hamlets in California. Before the road was built twelve thousand of Crocker's "pets," as they were dubbed, were at work, many brought from Asia by a concern in which Crocker had an interest. All of these were the normal problems of the railroad builder magnified into abnormal proportions by the peculiar conditions which faced the management of the Central Pacific in the mid-sixties.

As significant as any other problem which confronted them was the division which arose in their own ranks. Theodore Judah was the spearhead of the opposition to Crocker, Huntington, Stanford, and Hopkins. The latter, dubbed the Associates, or the Big Four, represented a locus of power of major proportions, for they manned the more important corporate posts of the enterprise and controlled a major part of the voting stock. Their emphasis in the early years was the construction of a road which would bring them the greatest immediate return in the form of the government subsidy and if this meant the sacrifice of quality, so be it. Judah, the engineer, on the other hand, was interested in building a road which would meet an engineer's rigid standards. When the Big Four organized a front, Charles Crocker and Company, to which lucrative contracts were to be awarded to build the railroad, the break between Judah and his partners approached. Crocker and Company, later reorganized as the Contract and Finance Company in 1867, owned lock, stock, and barrel by the Big Four, received $58,000,000 for the construction work, which is generously estimated to have cost $14,000,000.

When the final break came, Judah was given the opportunity of buying out his associates. Apparently convinced that eastern investors would provide him with the necessary capital, he hurried off to New York via the Panama route. In the crossing of the Isthmus he contracted a fever. When the ship docked in New York, Judah was carried ashore in a stretcher. A short time later on the eve of his thirty-eighth birthday, November 1, 1863, he died, and the problems of divided management in the Central Pacific were solved.

The men who survived were inexperienced in the building or the management of a railroad but each was suited in some special way to deal with some of the tasks at hand; the quartet made an effective team. Charles Crocker was a big man in every sense of the word. Heavy-set and energetic, he was the superintendent of construction who organized his subordinates and his labor force like an army. He drove himself almost all the time and drove others most of the time, and by voice and example he got the job done. Leland Stanford made a different contribution. He was a founder of the Republican party of California and a governor elected in the same year that Lincoln went to the White House. A politician by inclination and experience, Stanford could deal with officials—elected and otherwise. He was the man who could appear before a legislative committee as an effective spokesman of the railroad or draw up a piece of legislation which would serve the political interests of the road. Born in the same small town in New York, Troy, which had produced Crocker, Stanford had practiced law with indifferent success, and made a small competence in the profits derived from a grocery business which he and his brother operated in Sacramento.

Mark Hopkins brought a different set of talents to the enterprise. Older than his associates by ten years, Hopkins was paid a certain amount of deference by them. He, too, was a merchant, associated with Collis P. Huntington in a wholesale hardware business. A careful and precise man who kept accounts for the enterprise, Hopkins was the conservative voice of reason in the group whose opinion was valued by each of them. Huntington, his former associate in hardware wholesaling, was possibly the most talented of the Pacific Associates. He was astute and realistic in his dealings with people and likely to see them in an uncompromising and unsentimental light. He also had the capacity to look at a business proposition with pitiless objectivity and thereby avoid the illusory profit or opportunity. Late in life, a millionaire many times over, he was described as "A hard and cheery old man with no more soul than a shark." However objectionable to his friends and family, this characterization had an impressionistic truth to it. Each of the Big Four, then, contributed to the enterprise. Hopkins was the office manager and account keeper, Crocker the construction boss, Stanford the political manager who handled relations between the corporation and the many political entities with which it dealt, and Huntington the director of the enterprise who moved in and out of national legislative chambers and board rooms of Wall Street concerns, and dealt with the manifold problems of financing and supply.

The actual building of the Central Pacific continued through the Civil War years. The road was to run up 7000 feet through Donner

Pass and down the eastern slopes of the Sierras, the best route across the mountain rampart which guarded the eastern border of California. It was also a route filled with incredible obstacles of cliffs, mountain slopes, precipitous terrain, and granite barriers. So monumental were the problems that there was good reason to consider them insurmountable but the army which Crocker marshaled for the assault clawed its way upward through the mountains.

Before the work was over a number of prodigious feats were done including moving the Sierra Nevadas 40 miles westward. The move was accomplished by convincing local and national authorities that the western base of the mountains lay a few miles east of Sacramento where the soils of the mountains and the valley could be distinguished. The objective was the half-million additional subsidy which the railroad would receive as it built eastward through this newly discovered "mountainous" country. Judah objected to this sharp practice but he was overruled. The cash position of the railroad improved immediately.

Other problems confronted the builders of this 800-mile line. Money was a continuing problem, for the project consumed capital. A single mile of track required 2500 crossties and more than 100 tons of rails and spikes. The crews in the field consumed tons of foodstuffs and staggering amounts of blasting powder, tools, and equipment. Much of it came from the East Coast via a supply line of 18,000 miles which led around Cape Horn. As much as 10,000 tons of cargo a month was shipped out of eastern supply centers to the construction crews of the two railroads. Private capital, usually in short supply, was sometimes augmented with money supplied by state and local governments. The state of California undertook an obligation to pay the interest on $1,500,000 of Central Pacific bonds for twenty years on one occasion. Such steps were essential if the work would proceed.

It proceeded in spite of staggering obstacles. "Cape Horn," a giant cliff which reared skyward 1000 feet, was such an obstacle. It seemed impossible to carve a roadbed out of that granite cliff but hundreds of Chinese laborers, working with primitive tools from rude baskets suspended on cables, scratched an adequate road across Cape Horn. Beyond lay other problems. The Sierra crossing required fifteen tunnels, including a summit which was more than 1600 feet long. The summit tunnel work began in the spring of 1866 from four faces, one from each end and two more from a center vertical shaft. At times daily progress was measured in inches. Before it was finished, three locomotives, forty cars, and the tools and equipment of railroad building were hauled to the end of track, mounted on sledges, and hauled up and over the Sierra rampart. While crews continued their molelike pace through the granite top ridge of the mountains, advance parties were working on the roadbed which led down out of the Sierras in the direction of Lake's Crossing, Nevada.

In midsummer of 1865 as Civil War guns were cooling, the two concerns had laid less than 100 miles of track between them; a year later, Central Pacific tracks reached Dutch Flat, 67 miles east of Sacramento. At that rate it would take a generation to complete the railroad. It took five years of effort and the doubters had a field day predicting imminent disaster and inevitable failure, but in June 1868 Central Pacific rails crossed the state line and set out across the chaparral plains of Nevada. That the railroad survived is a tribute to the men who hunted down material in scarce supply during the Civil War years, squeezed money out of reluctant investors, summoned an army of Chinese laborers from near and far, and drove, cajoled, and persuaded them to do the impossible. When the roadbed was finished it was 800 miles long, 500 miles of its length was above 5000 feet, 200 above 6500. To cope with snow in the higher elevations almost 40 miles of snowsheds ·sheltering the track were built. Sixty-five million board feet of massive timbers and 900 tons of bolts and ironwork went into the gloomy galleries which guarded the track.

And while the Central Pacific hammered down a road toward the rising sun, once setting a record of 10.6 miles of track in one day, the Union Pacific was building west. Both corporations dealt with similar problems, and each had similar motives and goals. The Union Pacific assembled a labor force of Civil War veterans and Irish emigrants, contracted out the actual building to a dummy corporation, the Credit Mobilier, owned by insiders, and built rapidly rather than well, for their share of the public land and cash subsidy was also determined by the miles of track laid.

For a time it appeared that the two lines would never meet. The

8. The early prospectors in the California gold fields used various techniques in placer mining. They involved washing material from the streams with the aid of a pan, cradle, or sluice box and sifting out the gold.

9. As mining techniques became more sophisticated, rivers were often dammed, diverted into flumes, and power taken from them to operate mining machines in the exposed river beds.

10. Gold fever attracted thousands of prospectors from all parts of the world. Chinese miners are pictured.

11. Hydraulic mining, introduced in 1852, used water under pressure to wash gold-bearing deposits out of hills and into sluices where the gold could be recovered. It produced widespread ecological damage wherever it was practiced and was finally eliminated in the 1880s.

12. The 1850s were years of turbulence and violence in which vigilance committees were organized in San Francisco, Los Angeles, and a number of the mining towns. Depicted is a lynching conducted by vigilantes in Los Angeles.

13. The seal of the 1856 San Francisco Committee of Vigilance.

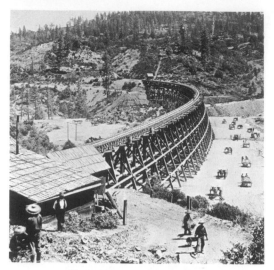

14. In its race with the Union Pacific construction teams, the Central Pacific bridged many of the high Sierra chasms it encountered with timber trestles. When tracks joined at Promontory Point in 1869, its crews returned to finish their work, filling in the chasms and stabilizing embankments.

15. Bucker snowplows of the Central Pacific were pushed by as many as eight wood-burning locomotives in order to ram their way through snowdrifts that sometimes reached more than 30 feet in height. This plow is pictured near Cisco, 92 miles from Sacramento, in the winter of 1867.

16. A scene at the gold spike ceremony, Promontory Summit, Utah, May 10, 1869, which joined the Central Pacific and the Union Pacific.

problem was not a surveying error but simply the desire of each company to get as much of the public land subsidy as possible. Congress hastily amended an oversight in not specifying the point of the juncture and the two lines joined at Promontory Point, Utah, in May 1869. A new day had dawned for California. It came one hundred years after the first Spanish settlement. The second hundred years would have a full measure of giant construction achievements but it was to be some time before anything like the Central Pacific Railroad was attempted.

While the management of the Union Pacific devoted itself to an exploitation of their road and the resources it commanded, the Big Four began to develop immediate as well as long-range plans. A matter of weeks after the ceremony at Promontory Point, another major transportation artery, the Suez Canal, was completed. The link between the Mediterranean and the Red Sea altered the relationships of transportation links which joined Europe and the Far East. Those who had envisioned a transcontinental railroad as a means of funneling that trade between Europe and Asia through the United States had reason to pause and reconsider. Evidently the Big Four continued to think in terms of a far-flung enterprise which would involve the trade of the Orient, for they began to supplement their transcontinental railroad with facilities that would lead to that end.

Even before the railroad was completed they were acquiring lines within California. By 1869 they controlled all rail routes into and out of San Francisco, operated ferry and steamship lines within the vicinity of the bay, and were in position to dominate further railroad development in California to either the north or south. By 1871 their subsidiary, the Southern Pacific, was alienating the population of some of the southern counties by switching routes from the coastal region to the inland valley. To the people of the coastal region who looked forward to a rail facility, the shift was a betrayal: to the Big Four it was a prudent move which enabled them to obtain a further land subsidy from the public domain through which the line passed. It would also enable the Big Four to move in the direction of shutting possible competitors out of California by seizing control of strategic railway gateways into the state at Needles and Yuma.

As the Southern Pacific came south, its work crews were directed by the Contract and Finance Company and its advance men squeezed special subsidies out of towns and counties en route by threatening to bypass them. Thereby, it created a body of new enemies. Los Angeles, the largest city in Southern California, was subjected to this extraction. To avoid being bypassed and left to languish without railroad service, Los Angeles acquired the Los Angeles and San Pedro Railroad and turned it, together with a 60-acre plot in the center of town and $600,000 in cash, over to the Southern Pacific. Cities which did not co-operate were left to stagnate and reflect on the penalties of crossing the Big Four.

As it built and consolidated its grasp on the railroads within the state, the Central Pacific also moved to meet the threats posed by rival transcontinental lines. It built northward from Sacramento toward Oregon, pre-empting that portion of the state. The Texas and Pacific under the astute leadership of Tom Scott, the Pennsylvania Railroad's chief, was the chief threat in the south in the early seventies. Operating under a charter from Congress which extended substantial subsidies, the Texas and Pacific snaked its way out of Texas toward a terminus on the Pacific at San Diego. Collis P. Huntington led the forces of the Central Pacific in this battle between two of America's biggest railroad titans and eventually emerged victoriously by combining advantages secured from the territorial governments of New Mexico and Arizona with efficiency in track laying which enabled him to outstrip his enemies. The two lines eventually met, not at Yuma but at El Paso. A short time later the Central Pacific continued its line on to New Orleans.

When the Central Pacific was confronted with a similar threat in the form of the Atlantic and Pacific in the south, Huntington pursued a similar strategy. By building more rapidly, the Central Pacific tracks reached Needles first and shut the door in the face of the A and P. In 1884 the Central Pacific and its various subdivisions combined under the corporate name of the Southern Pacific Company. It was incorporated under the laws of Kentucky which were comparatively lax, but in effect, the "Octopus," as it was called in popular parlance, was a phenomenon of California. The enterprise which had been launched in the summer of the first year of the Civil War with an initial capital investment of some $15,000 had become a gigantic railroad monopoly which sprawled across California and reached out to such far-flung cities as Canton, China, and New Orleans. It was the most powerful concern in the American West. Before long Lord Acton's axiom, "Power tends to corrupt; absolute power corrupts absolutely," was tested by the Southern Pacific Company.

CHAPTER XI

The Indian Confrontation

The Indians of California lived for centuries in a unique relationship to their environment. Blessed with adequate supplies of food, in little need of shelter, and isolated by geographic barriers from other peoples, they flourished. Their culture tended to be stable and unchanging. Pacific in behavior—only one Indian group, the Yuman, had a weapon clearly designed for war—they multiplied and prospered. When the Spanish arrived on the scene they found a land more densely populated with aborigines than any similar large area in what is now the United States.

The Spanish changed this to some extent, although when they left the scene, a great deal of California and its people were untouched by them. The greatest impact of the Spanish was on the fringe of land adjacent to the coast. Here the friars assembled large numbers of Indians into missions, as many as 21,000 at a given time, stripped them of their culture, and substituted another ill-fitting cultural cloak. The objective was "salvation" and the transformation of the Indian into a Spanish citizen, who would work and worship as his teachers. The process involved teaching the Indians the skills which sustained the missions as well as the rudiments of a creed which would sustain them in this world and facilitate their passage into the next. These were the basic objectives which dominated the Hispanic approach to the Indians of California. When the Spanish flag was replaced by that of Mexico and the missions secularized, there were major changes in policy and practice, but under Mexico as under Spain the Indian was regarded as a human being for whom there was a place in society. He was or he could become a communicant and there was a place for him and his labor in the ranches and fields.

In 1848 there were close to 100,000 Indians in California. They ranged widely in residence, culture, language, and appearance. Along the coastal region where the Hispanic impact was concentrated, the Indians had absorbed some of the culture of the newcomers but since the Spanish and Mexican population was limited to less than 8000 and concentrated on the coast, Indians of the interior valleys and the Sierra country remained largely untouched.

In the Spanish communities and ranchos along the Pacific fringe the impact of the Spanish brought mixed blessings. The Indians were stripped of their culture and provided with a new and alien culture. They were partially changed into citizens of the new society which was being established, but the process had not proceeded far enough or completely enough. They had learned some of the skills which were essential to the operation of the missions and ranchos and they had absorbed the fundamentals of the creed which the fathers brought them. They had, in short, taken several major steps in the direction of citizenship in the new society. They had also borne the full impact of the introduction of such European diseases as the cold, pneumonia, smallpox, and measles. A fearful mortality rate attested to the effectiveness of such diseases among peoples who lacked both natural and scientific defenses. From an estimated population of 133,000 in 1770, the Indian population fell to a little more than 85,000 in 1852. The damage which arose from changes in living habits and diet was as devastating as diseases spread by germs.

In effect, the Indians along the coast were demoralized and debilitated on the eve of the establishment of American rule. Dutiful and obedient, pious and uncomplaining, they were dependents who functioned when they were directed by the Franciscans but were incapable of performing as Mexican citizens when the missions were abolished. Thereafter they were cast adrift in a world which was not of their making and beyond their understanding. In theory they were liberated by secularization of the missions, but in practice they were reduced to a kind of forced labor on the ranchos. Clerical authority gave way to civilian but the lot of the Indian was largely unchanged.

The arrival of the Americans sharply changed this picture. The Americans were descended from generations which had followed much different approaches to the native Indian population. Almost

BREAKUP OF THE MISSIONS

*Nearly all the cattle in the country belonged to the missions, and they
employed their Indians, who became in fact their slaves, in tending their
vast herds . . . Ever since the independence of Mexico, the missions
have been going down, until at last a law was passed stripping them of all
their possessions, and confining the priests to their spiritual duties, and at
the same time declaring all the Indians free and independent rancheros.
The change in the condition of the Indians was, as may be supposed, only
nominal: they are virtually slaves as much as they ever were. But in the
missions the change was complete. The priests have now no power except in their religious character, and the great possessions of the missions
are given over to be preyed upon by the harpies of the civil power, who
are sent there in the capacity of* administradores *to settle up the concerns—
and who usually end in a few years by making themselves fortunes, and
leaving their stewardships worse than they found them. The dynasty of
the priests was much more acceptable to the people . . . than that of
the* administradores. *The priests were attached perpetually to one mission, and felt the necessity of keeping up its credit. Accordingly their
debts were regularly paid, and the people were, in the main, well treated,
and attached to those who had spent their whole lives among them.*

Richard Henry Dana, *Two Years
Before the Mast* (Doubleday, 1949),
pp. 164–65.

from the beginning of his contact with Indians in the early seventeenth century, the Anglo had displayed little interest in incorporat-
ing the Indian into his society. On the contrary, the Indian was
at best tolerated. He was a nuisance, an obstacle to settlement and
western migration, which was to be overcome, removed, or eliminated. When in 1848 American representatives came to California,
there was no change in this basic approach. The result was a period
steeped in tragedy for the Indian.

The first contacts between California Indians and Americans furnished a number of ominous portents of what was to come. The
mountain men who came to tap the fur resources of the inland
valleys were hard-bitten men who had little regard for the rights
of Mexicans and even less for the rights of Indians. A latecomer

to the scene, John C. Frémont exhibited a callous attitude toward the Indians: "We killed plenty of game and an occasional Indian. We made it a rule to spare none of the bucks," was the report of one of his party.

The Americans who came flooding in over the land during the gold rush accomplished in a few years that which the Spanish and the Mexicans had never been able to do—they penetrated into every nook and cranny of the state. They came in great numbers to claw at the gravel beds beside mountain streams, to fire the forest and cut it down, to dam and pollute the rivers, to fish for salmon and slay the deer. They went everywhere, and everywhere they went they took that baleful attitude of the Anglo toward the Indian expressed in the phrase "The only good Indian is a dead Indian."

There had never been but a fleeting and transitory place for the Indians in the Anglo scheme of things. From the beginning they had been tolerated when they were a necessary adjunct to the fur trade, but when the frontier passed beyond this first stage, the day of the Indian was numbered. He was tolerated no longer once the fur resources of his land were depleted and the cultivators of his soil appeared. Then he was to be removed from the scene, driven from the land of his ancestors. This had been the Indian experience with the Anglos since the early seventeenth century. There was no place for the Indian in this scheme of things. In California the Anglo response to the Indian was no different.

Over the years Americans had developed a way of dealing with Indians which followed a number of familiar lines. The Indians were regarded as people divided into a number of sovereign entities. Each was dealt with as though it were a nation and a "treaty" would be negotiated with the Indian nation by representatives of the United States subject to the same ratification by a two-thirds vote of the United States Senate as any other treaty. The agreement would provide for a cession of land, a relinquishment of rights in territory, and perhaps removal of the particular group of Indians to another location—perhaps a government reservation. If the group were fortunate they might be subjected to the process but once, although there were Indian groups who were removed and resettled on reservations as many as a dozen times.

In California representatives of the United States came early on the scene, eager to follow the paths of precedents in their search for an accommodation of Indian and white. That there was an immediate need for peacemakers was seen in a number of bloody Indian "wars" which took place in the gold country. The violence directed at the Indians was multifaceted. The traditional antagonism of Americans to Indians was reinforced by the overlanders' experience with Pawnees and Paiutes who stole their stock and harassed them as they made their troubled way to California in 1849–50. On the scene they found Indians in the country of the golden fleece—an uncertain threat to the gold seekers. Their response was violence, usually unrestrained. The Indians responded in kind, and, as the white raised his hand indiscriminately and the Indian responded in the same way, violence escalated and spread.

In 1848 and 1849 open warfare broke out in a number of places. More often than not the conflict could hardly be termed war, for whites set upon Indian rancherias and massacred dozens, scores, even hundreds of Indians, usually without provocation. In the Coloma district, in the Yuba and Kings River region, far to the south where the Yumans reigned, and in the Clear Lake area, whites chased Indians. When they stood and fought, the Indians paid a heavy price in blood. In 1850 the major effort in the South was led by Joseph C. Morehead, who ran up sizable bills in a campaign against the Yumans but won little glory on the field of battle. Subsequently he performed in an equally inept fashion as a filibuster in Baja California. In 1851 Luiseños and Yumans in Southern California again responded to provocations and organized outbreaks which ended with the capture and execution of the Luiseño chief.

In the same year an Indian trader, James D. Savage, who monopolized trade with the Indians by marrying five daughters of chieftains, led a force dubbed the Mariposa Battalion in action against Chief Tenieya and several hundred Yosemites. The most memorable event was the rediscovery of Yosemite Valley, long the stronghold of Tenieya. Captured and herded to a government reservation in the lowlands, the old chief brooded before slipping away to his beloved valley of Yosemite. Anyone familiar with the summer San Joaquin Valley and the valley of Yosemite can understand Chief Tenieya's preference. There, a number of years later, he was killed by rival Indians.

In northern California in 1852 there were several outbreaks in which whites conducted themselves with the kind of savagery which has been attributed generally to the Indians. When a butcher's body was found near Weaverville in the Trinity Mountains, a group of miners put down their tools, organized themselves into a volunteer company, and set out to avenge the murder. At daybreak when they found a rancheria peacefully stirring, they fell upon it and before the bloody work was done about 130 Indian men, women, and children lay dead. In September of the same year, an immigrant party en route from Oregon suffered extensively when it came under Indian attack. A young man, Ben Wright, organized a group of miners in Yreka and went forth for revenge. Luring a group of Indians to a parley, he waited until they were thoroughly disarmed and then fell upon them. When the massacre was over, more than forty Indians were "good Indians."

CALIFORNIA'S INDIAN "WARS"

Thus it is that the California valley cannot grace her annals with a single Indian war bordering on respectability. It can boast, however, a hundred or two of as brutal butcherings, on the part of our honest miners and brave pioneers, as any area of equal extent in our republic. The poor natives of California had neither the strength nor the intelligence to unite in any formidable numbers; hence, when now and then one of them plucked up courage to defend his wife and little ones, or to retaliate on one of the many outrages that were constantly being perpetrated upon them by white persons, sufficient excuse was offered for the miners and settlers to band and shoot down any Indians they met, old or young, innocent or guilty, friendly or hostile, until their appetite for blood was appeased.

Hubert Howe Bancroft, *History of California* (San Francisco, 1884–90), VII, p. 477.

And so it went. One clash followed another, each resulting in substantial losses in Indian life. As their homeland was overrun the Indians were forced to turn toward the stock of the newcomers if they would feed themselves. As a Santa Barbara ranchero, Pablo de la

Guerra, pointed out in a letter to Senator David C. Broderick in which he advocated the establishment of reservations, the Indians were forced to steal the cattle on the ranchos to survive. It is significant that these clashes of the 1850s were not confined to any section of California but took place wherever Indians responded to the invasion of their land in the only way they knew. The whites overwhelmed the Indians, driving them first from the fertile valleys and rich mining country. The natives fell back from their ancestral lands into the less accessible higher country of the mountains and the less desirable desert regions of the south. Everywhere the hand of the newcomer was raised in indiscriminate anger against the Indian. "Never before in history has a people been swept away with such terrible swiftness," was the judgment of an authority who looked carefully at this confrontation of white and Indian in California.

In the far north, a young newspaperman, Francis Bret Harte, was ostracized and driven from the community when he protested a massacre of some two hundred peaceful Indians. This particularly brutal affair took place on a small island in Humboldt Bay opposite the city of Eureka in February 1860. Two hundred Indians in a rancheria busily involved in religious ceremonies were set upon by a party of whites. They were surrounded and near midnight, while they slept in exhaustion from the singing and dancing, a methodical slaughter with knives, axes, and clubs began. Only a small number of men escaped. A similar massacre took place at two rancherias nearby, although the toll was limited to less than one hundred. Those who first came to the scene were sickened and horrified, but when an effort was made to bring the culprits to justice, the grand jury limited itself to condemning the "outrage." Not a single member of the secret organization which staged one of the most despicable crimes in the history of California was ever punished.

The final stand of the California Indians came in one of the most remarkable conflicts that ever took place between Indian and white in America. The Modoc Wars came late—in 1873—and under circumstances which caught the attention of a large part of the world. The events which precipitated this final conflict began shortly after the whites began traveling through the Modoc country in force in the 1850s. The Modocs lived for generations in the northeastern part of

California astride the California-Oregon border. Mount Shasta loomed high over a landscape of timber, lakes, and lava beds which teemed with fish and game and furnished the Modocs with sustenance in their golden years before the arrival of the whites.

The mountain men who traveled through this region and those who came in their footsteps antagonized the Indians. As the volume of travelers increased and the number of provocations multiplied the Indians became increasingly disturbed. The inevitable explosion took the form of an attack on an emigrant train in 1852. The party, en route to California from Oregon, was wiped out. When the news reached the mining settlements, retaliation was swift and brutal. Ben Wright played a role in the indiscriminate slaughter of some forty Modoc braves. Thereafter knife met gun and arrow met bullet until a peace of sorts was restored in 1864, and the remnants of the Modocs were moved to a reservation which they shared with their traditional enemies, the Klamaths. The result was friction and dissatisfaction which led a chief, Captain Jack, to return with a group of his people to their ancestral homelands on the Lost River. A few years later the dissidents were persuaded to return to the reservation but they stayed only a few months before departing once again in the spring of 1870. Once again efforts were made to persuade Captain Jack and his followers to return, but they had had their fill of white men's promises and the haughty disdain of their enemies, the Klamaths. When the Army was sent to enforce an order from Washington to the Indian agent to remove the Modocs to the reservation, "peacefully if he could, but forcibly if he must," the issue was joined.

Captain Jack had some fifty fighting men who were armed with muzzle-loading rifles and a few revolvers. To complicate his problems as a commander, he was responsible for a hundred and fifty women and children who were part of the party. They took refuge in an area of lava beds where the terrain resembled that of the moon. The military commander of the four hundred well-armed soldiers decided on a frontal attack on the Modoc stronghold in the lava beds. In January 1873 the attack began, the soldiers advancing toward an unseen enemy who picked them off from their hiding places. When the toll reached nine men killed and thirty wounded, the colonel saw his men fall back. Reinforcements were called up with additional artillery. From his stronghold, Captain Jack looked out at an enemy force of three hundred, which proved to be just as ineffectual as the smaller group in dealing with the Modocs.

The fighting continued for weeks without victory so the Army turned to a parley. When the principals came to the peace conference, Captain Jack was given the only terms which General E. R. S. Canby, the American commander, would consider—surrender. When the negotiators came together for a second parley on Good Friday, April 11, 1873, the Indians whipped out weapons, killed Canby—the only general who died in the Indian Wars—and a missionary-negotiator, then fled into the lava beds for a renewal of the battle.

More reinforcements were brought up and another disastrous assault on the stronghold of the Modocs attempted. It was as unsuccessful as the first, but the tactics of the Army were producing results. Supplies were running low in the Indian bastion. Artillery, including howitzers, Indian allies, and constant pressure first cut the Indians off from a water supply and then compelled them to split up. Eventually the various groups were captured. A short time later several of the Modoc prisoners were shot by settlers while being transported to imprisonment. Captain Jack and three other men were court-martialed and sentenced to death. When President Grant and Secretary of War William T. Sherman refused to intervene, the Indians were hanged from an improvised gallows. Sherman was a man of consistency. As a young shavetail lieutenant in 1847 he applied white man's law to Indians when he authorized shooting of those caught stealing horses.

Thus ended the Modoc Wars and the long period of armed conflict between Indian and white in California. The cost of the operations in lives and property was enormous. In about a hundred clashes, between 1848 and 1865, fifteen thousand Indians were killed and a considerable number of whites. In the Modoc Wars alone the United States lost eighty-three dead and numerous wounded and spent close to $1,000,000. In other wars, California state and local officials had spent money freely for salaries, supplies, stock, and munitions. The federal government reimbursed the state in the amount of $2,000,000 in the 1850s, an enormous sum for that time. A large part was squandered—in a sense the whole represented a waste, for little was accomplished but subjugating the Indian. That might have been avoided had an effort been made to bring him into the society which was being created.

While some pursued the Indian with sword, others sought a more civilized approach. The latter entailed dealing with the Indians by the usual treaty-making processes. Under these the sovereign Indian nations negotiated arrangements with the federal government. When ratified, the treaty arrangements were a framework which regulated relations between the two "nations."

The first steps in the development of Indian policy in California were taken by the military. Two proclamations in early 1847 were issued by the Army. The first provided for the establishment of a military group to keep the peace and "prevent and punish the aggressions of the Indians." The second ordered the release of all Indians held against their will. A few weeks later the military governor, General Stephen W. Kearny, appointed John Sutter and Mariano G. Vallejo, long-time residents, subagents to the Indians. They were to gather information, formulate necessary regulations, and look after the best interests of the Indians.

These positive steps by the Army were followed by several others which are less admirable. The shooting of Indians caught stealing horses was authorized and all employed Indians were obligated to carry certificates from their masters. "Wild" Indians who wished to visit settlements were required to secure passes from the subagents. Indians who were found wandering without passes and certificates were to be arrested.

In September 1850, some two weeks after California was admitted to the Union, the Congress authorized the appointment of Indian agents and two days later provided $25,000 for the making of treaties with the Indians in California. In January 1851 the three men, Redick McKee, George W. Barbour, and O. M. Wozencraft, arrived in San Jose to consult with representatives of the state government. They found the latter up in arms over Indian "outrages." The legislature had provided a war chest of half a million dollars to deal with the problem and established a militia system which provided for liberal salaries for volunteers who turned from panning gold to fighting Indians.

The commissioners in the following month assembled tribes and negotiated treaties in two areas which set aside reservations and provided for supplies in beef and foodstuffs. On the practical ground that it "is cheaper to feed the whole flock for a year than to fight them for a week," the commissioners divided the state into districts and each went forth to talk of peace and enduring friendship between the Great White Father and his Indian children.

The treaty writing proceeded with dispatch as the three agents fanned out over their assigned areas, assembled tribes, and negotiated agreements. In all, they made eighteen treaties affecting 139 groups or something in the nature of 25,000 Indians. Areas were set aside for the Indians which totaled 11,750 square miles or more than 7,000,000 acres. Some of it was the finest real estate within the borders of the state. The commissioners spent every nickel of the money which Congress appropriated, but in addition let contracts for supplies and incurred other expenses which totaled nearly $1,000,000. The reaction of disapproval from Congress was predictable. In California opinion was divided: a majority of the population disapproved of the commissioners and their work, but a tiny minority insisted that justice be done the Indians and that reservations and treaties were preferable to gauntlets and battlefields.

The state legislature probably reflected majority opinion. A state senate committee condemned the policy of the federal government, recommended that the Indians be removed from the state, instructed their senators to oppose the treaties, and called upon their congressional delegation to push for the adoption by the federal government of the same course toward Indians "as had been pursued in other states for the past quarter of a century." A minority report by J. J. Warner, one-time mountain man and long-time friend of the Indians, pointed out the injustice and impracticality of removal of the Indians from California and urged that they be treated fairly. Much of the opposition was based on the extensive reservations set aside by the treaties. The nearly 12,000 square miles included some of the richest agricultural and mineral land in the state. Critics said its potential would never be realized if it were to be set aside for the exclusive use of Indians, and as thousands of American citizens had settled on these lands prior to the treaties, it would be grossly unfair to evict them.

Two of the commissioners, Wozencraft and McKee, attempted to meet these objections but they had little success. The anti-Indian orientation of the California legislature had taken the form of a law passed in 1850 prohibiting the testimony of an Indian in a case against a white man. It had not changed in the interim but on the contrary had become more fixed. That the California legislature should take such a stand is understandable. A body of lawmakers in which miners and settlers were strongly represented could hardly take a different position. It tied its opposition to the treaties to its advocacy of policies which would divide the public domain in California into 160-acre parcels for distribution to settlers, and laws which would provide security of title to miners.

When the treaties came before the Senate for ratification they were considered in a secret session and all were rejected. The violent opposition in California, the unauthorized expenditures of the commissioners, and the incipient violence which would be spawned by the establishment of reservations on rich mineral land—all played a role in creating opposition. In retrospect it is easy to criticize the Senate's action. In effect the United States government had authorized a number of people to make agreements in its name. When its agents made such agreements, the government subsequently repudiated those treaties. Indians who had personally witnessed the perfidy of white men would find it difficult to view this repudiation as anything other than another example of white treachery. On the other hand, there can be little doubt that establishing reservations in attractive farming and mineral land was most unwise. In any case the treaties were discarded.

The government was still interested in developing a workable Indian policy. Even before the treaties were rejected, an Indian Superintendency was established in California and Edward F. Beale was appointed to fill the office. Charged with the responsibility of preserving peace with the Indians who had been dispossessed, until appropriate arrangements had been made, he came to California in September 1852 and set about the task of developing a workable program. Beale was a knowledgeable young man who had traveled widely in western America and was a veteran of the Mexican War, who after the Battle of San Pascual slipped through enemy lines to San Diego for help for the beleaguered Kearny. His knowledge and understanding of the realities of the Indian-white confrontation in California were broad and deep.

Out of such understanding came Beale's plan which called for the establishment of a number of small reservations on the public lands. By agreement the Indians would be invited to settle on them. They would enjoy the protection of a military garrison while they produced foodstuffs for themselves and the reservation establishment on the approximately 25,000 acres of land provided. Congress endorsed the plan and provided funds and Beale promptly established the first reservation near Tejon Pass in Southern California. From the first it flourished. Within a year 3265 acres of land were under cultivation by more than four hundred Indians. The similarities between this American establishment and the missions of Spanish days are obvious; J. Ross Browne, in an insightful report, declared the missions were copied deliberately.

Beale's plans for a chain of similar reservations reaching northward through California had not proceeded beyond the planning stage when he was removed. His successor, Thomas J. Henley, an able and talented Democratic politico, found little reason to change the basic outlines of Beale's plans. Under his direction a reservation was established at Nome Lake in Colusa County, another at Mendocino, and a fourth at Klamath on the river of the same name. A number of supplementary reserves or farms were also established on the Fresno and Kings rivers. From the glowing reports which issued from Henley's office all was going well.

A more critical look at the entire system by a special agent produced a disquieting report. It indicated that the reservations were not the prosperous establishments which Henley had described but a kind of almshouse where hapless and improvident Indians became permanent dependents of the government. They were not trained or educated to self-sufficiency "for there was nothing in the system, as practiced, that looked to the permanent improvement of the Indian, or that tended in any way to his moral, intellectual, or social elevation."

The system was continued, however, until the middle of June 1860, when a new tack was taken in Indian affairs. Under the new law the Secretary of the Interior divided the state into a northern district and a southern district, each to be supervised by an agent. The small reservation system was continued and the agreement rather than the treaty system was permanently adopted. Under the new policy, which was adopted in other western states, the Indians of California found their conditions little changed. The Indian service continued to be a refuge for political hacks who paid for their positions in that most durable of political currencies, past or the promise of future political service to the appointing political official. Contracts for supplies for the reservations continued to be a lucrative pot into which dipped Indian agents and their confederates. The Indians, their memories clouded with misty dreams of the golden days before the coming of the white man, lived out their days without dignity or purpose. Late in the nineteenth century literary champions such as Helen Hunt Jackson and Charles F. Lummis came to a belated awareness of how the California Indians, like Indians everywhere in the United States, had been victimized by a "Century of Dishonor."

Many California Indians were never part of a reservation system, but lived apart, subsisting not on government handouts but what their labor brought them. Working as vaqueros, herdsmen, and harvesters, they were the essential hewers of wood and drawers of water which are so plentiful in a pastoral agricultural economy. Early in the nineteenth century the mission Indians were the major source of labor on the ranchos. Acquisition of California by the United States did not change the situation. The Indians lived out their lives of hard but irregular employment, limited income, and curtailed dignity, essential to the agricultural system but enjoying few of its bounties.

In the 1850s city ordinances in Los Angeles provided for the arrest, imprisonment, and fining of any Indian "able to work who shall be found loitering, or drunk, making a noise or disturbance." The mayor was charged with examining the offender and if the alleged offense were established, the individual was subject to being "hired out within twentyfour hours, for the highest price that can be had, for any term not exceeding four months." The law provided a legal system whereby Indians were shamefully exploited. A vicious pattern developed in which the Indians worked for a time toward the binge when alcohol would make their dreary lot disappear for a time. Picked up and imprisoned in the local bastille, they were "hired out" to prospective employers. Set to work by their benefactors, they labored through another phase of the cycle toward

ISHI

In the latter part of August 1911 a sick, exhausted, and half-starved Yaki Indian was discovered cowering in fear before a band of watchdogs in a corral in the town of Oroville, California. Clad in a poncholike garment, obviously terrified at his prospects, the Indian was taken by the local sheriff to the local bastille and confined while the city's fathers pondered his fate. The news of his arrival in civilization made its way south via the press wires and eventually came to the attention of Alfred Kroeber, a University of California anthropologist.

A few days later, Kroeber rescued Ishi from his improvised imprisonment and brought him to San Francisco. There he lived for the next five years, this representative of the Neolithic Age who stepped out of the forest into the twentieth century at Oroville. He spoke no language other than his native Yaki. His contact with Europeans had been fleeting and sporadic since he and the remnants of his people sought survival in concealment and isolation in the early 1870s. For the ensuing near forty years, Ishi lived in the fastness of the forests of the Mount Lassen area. One by one the members of the tiny band were eliminated until only Ishi remained until illness and hunger drove him from his sanctuary.

In San Francisco, Ishi began his second life. A glossary of terms from his language which the anthropologists discovered enabled them to begin serious communication with him. Once this barrier was broken and Ishi came to understand that these men were not bent on his death, he began the exploration of the modern world of twentieth-century America. It was a unique and historic incident, for Ishi was like a visitor from another planet devoid of the most basic impressions of this society. And it was a reciprocal arrangement, for through Ishi, anthropologist Kroeber was able to learn things about Indian society and culture from a participant.

Ishi was not an exotic sideshow novelty during the five years that he lived and worked and played and discovered. His values of life and death, his simple dignity, and his human qualities attracted and made for lasting relationships with some of his associates. When he died, a victim like myriads of other Indians of a white man's disease, TB, grief was instant, profound, and extensive. One who knew him well wrote:

And so, stoic and unafraid, departed the last wild Indian of America. He closes a chapter in history. He looked upon us as sophisticated children—smart, but not wise. We knew many things, and much that is false. He knew nature, which is always true. His were the qualities of character that last forever. He was kind; he had courage and self-restraint, and though all had been taken from him, there was no bitterness in his heart. His soul was that of a child, his mind that of a philosopher.

(Kroeber, *Ishi*, pp. 237–38.)
The story of Ishi is told in Theodora
Kroeber, *Ishi in Two Worlds, A Biography
of the Last Wild Indian in North America*
(University of California Press, Berkeley, 1961).

---

their spree, imprisonment, and sale. The cycle, repeated through the year, provided those interested with Indian laborers at a nominal expense.

The net result of the American Indian policy in the first twenty years after 1848 was decimation of the native population. While it is difficult to obtain precise figures, the best estimates indicate that the decline in the Indian population of the state was in excess of 65 per cent. The population estimated at 100,000 in 1850 declined to 30,000 in 1870 and by a further 10,000 in 1880. By 1916 it had dropped to 16,000. Bullets account for part of the total decline, but disease was especially effective in curtailing their numbers. As deadly as these apparent factors was the insidious effect which came when the Indian was crushed in spirit. Deprive a man of soul and you strike at life.

In summary, American Indian policy in California had many flaws. In spite of some imaginative proposals and a few individuals of good will, a viable policy never emerged. In many respects the failure was the result of the incompatibility of two ways of life. The Indian society of hunting and gathering was simply incompatible with the society of mining, herding, grazing, farming, and manufacturing which overwhelmed it.

CHAPTER XII

The Seething Seventies

Californians hailed the 1869 joining of the rails of the Central Pacific and the Union Pacific at Promontory Point, and all save a group of naysayers said it marked the beginning of a new era. Politicians and newspaper editors alike found normal rhetoric inadequate to describe the multiple blessings which were to come to California and its people. Now the Atlantic states were just five days' travel away; henceforth, California would be linked immediately and permanently to the Union; from this time forward its economy would not be shackled for want of facilities to carry away its produce or bring it necessities. Henceforth, Californians would come and go in comfort—their travel speeded by thundering locomotives which intimidated Indians and whites alike as they lumbered across the wide stretches which lay between the Pacific coast and the Mississippi Valley. The days when travelers came via the pitching coaches of the Butterfield stage or the prairie schooner or perhaps an interminable sea voyage interrupted by a miasmic crossing of the Isthmus of Panama were, thankfully, gone forever.

Speed, comfort, and certainty of transportation and communication were but three of the benefits which the railroad would confer. There were a number of additional boons. The completion of the railroad to Ogden opened up a greater hinterland to the merchants and farmers of the coast. The Utah-Nevada market, still unproven, was a factor with which to reckon within the immediate future. And there was another economic gain, of uncertain but hopefully gigantic dimensions. The railroad was to channel a vast trade in the goods of Europe and Asia. Soon the exotic cargoes of the Orient would be wending their way to London and Paris across the prairies of western America. En route they would pass trains heavily laden with the output of Liverpool, Manchester, and Antwerp as well as many New

England centers of industry. A new era had dawned—a day of increasing prosperity, not only for the builders of the railroad but for the general citizenry of California.

Some observers were not so sanguine. Henry George, who was later to pen the most provocative book ever produced by a California writer, predicted that the coming of the railroad would heighten social tension when the Chinese laborers, some ten thousand strong, were thrown on the labor market. In an even more perceptive observation he declared that the California business community might be disadvantaged by the coming of the railroad, which would make it possible for the businessmen of the East and the Midwest to compete in the California market. George proved right on both counts. Before the echoes of the first train whistle across the junction point died away, representatives of the mercantile houses of Chicago and points east were soliciting orders for various kinds of merchandise from customers who had long been the exclusive concern of Sacramento, Stockton, and San Francisco houses. The merchants and budding manufacturers of California discovered that the railroad served them but also served their competitors.

A number of other factors were quietly shaping the immediate future of California as well as the nation. The panic of 1873 was on the horizon. Soon it would descend on the land. Ushered in by unbridled speculation in railroads, overexpansion in a number of lines of industry and agriculture, a declining European market for American farm produce, and triggered by a break in the securities market and the failure of Jay Cooke and Company, the panic brought widespread business contraction, unemployment, numerous bankruptcies, and general economic distress to wide segments of the United States. California was not spared, although her time of depression came later in the 1870s. It helped to make the seventies a decade of change and conflict.

California's problems in the "seething seventies" did not arise simply from the panic of 1873. They represented a matrix: some had national roots, others state; some existed independently, others were interrelated. A significant portion of the non-Chinese population believed the Chinese problem to be the most pressing one of the day. To others, the transportation monopoly and the political activities of the Big Four were the source of most problems. To the descendants of the National Reform Association, Henry George and James McClatchy, the source of most difficulties was the huge monopolies in land and water in California. To the farmers of the Sacramento Valley, the real difficulty was the failure of the society to protect them and their verdant fields from the debris which the hydraulic miners tore out of the foothills of the Sierras and sent downstream where it clogged channels, ruined fishing, and caused floods which deposited a layer of sterile slime over productive fields. To still others, the corruption, inefficiency, and insensitivity of local and state government were the paramount problems. Governmental inadequacy was difficult to tolerate at any time but particularly galling when it directly touched the lives of the general citizenry. The fruits of political corruption took the form of waste, extravagance, unjust assessments, excessive charges for governmental services, and a score of other abuses. The need for reform in government, in politics, and perhaps in the constitution itself became increasingly clear as the decade passed. In summary, there were a number of problems in California during the seventies—none of them minor—most of them interrelated.

CHINESE SCAPEGOATS

Portents of racial conflict appeared in the first twenty years that followed the gold rush. The first Chinese on the scene came in limited numbers: less than a hundred before 1849 and less than a thousand by January 1850. In the latter year the total Chinese population swelled to 4018 and this almost doubled to 7512 by January of 1852. With each passing year the Chinese population grew, almost all of the increase coming with emigration from mainland China. In 1860 there were approximately 45,000 Chinese in the state and in 1876 they numbered 116,000 in California and about 151,000 in the United States.

In the early years, although they were different in color, language, customs, and religion from the Anglo-Americans who dominated the California scene after the Mexican War, they received a measure of toleration. From time to time the special animosity of the Anglos for Negroes and Indians spilled over and affected the Chinese. Thus, they

were subjected to the discriminatory miner's tax in the early fifties
and in 1854 Justice Hugh C. Murray of the Supreme Court persuaded his fellow justices that the provisions in the constitution
excluding the testimony of Indians and Negroes in cases involving
whites applied to the Chinese as well. Toleration of the Chinese in
California continued so long as they were confined to working
played-out claims disdained by whites or so long as they were the
hewers of wood and drawers of water who did the work which
whites refused. They were the sober, thrifty, and industrious house
servants, launderers, gardeners, stablemen—in short, representatives
of a servile labor class. During the 1860s they began to move into a
broad variety of occupations. By 1869 they were employed in railroad construction, in textile mills, dairies, saltworks, liquor manufacturing, brickmaking, mining, and in the maritime industry. As long as
California was a land of opportunity in which jobs were plentiful
and wages high, there was toleration of the Chinese.

There was antagonism but it was controlled. Much of it sprang
from another form of racism, especially noticeable in the transplanted Southerners who comprised about a third of the state's population in the fifties. Accustomed to look upon those of darker hue as
inferior, they identified the Chinese as representatives of a servile
people who should be ruled. In the early fifties Archibald C. Peachy,
of Halleck, Peachy and Billings, a prominent law firm which specialized in land litigation, proposed the coolie bill. It would have established a system of servile labor in California under which laborers
imported from China would work in the fields of California for a
period up to ten years in exchange for "wages" of at least $10 a
year. Governor John Bigler's special message in 1852 called for restrictions on Chinese immigration. It earned for him a lasting reputation as a racist, but his antipathy was directed as much at the contract labor system of the Peachy bill as the Chinese themselves. The
bill was never passed but the support it received among the lawmakers and in the press indicated the role which a substantial part of
the population contemplated for the Chinese.

The coolie bill also indicated the source of the attitudes toward
the Chinese. To those who used them and their labor, the Chinese
qualities of patience, intelligence, docility, and frugality made them
quite acceptable as immigrants. To those who competed with them

for jobs, the ability of the Chinese to work as hard and perform as much on half the wages made them unacceptable as residents of California. One of the first organizations of anti-Chinese sentiment was the People's Protective Union, organized in 1859 in San Fran-

---

A POLITICIAN LOOKS AT THE CHINESE QUESTION

If I understand the avowed object of the so-called anti-coolie movement, it is an attempt by men of the European race to prevent, by all unlawful means, the employment at the various industrial callings in California, of men of the Asiatic race. I am in favor of such a scheme. If, as some believe, ignorant Asiatics are improperly induced to make contracts with capitalists of their own race, by the terms of which they are to owe service or labor in this state for a term of years, without a good consideration, I will aid by any proper means to remedy the evil. I am opposed to human slavery, and to all its substitutes and aliases; coolieism, peonage, contract systems in which one side makes the bargain for both —these are all abhorrent. But because I am an anti-slavery man, I am also an anti-slave man. Because I detest the overreaching man who would grind the faces of the poor, I do not also detest the poor. Because I am opposed to the coolie system, I am not the enemy of its victims. I believe in the Christian religion, and that rests upon the universal fatherhood of God and the universal brotherhood of man. The same God created both Europeans and Asiatics. No man of whatever race has any better right to labor, and receive his hire therefore, than has any other man. To controvert this is to contend with him who said to man: "In the sweat of thy face shalt thou eat bread till thou return unto the ground." As a question, then, of right and wrong, I am as emphatically opposed to all attempts to deny the Chinese the right to labor for pay, as I am to the restoration of African slavery whereby black men were compelled to labor without pay . . .

From a letter by George Gorham, candidate
for governor, to officers of a San Francisco
anti-Chinese organization, May 3, 1867.
Gorham lost to Henry H. Haight.

---

cisco out of protests against Chinese cigar makers. To Charles Crocker, who mustered thousands of them in the building of the Central Pacific, the Chinese were as good as most and better than a substantial portion of the white laborers he could hire. They were

"Crocker's pets," and he was pleased with them and what they did for him and for the Central Pacific.

Even before Chinese labor on the Central Pacific was finished, Henry George was speculating as to the impact of this new source of labor on American workers. That they would not be readily absorbed into the work force was obvious. On the contrary, instead of peaceful integration into the labor force, they met a renewal of the intermittent hostility which had been directed at them from the early eighteen fifties. Now, however, the antagonism was to become sharper and more pervasive, and the hostility and insolence of the white majority were to be transformed into injustice and oppression. In some instances the persecution of the Chinese took ingenious forms. In 1862 a "police tax" of $2.50 per month was assessed on every Chinese male over eighteen who was not paying the miner's tax. The Supreme Court later declared it unconstitutional. In the mid-sixties Chinese children along with black and Indian children were excluded from schools. In 1866 this was softened by adding the qualification that they might be admitted if there were no objection from the parents of white children. In the spring of 1867 an Anti-Coolie Labor Association was formed; many of its members came from anti-Chinese local clubs formed as early as 1862. The political power of prejudice was demonstrated when gubernatorial candidate George C. Gorham in 1867 denounced the association, saying, "The same God created both Europeans and Asiatics." He was resoundingly defeated. In 1880 in a San Francisco election only 229 votes out of 40,259 were cast for allowing the Chinese to remain in the United States. Before the discriminatory legislation against the Chinese had reached its peak in the form of provisions in the constitution of 1879, Chinese residents of California had been subjected to some of the most onerous restrictions ever applied to a peaceful minority in America.

Among others, Chinese could not be employed on the public works nor in the construction of the canals and dams of the great irrigation district organized in 1876, which sprawled across the counties of Alameda, Contra Costa, San Joaquin, Stanislaus, Merced, Fresno, and Tulare. They were excluded from citizenship, prohibited from owning or acquiring real property, and denied business licenses. In an outburst of mindless animosity, the supervisors of San Francisco forbade the use of Chinese granite on public works and specified that all prisoners in the local bastille must have their hair cut within one inch of the scalp. This "Pigtail Ordinance," although it applied to all, was directed at the Chinese.

Chinese residents of California were harassed in other ways as well. They were robbed, murdered, assaulted, and driven out of communities with apparent impunity. In the post-Civil War period, as the manifold problems of Reconstruction dominated public affairs, thinking on the Chinese question was affected. The safeguards of the Fourteenth and Fifteenth amendments, in some instances, strengthened the position of the Chinese as well as the Negro in American society. On the other hand, judicial decisions which limited federal jurisdiction over civil rights matters worked to the contrary. The treatment accorded the Chinese reflected such legislation and decisions but it was also determined by a number of economic factors. When the population was divided into competing groups scrambling for jobs and positions, verbal expressions of resentment and abuse became physical assault.

In 1867 when the Pacific Mail Steamship line initiated direct connections with a number of Far Eastern ports, its ships carried Chinese immigrants on return voyages. They were greeted upon their arrival in San Francisco by a mob which pelted them with cobblestones and debris from the streets as they made their way from the docks to Chinatown. Thereafter, assaults on Chinese by individuals and groups increased in number and spread over the entire state. In the wake of the celebration of the completion of the transcontinental railroad at Promontory Point in 1869, a disgraceful mob attack on Chinese residents of San Francisco produced considerable alarm and a disquieting feeling that there was tinder in the social milieu of California which could be fired. A few years later, in October 1871, in the city incongruously named the City of the Angels, there was a violent attack on the Chinese section. Houses were burned and looted, men, women, and children shot down, and a number of men methodically hanged from an improvised gallows. The toll was eighteen. A local newspaper commented, "We have often read of outrages being perpetrated upon Americans in China, but never, at any time, anything more barbarous than the hanging of children and brutally clubbing them till they were dead on the gallows." The grand jury indicted over 150 men. Six were convicted and then released on technicalities. Even this disgraceful episode brought no relief. On the contrary, throughout the decade Chinese residents of California were subject to varied harassment ranging from the vilest kind of verbal abuse to physical assault.

Ethnic conflict continued to mount. In part it was stimulated by the swelling immigration and the contraction of the economy which followed the panic of 1873. Throughout the seventies the Chinese came in growing numbers. Their passage was paid under a contract which provided that they were to labor for one of the six mercantile companies which operated as labor contractors. Archibald Peachy of the coolie bill fame would have recognized the system. In essence it was debt bondage or peonage, a system which was antithetical to the American system of free wage labor. In 1876 22,493 came and the books of the companies revealed that more than 150,000 Chinese had been brought to California under these arrangements. Although much of California's agriculture was undergoing a transformation toward intensive cultivation and thus absorbing substantial numbers of these new arrivals in the fruit orchards and vegetable farms of the Sacramento and San Joaquin valleys, there was growing friction between the Chinese and those who used Chinese labor and those who labored or spoke for them. In the same general period, there were waves of Anglo immigration to California. In the 1868–69 season almost 60,000 came, and in the period from 1873 to 1875 approximately 150,000 arrived. While it could be argued that Chinese labor supplemented rather than supplanted Anglo labor, in times when jobs were scarce and labor in plentiful supply, there was likely to be growing tension. The tension existed within the cities, since much of California's population in the sixties and seventies was concentrated in the urban areas of San Francisco and Sacramento. It was in the cities as well that the nineteenth-century migrant worker gathered in the fall when harvest was over and there was no role for him to play until planting time in the spring.

So long as the economy was booming there was a minimum of difficulty, but as the currency of the United States was deliberately curtailed, as the great railroad building was completed, as the output of the mines declined, and as the pace of economic activity in California and the nation slackened, troubles between the Chinese and their competitors for jobs increased. In the mid-seventies a number of developments portended trouble. A sharp break in the market for mining securities in August 1876 caught thousands of overextended Californians in a vulnerable position. For more than a decade speculation in mining stock, especially in the mines of the Comstock, intrigued thousands of people and enriched a small number of insiders who came close to managing the market in their interest. The break in prices wiped out $100,000,000 in security values, impoverished thousands of families, and brought immediate distress to a broad segment of the population. The winter of that year also brought a $20,000,000 disaster to the ranchers and farmers of the state. Prolonged drought extending through the winter months of 1876–77 withered the wheat in the ground and sharply curtailed the natural forage upon which cattle and sheep fattened. Sheep dropped to an incredible low of $1 a head. It was a bleak time generally for big segments of the population. One measure of the distress was the number of people in San Francisco who were dependent upon the charity of their friends and fellow parishioners for survival. In the period from 1876–78, the number of unemployed and the number of people being assisted by handouts rose steadily until in the spring of 1878 more than two thousand people were being fed daily by a church-organized relief program. And mounting distress in the form of more than four hundred business failures in a single year demonstrated the magnitude of the economic collapse.

The series of disasters which afflicted the state were in sharp contrast with what had once existed. High wages and working conditions superior to those which prevailed in the rest of the United States had been the general rule since 1850. In California the eight-hour day had been established on public works in 1868, and some twenty-five trade unions in San Francisco, some dating back to the early fifties, safeguarded the rights of labor. When the economic skies began to darken and real distress came to the work force of California in the mid-seventies, a number of people began to search for an explanation for the changes.

To the unsophisticated, an explanation came readily. In looking about the California scene one saw the thousands of representatives of the Orient. It was the Chinese laborer, "John," who was responsible. It was he who displaced the white worker and helped to undermine his wage level and his working conditions. Exclusion of new immigrants from China and removal of the Chinese would restore prosperity to California and the good life to its farmers and workers. The existing system under which thousands of Chinese were imported each year under labor contracts degraded labor. "The Chinese must go" became the war cry, and to hasten his going as well as restrict his activities in the interim, laws were passed restricting his employment on public works and the irrigation improvements in districts established under state law.

The restless and fearful spokesmen for labor and small-business men had found plausible explanation for their plight and they would take whatever steps they thought necessary to deal with the culprit. It was a classic example of scapegoating; an inoffensive and defenseless minority was to bear the responsibility for a multifaceted economic situation which was not of their making. If anything, the Chinese were as victimized by and had even less control over the economy of California than their Anglo counterparts. A kind of psychological imperative was operating, however, which allowed whites to deal with their fears and distress with animosity directed at the Chinese. This phenomenon had a major influence on all aspects of California life during the late seventies. It was especially evident in the political field. The Democratic party in 1869, for example, combined an appeal to workingmen with a denunciation of the Chinese, the railroad monopoly, and the Fourteenth and Fifteenth amendments.

To some observers, however, the Chinese were not nearly as responsible for the sad state of affairs as a group of potentates who possessed the riches and power of figures out of oriental mythology. They were the Big Four, Huntington, Stanford, Hopkins, and Crocker. It was they and their enterprises who were responsible, and it was they and their enterprises which needed to be curbed. In some respects, the animosity directed at the Big Four was as mindless as that directed at the Chinese, but in other respects, Huntington, Stanford, Hopkins, and Crocker fully deserved the hostility that came their way.

THE OCTOPUS

The Pacific Associates, from the beginning of their association, followed an independent course. The completion of the Suez Canal in late 1869 changed the relationship of geography and transportation routes of Europe and Asia. Apparently the dream that the transcontinental railroad would be the means whereby the commerce of Europe and Asia could be channeled through American commercial arteries was a dream and nothing more. However, the Big Four clung to the dream of creating a far-flung enterprise which would be based on trade with the Orient. When the joint Central Pacific-Union Pacific venture completed the 1776 miles of track between the Missouri and the Sacramento rivers and cut the travel time between Asia and western Europe nearly in half, the Big Four began acquiring supplementary facilities on the West Coast. Even before Promontory Point they were acquiring lines within California and establishing facilities which enabled them to dominate the transportation scene. By 1869 they controlled all railroad routes into San Francisco, operated ferry and steamship lines and facilities within the bay, and were in a position to dominate further railroad development within California. Before their work was done, the Pacific Associates controlled a vast railroad network of more than 9000 miles of track, several steamship companies, shipyards, millions of acres of public land, and their private fortunes varied from $40,000,000 to $65,000,-000. Well before the end of the century they were lords who controlled a vast domain, a sixth of the nation's area, which stretched from the Columbia on the north to the city of San Diego on the south! The tentacles of the Big Four, the Octopus, a term heard with increasing frequency in the seventies, stretched across the trans-Mississippi West to the Atlantic coast. So complete was their control over California that scarcely a passenger or a ton of freight moved without paying them tribute. They met and beat their competitors by seizing control of strategically located passes, harbors, river crossings, and railroad routes. They met and bested their rivals in political conventions, legislatures, and in the halls and committees of Congress. It wasn't until 1885 that they tolerated the entry of a rival railroad into Los Angeles. Fifteen years later they opened the city of San Francisco to a competitor.

That the railroad brought great boons to the people of California cannot be denied. Widespread economic development came in the wake of the track-laying crews of the railroad. For decades the potential of California in agriculture was imperfectly realized for want of means to carry away the produce of its verdant fields. Wheat and other grains were almost ideally suited to the hot, rainless summers of the great valley. The grains produced, especially wheat, were hard and dry and durable. They brought top prices in the wheat markets of the world, although until the appearance of the railroad on the scene, the costs of transportation constituted an insurmountable barrier to many California producers. The railroad brought new, and enlarged existing, opportunities to the California farmer, for now his grain and forage could reach markets at economic costs. The first cargo of fruit went east in 1869, and thereafter the tonnages grew as the technical problems of shipping delicate fruit without refrigeration were overcome. In the eighties the shipments amounted to thousands of carloads, and by the nineties, after the development of refrigerator cars, California fruit reached London and Paris markets. The railroad was an essential link between the producer and the market.

The railroad also worked to the benefit of Californians in other ways. It provided them with a means to travel in or from the state in comfort, certainty, and style. It brought large numbers of immigrants whose coming and presence stimulated the economy. It provided them with the means to draw upon the output of the factories of the East. The moguls who controlled and directed these railroad enterprises also accumulated capital which they invested in other fields. Land, lumber, agriculture, irrigation, urban transportation, and utilities all felt the benign hand of the Big Four. As the Pacific Associates looked at the West of their day they saw a community of interest which linked their economic destinies with those of the region. If the West grew and developed so did the enterprises of the Pacific Associates. As the population increased, so increased the rate-paying public. In short, the Big Four did much for the West, California, and themselves in the years that spanned the completion of the transcontinental railroad and the beginning of the twentieth century. Unfortunately the good which they did was often overshadowed in the public mind by the manner in which they operated.

In the interest of their railroads and associated enterprises, the Big Four used whatever means were necessary to fatten profit margins and extend their power and control. Operating on the axiom "what the traffic will bear" in setting rates, they sometimes demanded a look at a shipper's books before settling rates. Whenever they took that step, the customer was often left with the unsettling feeling that the rate was set to give the railroad the greatest possible return, but was not so high as to drive him out of business. Thus, the Big Four applied the old adage of the goose and the golden eggs. For more than forty years a disproportionate share of the profit of every business and industry in California was diverted into the pockets of the Associates through such practices.

The Big Four had little concern for public opinion when they built their railroad, and they had even less concern as they operated it. Sometimes they used raw economic power. They cowed and intimidated the opposition. If they couldn't deal with a competitor they might buy him out. In many respects they personified the predatory capitalist of the period whose civic conscience was stunted. In a time of robber barons, a Tweed ring, and corruption which touched the Supreme Court, intimates of the President, and members of both branches of Congress, they bought politicians, editors, members of regulatory bodies, congressmen, governors, and anyone else whose services were needed. They had power which rivaled that of government itself and in California far overshadowed any other locus of economic power. There were men whose personal fortunes approached those of Stanford, Huntington, Hopkins, and Crocker, but no other group controlled a facility which touched the life of every resident of California. Frequently they exercised their control with little finesse. From time to time the public was given glimpses of what was going on. To men reared in the democratic tradition, it was demoralizing to learn that one out of every three members of the state legislature were beholden to the Central Pacific. More vexing were the highhanded practices of the men who controlled the transportation system of California. With a battery of the best legal men on the payroll, with money and influence of considerable magnitude to exert in political parties, and by controlling an adequate number of newspapers, the railroad had its way. Frequently, it ran over somebody.

One such occasion involved a group of settlers in the San Joaquin Valley locale of Mussel Slough who came upon a barren land and spent lavishly of their labor and transformed it into a green and productive area of farms. After they had completed homes, farm buildings, 50 miles of irrigation ditches, fences, wells, and orchards, the settlers discovered that they and the railroad interpreted their agreements to acquire land differently. The former insisted that the railroad had committed itself to a sale at minimum prices of $2.50 an acre; the railroad denied any such agreement had been made and demanded payment at ten to twenty times the minimum offered. The settlers promptly accused the railroad of jacking up the price to reflect the improvements which they had built.

Positions hardened and settlers began to make preparations to resist eviction. At the same time the railroad began to bring heavy guns into play in the form of sales to outsiders. When the settlers resisted their displacement by such newcomers, the railroad brought the law down on them. In 1880, armed with writs of ejectment, the representatives of the railroad came into conflict with sun-tempered farmers who were determined. Shooting resulted, and seven men were killed in this dramatic episode which was later the focus of Frank Norris' *The Octopus*, a landmark in the literature of California. Subsequently the railroad had its way. Five settlers went to jail although when they were released they were greeted as public heroes when they returned to Tulare County. In the long run, the railroad lost a good deal in the Mussel Slough tragedy, for it convinced a great many people that the Octopus had no conscience and too much power. Something needed to be done to restrain this soulless monster.

MONOPOLY IN LAND

Another factor produced unrest and instability in the social order of the 1870s. Land monopoly, a fearsome specter which haunted the dreams of land reformers of the nineteenth century, came closer to reality in California than any other state. It was a product of a number of circumstances, and it affected Californians in different ways, but it touched the lives of most citizens. When the land monopolists and the Octopus merged in the public mind, one of the consequences of Mussel Slough, the demand for change increased. It was also fortified when the growing population increased the demand for land and more people became acquainted with the existing pattern of land ownership of the 1870s in which huge swaths of land were concentrated in the hands of small groups.

The pattern of land ownership was given a basic set during the Spanish and Mexican periods when extensive tracts of land were granted to deserving citizens—some eight hundred in all. They covered large areas of the richest and most productive land in the state—some 16,000,000 acres, of which approximately 8,800,000 was subsequently confirmed 521 claims. During the 1850s when average claims of more than 15,000 acres were being confirmed, the ownership of such property frequently changed hands in the course of the complex process of adjudication set up under the Land Act of 1851. Sharp-eyed land speculators and squatters, always present on the frontier, picked up some, shrewd moneylenders used mortgages and interest rates of 2 or 3 per cent a month to obtain title, and legal firms like Halleck, Peachy and Billings acquired a share, often in satisfaction for legal services for representing land claimants in proceedings before the land commission. Thereafter much of the public land of California was distributed so as to supplement the basic pattern. Some 9,000,000 acres of school lands, swamp and overflowed lands, Morrill Act land, and land purchased in extensive tracts by speculators came into the hands of great magnates. The disbursements, often accompanied by a full measure of fraud, facilitated the development of land monopolists. Almost a third of the state was disposed of in this fashion, the Southern Pacific alone benefiting to the extent of some 12,000,000 acres. Those who had looked at the golden land of California in 1850 and envisioned the realization of Jefferson's dream of a society of independent landed, yeoman farmers by its distribution among the landless had good reason to look with anger and regret on what had happened.

As farmers became aware of the manner in which tax assessments were made to benefit the big landowners, they became increasingly dissatisfied. When they learned at first hand how the major landowners dominated irrigation districts and companies and set water rates that penalized the small farmer and rancher and benefited the land speculator, they became enraged. As the 1870s passed, a substantial part of the population came at last to the conclusion that reform of the governmental system was essential. Soon the dissatisfaction of the agricultural hinterland of California was to unite with a volatile and restless political movement in San Francisco.

In ordinary times, the pattern of land ownership manifested itself in a number of ways. California had a latifundia pattern of its own, for half the agricultural land of the state was owned by a small number of men in feudal-like estates which covered literally thousands—even hundreds of thousands of acres. Farming and ranching were done on an extensive scale; 5000- to 125,000-acre tracts were not uncommon. California, far from being a state of small farmers, was a "country of plantations and estates." William S. Chapman amassed more than 1,000,000 acres; Henry Miller joined with Charles Lux in a partnership which also acquired more than 1,000,000 acres. Miller and Lux acquired not only land but riparian rights which enabled them to monopolize the life-giving water sources and on one occasion nearly 100 miles of both banks of the San Joaquin River. Miller proudly boasted he could ride from Oregon to Mexico and spend each night en route in a Miller-Lux ranch house. The extensive agricultural units were often owned by absentee landlords and worked by Mexicans, Chinese, or Indians, who labored for modest wages during the busy seasons and then spent the winter in unemployment in the cities. Often huge tracts of land lay fallow, the owners awaiting a rise in land value—their period of waiting made tolerable by a light tax load produced in part by underassessment of "uncultivated land." A pattern was established which is often seen today.

When times were not ordinary the pattern of land distribution and ownership was especially burdensome. When in the mid-seventies a break in the mining securities market coincided with agricultural depression sparked by a prolonged drought, the unrest in the agricultural hinterland became noticeable. Unemployment and unrest also grew in San Francisco. Anger and resentment of working people was vented in attacks on Chinese residents. So threatening was the situation that William T. Coleman of vigilance committee fame was called out of retirement to organize a new committee of public safety in the summer of 1877. The landless, floating agricultural laborers, supplemented by unemployed miners who sought refuge in the city of San Francisco in 1877, were interested in changing a social order which had promised them and their forebears so much and delivered so little. As they contemplated their misery, with unemployment reaching record levels and the echoes of labor strife in the East reaching the Pacific coast, they became increasingly impatient. When men began to appear before them with political solutions for social problems, they responded.

THE GENESIS OF THE WORKINGMEN'S PARTY

In the fall of 1877 a political party came out of this milieu, the Workingmen's party. Within a month its public meetings on the sand lots of San Francisco produced a leader, Denis Kearney, a self-taught former merchant marine officer who used effectively inflammatory rhetoric. From the platform he recommended "a little judicious hanging" for the nabobs of Nob Hill which included the Big Four and he raised the slogan "The Chinese Must Go!" The program of the new party, adopted in the spring of 1878, was far less truculent than the oratory of Kearney. In today's light such things as the eight-hour day, the direct election of United States senators, compulsory education, state regulation of banks, industry, and railroads, and a more equitable tax system seem eminently reasonable. To a great many people of the period, already alarmed by militant railroad strikes in the summer of 1877, the new party was an attack on the established order which must be resisted. And when the guardians of the old order considered the resolutions passed by the sand-lot gatherings of the Workingmen, their worst fears were realized. This was indeed a revolutionary movement which pledged itself to wresting "the government from the hands of the rich" and placing it in those of the people. They also proposed to deal with the "land monopoly in our state" and to "rid the country of cheap Chinese labor . . . because it tends to degrade labor and aggrandize capital." To accomplish all this, Kearney and his followers proposed to use votes, but if legitimate means failed then they would use whatever means necessary.

Attendance at the sand-lot meetings grew until crowds of several thousand were gathering in the Nob Hill neighborhood of the Big Four. In a meeting of early November 1877, Kearney was arrested for language tending to incite violence, and the militia of San Francisco was called out in anticipation of a violent outburst by the Workingmen. The following day several more leaders of the fledgling party were arrested, but all of them were released and the charges were dismissed. A tremendous gathering of ten thousand greeted them on the following Thanksgiving Day in the city. As the new year opened there was continued tension as demonstrations of the unemployed gathered on the steps of the city hall and demanded that the city provide them with either jobs or relief. Meanwhile, the conservative leaders of the community were organizing. A vigilance committee of more than five thousand members was set up, arms were gathered—the most popular a hickory pick handle—and plans were made for possible action. The Workingmen promptly responded by organizing military companies. When the grand jury voted indictments of Kearney and some of his associates, they were acquitted. The movement obviously had considerable support, for it elected officials of Sacramento and Oakland. The supervisors of San Francisco urged the legislature to enact a new law which would punish such revolutionary advocates as Kearney, and the mayor by proclamation urged the citizenry to avoid such sand-lot gatherings, but the party continued to grow.

The movement lost momentum when Republican and Democratic gatherings began to pass resolutions and take positions which were similar in tone and content to those of the Workingmen. They too began demanding constitutional reform, even a new constitution, as a way out of the crisis which California faced. Workingmen also had internal problems. New leaders and factions arose to compete with Kearney and his associates for place and advantage. It was even reported "that money and the promise of more" had been given to some of the leaders of the fledgling party in exchange for promises to disarm this radical movement. That it retained considerable strength and that it would play a major role in the forthcoming

WORKINGMEN'S PARTY RESOLUTIONS

The workingmen of California desire to unite with those of other states in effecting such reforms in our general government as may be necessary to secure the rights of the people as against those of capital, to maintain life, liberty, and happiness against land and money monopoly. Only in the people, the honest workingman can hope to find a remedy.

Chinese cheap labor is a curse to our land, a menace to our liberties and the insitutions of our country, and should, therefore, be restricted and forever abolished.

The land is the heritage of the people, and its appropriation by the government for the furtherance of the schemes of individuals and corporations is a robbery; and all land so held should revert to its lawful possession, to be held for actual settlement and cultivation, and individuals holding by purchase or imperfect title land in excess of one square mile shall be restricted to the use of that amount only for cultivation and pasturage; and all lands of equal and productive nature shall be subject to equal taxation. Our previous legislatures have abused the trust confidingly reposed in them by a misguided people, by allowing a corrupt ring of land monopolies to exist who have appropriated vast tracts of the fairest land on earth to themselves; we, therefore, in the name of humanity, consider a resurvey of the state necessary in order to ascertain as far as possible the extent to which the law in this instance has been violated. As the land is the natural heritage of the children of men, we deem, in the laws of equity and justice, that one section of six hundred and forty acres is a sufficiency for any one man to own or transmit to his offspring. All import duties on raw material not produced in the United States should be abolished.

The industries of the country are depressed or improved by the fluctuation in our financial system; and we therefore insist that the national government shall give to the people a system of finance consistent with the agricultural, manufacturing, and mercantile industries and requirements of the country, uncontrolled by rings, brokers, and bankers.

Malfeasance in public office should be punishable by imprisonment in the state prison for life, without intervention of the pardoning power.

We demand the abrogation of the contract system in our state prisons and reformatory institutions. They should be managed in the interests of the people, and the goods therein manufactured should not be sold at less than current market rates for the product of free labor.

All labor on public works, whether state or municipal, should be performed by the day, at current rates of wages.

Eight hours is a sufficient day's work for any man, and the law should make it so.

We demand that the constitution of the United States be amended to the effect that the president and vice-president of the United States, and senators of the several states, shall be elected by the direct vote of the people.

> The program of the Workingmen's Party adopted at its first state convention, January 24, 1878, in San Francisco. Winfield J. Davis, *History of Political Conventions in California, 1849–1892,* pp. 379–80.

---

constitutional convention was apparent to all in the spring of 1878. Faced with this new and still powerful political force, the conservative elements of both old parties hesitated for a time and then joined forces in a common front against the Workingmen. In April 1878, in San Francisco, an agreement was worked out under which a nonpartisan effort would be made. The principal objective was to prevent the Workingmen from dominating the convention.

That objective was realized. Of the delegates elected, seventy-eight were non-partisans, fifty-one Workingmen, eleven Republican, ten Democratic, and two Independent. Although they did not dominate the convention, the Workingmen, who represented more than seventeen counties, played a major role in the gathering. The group which assembled in September 1878 was drawn from the general citizenry. Although the legal profession was overrepresented, the delegates came from a variety of occupations and professions. Most were familiar with the broad problems of railroad monopoly, land and water monopoly, the Chinese, taxation, and assessment, which troubled Californians of this decade. For months, actually 156 working days, the delegates discussed and debated every aspect of government, practical and philosophical. Hundreds of resolutions were considered, millions of words uttered, and earnest attempts made to deal with the problems which had made the seventies a turbulent decade.

In the light of events since the work was completed and ratified by the electorate by a small margin in 1879, the problems of the decade were not resolved, but a workable framework of government was produced which survives to the present time. The constitution writers made valiant efforts to deal with the problems which had made the preceding ten years among the most trying in California history. New restrictions were put on corporations. Neither the state nor any public entity was to become a stockholder or make any gift of public funds to a corporation. The state was to enact laws limiting the charges of gas and telegraph companies and by inference other utilities. The books of corporations were to be open to everyone who had a legitimate interest. All railroad companies were to be considered common carriers subject to legislative control; they were forbidden to combine with navigation companies or any other common carrier. To eliminate some of the abuses which the railroad companies had visited on their rate-paying customers, a railroad commission was to be established. It was to consist of three elected members, for terms of four years, who were charged with the responsibility of establishing passenger and freight rates. It was given the power to examine books and witnesses as it set "reasonable" rates. Refusal to comply with the rates established could result in legal and criminal penalties against the company involved and its officials.

To deal with the land monopoly, the constitution specified that all property should be taxed according to its value and regardless of whether it was cultivated. Railroad property was to be assessed by an elected state board of equalization and the tax apportioned to the counties in which the property in question was situated. Lands of the state might be granted, but only to actual settlers and in quantities not exceeding 320 acres. Water use was also to be a public matter subject to state regulation, and water rates in cities and counties were to be regulated by city councils and boards of supervisors.

Not unexpectedly, the constitution dealt rather harshly with the Chinese. All contracts for "coolie labor" were declared void. All companies engaged in the traffic of bringing contract laborers to the state were to be subjected to whatever penalty the legislature should decide. To make it difficult for Chinese residents to stay, and to encourage them to leave as soon as possible, the constitution provided that no corporation could employ, directly or indirectly, any Chinese; nor should any Chinese be employed on public works except in punishment for crime. These provisions of the new document, among others, were subjected to considerable criticism; before long they were a nullity, for the courts quickly found them in conflict with the United States Constitution.

There were many criticisms made when the convention was done, and for some time it appeared that the voters would reject it. The press, except for the San Francisco *Chronicle*, bitterly opposed it. The Workingmen, by now divided into a number of factions, found it generally inadequate although Kearney supported it. Corporate and business spokesmen felt it went too far; but farmers, hopeful of a better day now that reforms in the field of railroad rates, assessment, and taxation had been written into the constitution, generally approved of it. As a result it was ratified by a vote of 77,959 to 67,134, and it remains today the basic organic law of California.

The Workingmen's party reached its zenith of power and influence in early 1879. By that time it was organized in forty counties and it had won major victories in a number of elections. Workingmen served as mayors of Oakland and San Francisco, twelve of the fifteen city councilmen of Los Angeles were Workingmen and they held seats in both branches of the legislature. But the fledgling party's spectacular growth was only the prologue to an equally spectacular decline. The formation of a New Constitution party was partially responsible. It appealed to all friends and supporters of the new fundamental law to come together, and a great many Workingmen flocked to its banner.

Almost as responsible was the division within the ranks of the Workingmen. It involved not only Kearney himself but men from all levels of the party. A prominent newspaper publisher of San Francisco, Charles de Young, shot the Workingmen's mayor of San Francisco, Isaac S. Kalloch, in the summer of 1879. While Mayor Kalloch tended his wounds, gathering sympathy and support which subsequently resulted in his re-election, his son planned revenge. Eight months to the day, Kalloch's son invaded de Young's office and fatally wounded the editor. He was subsequently acquitted after a sensational trial. Events of this sort sold newspapers and sapped at the party's unity. The Democratic party contributed toward the demise of the Workingmen by adopting much of its platform. By 1881 it was a vivid memory to most people who had witnessed its turbulent birth and death and Kearney himself was campaigning for other groups. When it proved to be impossible to revive the Workingmen in 1883, Kearney retired from politics. He lived in obscurity until 1907 when he died in well-to-do circumstances.

In the first few years following adoption it became apparent that the constitution fell short of dealing effectively with the railroad problem, the land and water monopolies, and the Chinese question. But as the depressed conditions of 1877–80 became a memory, there was evidently less sentiment in the body politic for change and reform. The period from 1880 to 1900 was generally quiet and stable, quite unlike the turbulent seventies. It was rather surprising, for many of the problems which had beset the state during the first ten years that followed Promontory Point remained unresolved.

CHAPTER XIII

Toward an American Economy

In 1839 British diplomat Alexander Forbes declared that "taking every circumstance into account, perhaps no country whatever can excel or hardly vie with California in natural advantages." Three years later Waddy Thompson, the American minister to Mexico, described California in similar terms as "the richest, the most beautiful, the healthiest country in the world." At approximately the same time a far better prophet than he could have realized wrote in *Hunt's Merchants Magazine*, "When we reflect that this superb region is adequate to the sustaining of twenty millions of people; has for several hundred years been in the possession of an indolent and limited population, incapable from their character of appreciating its resources—that no improvement can be expected under its present control, we cannot but hope that thousands of our fellow countrymen will pour in and accelerate the happy period . . . when Alta California will become part and parcel of our great confederation."

By the beginning of the twentieth century some of these lofty dreams were beginning to be realized, for a distinctly American economy had emerged. The bountiful agricultural wealth of the state became the true basis of the economic well-being of most of the people. Farming soon surpassed ranching and mining as the leading economic base. Manufacturing generally served such activities.

Gold, which had so profoundly altered the character of central and northern California, also influenced less directly the southern part of the state. Rancheros, who had only a few years before been content to sell their livestock for $2 or $3 in the hide and tallow trade, now drove them northward and in the early flush days of the mining camps sold some for as much as $500 a head. Such inflated prices did not last long, although beef brought from $50 to $100 throughout the early eighteen fifties.

The importance of livestock raising in California was reflected in a passage of the Trespass or "No fence" Act, originally passed in 1850 and not repealed until 1872. The net effect of this law forced farmers to fence their lands, as the law exempted the cattle owner from the responsibility of any damage done by his herds. The trespass law was bitterly resented by farmers, and John W. North, the founder of the Riverside colony, expressed this antagonism: "It is a contest between advancing civilization and obsolete barbarism." To a certain extent, these words are an accurate representation of the situation. The ranchos were a symbol of California's past and the cattle industry based upon them had to go before real agricultural settlement and development could be possible. North and other foes of the cattlemen little realized that there were forces at work which would do the task far more effectively than they could have hoped.

LAND TITLES

Questions arising over titles to the great Mexican land grants were to be one of the many factors that led to the demise of the great ranchos. The semi-feudal society of Alta California resulted from the accepted Hispanic practice of granting large amounts of land to those who served the state. A different cast was given society by established American practices. Generations of American frontiersmen looked upon undeveloped, uninhabited, unfenced, and uncultivated land on the frontier as theirs for the taking. Settlers or squatters (and often the terms are interchangeable) who had political muscle in their numbers had champions in legislative bodies. They looked after the interests of the squatters and in 1841 passed a pre-emption law which gave rights to settlers who squatted on public land. To the land-hungry settlers who swarmed into California after acquisition, the huge expanses of unfenced land of the ranchos were part of the public domain subject to pre-emption. A scrupulous examination would reveal the rights of the rancheros, but the Americans were little inclined in this situation to observe legal niceties which gave rights to a defeated enemy.

The Treaty of Guadalupe Hidalgo committed the United States government to giving full faith and credit to all of the acts under

Mexico. Such a commitment, of course, made grants of land under Mexico absolutely legal. In 1849 the Secretary of the Interior sent William Cary Jones, another of Senator Benton's sons-in-law, to investigate and report on the validity of the large landholdings in California. His report found that most of the grants were authentic. However, an earlier report by Henry W. Halleck had cast doubt on the validity of many land titles. The future Civil War general pointed out that Governor Pico, the last in the Mexican era, had made eighty-seven grants, most of them to his personal friends. Halleck reported hearing numerous stories about grants that were hastily drawn up with boundaries even more ill-defined than usual, and sometimes antedated before the entrance of the Americans. There was ample evidence that Mexican law governing such grants had been violated so extensively as to cast many of the holders in an illegal position even before the coming of the Americans. There were rumors that many foreigners had obtained extensive grants of land by the payment of small sums of money when it became obvious that American cession was imminent. In this, California was only following the practice that had taken place in New Mexico before the invasion of the United States.

Claims and counterclaims involving titles to vast tracts of agricultural and mineral lands, sometimes even including urban areas, with hundreds of millions of dollars at stake, made an early solution absolutely necessary. In an effort to handle this impossible problem, Congress passed an act in 1851 "to ascertain and settle the private land claims in the state of California." Although the land act was mostly engineered by Senator William Gwin, who was promoting the interest of American land seekers, it was probably the only possible approach to the problem. All who claimed land were compelled to appear before the commissioners who mainly met in San Francisco. Unfortunately, none of the members of the commission knew any Spanish, so the Californians were at a disadvantage. More importantly, even those who had held land for years sometimes had lost proof of title or had boundaries so ill-defined that it was impossible to ascertain with any degree of certainty just where their lands lay. With plenty of land available few of the ranchos had been adequately surveyed in the past and frequently had an oak stump, an ill-defined cowpath, or a boulder to mark their boundaries. In all, the land commission heard 813 claims in its four years of meeting, confirmed 521, rejected 273, and discontinued 19.

The greatest weakness in the land law was the fact that too much time was consumed in reaching a decision, thereby beclouding all titles and making land sales virtually impossible and thus materially discouraging settlement. Lawyers skilled in land law gained most from the hearings. Just how destructive of the economic position of the rancheros the hearings before the land commission were remains a problem about which there is little agreement. Some have contended that as much as 40 per cent of the land was swept away to pay lawyer's fees while other equally competent historians stress that the figure probably was not more than 5 per cent.

No fair-minded person can deny that many innocent rancheros were unnecessarily harmed by the hearings before the land commission, by the necessity of legal appeals, the payment of consequent lawyer's fees, and the uncertainty all of this involved. But the fact remains that fraud was so common that something had to be done to try to unravel the mess. Attorney General Black commented, ". . . the archives thus collected furnish irresistible proof that there had been an organized system of fabricating land titles carried on for a long time by Mexican officials." The most notorious of the many fraudulent claims was that of José Y. Limantour, a Frenchman who had been a merchant at Monterey. Two of his claims initially upheld by the land commissioners comprised large portions of the city and county of San Francisco as well as other valuable areas. The initial investigation resulted when one Auguste Jouan wrote the attorney general contending that he, as an employee of Limantour, had altered the date of one of the grants. This convinced Black that "the most stupendous fraud ever perpetrated in the history of the world" was being attempted.

Many people residing on the land claimed by Limantour accepted local legal advice and began paying rent to and buying quitclaim deeds from the Frenchman. To conduct the investigation, the attorney general's office sent Edwin M. Stanton. En route to California the future Civil War cabinet member occupied his time learning Spanish so that he could better study the records.

In spite of political pressure that tried to distract Stanton from the land claims inquiry, he proved fraud. Limantour had apparently obtained eighty blank petitions from former governor Micheltorena, who had signed all of them as blanks, supposedly in 1843. Stanton was able to prove that the paper used had been manufactured at a much later date and that the seal used was a counterfeit. Agents searching the archives of Mexico City were able to certify that there was no confirmation of the Limantour grants filed with the Mexican government. As the case evolved, the Frenchman's lawyers deserted him and he too fled to escape a prison term.

The unanswered question that remains in the contest over land titles is simply this: How many other grants were as fraudulently based as that of Limantour? The evidence is overwhelming that many such frauds were perpetrated on the United States government throughout the Mexican cession of 1848. Henry George in 1871 sensibly commented, ". . . if the history of Mexican grants of California is ever written it will be a history of greed, of perjury, of corruption, of spoilation and high-handed robbery, for which it will be difficult to find a parallel . . . It would have been better, far better, if the American government had agreed to permit these grantholders to retain a certain amount of land around their improvements, and compound it for the rest of the grants called for, by the payment of a certain sum per acre, turning it into the public domain."

THE PASSING OF THE RANCHOS

The passing of the ranchos and the end of the cattle base of California's economy was foreordained by the discovery of gold and the rapid influx of Americans. The increase in population led inevitably to economic changes that necessitated a broader economic base. The attack upon established California land titles did not by itself account for the elimination of the rancheros, but there is no question that it helped. As William Cary Jones correctly warned, "A title discredited is not destroyed but everyone is afraid to touch it, or at all events to invest labor and money in improvements that rest on a suspected tenure." For the ranchero, insecurity of land title drove prospective purchasers away and pushed interest rates up. It made development money scarce even for men who had extensive land claims.

The contest over who owned the land was initiated when many

disillusioned gold seekers attempted to seize land to cultivate. They
did this in the time-honored American way of simply squatting on
it and challenging the owners to do anything about it. In the early
1850s most of the land seized in such a manner was found in the
region adjacent to the gold fields. Unfortunately, those who claimed
land under such circumstances did little in the way of putting in
crops or making improvements until their titles could be proven.
Naturally, the settlers were able to find lawyers to plead their case
against the Californios. Some settlers formed leagues to protect
themselves and even provoked riots such as those which occurred
in Sacramento. Probably doing more damage to the rancheros in the
long run were not the squatters seeking to obtain a few acres for the
purpose of farming, but rather those who worked out techniques to
seize tremendous quantities of rancho land. The activities of Henry
Miller were perhaps the most notorious of this group of men.

The great prosperity brought on by the boom in the cattle industry saw rancheros enriched beyond their wildest dreams. Unfortunately, they lacked any real understanding of the money economy. Men bought expensive saddles trimmed in solid silver and had
their spurs made of gold. In some instances, the ranchero spent several
thousand dollars on a single costume and thus unwittingly "wore a
whole rancho on his back." Humble dwellings were suddenly adorned
with expensive furniture and women had to dress up to the new
station their husbands had attained. Such extravagance was also
frequently accompanied by extensive gambling. Obviously, the losses
through such practices can only be estimated. Similarly, the borrowing of money with interest rates as high as 8 per cent compounded
was alone enough to lead to ruin.

The friendly, easygoing dons did not comprehend the intricacies
of the money economy of the newcomers. They failed to adapt
themselves to the changes and innovations brought about by American rule, and clung to ranching practices of the past. Mormon
settlers who came to San Bernardino brought in livestock that was
much heavier than that of California. When crossed with the native
stock, the result was more appetizing beef as well as heavier beeves,
but the Californios did not adopt such new breeds; as shortsighted
was the practice of selling their breeding stock when prices were

LAND TITLES

Yet I cannot conclude this survey without alluding once more to the deplorable confusion and uncertainty of land titles, which has been, and still is the master-scourge of this state. The vicious Spanish-Mexican system of granting lands by the mere will of some provincial governor or municipal chief without limitation as to area, or precise delineation of boundaries, here develops and matures its most pernicious fruits. Your title may be ever so good, and yet your farm may be taken from you by a new survey, proving that said title does not cover your tract, or covers it but partially. Hence, many refuse or neglect to improve the lands they occupy lest some title adverse to theirs be established, and they legally ousted, or compelled to pay heavily for their own improvements. And, in addition to the genuine Spanish or Mexican grants, which the government and the courts must confirm and uphold, there are fictitious and fraudulent grants—some of them only trumped up to be bought off, and often operating to create anarchy, and protract litigation between settlers and real owners. Then there are, doubtless, squatters, who refuse to recognize and respect valid titles, and waste in futile litigation the money that might make the lands they occupy indisputably their own. I blame no party exclusively, while I entreat the state and federal governments and courts to do their utmost to settle the titles to land in this state beyond controversy, at the earliest possible day.

Horace Greeley, *An Overland Journey
from New York to San Francisco
in the Summer of 1859.*

good. Possessed of great herds of cattle, worked by hundreds of subordinates on extensive tracts of land, the rancheros operated like feudal lords of medieval France. Accounting practices were primitive, figures on costs or production were based on estimates of the crudest variety. On one rancho the proceeds from sales of land and cattle were dumped into a canvas bag, and members of the household helped themselves whenever they had a need for funds. That way of life could not survive long in a land dominated by cost-conscious and profit-minded Yankees.

Living for the present, the rancheros assumed that the inflated prices they obtained for livestock in the gold camps were permanent. The changes they did not foresee began in the early 1850s with the arrival of large numbers of cattle and sheep from New Mexico, Texas, and even from Missouri. Thus, the dependence upon range cattle in California declined rapidly after 1855. Indian raiding of livestock was another factor in the decline of the ranchos. Making the position of the California don even more troublesome was the development of American-style land taxes, a feature unknown under Spain and Mexico. The dons often lacked the ready cash to pay taxes on tremendous landholdings, a good percentage of which was non-productive. Sometimes by borrowing money to pay taxes they became enmeshed in the tentacles of the moneylender. The end result of borrowing at fantastic rates of compounded interest was forced sale and the breakup of another rancho.

As if man-made troubles were not enough for the rancheros of California, a series of natural disasters, flood, drought, and epidemic, added to their woes. In December 1861 tremendous rainstorms produced the worst flood in the history of California. Thousands of head of cattle were drowned and possibly a fourth of the state's total taxable wealth was destroyed. The disaster was most keenly felt in the great valley where continuous rainfall combined with the runoff from the mountain ranges created an inland sea "two hundred fifty to three hundred miles long and twenty to sixty miles wide." The devastation in Southern California was almost as extensive.

The floods of 1861 and 1862 were followed by several years of the worst drought in the history of the state. As little as 4 inches of rain was recorded in some areas in the course of twelve calendar months. Streams dried up, grass lay blighted beneath a pitiless sun, and rancheros were forced to dispose of cattle for whatever they would bring. The de la Guerras in Santa Barbara sold a large herd for $.37 a head. Other rancheros gathered their cattle and trailed them to sanctuaries in the mountains. Carcasses of dead cattle lay in huge piles about parched water holes and it was not long before the former grasslands were strewn with skulls and skeletons of the once great herds. Cattle that lived were so weakened that they fell easy prey to predatory animals. Between 1860 and 1870 the official drop in the

THE DROUGHT OF 1863–65

Two successive years of drought have almost swept the country clean of cattle, horse, and sheep. Out of seventy thousand head of stock cattle existing a few years ago, only twelve thousand seven hundred and twenty-four . . . are left . . . The total absence of rain during the greater part of the winter of eighteen hundred and sixty-three and eighteen hundred and sixty-four, made pasture last year exceedingly scarce; its scarcity was felt as early as the month of May, when already valleys and hills were bare, and the cattle and horses left for the mountains, where, among the shrubbery, they did well during the summer, but when in the month of December they were visited by severe weather, snow, and hail, all that were not too weak moved to the valleys again, the rest, with few exceptions, died from exposure. A great number of those that had come down again to the lowlands died of starvation, or were killed by the owners in order to save the hides.

About five thousand head have been killed during last summer, at an establishment erected near Monterey, for their hides and tallow. Their average value was from two dollars to four dollars per head.

California State Agricultural Society
Transactions 1864–65, p. 227.

number of cattle in California was some 46 per cent, with some counties suffering a drop of 75 per cent. Few of the great grant holders were able to withstand such losses; many sold their holdings for what they would bring.

To add to the troubles of this ravaged land came a smallpox epidemic which made its first appearance in the fall of 1862 and went on to afflict communities which were scattered throughout Southern California. As the disease spread, it paralyzed the normal activities of the rancheros, for the approach of every man might well be the visitation of the plague. A grasshopper plague in 1863 provided another devastating touch. To those who survived this time of flood, drought, and epidemic, the era of the sixties was remembered as a time of unmitigated disaster. Not only were individuals sorely afflicted, but the society itself was transformed.

THE DIVERSIFICATION OF AGRICULTURE

Cattle raising did not end with the decline of the great California rancho. It only declined in relative importance. In some instances, descendants of the original grantees held onto their property, but more often large landholdings were accumulated by entrepreneurs who proceeded to put cattle ranching on the kind of sound financial basis that was in the process of developing in other parts of the nation. The introduction of blooded stock from England made fencing an absolute necessity. Ranching became an organized business instead of the romantic way of life that it had been in the earlier epoch.

Sheep raising was another part of the livestock industry that had its origins in the days of the missions. It is estimated that by 1825 there were more than a million head of sheep in California but this number had drastically declined after secularization. One estimate placed only 150,000 in the state in 1851 and these were described as very poor in quality for both wool and mutton. From this low point, sheep raising grew in importance until 1876 when there were about 7,700,000 head in the state. Sheep raising was favored by natural conditions in California. Vast areas of range land that were unsatisfactory for cattle provided enough grass for close-grazing sheep. The dry climate of the state discouraged foot rot and other sheep diseases common in more humid areas.

Prior to 1848 sheep too were killed chiefly for hides and tallow, but with the gold rush mutton brought a high price. Thousands of head of sheep were brought into California from New Mexico and even from as far away as Chihuahua, Mexico, to fulfill the demand. After the Civil War the shortage of cotton helped increase the price for wool, and California, needing a commodity that could be easily shipped, took advantage of the hospitable environment to raise tremendous flocks of sheep. In fact, overstocking of the range led to overgrazing, the destruction of some range land, a market glut, and a collapse in wool prices. Prices were further depressed by the panic of 1873. An abnormally dry winter in 1876–77 dealt sheep raising a severe blow, and it never regained its former prominence although it continued to be a significant part of the state's agriculture. Spanish instead of English traditions still prevail, wool being the general objective rather than mutton, and many modern shepherds are Basques from Spain.

Dairy products had not been totally unknown during the mission period, but were simply not in great demand. They did not figure prominently in the diet of the native Californian. Then too, the wild range cattle were not milk producers even if one were able to tame them sufficiently for the purpose. The influx of American miners established a market for butter, milk, and cheese. Hence, there were soon farmers who brought in cattle from the Midwest to fulfill these demands. In the post-Civil War period dairying initially developed north of San Francisco Bay. By the end of the century dairymen from Switzerland and Holland established "milk factories" around the major population centers of the state.

Farming in California dated back to mission days, but after secularization, the fields, vineyards, and orchards formerly cultivated under the supervision of the Franciscans were neglected. Modern crop agriculture revived upon the invasion of the Yankee. The revival of agriculture was delayed, for many of the early migrants believed that California was a sterile, mountainous, sandy region, which was parched with drought during one half of the year and drenched with floods during the other half. Those few early miners who planted fruit trees or raised crops were considered "utter fools." The San Joaquin Valley, perhaps the greatest agricultural region known to man, was initially considered a desert. The prevailing belief that farm produce grown in other parts of the United States would not prosper in the inhospitable soil of California must have been strong indeed when one considers the exorbitant prices paid by the hungry miners: "watermelons at from one to five dollars each, apples from Oregon at one and two dollars each, potatoes and onions at fifty cents to one dollar a pound, barley at ten to twenty-five cents a pound, hay at one-hundred dollars a ton, eggs at two dollars a dozen, milk at one dollar a quart." Onions were especially in demand by the miners and one enterprising individual who planted two acres obtained a return of $8000 in 1852. Naturally, the amount of money in circulation influenced the scale of prevailing prices.

These high prices must have been what one old man had in mind when he admonished his son: "Plant your lands; these be your best gold fields, for all must eat while they live." Many others obviously heeded such advice because by 1862 the state was producing a surplus in such basic crops as potatoes and onions, and within a few years the price of most farm produce had declined rapidly. By 1860 wheat was being shipped out of San Francisco and one official reported that in California "riches, other than gold, have been found in the soil." The number of farms in the state grew from 872 in 1850 to 18,716 in 1860; most of these early farms were to be found in the Central Valley.

The pioneer farmer in California faced many very difficult problems. First of all, he had to forget most of the agricultural background he already had, for farming in this strange land was much different. He had to learn to adjust to the two seasons, the wet and the dry, instead of the four of the Midwest and East. Once the limited demand on the local scene was met, he had to raise crops that would stand the high transportation cost to population centers. Hence, most farms were located along streams before the coming of the railroad, where nature's water highway was used to transport produce to market. In 1854 Governor John Bigler highlighted one of the problems these early farmers faced when he stressed that the unsettled condition of land titles was holding back the development of the state's agriculture. Few dared make improvements on lands that had an insecure title. Except for grain the expansion of farming was tied to the development of irrigation, which entailed large capital outlays. Extensive capital for development was also a prerequisite in citrus because of the long waiting period before a crop could be marketed. The state had many natural peculiarities that only painful experience would reveal to the pioneer farmer. Most citrus fruits could only be grown on hillsides where air drainage prevented frost, in desert valleys, or along the seacoast where the ocean breezes moderated temperature fluctuations. The unusual nature of the soil also dictated what crops could be grown in a specific area. Thus, the state developed specializations in certain areas dictated by the natural environment and arising out of a period of trial and error. Many a farmer went bankrupt before he understood such natural selectivity.

The first dominant commercial crop of California's agriculture was wheat. Much of the great Central Valley was naturally suited for the growth of this important grain. Wheat prospered in areas where annual rainfall varied from 8 to 30 inches and it also adapted readily to the hot, dry, summer conditions of the inland valley. Its early, important growth came in the mild, wet winter. During the long, hot summer, it matured. The ripe kernels, encased in husks that were hard and durable, took readily to the long ocean voyage to market. It was especially prized by British millers who found that it produced a superior flour. This combination enabled California farmers to produce a crop which would offset California isolation from world markets.

Wheat growing caught on during the late fifties as the advantages of the California scene became known. It became an export crop in the sixties which was spurred on by a shortage of grain in England during the Civil War period. The wheat of California was found in the grain markets of the world and for a time the rewards of wheat farming rivaled those of mining.

The triumph of wheat lasted until 1879, when production declined sharply. Worldwide overproduction and the declining price on the export market were partially responsible, but the coming of the railroad also undermined bonanza wheat growing. Better transportation east made it possible to grow crops of higher return per acre. The extension of irrigation also influenced the decline in wheat acreage. But just as in the case of the cattle industry, wheat production continued to be important in California, especially where irrigation is not feasible.

Wheat was produced in what one author terms California's "factories in the fields." Thousands of acres were sown to this single grain and as Frank Norris described it, "like a gigantic carpet, it spread itself over all the land. There was nothing else to be seen but the limitless sea of wheat as far as the eye could reach." Some landholdings were so large that when men started to plow in the morning they had their lunch at a midway point and only reached the end of their field at nightfall. There they stayed all night and plowed their way back home by the end of the next day. California's farmers learned to develop machinery for their purposes unlike that found elsewhere. The pattern established in wheat production was later repeated for other crops and continues down to the present time with the state taking the lead in innovating new agricultural equipment. Huge gang plows, broadcast seeders, and combines were widely used in California when they were novelties elsewhere. The level topography of the inland valleys, the substantial size of the typical "farm," and the desire to minimize farm labor costs encouraged the use of modern, efficient farm machinery.

Diversification came to California's agriculture in many ways; great interest developed in the raising of cotton, especially as the result of the shortage during the Civil War. In spite of an almost perfect natural environment that was to cause cotton to be the state's number one crop in the mid-twentieth century, the lack of improved irrigation technology retarded its early development. By 1870 only about 2000 acres were planted in cotton; most of this was in the southern part of the state; much of it in the confines of present-day Los Angeles. The lack of a home market, the high cost of irrigated land, and the lack of cheap labor at harvesttime inhibited the growth of cotton. Indians were used to pick cotton but never proved satisfactory. Some efforts were made to entice the newly freed Negroes of the American South to California for such labor in the post-Civil War years, but the few that did come opted for the cities and turned their backs on the fields.

Another unique effort to find a crop that would supply material for clothing was that of sericulture. Louis Prévost, a French immigrant, introduced the raising of mulberry bushes and silkworms to California in 1854. Sericulture never got beyond the status of a fad in spite of the fact that the state legislature in 1866 subsidized producers of mulberry trees and merchantable cocoons. The solvency of the state was threatened because so many people qualified for the bounty of $250 per every five thousand mulberry trees two years old and the $300 for every thousand cocoons. One serious effort was the establishment of a colony of growers known as the California Silk Association who had a ranch in the present Riverside County. The untimely death of Louis Prévost, who apparently had the only real knowledge of silk culture, in August of 1869 doomed the effort. In addition, the state legislature withdrew the bounty, causing much of the early enthusiasm to evaporate. Although some have contended that California's climate was not conducive to sericulture, unquestionably the biggest hurdle to such economic activity remained the high cost of labor.

Efforts to irrigate California were as old as the Spanish settlement, and were probably practiced in a primitive way even by the Indians. The Franciscan friars who developed the missions were frequently from Spain and were well aware of the necessity of providing some water for their crops in the long, hot, dry summer. However, the number of acres developed under their direction was never large and the real expansion of irrigation occurred with the coming of the more resourceful Americans. Most of the better land had already been occupied and new settlers were forced to farm land that was less desirable or which had to be irrigated. One established rancher told an Englishman interested in sheep farming: *"Too late, sir! Too late, sir!* Six years too late, sir. There is not a patch of Tulare, Kern or Fresno [County] left. If you had had capital to invest in it six years ago, you could have secured your [sheep] run, made a pile out of sheep, & sold every acre you bought for one dollar for eight dollars and lived independently all the rest of your life." The increasing shortage of land for ranching purposes or for dry-land farming made irrigation a matter of statewide concern. Unless the land could be "redeemed by baptism" California agriculture would not expand. Californians in the early seventies embarked seriously on the development of irrigation facilities.

In the 1870s an English newcomer was advised "that by purchasing land on either side of a stream, that one effectively prevented anyone else from using the surrounding country." This advice illustrated a basic problem of the early irrigationists. The Americans retained from the English common law the doctrine of riparian rights. This concept permitted those who owned the land along the banks of a stream to have the right to full use of water, even to the exclusion of others. The acceptance of such a legal concept made it possible for farmers and ranchers to control the entire countryside and dominate vast feudal-like estates by the simple procedure of obtaining control of water rights.

Further complicating the water situation was the development of the doctrine of prior diversion or appropriative rights in the mining camps. Under this doctrine the first priority in the use of water went to those who established the initial appropriation. Thus, irrigation was molded under the common law of riparian rights and the statutory code of appropriation. These two concepts were contradictory. This was evident when the mining companies began diverting much of the water for hydraulic mining purposes, leaving little water for downstream users. The courts were swamped with lawsuits by rival claimants. It was not until the passage of the Wright law in 1887 that much of the conflict was eliminated. As its author, C. C. Wright, commented, this law was passed "with the object in view that there might be created a special government for the one purpose of developing and administering the irrigation water for the benefit of the people." This law made possible the development of irrigation districts composed of the landowners in a particular area and helped provide the life-giving sustenance of water to the dry but fertile plains that were sometimes remote from the river valleys. The special irrigation districts had eminent domain powers and by condemnation suits could overrule riparian rights. In the years following the passage of this law, irrigation districts sprang up, especially in the San Joaquin Valley and in Southern California. By 1911 the fiftieth district was formed and its general success has been a testimonial to the pioneers who were willing to initiate changes and thus make possible the emergence of agriculture as the state's greatest industry. The effect of the irrigation on the land was far more significant than the crops that could be produced. The delivery of water to arid land caused its price to increase in value at an unbelievable rate. Acreage that had previously been sold for $5 was valued at $200 and more once irrigation projects were built.

Irrigation projects were not confined to the great Central Valley. As early as the 1850s William Wolfskill in Los Angeles County had a large vineyard, numerous orange trees and other fruit trees under irrigation. The German settlers at Anaheim and the Mormons who briefly established a colony in San Bernardino were among the first to irrigate crops in Southern California. Some farmers around Sacramento were also utilizing irrigation for fruit and vegetables as early as the 1850s.

The success enjoyed by many farmers in their development of irrigation facilities was largely a result of the examples set by enterprising pioneers. John Wesley North, who in 1870, founded the community that was ultimately to be Riverside, was the first of these pioneers. A New York lawyer whose multifaceted career involved him as a founder of the University of Minnesota and the nearby town of Northfield in that state, North was also instrumental in the emergence of Nevada as a state. He envisioned, as an enlightened carpetbagger, a South of racial harmony in the post-Civil War period. His aspirations for the South were never realized but he left an enduring imprint in California. His claim that irrigated California land planted in citrus fruits or vines would net an annual return of $100 per acre sounded like a promotional gimmick, but history has more than endorsed his foresight. North's Southern California Colony Association constructed an irrigation network which made Riverside a leader in the raising of citrus fruits.

George Chaffey, a Canadian engineer, whose previous work had been devoted to designing lake steamers, studied irrigation developments at Riverside and improved upon them in the development of the agricultural communities at Etiwanda and Ontario in the 1880s. His success in establishing mutual stock companies as a basis of the agricultural communities was widely copied. Chaffey correctly saw that the flow of water could be used to produce electricity and he was successful in establishing the first commercial hydroelectric plant in the West, as well as the first electrically lighted homes. The college he established is still in existence. After a less than successful business effort in Australia, Chaffey returned to California and his program for the diversion of Colorado River water to the valley which he renamed Imperial.

By 1890 one fourth of all of California's farms were irrigated. In addition to water obtained from rivers and streams, farmers drilled hundreds of deep wells to tap sources of water. The rapid increase in irrigated acreage led to a substantial change in the type of crops produced. Indicative of the kind of change which had occurred in the state's agriculture was the fact that by 1899 64 per cent of the value of all crops came from non-cereal commodities. Acreage previously devoted to wheat was changed to orchard products. Every decade saw a substantial increase in the value of such produce, and by the end of the century, California was a leading producer of apples, apricots, cherries, peaches, pears, as well as plums and prunes. But the value of the products from the vineyards and from the citrus groves was so great that they were in a class by themselves.

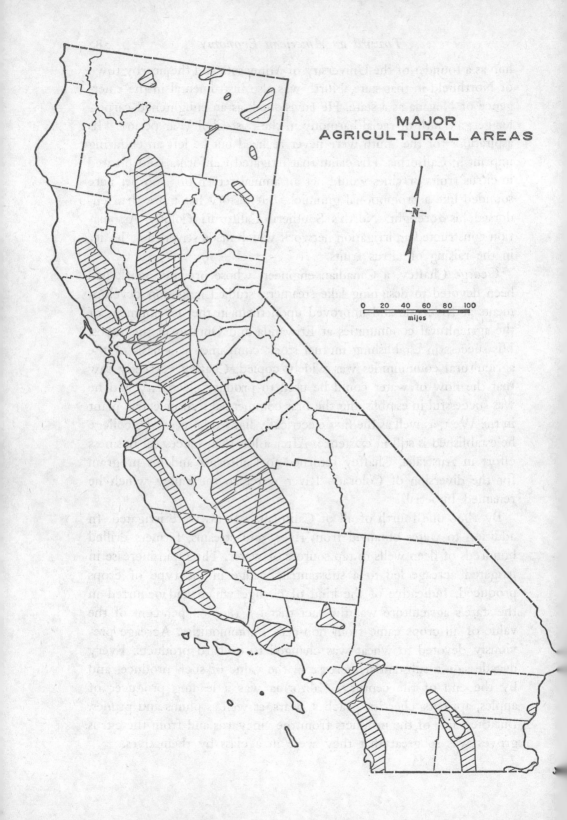

MAJOR
AGRICULTURAL AREAS

-N-

0   20 40 60 80 100
miles

THE SUN AND THE GRAPE

Like much of the state's agriculture, viticulture was started by the Franciscan friars. The modest amounts of wine produced at the missions by primitive methods had little importance to the provincial economy. The mission located in the Sonoma Valley was the first to produce and sell wine commercially. As early as 1847 California-produced wines and brandies were sold in the saloons of San Francisco to appease the thirst of sailors. The market was enlarged soon after during the gold rush when hard-drinking miners demonstrated a prodigious capacity.

Commercial wine production began in Southern California when a French immigrant brought cuttings from his homeland, but the first vineyard of any real size and productivity in the area was that of William Wolfskill. A former Kentucky trapper and mountain man, Wolfskill became one of the more successful growers in Southern California. The vineyards of Southern California were further expanded by a group of Germans who settled at Anaheim in 1857. The Los Angeles Vineyard Society which they formed was expected to be the nucleus for a great German colony. Many Germans had become interested in California as a possible site for a colony from the writings of the famous Prussian scientist Alexander von Humboldt.

Much of the success of viticulture was the result of the contributions of Agoston Haraszthy, a Hungarian who introduced a superior type of grape in his vineyards at Sonoma in 1851. In 1862 the state appropriated funds to send "Count" Haraszthy to Europe in a search for better varieties of grapes. He returned with some 100,000 cuttings of more than three hundred different varieties of European grapes. A rapid increase in acreage planted in vineyards was the result. One writer described the boom as a "growing wine fever which penetrated every county of the state."

The industry encountered many problems before it reached maturity. Diseases were a considerable problem. In the 1870s phylloxera, an infestation of microbelike aphids, appeared and wiped out a high percentage of the viticulture. The disease was generally a greater threat south of the Tehachapi Mountains. Consequently Southern California, except for the San Bernardino area and a small area around Indio, has limited vineyard acreage. Most of the production of grapes has been in the Delano area, the Lodi-Stockton area, and the area north of San Francisco Bay. By the end of the nineteenth century the major problems of disease and marketing were solved and the wine industry was firmly established. Wine making continued its expansion in the early twentieth century as its market grew with the immigration of millions of wine-drinking eastern and southern Europeans. It survived the lean years of the prohibition era and expanded in the years that followed repeal of the Eighteenth Amendment. During World War II the destruction of European vineyards and the disruption of European wine markets accelerated the growth of California's wine industry, and California emerged as one of the world's most important wine-producing regions. At one time known only for her low-grade, inexpensive wines, by the middle of the twentieth century California produced some of the finest wines in the world. As is true of much of California's agriculture, the success of the wine industry can be attributed to improved technology which reduced costs and enabled the state's vineyards to produce a superior product.

Although California grapes were early used as fresh fruit and continue to be significant as table grapes, the state produces more than one half of the world's supply of raisins. Agoston Haraszthy was the first to introduce the seedless grape essential in raisin making. The cultivation of raisin grapes was first introduced at Riverside in 1873. From that point it spread over Southern California. Its decline in Southern California was caused by early rains that sometimes ruined the entire crop in the Riverside area. Weather drove the industry north to Fresno.

It was soon proven that much of the state was as well suited to the production of raisin grapes as Spain, the world's leading supplier. During the 1880s growers realized profits in excess of $400 per acre which raised the price of good vineyard land to as much as $1000 per acre. A general market collapse, triggered by the panic of 1893, caused the raisin producers to combine in co-operatives in much the same fashion as citrus growers. The California Raisin Growers Association was organized to control marketing and to reduce production and transportation costs.

THE GOLDEN GROVES

The most distinctly Californian of the State's agricultural produce is the orange. Efforts were made to regenerate the deteriorated mission stock by using seedlings from Hawaii and Central America with limited success. In the 1850s William Wolfskill purchased orange groves, planted his own trees, and became the largest citrus grower in the United States. However, the citrus industry languished in the first generation after American acquisition. Hawaiian oranges dominated the small market in San Francisco. In 1875 Theodore Van Dyke observed, " . . . nothing worthy of the name of orange could be seen in California. Thick-skinned, sour, pithy, and dry, it was an insult to the noblest of fruit to call the California product by that name . . . The lemons, great overgrown things, with skins half an inch thick over a dry and spongy interior, were more worthy of pity than contempt." Judge North in planning the development of his Riverside colony believed that oranges could be grown with great profit. North did not succeed but appropriately it was in his colony that the modern citrus industry was born. In 1873 Luther Calvin Tibbets received seedlings of navel oranges from Bahia, Brazil. Carefully cultivated by him and his wife, the first fruit did not ripen until the winter of 1878, when "it required but one taste to reveal that a star of first magnitude had arisen in their midst." The offspring of that celebrated tree transformed the industry. There was such a great demand for buds that the Tibbetses' trees were kept for propagation rather than for fruit bearing. When the first of the navel oranges were marketed in the East they were identified with wrappers stating that "I am a Riverside Washington navel orange. I have no seeds to choke the young or worry the old." To promote the navel orange, Riverside sent a delegation to the Chicago World's Fair of 1893 with an assortment of citrus fruits. This effort was so successful that other delegations were sent to New York and other cities to promote California oranges.

The new oranges, the expansion of the market, and the resourcefulness of the growers combined to push profits up. Orange growing eclipsed grape production. This transition was helped by the problem of disease, which plagued Southern California vineyards. The rapid growth of the orange industry is revealed by production figures. In the 1880–81 season, 4290 boxes of the fruit were produced. Eleven years later more than 400,000 boxes were picked and marketed. By the end of the century there were some 5,500,000 navel orange trees in the state.

The production of oranges is typical of much of California's agriculture. The production unit is seldom a "typical, family-sized" farm characteristic of Midwest agriculture. A wait of five years for a marketable product, a high land cost, irrigation and other production expenses necessitate a large initial investment. Most of the early orange growers were not really farmers. This was a pronounced asset because it meant that they did not have anything to unlearn. The pioneers in citrus were frequently men who had earned substantial money in other businesses. Therefore, they were predisposed to experiment in the production of oranges. Pioneer citrus men had to evolve their own system of irrigation, cultivation, pruning, the treatment for diseases, protection against frost, and even harvesting. Although William Wolfskill had shipped oranges east with profit in the 1870s, the high cost of transportation was a major obstacle that had to be surmounted. More importantly, a market had to be expanded and developed. The orange was traditionally a novelty, or a luxury to be enjoyed during special occasions. Inadequate methods of packaging and preservation resulted in a high spoilage rate. Faced by common problems, growers began exchanging ideas on production techniques, irrigation, cultivation, etc.

In the initial stages it was the grower who took almost all of the risks but realized little profit. Agents bought fruit for such low prices that they ran little or no risk. During the mid-1880s efforts were made to control shipments so as to avoid a glut in any one market area. To this end, growers formed local associations, built packing houses, and attempted to establish standards. The first of these groups was the Orange Growers Protective Union of Southern California, organized in 1885. Its objective was to prevent the citrus growers from losing "the reward due to their labor," and "proposes to market your fruit by so distributing it that no market shall be glutted but every market supplied." This organization was succeeded by the Pachatta Orange Growers Association of Riverside, out of which the Southern California Fruit Exchange came in 1893. It in turn was succeeded by the California Fruit Growers Exchange in 1905 when central California growers joined the organization. Its ability to market the higher grade of oranges under the Sunkist brand is one of the most remarkable stories of advertising promotion in the history of the nation. In a very few years the dietary habits of the American people were altered so that oranges played a key role. The market was broadened and stabilized as self-styled champions of "rugged individualism" came together in producer co-operatives. Step by step the industry progressed. The demand was increased as the introduction of the Valencia orange made fruit available the year round. Refrigerated cars, better packing, improved fertilizers, more efficient insecticides all contributed.

THE ORANGE TREE

Carefully trimmed and corseted, the orange tree is like a rather plump middle-aged dowager bedizened with jewels and gems and a corsage of gardenias. The typical grove is as immaculately kept, and as orderly, as the parlor of such a dowager. Plebeian weeds are removed as rapidly as they have the impudence to intrude upon these elegant preserves. Delicate in health, the dowager-orange is carefully protected against even the mild rigors and hazards of climate in Southern California. Elaborate windbreaks of cedar, cypress, and eucalyptus protect the sacrosanct groves where the smudge pots are lighted at the first threat of frost. The water brought to the trees is examined as carefully as the diet of a diabetic patient in a Santa Barbara hospital. The armed might of California, represented by its famous highway patrol, guards the borders of the state to prevent the invasion of bugs, insects, and blight. A whole retinue of servants waits upon this perennially pregnant lady. The grove in which she lives is not a farm, but a kind of outdoor hothouse guarded as jealously as a Scottish lord's hunting park. (If you doubt this statement, try to pick an orange, sometime, in Southern California.) The dowager-orange is always well groomed, carefully manicured, and willing to receive guests—provided they remain at a distance and admire her discreetly. Like most dowagers, her perfume is heavy, rich, a little overpowering.

Carey McWilliams, *Southern
California Country*, pp. 207–8.

While orange production was climbing to its dominant position, lemon production was also growing. The market for California lemons in the eastern United States grew slowly principally because of competition from Italian lemons. However, the political influence of California led Congress to enact high protective tariffs which eliminated such competition. Although California oranges have to compete with the oranges of Florida, Texas, and Arizona, the state has a virtual monopoly on lemons today. Lemon trees, more sensitive than orange trees, can be grown only in areas that do not have excessively high or low temperatures or severe wind conditions. However, they are marketed in much the same way as oranges.

CROP DIVERSIFICATION

Walnuts may have been brought to California by the French voyager La Pérouse in 1786. Many early visitors to Spanish California observed walnut trees at the missions. Colonel J. J. Warner planted walnut trees near San Diego in 1843 and walnuts were exhibited at agricultural fairs in Sacramento in 1852 and in San Francisco in 1853. They took readily to California and prospered in much of the state.

English soft-shelled walnuts were first planted in Santa Barbara in 1867 and in Los Angeles in 1873. During the 1880s they were produced on a commercial scale. By 1883 production of 250 tons was reported. Just as in the case of citrus, walnut growers initially combined in many different marketing groups, ultimately joining together in the California Walnut Growers Exchange with the Diamond Brand as their trademark. The exchange continues to be a significant part of the state's agriculture with production directed by men specializing in walnut culture. Their business practices have enabled them effectively to market their product, and the development of scientific knowledge has made it possible for them to locate walnut production in areas of the state where it is most feasible and to control diseases that beset the trees. Almonds and many other nuts are likewise effectively grown in California.

The production of olives also dates from the Spanish period. The importance of olive oil to the diet made this a significant commercial item during the mission period. Both olives and olive oil continue to be important agricultural products; however, lower Spanish production costs inhibit the expansion in California. Dates and figs were not produced until the Coachella Valley near Indio was irrigated. Like other exotic fruits they are luxury items and have never become popular in the United States. The production of avocados is likewise more a phenomenon of the twentieth century than the late nineteenth.

ECONOMIC DIVERSIFICATION

In the process of developing an American economy in the half century between 1850 and 1900, California emerged as a predominantly agricultural state. This is not to suggest, however, that other economic activities were overlooked. For example, although mining underwent a slow but steady decline both in relative and absolute importance, it nevertheless continued. California probably possesses a greater variety of minerals than any other similar area on earth. The state is a leading producer of sixteen of the sixty major commercial mineral commodities mined in the United States. In the half century between the discovery of gold on the American River and 1900, there were periodic flurries of mineral activity in various parts of California.

Gold continued to be of greatest interest and hardly a decade passed without new discoveries in different parts of the state. Many of these gold sites were either in nearly inaccessible mountains or inhospitable deserts. Gold was found in the San Fernando hills, the Kern River Canyon, the mountains north of San Bernardino, the San Gabriel Canyon, San Diego County, to mention but a few areas that are not normally considered gold-producing regions. Even the mountains of Orange County experienced their short but exciting moments of "gold rush."

Silver was also found in much of the state and numerous mines were worked in scattered areas until well into the twentieth century. The great Comstock mining story is not properly a part of California history, but the wealth of that rich silver mine induced many to seek similar bonanzas in California.

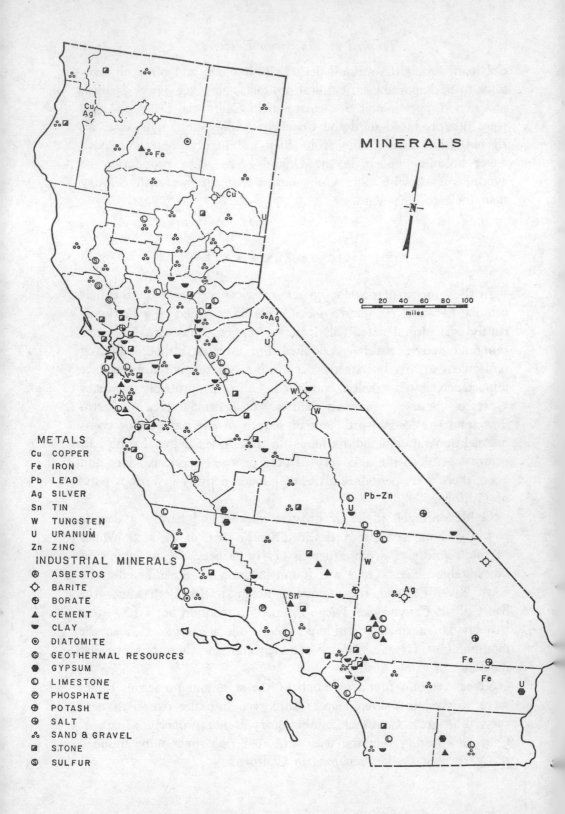

MINERALS

N

0 20 40 60 80 100
miles

METALS
Cu COPPER
Fe IRON
Pb LEAD
Ag SILVER
Sn TIN
W   TUNGSTEN
U   URANIUM
Zn ZINC

INDUSTRIAL MINERALS
Ⓐ ASBESTOS
◇ BARITE
⊕ BORATE
▲ CEMENT
▼ CLAY
◉ DIATOMITE
Ⓖ GEOTHERMAL RESOURCES
⬣ GYPSUM
Ⓛ LIMESTONE
Ⓟ PHOSPHATE
⊕ POTASH
⊕ SALT
⸪ SAND & GRAVEL
◪ STONE
Ⓢ SULFUR

The census of 1870 revealed that 36,339 miners were in California, with this number increasing by 1880. Much of their effort was expended in mining the less valuable minerals such as copper, tin, and lead. None of these were ever found in really rich deposits but the search for minerals led miners into many isolated valleys of the state. Manufacturing and hauling supplies to these mines became a significant part of the state's economic activities. The mining of borax in Death Valley turned out to be very profitable as well as a rigorous test for Yankee technical ingenuity. The processing of the borax in Death Valley itself was difficult enough but hauling it 165 miles to the railroads at Mojave was far more difficult. To accomplish this huge wagons capable of carrying 10 tons were developed. As every school child and television viewer knows, they were pulled by a twenty-mule team, at least until the coming of the railroads.

BLACK BONANZA

Petroleum, which was ultimately to be the most significant of all California minerals in terms of value, dated back to Indian days. The natives used it to line their cooking baskets and waterproof their boats. The Spanish and Mexicans use brea to waterproof the roofs of adobe houses. Once petroleum had been successfully used for illumination, interest in refining it for such use in California grew. California experienced its first petroleum boom in the 1860s and thousands of dollars' worth of stock was sold in wildcat companies. Many prominent citizens, such as Colonel R. S. Baker, "spent fortunes in an effort to find the black gold." Wells were sunk in many areas of Los Angeles, along the waterfront between Ventura and Santa Barbara, and in Humboldt County a town was optimistically named Petrolia. The initial failures caused many to lose confidence in the potential of petroleum and to ignore the findings of Professor Benjamin Silliman, a trained geologist who made a survey of the oil resources of California in 1865. Silliman concluded: ". . . the small quantity of petroleum received may be the forerunner of many millions which will, at some future time, lubricate the wheels of commerce." However, few people believed Professor Silliman's claim that California would be found to have "more oil in its soil than all the whales in the Pacific Ocean." In spite of such pessimism, production rose slowly but surely, and by the middle 1880s the industry was on a firm foundation. In the 1890s Edward L. Doheny brought in the Los Angeles field and convinced the Santa Fe Railroad to switch from coal to oil. Thereafter the railroads provided an ever increasing market for California's black gold and made it a leading industry before the turn of the century.

MINING THE SEA

Prior to the 1880s most of the illuminating oil used in California came from whales. Whaling fleets, largely manned by the Portuguese, sailed out of San Francisco into the Pacific to bring back oil and whalebone. Such fleets traveled in the wakes of hundreds of whaling vessels which served the Pacific during the first half of the nineteenth century. The decline of the whaling industry of New England preceded the Civil War. A similar decline came to California's whaling industry before the end of the century.

As Portuguese whalers disappeared from the California coast, Chinese fishermen took their place in "mining the sea." Chinese fishermen operated off the California coast as early as the 1860s. They shipped abalone to China, but they also fished for cod, halibut, flounder, mackerel, sardines, and shellfish. A great part of the catch was salted or dried in the sun and brought to San Francisco. Much of it found its way to the mines as well as to the southern part of the state. These enterprising Chinese, who dominated the fisheries, were largely concentrated at Carmel and Monterey, where they made fishing a significant early California industry.

MANUFACTURING

Manufacturing which developed between 1850 and 1900 was that which could be expected in a society where agriculture and mining predominated. The state was forced to develop its own special agricultural implements to satisfy unique needs. They could not be purchased elsewhere because there was no understanding of the way in which they had to be built. Interrelationship between manufacturing and agriculture was displayed frequently. The lumber industry, for example, faced an expanding market for boxes to ship oranges.

The initial impetus to manufacturing came from the needs of the mining community. Mining required lumber and the timber resources of the northwestern counties developed rapidly in the 1850s to fulfill this demand. Then too, the Yankees, uninterested in adobe houses, continued to prefer the wooden dwellings with which they were familiar. Railroad construction also provided a significant market for ties and timber for the building of bridges. Lumber was also necessary to build the schooners used to transport the timber from the mills located in Humboldt and Mendocino counties to San Francisco.

Other manufacturing developed in the realm of the consumer commodities. Meat packing, milling, and the processing of fruits and vegetables were examples. There was an extensive production of leather goods to provide harnesses and saddles, as well as some boots and shoes. Textiles were produced in a limited fashion before the Civil War, but most goods of this nature were imported. Blacksmiths, who were among the early arrivals in California, soon developed flourishing businesses making wagons and carriages. The processing of steel was limited, but there were ironworks in San Francisco, largely to produce equipment for the mines or the railroads. There was hardly a sizable community that did not have its own brewery or distillery, those indispensable institutions of frontier America. The maturity of California's manufacturing was seen when the "California column" commanded by General James Henry Carleton left the state in 1862 to check the Confederate advance into New Mexico. A large part of its supplies and equipment had been manufactured within the state.

FINANCING A FRONTIER COMMUNITY

The early financial history of California is another unique phase of California's development. California has always benefited by in-

CHAPTER XIV

Boom!

By the beginning of the twentieth century, California was on the threshold of the tremendous growth and development which were ultimately to see it as the largest and in many respects the most important state in the nation. The coming of the railroads played a vital role in triggering the great influx of population into the area south of the Tehachapi Mountains in the 1870s and '80s. It was now possible for settlers from other parts of the country to find their way to California with a minimum of discomfort. In addition, the railroads made it possible to get farm produce to the eastern markets. The solution of the water problem was fundamental to the rapid growth in population and also indispensable to the development of the citrus industry. The transition in the status of California was also aided by the growing interest of the nation in the Orient, to some extent an outcome of the Spanish-American War. The United States was now concerned with the great markets of China and Japan, and as the attention of the nation shifted toward the Orient, California became less isolated than she had been in the past. Finally, the great boom in California in the late nineteenth and early twentieth centuries was aided by the development of the oil industry, an extractive industry which soon passed gold as the most important in the state.

SOUTHERN CALIFORNIA COMES OF AGE

When the Americans first came to California, they settled largely in the central part of the state because of the magnet of gold. Towns like Santa Barbara, Los Angeles, and San Diego languished and were considered little more than fossilized cow towns for a generation. Some Anglos did make their way into the southland but, in the main,

Southern California was a pastoral region relatively isolated from the dynamic society of the northern part of the state. The semi-isolation of Southern California was to endure until the close of the Civil War. In the decades that followed new circumstances triggered a period of rapid growth. The influx of population into the region south of the Tehachapi Mountains since 1870 was not uniform but in the words of one observer, "should be regarded as one continuous boom punctuated at intervals by major explosions." The new arrivals to Southern California in the 1870s made their way from San Francisco via stagecoach or steamer to Los Angeles or San Diego. Some were former miners who were looking for economic opportunity. Others came as colonists in organized projects, some of which originated abroad. Many town sites were laid out, such as the Centinela colony near the present city of Inglewood, the Westminster colony, and others. Some were to be utter failures, such as the city of Savana near Santa Ana. The historian James M. Guinn visited the Savana site some weeks after it had been abandoned and described it as follows: "A solitary coyote on a round-topped knoll, possibly the site of a prospective city hall, gazed despondently down the street on the debris of the deserted sheep camp. The other inhabitants of the city of Savana had not arrived, nor have they to this day put in an appearance." The early population influx was slowed by the panic of 1873 and the economic dislocation which followed.

The great boom of the 1880s picked up where the earlier one had left off. It was essentially a product of the railroads. The Central Pacific had little initial interest in Southern California and was slow to extend a branch in that direction. Only the economic growth of the area and the possibility of outside competition prompted it to build southward in 1876. The monopoly practices of the Southern Pacific and its high freight rates made its coming a mixed blessing to the southland. It was not until the Santa Fe reached Southern California in 1885 that the railroads contributed to the economic development of the area in a manner that had been long anticipated. The competition between the two lines triggered the great migration of the eighties. Normal fare from the Mississippi Valley to Southern California had been approximately $125. Once the two competitors locked horns, this rate came tumbling down to as little as $32.50. The result was that anyone with even the slightest curiosity about California was able to come, and both railroads ran large excursion trains from Chicago.

Reduced fares, special trains, and sharply increased numbers of passengers were accompanied by a massive promotional campaign. In the 1880s the greatest endeavor to advertise the attractions of a region in the history of man began. In 1882 Helen Hunt Jackson discovered the California Indians and began writing articles for eastern magazines about them. She was soon joined by Charles Fletcher Lummis, who also stressed the romantic Spanish-Mexican past of California. Harrison Gray Otis, an Ohioan who arrived in Los Angeles in 1882 at the age of forty-four, became an even more important champion of things Californian. Otis, the widely known editor-publisher of the Los Angeles *Times*, had formerly been editor of the *Grand Army Journal*, the veterans' newspaper of the day. Taking advantage of his many connections within the Grand Army of the Republic, he organized a national letter-writing campaign stressing the glories of California. His numerous contacts and great personal prestige ensured its success. But of all of those who wrote about California, none was as successful as Charles Nordhoff. His book *California: For Health, Pleasure and Residence*, as one author has put it, "had a more far-reaching effect on the fortunes of Southern California than anything that has ever been put into print." Important eastern newspapers like the New York *Times* and many magazines also sent members of their staffs to write about this romantic area of the nation, thereby furnishing it with free publicity. The disadvantages of life in California were not mentioned, and instead the state was depicted as a romantic land of sunshine, filled with the scent of rose and orange blossoms. Efforts to promote California were greatly assisted by comparisons to romantic Italy. New cities were named after the Mediterranean nation, and even architecture often followed the Italian style. The advertising campaign was naturally assisted by both the Santa Fe and the Southern Pacific Railroad, which stood to benefit from the influx of settlers. No one can question the truth of much of this promotional endeavor, but unfortunately the exaggerations helped associate Californians with boosterism in the rest of the country.

Those who listened to the siren call of the promotional literature came from all walks of life. They were homeseekers who believed, in the best traditions of the development of America, that there was economic opportunity in California. Some were transient merchants who moved into any boom area hoping to profit from the period of rapid change. Some were land speculators looking for an opportunity to make a fast dollar. A large number of them were health seekers, who first began arriving in California in the 1870s.

The climate of California has always been, and remains, one of the primary attractions. Enthusiastic letter writers to the East and the Midwest extolled the healthful benefits derived from living in this land of eternal sunshine. Unfortunately, much of the promotional literature stressed the health-giving benefits of the state in terms that stretched the truth out of all proportion. Many health seekers came in the expectations that a magical cure would be effected for tuberculosis. In fact, so many came that San Franciscans referred to Los Angeles as "a one-lunged town." Although the Southern California climate did not necessarily cure those suffering from tuberculosis, there is no question but that many people cursed with respiratory disorders have been benefited by the mild climate of the area. Others with rheumatism and arthritis have found living easier in this land of sunshine. Unfortunately, medical quacks operated and exploited the afflicted. In summary, the health seekers provided a significant portion of the population influx into Southern California in the closing decades of the nineteenth century. Some went into white-collar work, while others invested in small farms. Many in this group were also retired people whose earnings amassed in other parts of the nation contributed to the growth of California's economy.

In 1884 Los Angeles had a population of 12,000. Two years later this number had swollen to an estimated 100,000. Santa Barbara, San Diego, and San Bernardino also grew. In addition to the rapid expansion of existing cities, new towns were born overnight. From Los Angeles to the San Bernardino county line, a distance of 36 miles, to cite one example, twenty-five towns were laid out within a single year. Many real estate promoters learned their trade in the boom periods of Midwestern cities and adapted readily to the California scene. Perhaps most of these men honestly believed in their zealous promotion of California real estate but there were far too many "escrow Indians" waiting to scalp the innocent newcomer. A general intoxication permeated the atmosphere. Promoters promised everything: the land would grow anything and some even went so far as to hang oranges on Joshua trees so as better to sell land at inflated prices. Sales promotion took place by escorting customers to the land free of charge, usually with a free lunch, and at the site there would be brass bands playing martial music and even animals from a circus. California real estate promoters have never been known for their modesty, but their advertising reached ridiculous heights in the 1880s.

TYPICAL ADVERTISING OF THE BOOM

GLENDORA

This is where the orange groves are loveliest!
This is where the grapes are most luxuriant!
This is where the vegetation is grandest!
This is where the flowers are prettiest!

WHITTIER! WHITTIER! WHITTIER!

Queen of the Foothills and Crown of the San Gabriel Valley

VERNON

Go wing thy flight from star to star
From world to luminous world, as far
As the Universe spreads its flaming wall—
One winter at Vernon is worth them all!

Morrow Mayo, *Los Angeles*, pp. 81–83.

A typical operator got into the real estate "business" by putting $500 down as an option on a tract. He would then lay out a town and sell lots for $600 each. The usual way was to lure customers with flamboyant promises, build a hotel (the landscape of Southern California was dotted with abandoned hotels once the boom was over), and even promise a college, some of which did materialize. The wilder the name the more attractive the enterprise. For example, Azusa had "everything from A to Z with the rest of the USA thrown in." As one student of the period described a typical development: "The town of Border City was most easily accessible by means of a balloon, and was as secure from hostile invasion as the homes of the cliff dwellers. Its principal resource was a view of the Mojave Desert."

In 1887 real estate sales in Los Angeles County reached $200,-000,000, but by 1888 the boom had spent itself. It began dying when the banks sharply curtailed lending; without money for speculation, the land craze was over.

The effects of the boom are not easy to gauge. A character in a novel commented that "I had half a million dollars wiped out in the crash, and what's worse, five hundred dollars of it was in cash." This suggests that the amount of money that was lost at the conclusion of the boom was limited, but there is no question that some lost more substantial sums. Glenn Dumke in his study *Boom of the Eighties* contends that "the great boom was the outstanding event in Southern California's history. By bringing in a new population, it forced the region one step further away from the mellow Spanish-Californian culture which had so tinged its early development, and as the third and final step in the break-up of the ranchos, completed the transition from range land to agricultural economy." Los Angeles County tax assessments that had reached as high as $63,000,000 dropped back to $20,000,000. In all, some sixty ghost towns theoretically capable of supporting a population of two million dotted Southern California. Some towns lacked the tax base to carry on the municipal services which the swollen population needed. Many fertile farms had been converted into town lots and it took years to get them back into production.

The boom produced some benefits, however. By 1888 Southern California towns probably had more municipal services than most other cities of the nation. The transportation network was rather complete, city streets were paved, and most had sidewalks. A superior domestic water service, efficient police and fire services were off-shoots of the boom. It also brought large numbers of people into the southland with capital which had been accumulated elsewhere. The extensive advertising campaign emphasizing the charms of the area started the pattern of tourism that was to continue to constitute a significant element in the economy of the state. As the gold rush had populated central California, so the boom brought people to Southern California. When it was over, the wide discrepancy in population between the two areas was substantially reduced. The boom also helped higher education since many of the promoters used the promise of the establishment of a college to help sell tracts of land. Some of the institutions founded lasted little more than a year, but others remained, such as the University of Southern California, Chaffey College, Occidental College, Redlands University, Whittier College, La Verne College, Pomona College, and Throop University (which ultimately became the California Institute of Technology). The boom demonstrated in graphic ways the benefits of boosterism. Thereafter the ranks of the promoters of Southern California grew steadily. The Los Angeles Chamber of Commerce embarked upon a system of organized advertising to sell the area to potential settlers and investors from other parts of the nation.

IMPERIALISM AND CALIFORNIA

The growing interest of the United States in the affairs of the Orient, which was climaxed by the Spanish-American War, had a most significant impact upon the development of California. The annexation of Hawaii and the cession of the Philippines in 1898 caused the nation to look out over the Pacific toward the Orient. Increased trade with Hawaii, the Philippines, and China was reflected in the activity of California ports. The military campaign to subdue the Filipino insurrectionists made San Franciso an important staging area. The development of interest in the Pacific was accompanied by a growth in the United States Navy. And naval installations, principally in the San Francisco area and in San Diego, had an economic impact.

More importantly, the United States' newly awakened concern with things oriental helped end the long period of isolation for California. The state was no longer on the periphery of action, and with the eyes of the nation focused across the Pacific, California moved into the center of events. The completion of the Panama Canal in 1914 further enhanced California's position in the nation's affairs.

WATER

Water is the lifeblood of California. The growth of agricultural productivity and profits was directly tied to the ability to irrigate, and the growth in population was dependent upon the water supply. Without this life-giving fluid, the rapidly emerging metropolitan centers of the state would have found their growth stunted. That the cities were able to obtain the water they needed stemmed from the imaginative resourcefulness and, some would even say, unscrupulousness of a small number of individuals.

Charles Mallory Hatfield attempted to solve California's water problem in a most unusual way. He personally denied his title of "Hatfield, the Rainmaker," and contended that he only assisted nature. Beginning his career in 1903, Hatfield spent several years conducting some five hundred rain-making demonstrations for fees ranging from $50 to $10,000. His customers were usually farmers who took up collections, but he also counted city governments among those who signed contracts with him. Of all of his heralded feats none was more famous than his arrangement in 1916 with the city of San Diego to fill its giant reservoir by a specified date. Near the end of the time limit the greatest rainfall in the history of the city occurred, with more than 16 inches falling within a two-day period. To Hatfield's chagrin, the city refused to pay his fee on the grounds that he was only supposed to fill the reservoir and not to flood the community. Whether Hatfield was a great scientist ahead of his time or a clever charlatan has not yet been decided. Some critics maintain that his basic technique was to wait until the dry season was well advanced and then when rain was about due naturally, Hatfield would appear and contract to produce it within thirty or sixty days. Thus, he seldom failed to work his "miracle."

As the largest city of the state, it was only natural that San Francisco would be the first to attempt to solve its water problems by more conventional methods. It had long been dependent upon the Spring Valley Water Company, a privately owned firm, which obtained water from nearby lakes and reservoirs. By the end of the century, the Spring Valley Company came in for much criticism and charges, probably correct, that its high rates resulted from the company's ability to bribe members of the city board of supervisors. By 1900 most civic leaders of San Francisco were convinced that the city should acquire its own water supply in the not too distant Sierra Nevada mountains.

In 1901 the city engineer recommended that San Francisco secure water rights along the Tuolumne River and build its own dams and reservoirs. The proposed site was in the Hetch Hetchy Valley of Yosemite National Park, then under the jurisdiction of the Department of the Interior. In 1903 the Secretary of the Interior, E. A. Hitchcock, rejected the city's application, thereby setting the stage for a ten-year struggle between the advocates of the Hetch Hetchy project and its opponents. Vigorous opposition came from the stockholders of the Spring Valley Water Company, who maintained that it was totally unnecessary to acquire more water. Other militant foes of the Hetch Hetchy project were those interested in the Bay Cities Water Company, which controlled water rights near Lake Tahoe. Representatives of the Bay Cities organization proposed to sell such rights to the city of San Francisco in 1906 for $10,500,000. Out of this sum Abraham Ruef was to obtain a modest attorney's fee of $1,000,000 to be divided among "interested parties." Bay Cities spokesmen argued that the Hetch Hetchy project was finished because of the action of the Secretary of the Interior, and lent monetary and moral support to those who opposed the site in the Yosemite National Park. The tactics of the Bay Cities Water Company were exposed in the sensational graft trials in San Francisco in 1907 and 1908. Their revelations destroyed its chances to become the dominant water company in San Francisco.

Leading the opposition to what they considered the desecration of the beauties of Yosemite were John Muir, the celebrated naturalist, the powerful Sierra Club, and the editors of many nationally prominent magazines and newspapers. Muir described the beauties of Hetch Hetchy in this manner: "No holier temple has ever been consecrated by the heart of man."

Proponents of the Hetch Hetchy project were led by Mayor James Phelan of San Francisco, who enlisted the backing of Gifford Pinchot, America's leading forester, and Theodore Roosevelt, a conservation-minded President. The President and Pinchot believed that the land area involved should be utilized and that there was no reason why natural beauty could not be preserved at the same time that water, which might otherwise be wasted, was impounded for the benefit of the city. The proponents of Hetch Hetchy were greatly assisted by the earthquake and fire in 1906, for many believed that the fire would not have gotten completely out of hand if an adequate water supply had been available.

The Secretary of the Interior, James R. Garfield, reversed his predecessor's decision in 1908 and granted permission to utilize the waters of the Hetch Hetchy. However, when the Taft administration took over, the legalistic Secretary of the Interior, Richard A. Ballinger, again reversed the decision. The stalemate lasted until the Wilson administration. The President's appointment of Franklin K. Lane as his Secretary of the Interior was to prove decisive. Lane, a Californian, had long favored the proposed Hetch Hetchy project. In December 1913 the Raker Act was finally signed into law and the long legal struggle was over. But private electric companies bitterly opposed public power facilities and caused bond issues to be defeated, so it was not until 1931 that the 186-mile aqueduct to San Francisco was completed.

THE OWENS VALLEY PROJECT

Because of its location in a more arid part of the state, Los Angeles faced more serious water problems than San Francisco. By the turn of the century it was obvious that the wells and the Los Angeles River would not furnish an adequate supply for the growing metropolis. In 1902 the city purchased a major private water company and instituted an aggressive search for a greater supply. William Mulholland, a self-trained engineer, and Fred Eaton, former Los Angeles mayor, were convinced that Owens Valley would satisfy the city's growing water needs.

This valley, located some 240 miles from Los Angeles, was predominantly a cattle and ranching community with some mining. A long period of drought influenced Los Angeles leaders to accept Mulholland's recommendation that an aqueduct be built to bring Owens Valley water to Los Angeles. Mulholland estimated the cost at $24,000,000, almost precisely the cost of construction. Work began in 1908 and was completed by 1913. Built over some of the roughest terrain in the country, across the blistering sands of the Mojave Desert, under and over mountains, its completion must rank as one of the great engineering feats of its time. The construction of additional reservoirs assured the city of enough water for an estimated population of two million. In addition, the electricity generated by the gravity flow of the water made it possible for the city to develop its own electrical facilities and, in spite of vigorous opposition, ultimately to have the lowest electrical rate of any major city in the nation.

Unfortunately, the tremendous feat of providing adequate water for the city was marred by the ill will engendered by the city's contempt for the rights of the residents of Owens Valley. It has been contended that landowners of the valley were duped of their property by an employee of the United States Reclamation Service who was actually in the pay of the Los Angeles Water Department when the project was first organized. Particularly galling to the farmers and ranchers of Owens Valley was the fact that this water was originally delivered to a reservoir where San Fernando Valley ranchers and farmers used it to irrigate thousands of acres of land. Some authors have claimed that Harrison Gray Otis and Harry Chandler, of the Los Angeles *Times*, along with other leading Los Angeles citizens, made fortunes out of the happy "coincidence" that the Los Angeles aqueduct brought water to their arid tracts in the San Fernando Valley.

The long-standing hostility of the residents of the Owens Valley to the representatives of the Los Angeles water program continued for two decades. At times it broke into open warfare. Dynamiting dams and flumes by the ranchers of the valley became a periodic feature. In the 1920s when Los Angeles sought additional water rights in the Owens Valley, its residents fought back with fists, guns, and dynamite but the City of the Angels sent in bands of detectives and guards armed with machine guns. In the long run, as is usually the case, the city had its way and the farmers and ranchers were forced to move. The callous attitude of city officials toward the rights of the valley dwellers provoked anger and held Los Angeles up to the wrath of the entire nation. National magazines and newspapers sent in reporters to learn the truth about "the rape of Owens Valley." Although it was undoubtedly true that many of the local people were unreasonable in their demands, the city of Los Angeles fully deserved the criticism it received as a result of this episode.

Although the water seekers of Los Angeles had their way in Owens Valley, the water they brought to the city triggered a major catastrophe. On March 12, 1928, a dam which William Mulholland had built in San Francisquito Canyon, a short distance from Saugus, collapsed. The resulting disaster was the worst in the history of the nation. Some four hundred and fifty lives were lost and property damage was reckoned in the millions. State investigation revealed that the dam was built on a fault and that even the most cursory geological survey would have prevented the mistake. The city admitted its blame and paid more than $15,000,000 in damages.

COLORADO WATER

It was inevitable that water-starved Southern California would ultimately turn to the Colorado River, the one stream in all of the Southwest worthy of being termed a river. Probably the first use of Colorado River water by Californians occurred in 1877 when Thomas Blythe used it to irrigate some of the 40,000 acres he acquired in the Palo Verde Valley.

As early as 1849 a physician, Dr. Oliver M. Wozencraft, suggested the possibility of diverting Colorado River water to the desert regions of Southern California, but he was unable to find financial backing to support such a project. A company headed by Charles R. Rockwood began irrigation from the Colorado on May 14, 1901. The entry of Colorado water into the Imperial Valley was followed by swarms of settlers. New towns such as Raleigh, Holtville, and El Centro sprang up overnight. The newcomers experienced the problems typical of frontier America. Initially they lived in tents without any of the comforts of life. Their greatest hardship came in the summer when temperatures sometimes reached 125°. At times wild ducks destroyed the crops in the same manner as did the swarms of grasshoppers in Kansas. The settlers suffered from either too much water or too little, but such hardships were nothing compared to the promise of the area. Melons, tomatoes, lettuce, cotton, grapes, and almost every other farm product could be grown in abundance.

But the early promise of the region was not to be fulfilled until the area had undergone unbelievable privation. Through many centuries, the Colorado River carried in its stream tons of silt. As a result of depositing this silt, the river had cut off an extension of the Gulf of California that at one time extended as far north as the present city of Indio. The water evaporated from this vast area, which embraces today's Imperial and Coachella valleys, and it became a dry basin well below sea level known as the Salton Sink. Cutting its way through to the ocean, the Colorado River remained unstable, and several times had left its usual channel to the sea and swung northward into the sterile depression it had itself created. After refilling this area the passageway would become so choked with silt that the stream would again be obliged to swing toward the sea, leaving the inland lake to evaporate again. Apparently these geological facts were unknown to engineers Rockwood and Chaffey although they were a part of Indian legend.

One of the many ancient overflowed channels recognized as a natural canal was the Alamo River. Starting near a promontory called Pilot Knob just above the Mexican border, this ancient stream ran westward for about 50 miles after a slight dip below the Mexican border, finally crossing the border on its way to the Salton Sink. In order to increase the flow to satisfy the demand for water, an additional cut was made below the international line to divert more water from the Colorado River into the main Imperial canal. Obtaining the necessary Mexican approval to build the needed control gates was delayed, and in the spring of 1905 heavy floods occurred. By the time the water had subsided in October, the Colorado River had abandoned its old course to the Gulf and had returned to empty into the Salton Sink, thereby creating the Salton Sea. With the whole of the Colorado River emptying into the valley, the river spread to a width of 8 to 10 miles, forcing the Southern Pacific Railroad to move its tracks to higher ground five times that season. Approximately 400 square miles in the Imperial Valley were flooded, and most of the farmers were ruined.

For two years men struggled to control the rampaging Colorado. Rockwood's California Development Company went bankrupt and the Southern Pacific assumed the very difficult engineering tasks involved. The railroad had taken over the defunct irrigation company but was also trying to protect its own right of way. Efforts to obtain financial assistance from the federal government failed, but the Colorado River was ultimately turned back to its former route to the sea. Additional stability came when the Imperial Irrigation District was organized in 1911, with an area of 523,000 acres.

It was obvious to many that the work in the Imperial Valley was only the beginning of the utilization of the Colorado River. Furthermore, its frequent flooding made control absolutely necessary especially in view of the fact that the river annually carried past Yuma an average of 200,000,000 tons of silt. The only solution was a series of dams upstream. Progress in developing a Colorado River program was slow, partially because of the necessity of obtaining Mexican approval, but also because of the necessity of getting the representatives of seven states to agree to a division of the water. In addition, many private power companies were opposed to Colorado River development. In 1923 the Swing-Johnson bill, providing for Colorado River development, was introduced into Congress, but it was not passed until 1928. The construction of the first dam began in 1931 and was completed in 1936. Ultimately named for President Herbert Hoover, it is another of the great feats of American engineering. To utilize the water impounded by Hoover Dam, the Colorado River aqueduct was planned in 1928. To bring it to fruition, the Metropolitan Water District of Southern California was formally organized in 1928 with Los Angeles taking the lead. Ultimately it was joined by most of the cities in the southern part of the state. The first delivering of water via this aqueduct began in 1940. Thus, Southern California's quest for an adequate water supply had been realized. More than enough water was now available for irrigating once barren deserts and turning them into lush farmland. More importantly, sufficient water for the needs of rapidly growing cities was also available.

THE QUEST FOR A HARBOR FOR LOS ANGELES

The full economic development of Southern California awaited not only an adequate water supply but a harbor and the related facilities to handle incoming and outgoing freight. The existing freight facilities, monopolized by the Southern Pacific and inadequate to some tasks, drove the price of imported goods upward and limited the volume of outgoing produce. Trans-Pacific shipments which originated in Southern California traveled by rail to San Francisco for transshipment via ocean freighters. Costs often became prohibitive.

San Pedro served as a harbor of sorts into the 1880s with little improvement since the time when Richard Henry Dana first anchored there in 1835. The entrance was very hazardous and ships of any size had to anchor in the ocean and send their freight and passengers ashore by lighters. Such practices were not only expensive but also dangerous if any kind of a storm developed.

The decade between 1889 and 1899 was spent in a fruitless attempt to locate and build an adequate harbor. During this period the city was to contest again with the power of Collis P. Huntington and the Southern Pacific Railroad. The basic question was control of the harbor. The Southern Pacific preferred Santa Monica, the Santa Fe preferred Redondo, while the city preferred San Pedro.

After three boards of army engineers investigated possible sites for the harbor, and after the United States Senate spent substantial time in debating the location, San Pedro was chosen. It was not until 1910 that the original breakwater, upon which construction had started in 1899, was completed. With the opening of the Panama Canal in 1914, Los Angeles was in a position to handle large amounts of ocean shipping. By 1924 Los Angeles passed San Francisco as the leading port on the West Coast, thus realizing the high hopes that many had held for the harbor at an earlier date. To extend city control, a consolidation in 1909 joined San Pedro and Wilmington with Los Angeles. To connect with the port, Los Angeles simply annexed a narrow strip of territory running from its southern boundary to the limits of the seacoast cities.

BLACK GOLD

The pioneers in California's oil industry came to be highly skeptical of Benjamin Silliman's 1864 prediction of a rosy future for the state's oil wells. Skepticism was founded on realism, for many a fortune was to be lost before the predicted promise was realized. Silliman described the oil field at the Ojai Rancho: "The oil is struggling to the surface at every available point, and is running down the rivers for miles and miles . . . as a ranch, it is a splendid estate, but its value is its almost fabulous wealth in the best of oil." It is entirely possible that the renowned Yale scientist based this evaluation upon an oil sample brought from Pennsylvania and was the victim of a brother-in-law's attempt to promote the sale of oil stock.

The Civil War saw the first great oil boom when turpentine and kerosene from the East were cut off. The main fields of this first boom were in Humboldt County, in the San Francisco bay area, and at the Ojai Rancho. In all some seventy-five groups of promoters were involved in this first boom; many were paper organizations and some were mere speculations.

The initial boom in California petroleum in the 1860s went into a sharp decline after the Civil War. The pattern established was followed in each of the decades until the 1890s. There would be many promising signs of oil, an infusion of men and money from the East, and an initial amount of local excitement. All this would fade in a short period of time with many a would-be venturer in California oil staring bankruptcy in the face. The principal weakness of the oil industry in the nineteenth century arose from the assumption that the surface indications of oil made it as easy to obtain as it had been in Pennsylvania and Ohio, and as easy to process for market. Many an oil expert imported from the East discovered, however, that drilling techniques developed there simply were inadequate when confronted with highly faulted, fractured, and folded source rocks through which wells had to be drilled. One oil hunter moaned that "a more difficult formation through which to bore can scarcely be imagined." The simple techniques and relatively light tools of the

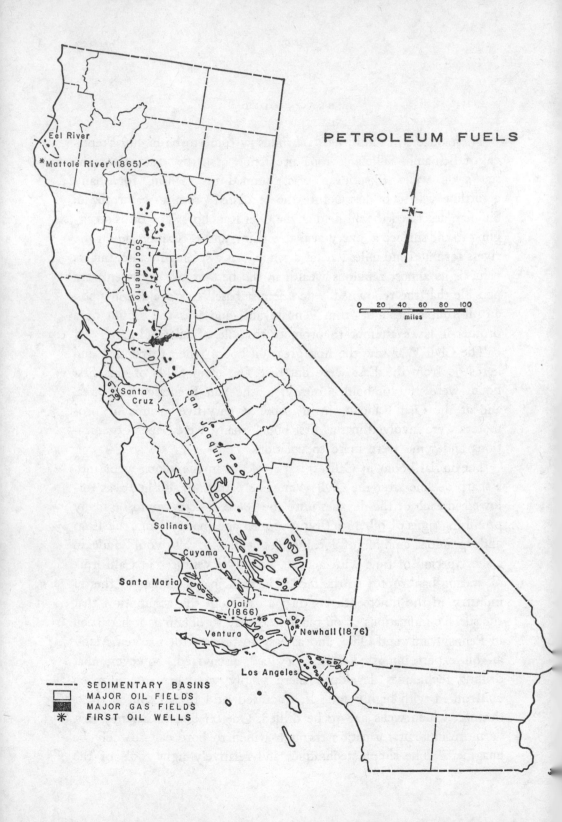

PETROLEUM FUELS

N

0   20 40 60 80 100
miles

Eel River
*Mattole River (1865)

Sacramento

Santa
Cruz

San Joaquin

Salinas

Cuyama

Santa Maria

Ojai
(1866)
Ventura   *Newhall (1876)

Los Angeles

```
------   SEDIMENTARY BASINS
□        MAJOR OIL FIELDS
■        MAJOR GAS FIELDS
*        FIRST OIL WELLS
```

eastern oilmen had to be completely reworked before California oil could be tapped.

Then too, California oil had mainly an asphaltic base and a low paraffin content. This made the oil very heavy, and the excessive carbon in it made it most unacceptable for either lighting or heating purposes. A succession of individuals and companies endeavored to solve these problems of California oil, and though none were totally successful, a great deal of progress was made. By 1890 the Union Oil Company emerged as a leading producer, refiner, and distributor of petroleum products.

Much credit for the revolution in the California oil industry goes to Edward L. Doheny. A prospector who had enjoyed both success and failure in the gold mines of New Mexico, he came to Los Angeles virtually broke in the fall of 1892. Although without experience in oil, he recognized that the material hauled from the Brea tar pits must be close to an oil source. With his partners he sank a shaft in a promising site near Second Street and Glendale Boulevard. Starting with a pick and shovel, he penetrated some 155 feet downward when gas forced him to stop digging. Then, remembering the way that water wells had been dug in his native Wisconsin, he began drilling for oil instead of digging for it. This approach cuts costs sharply in this field. As a result, by 1895 Los Angeles production alone was many times that of the other areas of the state. It came from some three hundred wells that were bunched together in an area that did not total more than 160 acres. As one oilman put it, "Wells were as thick as the holes in a pepper box."

The sharp increase in the production of oil meant that for the first time, California had an unlimited quantity available. Now the problem became one of marketing rather than production. Doheny pioneered here as well, when he convinced the Santa Fe Railroad to use fuel oil instead of soft coal. Efforts to utilize fuel oil in place of coal aboard ship were renewed and finally were successful. In addition, the ingenious Irishman introduced the use of oil in the form of asphalt for paving purposes.

The increase in population in California at the turn of the century led to a greater demand for petroleum by-products such as kerosene, but most important were the improvements in refining that enabled people to utilize the petroleum products more completely than ever before. Innovations in the processing of oil were coupled with changes in drilling procedures, such as the introduction of the diamond drill, making it possible to get at more of the state's oil. The completion of the Panama Canal made it possible for the state to ship its petroleum great distances, and the coming of the automobile and the ancillary needs for roads further caused market demands to soar.

For a time the Los Angeles area held the lead in California oil production as the result of Doheny's discovery, but by the beginning of the century, new fields were brought into production. The most notable of these was in Kern County near the present site of Taft in 1910. During the 1920s new fields were exploited near Huntington Beach, Santa Fe Springs, Signal Hill, and in many regions of the San Joaquin Valley. By 1924 the state led the nation in petroleum production, a position it held until it was surpassed by Texas in 1936. The amount of wealth realized from the oil fields has been many times that of the value of the total gold produced, and justified oil's designation as "black gold."

Fundamental to the oil boom was the growth in the use of the automobile. Initially considered a rich man's toy, by World War I it became a necessity for many people. In the Los Angeles area the "big red cars" of the Pacific Electric Railway provided quick, inexpensive, and convenient transportation to the general public. The need for cars was limited in Southern California by Henry E. Huntington's interurban railroad. But immense distances within the state had not been bridged either by the railroads or the interurban electric lines. Here was a real and immediate need for the automobile and truck. The tremendous growth and development of modern California was made possible by the automobile and the motor truck. Without them, and the highway system, such development would undoubtedly have been a great deal slower. Not only did Californians soon have more automobiles than any other state in the union, but most families eventually had more than one. The social significance of the motor car has altered family life and dating habits, as well as the choice of where a man lives. Thus, the development of the petroleum industry has assisted the automobile in making possible man's conquest of the tremendous space that makes up the state of California.

The oil industry has always had much of the speculative flavor associated with mining. Most people realize the element of risk involved and accept it for what it is. Unfortunately, the state has been the scene of scandals growing out of the irresponsibility of some oilmen. Edward L. Doheny, who was so instrumental in establishing petroleum on a sound basis in California, was involved in one of the most prominent of all national oil scandals. Doheny, a civic-minded philanthropist who gave away a fortune to his church, the University of Southern California, and countless other civic enterprises, bribed Secretary of the Interior Albert B. Fall during the Harding administration. Fall had been an old friend and mining partner of Doheny in their New Mexico days. When the government official found himself in dire financial circumstances, the oilman loaned him $100,000 in cash, accepting a note only when Fall insisted on giving him one. Shortly after this loan was made, Fall signed over the oil lease rights to the military reservoir at Elk Hills. The fact that no competitive bids were allowed put the transaction in the worst possible light.

Ultimately the Secretary of the Interior was convicted of receiving a bribe and went to prison, but Edward L. Doheny was not convicted of having offered one. This curious turn of American justice prompted Senator George Norris (Neb.) to comment sarcastically that "It was a waste of time to try any man in America for a crime who was worth one hundred million dollars." In spite of Doheny's acquittal, the resulting notoriety broke his spirit, and he lived out the remainder of his days an ill man.

The story of Chaucey C. Julian, a Canadian-born oilman, was another example of the unfortunate corruption which frequently crept into the oil business. A born promoter, he launched his own oil company with the kind of flamboyant publicity dear to the hearts of Angelenos in the 1920s. With full-page ads he advised people that "We are all out here in California where the gushers are and we just ought to clean up!" In a short time he had about $11,000,-000 from over forty thousand stockholders with which to carry on more prospecting.

Julian was forced out of the control of his oil company by two unscrupulous promoters, S. C. Lewis and Jack Bennett. These two, in collaboration with normally respectable Spring Street financiers, overissued Julian Oil securities, or engaged in stock watering until the total reached a reported sum of $150,000,000. In all, it constituted one of the largest stock swindles in American history. Forty of Los Angeles' leading financiers were indicted for conspiring to violate state usury laws as a result of their stock-pooling efforts but they never stood trial. Bennett and Lewis, along with nine others, were tried for obtaining money under false pretenses. They were acquitted, possibly as a result of their bribery of the district attorney. However, they were later sent to prison for another stock-rigging case. The flamboyant Julian, who had been wiped out in the failure of his oil company, tried to recoup his fortunes in China but ended a suicide.

CHAPTER XV

The Progressive Era

Many Californians contemplated their world with satisfaction in the first year of the twentieth century. If they lived in the city of San Francisco, and 25 per cent of the state's residents did, they resided in an urbane and sophisticated city which lived well, graciously, and earnestly. The hard times of the nineties, which had been difficult for most of the country after 1893's recession, were behind them, and the new century opened with an outburst of economic growth. The Spanish-American War and the Alaska gold rush were partially responsible. The people of the city, and for that matter the rest of the state, were almost complacent. Life was good and it was especially sweet in the "Paris of the West."

Life had not always been this way. The turbulent seventies had passed, the decade's closing marked with the writing of a new constitution and Henry George's monumental study, *Progress and Poverty*. The first was intended to deal with a number of problems in the form of railroad monopoly, land and water monopoly, and the Chinese problem; the latter was an indictment of existing society as well as a prescription for what must be done. Both survived. The constitution remains, albeit much amended, the basic framework of government in California. Henry George did not live to see the opening of the new century, but his name became a household word, and his philosophy and program survive in the world of today in the form of Henry George Schools of Social Science, found in most major urban centers of the United States. While both the constitution and George's work endured, neither accomplished much in the form of solving the great problems which California faced in the final two decades of the nineteenth century.

Land monopoly and the oppression of the Big Four made an ugly appearance in Mussel Slough in 1880, and for the next twenty

THE PROPHET OF SAN FRANCISCO

One of the most remarkable of the writers who came out of a California setting was Henry George, best known for his book Progress and Poverty, *which appeared in 1879. George was born in 1839 in Philadelphia. While still a boy he sailed to Australia and the Far East, where the scenes of widespread poverty made a deep impression on him. He landed in California in 1857 and in the course of the next few years he participated in a short-lived gold rush to British Columbia and earned a precarious living as a printer and agricultural laborer. Some eleven years after he arrived in San Francisco he attained a measure of security as a printer on the San Francisco* Times.

His new position took him to New York City in 1869, where he observed at first hand the slums, poverty, and hunger which existed in the midst of opulence. His reflections on the causes and consequences of poverty in the midst of wealth led to the conviction that the two phenomena were related to the ever increasing value of land as society and civilization developed. Land increased in price and as it did so, "men who worked it must pay more for the privilege." Since land was the free gift of nature, it was manifestly unfair for men to acquire great wealth by holding on to land which increased in value independently of anything the landowner did. To remedy this injustice and break the chain that bound "progress and poverty" George proposed a "single tax" on the "unearned increment" that is the increased value to land which arose out of the development of society.

Economists then and now doubted the validity of his ideas, but a large number of people found them logical and attractive. When his book Progress and Poverty *was finished there was some difficulty in finding a publisher, but once it appeared in print, it became a best seller. From that time to this it has never been out of print. Not only did it circulate in great numbers, in English as well as in translations into the more important languages of the world, it also had a major influence on the thinking of economists and political leaders.*

For the balance of his life George was a popular lecturer who traveled throughout the United States and Europe expounding his basic ideas. He was a most effective speaker, who pursued a line of argument step by step in clear, concise prose. A popular movement, the single tax became a powerful political force, and George himself became a politician in New York State. It was there, while running for mayor of the city of New York, that he died. Millions mourned him, hundreds of thousands of followers pledged themselves to the perpetuation of his ideas, and three quarters of a century later, Georgian ideas have considerable impact on the thinking of economists and political leaders.

17. Traffic posed no problems and transit was leisurely in San Francisco in 1880. At that time, cable cars operated over eight lines and traversed 112 miles of the city.

18. The establishment of the free port of Los Angeles at San Pedro came only after a long struggle between the owners of the Southern Pacific and the city of Los Angeles.

19. Los Angeles, located hundreds of miles from natural sources of water, built the Owens River aqueduct (1907-13) to meet the needs of her growing population. Owens Valley residents later dynamited the facilities because of the devastation it caused to their farmlands and homesteads.

20. When the Colorado River broke its banks in 1905 the resultant flood formed the Salton Sea. The Southern Pacific fought to control the river and reclaim the land that its main line to New Orleans traversed.

21. California's "factories in the fields," raising wheat in huge, sprawling farms, made the use of modern machinery a necessity to keep costs down and production high. As early as the 1890s harvesters were used.

22. April 18, 1906, was the date of San Francisco's greatest ordeal. The earthquake and fire which followed destroyed 28,000 buildings and 4 square miles of the city.

23. Discovery of oil in Southern California at the turn of the century helped to change the area dramatically from an agricultural to an industrial center.

24. In 1916 the Lockheed brothers established Lockheed Aircraft Corporation. The model shown is the first of a long line of military planes manufactured for the U. S. Navy.

years the railroad was repeatedly involved in incidents which disturbed most concerned people. The Big Four went their merry way using their monopoly of transportation in the state to exploit one sixth of United States residents. From time to time the public was given an insight into the operations of the Pacific Associates. One such view from the inside was provided by the widow of one of the intimates, Mary Ellen Colton.

Mrs. Colton was widowed when David D. Colton died quite unexpectedly in the late seventies. Colton was a long-time resident of California who had been in the course of a busy life the sheriff of Siskiyou County and an associate of Senator David C. Broderick in the Democratic party. In 1859 he served as Broderick's second in the famous duel with David S. Terry which cost the senator his life. A few years later Colton was the principal beneficiary when Broderick's estate, consisting of about $800,000 worth of land, was distributed by means of a forged will. In the early seventies he became an associate of the Big Four, brought into the enterprise by Mark Hopkins. His role was that of political manipulator on the state scene, and he served them so well that he began to use a collective "we" in letters to them. The press began to refer to the "Big Four and a Half," the fraction representing Colton.

When Colton died in October 1878, his associates were saddened, and after an appropriate period of mourning they made a settlement with their late partner's widow. It amounted to a half-million dollars, not an immodest sum for an ex-sheriff to acquire. That might have been the end of the matter had not Mark Hopkins died about the same time. Mrs. Colton was first intrigued and then outraged when she learned of the terms under which Hopkins' estate was distributed. Evidently securities were valued differently when they were owned by a Hopkins rather than a Colton. Convinced that she had been defrauded by her late husband's associates, Ellen Colton sued in 1883 to set the argreement aside. In court, to establish the degree of intimacy which existed between her husband and the Big Four as well as the key role which David D. Colton played, she had read into the record of the trial some six hundred letters which Collis P. Huntington had written to her husband. Almost all began with "Burn after reading," or something similar.

The fact that the letters had not been burned revealed something about Colton; the fact that Huntington had written him some six hundred letters with that salutation revealed something about him. And the contents of the letters revealed a great deal about American and California politics and the manner in which the Big Four used the American political system in whatever way they found necessary to further their own interests. The *Chronicle* in San Francisco and the New York *World* published each letter as it became available. Other newspapers also printed them in their unexpurgated versions, and from one end of America to the other the general public became aware of the manner in which the money of the Big Four had corrupted congressmen, senators, judges, commissioners, cabinet members, and even a justice of the U. S. Supreme Court. The sights that were revealed were enough to sicken a man and undermine the faith of a people in the democratic system. The eventual loss of Mrs. Colton's suit after some eight years of litigation was scant solace to the leaders of the Southern Pacific. While they were not obligated to rewrite the agreement with Mrs. Colton, they lost a great deal in the eyes of the public. Not only had they been exposed as corrupters of democracy on a vast scale, but they had also been convicted in the court of public opinion of taking advantage of a former business associate's widow.

Two other incidents in the nineties did much damage to the Pacific Associates. The first involved the selection of a harbor for the city of Los Angeles, and the second involved the funding of the approximately $27,000,000 debt created when the U.S. government advanced money to the Central Pacific Railroad to finance initial construction. Each brought into being groups of diverse outlook which were determined to block the plans of the Southern Pacific. Each contributed in the long run to the creation of an effective opposition which eventuated in the political downfall of the Southern Pacific.

The Free Harbor fight began as a conflict over the location of a harbor for the city of Los Angeles. San Pedro had been for generations the nearest thing to a harbor that the region had. Improved by Phineas Banning, who developed facilities and established a stage line and later a railroad to carry freight inland, it was the preferred harbor site for the residents of Los Angeles when they began to think seriously of the future and catch some glimpse of what their city would be. Southern Pacific directors once looked upon San Pedro as the best site, but when they acquired a railroad which joined the city of Santa Monica with Los Angeles as well as substantial amounts of its waterfront property, they changed their minds. Santa Monica furnished them with the opportunity to dominate the harbor of the major city of the south in the same way that they dominated the harbor of the north. Accordingly, Huntington began to marshal his resources in an effort to procure federal appropriations to develop the harbor at Santa Monica. The battle was joined.

The group which coalesced in an effort to frustrate Huntington included the Los Angeles Chamber of Commerce, the Santa Fe Railroad, Harrison Gray Otis of the Los Angeles *Times*, and most people who were not beholden to the railroad interests. Outnumbered but never outfought, Huntington used his considerable influence in Washington in behalf of his objectives. The day when he and his associates had overwhelmed any opposition was past, for by now the state, once dominated by a single giant center of economic and political power in the form of the Big Four, had matured. The rate-paying public and the manufacturers, citrus growers, oilmen, maritime interests, agriculturalists, etc. of Southern California had the strength as well as the will to contemplate war with the Southern Pacific.

Before the issue was resolved in favor of the site at San Pedro in 1899, a great deal of conflict had taken place and the railroad had been revealed once more as a grasping corporate entity which subordinated all other things to the welfare of the Southern Pacific. In the process as well, the enemies of the railroad were not only increased but emboldened, for they demonstrated rather effectively that the power of the railroad was limited.

The battle over the funding bill again pitted the railroad against a large part of the general citizenry. In this instance, the railroad sought a refunding of their debt to the United States government incurred when they accepted approximately $27,000,000 of federal aid in the construction of the Central Pacific. The aid took the form of 6 per cent bonds with a thirty-year due date. As the fateful day approached when the bonds were to come due, Huntington and his associates sought to evade the obligation in a variety of ways. Arguing that the railroad had rendered valuable and important services to the government over the years, they sought first cancellation, then scaling down of the debt, and if neither of these options were available, refunding of the debt in the form of seventy-five-year bonds of 2 per cent interest.

The negotiations between the company and the government went on for years before a settlement was reached, under which the debt, by now almost $60,000,000, was to be repaid over a period of ten years. During the battle, Ambrose Bierce and Homer Davenport worked with acid-tipped pens to fix in the public mind an image of the Southern Pacific. Bierce produced prose which indicted; Davenport, the cartoonist, illustrated his themes with pictures which swelled the circulation of William Randolph Hearst's newspapers and inflicted serious damage on the railroad and its interests. When the fight was ended, the railroad paid dearly.

The final negotiations came just two years before the death of Collis P. Huntington, last of the Big Four to die. When they were reunited in the next world, predicted a wag, the Pacific Associates would build another railroad. Who would finance it and provide it with fuel and a subsidy of the public domain was a matter of speculation. The old order's passing was signaled by the deaths of two very different types, Huntington and Mariano G. Vallejo, both symbols of another age. However, the efficient political machine of the Southern Pacific did not disappear with Huntington. Railroad politics survived, for the railroad itself survived. A new titan of the rails, Edward H. Harriman, purchased Huntington's stock in the enterprises of the Southern Pacific in 1901. For the next few years he busied himself with rebuilding the road and co-ordinating its activities with other parts of his railroad empire.

In California, the efficient political machine headed by William F. Herrin and his subordinate in Southern California, Walter Parker, continued to operate. Railroad politics, as essential as coal in running a railroad, continued. Free passes to state and local legislative representatives, cash subsidies to friendly newspapers, campaign contributions to aspiring politicians, investment opportunities afforded officials, rebates to co-operative shippers, a battery of the best legal talent in the state—these were the techniques which the railroad used to influence, control, or dominate government. For the most part these techniques had served the railroad well since the days when

Theodore Judah sought the passage of a Pacific Railroad Act in 1862, and there was no reason to change.

Nevertheless, a new day was dawning with the new century. Life in California was a far cry from the society which had welcomed the railroad's completion at Promontory Point. As significant as any other change was the new economic milieu which existed. For years the Big Four had towered above their contemporaries' enterprises. Each year brought maturity to the economy and each year brought diversity and sophistication to the society. Now there was not one but a number of enterprises in the state. Each was joined in a community of interest around a nexus of rate paying. For years they had seen the railroad dominate the state, squeeze its entrepreneurs, and exploit its farmers. They lusted for an opportunity to strike back at the Octopus and free themselves of its grasping tentacles.

The opportunity came early in the twentieth century and as a result of some dramatic and surprising incidents in the restless and cosmopolitan city of San Francisco. San Francisco had matured in the last twenty years of the nineteenth century. In line with most United States cities, it grew very rapidly as the population of the United States climbed from 62 to 75,000,000. In California eleven counties declined in the last decade as mining lost importance and agriculture changed in character. The city beside the bay absorbed a share in the closing decades of the nineteenth century. San Francisco's population reached a half million before 1900, making it the sixth largest city in the United States, while its rival in the south, Los Angeles, lagged far behind.

As the residents of San Francisco looked about them, they saw a cosmopolitan, energetic, and creative society. Their city was the social, financial, and commercial capital of a great agricultural empire. But they also saw a society which was divided into antagonistic groups, each ready to do battle with the opposition. Conflict between labor and capital had roots which reached back into the gold rush period. In the seventies, the sand lotters had made the moguls of capital tremble with huge mass meetings that threatened violent action if their demands were not met. In the mid-eighties the first of a series of strikes in San Francisco featuring the maritime and brewery workers took place. Thereafter at periodic intervals there were similar episodes.

Out of a mosaic of strike, lockout, boycott, and picket line violence came rapid growth for the labor movement, and by the turn of the century, organized labor exerted more influence in San Francisco than in any other city in the western world. As the unions grew in numbers and influence, groups of employers also began to unite. Soon federations of unions were matched by associations of employers. In each case, unity improved the bargaining position of each side and provided for an escalation in the intensity and duration of conflict. In 1890 and again in 1893, bitter battles between labor and management produced much violence and a serious setback to the unions.

The next test came in the flush times which followed the Spanish-American war and the rush to the Klondike. In 1901 the California State Federation of Labor was launched, and the same year brought an alliance of waterfront workers, the City Front Federation. It was also the year in which an employers' association, the Employers' Council, was formed. Both sides girded for battle which came in the spring when cooks, waiters, machinists, teamsters, and carriage and wagon makers struck. As the battle continued, it became a campaign and then a war as each side committed additional troops. When the eighteen unions of the City Front Federation walked out, San Francisco was gripped by what was close to a general strike. As it continued, it changed in character: violence became commonplace, hundred of assaults and arrests were made, and five men died. The Employers' Council fought with every available weapon. With 60 per cent of the city's businesses closed, and strengthened by allies who were directly affected by the closing of the harbor, the employers fought doggedly. In October peace of a sort was restored, but it was little more than an armistice and an interlude in the violence in which each side could gather its strength for a renewal of the conflict. As the union looked back over the episode they were particularly incensed at the role which the city authorities played. Labor felt that the incumbent reform mayor, James D. Phelan, scion of a wealthy San Francisco family, had not been neutral, but on the contrary, an open ally of the enemy who used the city police against the strikers. The lesson was clear. So long as the money interests controlled the city government, labor would fight not only the employers but the city authorities. If labor would avoid such a confrontation, it was essential that it control the city government.

Father Peter C. Yorke, a Catholic priest, had become a spokesman and champion of labor as well as the first to urge political action on the unions. Plans were laid, an organization established, candidates located, a convention of delegates from unions scheduled, and the Union Labor party was launched, the first distinct, separate union labor political organization in twentieth-century America. Democratic and Republican professionals and some major union officials jeered, while in the background a minor but experienced political worker sensed that the new movement had considerable potential.

Abraham Ruef was a native son, born in San Francisco in 1864. He was a bright young man who had graduated with honors from the University of California at Berkeley at eighteen, going on to pick up a law degree and win admission to the bar when he was twenty-one. He had cut his political eyeteeth as a liberal and reformer in the university, where he authored a senior thesis entitled "Purity in Politics" and had helped to organize a students' co-operative which made books available at reasonable prices. But when he went into the world of real politics soon after he began the practice of law, he quickly learned that politics of his time had a hard, cold, cynical core. Elections were a sham and a curtain; from behind the façade, the political bosses nominated, manipulated, and controlled the machinery of government, and more often than not the little bosses did the bidding of larger bosses, and they in turn obeyed the instructions of the leaders of the hierarchy. At the top in the eighties as well as the nineties was the political organization of the Southern Pacific. As Dr. John R. Haynes described the situation, the final selection of public officials from the village constable to the governor was made by the railroad. The machine of the Octopus was non-partisan when it was convenient, although at times it could be found in the corner of one party or the other. William F. Herrin, the leader of the "Southern Pacific Political Bureau," was also the key in the co-operative arrangement which joined the leaders of each party and the railroad organization. To anyone who aspired to the top in the political world of San Francisco, the route was long and filled with hazards.

Abe Ruef saw in the Union Labor party a shortcut to power. While others turned their backs on the fledgling organization, Ruef stepped to the foreground. Within days he was the behind-the-scenes boss of the new organization, head of a group within the party which could act decisively when necessary. By the time the November 1901 elections were at hand, Ruef and his henchmen were in full charge of a party which had considerable potential.

The first test at the polls pitted Ruef's carefully chosen and groomed candidate for mayor, Eugene E. Schmitz, against Democratic and Republican candidates. In the three-way race, Schmitz won—the first Union Labor mayor in the United States. Some anticipated Red revolution as a result, but those who knew Schmitz and Ruef should not have been so alarmed. Both were essentially conservative, Republicans of some experience, and as intent on feathering their own nests as bringing about changes in the society. Soon it was apparent to the knowledgeable citizens of the city that the Union Labor party would operate in much the same fashion as other political organizations of the time; the major difference between what was and what had been was the systematic manner in which the bosses of the Union Labor party went about their business.

Their business was trading in the favors and privileges which the municipal government could confer. They were handicapped by their lack of complete control of the municipality (only three members of the board of supervisors were Union Labor in 1901), but aided by a new city charter which strengthened the hands of the mayor, Ruef and Schmitz planned carefully as they felt their way. Changing conditions in the city provided them with opportunity, for not only was the city growing very rapidly, but technical innovations in communication, power, and transportation demanded not only new approaches on the part of capital but as well the co-operation of the city government. Telephone companies, electric power enterprises, traction railroad systems—all required the co-operation of the city authorities. Franchises which authorized them to run their lines through the streets and use the public thoroughfares for their facilities were essential.

Schmitz, a long-time musician who conducted when he wasn't playing the violin, took readily to the job of running the sixth largest city in the United States. With Ruef in the background to turn to when necessary, he gathered the strings of power until he had the city in his grasp. Soon it became known that the city government trafficked in many things and the chief broker was Abe Ruef, the "Curly Boss," as he was dubbed by an opponent. To see Ruef, alumnus of the university and the Hastings School of Law, entailed a business arrangement with lawyer Abraham Ruef. Soon the Pacific State Telephone and Telegraph Company, United Railroads, and the Home Telegraph Company were paying Ruef a monthly retainer. The boodle, disguised as payments for legal services, began to mount.

Boodle came from other sources as well. The city licensed more than two dozen kinds of businesses, ranging from auctioneering, through carpet cleaning, real estate broking, debt collecting, insurance adjusting, to restaurants and theaters. Thousands of people employed in hundreds of enterprises depended upon the good offices of the men who ran the city. No outright bribes were solicited, but the squeeze was put on them all. The response swelled the volume of business transacted by Abe Ruef as clients came forward to employ the Curly Boss to represent them. Eventually Ruef and his organization were drawing tribute from hundreds of legitimate and illegitimate enterprises. Not only did they exact payment from dairies, theaters, and produce dealers, but saloons, French restaurants (San Francisco's institutionalized houses of assignation), gambling houses, brothels, and so on.

From the initial victory of 1901, Abe Ruef and his associates built other victories. In 1903 a divided opposition in the form of a Republican as well as a Democratic candidate paved the way for Schmitz's re-election. In 1905 Fremont Older, battling editor of the *Bulletin*, led a crusade of reform which seemed promising. He was joined by the *Chronicle* and the *Call*, and the newspapers of San Francisco launched an all-out assault on Ruef and his organization. Uniting behind a single candidate, the reformers were so confident that Fremont Older claimed victory on the eve of election. To the amazement of all observers, the Union Labor party won a smashing victory. Not only was Schmitz re-elected, but the entire slate was victorious. Henceforth, every major post in the city and county government, eighteen supervisors as well as the city treasurer, district attorney, city attorney, county clerk, and even the coroner, was to be a Union Labor party man. The victory was an over-whelming landslide, and it gave Ruef full control of the government of San Francisco.

Meanwhile, the opposition was gathering its forces. They included public-spirited citizens as well as representatives of the political rings that formerly ruled the city and propertied interests who were dis-advantaged by the new locus of political power which Ruef had created. The Political Bureau of the Southern Pacific hesitated at times, but for the most part it took a pragmatic approach, made its peace with Ruef, and went along. James D. Phelan, predecessor of Schmitz, and Rudolph Spreckels, another scion of an affluent and socially prominent family, joined hands with Fremont Older. They faced imposing tasks, for Ruef had planned well, and after the tri-umph of 1905 he appeared to be nearly invincible.

Unfortunately for Ruef, his overwhelming success was the portent of his eventual downfall. In that election, the Union Labor party slate swept the field and swept into office a number of men who had more than their share of human weaknesses. Of the eighteen super-visors elected in that landslide, there were a drayman, a blacksmith apprentice, a shoe machine operator, a drummer, and a piano polisher. All were men of modest background and experience, and immodest aspiration. They were a difficult crew for Ruef to command, but eventually he worked out a method of operations. The board of supervisors would meet unofficially and there in caucus take a position on questions which were to be decided subsequently in a formal meeting. Ruef and his associates would work out the preliminaries, even drafting the text of a proposed ordinance. Then in the formal meeting, each supervisor would cast his vote according to the manner in which he voted in caucus. Furthermore, no supervisor was to take so much as a free cigar from anyone interested in any of the matters which appeared before the board. The collection of boodle, generally in the form of legal fees paid to Ruef, was to done by the Curly Boss himself or one of his trusted intimates. Subsequently it was to be divided among the supervisors and other members of the ring. This was the system—apparently a flawless arrangement which allowed the Ruef organization to have its way with San Francisco without running the risks that a more direct form of "influence broking" entailed.

In the first few months of the administration, the system worked well as it dealt with a number of matters involving utility rates, real estate development, and traction railroads. A more important matter involving the United Railroads combine awaited settlement. Headed by Patrick Calhoun, a grandson of the "Great Nullifier," this aggressive concern had acquired a collection of urban transit systems and was interested in making the whole system uniform and efficient by converting it to an overhead electric streetcar system. It sought a new franchise for its operation; apparently it would soon acquire such a franchise, for Abraham Ruef was on its payroll.

However, a sizable and important group of property owners in the city objected to an overhead system on the grounds that it would deface the streets and depreciate property values. Two of the largest property owners involved, James D. Phelan and Rudolph Spreckels, spearheaded the opposition to this proposal and demanded that the city look to the development of a system which would place the power lines in conduits in the street. Thereby the city would be beautified and property values improved. When the United Railroads refused to consider underground power lines, Spreckels and Phelan took the matter to the public. They organized a rival concern, the Municipal Street Railway of San Francisco, capitalized at $14,000,-000, met with some encouragement from City Hall, and filed formal incorporation papers the day before the city was rocked by the earthquake of April 18, 1906.

The earthquake and fire which followed almost destroyed the city and drove from the minds of most people all thought about a conflict over transit systems. Within a month, however, while most of the city was preoccupied with rebuilding, the city authorities passed an ordinance which authorized the United Railroads to convert to an overhead trolley system. The howls of outrage which followed were heard from one end of the city to the other. Mass meetings were held where the citizenry vented its anger at the venal city government, and District Attorney William H. Langdon announced that he was taking charges of graft and malfeasance to the grand jury. Langdon, though elected on the Union Labor party ticket, was a man of principle and integrity.

Behind the scenes, Phelan, Spreckels, and Older were organizing quietly but efficiently for an assault on the Ruef organization. With

SAN FRANCISCO EARTHQUAKE AND FIRE 1906

The San Francisco earthquake and fire remains the most spectacular disaster in the history of the state, and perhaps of the nation. The earthquake struck at 5:12 A.M. April 18, 1906. The first shock lasted for some forty seconds, ceased for ten seconds, and returned for another twenty-five seconds; aftershocks continued for much of the day. It has been estimated that the earthquake measured 8.4 on the Richter scale. The quake felled some five thousand buildings, twisted roads, railways, sidewalks, and gas, water, and electric lines into useless shapes. An estimate of the number of lives lost in the quake itself was impossible because of the fire which followed. The worst damage was caused to buildings erected on fill; where structures were anchored in solid rock, damage was less severe. Disaster was not confined to San Francisco: an area 20–40 miles wide stretching for 200 miles from Salinas to Fort Bragg was devastated.

Sporadic fires broke out shortly after the quake but it was two or three hours before authorities realized a major conflagration was at hand. The earthquake had shattered the pipes leading from the basic water supply at Crystal Springs Lake and San Andreas Lake. The undermanned fire department of only 585 men and some fifty pieces of equipment relied on the little water available from cisterns, reservoirs, and what could be pumped from the bay. Desperate initial efforts to contain the fire by dynamiting buildings were usually ineffective because of the lack of experienced personnel. Seventy-four hours after it started, the fire ended. Dynamite, heroic firemen, a change in the wind, and hasty repairs to the water system combined to produce victory. In the smoldering city a tally of the disaster was made.

The fire cost some 450 lives, destroyed 28,000 buildings (about one third of San Francisco), 490 blocks, totaling more than 4 square miles. Property damage was estimated from $350 to $500 million. Gone were the city's financial district, its retail district, Chinatown, the City Hall with its records, the city's libraries and art collections, and many of its schools and churches. Many businesses were totally destroyed and prominent families financially ruined. Some 80 per cent of the $229,000,000 in insurance helped ease the burden, but some companies refused to pay, claiming fires caused by earthquake were not covered. Even today, less than 5 per cent of Californians have earthquake insurance, although periodically the earth trembles and shakes ominously.

Theodore Roosevelt's co-operation, they secured the services of Francis J. Heney, who had made a reputation as an investigator and prosecutor of public officials who had been involved in timber frauds on the public lands of Oregon. Heney was to serve as a special deputy to Langdon. William J. Burns, a former member of the Secret Service, was to direct the investigation, and a purse of more than $100,000 had been pledged to underwrite the campaign. Before the work was done, every dime was spent.

Meanwhile, Ruef was busy running his organization. Minor rebellions within the ranks were dealt with, the rebels being dismissed from their posts. In midsummer 1906 Ruef won a smashing victory in the election of delegates to the Republican state convention by capturing complete control of the San Francisco delegation. That coup enabled him to deal with Herrin from a position of strength. In exchange for $14,000 for expenses, Ruef voted the San Francisco delegation for James N. Gillett, the Southern Pacific candidate for governor. That night the luminaries of the convention gathered around the festive board of a victory celebration. While they were enjoying fine food, good cigars, and vintage wines, a photographer snapped the affable group. Seated in the center was the Curly Boss. To his rear and with a hand casually resting in friendship on his shoulder was the candidate for governor, Gillett. The rest of the group included Walter Parker, Southern California section boss of the railroad political bureau, judges, congressmen, lobbyists, and politicians who served the railroad interests. The photograph soon appeared in a San Francisco newspaper, where it made a small immediate impression. Before the saga of the Curly Boss ended it was to make a major impact.

Fresh from his triumph in the convention, Ruef returned to San Francisco to find himself and his associates under increasing fire. An attempt to depose District Attorney Langdon and replace him with Ruef failed when the presiding judge refused to recognize the machine's dismissal of Langdon. When the grand jury heard some of the evidence which Burns and Heney assembled, it handed down five indictments against Ruef and Schmitz for extortion. Technicalities of various kinds postponed the trial for months. The delay merely strengthened the case against Ruef, for in the interim, seventeen of the eighteen members of the board of supervisors confessed to accepting bribes from the Pacific Gas and Electric Company, the United Railroads, the Pacific States Telephone Company, and the Parkside Transit Company. Additional indictments of Ruef and some of his associates followed. When a court finally heard the evidence, Schmitz was convicted and Ruef pleaded guilty to extortion, but on appeal, the decisions were reversed and both men were released. Ruef was tried a second time and the jury deadlocked. In the course of the third trial, Heney was shot down in open court by a prospective juror he had exposed as a former convict. A short time later, the would-be assassin was himself killed in a cell while in the custody of the police. To this day the question of whether it was suicide or murder is unresolved. A prominent young man named Hiram Johnson replaced Heney and won a conviction, and Ruef was sentenced to fourteen years, but he was later released after serving four years and seven months.

During these trials of the bribetakers the city's newspapers cheered Heney and company on. Throughout the state, demands that the criminals who had dominated San Francisco through the Union Labor party be brought to justice were repeatedly featured in the editorial pages. A large part of the "respectable elements" of the city joined in the chorus, but when Heney, Johnson, and Matt Sullivan turned their attention from the bribetakers to the bribers, the newspapers of the city and state changed their views on the trials. The very people who had thundered "justice must be done" in the case of Ruef and Schmitz began to see things in a different light.

Patrick Calhoun, president of United Railroads, was one of the first of the "socially prominent and propertied defendants" to be brought into court. Defended by a staff which included the best legal minds of California, including the famed Earl Rogers, perhaps the most gifted trial attorney to practice law west of the Mississippi, Calhoun's trial consumed more than five months. It ended with a deadlocked jury in the fall of 1908. A second trial was scheduled, but before a jury could be selected, Heney ran for district attorney of San Francisco. When he was defeated by an opponent running on a Republican-Union Labor party ticket, a great deal of steam went out of the effort to bring Calhoun to justice. Eventually the case was dropped, and further legal proceedings against Calhoun and other defendants ended.

The city had been through an unprecedented period. It all began when the Union Labor party elected Schmitz in 1901 and it came to a close at the end of the decade. Hundreds of indictments resulted in four convictions, three of which were reversed. The graft trials had been enlivened by a variety of miscellaneous developments ranging from the courtoom shooting of Heney, to his assailant's murder or suicide in the city jail; the death two weeks later—possibly by suicide, perhaps by accident—of the chief of police; the bombing of a key witness' home; the kidnapping of Fremont Older, champion of the prosecution; the disappearance of witnesses; jury tampering; concealment of material evidence; and the appearance in the dock of Patrick Calhoun, associate of J. P. Morgan, financier.

That something positive had been done in the form of removing from office some of the prominent grafters was doubtless true. On the other hand, little permanent improvement in San Francisco's political scene was noted. In the course of the five years that passed from the beginning to the end of the trials, public opinion had done an about-face, and people who once had clamored for quick justice were speaking out for "let's forget the whole business." Phelan and Spreckels were transformed in the press from public benefactors to capitalists who used the law to ruin business competitors, and Heney was even portrayed as a vindictive and ruthless troublemaker. But if little significant improvement could be seen in San Francisco, the trials made an impact on other parts of the state, and in the long run they contributed to the building of progressive sentiment in California that eventuated in a statewide movement to create a better political climate. The reign of the Political Bureau of the Southern Pacific had not ended, but the trials in San Francisco had graphically demonstrated the need for change. The men who would lead the forces for change were in large measure the supporters of Heney, Spreckels, and Phelan.

Los Angeles went through a similar period of turmoil and drama in the opening years of the twentieth century. Although the circumstances were strikingly different in many ways in the two cities, there were similarities as well, and the result was the swelling of

HARRISON GRAY OTIS

Probably the most influential man in Southern California during the generation which spanned the closing decades of the nineteenth century and the first twenty years of the twentieth century, Harrison Gray Otis was born in Marietta, Ohio, in 1837. A veteran of the Civil War, Otis came to Southern California and settled in Santa Barbara in 1876. For a short time he was unsuccessfully involved in newspaper publishing before becoming a special agent of the Treasury Department in 1879. His work took him to Alaska for several years. In 1882 he returned to Southern California, settled in Los Angeles, and acquired a part interest in a small weekly newspaper, the Los Angeles Times. By 1886 he had acquired control of it. Thereafter the paper became an extension of Otis, reflecting his values and views and his unrestrained optimism in the future growth and development of Southern California.

The collapse of the boom of the eighties drove many of Los Angeles' public figures into a slough of despair, but Otis never hedged on his bet that the city had a bright future. In 1888 he committed the Los Angeles chamber of commerce to a program of expansive publicity and for the rest of his life he was involved in making a reality of his vision of Los Angeles. He was a strong-willed man, who cherished the military titles he accumulated (he was breveted a general in the Spanish American War), collected knives and swords, and was accustomed to command rather than lead. Those who opposed Otis quickly came to understand that he was a formidable opponent.

When Otis' battle with organized labor began in 1890 there were few who understood that this was the beginning of a forty-year war which would shape in a basic way the future of Southern California. In the course of that war, Otis was the commanding general who not only reported the news of each battle, but marshaled and directed the armies of management. In 1910 the bombing of the Times building and the subsequent conviction of the McNamara brothers were the decisive events which heralded victory for General Otis. For the ensuing thirty years, Los Angeles was the citadel of the open shop, and the largest city in America relatively free of labor unions.

During the time between Otis' arrival in Los Angeles in 1882 and his death in 1917, his dreams for Southern California came to fruition. The city grew steadily in population and size, his newspaper came to tower over its rivals, and Otis' personal fortune, derived from the profits of publishing as well as investments in land and development, made him one of the wealthiest men in the community. The term "Otistown" was fastened on Los Angeles by his union labor opponents. In some respects it was an apt name, for Otis left an enduring mark on the city and on Southern California.

---

progressive ranks and progressive political influence. Before the denouement, the City of the Angels was to make a full contribution to the dethronement of the Political Bureau of the Southern Pacific and the birth of a period of honest politics in California.

For years there had been repeated attempts to curb the power of the Southern Pacific over the life and society of Southern Californians. A leading opponent of the railroad was Dr. John Randolph Haynes, an M.D. in ill health who had migrated to the land of the sun in 1887 and built a prosperous practice which included as a patient Harrison Gray Otis. When Haynes coupled the practice of medicine with oil investments, he quickly accumulated a large personal fortune. He also acquired a consuming interest in politics and government. That interest is presently reflected in the John Randolph and Dora Haynes Foundation, which he established to finance continuing research in social, political, and economic aspects of Southern California. As Haynes studied the political world of his time, he saw many evils and flaws and the fountainhead was the Political Bureau of the Southern Pacific, directed by Walter Parker. He felt that the solution was to place in the hands of the people direct control over their government. His prescription for the illness of democracy was more democracy.

To popularize his prescription, Dr. Haynes organized a Direct Legislation League in 1895. Essentially it was devoted to the adoption of initiative, referendum, and recall by local as well as state governments. Four years later San Francisco adopted some of its ideas, and in 1902 Los Angeles' new city charter included all three of the league's reforms. Thereafter one or more of them were used at periodic intervals, but progress was slow, and the Southern Pacific remained a powerful influence in the political life of Los Angeles in mid-decade. However, the reform organization was gathering its forces. A Good Government League brought the new-breed civic reformers together. Haynes was joined by Marshall Stimson, Russ Avery, Meyer Lissner, Edward A. Dickson, and Charles Dwight Willard. Bright, creative young men who were devoted to the objective of good government, they worked hard to win a major victory in the election of seventeen of their twenty-three-candidate slate in 1906.

This first great election victory was won in spite of the opposition of the Los Angeles *Times*, the Southern Pacific, and the labor unions, but it was not enough to give the reformers full control of the city government. Nevertheless, they proceeded with such changes as the elimination of the ward system and the adoption of non-partisanship in municipal elections. Mayor Arthur C. Harper co-operated at times, albeit reluctantly. A member of a distinguished and wealthy family, he led many people to believe that he was a man of integrity. In fact, he was a key member of an organization which had developed a way of collecting boodle in Los Angeles which was almost as foolproof as Abe Ruef's "payments for legal services" system. Harper and his associates organized a number of bogus corporations and then sold stock in the Pacific Sugar Company or the Utah-Los Angeles Oil Company to citizens who were interested in political favors or protection.

When this novel system was exposed, Harper's chances for re-election dropped, and when the Southern Pacific decided to support another candidate in view of the threatening political picture, the mayor dropped out of the 1909 race. This left the field to George Alexander, candidate of the reformers, and Fred Wheeler, a Socialist. Alexander won the election, but as Harrison Gray Otis and the *Times* noted, the reformers had so mismanaged things that the Socialist ran only sixteen hundred votes behind. Nevertheless, the "Goo-Goos," as the Good Government League reformers were called, were in command of the city government in 1910. Los Angeles and San Francisco alike were delivered from the iron grip which corrupt political machines had fastened on them. Other cities also came over into the ranks of the purified municipalities—Sacramento, Palo Alto, and Santa Barbara. But in spite of such changes in the cities, the Southern Pacific, now directed by the Harriman interests, was still firmly in control of the body politic of California—administering state government primarily in the interest of the railroad.

The men who had brought reform to Los Angeles and San Francisco were not inclined to sit on their laurels. The cities had been delivered, the state awaited. Reform was in the air. Throughout America Theodore Roosevelt and the muckrakers were joined in an uneasy and involuntary alliance against corruption and for reform. Men like Lincoln Steffens produced such studies as *Shame of the Cities* and exposed in pitiless detail the venality and corruption of city government in the United States, and newspaper editors like Charles Dwight Willard drew inspiration from the writings of the muckrakers and letters he exchanged with Theodore Roosevelt. Corruption and malfeasance were not confined to the city halls of California but on the contrary were found on all levels of government. Even before the liberations of the cities, the middle-class, urban, educated reformers who were the leaders of progressivism were organizing for a statewide operation. The fountainhead of corruption was still the Southern Pacific, which generally ran a bipartisan operation, although it was most frequently aligned with the Republican party. To break that alliance, to bring reforms to state government, to restore the rule of the people, and to end the domination of the Southern Pacific, the reformers turned their eyes to Sacramento.

That the state government was in need of the attention of the reformers was seen in a number of developments in the first decade of the twentieth century. The domination of the Southern Pacific was nearly complete. Walter Parker, director of the Southern Pacific Political Bureau, Southern California branch, sat in the assembly and directly looked after the interests of the railroad. Governor George C. Pardee had been the pliant tool of the railroad, selected by them in 1902. He had served the railroad well but outlived his usefulness after he helped to depose Senator Thomas R. Bard, the sturdy, conservative, and independent incumbent, for the Southern Pacific candidate, Frank P. Flint. Renomination was denied him in 1906 when the railroad chose Congressman James N. Gillett to replace him. It required a major effort to win his nomination over Pardee and election over Theodore A. Bell in a three-corner race which included William Langdon, former district attorney of San Francisco. However, the Union Labor party of Ruef and the Political Bureau of the Southern Pacific directed a successful campaign which met the challenge posed by Bell. In part the victory was due to the reluctance of a number of Progressive and anti-railroad papers to support the young and outspoken Progressive, Bell.

The legislature of 1907, dominated by the railroad interest, gave additional evidence of the need for reform. Expense allowances were increased, the payroll of the legislature padded—ten door-keepers in the house for four doors—and no reform legislation which adversely affected the interests of the railroad was considered. The railroad, content with the status quo, was not interested in change, and it fought off all challenges. When the legislature was adjourned, Progressives generally heaved a sigh of relief and then pledged anew their determination to end the domination of the state government by the Southern Pacific. A necessary first step was marshaling the opposition. Even while the legislature was meeting, plans were going forward, and shortly after it adjourned a group of reformers met in Los Angeles, drew up a program, and called for a summer meeting in Oakland where a permanent organization would be launched.

The Oakland conference brought together a small group of extremely talented men who gathered under the banner of the League of Lincoln-Roosevelt Republican Clubs. The fundamental objective was curbing the power of the railroad, although a platform of aims included such things as regulation of utility rates, a minimum-wage law, the vote for women, and a direct primary. Building on existing reform organization in Southern California, the Lincoln-Roosevelt Republicans went forth to do battle with the enemy. The first skirmishes in 1908 produced modest victories in Alameda and Oakland and promising portents in election victories in the fall which shook the Southern Pacific's machine.

The Political Bureau of the Southern Pacific still controlled the legislature which met in January 1909. It passed a number of reform bills including a primary law, which was a considerable improvement although not all the reformers wanted. Other measures which were proposed by the Lincoln-Roosevelt crowd were rejected out of hand. When the legislature adjourned, it was considered a sizable improvement over its predecessor but there was still much work to be done.

In November 1909 an Oakland conference of the Lincoln-Roosevelt League produced a plan for the coming election. The principal objective was to kick the Southern Pacific out of California politics; every other objective would be subordinated to this goal. At the same time, the California insurgents began to talk in terms of their role in a national party which would do battle with the stand-patters where they might be found. In January the search began for a gubernatorial candidate. Heney's name came up but the identification of the famed prosecutor of San Francisco as an extremist who was friendly to labor and an enemy of conservative interests made him unacceptable. The decision was eventually made to back Hiram Johnson, the battling son of a onetime stalwart of the railroad machine, Grove Johnson.

Reluctant to accept the nomination of the league, but determined to do whatever he could to win the nomination of the Republican party once he accepted, Johnson set out on a whirlwind, four-month campaign that took him into every part of California. Twenty thousand miles after he started he was the official Republican nominee. In the general election of 1910, Johnson competed with Theodore A. Bell, the Democratic standard-bearer of the preceding election. Both campaigned vigorously on anti-railroad and thoroughly Progressive platforms. Johnson won by a margin of 23,000 votes and promptly set out to bring about a realization of the Progressive platform. Four years after its founding, the Lincoln-Roosevelt League was in power in California. A series of post-election meetings in San Francisco began drafting constitutional amendments and legislative proposals for the forthcoming meeting of the Progressive-dominated legislature. While the opposition sniped, the assembled lawmakers enacted one of the most comprehensive reform programs that was ever passed by an American legislature.

Still convinced that the ills of democracy should be cured by more democracy, the Progressives brought initiative, referendum, recall, and the direct election of senators to the state political world. To the alarm of conservatives generally, over the opposition of some Progressives, and on the heels of a reversal by the Supreme Court of Abe Ruef's conviction, recall of judges was enacted into law. A new commission to regulate not only the railroads but all public service corporations except municipal utilities was established. A maximum workday of eight hours was established for women and a workman's compensation law became part of the code. To cap the work of reform, the legislature enacted several conservation acts, a resolution endorsing woman suffrage, a bill to provide free schoolbooks, and an act to improve the moral climate of the state by restrictions on slot machines. In all, the legislature passed more than eight hundred bills and twenty-three amendments to the constitution, nearly all of which were subsequently ratified by the electorate in the election of 1911.

When the lawmakers assembled in special session in the fall, they enacted a comprehensive law governing utilities which was described by Governor Johnson as a fitting end to the reform program of the Progressives, but when the lawmakers assembled in Sacramento in 1913, the work of reform continued under the zealous supervision of the governor. A state conservation commission was established, a new commissioner of corporations set up to safeguard the public from unscrupulous securities operations, pipelines were brought under the jurisdiction of the railroad commission, civil service was extended, and new measures for regulating wages, hours, and working conditions of women and children were enacted. To flesh out the program, an anti-usury law was passed and a pension system set up for schoolteachers as well as the aged. Criminal procedures were modified, a weights and measures bill was passed, and state budget reform was adopted.

In all this the Progressives had been guided by reason, and while they were assailed by their political enemies of both right and left, few could deny that the over-all impact of the program was the betterment of California. In one area the Progressives of California acted out of the blind and unreasoning racist hostility which was directed at the Japanese. A handful of Japanese residents in California owned several hundred farms. The Progressives were determined to restrain their numbers and if possible drive them out of the state. The device selected was the Heney-Webb bill, which restricted the right of Japanese to own or lease land. The anti-alien land law was purely racial in character (European corportions were not affected), and an exercise in demagogy that reflected little credit on the Progressives.

Even while the work of reform was proceeding, the divisions within the Progressive camp were increasing. Conservative members of the Johnson movement objected to such things as the recall of judges, and repesentatives of organized labor, distrustful of the Goo-Goos who had been unfriendly to their aspirations as members of the municipal government, complained of the failure of the Progressives to restrict the use of the anti-labor injunctions. They were divided as well by the ambitions of some of the more prominent members of the Progressive camp, and it became difficult to keep the movement together after their program had been enacted into law. The breach with Harrison Gray Otis had never been healed completely.

National politics also divided the ranks of the Progressives in California. In 1912, for example, when Theodore Roosevelt and Johnson ran on the Progressive ticket in a three-way race with the Democratic and Republican standard-bearers, the Progressives forced the Republicans to run on a write-in basis in California. Taft picked up a handful of votes; the Progressives captured eleven of the state's electoral votes and the undying enmity of the old guard Republicans, who thirsted for revenge. Four years later, when Republican presidential candidate Charles Evans Hughes campaigned in California, they saw their opportunity. From the time that he arrived until he departed, Hughes was closeted with representatives of the old guard who excluded Johnson and other Progressives. Johnson ran a separate and typically vigorous campaign for senator, doing little to bolster Hughes. When the votes were counted, Johnson had won a 300,000-vote victory, but Hughes lost the state by less than 4000 votes. To make the outcome in California especially galling, Hughes went to bed on election eve thinking he was the President-elect only to awaken in the morning to the shocking news that the returns from California and the Far West had thrown the race to Wilson. Republican regulars blamed Johnson personally although an objective analysis of the returns indicates that Hughes and his advisers were responsible for alienating a sizable number of voters in California, and for that matter in other parts of the nation as well. Meanwhile, Wilson put together a winning conglomerate which included independents, Socialists, and women, on a program of peace, prosperity, and progressive reform. Johnson and the Progressives received a similar combination of support in California.

There were other repercussions from the election. William D. Stephens agreed to run for lieutenant governor to strengthen the ticket with the understanding that Johnson would resign upon his election to the Senate so that Stephens could move up. After the election, Johnson delayed his resignation, whereupon some of Stephen's associates initiated legal action. Johnson, who once publicly excoriated a prominent opponent as "a creature who is vile, infamous, degraded, and putrescent," was apoplectic with rage. He refused adamantly to step down until the following March when Congress met. This was but one instance when the stubborn pride and conflicting ambitions of the Progressives were manifested.

Nevertheless the Progressives had made a contribution. They had literally transformed the political scene in California. Where once the Southern Pacific ruled arrogantly and in behalf of the railroad, a new order existed. Built upon the notion that the people would rule wisely if the reins were placed in their hands, the Progressive edifice stood. For more than a decade it dominated the state. It brought integrity and intelligence to the governance of California and even as it receded into oblivion, it left a heritage which lingered. In California the Progressives under Johnson had combined idealism with hard, cold, practical politics. Among the more successful of the men who led the movement was Hiram Johnson, who remained a national figure until the close of World War II. Earl Warren always looked upon him as a giant figure of California political history. In many ways, California and Californians of today are indebted to him and to his associates who dared to challenge a formidable locus of political power and went on to "kick the Southern Pacific out of politics."

CHAPTER XVI

The Labor Story

By the turn of the century, organized labor walked tall in San Francisco. Its heritage stretched back to the gold rush, when draymen, dock workers, and printers organized the first unions on the Pacific coast. From that time onward, as the city grew, organized labor played a prominent role. While it suffered its share of defeats, by the close of the nineteenth century labor was a major force. In fact, in terms of numbers and influence, organized labor was as strong in San Francisco as it was in any city of the United States.

The situation was far different in Los Angeles. There, no traditions dating back to the gold rush sustained the organized labor movement. On the contrary, labor came late to the scene and its arrival coincided with the appearance of social forces which were antagonistic to its growth. As the area was transformed from a ranching and pastoral economy by thousands of newcomers, the result was hardly conducive to the growth of labor unions. A great many of the new arrivals were interested in small farms, many were retired, some were invalids interested in the medical panacea of sunshine. All contributed toward building a stock of surplus labor and this in turn tended to keep wages low. Wage rates which ranged as much as 40 per cent lower than those prevailing in San Francisco characterized the Southern California labor market. And of course the continuing influx of newcomers, indifferent and sometimes hostile to unions, tended to keep the labor pool full and perpetuate the situation.

As influential as any social force in curbing the growth of labor was Harrison Gray Otis, who came on the scene in the 1880s and for the next forty years cast a giant shadow. Otis was many things in the course of his career: a soldier in the Union Army, a newspaper publisher, clerk of the Ohio House of Representatives, a printer in the Government Printing Office, and onetime editor of the *Journal* of the Grand Army of the Republic. Just before he came to Los Angeles he was also a special agent of the United States Treasury Department who safeguarded seals in Alaska against poachers. On arrival in Los Angeles he acquired a quarter interest in a struggling weekly newspaper called the Los Angeles *Times*.

To his admirers and emulators, Otis in his heyday was the courageous leader of the forces of law and order against the "criminal union scum" who used the boycott and bomb. To others he was a benighted and backward champion of predatory capital, a "surly old swill dispenser." While there were differences in the descriptions of Otis, all understood that he was the unyielding, determined, and enduring foe of organized labor. Since he combined implacable determination with power, Otis came close to being a social force himself, a force which molded his times and shaped the future of Southern California.

Otis' forty-year war with the unions began as the last decade of the century opened. That final decade was a period of general industrial discontent and upheaval marked by great contests between capital and labor. The first of these, at Homestead, Pennsylvania, in 1892, scarcely touched Los Angeles but the second, the great Pullman strike of 1894, brought pickets and strikers into the city's streets and disorder that brought federal troops into action. In this strike, a boycott by the National Railway Union of Pullman cars brought most of the railroads of northern and western America to a standstill. Scores of freight carloads of fruit and vegetables spoiled on sidings and underscored for Otis and his followers the need for curbing the power of labor. To Otis' chagrin, during the strike cordons of pickets circled the *Times* building, intimidated the carriers and destroyed every copy of the paper they could find. Otis needed no convincing, for his own war with labor began several years before in 1890 when the printers of Los Angeles denounced a proposed wage cut of 20 per cent and went on strike. Other publishers came to an agreement with the striking union, but days, weeks, and then months passed without a settlement by the *Times*.

Otis' stubborn resistance was somewhat surprising, for he had been a union printer himself. As the contest continued, positions hardened, and rhetoric of labor and management alike changed. What had begun as another contest of wills became the opening battle in a campaign, and what became a campaign was transformed into a forty-year war of capital and labor. At first a local matter, it became statewide and finally a matter of national importance. The International Typographical Union was one of the oldest of American unions and printers had been one of the first of the trades to organize in California. Tempered in a hundred battles with recalcitrant employers, the ITU was a formidable opponent.

But Otis too was tempered. A onetime Union Army private who had clawed his way to the military eminence of a captaincy during the course of the Civil War, Otis had never asked quarter of any man in any fight in his life. And not having asked, he was equally reluctant to give. Battles were not to be avoided but won; enemies were not to be forgiven but beaten. These were the fighting principles of Otis, the champion of "industrial freedom," as he designated life free of unions. From the beginning in the spring of 1890 Otis marshaled his forces and struck back at the men who had the effrontery to tell him what wages to pay and which men to employ. To counter union strength which arose out of joining and working together, Otis organized employers into the next thing to an employers' union, a Merchants and Manufacturers Association.

Having mobilized his troops, General Otis turned to tactics. To counter the union boycott, which cost the *Times* dearly in advertising and circulation, Otis organized a counterboycott in which employers who were not boycotted by the unions were boycotted by the M and M. Among other curious results, which testified to the effectiveness of the M and M boycott, was a court case in which an employer sought to have a court order his name stricken from the "fair" list of organized labor. To ensure the impact of his legions, Otis policed the ranks of the M and M, encouraging those who exhibited signs of weakness and stiffening the backbones of those who thought in terms of negotiations with the unions. If persuasion could not keep a member in line then he was threatened with loss of credit or sales. Most were persuaded, some were coerced.

The battle came at a time when American labor and the American economy were being transformed by the industrialization of American society. Those who clung to the past and blindly opposed the organization of labor unions were grappling with powerful social and economic forces. Inadvertently those who opposed labor spurred the growth of other organizations which sought to alleviate some of the ills of the modern era. Industrialization and class strife brought in its wake a sharp rise in the utopian socialism of Bellamy's *Looking Backward* as well as a sharp rise in the Americanized socialism of Eugene Debs. The Socialist party in Los Angeles and Southern California grew in numbers and influence. In the absence of a system of mediation and arbitration as well as a means for collective bargaining, each battle between capital and labor was a contest of wills determined by raw power.

In San Francisco, the growth of the labor movement continued. Not only did it survive a series of great strikes in the first years of the twentieth century, but when it turned to political action via a Union Labor party, it made further gains. Eugene Schmitz, union musician, came to sit in the mayor's chair and eventually the Curly Boss, Abraham Ruef, obtained complete control of the government for himself and the labor movement. Even the fire and earthquake inflicted but minor damage to the edifice that Ruef built, although the revelations of the graft trials eventuated in the trial and conviction of a number of Union Labor party leaders. But Union Labor continued to loom large in the city. Soon after Schmitz and Ruef were deposed, Patrick "Pinhead" Henry McCarthy, president of the Buildings Trades Council, took over the reins of power. The net result was great power for the leaders of organized labor and wages and working conditions which made the union laborer in San Francisco the envy of his counterpart in Los Angeles, Portland, and Seattle.

But of course such wage levels put San Francisco employers at a competitive disadvantage with their counterparts in Los Angeles and other cities. They grumbled from time to time and about the close of the first decade of the twentieth century, they decided that something would have to be done to bring labor costs in San Francisco into line with those prevailing in other cities. The stage was set for one of the more violent episodes in California labor history when the employers of San Francisco flatly declared that they could not continue to pay wages that averaged 30 to 40 per cent higher than those of their Los Angeles competitors. If organized labor didn't do something to bring wages in the two cities into line, management in San Francisco would do the job by cutting wages back to the Los Angeles level. Faced with this ultimatum, organized labor in San Francisco turned their attention to "Otistown."

The International Typographical Union, at war with Otis since 1890, had previously sought and secured assistance from San Francisco. In 1907, for example, they successfully focused the attention of the national AFL on the Los Angeles situation and secured a commitment for assistance in the battle against the *Times*. About the same time, the labor movement purchased a newspaper, renamed it the *Citizen*, and used its columns to vent its hostility to Otis. The *Times* smarted from such verbal blasts and a local and national boycott of the newspaper and its advertisers. It fought back, and Otis became more convinced than ever that he was the leader of a great crusade to preserve "industrial freedom."

As the decade came to a close, new forces and allies were entering the fight. By 1910 the Socialist movement and the labor movement were working in friendly harmony in Los Angeles. One of the newer unions, the Structural Iron Workers Union, born in 1896, also entered the battle. Men who made a precarious living in the erection of the steel framework of the new architectural form, the skyscraper, iron erectors were usually itinerant workmen who followed a rough and hazardous trade from job to job. They were tough men who spoke with their fists and when they deemed it necessary, they were not above the use of violence to achieve their ends.

Their goal in 1910 in Los Angeles was a labor movement which had strength and purpose enough to bring them the hours, wages, and working conditions which prevailed in San Francisco. To this end they went on strike in 1910, separately and in concert with brewery workers, butchers, and other metalworkers. The City of the Angels was transformed almost immediately into an arena. Strikebreakers were recruited locally as well as imported from out of state. A city anti-picketing ordinance and injunctions secured from compliant courts forbidding picketing frustrated and restrained the unions. Hundreds of men were arrested for violating the injunctions and ordinance, scores were convicted and fined but when jury trials were instituted, many of those arrested were promptly acquitted by their peers. It was a most significant development since it revealed that there was public sympathy for the strikers.

There were other portents of trouble for Otis and the M and M. Membership in the Socialist party and the circulation of its publication, *Appeal to Reason*, climbed sharply. Moreover a new political organization called the Union Labor party began to organize clubs in Los Angeles. The political milieu of the city had recently been reshaped by Dr. John Randolph Haynes and the Good Government League. A new charter provided such things as initiative, referendum, and recall which democratized the municipal government and provided opportunity to the new party of labor.

The battle continued on the dark and bloody ground of Los Angeles during the spring and summer of 1910. Labor fought with their traditional weapons of strike, picketing, and boycott. There was much violence in clashes between non-strikers and pickets and police and strikers. Even more violent means were in the offing. The ironworkers had long looked upon dynamite as a legitimate weapon to use against recalcitrant employers. A blast that leveled a factory, a half-completed building or bridge was oftentimes most persuasive. Leaders who denounced the "soft, womanly, political action policies" of the Socialists had their own version of Theodore Roosevelt's "Speak softly and carry a big stick."

Complicating the confused capital-labor strife picture was a campaign for mayor of Los Angeles. The incumbent, George Alexander, re-elected following the recall of his scandal-tinged predecessor and the preferred candidate of the Good Government League, came out of the primary election trailing Job Harriman, a young attorney and organizer of the Socialist party. The consternation of Otis and other conservatives was unbridled when the primary results became known. Here in the capital city of his dreams came an apparition to haunt General Otis: Job Harriman, attorney of the labor bosses and chief organizer of the Socialist party, mayor of Los Angeles! It was almost enough to compel Otis to seek terms with the enemy.

But Otis did not seek terms. Instead he mobilized his resources behind Alexander. Joined in an uneasy alliance with his old enemies in the Good Goverment League, the publisher of the *Times* described the future if the battle were lost: "All decent people must rally around the flag of industrial liberty in this crisis, when the welfare of the whole city is at stake. If the San Francisco gorillas succeed, then the brilliant future of Los Angeles will end, business will stagnate; Los Angeles will be another San Francisco—dead."

The blow which Otis and a number of others feared came shortly after 1 A.M., October 1, 1910, when a deafening explosion ripped through the *Times* building. About a hundred people were in the building putting the morning edition of the paper to bed. Twenty paid with their lives in the explosion and fire which followed. Less than a score of those in the building escaped uninjured. The building itself was reduced to a smoldering pile of ruins.

Otis, in Mexico at the time of the explosion, came back to thunder: "O you anarchic scum, you cowardly murderers, you leeches upon honest labor, you midnight assassins, you whose hands are dripping with the innocent blood of your victims . . ." for openers. The first post-explosion issue of his paper carried a banner headline: "Unionist Bombs Wreck the *Times*." Before long some $300,000 in rewards was offered for the apprehension of the bombers. While General Otis had a full share of sympathizers, there were a considerable number of people who said no rewards would ever be paid, for the *Times* building had not been bombed but had been demolished by an explosion of escaping gas. If there was a criminal involved it was Harrison Gray Otis, who had worked his employees in a deathtrap.

A number of investigations followed. The police, a mayor's committee, the grand jury, and the city council agreed that the building had been dynamited and the gas set afire by the explosion. The labor council conducted its own investigation and came to quite different conclusions. Job Harriman reported that the building was demolished by a gas explosion. To support that conclusion, he presented a number of allegations which ranged from the fact that for weeks there had been problems with the gas system which sickened employees in the building, to the pattern of damage which was not characteristic of a dynamite explosion. The people of Southern California accepted or rejected the reports of the investigators according to their feelings about the *Times* and organized labor.

Some seven months after the explosion, three active figures of the labor movement, Ortie McManigal, John J. McNamara, Secretary of the Iron Workers Union, and his brother, J. B. McNamara, were arrested and returned to Los Angeles for trial. Tracked down after a nationwide manhunt by the famous William J. Burns detective agency, the trio had been seized and returned to Los Angeles under quite irregular circumstances. Organized labor charged immediately that they had been kidnapped as the first step in a replay of the 1907 notorious attempted frame-up of a group of leaders of the Western Federation of Miners. Labor leaders denounced the "corporate interests" who were responsible and the American Federation of Labor issued an official appeal for funds to defend "these victims of another conspiracy to fasten the crime of murder on the labor union officials to discredit and destroy organized labor in the United States."

Labor was determined to spare no expense. Clarence Darrow, the most renowned trial attorney of the day, was retained to defend the McNamaras. A huge defense fund was made available and a staff of investigators and attorneys to assist Darrow was hired. Job Harriman, odds-on favorite to win the current mayoralty election, assisted Darrow and thereby in the public mind became completely identified with the McNamaras. AFL president Samuel Gompers came to Los Angeles, visited the McNamaras, called for the election of the "people's candidate," Harriman, and left no doubt in anyone's mind that the McNamaras were labor's own. On Labor Day thousands marched in Los Angeles beneath banners which denounced Otis and the "McNamara Frame-up" and acclaimed Harriman. Meanwhile, the circulation of the Socialist newspaper, *Appeal to Reason*, in Los Angeles began to rival that of the *Times* itself.

Defending the McNamaras in the court of public opinion was easier than defending them in a court of law. The general citizenry of Southern California included large numbers of people who believed that they were the victims of a frame-up. They accepted uncritically and enthusiastically every statement that reinforced their basic beliefs. However, the case against the McNamaras was based upon some hard evidence which included a confession of Ortie McManigal. An unfriendly judge and a determined district attorney combined with the evidence to reduce the McNamaras' chances of acquittal. The prosecution went beyond normal bounds which governed their behavior by planting spies on Darrow's staff and dictaphones in his rooms.

The denouement came as a great shock to the friends and allies of labor when the McNamara brothers through their attorneys made a deal with the prosecution under which they confessed in exchange for promises that their lives would be spared. Lincoln Steffens, prominent muckraking journalist, played a role in the affair by hammering out the agreement and bringing together a diverse group of prominent businessmen which included Otis as well as a number of Progressives. Under it, J. B. McNamara pleaded guilty to the dynamiting of the *Times* building and John J. McNamara to the bombing of the Llewellyn Iron Works. John J. was sentenced to fifteen years, his brother to life imprisonment. McManigal, the prosecution's star witness, went off to Honduras to live for a time under an assumed name. He later became a watchman in the Los Angeles Hall of Records, where he found security and obscurity until his retirement in 1944.

The confession came just four days before the election. Its immediate result was the defeat of Job Harriman, the Socialist who was expected to win the mayoralty of Los Angeles. His complete identification with the McNamaras cost him dearly. Outraged supporters littered the streets with discarded Harriman buttons and banners and became so threatening that the candidate literally fled his campaign headquarters. The Socialist party, which had been growing spectacularly, its newspaper challenging the *Times* for circulation, went into eclipse. Otis for a time slept easier, his dreams no longer troubled by the prospect of a Socialist mayor presiding over Los Angeles.

Clarence Darrow was discredited. Some of his closest friends held him responsible for the sorry outcome and it was charged that he had pled his clients guilty in order to escape the consequences of a jury-bribing charge that the district attorney had brought against him. Darrow later said the deal was made because "I have known for months that our fight was hopeless." He had made the best settlement that was possible and "we did not wait for the consent of any of the labor leaders or others interested in the defense." Among those kept in the dark was Harriman. While Darrow subsequently went on to other great triumphs as a trial attorney, the impact of the McNamara case left an indelible impression on him. Lincoln Steffens acted as a catalyst in working out the arrangements under which the case was resolved. He was convinced that it was essential for the men gathered around Otis to put their bitterness behind them and usher in a period of peace by working out a modus vivendi with labor. He thought he had a commitment from the figures involved to follow up the settlement with a conference of all the parties involved but the conference never took place and the period of harmony never began.

The cause of organized labor in Southern California was set back a generation. From a promising beginning when the Socialist party and the AFL in Los Angeles combined to work for common objectives, came a long period of stagnation. The countervailing power of organized labor, which was present in most American cities in the twentieth century, was conspicuously absent in Los Angeles. Consequently, the city was a community unbalanced in structure and dominated by combinations of capital bent on the unbridled exploitation of its labor and resources. Wage scales lagged in the city, where chamber of commerce advertisements to prospective industrialists emphasized that "cheap non-union labor is plentiful." It was not until the late 1930s that the organized labor movement of Los Angeles earned a respectable place in the sun.

There were a number of unresolved angles to the McNamara case. Since the evidence was never presented in a court of law, there are still questions about the completeness of the case as well as how the evidence was assembled. There are as well contradictions between the various versions of the planting of the bomb as it was described in the McNamara confession and in published accounts. In 1929, the *Times* declared "only six men know all the facts and they have guarded the secret well."

LABOR CONFLICT IN FIELD AND FOREST

About the same time that new forms, organizations, methods, and militancy came to the fore in labor-capital conflict in the cities, similar changes came to the countryside of California. The new organization, the Industrial Workers of the World, was an anarchosyndicalist-oriented radical group which was born in Chicago in 1906. Its founders, a diverse group of radicals, included several academics, many figures from organized labor, Eugene Debs, and "Big Bill" Haywood. The preamble of their constitution boldly announced: "The army of production must be organized, not only for the everyday struggle with capitalists, but also to carry on production when capitalism shall have been overthrown. By organizing industrially we are forming the structure of the new society within the shell of the old." Denounced by the established order of the American Federation of Labor, the "Wobblies" went forth to organize the proletariat of factory and field into one big union against the time when a series of strikes would merge into a general strike and force the capitulation of the capitalists.

In its first ten years, which coincided with a national upsurge in radicalism, the IWW became a powerful force although its membership never exceeded 100,000, less than 5 per cent of the total trade unionists in the United States. The turnover in its membership was very high, frequently more than 100 per cent a year, so that as many as one million workers held red cards at one time or another. Its influence was not determined by numbers alone but reflected a matrix of factors. It molded its times because it concentrated on organizing the unskilled, foreign-born, unwanted, poorest and weakest, "submerged fifty" of the working class. This field of much promise was neglected by the AFL. The IWW also included in its ranks the most articulate and resourceful of labor organizers of the time, men and women who often possessed more courage than discretion and needed much convincing before they would agree that they were unwanted, unneeded, or beaten.

They were also influential beyond their numbers, because their tactics included civil disobedience long before Gandhi or Martin Luther King, Jr., came along. They understood that the resources of a local establishment might not be sufficient to withstand a challenge provided a determined band of dissenters could be assembled. A number of communities in the West were the scenes of conflict between the IWW and its opponents. Several of the most notable encounters took place in California, although IWW state membership leveled off at five thousand, about 8 per cent of the farm labor force.

The Wobblies invaded California in force in the decade that followed their founding convention. They came to organize in the lumber camps, on the docks, in the mines, and above all in the fields. Seamen, lumberjacks, fishermen, hard-hat miners, and bindle stiffs, as single migratory farm workers were called, long neglected by the AFL responded to the rhetoric of the Wobbly organizers. They also joined in increasing numbers and became practitioners of the Wobbly approach to labor disputes. "Direct action" was a catch phrase which described the essence of their approach. It meant organization of the workers involved, marshaling their forces, and then hitting the employer with a strike. The aim was to shut the plant down, win concession in the form of wages or improved working conditions, and educate the rank and file in the ways of class warfare. Direct action also meant "striking on the job that is working slowly or inefficiently, hitting the employer in the most sensitive part of his anatomy—his pocketbook. Wobblies disdained the "soft" unionism of Gompers and its emphasis on boycott and appeals to the good nature of employers. "One must not supplicate but demand, one gets not justice but what one can command."

However, they had other tactics and weapons. When the authorities in Fresno in 1910 attempted to restrain Wobbly activities focused on the organization of orchard workers by prohibiting meetings and street corner soapbox oratory, the IWW responded by bringing hundreds of members from all parts of the West. They courted arrest. The authorities accommodated them readily at first but with increasing reluctance as the jail was filled. The prisoners were a difficult lot who propagandized their fellow inmates and guards and sang songs of revolutionary defiance. A bread and water diet failed to curb their enthusiasm. When fire hoses were brought into use to "drown" out the strains of revolutionary songs, the Wobblies took mattresses to shield themselves from the streams and sang louder. The city authorities desperately sought for a way to let go of the tail of the Fresno Wobblies, whose ranks were swollen with new reinforcements. Despite the opposition of the city's press, the mayor lifted the ban on public meetings in March 1911. Shortly thereafter prisoners were released from the jail in small groups and encouraged to depart. They went their way, emboldened by the victory that their new tactics had won.

Similar encounters between IWW organizers and local authorities took place in a score of towns and cities in the West to be exact twenty-six. San Diego was the site of a second California battle for free speech in 1912. It began in 1911 when an ordinance, No. 4660, was passed banning demonstrations and street corner soapboxing shortly after the McNamara brothers had been arrested for the bombing of the *Times*. This blanket injunction antagonized not only IWW spokesmen but representatives of the Socialist party, labor unions, and single taxers. As the battle continued, other groups entered the lists. Vigilantes appeared, threatening and intimidating sympathizers of the free speech campaign. Before long something more than intimidation was used. The Wobblies mobilized members from all parts of the state and turned to the tactics which had won victory in Fresno. The objective was to overwhelm the local police and judicial system by courting arrest and demanding separate trials. Before long the jails were bulging with guests who strained the budget and pushed the city toward bankruptcy.

Fresno authorities had been unable to cope with such problems but the power elite of San Diego found an effective expedient by turning prisoners over to a vigilante committee. Unrestrained by such legal concepts as fair trial and the like, the vigilantes took their prisoners, made them kneel and kiss the American flag, marched them considerable distances to the track, which led northward, and forced them to run a gauntlet of vigilantes armed with clubs and whips. The city's press applauded, aside from one courageous editor who was himself kidnapped and threatened with like treatment if he didn't end his support of the free speech movement.

The reports which reached Governor Hiram Johnson indicated that the situation threatened to get completely out of hand. He sent an official investigator who reported that the respectable businessmen of the city were working hand in glove with the vigilantes and the latter were acting as an auxiliary of the police. The rights of the protesters had been violated on a wholesale scale. The governor supported the work of his investigator and tried to mitigate the violence in the sun at San Diego. The battle did not end in the clear-cut victory which came out of the encounter in Fresno, although a considerable number of people in San Diego, sickened with what was being done in the name of "law and order," quietly forced a change on the city's authorities. When Emma Goldman, a noted anarchist who had been deported from San Diego in 1912, returned in 1915, she was unmolested although she delivered a series of lectures on such objectionable topics as anarchism, birth control, and the like.

The Wobblies who were veterans of Fresno and San Diego were bloody but unbowed, and ready for further tests. The next battle came at Wheatland in the summer of 1913. On a hop ranch owned by the Durst family, largest employers of agricultural labor in the state, several thousand hop pickers were assembled in blazing heat to labor for up to a dollar a day. There were more pickers than hops, a deliberate imbalance created to keep wages at a minimum. Piece rates were set daily, downward when pickers were plentiful. The workers patronized a company store where they were gouged, purchased "lemonade" from a vendor who was a member of the Durst family, and lived in a filthy collection of tents rented from Durst which had inadequate water wells to serve scores of families and the most primitive of toilet accommodations, nine to serve 2800 people. A hot spell which drove the thermometer to 105° in the afternoon made work in the fields a living hell.

The heat, exploitation, and hopelessness combined to produce rising resentment. A dozen IWW members, some veterans of Fresno and San Diego, began the work of building a local. A few days later they called a meeting for the obvious purpose of organizing to better their wages and conditions, if necessary by strike action. Toward the close of the meeting the district attorney, who also served as Durst's private attorney, showed up, accompanied by the sheriff and a posse. When a deputy fired a shotgun in the air to "sober the mob," a riot began and before the shooting and fighting ended, the sheriff and district attorney and two workers lay dead in the dust. Dozens more were wounded and injured.

Before the last echoes of the shots had died away, a general exodus from the camp began, the workers fleeing in every direction and in every feasible way "from the spontaneous, unpremeditated explosion." The National Guard was called out to patrol Wheatland while a general manhunt for the members of the camp began. Scores of bindle stiffs, many of them IWW members, were rounded up in widely scattered parts of the state but the "ringleaders" of the IWW local at Wheatland, Herman Suhr and Blackie Ford, initially eluded capture. Suhr was taken in Arizona and without the niceties of legal extradition shipped back to California. Here some eight months after they had attempted to organize to better the working and living conditions of an exploited and friendless group of migrant pickers, they were tried on homicide charges. Suhr, who left the camp before the riot took place, was convicted with Ford and both were sentenced to life imprisonment although no one testified that either had lifted his hand in anger. In fact, both consistently advised against violence. They remained in prison for years, martyrs to labor's cause although many from the organized labor movement in the country turned their backs on these organizers of the bindle stiffs.

An immediate result of Wheatland was the investigation conducted by the Commission on Immigration and Housing, which publicized not only the spontaneous revolt on Durst's ranch, but the deplorable conditions under which the 75,000 migratory farm workers of California lived. Headed by Simon J. Lubin, the commission made strenuous attempts to paint a realistic picture of the life and times of the bindle stiffs of California, more than half of whom were aliens from more than a score of nations. Provided with irregular employment at miserable wages, they wandered about the countryside, exploited and friendless until the Wobblies took up their cause. And even after the publicity attendant to the Wheatland riot and the reports of the commission, their lot was basically unchanged. Commission reports had limited effect. The IWW continued to operate, even growing sharply in numbers and influence.

In San Francisco during the winter of 1914, a short-lived army built of migrants wintered in the city. Organized into military companies by a "General Kelley," they became increasingly menacing with their demands on the city's authorities for adequate relief. Encouraged to leave San Francisco for a march on Sacramento, they left by ferries for Oakland, where they were also "welcomed" and encouraged to leave for Sacramento. At the capital they were met by an army of eight hundred special deputy sheriffs. Kelley's "army" was driven out of its encampment by brute force. None were allowed to return even to reclaim their miserable packs, and in a matter of days, the army, wet, hungry, and forlorn, slipped into oblivion.

FRAME-UP

The next great episode involving the radical figures of labor came during the prologue to American participation in the "war to end wars and make the world safe for democracy." A vast upsurge of patriotism came as the nation marched toward entrance. Civic and political leaders in major cities whipped up public sentiment for the inevitable by staging parades and exercises which supported "preparedness," that is, getting the United States in the proper posture for war. In Los Angeles, getting ready for a foreign war brought an armistice to the war between capital and labor and a growing tolerance for unions. In San Francisco, on the other hand, preparedness entailed further restrictions on the power of unions. The anti-war sentiments of a number of northern California labor radicals may have been partially responsible.

Labor had taken a series of setbacks since its heyday when Ruef and Schmitz ruled the city and hardly a wheel turned without labor's sanction. Labor's hold on the city government was broken in 1912. Some labor leaders took their lumps as a result of their identification with the McNamara brothers and at least one, O. A. Tveitmoe, went to jail, as a result of his involvement in the "dynamite conspiracy." The executives of a number of utility companies pressed their advantage and cowed some labor leaders. The more left and more militant arm of labor, which included an articulate and energetic organizer named Thomas J. Mooney, became more defiant.

The denouement came on July 22, 1916, when a Preparedness Day parade in San Francisco was bombed. The toll was ten dead and two score wounded. To the great leaders of commerce and industry, there was little doubt that the radicals were responsible, and it was equally certain to them that Thomas J. Mooney was involved. An associate of anarchists in philosophy and deed, vehemently anti-war, Mooney had been tried but acquitted on several occasions for dynamiting the property of utility companies. He was, to the corporate interests, almost an ideal defendant, an outspoken, young, radical "Don Quixote" who had fruitlessly challenged the power of the United Railroads in 1916 by trying to organize the underpaid carmen. Five days after the bombing, Mooney, his wife, Warren K. Billings, and two friends were arrested. Charles M. Fickert, the district attorney, long known for his antipathy to unions and radicalism, mobilized the resources of his office to prove that Mooney and Billings and their associates were responsible.

Billings was tried first, convicted, and sentenced to life imprisonment after a parade of witnesses testified that he had placed a suitcase against a wall a short time before the explosion. Mooney was also there, his presence fixed by the testimony which had the two men conferring at the scene. However, when Mooney was tried in early 1917 photographs were produced which showed by a clock in the background that Mooney had been a mile from the scene of the explosion when the witnesses in the Billings trial fixed his presence at the scene. That problem was met by having the witnesses change their story. A new witness was produced who also testified that Mooney had been on the scene, driven there in a taxi. Furthermore, he produced the license number of the vehicle and it proved to be that of one of the accused. Mooney was convicted and sentenced to death but his wife, the taxi driver, and a third defendant were subsequently acquitted or discharged for lack of evidence.

From the first, large numbers of labor people believed that Mooney had been framed, and they mobilized, first for a new trial, then clemency, and finally a pardon. In the course of the effort for Billings and Mooney it was proven beyond a shadow of a doubt that they had been convicted by perjured testimony and fabricated evidence. The most impressive witness of the Mooney trial who had provided the license number was in fact almost 200 miles away when the explosion took place and letters in which he acknowledged his perjury were revealed. It was also shown that the prosecution had used some highly unprofessional methods to swear away the freedom of Billings and the life of Mooney.

President Woodrow Wilson successfully sought commutation of Mooney's sentence to life imprisonment for fear of the worldwide reaction which would follow execution, but the two men languished in prison. The trial judge and the jury sought to redress the crime in which they had participated and even the staff of the prosecution became belated allies of the two men, but every effort to secure a reversal or new trial met with defeat. Every California governor for the next twenty years considered the Mooney case, but none took action until Governor Culbert L. Olson in January 1939. Mooney was given an outright pardon and Billings, "a second offender" who could not be pardoned, had his sentence commuted to time served. The two men who entered prison as young adults and emerged in late maturity went their separate ways, two symbols of the injustice which can be visited upon men when those sworn to uphold the law instead manipulate the machinery of justice to their ends.

DECLINE OF THE WOBBLIES AND ORGANIZED LABOR

The Wobblies continued to operate in the fields and forests of California during the decade which followed Wheatland. After their 1914 convention, they turned increasingly to the more orthodox forms and methods of trade unions. The Agricultural Workers Organization launched an organizing drive in the Midwest wheat belt that drove the membership of the IWW upward to nearly 100,000 in 1917. The success of the AWO led to similar efforts among the lumbermen, the construction and road-building crews, maritime workers, and miners. On the eve of the war, the IWW was achieving a degree of respectability and stability. It had major representation in a number of places in the nation, virtually controlled the Philadelphia waterfront for example, and was bringing the benefits of industrial unionism, despised by the AFL, to the underprivileged workers of the United States. Once determined to go it alone, it now reached out a fraternal hand to other organizations and whereas once it despised collective bargaining agreements, it now signed dozens of such agreements.

The wartime years were to bring a halt to this spectacular growth and a precipitous decline in the membership of the IWW. Its identification with militant opposition to the war was partially responsible. The organization never officially took such a position, but it was convicted by the public media. The full force of the federal government came down on the Wobblies in September 1917 when 165 leaders of the IWW were indicted and charged with conspiracy to "prevent, hinder, or delay the execution of" acts related to the prosecution of the war. In the trial in Chicago, the prosecutor stated at the outset that "It is the IWW which is on trial here." Five months later, after a million words of testimony had been heard, the jury required less than an hour to find 101 defendants guilty. It was a body blow for the IWW, for almost its entire leadership was lost.

In the summer of 1918, Sacramento, California, was the scene of a great conspiracy trial of forty-six IWW members, arrested and held for as long as thirteen months preceding trial. Defense efforts were hampered in a variety of unusual ways. Federal agents raided local defense headquarters seven times in six months, seizing all records and papers. A secretary of one of the committees was arrested and held incommunicado for eight months and another individual who came to the jail to post bail for several prisoners was herself arrested, subjected to the medical examination reserved for prostitutes, and subsequently indicted. Most of the defendants refused to take part in the proceedings. Their "silent defense" based on their stated belief that they would inevitably be found guilty had a ring of prophecy when the trial ended with guilty verdicts for all forty-six defendants. The guilty verdicts came in spite of the fact that the evidence was decidedly circumstantial. Twenty-four were sentenced to ten years, others received from one to five years in the state prison.

The trial had been a showcase proceeding in which the objective was to show the lawless character of the IWW and the need for new legislation to deal with it. The new statute, enacted in 1919, was a criminal syndicalism law. Twenty-three other states copied the California model in the next few years. This law defined the new crime of criminal syndicalism as "any doctrine or precept advocating, teaching or aiding and abetting the commission of crime, sabotage . . . or unlawful acts of force or violence or unlawful methods of terrorism as a means of accomplishing a change in industrial ownership or control, or effecting any political change." Guilt was attached to doing, advocating, or belonging to an organization that advocated such politics and penalties of up to fourteen years were provided. In the next five years, more than 500 arrests were made on criminal syndicalism charges in California and 164 Wobblies were sentenced to long terms in prison. Professional witnesses, two of whom learned their craft in the Sacramento trial, practiced it in one case after another.

The statute proved to be an effective cudgel against the IWW. The Russian Revolution precipitated a national paranoia about Bolshevism which intensified anti-radicalism sentiment generally. In the year of the Armistice, United States Attorney General A. Mitchell Palmer launched nationwide raids which rounded up thousands of people and deported hundreds of foreign-born radicals and their sympathizers. Substantial numbers of IWW members were caught up, but it was the criminal syndicalism law which struck effectively at broad segments of the liberal and radical movement in America. The act was used to indict Anita Whitney, whose Socialist convictions led her to involvement with the founding convention of the Communist party in Oakland in 1919. There she spoke out for reform through the ballot and against revolutionary activities, but a short time later she was indicted under the criminal syndicalism act for associating with a group which advocated, taught, or aided and abetted criminal syndicalism. Appeals took the case to the Supreme Court, where the justices decided by a split vote to affirm the decision. Whether any of them knew that she was the niece of Stephen J. Field, appointed to the Supreme Court by Lincoln, is unknown. Governor C. C. Young intervened at this point, declared it was unthinkable that a woman like Anita Whitney should be confined to a prison, and pardoned her.

The criminal syndicalism act was also used in other settings. Thus, when a waterfront strike led by the IWW began in San Pedro in 1923, the authorities used the act and indicted the strike leaders. Moreover, direct action was taken. Wholesale arrests of hundreds of strikers and their sympathizers took place. When civil libertarians mobilized against the reign of terror, they too were arrested—Upton Sinclair for reading part of the United States Constitution, a second speaker for reading the Declaration of Independence, and a third for announcing from the same podium, "This is a most delightful climate." The strike ended in late May 1923. Although defeated, the IWW remained a power in San Pedro for a short time, until vigilantes and the police drove the Wobblies from the water-front.

This was the twilight period of the IWW, although there were some superficial signs of vitality. Internal dissension cost the movement dearly and perhaps was as effective as the criminal syndicalism act in curbing its growth and activities. When the organization divided into three major factions and expended traditional energy and dedication fighting one another, the IWW's days were numbered. As it declined in membership and activities, it became more tolerable and there was much talk of repealing the criminal syndicalism statute. However, repeal never got beyond the talking stage. The act did not become a nullity until the United States Supreme Court struck it down in 1969 after it had been revived for use against a black militant in a Los Angeles case.

As the IWW declined, so the labor movement of the United States and California declined. By the end of the twenties, the AFL had dropped sharply in membership in California and the nation. Periodically during the twenties a criminal syndicalism trial featuring a group of professional witnesses was staged. Vigilante groups periodically took action against a radical group. Their efforts in Los Angeles were supplemented by a "Red Squad" of the Los Angeles Police Department which harassed radical and liberal organizations. The methods were frequently highhanded and more often than not they elicited cries of outrage from those involved. Some say that the stout hand of the police created a full share of radicals, but the figures seem to show that by the end of the decade, the IWW and kindred organizations were well in hand. One stage in California labor history had come to an end. The IWW sun had set.

CHAPTER XVII

The Age of Prosperity

The prosperity of California in the 1920s paralleled that of the nation as a whole. There was the same kind of feverish expansion in existing industries, the rise of new industries, and much unwholesome speculation. But the economic upturn of the state was also very different; many of the new industries were to be peculiar to California.

The continual growth in the movie industry brought a substantial flow of investment capital into the state from eastern money sources. Perhaps rivaling or even exceeding the motion picture industry in the 1920s was tourism. The continual magnet that the state provided for health seekers and the retired now had the glamour of the movies to prompt a new flood of visitors, usually in the winter. In fact, by the end of the decade many communities had row upon row of small one-bedroom homes especially designed to be rented or sold to the aged, the precursors of the modern retirement centers. Many of the tourists invested in California real estate, and large numbers became permanent residents.

To finance the housing boom that accompanied the influx of population, the financial community of the state expanded. Building and loan companies grew rapidly in number and in resources in the two major metropolitan centers, as did also trust and title guarantee companies. Bank deposits increased from $1,890,000,000 in 1920 to over $3,000,000,000 in 1930. The decade saw the emergence of gigantic banking organizations such as the Bank of Italy, which had been founded in 1904 by Amadeo Piatro Giannini. Later, renamed the Bank of America, it expanded from its headquarters in San Francisco into the rest of the state, sometimes ruthlessly squeezing out its smaller competitors. When the First National Bank of Los

Angeles and the Security National Bank merged, another giant following the same pattern of expansion was created.

The rapid growth of population from 3,426,861 in 1920 to 5,677,-251 in 1930 had a resultant impact upon the consumer industries of the state. The greater market prompted the major manufacturers of the country, led by the automotive industry, to establish assembly plants close to such a growing market. Others established branch plants and service facilities. These in turn attracted more people who found it easier to come to California because of the growing network of national highways and improved rail transportation. And the more people who came the more industries were necessary to satisfy their consumer wants.

The expansion of the movie industry continued influencing the growth of a specialty garment industry. The lumber industry of the northern part of the state expanded to meet the building needs. The dawn of the automobile age further increased the demand for oil. The fact that the eyes of the United States Navy were on the Pacific created a further demand for petroleum products. The fear of Japan made San Diego in a few short years the greatest naval port in America. That city also became one of the nation's leading fishing centers partially as a result of the demand created for tuna during the meatless days of World War I. San Francisco and San Pedro also continued as important fishing ports. Improved technology made it possible to ship the fishing products of the Pacific Ocean throughout the nation.

THE GENESIS OF THE AIRFRAME INDUSTRY

One of the glamour industries that had its real beginning in California in the 1920s but was not to emerge as one of the giants in the state until some two decades later was the aircraft industry. It was attracted to California by factors similar to those that lured the motion picture industry. California weather made it possible to fly almost the entire year in an era before advanced instrumentation. The possibility of building planes outdoors most days lessened the initial investment for factories when the infant industry could ill afford such expenditures. The presence in the state of a few daring entrepreneurs who saw the potential in air flight and, equally important, the presence of the necessary financial backers who were willing to risk venture capital helped to make California the aircraft-manufacturing center of the world.

As early as 1907 Glenn L. Martin made gliders in Santa Ana. He later converted an abandoned church into an airplane factory in that city. By 1912 his planes carried airmail from Compton to Santa Ana, perhaps the first such service. Martin later moved his operation to what is now Los Angeles International Airport, and after World War I Martin relocated in the East. But there were many more aviation pioneers in California to pick up where he left off.

Donald W. Douglas, who had started his career with Martin, established a company of his own in 1920, on Pico Boulevard in Los Angeles, which was probably the first permanent-based California aircraft plant. Soon moving to Santa Monica, he turned out an airplane a week by 1922, most of them for the Armed Forces. The prestige of Douglas' operation was greatly aided by his production of four "world cruisers," three of which successfully circumnavigated the globe in 1924. But the future of his company lay not in producing planes for the Army or the Navy, but instead in the design of civilian passenger transports. With the building of the DC-1 in 1933, as one observer puts it, "air travel came of age." Carrying fourteen passengers, the soundproof cabin and numerous safety features put aviation passenger travel on a solid foundation. The Douglas achievement resulted from the challenge of the Boeing 247. The latter plane was so superior to other transport planes that the airlines faced the choice of replacing their fleets with 247s or, preferably, finding a better plane. Transcontinental and Western Airlines (TWA) asked for bids on a plane that would outperform the Boeing craft. Douglas accepted the challenge by designing a similar but superior plane.

The DC-1 (Douglas Commercial) was larger and faster and was equipped with a more powerful engine than the 247. More importantly, it was fitted with wing flaps. These brought the landing speed down to 60 m.p.h., making it possible to handle the larger and heavier plane safely. The slower landing speed also permitted the use of shorter runways. The only DC-1 ever built was test-flown on July 1, 1933, and successfully flown by TWA on its transcontinental route in September 1933. A larger and improved DC-2 was the production model: 190 of these planes were built. To meet the demands of American Airlines for a sleeper plane, the DC-2 fuselage was widened to accommodate berths. Only a few of these modified planes were sold and Douglas feared it would lose the costs of the model change. However, four seats were placed in a row with an aisle down the middle and the DC-3, the most successful plane in aviation history, was born. This was the first airplane to support itself economically as well as aerodynamically; airlines could now operate by carrying passengers alone and did not have to rely on a government mail subsidy. Within two years DC-3s were carrying 95 per cent of the nation's civil air traffic.

San Diego shared with Los Angeles the privilege of giving birth to the aircraft industry. Ryan Aeronautical Company was the second airframe manufacturer to go into business in Southern California and remain in it.

T. Claude Ryan, an army pilot, left the service for a try in commercial aviation. In 1925 Ryan Airlines inaugurated a regular service between San Diego and Los Angeles, the first regularly schedule year-round passenger airline in the United States. This service grew to fifteen planes, the largest being a twelve-passenger "airbus." Ryan believed that there were no suitable planes available for the needs of his airline and designed his own high-wing monoplane. Convinced of the future potential of his new plane, Ryan sold his interest in the air service and concentrated on plane production. That his confidence was not misplaced was illustrated by Charles A. Lindbergh's selection of one of Ryan's planes for his historic trans-Atlantic flight in 1927.

Lockheed Aircraft Corporation was third in terms of continuing corporate existence in Southern California. Originally founded by the Loughead brothers (their name was legally changed to Lockheed) at Santa Barbara in 1916, the firm had gone into bankruptcy and was reorganized many times. Like Douglas during the 1920s it had concentrated on building single-engine planes. By the early 1930s the Electra, an all-metal craft, began to be used for transport plaens. It was not until production for World War II that

Lockheed emerged as one of California's, and the nation's, leading aircraft manufacturers.

The early days of the aircraft factories were similar to those in the movie industry. Frequently, employees had to tighten their belts while waiting for a payday that was dependent on a customer paying for a plane on schedule. Most aircraft manufacturers operated one jump ahead of the sheriff and many companies have been consigned to oblivion because they failed to keep ahead. Some employees of the early companies struck out on their own, and some, like Jack Northrup, were successful. Other companies, like North American, Consolidated, and Vultee, moved from the East to California because of the concentration of talent in the Southern California area along with other advantages. Thus, the nucleus around which the mighty aircraft and space industry which emerged during World War II was being put together.

THE MOVIES

California's most important industry of the 1920s was the production of a make-believe world. The making of movies was the state's unique contribution to the world, as well as to the nation, and for many years California reigned supreme in this area. In the production of motion pictures, an art and a business was created that has influenced the world for both better and ill in the twentieth century. The making of movies has remained a unique enterprise. It is an industry that has relied heavily upon the innovative inventor, the creative artist, and the businessman as entrepreneur; and in many instances, all three of these were combined in the same person.

The technology of motion pictures dates back to the second century A.D., but ultimate success was the result of a series of inventions of the nineteenth century. Scientists, led by Peter Mark Roget of Roget's Thesaurus fame, long recognized that the eye retains an image for a split second after a picture is removed. If a series of pictures of an action are shown in succession at the rate of sixteen separate images per second, the eye's retention of the images produces an illusion of continuous action. Many men put together a variety of devices which moved pictures at a rapid rate, producing the illusion of constant motion. Most of these were mere toys, but some of them anticipated the movement built into the animated cartoons of our own day. Such devices were finally linked with improvements in the camera to produce the motion picture. In 1877 Eadweard Muybridge on a Palo Alto ranch used a series of twenty-four cameras to photograph Leland Stanford's race horse in motion. With an electrical timing device to trip the shutters as the horse ran past, he produced the pictures needed to stimulate motion. Incidentally, he won a wager for Stanford, who bet an associate that a horse sometimes has four feet off the ground when running. A Frenchman used a camera to accomplish the same objective by shooting a series of pictures upon a revolving drum set in its chamber.

The experiments of many others were put together by William Kennedy Laurie Dickson, an employee in Thomas Edison's laboratory. Dickson solved the problem of putting film through a camera by devising the sprocket that is still used on many cameras. Edison's talented assistant was even able to show a brief film in 1889 with a record synchronized to it, perhaps marking the first appearance of the talkies. Basic to Dickson's innovation, of course, was celluloid-type film perfected by George Eastman.

Edison, however, was not interested in motion pictures as such but was mainly concerned with the kinetoscope, which was a peep show displaying pictures for about a minute. For these crude devices, which could be used only by one person at a time, Dickson photographed portions of vaudeville, one of his most remarkable presentations being a graphic re-creation of the execution of Mary, Queen of Scots. Edison's failure to take out European patents made it possible for the Lumière brothers, Auguste and Louis, to improve upon the American inventor's design and make the first effective projector that could be viewed by a large audience. Edison ultimately combined the improvements of several Europeans with his own device and made the first regular projector in 1896. The movies' "first night on Broadway" occurred on April 23 of that year. The early films ran only a minute or two and depicted simple scenes and were a great attraction as long as they were a novelty.

A modern motion picture emerged under the leadership of Georges Méliès, a professional magician, whose movies told a narrative sometimes running as long as fifteen minutes. A series of productions beginning in 1900 showed that Méliès was able to perfect most of the basic camera tricks, such as slow motion, fade-ins, fade-outs, and the movement of the camera backward so as to dissolve one scene and then forward for the new one so that the two scenes appeared to merge together. Following the realistic traditions developed in the theater, Méliès devised elaborate stage settings, but his weakness lay in the fact that he could not free himself from the traditions of the stage. He failed to utilize close-ups for singling out individual actors for significant scenes, but instead photographed the entire group on stage.

The success of Méliès led to the pirating of many of his films in the United States, but, more importantly, prompted others to duplicate his success. Edwin Porter, a cameraman for Edison, began in 1903 to improve upon the Frenchman's films. Porter is credited with being the first to realize a simple story could be told by means of chronologically arranging the scenes. By cutting film he was able to present scenes for maximum effect. Thus, what the audience saw on the screen was selected views of the action that had been edited in a way best calculated to achieve the dramatic quality desired. Porter was also the first to use the close-up.

Porter's innovative techniques were best revealed in *The Great Train Robbery*, which was based upon a successful stage play. Crudely done by modern standards, it is generally acknowledged as the first real movie. It brought to the screen the Western, and the suspense of the chase, both of which were to be long-time stand-bys of the movie industry. Only ten minutes in length, most of the scenes were shot outdoors, itself an innovation. By means of careful editing, Porter conveyed to the audience the impression that action was taking place simultaneously in different places, a technique basic to the movies from that day on. *The Great Train Robbery* was not just an artistic success but was also a great commercial one. It led to the development of film exchanges wherein prints were rented to exhibitors, thereby reducing the possibility of pirating and assuring a greater return to the producer. There were no places designed specifically to show movies at the time. There is some doubt as to who established the first motion picture theater but the honor is generally accorded to Thomas L. Tally, who opened an "electric theater" in the back of a Los Angeles amusement parlor in 1902. Two years later such houses were taking in as much as $1000 a week at a nickel a person to view *The Great Train Robbery*.

The profits from the early movies were sometimes unbelievable. One company started in 1905 with an initial investment of $6000 and expanded this capital to a total of $4,000,000 within three years. Such profits and the seemingly insatiable demands of the viewing public resulted in the efforts of a few producers to develop a monopoly. Several pioneer companies claiming a legal right to the parents organized the Motion Picture Patent Company, which attempted to control the industry totally. Pooling their patent claims, each received a license to manufacture motion pictures. The agreement stipulated that no additional licenses would be issued. Originally organized in 1909, the trust was soon doing battle with any new member trying to produce films. Most exhibitors signed with the trust with the notable exception of William Fox, who controlled many theaters in New York City and who went on to challenge successfully the group in the courts. The trust businessmen were interested in profits only and tried to block artistic innovations, fearing that they might distract the public from paying to see movies already produced. In addition, the trust tried to keep the actors as anonymous as possible so that they would not have to pay them large salaries, seldom even announcing the cast.

Independent companies, to counter the power of the trust, signed prominent stage actors to star in their films. The independents also stressed improvements in techniques and it was this group that was creative and progressive. The trust countered with acts of sabotage against equipment, against film already produced, or intimidated exhibitors in an effort to keep them from showing the films of independents. After the deliberate destruction of a film, Cecil B. De Mille took far-reaching precautions. His brother described De Mille's security in the following fashion: "No one could get a job in the laboratory without showing his birth certificate, a portrait of his mother and a letter of praise from his village pastor."

The independents looked for sanctuary free of harassment. Cuba was tried, and proved to be disease-ridden; Florida was abandoned as being too warm. San Francisco and Oakland flourished momentarily, but climatic problems caused them to be bypassed. As early as

1907 a studio had been established in Los Angeles. By 1909 a general movement of the movie industry to Southern California began. Los Angeles had the advantage of being close to Mexico, where one could escape injunctions and subpoenas. Producers began to concentrate in Hollywood, where land was cheaper than in Los Angeles, then a city of some 250,000. The pioneer movie producers soon discovered that Southern California had other advantages. The all-year weather in an age before artificial lighting was most important. Then too, "within a two-hundred mile radius of Los Angeles was to be found every variety of natural scenery from the Sahara Desert to the Khyber Pass." Southern California was also most receptive to this new industry which received the co-operation of the business and financial community. By 1913 Hollywood was firmly established as the home of the motion picture industry and the site of most of the world's movie production.

The first producers who came to California were frequently in "something of a race between the completion of the picture and the extinction of the bank account." In addition to operating on the proverbial shoestring, the first generation of Hollywood producers was a motley crew which included former newsboys, garment-workers, bouncers, bookmakers, and even butchers. They used every means at their disposal to cut costs, some even going so far as to turn in false alarms so that they could shoot a mob scene without cost. The tactics of the movie makers plus the curious assortment of individuals making up the fraternity caused them to be so rejected by Los Angeles that some apartment house owners posted signs reading: "NO dogs or actors allowed." David Wark Griffith thought so little of moviemaking that he said to his wife on one occasion, "In one way it's very nice to be making money . . . but you know we can't go on forever and not tell our friends and relatives how we are earning our living." It is ironic that the movie industry should finally settle in Hollywood, a community originally founded in 1903 by a Kansas prohibitionist. But the earlier ostracizing of the movie-making fraternity by Los Angeles ended by 1915. Nothing succeeds like success and by that year the industry had an annual payroll of some $20,-000,000. Southern California was happy to accept the industry and the elite of the movies.

The success of the industry was greatly helped by the emergence of the star system. Carl Laemmle, a leading independent, made the first Hollywood star to draw customers. He signed Florence Lawrence, a popular stage player who was also famed as the "Biograph Girl," to an exclusive contract, offering her a large salary but also publicity. By means of a fake death, conveniently blamed upon competitors in the industry, Florence Lawrence received publicity from one end of the country to the other. Perhaps the greatest of the early female stars was Gladys Smith, who became America's sweetheart as Mary Pickford.

In 1908 the cowboy was introduced to the American public in the "Bronco Billy" series, which exalted the frontier and led to a lasting craze for Westerns. Emphasizing honesty, hard work, and the rugged individualism of the West, traditional all-American values, these stereotypes became part of American movies. With little in the way of plot but emphasizing action and simple virtues, Western movies became standards of Hollywood. G. M. Anderson, the original Bronco Billy, was joined by William S. Hart, Tom Mix, Harry Carey, Hoot Gibson, Buck Jones, and a host of other strong, silent Western heroes. The coming of sound left the Westerns unchanged except for the addition of the guitar and cowboy ballad. Comedy saw the emergence of Charlie Chaplin, Mack Sennett's Keystone Kops, Harry Langdon, and Harold Lloyd along with Buster Keaton also brought sidesplitting laughter to motion picture theaters.

Probably the greatest of the early producers was David Wark Griffith. Most of the techniques associated with movie production had already been developed before he arrived on the scene, but he put them all together into the distinct visual style which gave film drama its unique characteristics. The limitations placed upon film making by attempts to follow techniques of the Broadway stage were eliminated by Griffith. Besides being a master in the improvement of existing filming techniques, he was the first to make a great spectacular.

His most famous movie was *The Birth of a Nation*, a film which ultimately grossed $18,000,000. Son of a former Confederate colonel, known as "Thunder Jake" because of the wild tales he told of the old South, Griffith brought from his Kentucky background a romantic concept of the antebellum South that was reflected in his movie making. He also accepted the Southern version of Reconstruction depicted in the popular novel and stage play by Thomas Dixon, *The*

Clansman. This portrayal of the chivalric life of the South appealed to Griffith and he decided to film it. *The Birth of a Nation* ran three hours, an exceptionally long film for that day. An artistic success, it glorified the role of the Ku Klux Klan, created a favorable image of the society of the pre-Civil War South, and strengthened an unfortunate stereotype of the Negro. The public in general agreed with the conclusions of President Woodrow Wilson, who declared it was like "writing history with lightning." Negro leaders, justifiably outraged by the film's distortions and exaggerations, tried to have the film banned. Inadvertently they may have increased its popularity. In spite of its racial bias and its extensive perversion of the facts of history, *The Birth of a Nation* served notice that the movies had arrived as an art form as well as a powerful social force.

World War I greatly aided the development of California's movie industry. Film producers quickly realized the salability of movies devoted to patriotic themes. Leading actors and actresses devoted much of their time and energy to assist in the sale of Liberty bonds. In addition, the war aided the financial development of Hollywood by curtailing the production of European competitors. German, French, Italian, and English movie makers virtually went out of business. In 1919 American motion pictures accounted for 90 per cent of those shown in Europe and virtually all of those presented in South America, India, western Asia, and Africa. The impetus provided by the war years was not lost in the era of the 1920s, which saw Hollywood become the unquestioned motion picture center of the world.

For the first time in history actors and actresses did not have to follow the theater from town to town. No longer transient workers, they were able to put down roots and establish permanent homes in Southern California. As the industry matured it became increasingly complex. The staff that was necessary to handle cameras, develop and print film, erect sets, provide wardrobes and administration soon made the movies a bigger industry in Southern California than even the orange.

The fantastic profits made in film production and the larger outlets necessary for financing in the 1920s brought about significant changes in Hollywood. The banking fraternity of Wall Street poured millions of dollars into the film companies to meet their constantly growing needs. This infusion of money brought in men trained in management rather than movie production. For example, a new director of Loew's was William C. Durant, then head of General Motors Corporation, who was experienced in automobile production. By the end of the 1920s, representatives of New York banks were found on the board of directors of most of the leading motion picture firms. Businessmen and not artists determined what movies would be produced and decisions were determined solely on the basis of their salability. Producers increasingly turned to imitation and the duplication of the most recent successes of their competitors. Thus the formula picture was born. Production methods themselves were mechanized and Hollywood virtually went on an assembly line. The creative talents of producers became subordinate to the dictates of those who financed the costly production of films.

With movies becoming big business, expensive theaters were erected in the downtown districts of leading cities. In 1928 $161,930,-000 was spent on new theaters, but this was money well invested, for more than 100,000,000 people attended the 20,000 movie houses in the nation every week. The plush downtown theaters charged as much as $3 for a premiere, while the neighborhood houses charged only $.25 or $.50. But there were few cities that did not have movie houses on side streets where admission was only $.10. Although every large city had lavish theaters with carpeted floors, ushers attired as if they were guards in a White Russian army, upholstered seats, and crystal chandeliers, Sid Grauman's Egyptian Theatre in Hollywood was the Taj Mahal of movie houses. It prompted one commentator to say that "the mezzanine floor looks as if it had been designed for eight-day bicycle races." This effort to conjure up visions of ancient Egypt by building a replica of the palace at ancient Thebes reflected the judgment of many movie moguls.

A brief downturn in attendance in 1927 was more than offset by the revolution of sound movies. Within two years silent movies were a memory to be reproduced only as novelties. Many established actors, lacking essential vocal talents, failed to make the adjustment to the new audio world of the movies. Some will contend that the art that went into the silent movies was superior to that needed to get by once the spoken word was utilized. But innovation has been the keynote of the movies and the introduction of sound was only a significant phase of this continually changing industry.

In the 1920s producers catered to the public desire to be titillated by suggestive films. Contrary to the opinion of many, motion picture producers were following public tastes rather than changing attitudes. When the public had desired sweet, simple heroines and the exalting of the Victorian code on the silver screen, Hollywood was happy to oblige, but with the revolution in sexual mores following World War I, movie producers climbed on the bandwagon. As one observer put it, "modesty and virginity became absurd as love-making took on the appearance of a wrestling match. The movie woman was now thrown around, carried off, or flung on the couch by her man in the holocaust of primitive passion." Films with suggestive titles were common: *Lying Lips, Mad Love, Passion Flame, More Deadlier Than the Male, Love Is an Awful Thing, One Week of Love, Twin Beds, Why Be Good,* and *Paid to Love.*

The American public apparently wanted such movies because they flocked to them in large numbers. Movie magazines recorded the private lives of the screen's "hot mamas" in a manner that satisfied the modest tastes of the nation's shopgirls. However, a series of scandals endangered the industry in the early 1920s. The still unsolved murder of a popular director, manslaughter charges against the leading comedian Roscoe "Fatty" Arbuckle, and several other incidents put the movies on the defensive. There was much agitation for national regulation and some states even wrote legislation to clean up the movies. Baseball owners appointed a commissioner of impeccable credentials to clean up the professional game in the aftermath of the "Black Sox" scandal. The movie moguls took a similar tack when they drafted Will H. Hays as their "czar." The former postmaster general's principal task was to appease those demanding that the government regulate movies by enforcing the anemic code which industry members drafted for self-regulation. Hays' main contribution was in public relations and thereby the image of the movie producers was improved.

Although most California industries were hard hit by the Depression, the movies continued to prosper. The advent of sound greatly increased the need for investment capital but returns more than offset this; movies were apparently untouched by the vagaries of the economic world. No matter how limited the family budget may have been during the Depression, funds were found to attend the movies.

The profits of Hollywood helped California weather the nation's economic debacle. Then too, the state's leading manufacturing industry, until the changes brought about by World War II, was peculiarly suited to California. It was not dependent upon the availability of raw materials, nor was it hampered by great distances from markets, for its products had a high value per unit of weight and were untouched by discriminatory freight rates. Hollywood also aided in the development during the 1920s of California's other leading industry, tourism. Movies added to the established appeal of climate as an attraction to draw people from the rest of the world.

The relative importance of movies to the state's economy began to decline during World War II as a result of the growth in importance of aircraft, shipbuilding, and other defense-related industries. The absolute importance of movies in California began to decline as a result of changes brought about by World War II. First of all, the entertainment tastes of the American people entered a period of change after 1945. A more mature society was no longer ready to accept the "escapism" which was too frequently all that Hollywood had to offer. Good reading, good music, camping, or boating could now be afforded by a more affluent people and competed with the movies for leisure time. Foreign films frequently offered greater depth and perception than the staid, tired formula films of Hollywood. The destruction of much movie production in Europe led to technical innovations, dictated by necessity in most cases, which were fresh and exciting. Above all, the coming of television led to a revolution in the entertainment world, the effects of which are still not completely understood. Postwar movie making was also altered by the end of efforts to control the type of films produced. Foreign films, which ignored the traditional taboos of Hollywood, started this trend and the courts, by virtually ending censorship, have furthered it.

The years since 1945 have also witnessed the demise of Hollywood as the movie capital of the world. Improvements in techniques of foreign film making and the availability of air transportation have prompted many firms to produce their movies abroad. The fact that unions had effectively protected the interests of labor in Hollywood led to an effort to cut labor costs. Even when movies are produced in California many scenes may be filmed in other countries. Real estate values were so high that expansion in Hollywood was impossible.

Hence, many companies which have remained in Southern California have moved to the suburbs.

It has long been accepted in evaluating the role of movies in American life to denigrate them as a "fairyland on a production line." There is no question but that most movies present stereotyped views of society that bear little or no similarity to reality. There is also no question but that most movies are designed to appeal to the twelve-year-old mind, but much literature also depicts society unrealistically and most books and magazines are intended to appeal to a similar lowest common denominator. Perhaps the reason most movies have not had greater intellectual content has been because producers gave the public what they wanted. Possibly the greatest weakness of Hollywood has been that it is too typically American, or as one observer put it, "The Hollywood sophistication was painlessly absorbed because it was, after all, little more than Iowa-on-the-loose."

REPUBLICAN ASCENDANCY

Republicans dominated the political life of the nation as well as California during the 1920s. Their sway was so complete that the state was almost a one-party state in the tradition of the Deep South. During the six elections of the decade, Democrats won but 9 of 66 seats in the House of Representatives; 11 of 120 seats in the state senate; 38 of 480 seats in the assembly. By 1930 statewide Democratic registration had shrunk to only 22 per cent. The Republicans were in such complete control of the state machinery that they could indulge themselves in the luxury of intraparty feuds.

Contributing to the demise of the Democratic party was the Republican orientation of the state's newspapers. Led by the Los Angeles *Times*, the San Francisco *Chronicle*, and the Oakland *Tribune*, most of the journals of the state simply ignored Democratic political news so that that party was unable to present its case to the public. By 1924 only 7 of the 120 seats in the legislature were in the hands of Democrats and it was ruefully observed that "there were no Democratic politics to speak of in California throughout the 1920s. Republican nomination was tantamount to election." Republicans elected were generally those of the old guard. Cross-filing, which allowed candidates to run on both tickets, also hurt the Democrats.

The administration of Republican William D. Stephens extended the program of the Johnson Progressives. Stephens replaced Johnson, who had gone to the United States Senate and was elected in his own right in 1918. Long after the Progressive spirit had died elsewhere, Stephens managed to keep it alive in California. He raised taxes for needed improvements in the face of vigorous opposition from corporate groups and reorganized state government to bring more efficiency and economy to Sacramento. His work in this area was so effective that it stood relatively unchanged until 1961.

Friend William Richardson, whose Quaker origins are suggested by his name, defeated Stephens in the GOP primary in 1922 and was elected governor. Many Republicans in the state still look back longingly at the Richardson administration as an example of an ideal state government. Economy was the watchword of his administration and the state budget dropped from the $91,000,000 that it had been under Stephens to $78,974,628.55 for 1923–25. In his inaugural address, Richardson denounced Stephens as a "spendthrift of the people's money," and as "the builder of a great, expensive, and wicked political machine." Convinced that "extravagance in educational matters has run riot during the past few years," Richardson attempted to close California Polytechnic School (San Luis Obispo) and Humboldt State Teachers College as well as slashing the budgets of other educational institutions. In the budget slashing, some observers discerned political motivation as most of the jobs eliminated were Stephens' appointees. Drastic budget cuts produced wholesale resignations by outraged public servants who felt they could no longer function effectively. Economy was the watchword of Richardson, but he also stressed law and order. Few pardons were made by the governor, the champion of law and order.

The highhanded tactics of Governor Richardson created a split within his own party and led to a revival of the Progressive wing of the Republicans in 1926. In that year his lieutenant governor, Clement Calhoun Young, a onetime bay area high school teacher who had prospered in the business world and who had been speaker of the assembly under Johnson, unseated him in the primary. Senator Hiram

Johnson campaigned extensively on behalf of his protégé. Educational leaders of the state also opposed Richardson. Far more potent than college professors or members of the board of regents of the university was A. P. Giannini of the Bank of America. Richardson, a career journalist and member of the California Press Association, had been brought into close contact with many local banks. At that time the Bank of America, expanding rapidly by establishing branches in widely scattered parts of the state, alienated many of these local banks. Richardson championed the local banks and opposed the granting of branch permits to the Bank of America. Giannini and the bank's stockholders reinforced the opposition to Richardson. The bank stockholders may well have been the decisive factor in Young's narrow defeat of Richardson in the primary by a margin of about fifteen thousand votes.

As governor, Young announced a Progressive program and identified with Theodore Roosevelt and his "square deal." In addition to being more friendly to education, Young was concerned with agricultural problems. He encouraged teachers' retirement programs, as well as pensions for other state employees, and helped establish a California merit system and old age pension law in 1929. Unfortunately, neither he nor his predecessor did anything about the pressing problem of reapportionment that had grown more serious during the decade because of the rapid increase of population in Southern California. At the close of the decade Republicans of Progressive and more orthodox stance shared control of the state government.

CALIFORNIA CULTS AND SECTS

Early in the morning of December 10, 1958, a tremendous explosion shattered the main building of the WKFL (Wisdom, Knowledge, Faith, and Love) fountain of the world located in a box canyon north of Los Angeles. Krishna Venta, seven of his followers, and two strangers died in the blast. The notoriety associated with it reminded Californians of the reputation the state had earned in the 1920s as the cult capital of the world. The state's citizens would like to forget that religious faddists had been part of the scene for years. The investigation into the disaster revealed that the WKFL was another of many religious cults. Its leader, Krishna Venta, claimed to be the reincarnation of Christ. He had a flowing beard and wore white gowns. He identified himself as the prophet and claimed to have come to America in a spaceship from an area near Mount Everest in Nepal. Scoffers noted that someone with his fingerprints had a lengthy police record but this did not shake the faith of his converts. Only when he paid undue attention to the wife of one of his followers was his divinity questioned. What led from scoffing to bombing is imprecisely known. More relevant is the manner in which this cult and scores of others added spice, zest, and intrigue to the California setting.

Just why men like Krishna Venta and others like him have flocked to California has been a matter of speculation. Some have suggested that the health seekers were principally the cause. "They come to California to die, and, dammit, they don't." When the climate fails to cure their many ailments they turn to the quacks and charlatans. As Morrow Mayo commented, "Los Angeles leads the world in the advancement and practice of all the healing sciences except perhaps medicine and surgery." Thus, nostrums, health cures, and freak brands of medical science abound and many of the cults are associated with them. Some have suggested that the quacks and faddists flee westward from the law and when they reach the Pacific coast there is no place else to go and hence they settle down there. The abundance of potential followers and recruits makes Southern California attractive. California is a modern Zion for the restless multitude in quest of something more in life than their dull, prosaic routine. They are easy prey to purveyors of religious nostrums. The mere migration of people is enough to cause the corruption of traditional religious faith, as any reader of the Old Testament is only too aware. Perhaps the failure of the conventional Churches to provide a spiritually satisfying message induces them initially to search elsewhere, and the fact that California provides ready incorporation of a new Church encourages the organization of new cults and sects.

A casual glance at the advertisements in a leading newspaper shows a strange mixture of Churches unknown in the rest of the nation. On a given day the following advertise: Church of the Open Door, Christadelphian Ecclesias, Mercenary Missionaries, Church of Scientology, International Wings of Healing, Esoteric Transcendentalism,

Self-Realization Fellowship, Temple of Tarot and Holy Qabalah, Pillar of Fire.

Among the more important of the cults has been that of Theosophy established by the "Purple Mother," Katherine Tingley, at Point Loma in San Diego in 1900. Its curious collection of Egyptian- and Greek-style buildings ultimately formed the nucleus of the campus of the present United States International University. The Theosophists made their permanent home in the Ojai Valley, but their influences ranged throughout California, for many cults drew heavily upon their basic ideas. Most cults in California have lasted about twenty years, their ebb and flow usually coinciding with the career of the leader.

Perhaps the most distinctive of all of the cults is Mankind United, which was officially begun in 1934 and was still prospering in 1970. Mankind United was organized by Arthur L. Bell. It borrowed heavily from the philosophy of the Theosophists, the Rosicrucians, the Self-Realization Fellowship, but also from the technocracy of Howard Scott. In other words, it offered its followers an opportunity to solve economic as well as spiritual problems within a single organization. Borrowing heavily from the science fiction of the day, a book by Bell, *Mankind United*, declared that the world was really run by "hidden rulers." This unsavory clique "financed and prepared revolutions, sometimes under the guise of establishing world brotherhood [as in Communism], and carefully selected each dictator—Nazi, Fascist, or Communist." This concept probably comes from the infamous "Protocols of the Elders of Zion" which purported to reveal a Jewish plot to dominate the world. Bell's hidden rulers were accused of being at the root of all of the troubles of the world. They were accused of regulating the mentality of people through the use of drugs put in drinking water. (Such an idea probably influenced the anti-fluoridation campaign of later years.) The hidden rulers were also accused of holding off the world market a large number of inventions that would make life easier for everyone and solve most of the world's technological problems. To counteract this insidious influence a group of men in 1875 made contact with a superhuman race from outer space. These superbeings had superbrains which were encased in metallic heads. These astral beings were to assist in the creation of a better world for those who joined Mankind United. Such assistance would make possible for those who joined ultimately to have an exalted living standard that included an expensive air-conditioned home equipped with unlimited gadgetry. In return for these promises prospective members surrendered their worldly possessions and worked for the order. A state investigating team estimated that Mankind United took in some $4,000,000 between 1934 and 1944 in dues, contributions, and books sold to the faithful. Among other items they sold a ring guaranteed to restore virility. In addition, the group received control of a large number of business enterprises and farms throughout the state, so its economic power was extensive.

A study of this California cult throws much light on all California cults. Membership in Mankind United gave purpose to life that had been lacking. Those who joined were assured of steady work and of course great wealth if they remained faithful. Its maximum membership probably reached 75,000 in 1939, but the distribution of 220,000 copies of Bell's book indicates a wider influence.

Those who joined Mankind United did not follow the usual stereotype of the "zany crackpot" who joined such groups. Most of its members were from northwestern European stock. In terms of religion they were usually from the more fundamentalist churches. Most were not newcomers to California. The membership averaged 24.4 years' residence, a surprising statistic which undermined the view that most members of the cult were drawn from California newcomers. Many members had a limited education. No liberal arts graduates and no real businessmen were found in their ranks.

The simplistic solutions to the complex problems of California appealed to the faithful. In those Depression years the view that the troubles of the age could be blamed upon the hidden rulers was especially comforting. The theology of Mankind United retained the ethical precepts of Christianity but, like most California cults, was polytheistic in nature. It borrowed from Christian Science. Pain, suffering, and disease existed only in the mind and all one had to do was think properly to cure such things. In addition to such spiritual solace, the followers of Mankind United eagerly awaited the Messianic Age. As one observer puts it, "Much of the attraction of Mankind United lay in the fact that not the past, but the present was the history-making era, and not Palestine, but California was the Holy Land."

The pacifism of the sect led to difficulty with the FBI during World War II and its extensive economic holdings led to investigation by state and federal tax authorities. On January 20, 1944, Arthur Bell incorporated the organization as Christ's Church of the Golden Rule for tax purposes. In 1970 the group was still in existence. In 1962 it bought a large ranch in northern California for $1,000,000 cash and operated, according to a news story, "an ultra-modern $500,000 motel, restaurant and gift shop, a new garage-service station, a sawmill and a large cattle operation on their property, Ridgewood Park, six miles south of Willits." The spokesman for the group, Harold Von Norris, claims to have been in the organization when Bell incorporated the Church. It still maintains that it lives by the golden rule and all that enter must give all of their property to the group and do the necessary work assigned for nothing. In 1968 it again attracted the attention of the authorities because about one third of its members were receiving welfare checks in spite of the relative affluence of the organization.

Among the multiplicity of more orthodox Christian sects in California, easily the most important was that of the evangelist Sister Aimee Semple McPherson. After a career as an evangelist in the United States as well as the Orient, she arrived in Los Angeles in 1922 virtually a pauper. In a few years she amassed a personal fortune and built a large, expanding Church. A born showwoman, her name appeared in front-page headlines, at least according to her biographer, "on an average of three times a week for five years." No one would deny that she was truly the Barnum of religion.

Her theology was essentially orthodox, what there was of it. Her four-square gospel stressed conversion, physical healing, second coming, and redemption. When she found that the emphasis upon physical healing might get her into much difficulty she dropped the stress upon it. In a matter of a few years she built the huge Angelus Temple, which would seat five thousand. A college was attached to it. She had "a brass band bigger and louder than Sousa's, an organ worthy of any movie cathedral, a female choir bigger and more beautiful than the Metropolitan chorus, and a costume wardrobe comparable to Ziegfeld's." Most orthodox clergy were furious with her as she enticed their membership away with flamboyant preaching in sharp contrast to the dull sermons that they were offering. In fact, it was claimed that one Hollywood producer used to study her techniques in order to get new ideas. In her sermons heaven became "a cross between Pasadena, California and Washington, D.C." On one occasion she chased the devil across the front of the church with pitchfork in hand; on another, she raced onto the stage on a motorcycle dressed as a policeman, skidded to a stop and shouted "Stop, ye sinners." Perhaps her most famous scene was built around "the gospel lighthouse." The ladies in the chorus were clad in blue uniforms not unlike those of the Navy itself. The grand finale came when a dozen nightgowned virgins appeared "clinging to the rock of ages, while the wind howls, the thunder rolls, the lightning flashes, and the waves beat about them." Naturally, the virgins were saved and the curtain descended as the band reached a crescendo. When she preached she stressed heaven, asking, "Who cares about old hell, friends? Why, we all know what hell is. We have heard about it all our lives. A terrible place, where nobody wants to go . . . let's forget about hell. Lift up your hearts. What we're interested in, yes, lord, is heaven, and how to get there!" She was at her best when it came to taking collections. On one occasion the ushers simply went through the aisles carrying lengths of ribbon to which the faithful were expected to pin their dollar bills. On another, she exhorted the congregation: "Let us not hear the vulgar clinking of coins, but rather the soft rustle of paper."

Although Sister Aimee gloried in publicity, when she disappeared on May 18, 1926, she received far more than she had desired. It was popularly assumed that she had been drowned while bathing near Ocean Park but she turned up near the Mexican border with a hair-raising tale of having been abducted and forced to flee in the desert. Skeptical newsmen provided evidence that she had actually spent the interim with a handsome radio operator at Carmel. To the scoffers who raised questions about why her shoes were not marred by the desert journey, she replied scornfully that the "three Hebron children came out of a fiery furnace even hotter than the Sonora sun, without their garments being singed!" Indicted for making false reports to the police, she was acquitted. Her faithful followers took this as a complete vindication and their faith in Sister Aimee was stronger than ever.

The evangelist continued in and out of the courtroom as the result of frequent conflicts with her mother, her employees, or as a consequence of her marital difficulties. But her legal troubles and the accompanying publicity failed to diminish her hold on the faithful. She remained in full charge of her large Los Angeles congregation and the growing number of branch churches and even held successful revivals in the United States, Canada, and England. Her death from an overdose of sleeping pills in 1945 removed a colorful and controversial personage from the California scene and initiated a period of mourning for thousands of her supporters.

CHAPTER XVIII

The Depression Decade

Californians, like most Americans, reveled in the prosperity of the twenties, forerunner, said some, of an economic millennium which lay in the immediate future. Herbert Hoover, the first Californian to occupy the White House, declared at his 1929 inaugural that the country was on the verge of winning the long battle that mankind had waged against poverty. Everywhere the signs of affluence abounded and manifested the concrete reality which apparently underlay this prediction. In California, roads and streets were extended and improved, public buildings were constructed, factory payrolls climbed, the motion picture and the oil industry boomed, bank clearances mounted, the volume of business and trade of all kind increased, and county assessors were hard pressed to keep abreast of rapidly increasing property values. In the countryside, things were somewhat difficult for California farmers and ranchers, for agriculture was one of the major segments of the economy which languished during the decade, but for most of California, the "roaring twenties" were prosperous years.

There were a few signs of impending trouble during the twenties. Such things as prolonged farm depression, an inequitable distribution of the national income, unbridled speculation in securities, an unstable international economy, an awkward and unwieldy domestic monetary system, all indicated that the underpinnings of prosperity were fragile. The situation began to change in the summer of 1929 when the contrived economic structure of Europe, constructed by the peacemakers at Versailles and supported by massive infusions of American capital, began to totter. A bank in Austria triggered the crisis in Europe which spread in ever widening waves until it engulfed the stock market in New York in October. Thereafter financial news featured an apparently endless succession of bank failures, business bankruptcies, and general economic collapse. National income dropped from 87.8 billion to 40.2 billion in four years, salaries decreased 40 per cent, dividends nearly 57 per cent, and manufacturing wages 60 per cent. California and the nation were in the grip of the most profound economic crisis which ever gripped the United States.

The crisis demanded leadership, but for the most part in California and the rest of the nation, leaders wrung their hands and made brave predictions of a brighter tomorrow. "Prosperity is just around the corner" became the favorite phrase of those who imperfectly analyzed the nation's ills. In Washington, Herbert Hoover made valiant and vain efforts to stem the general loss of confidence which he thought was responsible for the crisis. In Sacramento, Governor James "Sunny Jim" Rolph, onetime mayor of San Francisco, brought affability to the crisis and little else. Meanwhile, unemployment grew, the toll of bankrupt businesses increased, and foreclosures multiplied. California crops went unharvested: thousands of tons of peaches and pears, tomatoes, and onions. In the cities nearby, want and hunger stalked the streets while in the fields and orchards crops went unharvested for want of a market.

The Depression affected every state in the Union, but neither in a uniform manner nor to the same extent. It touched California in special ways, for its economy had long been shallow-rooted, and its industries like tourism and real estate development were particularly vulnerable to an economic downturn. During the twenties prosperity in motion pictures, real estate, and tourism had not only doubled the population in Los Angeles, but almost doubled the usual proportion of white-collar workers. This group—the white collar, lower middle class—was severely affected by the Depression, which brought the total unemployment in Los Angeles County to 300,000 by mid-1934. Furthermore its golden climate made California an attractive refuge for the nation's unemployed and disadvantaged. They came by the thousands to swell the rolls of residents who found themselves in difficulty. A great many of the latter were retired farmers and professionals who had come to spend their declining years on the Pacific coast. The Depression hit them hard, wiping out retirement nest eggs, and pushing once comfortable people into penury. Everywhere public officials wrestled with such problems; in California they were especially numerous and enormous.

Governor Rolph in Sacramento and President Hoover in Washington made efforts to deal with the emergency, but it was not until the advent of the Roosevelt administration in 1933 that a comprehensive program of relief, recovery, and reform was initiated. In the years that remained before a new European war quickened the economic pulse of California and the nation, the New Deal touched the lives of millions in California. Late in the decade, the New Deal, or a reasonable facsimile of it, came to Sacramento in the form of Culbert Olson's administration, but for the distressing depressed years of the early thirties, politicians like Rolph and his successor, Frank Merriam, provided little leadership.

ORGANIZED LABOR AND THE ANVIL OF DEPRESSION

Past depressions had generally been trying periods for organized labor, in which membership usually declined. However, the Great Depression produced a new pattern in California as well as the United States. Agricultural and factory workers combined to make this a decade of considerable labor activity. Strikes, pickets, injunctions, strikebreakers, boycotts, and concomitant violence were seen throughout the state. On the waterfront, in the great "factories in the fields," and in the cities, labor was actively engaged in an effort to organize for better wages and working conditions, and to resist the wholesale layoffs and wage cutting that were characteristic of the Depression.

Out of the experiences of the thirties came new methods of organizing, negotiating, and operating. The general result was a much larger voice and role for organized labor in California, especially for the unions in the urban centers. Agricultural unions were also involved and played a prominent role in the labor activity of the decade, but at the end of the period there were few gains from the major efforts made to organize farm labor.

The pattern of relationships between farm laborers and their employers in California existed for many years. It was the product of a number of circumstances. The typical farm laborer followed the crops, moving in response to the changing needs imposed by farming operations involving more than two hundred crops. He was periodically welcomed and then rebuffed. When his labor was in short supply and essential as a ripening crop neared harvest, he was not only tolerated but sought out. When the crop was in, his welcome was likely to become frosty and he was encouraged to move elsewhere. In general, farm costs were fixed, but agricultural wages were flexible. Labor costs can be manipulated by the farm operator although his effort to fix them at the lowest optimum point is likely to bring him into conflict with his migrant workers.

In the early thirties there were some 200,000 farm laborers in California who followed this nomadic life which provided them with irregular employment at miserable wages and no permanent stake anywhere. The migrant worker was an essential part of California's unique agricultural system. Here the average-size farm was larger than in most states and here some 2800 giant farms dominated the agricultural sector. About 2 per cent of the total number of farms in the state employed the bulk of the migratory labor, made more than half the farm profits, and owned more than 60 per cent of the total farm acreage. They were the "factories in the fields," huge combinations of capital which exercised tremendous influence in the social, political, and economic milieus of which they were a part.

The men who ran these corporation-farms tended to look upon the migratory labor which tilled their fields as a factor in production. Like managers everywhere, their prime objective was the organization of an efficient and inexpensive labor force. Migrants, on the other hand, were prone to make the job last in order to obtain maximum wages. The objectives clashed and produced conflict. Potentially, the farm workers possessed great power especially at harvesttime, when a labor stoppage could have left crops rotting in the field at great cost to the grower. Accordingly, operators and growers through the years have been concerned with their labor force. Essentially they seek to ensure that it will be available at the right time, for the right price, and in the right place. The problems the growers faced became acute with the onset of the Depression. Farm prices dropped abruptly whereas farm costs declined moderately and some—mortgage payments—remained fixed. Agriculture in California is generally large-scale, dependent upon heavy capital investments and high operating costs. The grower's solution to his problems of high fixed costs and declining farm prices and income was wage cuts. As farm wages fell, farm labor became increasingly restive, and from 1929 onward there was unprecedented farm labor strife in the agricultural hinterland of California.

There had been any number of attempts to organize farm labor prior to the advent of the Great Depression, but most of them produced scant results. The IWW had once been a potent influence, but its power had been broken in the twenties. The AFL operated differently from the Wobblies, but its efforts were halfhearted, and while appropriate to the organization of craft workers in the building trades, were unsuitable to the migrant workers of California's fields.

The failure of the AFL and the Wobblies to make any permanent organization of farm workers provided opportunities for the Trade Union Unity League. Distinctly left wing in its orientation, the league began the organization of an industrial-type union which would unite all agricultural workers of the Imperial Valley in a single union. Two abortive strikes which followed wage cuts were ineffectual in winning wage gains and improvements in living and working conditions, but they laid the groundwork for the organization of an Agricultural Workers Industrial League. In the spring of 1930 a number of the leaders of this fledgling union were charged with violations of the criminal syndicalism act, convicted after a brief trial, and sentenced to San Quentin.

This setback was soon followed by the open participation of Communist party organizers, who broadened the effort to include cannery as well as field workers in the union. Several years of effort produced limited results, but in 1932 a series of strikes took place in California. Each clash produced arrests, intimidation, and sporadic violence. In the spring of the following year their efforts continued as pea, cherry, apricot, grape, peach, and pear pickers were involved. Most of the work stoppages produced limited gains plus an assortment of intangible benefits in the form of increased knowledge and understanding of trade union tactics. In the summer of 1933 a statewide convention consolidated these scattered efforts into a new union, the Cannery, Agricultural Workers' Industrial Union, which was open to any worker in the agricultural industry without discrimination as to race, color, creed, or sex. Dues of $.25 per month were set for employed workers, $.05 for unemployed. Their objectives were $.75 an hour for skilled labor, an eight-hour day, time and a half for overtime, wages to be set by the hour, and an end to piecework.

That the new union had potential was apparent to all observers. It demonstrated its strength graphically in the fall of 1933 when it organized a strike of cotton pickers in the San Joaquin Valley which involved eighteen thousand agricultural workers in a contest with some of the more powerful corporate farms in the state. At the end of three weeks, they went back to work under a compromise worked out by a state mediation board. Less than four months later the CAWIU struck against pay that averaged $.56 a day and living conditions that were deplorable. The strike produced no lasting benefits although it tempered the union's membership, which survived a formidable combination of brutal vigilante and police harassment. The union continued to build its membership in the spring and summer of 1934. That summer the unions of San Francisco called a general strike. It triggered a massive response in the form of a roundup of hundreds of union members and organizers in a statewide attempt to curb the rising trade union movement in California. The day after the general strike of San Francisco began, eighteen members of the CAWIU were arrested on criminal syndicalism charges in Sacramento. Subsequently eight were convicted and sentenced to prison. The arrests and trials were a body blow from which the union never fully recovered. The union went into eclipse, but its pioneering work paved the way for other efforts to organize the migrant workers of California.

While farm labor was turning to new organizations in an effort to deal with its problems, farm operators and growers also turned to new organizations. The rising militancy of the unions, the wave of strikes, and the inability of the accepted organizations to deal with the situation pushed the farmers toward a new voluntary association, the Associated Farmers. Financed in the beginning by corporations which were interested in large-scale food production and processing, it became a statewide organization which drew its funds from a levy on wages paid to farm labor or on agricultural produce. From the outset, the prime function of the Associated Farmers was to curb the growing influence of unions. Comprised of the propertied interests of the community, the organization pushed the enactment of anti-picketing ordinances in every town, and on the state level it pushed a massive anti-labor legislative program.

In the years that followed the organization of the Associated Farmers, its value to the growers was demonstrated repeatedly. In 1935 it was instrumental in smashing a strike of apple pickers and packing house workers in Santa Rosa, by the use of such vigilante tactics as tar and feathering and brutal beatings. The mob in Santa Rosa was so effective that an actual shortage of farm workers developed as migrant workers fled the scene. In 1936 the action shifted to the citrus groves of Orange County where a $20,000,000 crop was threatened by a walkout of pickers. The "Santa Rosa treatment" was utilized to break the strike. Mass violence, intimidation by vigilantes and "special deputies," and hundreds of arrests deprived the pickers of the $.40 wage they demanded, and they returned to the groves at the old rate of $.20 an hour.

In 1936 and 1937 there were major strikes of farm workers, the first by lettuce packers in Salinas and the second by cannery workers in Stockton. In each case the Associated Farmers mobilized the citizenry of the community against the union. Asserting that the unions were led by Communists and radicals, the farmers' organization in Salinas raised a war chest by levying a charge on each boxcar of lettuce shipped out of Salinas. Newspapers in the communities helped to whip up public opinion against the unions, special guards participated in arrests and raids on union members' homes, and violence and intimidation were freely used to break the strike. In Stockton pitched battles between the strikers and police and special deputies took place, and the casualty lists of the injured were those of a small war.

During most of this long period of farm worker strife, the agricultural workers' unions received nominal support from the American Federation of Labor. Beset with problems of their own and frequently convinced that the workers in the factories in the fields could not be organized into viable labor unions, the leaders of the AFL remained indifferent, sometimes actually hostile, to the aspirations of the farm workers. But the experiences of the 1934 strike in San Francisco gave new perspective to some labor leaders, and with the formation of the CIO, there appeared a new national union of farm workers, the United Cannery, Agricultural, Packing and Allied Workers of America.

The appearance of UCAPAWA was a hopeful portent of those interested in farm labor organization. Locals were organized in a number of communities, a membership drive among field, shed, and cannery workers initiated, and optimistic predictions made of rapid growth. As the decade came to a close, however, the optimism of 1937 faded. Obviously conditions still furnished opportunities to those who would organize the farm workers of California. Almost a quarter of a million strong by the close of the thirties, the farm workers represented a formidable bloc which, if organized, would make up one of the largest unions in the West. But as the thirties came to an end, farm workers were still unorganized for the most part. Growers and farm operators were adamant in their opposition. Tempered in hundreds of strikes, they had developed effective techniques for blocking the organization of farm workers. So well had the Associated Farmers done their work that at the end of the decade only a small portion of the agricultural workers of California were organized. That was the situation in spite of the deplorable conditions of life and labor in the fields of California, publicized so well by John Steinbeck in *The Grapes of Wrath* and Cary McWilliams in *Factories in the Fields*. Steinbeck's novel dramatized the reality of the fields, but McWilliams produced a scholarly examination which demonstrated graphically the plight of the migrant worker and his need for the benefits of organization.

One of the factors which made the unionization of farm workers more difficult, and at the same time was responsible for the conditions described in vivid detail in *The Grapes of Wrath*, was the heavy influx of newcomers to the farm labor scene during the Depression decade. "Tractored out," that is, forced off their farms through technological change, or "dusted out," that is, forced out by prolonged drought on the Great Plains in the thirties and its accompanying dust storms, they came to California by the hundreds of thousands. This army of the dispossessed (350,000 came in the period from 1935–39) was mainly from the southern Plains states. Most of them had once been farmers, part of the sturdy landed yeomanry, and this is the way of life which most of them preferred.

When they arrived in California, more than two thirds of them went into the San Joaquin Valley in search of opportunity. What opportunity existed was work as migratory laborers. There were no farms available in this land dominated by great corporation farms. Less than 10 per cent of the population of California produced not only all the food that the state consumed but great quantities for export.

Half of this army was drawn from Oklahoma, Arkansas, Texas, and Missouri; the other half came from adjacent states. Most of them were native white Americans, members of family groups rather than single men, literate, solid citizens who were victims of the Depression, drought, and technological change. Few of them owned much beyond their ancient flivvers and whatever necessities in the form of bedding, furniture, and personal effects they could carry. Few of them had much cash. Most sought work, not charity, but the only work which was available was in the fields as farm laborers. In spite of the departure of an estimated 200,000 Mexicans in the period from 1929 to 1939, the arrival of "Okies and Arkies" inundated the labor supply, depressed farm wages, handicapped the work of labor organizers, and overwhelmed local authorities who were responsible for relief programs and the like.

To deal with the situation, the authorities devised a number of programs. Perhaps the most direct method was establishing control stations at the border of California to bar the entrance of migrants who were not sufficiently prosperous. Los Angeles policemen enforced this prohibition, and the state legislature passed laws to close the border. The U. S. Supreme Court declared this unconstitutional, however, in the same year in which the problem began to disappear. Its departure coincided with the entry of the nation into World War II. Once the country was transformed from a neutral to an arsenal of democracy, and then into a full-fledged belligerent, the surplus labor of California disappeared. Airframe factories, shipyards, textile factories, and the Armed Forces all absorbed great quantities. Eventually a number of the despised Okies and Arkies proved that they were what they had always been, as they became shippers, growers, and operators themselves. Today a number of the leading families of such towns as Bakersfield,

Delano, Hanford, Madera, Fresno, and the like are representatives of the army of dispossessed who came out of the Dust Bowl of the thirties.

ORGANIZED LABOR AND THE CITIES

While agricultural labor was making little progress, other segments of organized labor in California marched ahead in the Depression decade. In the van of labor's parade were the maritime unions led by one of the more colorful and controversial labor leaders of the modern era, Harry Bridges. Bridges, an Australian who came to the United States as a merchant seaman, settled in San Francisco in 1922 where he was employed on the docks as a winch operator. A slim, intelligent, and articulate man who could speak of "pork-chop issues" so that you could smell the aroma of frying pork, Bridges came from a seafaring background. He had once sailed aboard a U. S. Coast and Geodetic vessel, he had been a member of the IWW during the twenties, and he was a calculating and cold-blooded radical who championed the interests of the longshoremen. He also took positions on a variety of other issues and publicly announced his willingness to work with Communists or representatives of any other groups.

During the twenties and early thirties the once vaunted waterfront unions had been reduced to impotency. Wages and working conditions deteriorated. In 1933 the average wage of longshoremen at a major port was $10.45 per week, employment was irregular, and longshoremen were subjected to a long string of abuses. Speedup that had men running at their work, hazardous conditions which made longshoring among the most dangerous of all employment, miserable wages, and hiring through a daily "shapeup" where men gathered around a straw boss and were assigned jobs provided they were properly subservient or paid kickbacks—these were some of the conditions which finally drove the longshoremen to rebel.

The chance to break the domination of the companies on the waterfront came with the New Deal's famous National Industrial Recovery Act. To ensure the co-operation of organized labor in the Blue Eagle programs which were designed to revive the American economy, Section 7A was added. It encouraged employees to organize unions for the purpose of bargaining collectively with their employers. Democratic elections, as American as apple pie, were to be used to select a bargaining agent from competing labor unions and employers were obligated to deal with the union chosen by majority vote. The longshoremen promptly organized a new local of the International Longshoremen's Association. When the union in 1934 presented a list of demands which included a minimum wage of $1 an hour, a six-hour day, a thirty-hour week, and a hiring hall controlled by the union to replace the hated shapeup system, the Waterfront Employers denounced the union as Communist-led and refused to bargain with it. The issue was joined when the long-shoremen struck on May 9, 1934. The next day a seaman's local walked off the ships; radio operators, officers, and engineers followed. Within a month the maritime industry of the coast was at a standstill.

From the outset it was apparent that this would be a major battle. The strike spread to other ports. Tough, lean longshoremen, reinforced by teamsters, sought the support of other waterfront workers as well as the general public. Cargo piled up on the docks after warehouses filled. The day after the Fourth of July the employers made an effort to move cargo through picket lines by using strikebreakers. A pitched battle was the result as longshoremen and teamsters resisted, overturned and burned trucks, dumped cargo into the streets, and answered tear gas and pistol fire with barrages of bricks and stones. Before peace was restored, two strikers lay mortally wounded and scores from either side were nursing an assortment of injuries. The toll of casualties reached 266 by July 9. The longshoremen named the incident "Bloody Thursday" and from that day to this they have observed it as a day of mourning. The dead were buried in an impressive funeral as ten thousand longshoremen marched down Market Street behind the coffins.

News of the "battle of Rincon Hill" traveled swiftly. "Red revolution" was at hand, said some; civil war impends, said others. A governor on the Pacific coast described it as "insurrection which will lead to Civil War" and tentatively called for the intervention of federal troops. Even before that message was delivered in Washington, troops were entering San Francisco. Governor Merriam, when the battle dispatches from the city reached him, sent in the

National Guard to preserve order and "protect state property." The response of the labor unions was a general strike. Called in spite of the opposition of conservative union leaders, it caught up the organized labor movement as one union after another voted to participate. On July 16 most of the unions of the bay area were on strike. At the end of the fourth day, the general strike was terminated, but the waterfront unions stayed out a few more days until an agreement was reached to refer all issues to a federal arbitration board.

The general strike brought tremendous changes to the labor movement of California. When the settlement was announced in October, it provided for control of the hiring halls by the longshoremen's union, perhaps the most significant single gain ever made by the union. In California the new groups in labor, which spurned the staid craft unionism of Sam Gompers and the AFL for the vibrant new industrial unionism of the CIO and John L. Lewis, had won a tremendous victory. In San Francisco, Harry Bridges, the chief proponent of the new militancy, led the longshoremen and warehousemen into the CIO. As the West Coast director of the CIO, he directed "labor's march inland," as the foothold that the CIO and the maritime unions won in the ports and harbors of California was expanded by an organizing drive that led into the hinterland. Aided by a "neutral and even friendly" national administration, the CIO took full advantage of the National Labor Relations Act to win elections that eventually posted its standard in every major community in the state.

The 900 per cent growth of labor in the thirties was not accomplished easily. While left, right, and center unions combined in general strike in San Francisco in 1934, they frequently worked at cross-purposes. Sailors Union of the Pacific president Harry Lundeberg, whose sailors joined with the longshoremen in 1934, thereafter remained aloof and even antagonistic. Frequently the AFL sailors and the CIO longshoremen clashed in jurisdictional strikes which sapped the strength of labor and vexed alike its friends and enemies. Vigilante activities characterized much of the anti-labor movement in the thirties and were a major factor in blunting labor's organizational drive. While San Francisco was being reorganized into the solid union town it promised to be around 1900, Los Angeles remained the open shop city which Harrison Gray Otis had blueprinted. Even in the South, however, labor was making strides in oil, aircraft manufacturing, trucking, building, and motion pictures. But much remained to be done; the total labor membership was 200,000 in 1940, a small part of the total work force.

DEPRESSION POLITICS

The Depression touched every aspect of life in California and the United States. As men looked at the crisis in which they were involved, they saw problems which were immense: poverty in the midst of plenty, great financial institutions plunged into bankruptcy, the industrious forced into idleness, the thrifty reduced to want, and the world of opportunity transformed into a world of closed doors. And as they contemplated the world which they had not made, an absurd and anachronistic world which placed intolerable burdens on them, they became increasingly determined to do something about that world. Some looked back to the golden twenties, most looked forward and hoped for a new world, some listened to the oily spiels of demagogues who preyed on the fears and the pocketbooks of the distressed citizenry of California. A new politics appeared, Depression politics. The times cried for new changes; political voices and political figures answered.

California had produced its share of unusual politics and political figures in the past. In the 1850s it produced a dominant Democratic party which was as pro-slavery as the ultra pro-slavery parties of the South. In the seventies it produced a Denis Kearney and the sand lotters, and it also produced the Union Labor party of San Francisco at the turn of the century. Once a stronghold of Progressivism, and before that a battleground for the Populists, the state often followed the national pattern, but at times deviated sharply from it. The thirties were a period of panacea and pension politics when California produced a number of political and social movements which attracted national attention and a multitude of followers in the Golden State. A case in point was Upton Sinclair's EPIC movement.

Upton Sinclair was one of the original muckrakers whose rise to national fame or notoriety came with the publication of *The*

Jungle in 1906. That book not only made his reputation but played a major role in furthering the passage of the Pure Food and Drug Act. Thereafter Sinclair produced at regular intervals tracts of various kinds on various subjects. He had the great gift of writing clean, concise, understandable prose, and he used that gift to expose the defects of the capitalist system and propagandize in behalf of the socialist system which he fervently believed would replace it.

In the fall of 1933 the old Socialist reluctantly changed his party registration and announced that he would be a candidate for the Democratic gubernatorial nomination in the 1934 election. From the outset he was ridiculed by the party professionals who could scarcely believe that the party faithful would follow this latter-day self-anointed messiah. In ordinary times his campaign would not have gotten off the ground, but these were desperate times for most people, and soon the muckraker turned gubernatorial candidate was besieged with volunteers. Many of them read a book which Sinclair wrote in the beginning of the campaign, *I, Governor of California and How I Ended Poverty: A True Story of the Future*, in which he engagingly and persuasively described how he would tackle the Depression-spawned problems of California. Sales mounted and it became the source of campaign funds as well as inspirational tracts which mobilized hundreds of thousands of the white-collar, lower-middle-class folks who were victimized by the Depression. Organized into over eight hundred EPIC clubs (for the "End Poverty in California" slogan), they licked stamps, contributed nickels, dimes, and quarters, and cajoled and persuaded their friends and neighbors of the righteousness of the cause. To the consternation of the professionals, Sinclair won the Democratic nomination in the August primary, amassing a grand total which exceeded the vote of his eight opponents.

To the faithful, the primary victory was a sign from heaven and they redoubled their efforts. To the conservatives, the prospect of having Sinclair as the governor of California was enough to boggle the mind. To California's doctrinaire radicals of varied hue, Sinclair was a well-meaning, fuzzy-minded crackpot. To the impoverished and dispossessed, however, he was the man of the hour who would lead them out of the wilderness and they dedicated themselves to the cause. They studied their leader's plans carefully and found them increasingly attractive in the light of the absurd Depression-born situation of the country where people went hungry while crops rotted in the fields. Sinclair advocated the operation of farms by the state on tax-delinquent land as well as the acquisition and operation by the state of deserted factories. In short, he would establish a dual economic system of public-owned industry beside a private enterprise system. Production for use would compete with production for profit. "Let the people go to work again, and take themselves off the backs of the taxpayers." The persuasive prose of Sinclair was most effective in mobilizing thousands of people in behalf of his candidacy.

While the orthodox leaders of the Democratic party grappled with the problem of Sinclair after he won the primary nomination, California opposition to him mounted. He was a most vulnerable candidate because he had produced in the course of a generation of muckraking a Niagara of prose, most of which had found its way into print. He had dissected, criticized, muckraked, and attacked many of the most sacred institutions in America in such books as *King Coal, Oil!, The Wet Parade, The Goose-Step, The Goslings, The Brass Check*, and *The Profits of Religion*. Ministers were horrified by the latter, newspapermen by *The Brass Check*, educators by *The Goose-Step* and *The Goslings*. "Would that my enemy would write a book!" was an axiom of the political world. Sinclair had not written one but many, and his opponents sifted from them damaging extracts which they trumpeted to the winds as evidence of the thinking of the man who would be governor.

Sinclair had two rivals in this race, an ex-Iowan and onetime realtor from Long Beach, Republican Frank Merriam, and Progressive Raymond L. Haight. The latter ensured a division of the anti-Republican vote, but it would take much more to cope with the great coalition of dissident opinion which gathered behind Sinclair. The means appeared in the form of an unprecedented campaign in which the public relations and advertising experts organized under the leadership of movie mogul Louis B. Mayer. Spending huge sums of money, they distributed thousands of campaign documents, produced scores of movie trailers and fabricated newsreel shots which were exhibited in most of the state's motion picture theaters. They persuaded the major newspapers' editors to "black out" the Sinclair campaign, deprived Sinclair of Democratic party support, and in a matter of weeks changed the image of Sinclair for a vast number of Californians. The old muckraker was transformed from a gentle, well-meaning advocate of "socialistic remedies for capitalistic ills" into an atheistic Communist, an advocate of anarchism and free love, an enemy of organized religion, a vegetarian, and a man who would throw open the gates of California to the unwashed multitude of bums who waited outside for the victory of Sinclair. One of the architects of this victory later explained, "He was a good man and we were sorry to do it that way." Meanwhile, Republican conservative Merriam was endorsing the Townsend plan and expressing guarded approval of Franklin D. Roosevelt's New Deal. The result was a Merriam victory with the votes falling 1,138,000 for Merriam, 879,000 for Sinclair, and 302,000 for Haight.

Sinclair's response to defeat was another book, *I, Candidate for Governor: And How I Got Licked*. It was not a manifesto but a review in which he expounded his philosophy anew. He never again ran for political office. His campaign, however, had several long-lasting results. For one thing it brought into the Democratic party thousands of new faces and minds which transformed it and brought to the fore liberal-minded politicians (twenty-nine EPIC-endorsed candidates were elected in 1934) in place of the orthodox Democrats of yesteryear. It pushed a major part of the electorate to the left and activated thousands of people who had never before done much more than vote in an election. The EPIC movement laid the basis for Culbert L. Olson's successful gubernatorial campaign in 1938 and the election of U. S. Senator Sheridan Downey, Sinclair's running mate in 1934. It also provided a springboard for the career of Jerry Voorhis, whose distinguished congressional career was brought to a close by a young Republican leader named Richard M. Nixon in 1946. Perhaps the most significant result, which reached far into the political future, was the effective showing made by the public relations and advertising men. They had demonstrated concretely their ability to shape and mold public opinion. From the 1934 campaign onward, the advertising men had played an important role. Their tools are the public media, their technique is their manipulation; and they have become indispensable. In modern campaigning, the first step is the candidate, the second is the selection of an advertising agency to handle the packaging and sale of the candidate.

Governor Merriam's term was marked by little that was noteworthy. While the federal government launched bold new programs in 1933, designed to bring relief, recovery, and reform to the national scene, Merriam remained the conservative although his administration co-operated, sometimes reluctantly, with new federal programs. National policies had their impact on California, however. The CCC built roads in forested areas, constructed campsites and firebreaks, and took thousands of young men off the streets of California cities. Other New Deal alphabet agencies changed the face of California. The WPA, CWA, PWA all contributed in the form of various programs. Some were make-work projects, but others funded by federal, state, and local governments were public works projects. Schools, public buildings, streets, highways, sewer systems, parks, airports, storm drains, in short hundreds of projects were involved. They gave millions of days of employment and pumped millions of dollars into the economy in the form of wages and payments for building material. Labor relations in California reflected the changes brought first by Section 7A of the National Recovery Act and then by the Wagner Act. The farm programs of the New Deal, devaluation of the dollar, a new approach to tariff questions, and agricultural benefits of various kinds all had an impact on the state.

In 1938 Culbert Olson, who had made a major step in the direction of the governor's mansion as a Los Angeles County state senatorial candidate of the EPIC movement in 1934, replaced Merriam. California had its first Democratic governor in the twentieth century. By then the flush times of the first New Deal were over. A committed New Dealer had come to power in the state, but he arrived on the scene as the national New Deal tide was ebbing. Thereafter Olson worked long and hard to make a New Deal for California, but his achievements were modest. His political problems were numerous: a senate dominated by the conservative representatives of the cow counties; divisions within his own party; and the state press unified in opposition to him. He also was handicapped by a number of personal problems, not the least of which was poor health, which may have also been a factor in his inability to administer well and to utilize his associates in the best way.

But on the other hand, Olson was sincerely interested in bringing progressive changes to California. He pardoned Tom Mooney and commuted the sentence of Warren K. Billings; he was an outspoken defender of minority rights, civil liberties, and the rights of labor; he brought new and higher standards of care and operation to California's mental hospitals and prisons. It is significant to note that his successor in the governor's mansion, Earl Warren, followed many of the precedents which Olson established.

DEPRESSION PANACEAS

While some Californians channeled their frustration and desperation into the EPIC campaign, others directed their energies into diffuse programs of reform. Some programs born elsewhere flourished in the California Depression sun, others were conceived in the visionary minds of California promoters. Here they were spawned and nourished before they went forth to touch the lives of millions of Americans. Technocracy was of the former mold. It was born in the rarefied intellectual atmosphere of Columbia University in New York, coming out of a study of the impact of technology on the modern era. Howard Scott, much impressed by the writing of Thorstein Veblen, and Manchester Boddy, publisher of the Los Angeles *Daily News*, both contributed toward making technocracy a prominent movement of California in 1933. With Scott as a spokesman and the *Daily News* as an outlet, the movement captured the imagination of thousands of Southern Californians. Organized into hundreds of clubs, some of which survive to the present time, technocrats gathered to listen to and expound an integrated set of ideas which attracted engineers and technicians who were convinced that scientific management of the productive system of the United States would produce "plenty for all."

A rival set of promoters of panacea formed the Utopian Society in 1933. Borrowing freely from the basic ideas of technocracy, the promoters combined them with colorful pageantry, rituals, and initiation ceremonies with vague religious overtones. Almost before they knew it, the founders of the society had enrolled hundreds of thousands of members. In its abbreviated life span of two years, it enrolled a half-million members although it never spread beyond Southern California. In hundreds of meetings, audiences assembled to witness pageants which combined morality with visits to a future utopia, where men worked but three hours a day and were retired at forty-five. It was a utopia where there was work for all and plenty for everyone.

The Utopian Society, the technocracy boom, and the EPIC movement were all born of depression. Each reflected the bitter circumstances of that time when men who believed in the eternal verities of the free enterprise system found them contradicted by the harsh realities of life. While some men turned to such movements, others turned to co-operatives in their time of need. The interest in co-operatives was statewide, although like other Depression-born social phenomena, it was especially strong in Southern California. Essentially this phenomenon took the form of individuals and small groups working together in canning food acquired as surplus from farmers or marketing necessities in a co-operative venture. It wasn't the first co-operative venture, nor was it to be the last, and many of these self-help groups did not last beyond the Depression. During their existence, however, they channeled the energies of people into constructive lines and they gave people hope. They also contributed considerably to the building of sentiment and opinion which supported the EPIC movement.

The Townsend movement was also born in the depths of depression when a Long Beach physician and realtor turned in revulsion from the sight of several old women rummaging in garbage cans for food. Revolted as well as angered by the sight, Francis Townsend, ordinarily a gentle man, bellowed with rage and resolved to do something about the plight of the older people, for "after all, they built our country and made it what it is." This apocryphal story, devised after the fact as a plausible explanation of the genesis of the plan, glosses over the facts of its intellectual birth. Townsend's solution of dubious and mixed intellectual ancestry was simple. He wished to establish a pension system and pay everyone over sixty $150 or more a month (later $200) on the condition that they would spend the money as they received it. The program, financed by a 2 per cent tax on commercial transactions, would open up new job opportunities to the young, provide the aged with the rewards they deserved, and pump new purchasing power into a stagnant economy.

The idea caught on. Soon several dozen old men and women were put to work circulating petitions, an office was opened, and Townsend and an associate incorporated the organization as Old Age Revolving Pensions Ltd. With an efficient associate, Texas-born Robert E. Clements, as an aide, the movement began to gather steam. As it captured the allegiance of thousands of the aged in California, it became a political force. Republican candidate Frank Merriam endorsed the Townsend plan in his race with Sinclair. He was elected. Soon other political aspirants indicated interest in the movement, now organized into hundreds of clubs scattered throughout the state and the nation. The headquarters, nearly overwhelmed with applications for membership and club charters, hired additional help to keep track of a swelling volume of nickels, dimes, and quarters which came pouring in. In January 1935 *The Townsend National Weekly* appeared, and before the year was out its circulation exceeded 200,000. Its advertising income mounted and supplemented the income from the contributions of the membership, which by 1935 was nearly $2,000,000. And as the founder began to sense the political strength of the movement—"We have at least thirty million votes"—politicians everywhere began to treat it with appropriate deference.

By the time the preliminaries of the 1936 election began, the movement was a national political force. Estranged from Roosevelt because of his coolness, Townsend began turning to other political alternatives. In 1936 he joined with Father Coughlin of the National Union for Social Justice, the Reverend Gerald L. K. Smith, who took over Huey P. Long's Share Our Wealth movement and was a notorious anti-Semite and admirer of Adolph Hitler, and Congressman William Lemke of North Dakota in launching the Union party. With William Lemke as the presidential nominee, it ran a poor third in the Roosevelt-Landon race of 1936. Thereafter it lingered on. Townsend clubs met and heard speakers describe the merits of $200-a-month pensions and the newspaper continued to circulate, each issue featuring news about the movement and advertisements for the multiple medicines and devices which would appeal to the aged. The passage of the Social Security program of the New Deal took some of the momentum out of the movement, and the gradual improvement of economic conditions sapped at its constituency, which was largely drawn from the bankrupt lower middle class.

But "pension politics" continued. Robert Clements was not the only one to realize the profits which might be derived from a mass movement which promised aid to a major segment of the citizenry distressed by the collapse of values in the Depression. In the footsteps of Townsend came Robert Noble, who captured a portion of the Townsend following and additional recruits who flocked to what became a "Thirty Dollars Every Thursday" banner. The scheme was taken over by Willis and Lawrence Allen, who had been hired by Noble to handle his advertising. It promised a weekly pension in warrants to everyone over fifty who was not employed. The money was to be financed by a weekly stamp tax of $.02. At the end of the year, the warrant would be retired, hopefully with $1.04 attached, the four cents covering the administrative costs.

Launched in 1938 with an initiative campaign which quickly secured more than 789,000 signatures, a record total which was approximately one fourth of the total registration, "Thirty Dollars Every Thursday," or "Ham and Eggs" as it was known, swept the state. A newspaper entitled *Ham and Eggs*, a membership topping 200,000, and endorsement by the Democratic senatorial candidate, Sheridan Downey, produced 1,143,000 votes in the 1938 election, but the opposition obtained 1,398,000. Undaunted by the setback, the promoters returned to the battle. This time their petition campaign produced more than a million signatures requesting that the proposition be placed on the ballot at a special election. By now the organization was better financed and organized. A young promoter, George McLain, helped to organize the campaign. With twelve radio stations broadcasting fifty-two programs a week, a newspaper weekly of twenty-eight pages, a membership of 331,000, and an income of $55,000 per month, there was apparently no way the scheme could be defeated. Culbert Olson delayed for a time but eventually set a special election for November 1939 after the organization gathered more than a million signatures on a petition which they presented to the governor in May. Olson owed his election in part to his straddling position on the issue, but after he set the election date for November, he came out flat-footed against the scheme. By the time the election rolled around in 1939, a great deal of steam had gone out of the movement, the opposition was organized, and the proposition was defeated by a quarter of a million votes. The exposure of the profiteering of the Allen brothers was partially responsible, but the war in Europe, improving economic conditions in the United States generally, as well as the enactment of Social Security, all worked to bring defeat and the eclipse of pension politics.

Interest in pensions lingered on. McLain remained a major figure in pension politics until his death in the sixties and the organization he founded is still active. Several radio broadcasts a week followed the format of the 1938 campaign. A speaker, usually McLain himself, commented on the current scene as it related to the problems of the aged and the pensioners, pleaded for support so that the broadcasts might continue, and announced forthcoming meetings in each broadcast. The interest in pensions and problems of security for the aged is likely to persist in California so long as a sizable portion of its population finds itself in distress in the twilight years of life. More recently, private and public pension programs have made the insecurity of the aged a problem that has little of the significance it had in the Depression decade. But even now, although the population of the state tends to become younger, one sixth of the population is over fifty-five, and the problem remains. If the state were to experience another major setback comparable to the Depression, there can be little doubt that a new crop of promoters would come forth with new schemes and pension and panacea politics would be prominent again.

The end of the Depression decade and the outbreak of World War II in Europe coincided. The two events were distinctly related. It had been a time of tremendous change. The nation and the state which began the decade were vastly different. California had grown considerably in population, with a 20 per cent change to 6,900,000. More important than population change were the changes which had taken place in the industrial, social, political, and economic spheres. The development of the aircraft industry, continued growth of motion pictures, the unionization of great segments of industry, the extension of highways, streets, and roads, the construction of great bridges in San Francisco and the Hoover Dam on the lower Colorado were some of the changes. A new political climate had also appeared. The time when Republicans monopolized the state government was no more. But great new changes were in the offing; California altered as much in the forties as she did in the thirties.

CHAPTER XIX

Arsenal of Democracy

War came suddenly to California and the nation on December 7, 1941, with the Japanese assault on the mid-Pacific bastion of the American Navy at Pearl Harbor. Its coming had long been predicted. From the time that America sought international action to restrain the Japanese invasion of Manchuria through the bombing of the *Panay* in 1937, to the freezing of Japanese assets in the United States in July 1941, the two countries had been on a confrontation course. The European war and the string of Nazi victories emboldened Japanese policy makers and strengthened the Berlin-Rome-Tokyo Axis. The American response was renewed effort to aid the Allies. Both developments tended to accentuate the antagonistic posture of the United States and Japan. When the radio bulletins announcing the incredible attack of the Japanese Navy came, Californians like most Americans were caught by surprise. If they thought about it in retrospect, most concluded that they had long seen but ignored the shadow of war.

The war which had been raging since September 1939 on European battlefronts had already touched California—spurring its depressed economy. Now the war and its impact was to enlarge. California and its citizenry were to be profoundly affected; the war years did more to shape California than any other similar period in the twentieth century. When it began, California's senior senator, Hiram Johnson, dean of Progressive Republicans, symbolized the isolation of California and the nation from world affairs. His general reputation as a vehement opponent of American involvement in the European war made him a national figure. When the war came to a close, his retirement, the explosion of nuclear bombs at Hiroshima and Nagasaki, and the founding of the United Nations in San Francisco served as multiple portents of the coming of a new age for California, the nation, and the world.

Before the Japanese militarists decided to measure swords with the United States, California was being transformed into an "arsenal of democracy." Even before World War II began the state's economic pulse was quickened as a result of military orders from Britain and France. Among the major industries to be affected were aviation and shipbuilding; before the signing of a peace, every business and enterprise was affected directly or indirectly. Year by year the impact of the war mounted although when the tide of victory seemed assured, the total involvement of the airframe industry and shipbuilding began to change, payrolls were cut, and planners began to look ahead to peacetime conversion plans.

World War II affected California profoundly for a number of reasons. Geography was partially responsible. Fronting on the Pacific, a major theater only an ocean away, it was quite natural for California to be the staging area for the armies and fleets sent forth to do battle with the enemy. California also became a vast supply base from which far-flung forces drew necessities of every kind and sought sanctuary where the ravages of battle could be remedied. The state's varied topography also provided commanders with natural sites which resembled the varied battlegrounds where armies would clash. In the deserts of Southern California, General George S. Patton's famed armored legions tested the tanks, weapons, and tactics which they later employed in North Africa. On the coast nearby Marines practiced the amphibious landings which were to be essential in the island-hopping campaigns in the far Pacific. Along the coast the Navy trained its ships and crews in the multiple skills of the modern sea force.

The far-flung nature of the war also determined the nature and magnitude of California's involvement. Separated by vast oceans from the immediate battle fronts in Europe and Asia, it was imperative to provide the ships, planes, and men to man them if American military power was to be effective. The output of ships and planes to offset such distances was increased enormously during the war. By the time peace had been restored, ships and planes built in California were found in every theater of the war.

The nature of the war also determined the degree to which California would be involved and the manner in which its future would be molded in the wartime years. World War II was fought with tactics and weaponry which emphasized the role of tactical aircraft, powered landing craft, amphibious vehicles, automotive transport, and the tank. Military forces, highly mechanized and mobile, were coordinated in operation with complex and sensitive electronic communications systems. California geography provided stages where armored divisions and amphibious forces could test their tactics and equipment; the state's industry, paced by aircraft, electronic, and shipbuilding companies, furnished much of the equipment and some of the innovations in technology and weaponry which contributed to victory. The war was fought and won, then, not only by the Armed Forces of the United States and its allies, but also by the men and women on the home front. Mobilized as never before by the federal government, the American citizenry built not only a vast military force which waged global war, but also a complex technology that sustained the military system. California contributed to each.

Evidence that this was a new kind of war came with Pearl Harbor, where a force of 6 carriers struck with 450 planes and inflicted massive damage on American battleships, cruisers, and destroyers. The Battle of Coral Sea of May 1942, fought with carrier aircraft over distances of hundreds of miles, emphasized the new role of aircraft. Less than a month later a Japanese force of carriers met with a massive defeat in the Battle of Midway. The Japanese loss of four flat-tops was a body blow from which they never recovered. Each of these engagements demonstrated that the war would be fought with the weapons which California produced in abundance—aircraft.

WINGS FOR VICTORY

California's airframe industry had origins which stretch back to the first decade of the twentieth century. Among the Californians who were involved in the founding, growth, and development of the industry were the three sons of Flora Haines Loughead, novelist and feature writer of the San Francisco *Chronicle*. The first contributions of this remarkable family (which eventually tired of correcting misuse of their name and changed it to Lockheed) were two books published in 1909 by Victor Loughead, *Vehicles of the Air* and *Aeroplane Designing for Amateurs*. A year later, his brother Allan first flew one of the primitive aircraft, a kitelike device hitched to a gas engine. On June 15, 1915, the two brothers Allan and Malcolm launched a seaplane in San Francisco Bay of their own design and creation. It was a remarkable plane for its time which flew some twenty minutes over the bay in its initial flight at a speed of 60 miles an hour. There was little return from the plane until the Panama-Pacific Exposition in 1915 when it was used in exhibition flying. A year later the two brothers shipped their plane to Santa Barbara where they organized the Loughead Aircraft Manufacturing Company in the rear of a garage near the waterfront. The war soon brought encouragement in the form of military contracts but prosperity was short-lived. In the immediate postwar years the government disposed of surplus aircraft at bargain prices and thereby destroyed prospective markets. In 1921 the company was liquidated, only to be reborn in 1926 under the corporate banner of Lockheed Aircraft Company. The company's Vega design brought it a spate of orders and not long thereafter a merger into a holding company, Detroit Aircraft, based in the auto capital. Less than a year later the collapse of the stock market brought general ruin to the airframe industry and bankruptcy to the parent concern. In October 1931 the Lockheed unit went into receivership; six months later a new management group of the company purchased the assets in an auction in federal court for $40,000.

To the surprise of some skeptics, the company not only survived the lean Depression years but actually began to prosper. The design and development of a new twin-motored transport gobbled up cash and necessitated the sale of additional shares in the depressed Los Angeles securities market, but when the Electra flew for the first time in 1934, it brought in a number of orders from airlines and put the corporation on a sound footing. A sturdy plane which was adaptable to many uses (the XC-35, built for the Air Corps, was the world's first successful pressurized substratosphere airplane), the Electra brought great growth to the company. The early bleak years of the Depression behind them, the firm forged ahead. By 1937 total sales had reached $5,000,000. In the next few years the company experienced phenomenal growth, sales rose to $145,000,000, employment increased more than forty times to 53,000, and production in one month totaled 325 planes—four times as many as had been produced in the entire year in 1937.

The phenomenal growth began after Munich with an order for two hundred modified Electras for use as Hudson bombers by the British Royal Air Force. The order came at a fortuitous time. Lockheed management learned of the prospective arrival of a British purchasing mission as they were putting the finishing touches to a group of commercial planes for a Japanese concern. Working around the clock, the company's engineers produced drawings for a modification of the Electra. The result was the Hudson, a tough and versatile bomber which the British prized. Thereafter the orders for Hudson bombers came at periodic intervals until they totaled three thousand. They were joined by other Lockheed-produced planes which included the remarkable fighter pursuit plane, the twin-boomed P-38. Toward the close of 1941, the payroll rose to fifty thousand and Lockheed was the largest company in the industry. From a bankrupt company in 1932 had come a modern corporate giant.

All this was prologue to the tremendous expansion of Lockheed and the industry that came with Pearl Harbor. When the war began Lockheed was less than ten years away from bankruptcy proceedings in a federal court. Employment in the aircraft industry, which stood at 30,000 in 1937, soared to more than 2,100,000 at its peak. President Franklin D. Roosevelt in 1940 called for the production of 50,000 planes a year. In 1944 alone the industry built more than 96,000 planes and during the wartime years it built more than 300,000 aircraft. Lockheed contributed significantly to the totals. Production of P-38s mounted, 387 in a single month in 1943, more than 10,000 in all. By mid-1943 the Lockheed payroll had reached 94,239. By the time peace came, the company had built nearly 10 per cent of all United States aircraft. The total included not only 10,000 P-38s but about 5600 patrol bombers and 2750 four-engine Boeing-designed B-17 bombers.

While Lockheed was the biggest concern, a number of other major corporations comprised California's airframe industry. The Douglas Corporation built thousands of planes in dozens of plants scattered across the nation from Santa Monica to Chicago. In its peak year, 1944, Douglas produced more than $1,000,000,000 of aircraft, out of the $9,000,000,000 of contracts let in Southern California during the wartime years. North American, Northrop, Consolidated Vultee were other names which loomed large in the planning of the wartime aviation industry, but hundreds of smaller concerns were also involved. The smaller companies frequently operated as subcontractors, each producing parts or subassemblies of a plane. The moblization of production resources was nearly complete. The result was the transformation of California's airframe industry into a modern industrial giant. A great new plant was built, a modern technology of production was created, and an experienced and highly trained work force assembled which provided for a massive new advance in the industrialization of California. The implications were enormous. When weaponry underwent further fundamental changes with the appearance of the first atomic bombs, followed by hydrogen bombs and finally intercontinental ballistic missiles, California, in large measure because of World War II experiences, had the know-how as well as the capability of dealing in such weaponry.

ARMADA FOR VICTORY

California shipbuilding underwent a similar transformation during the war. Payrolls climbed from thousands to more than a quarter million. While the aircraft industry in Southern California obtained the bulk of the contracts, the opposite was true of shipbuilding. It was the San Francisco Bay area which obtained the greater share, almost $3,000,000,000 of the $5,000,000,000 committed by the federal government. In private shipyards at Richmond, Sausalito, Oakland, Vallejo, and in naval shipyards at Mare Island, men worked around the clock, building new craft to carry the men and munitions to the scattered battle fronts of World War II, as well as repairing the damages inflicted by enemy action. Wartime demands not only brought great growth of plants, financed in large measure by the federal government, but also new changes in shipbuilding practices.

Among the major innovators was Henry Kaiser, who had assembled and tested a great peacetime production team on vast construction projects like Boulder Dam. Out of that experience had come renewed conviction that production of almost anything required careful planning and organization, a knowledgeable work force, and responsible and informed management. When the demand for ships appeared, the Kaiser team tackled the problems involved in building ships in much the same way they tackled other tasks. In Richmond, where Kaiser employed more than 100,000 shipbuilders, they built hundreds of Liberty ships. Like the Model T Fords, the Liberty ships were ugly but durable, and Kaiser built them as Ford built cars. Fabrication of standardized parts was one of the basic changes in shipbuilding. In sequences planned and co-ordinated, parts of the ship were brought to the hull site by massive gantry cranes and there made part of the ships through welding or riveting. Using techniques of this kind, more than two thousand Liberty ships were built in the United States; more than half of them on the West Coast and almost a fourth of them in the Richmond yards of Kaiser. The shipyards of California turned out a diversified line during the war years. Liberties were built in abundance but other kinds of vessels were built as well, Victory ships, tankers, and C-2 and C-4 freighters, designed and approved by the United States Maritime Commission. Naval vessels of several sizes were manufactured, ranging upward from seagoing tugs. Amphibious craft consumed in great numbers especially in the Pacific were built by the thousands by a hundred California concerns.

WARTIME FACTORIES AND FARMS

The war brought expansion to several other industries. The steel industry, essential in a modern industrial society, infant in size before the war, grew substantially after Pearl Harbor. Henry Kaiser was also prominent in this development. Near Fontana he built the state's first completely integrated steel operation which produced raw steel in its blast furnaces and semi-finished steel in its mills. Although its capacity, subsequently enlarged several times, was limited to 700,000 tons, it represented a sharp increase in the state's prewar capacity of about 1,000,000 tons. In the course of the war, existing producers enlarged and modernized their plants, Bethlehem and United States Steel among others.

The war brought major change to a wide range of California industries. The petroleum industry, for example, increased production by more than 50 per cent. The demands of the fleets and squadrons in the Pacific required not only more fuel, but different kinds of fuel. The production of gasoline, especially high-test aviation fuel, climbed sharply, a reflection of the widespread use of aircraft and motor vehicles. Within the oil field and the refineries improvements of various kinds brought increased efficiency. When the war came to an end in 1945, California was producing record quantities of petroleum and petroleum products although its work force had been reduced.

Agriculture, the biggest industry in the state in peacetime, was confronted with a number of major problems as well as opportunities in the form of unprecedented demands for its produce after Pearl Harbor. A shortage of labor was its biggest problem. The mobilization of young men for military service, which eventually put more than 700,000 Californians into uniform, was partially responsible. War-swollen industries also absorbed a substantial part of the migrant work force—the much maligned Okies and Arkies of the thirties—and the "relocation" of the Japanese-American population also contributed to the acute shortage of farm labor during the wartime years. The shortage brought a number of changes to the agricultural scene. One was increased status for the migrant worker, another was the more extensive use of labor-saving machinery, and a third took the form of changes in operations and an emphasis on the production of crops which involved less labor. A number of alternate sources of labor were tapped. Thousands of black workers, many migrants from the South, joined the California labor force. Not only were Italian and German prisoners of war used, but prisoners from San Quentin and Folsom, and young people from the public schools. A real dent in the labor shortage was made by importing thousands of Mexican *braceros*, who came and labored in the fields and returned home under the terms of an agreement between the United States and Mexico.

In spite of the shortage of labor, complemented by shortages of gasoline, rubber tractor tires, and the like, California's agricultural system made a substantial contribution toward victory. The total tonnage of California's crops jumped sharply; the total acreage devoted to farming climbed, and the value of agricultural output set new records each year. There were changes in the patterns, exotic crops like strawberries were cut back, in part because of their dependence upon extensive use of hand labor, but the total acreage devoted to prosaic crops like potatoes climbed sharply. The prosperity of the wartime years provided expanded markets for California growers and the insatiable appetite of the Armed Forces for the diverse output of the state's agricultural producers made for general prosperity. The total value of California farm produce tripled in the period from 1939 to 1944. The respective dollar amounts in round numbers are $625,000,000 in 1939, $1,700,000,000 in 1944.

SCIENCE AND VICTORY

California's scientific community also made a considerable contribution to the war effort. Gathered in such institutions as the California Institute of Technology, Stanford University, and the campuses of the University of California, they played a variety of roles. Some served as technical experts of one kind or another, others organized and participated in research focused on electronic development or some phase of science which had application to military problems. The rocket jet assist takeoff and a torpedo which zeroed in on the noise emanating from the target were perfected in California laboratories. In many colleges and universities training programs designed to produce officers and specialists of various kinds for the Armed Forces were set up.

The most spectacular contribution of the scientific community was in atomic research. For a number of years, research in this new field had been conducted at the University of California at Berkeley where a number of basic discoveries were facilitated by the first cyclotron. The Radiation Laboratory of the university produced several basic discoveries, such as U-235, neptunium, and plutonium, but it also developed a number of scientists who were expert in this field. J. Robert Oppenheimer and E. O. Lawrence were prominent in this group which was subsequently enlisted in the Manhattan Project. This proposal to produce a new kind of bomb was first brought to Franklin D. Roosevelt's attention by Albert Einstein in 1939 but it was not until 1942 that the government initiated a crash program to produce a bomb. Much of the work was done at Los Alamos in

New Mexico by scientists who had trained at Berkeley. The project culminated in the production of the first atomic bombs, which ushered in the nuclear age.

THE POLITICS OF PREJUDICE

The full weight of the war descended in the early spring of 1942 on 110,000 Japanese-American residents of California who were quietly stripped of their constitutional rights and transported for the "duration" to a number of improvised internment centers. That they were singled out in this way, while aliens of German and Italian origin were ignored, is partially due to the deep-rooted prejudice against Orientals which stretched back to the mid-nineteenth century. In the beginning, Chinese took the brunt of the unreasoning bigotry, but in the twentieth century, the Japanese became the focus of the mindless animosity of the nativists. It was their distinctness as an ethnic group; their identification with the Empire of the Rising Sun; their general inclination to compete directly with whites in business, professional, and agricultural fields which accelerated the growth of prejudice. Concentrated in California, this minority whose members seldom ran afoul of the law were rounded up in early 1942 in "the worst single violation of the civil rights of American citizens in our history."

Although the basic decision to relocate the Japanese was made by the military under the authority of an executive order promulgated by President Roosevelt, there can be little doubt that political leaders of various levels and ranks, Governor Culbert Olson, Attorney General Earl Warren, and Los Angeles mayor Fletcher Bowron supported the basic decision made by General John L. DeWitt of the Western Defense Command. For that matter a great many lesser figures, congressmen, legislators, newspapermen, and a substantial part of the general citizenry, implicitly condoned the injustice visited on the Japanese-Americans in this program.

DeWitt was an army career officer of varied experience. In the weeks that followed Pearl Harbor and the subsequent investigations which seemed to point an accusing finger at the commanders who were caught napping on December 7, 1941, men like DeWitt were determined to avoid similar lapses through supervigilance. There was reason to be tense as the war came close to home through the sinking of an oil tanker off Crescent City, the shelling of a small cluster of oil field installations at Goleta, and the "battle of Los Angeles." The latter conflict took place on the night of February 24, 1942, when batteries of anti-aircraft guns in and around the city fired upon a phantom enemy. No enemy planes were shot down, but many reports of hostile aircraft were turned in. When the War Department and the Navy Department issued conflicting reports on the presence of Japanese planes in the skies over Los Angeles a great many people concluded that an invasion was at hand and began to make plans to meet it. Much of the population was semi-hysterical. The public media contributed by whipping up anti-Japanese sentiment and ignoring differences between the local population of Japanese descent and citizens of the Empire of the Rising Sun. The evacuation found widespread support in the general citizenry. When DeWitt's report on the manner in which it was carried out was subsequently made public it was found to contain a number of bigoted sentiments, although he generally defended his decision on the grounds of military necessity.

The removal of the Japanese began shortly after Pearl Harbor when some fifteen hundred "enemy aliens" were incarcerated by the Justice Department. The balance of the Japanese-American population, regardless of citizenship, was required to register and surrender their cameras, binoculars, radios, and firearms. This was followed by the creation of a "military area" by proclamation of DeWitt and the banning of all Japanese from it. At first the migration out of the area was voluntary but in late March 1942 compulsory internment for the Japanese population was decreed. The United States Army carried out the forced migration. Each family was given some notice but seldom did the time allowed provide for an orderly disposition of property. Accordingly, the evacuees incurred huge losses as they wound up their business affairs and disposed of their homes or land at bargain prices to brokers and dealers who hovered buzzardlike around the family subject to evacuation. The total of their financial losses shall probably never be accurately determined. Conservative estimates place their losses at $350,000,000 to $500,000,000. In 1948 Congress passed legislation to compensate partially for the losses and this produced some $38,000,000 for the approximately 75,000 evacuees who were American citizens. Other steps were taken in the postwar period to compensate the individuals who had been victimized by the relocation, but in almost all cases the relief was a small fraction of the monetary losses incurred.

For most of the evacuees the wartime years left scars which may never be healed. Rounded up, provided little time to make necessary arrangements, temporarily housed, in some cases in improvised quarters such as the stalls of horses at the Santa Anita race track, transported to distant and forlorn internment camps such as Tule Lake or Manzanar, the whole experience was a traumatic ordeal for thousands of Japanese-Americans. And that it should impose financial burdens of some $350,000,000 on the United States government is a final touch of irony.

A JAPANESE STUDENT'S VIEW OF EVACUATION

The violation of human personality is the violation of the most sacred thing which man owns. This order for the mass evacuation of all persons of Japanese descent denies them the right to live. It forces thousands of energetic, law-abiding individuals to exist in miserable psychological conditions and a horrible physical atmosphere. This order limits to almost full extent the creative expressions of those subjected. It kills the desire for a higher life. Hope for the future is exterminated. Human personalities are poisoned . . . If I were to register and cooperate under these circumstances, I would be giving helpless consent to the denial of practically all of the things which gave me incentive to live. I must maintain my Christian principles. I consider it my duty to maintain the democratic standards for which this nation lives. Therefore, I must refuse this order of evacuation.

By Gordon Hirabayashi in Anne R. Fisher, *Exile of a Race*.

The ludicrous nature of the evacuation is highlighted by several wartime developments. One such is the magnificent record of the 442nd Regimental Combat Team, comprised of Japanese-Americans who were permitted to serve in the United States Army in 1943. It won almost four thousand medals—more than any other unit of that size; its five thousand men were in the thick of some of the bitterest fighting in the Italian and Southern France campaigns where their sacrifice of life and limb is an eloquent reproach to all those who labeled all Japanese-Americans suspect. Furthermore, the fact that not a single case of sabotage or espionage involving Japanese-Americans came to light in California or in Hawaii, where they represented more than a third of the population, is another reproof to those responsible for inflicting this massive hurt on more than 100,000 American citizens.

Even before the war ended, some people were having sober second thoughts about the evacuation. As a result some internees were allowed to leave the centers for work in other cities and states and others were allowed to serve in the Armed Forces. When the war ended, the evacuees returned to their homes in California, where they attempted to pick up the shattered pieces of their lives. A number of studies were made of the episode but none seems to have satisfactorily answered one of the most important questions of the evacuation: "Why did it take place?" A complementary query which persists in many minds is: "If a democratic society tolerated such a thing once, might it condone it again?"

WARTIME SOCIAL CHANGES

The war brought a full measure of change to the lives of other ethnic groups in California. The ranks of migratory labor were depleted as Okies and Arkies went into the aircraft plants and shipyards in swarms. They were replaced in part by Negro migrants who came out of the South and found employment not only in the orchards and fields but also in war-swollen industries. Migrants came from Mexico as well as the general Southwest. They joined a substantial ethnic bloc in California whose members were themselves becoming increasingly prominent thanks to the general wartime prosperity.

During the wartime years there were other groups represented in the migration to California. Some came involuntarily as members of the Armed Forces. Gathered in great training centers like Camp Pendleton, the San Diego Naval Training Station, Camp Roberts, and the like, they endured the arduous routine of military training broken periodically by "passes" or trips into the cities for recreation. There they frequently came into contact with Mexican-Americans, who were numerous and distinctive. To some members of the Armed Forces in whom prejudice was ingrained, the Mexican-American youth was objectionable in language, appearance, and dress, which frequently featured an extravagantly cut suit of long coat and tightly cuffed pants. To other members of the Armed Forces he was objectionable because he was a civilian while they were ex-civilians in uniform. Relations between such groups became increasingly strained and the press contributed to the situation by its sensationalizing of crime news featuring servicemen and Mexican-Americans. The climax came in early 1943 in another episode which Axis propagandists declared revealed the basic hypocrisy of American society. The trouble took the form of gangs of servicemen assaulting Mexican-American young men in the streets of Los Angeles. The victims were beaten, stripped of their "zoot suits," and arrested for disturbing the peace. Before the episode came to a close, scores of young men had been treated in this fashion and thereby had their faith in the democratic order tested. That the group tested, the Mexican-American, has earned a greater number of Congressional Medals of Honor than any other such group in American society is a final touch of irony.

The war brought all sorts of change to the California scene. Not only was there tremendous growth of population, almost two million, but the manner in which the newcomers came, the centers of greatest expansion, and the measures taken to accommodate them all had extensive impact on the present as well as the future of California. As the rapid growth of the industrial establishment took place, it brought thousands of newcomers to California. It also forced or induced thousands of people to change occupations as some industries, especially service industries, were cut back while others expanded. The mining industry, for instance, cut back sharply, and construction, except for the most essential building, was curtailed.

Such changes transformed construction workers into shipyard riveters and hard-rock miners into aircraft builders. The general industrial work force nearly tripled from its peacetime level of 380,000. The almost insatiable demand for workers in the industrial area was

met in a variety of ways. Migration into the area in response to the
need for wartime workers brought large numbers of Negroes, Mexicans, and a representative cross sampling of the population of the rest
of the nation, especially the West and the South. A great many
women joined the work force as well, as "Rosie the riveter" made
her appearance and working mothers became a commonplace.

The shifts within industries and the influx of great numbers of
people, as well as the social changes incident to the entry of large
numbers of Negroes and Mexicans and working mothers, posed
problems of considerable variety and magnitude. While construction
housing had been sharply curtailed there were unprecedented
demands for housing. Improvised housing in the form of trailers,
prefabricated homes, and temporary housing units adjacent to war
industries were built, but none of these approaches did more than
meet a part of the total demand. The result was crowding as several
families moved into a home or apartment built for one. Waiting lists
for housing became common and the practice of paying "under the
table" for the privilege of renting a home or apartment occurred frequently.

The demands placed on utilities—light, telephone, gas, sewer, and
water—were unprecedented and in many instances were beyond the
resources available. Rationing of such services was attempted to
stretch the resources. Public schools which were especially burdened
by the new population went to double sessions, wherein an existing
school plant did double duty by having two sessions a day. But such
expedients met but a part of the problem. Throughout the wartime
years the facilities available for such services were insufficient but a
major effort was made to stretch resources to meet demands.

Gas rationing in sprawling Southern California imposed especial
burdens, but here again attempts were made to make the best possible
use of what was available. Car pools were set up to offset shortages of
gasoline and tires. A lively black market developed in these essentials
and Californians, generally more dependent on private automobile
transportation than the populace in other areas, supplemented rations
of gas and tires by patronizing such outlets. A surprisingly large proportion of the general citizenry responded to government appeals,
however, and simply made their legitimate share go further by re-

THE PORT CHICAGO EXPLOSION AND MUTINY

A glimpse of the devastation of war in all its fury came to Californians on July 17, 1944, when a fully loaded ammunition ship, the S.S. E. A. Bryan, blew up. The blast of 5000 tons of explosives took 323 lives and injured 58. Some 350 homes in Port Chicago, just off San Francisco Bay, were destroyed along with most of the business district. The streets were strewn with timbers, telephone wires, glass, and bricks; fifty parked automobiles were totally destroyed and countless others severely damaged. Pieces of steel from the ship's hull and superstructure showered the town, perforating roofs, walls, and sidewalks. Live shells fell everywhere. People 10 miles distant were cut by flying glass, and windows were broken 35 miles away. Several ships in the channel were damaged or destroyed. In all, property damages totaled $12,521,333. A naval board of inquiry concluded that the most probable cause of the disaster was an accident.

In the aftermath of the Port Chicago disaster came the first mass mutiny in the history of the United States Navy. On August 9, 1944, some four hundred black sailors refused to obey a command to load ammunition ships. Most of them changed their minds when confronted with Navy authority, and received summary court-martials or brief sentences in the brig. However, on September 15, 1944, the Navy announced a general court-martial of fifty seamen for "conspiracy to commit mutiny" and "mutiny in time of war." All those charged were black (as were all of the personnel who handled explosives). Of the 4000 sailors stationed at Port Chicago, 2500 were black. Theirs was the hazardous, backbreaking task of unloading ammunition, shells, and powder bags from boxcars, moving them to the pier and then stowing them into the hot, crowded holds of the ships. The supervisory personnel, naval officers and merchant seamen, were 99 per cent white.

The court-martial revealed that the morale of the black seamen, which had always been low, had plummeted after the Port Chicago explosion. Most were between seventeen and twenty-seven years old and had come from the Deep South. Under the best of circumstances it was nerve-wracking to handle live ammunition, knowing that one mistake might well be your last. Most of those court-martialed had lost friends in the explosion and many had been injured—one of those accused of refusing to load ammunition had a broken arm! Others had worked cleaning up the wreckage and often found an arm, a foot, or pieces of flesh in the debris. (Only thirty of the eighty-one recovered bodies could be identified). Hence, their reluctance to return to their hazardous duty was understandable. The blacks were also discriminated against in the local community. Port Chicago was a small, isolated white town with limited recreational opportunities and blacks were not welcome there or in adjacent cities. They suffered insults and harassment by their own officers and by Marine guards. The court-martial revealed that many of the incriminating statements introduced into evidence were obtained by officers who threatened to shoot the accused unless they signed the documents thrust into their hands. One poor seaman who was completely illiterate confessed that the interrogating officer signed his confession for him. The Navy prosecutor, who had been a district attorney, lost no opportunity to belittle the accused. Thurgood Marshall, an observer at the proceedings, bitterly criticized the blatant discrimination practiced by the Navy. Despite the fact that the black seamen sought only a change of duty by their action and did not realize their actions constituted a mutiny, they were found guilty as charged. Harsh prison sentences of fifteen years were first meted out to all. However, forty men had their punishment reduced to eight to twelve years by appeal of the Navy Judge Advocate General, and later Secretary of the Navy James Forrestal further reduced the sentences of seven men to twenty-nine months and forty-three men to seventeen months.

---

fraining from pleasure driving and sharing their mileage expended in business and essential driving with friends and neighbors.

The war often brought forth from the citizenry a sense of community which had seldom been realized. The support of the war took many forms, which ranged from the acceptance of the inconveniences of price control, rationing, selective service, rationing of essentials to active participation in Red Cross and USO programs, donation of blood, and the purchase of war bonds. Hollywood made a typical contribution in the form of stars who traveled widely to entertain troops and pin-ups of glamour girls to brighten barrack walls. The motion picture industry also contributed funds and purchased substantial amounts of war bonds. It also produced great numbers of training films. Among the members of an army unit which produced training films was Ronald Reagan, who went on to become a prominent political figure in the postwar period. Although they frequently lacked the dramatic and entertainment values of the peacetime product of filmland, they were an effective educational device which the military used extensively.

The lessons of beleaguered Britain during the blitz brought into being a widespread civilian defense system. Thousands of Californians participated as wardens who organized communities in anticipation of attack by gathering fire-fighting equipment and setting up warning systems and airplane-spotting groups. As things turned out, there was little need for their services, although some were given a graphic example of their need when the "battle of Los Angeles" took place in early 1942. Perhaps the greatest benefit of the entire civil defense effort was the manner in which it brought people together, laboring in a common cause, each concerned with the general good, each sharing to a degree the sacrifices of the GI.

When the war came to an end and there was time for a sober estimate of its impact on California it became readily apparent that the state had been profoundly affected. Its industrial as well as its general economic growth had been tremendous. The total work force had risen from 3,080,000 to 3,880,000. This growth cut across a number of industries, although aircraft and shipbuilding were the outstanding examples of growth and development. An economic base had been constructed which had enormous potential for future growth. A number of pessimists predicted that the postwar readjustment would produce crisis for California and the nation as wartime industries were forced to grapple with the problems of conversion to a peacetime economy. A material fact which many of these projections overlooked was the general prosperity of the war years and the manner in which pent-up consumer spending in the form of savings and war bonds would sustain the economy. California's citizenry increased their general income from $5,000,000,000 to almost $13,-000,000,000. Average annual wages rose from $1931 to $2961. While much of that income had been spent, some of it absorbed by inflation, the total in liquid assets at the war's end was more than $15,000,000,000. To those who took a long look into California's past record of impressive economic growth, there was good reason to be optimistic as far as the future was concerned.

CHAPTER XX

The New Age of Technology

John Bidwell, who guided the historic immigrant train into California in 1841, lived to see the beginning of the twentieth century. In the sixty years he spent in the state, he saw California altered from a sparsely settled Mexican cattle country to a populous and booming state in 1900. But as fantastic as the changes packed into those sixty eventful years were, they cannot compare to what has happened in California since 1945. A person who left the state at the conclusion of World War II and returned a generation later would hardly recognize California, so momentous have been the changes. In fact, it is no exaggeration to say that what has happened in the state in the past twenty-five years dwarfs anything of the almost two centuries that passed since its founding.

What has been the nature of these changes? The most spectacular has been the rapid increase in population. The 1940 population of 6,950,000 soared to 10,586,000 in 1950. The 1960 figure of 15,717,000 increased to 19,953,134 in 1970. In 1962 the state surpassed New York as the nation's most populous. This "greatest mass-migration in history" has seen the elimination of once prosperous farms and their replacement by "instant cities" virtually overnight. Once placid rural villages which serviced local citrus farmers have undergone spectacular growth. Garden Grove, for example, grew from 4000 to in excess of 100,000 within the short space of five years. In some areas of the state as much as 250 acres a day are urbanized. Some of this land long used in agriculture is converted to residential areas, shopping centers, industrial parks, freeways, office building sites; all have taken a toll of California farmland. The growth has been much more than horizontal; it has also been vertical, with huge skyscrapers and apartment buildings being built to accommodate the ever increasing numbers of people. Thousands of miles of eight- or

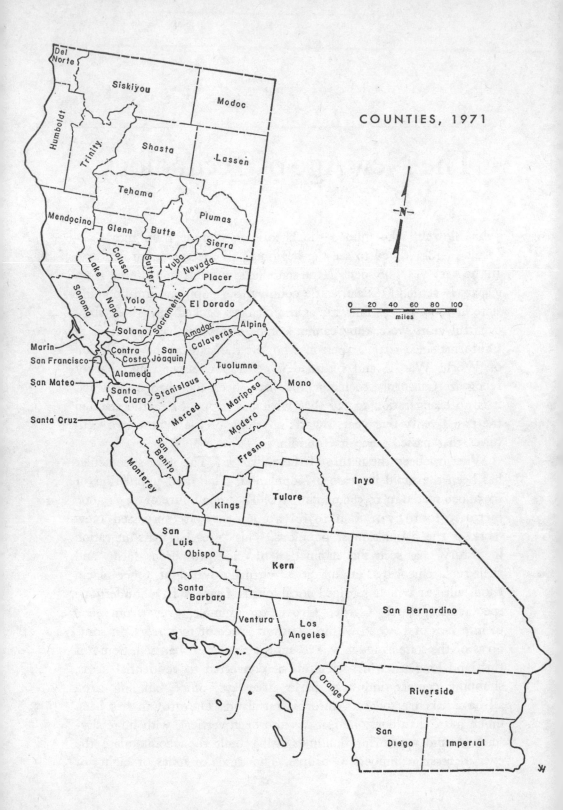

COUNTIES, 1971

ten-lane highways have been built to handle the cars and trucks which service the newcomers. Interchanges, sometimes taking up many acres, have emerged as a new kind of architectural form.

Some hail this incredible growth and dub California "the spectacular state" or "America's window to the future," but others have seen the continually growing population as anything but an unmixed blessing. Being first in the nation has brought with it the disadvantages of traffic congestion, long common to eastern cities, the pollution of air and water; and the increasing demand for public services has led to ever higher taxation. Nor has life in the "instant cities" brought happiness to the citizenry who have poured into California. Their restlessness has been reflected in the divorce rate, the growing crime rate, the prevalence of drug addiction and alcoholism, and the high suicide rate. Whether the problems reflected in these statistics are the result of the state's ability to attract malcontents from elsewhere or whether the conditions of life in California cause such irrational conduct remains an unanswered question. Over everything hangs an air of impermanence.

Why has the populace of the rest of the nation migrated to California at such a phenomenal pace? They have come for all of the historic reasons. Some to enjoy the weather in preference to that of the Midwest or East; others developed a lasting attachment to California during World War II service and returned to it. Others have come for the same reason that the forty-niners came, not to seek gold in the placers but to seek greater economic opportunities. To most, the magnet drawing them westward is usually a combination, or as one person put it: "It's not the better job that I'm interested in alone. It's the way of life."

This mass response to Horace Greeley's advice to "Go West, young man, go West," has been a phenomenon of the westward movement for generations. The boom has developed a momentum, for the constant influx of people has created constantly growing needs for new housing, new services, and even new cities, all of which have created more and more jobs. California has led the nation in the new kind of manufacturing that has emerged since World War II and which in turn has made it possible to sustain the population. While much of the growth has been associated with defense, the spectacular advancements in peacetime industry have more than kept pace. While

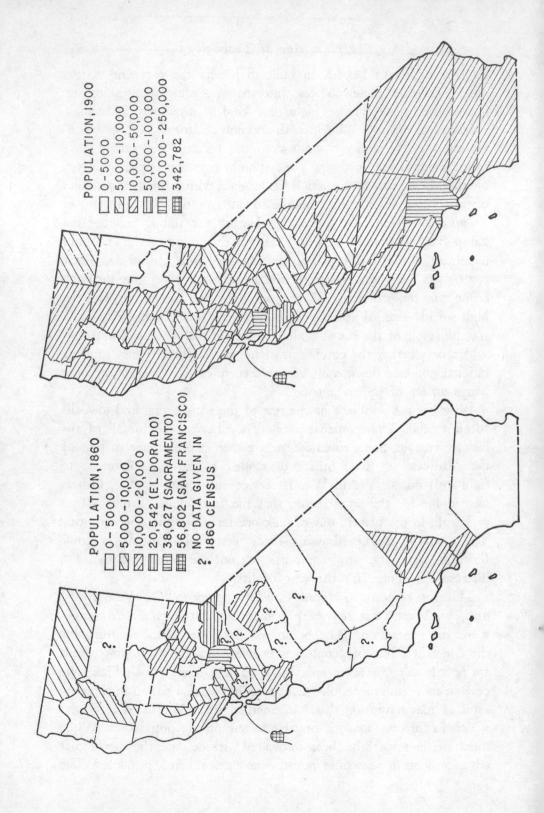

POPULATION, 1900

0–5000
5000–10,000
10,000–50,000
50,000–100,000
100,000–250,000
342,782

POPULATION, 1860

0–5000
5000–10,000
10,000–20,000
20,542 (EL DORADO)
38,027 (SACRAMENTO)
56,802 (SAN FRANCISCO)
NO DATA GIVEN IN 1860 CENSUS

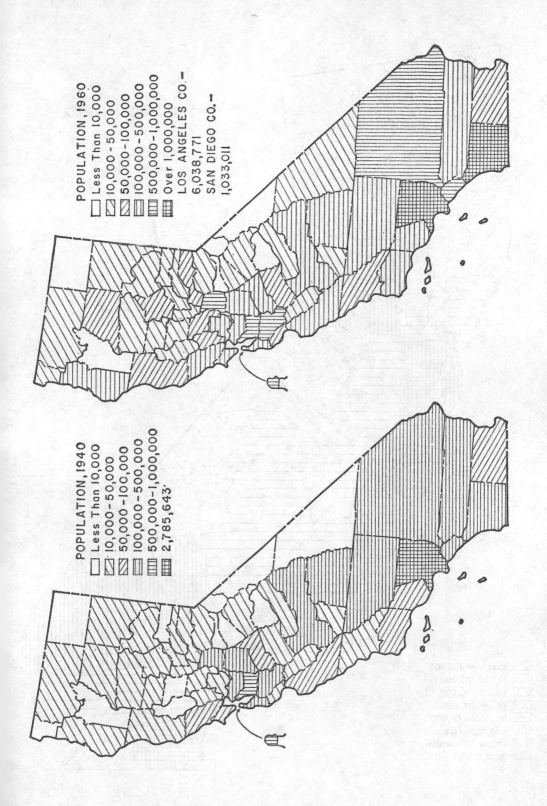

POPULATION, 1960
Less Than 10,000
10,000 – 50,000
50,000 – 100,000
100,000 – 500,000
500,000 – 1,000,000
Over 1,000,000
LOS ANGELES CO. –
6,038,771
SAN DIEGO CO. –
1,033,011

POPULATION, 1940
Less Than 10,000
10,000 – 50,000
50,000 – 100,000
100,000 – 500,000
500,000 – 1,000,000
2,785,643

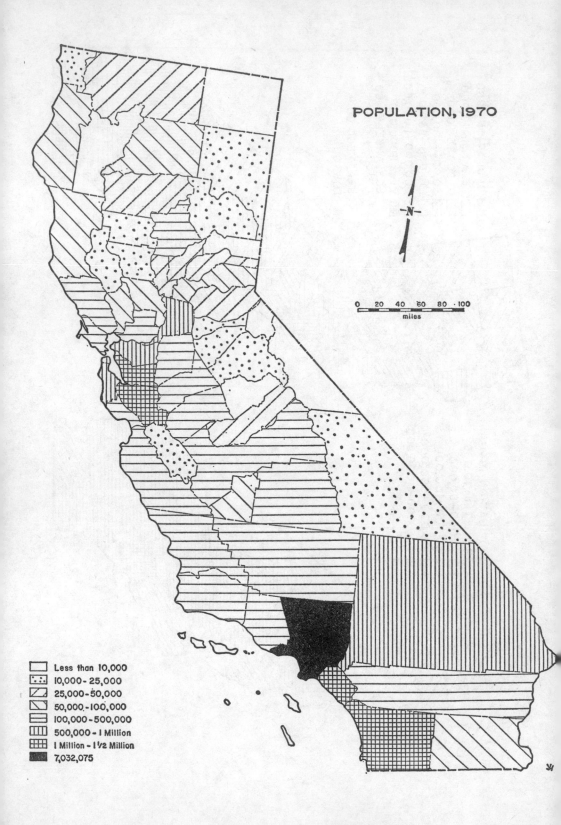

POPULATION, 1970

-N-

0   20   40   60   80 ·100
              miles

☐	Less than 10,000
	10,000 - 25,000
	25,000 - 50,000
	50,000 - 100,000
	100,000 - 500,000
	500,000 - 1 Million
	1 Million - 1½ Million
■	7,032,075

old established industries, such as the movies and the aircraft industry, have been declining, the growth in electronics and aerospace has offset such losses. The factories in the fields of the 1930s have been replaced by agribusiness complexes which have ensured California's primacy in agriculture. But just as the cities have had to contend with the new problems of the urban age, so also has the state's agricultural industry faced new problems. Efforts to solve the perpetual water problems of the state have been conspicuously successful, thus ensuring the continual growth of agriculture, industry, and the cities. Although most of the newcomers have participated in the prosperity of the era, affluence has not been distributed uniformly; members of ethnic minorities frequently had good reason to complain. The politics of California in the new age of technology have continued to bewilder the outside observer as well as the native Californian.

MANUFACTURING FOR A NEW AGE

Those who predicted that the war-inflated industries, such as steel making, shipbuilding, aircraft, and others, would go into decline once peace with Japan became a reality appeared to be able prophets between 1945 and 1950. Unemployment remained relatively high during this period and there was a small exodus from California. Although many left the state, new migrants continued to come, so that the building trades and service industries prospered. The construction industry was stimulated by federal legislation which provided veterans with the opportunity to purchase homes without down payments and at low rates of interest of 4 per cent. FHA and a California veterans housing bill worked in a similar way.

However, it took another Pacific war, this time in Korea, to start the state's economy booming again. Once more defense industries produced for war, and California again became the staging area for a military effort. After halt of that conflict in 1953 with its resulting effect upon the economy of the area, a major build-up of missiles began. The continuation of the Cold War and the development of new technology which demonstrated that nuclear warheads could be made small enough to be carried by the intercontinental ballistic missiles dictated a substantial change in America's defense spending. And California was able to adapt itself to that change.

The development of the intercontinental ballistic missile (ICBM) came to California because the state's industries were not as fully committed to a traditional production-line psychology as were industries in other regions. Manufacturing in this new age required human rather than natural resources and put a premium upon new ideas and technology. In the absence of a hidebound industrial tradition, Californians were willing to try new methods to produce sophisticated military items. California's life-style attracted young technicians whose minds bulged with new ideas and who preferred working in an informal atmosphere where new ideas were welcome. In the period between 1955 and 1965, employment in the state's manufacturing industries rose by more than 25 per cent, while the rest of the nation had an increase of only 6.5 per cent. This sharp increase in industrial production featured exotic military devices. California's industry was not significantly handicapped by a lack of raw materials and a distance from markets.

The new defense industries needed fewer blue-collar workers and an ever increasing force of white-collar specialists. This is reflected in the fact that almost 40 per cent of the work force of California's manufacturing establishment consisted of managers, technicians, highly skilled experts, and professionals. While the average American factory worker added $7.68 value to a product every working hour, the Californian added $9.55. Twenty-six Nobel prize winners resident in the state indicates the emphasis upon the sciences. Manufacturing for a new age needs the specialists that California both had and has been able to attract.

To design and plan the new kind of equipment dictated by the growing complexity of the scientific world, numerous "think factories" have been established in California. Most important is the Rand Corporation (from R and D, research and development). Located in Santa Monica, its physicists, chemists, mathematicians, astronomers, and social scientists are engaged in research primarily for the Air Force. Aerospace Corporation, located in Los Angeles, supervises missile design for the Air Force. Jet Propulsion Laboratories grew out of research performed by technicians at the California Institute of Technology and has continued to play a key role in the design and construction of rockets.

Private aircraft manufacturers also developed their own laboratory installations in which to carry out research for the government in aerospace problems, but their primary task is in manufacturing. Douglas, Hughes, North American, Northrup, Aerojet, Convair, and Lockheed all played leading roles, with the latter obtaining the largest share of government business. The excellence of California's system of higher education, as well as its ability to draw scientists and technicians from the rest of the nation, makes it possible for the state to attract about a fourth of all the nation's military contracts. In the 1964 campaign President Johnson called attention to the fact that "defense personnel in the state represent an annual payroll of almost two billion a year." The National Aeronautics and Space Administration (NASA) placed more than 50 per cent of all its contracts in California.

In the 1960s the building of missiles and the production of jet planes for both military and commercial uses were fundamental for the state's rapid growth in manufacturing. Perhaps one third of the total employed in manufacturing were kept busy on defense contracts. The San Diego area had more than 70 per cent in defense employment, while the Los Angeles-Long Beach area could count 59 per cent. America's involvement in the Vietnam War saw military spending in California increase sharply.

Californians could be justifiably proud of the fact that all major components of the Apollo spacecraft which was orbited in October 1968 as part of the first manned flight of the lunar landing program were developed in California. However, some economic authorities were concerned about the heavy dependence of the state's economy upon defense spending. Any substantial reduction in the nation's spending for military equipment could spell trouble for California's economy, as such changes have created problems in the past. The downturn in the state's economy between 1945 and 1950 was repeated in the late 1950s in those areas of the state with a heavy dependence upon the manufacture of aircraft. The San Diego area was especially hard hit by the cancellation of contracts and the changeover from piston to jet engines. Some aircraft manufacturers reduced their working force by more than one half. Again in 1964 when a major phase of the missile program was completed there was a comparable downturn in the economy. When a major manufacturer such as Aerojet-General in Sacramento or Convair in San Diego sharply reduces its work force, the entire area's economy is promptly depressed. Employees leave the region, abandoning homes and furniture bought on the installment plan. Banks, credit unions, savings and loan institutions are also affected. Schools have been known to lose half of their students while many churches, built on the assumption that the population pattern would remain stable, have been forced to close. Countless small-business men have been forced into bankruptcy.

This dependence of California upon the whims of Washington and the winds of technological change has long been a matter of concern. In 1964 Governor Pat Brown enlisted the co-operation of aerospace firms to deal with domestic problems such as smog control and traffic management, but with limited success. Men who use their minds in aerospace work have been slow to adjust their thinking to the mass production needs of the peacetime world. Those who have been concerned only with getting results, regardless of costs, have found it difficult to adapt to the kind of cost accounting characteristic of the peacetime production line. In spite of the insecurity that arises from the possible termination of a contract, employees cling to their positions in defense-oriented industry. Sometimes employees shift from company to company as contracts are awarded to one and denied another. A group of engineers from San Diego commuted to Los Angeles for more than a year until they found positions closer to home.

Despite frequent predictions of disaster to California's economy when federal defense spending declined, few anticipated the debacle which began in 1968. Since that year disillusionment with the Vietnam War and public disenchantment with technology in general have triggered a sharp reduction in defense spending. Nationally, this has caused a downturn of some 30 per cent in government appropriations. As the nation's leader in the production of military equipment, California has been particularly hard hit. Scores of aerospace-related firms have gone bankrupt. Once thriving "think tanks" are deeply troubled and have reduced personnel by as much as one third, and their future prospects are not bright. Giants of the California aircraft scene for years such as Douglas and North American have been forced into mergers and all have had to retrench in order to survive. Lockheed, the nation's leading defense contractor, was forced to seek a government-backed loan in an effort to avert bankruptcy. In human terms, the state was plagued with a new kind of unemployment. Layoffs have traditionally hit the blue-collar workers first. However, California industry's growing sophistication produced a highly educated, professional work force. It has been these white-collar workers, engineers and management personnel, with annual salaries often from $16,000 to $25,000 per year, who were suddenly jobless. In previous slack times, layoffs at one company were balanced by hiring elsewhere of aerospace personnel. Unfortunately, since 1968 there have been few positions available regardless of the willingness to commute. There has been a growing exodus from the state as all of California's economy has suffered from the reduction in government defense spending.

However, the state's economy is not solely dependent upon the defense dollar. Of fifteen of the largest corporations based in California in 1970, only four could be classified as predominantly military. The fact that five of the top ten in this group were Standard, Occidental, Union, Getty, and Signal is evidence of the continued importance of petroleum to California. The continual upward surge of population has itself provided a continual stimulus to manufacturing. More people create an ever growing market for goods and services. Each new family which arrives in California has a set of economic wants to be satisfied. Housing, municipal services, food, clothing, personal services are among the needs of each family. Established national companies have set up branch factories or assembly plants on the Pacific coast to provide for some of these needs. The high cost of freight also dictates the establishment of such branches.

Thus, California's prosperity, while primarily associated with the defense dollar, has also been self-generating. The building industry, financed by the savings and loan associations with substantial investments from the rest of the nation, has been busy creating new dwellings and even new cities for the migrants. To other parts of the United States California must appear as a parasite state, for it has continually drained other areas of its best-educated and its most talented citizenry as well as substantial amounts of capital. As the state's per capita income averages some 25 per cent higher than elsewhere in the nation, the newcomers usually find the affluence they seek. This in turn has led to a steady decline in labor strife as the income of many wage earners has lifted them into the middle class, some even into the upper brackets of that class. Unfortunately, most of the demands of California's industry have been for well-educated or highly trained technicians, and thus those who don't meet these qualifications have been barred from enjoying the prosperity. As most of those who lack education and training were Mexican-Americans or black Americans, they gravitated to low-paying jobs and to an inadequate living standard and housing ill-suited to their needs. From their ghettos they provided an exception to California's normally rosy picture of affluence and this helped to trigger much racial disorder in the 1960s.

AGRICULTURE

The state's leading industry, agriculture, was, however, to face a continued and perplexing labor problem in the second half of the twentieth century. To generalize about California's agriculture is just as difficult as generalizing about much of the rest of the state, for the exception is the rule. There are many small family farms which employ little or no hired labor and thus are not unlike farms in the Midwest. The fact that the farms of California average 372 acres supports the fallacious belief that farming is a way of life, but the reverse is true: farming in California is a business and not a way of life.

Agribusiness is the term used to describe this peculiarly California phenomenon. The magnitude of the typical agribusiness unit is reflected in several statistics: 6 per cent of the state's farmers own 75 per cent of the farmland and 5 per cent of the farms pay 60 per cent of the farm labor wages. Landholdings in Kern County, in the heart of the rich agricultural San Joaquin Valley, average 2279 acres. The California Packing Corporation, the world's largest packer of fruits and vegetables, principally under the Del Monte brand name, ranks seventeenth among California's industrial giants (in 1970) with sales nearing the half-billion-dollar mark annually. Further evidence

25. San Francisco as photographed from Telegraph Hill in 1858 (*above*) and as seen today (*below*).

26. This small hydroelectric plant at Highgrove in Riverside County, established in 1886, was a cornerstone of the present Southern California Edison Company.

27. Today, the San Onofre nuclear generating station is one of the nation's largest nuclear power stations.

28. California's water problems have been partially solved by a system of dams, canals, and other irrigation facilities. Depicted is the Oroville Dam, the keystone in the massive state water project designed to provide northern California water to portions of central and Southern California.

29. Irrigation makes it possible to grow many crops which would be impossible to produce under natural conditions. Pictured is a strawberry field in Southern California absolutely dependent upon irrigation.

30. Troops came to the docks during the violent turmoil of the waterfront strikes of the 1930s. Out of the conflict came a new and vibrant labor movement that, spearheaded by the longshore union, "marched inland" on an organizational drive.

31. Unlike many other crops, grapes require attention ten months a year. They must be sprayed, trimmed, and girdled. As a result, the average grape picker is a skilled worker. With Cesar Chavez as its leader, the United Farm Workers Committee negotiated a labor contract in 1970 to improve his working conditions.

of the size of California's agricultural enterprise is revealed in the subsidy payments of the federal government. In 1967 a Fresno County farm received almost $3,000,000 in such payments, while one in Kings County received some $1,300,000. Of fifteen farms in the nation receiving $500,000 to $1,000,000, five were located in the San Joaquin Valley. Such size usually means a high percentage of absentee ownership and the existence of hired managers who are paid to get results regardless of the human equation.

Size has helped make California the nation's leading agricultural state since 1943, and one of the wealthiest such areas in the world. Technological innovation, as in industry, has played an equally important role, for the state is "a vast controlled hothouse." Nature is manipulated on a scale not duplicated elsewhere. Farms usually specialize in the one or two crops which scientific experimentation has shown would make the most profitable use of the local soils, climate, and water supply. One farm specializes in the production of lettuce, another carrots, and still another artichokes. These decisions are frequently made with the assistance of agronomists at the University of California. The university specialists have made possible a wine industry which produces 85 per cent of the nation's total; they saved the citrus industry from a devastating disease and have developed automated chicken farms where no human hand touches the egg until the consumer cooks it. In addition, university research has grappled with the historic problem of farm labor. Machines to shake walnuts from trees, a device to "feel" heads of lettuce and activate a cutting knife if they're ripe, and an electronic eye that will pick only ripe strawberries have been a few of their contributions. When technology was unequal to the task of developing a machine to pick the existing breed of tomatoes, plant specialists bred a new tomato to fit their machine.

Mechanization, combined with government subsidies in the form of water for more than 8,000,000 acres at less than cost, has helped make agriculture California's leading industry, but critical problems remain. Rapid urbanization has meant that productive farmland is being converted to highways and cities at the rate of more than 150,000 acres per year. Citrus growing has been forced to relocate, sometimes out of the state into Arizona. Some tomato growers have successfully developed large-scale operations in Mexico. How to

curtail urban encroachment upon the richest farmland has not yet
been decided. A promising development came in 1965 when the legislature provided deferred taxes for agricultural land which was kept
in farm use for a ten-year period. Under this land conservation act,
farmland threatened by urbanization is protected for a time. Smog
has also led to the abandonment of some farmland or changing to
crops less susceptible to the polluted air. The most perplexing agricultural problem remains a source of cheap labor at harvestime, for
in spite of the many machines that have come into use, human hands
are still indispensable.

Because of crop specialization, there is an intense demand for labor
at a given time. The perishability of peaches, pears, grapes, strawberries, and apricots makes it imperative that the labor to harvest
them be available when needed. Moreover, weather frequently de-
termines when picking shall begin. To a farmer who must bring in a
crop within a matter of a few days or lose the fruits of a year's labor,
it is inevitable that he would be concerned only with the harvest. The
farmer is little concerned that there is a wide fluctuation in demands
for workers and that those who labor in his fields or orchards may
be unemployed more than one half of the year.

The Chinese were first to furnish such labor in the Anglo period
and by 1880 they constituted 90 per cent of the field labor hands.
To the growers they were most satisfactory as they were available
when needed and disappeared to their ghettos once the harvest was
over. However, the resistance of organized labor, which resented
the competition of coolie labor, led to their exclusion. The Japanese
were the next to furnish an inexpensive and available source of
labor. They were even more satisfactory to the growers than had
been their fellow Asiatics. They were more industrious, and as they
brought their women with them, they had fewer bad habits. Organized labor again worked for their exclusion, but the growers
themselves came to resent the Japanese, because they saved their
money to buy land and entered into competition with their former
employers.

The period of World War I saw an acute crisis created in the farm
labor situation. Black Americans from the South were imported to
work in the fields, but this was unsuccessful because such labor was
little more rewarding in California than it had been in Alabama. The

newcomers usually worked in the fields for a single season and then went into the cities in search of better opportunities. The critical shortage of farm labor brought about a mobilization of a "Women's Land Army" to keep food from rotting in the field. It was more patriotic than effective.

Mexican labor began to play a predominant role in California's fields after the outbreak of the Mexican Revolution in 1910. The subsequent anarchy that peaked in 1915 and did not subside until the 1920s drove large numbers of Mexicans to seek refuge in the United States. Their cheap labor was a boon to the California growers and was so important in 1920 that the harvest of that year became known as "the Mexican harvest." The depressed living standards that the average Mexican knew in his homeland conditioned him to substandard wages and conditions. Having been used to a system of peonage in Mexico, he accepted a California substitute. To the grower, the Mexican worker was most satisfactory. They were more tractable than Anglos, and their large families meant more labor was available to get out the crop. A gang boss speaking to a Mexican manifested his contempt for Mexicans and his belief in their subservience when he said, "When we want you, we'll call you, when we don't—git." The Mexicans were the principal fieldworkers of California into the 1930s, although Hindus and Filipinos labored alongside them.

The Depression caused many Mexicans who had lived on the margin of subsistence to become welfare recipients. Federal and state authorities financed the repatriation of some 200,000 Mexicans in the 1930s, perhaps 75,000 from California. Depressed economic conditions brought more than 200,000 Arkies and Okies to do the stoop labor of the fields, so Mexican labor was no longer needed. The conditions under which the Mexicans had worked were probably worse than those of the Okies and Arkies, but the nation did not get indignant until Anglos were exploited in a similar way.

When World War II enabled the Okies and Arkies to desert the fields for the shipyards, Mexicans were again in demand. By 1942 "there was a most acute and disastrous shortage of farm labor in the state of California." Recalling the haste with which their nationals had been shipped out of the country a decade before, the Mexican government was reluctant to permit their citizens to come north to labor in the factories and the fields of California. Wartime agreements were made and large numbers of Mexicans also illegally made their way into California, sometimes with the open connivance of the border patrol. In 1951 a *bracero* program was formally inaugurated wherein Mexicans came to work in the fields of the United States as the result of a formal treaty. To the growers of California, the *bracero* program was always popular. It provided unlimited supplies of labor when it was needed. Once their tour was completed, the Mexican workers took their earnings back home with them and did not linger to provide an embarrassment when their labor was no longer needed. Many Mexicans returned year after year to work for the same growers. The earnings of the *braceros* permitted many to buy land or start small businesses in Mexico and the influx of their earnings provided a significant part of Mexico's national economy. What little opposition to the program existed in Mexico was concentrated among intellectuals who were affronted by the image of their country as a nation of serviles.

Most of the opposition to the *bracero* program was to be found in the United States. Its popularity in Mexico was attested by the large numbers of candidates for the program. The conditions of work were established by international treaty, and made United States officials responsible for the enforcement of work contracts. Growers had to provide acceptable barracks, proper food, and insurance protection. Although there were violations of the contract terms, the standards under which the *braceros* worked were invariably higher than those enjoyed by domestic labor. Mexican-Americans frequently worked in the fields for less money and lived under harsher conditions than did Mexican nationals. But the *bracero* program would not have been terminated had it not been for the undying opposition of America's labor unions. It had been organized labor that drove the Chinese and the Japanese from California's fields, and it was organized labor which terminated the *bracero* program. Many efforts to unionize farm labor had failed in spite of the backing of some of the nation's leading unions. Just as labor had once fought to check the influx of cheap labor from Europe, now it would end the cheap labor from Mexico. And once the program was terminated, as it was on December 31, 1964, the effort to unionize farm labor was inevitable. Some *braceros* continued to come to California after that date under special arrangements, but the Democratic administration in Washington, indebted to its labor constituency, was bent on abolishing the program.

After its abolishment, the growers sought to have it renewed by claiming its end foretold disaster for them. Although it is true that some crops such as asparagus and strawberries could not be completely harvested, it is also true that the average agricultural return in California increased slightly in 1965 over the preceding year when *braceros* were available. Thus, it was proven that there were enough domestic agricultural workers available. The primary reason for the growers' opposition to the end of the *bracero* program, of course, was the fear of organization. As one Salinas Valley grower put it, "The handwriting may be on the wall, but we'll do everything possible to slow down unionization."

The efforts to organize began in 1962 with the establishment of the National Farm Worker's Association in Fresno. Under the leadership of Cesar Chavez the movement had a competent leader of charismatic charm. Larry Itliong, a Filipino organizer, also established an organization, called the Agricultural Workers' Organizing Committee. Both organizations eventually joined forces to become the Farm Workers Organizing Committee. By 1965 worker credit unions were established, along with a newspaper, co-operative insurance program, and other such self-help services.

On September 8, 1965, six hundred Filipino farm workers went on strike, initiating the longest continuous agricultural strike in California history. Within a week, the National Farm Worker's Association members, most of whom were Mexican-American, voted to support the Filipinos and demanded recognition. The Delano grape strike was on. The stakes were great and well understood by both sides although initially the growers did not take the strike seriously since they had been able to break most such efforts in the past. Reinforced by representatives of the civil government, and possessing ample funds with which to carry on the struggle, the growers were a formidable force. Assisting the farm workers were idealistic churchmen, liberal-oriented individuals and groups, and many who sympathized with the plight of Mexican-Americans and Filipinos. More importantly, the farm workers had the backing of the major labor unions of the nation and political figures such as the late Senator Robert F. Kennedy of New York.

National publicity won many adherents to the cause of the farm workers and enough financial support to enable them to continue their struggle. Their principal tactic was a national boycott of the grape growers. These tactics prompted the Schenley Corporation to accept the union as its sole bargaining agent, a major breakthrough in the solid front of the agricultural interests. The DiGiorgio Corporation followed, and the possibility that the farm workers had finally been able to organize California's agribusiness became very real. While the strike was in progress, many growers simply tried to wait it out in the hope that technological innovation would provide machinery that would make obsolete field hands in the vineyards.

However, the national boycott forced down the demand and hence the price of grapes. Table grapes were processed as wine early in the strike but its prolongation exhausted storage facilities and helped force a decision. Growers in the Coachella Valley yielded early in 1970, and most table grape growers in the Delano area followed suit in August 1970. The end of the nation's longest agricultural strike brought recognition to Cesar Chavez's United Farm Workers Organizing Committee and wages of $1.80 per hour (going up to $2.10 by the third year) and $.20 for each box of grapes. When the strike began, the going rates were $1.10 per hour and $.10 a box. After this historic triumph Chavez and his UFWOC contested with the powerful Teamsters Union for the right to organize some eight thousand lettuce and vegetable workers in the Salinas Valley. A truce in March 1971 gave Chavez the right to organize field hands while the Teamsters represent shed workers, truckers, and other agricultural labor. An effective lettuce boycott helped force the growers to accept the union. Apparently Chavez had made an effective start toward the unionization of California agriculture.

POLITICS SINCE WORLD WAR II

Since World War II California politics defies precise analysis. One observer describes the scene in the following words: "Its character is as diverse as the varied topography of this state of mountains, deserts, forests, and shoreline. Politics . . . like every other element of the State's society and culture, is almost constantly in flux—changing, growing, sometimes slumbering, usually temperamental, and often apparently shapeless."

The same forces which gave the state's economy its distinctive character have also been at work in the political arena. Most important has been the constant influx of population. A frontier society like California's attracts a diversity of people. Among them are those with a sense of adventure and those who are looking for an escape from their past. The same kind of devil-may-care spirit which has characterized the state's business entrepreneurs has also marked the sometimes bizarre politics of California. In fact, one might even attribute the vagaries of political fortunes in the state to the almost schizophrenic search for security on the one hand and the willingness to take a chance on the other.

Those who migrate to California (and in 1970 some three fourths of the population was not native-born) have found it easy to free themselves of former conventions. Many shed church, social connections, previous patterns of behavior, mates, and even their political affiliations. A populace that is highly mobile—and it must be remembered that a California family averages a move every four years—does not have deep roots in any community and has limited interest in civic affairs. Thus, it is impossible to create the kind of partisan political organizations which are found in other parts of the nation. Moreover, the very size of the state makes this difficult. Then too, racial and religious block voting is not as concentrated in California as it is in the cities of the East and the Midwest.

Geography contributes to diversity in politics. It spurs competition between northern and southern California and also between regions within these two sections. The political arena is also marked by competition between urban and rural regions. Voter registration is nominally Democratic, along with the rest of the nation, but when the impoverished newcomer partakes of the affluence of the Golden State, he tends to vote Republican without changing his registration. He frequently votes a split ticket, making a shambles of predictions by political pundits and defying any kind of party loyalty. Party lines were deliberately blurred by the Progressives, who championed no "partisanship." The development of a strong civil service system has deprived would-be political bosses of the "loaves and fishes" of patronage so useful in building an effective political organization. At one time laws banned party designations on the primary ballot, but this practice was eliminated in 1954. Another feature of California political life was cross-filing, which allowed candidates to appear on the tickets of all parties in the primary without revealing their real party affiliation. Such practices provided the public personality—the candidate with a public name—with real advantages. Cross-filing further tended to erode party loyalties. Winning nomination in the primary on both major tickets constituted election. Democrats who believed this worked to their disadvantage repealed cross-filing once they were in control in Sacramento in 1959.

Without a viable party structure candidates are usually on their own and often run without stating their political affiliations in campaign material. Left to their own devices, they are forced to hire public relations firms which "sell" candidates to the public, in much the same way soap is sold. Some individuals have effectively built independent political organizations, usually to promote their own candidacy, but often effectively disguised as entities created to serve the best interests of the party. Many such groups have been started only to die an early death but others have been most enduring. Most successful have been the California Republican Assembly (CRA) and the California Democratic Council (CDC). Voters who have been attracted to such organizations regularly desert once the cause they favor has been disposed of or the candidate they have backed has been elected (or defeated). These structures have sometimes started as liberal bodies only to become reactionary or have been taken over by dissident amateurs who have used them to embarrass elected officials of their party.

All these factors have combined to make the individual candidate the most important ingredient in California politics. The strong magnetic personality who can project the image of the "good guy" is the usual candidate. Such men can effectively raise money, attract a personal following, and be successfully "merchandised" by political public relations firms. A formal ideology is not important; appearance and image are essential. As a result, the politics of the

Golden State since World War II has been dominated by a series of individuals.

The first of these, and one of the most important, was Earl Warren. Defeating the Democratic governor Culbert L. Olson, who had the misfortune of being elected in 1938 when the New Deal fervor was already dying, Warren's talents made him the most successful, and perhaps the best, governor in the history of the state. First elected in 1942, he was re-elected four years later in the primary by obtaining the nominations of both the Democratic and Republican parties (through cross-filing). He won re-election to a third term in 1950. Warren is the only man to win the gubernatorial nomination in the primary and the only governor to be thrice elected. He was the GOP vice-presidential candidate in 1948, and in 1953 he became Chief Justice of the United States Supreme Court. From that time until 1969 when he resigned he directed the Court's epoch-making role in civil rights and the protection of individual liberties. Ironically, these accomplishments made him the target of abuse from many extremist groups based in California, notably the John Birch Society.

As governor, Warren first resisted efforts to slash taxes and built substantial surpluses for construction projects once World War II was over. Such reserves provided for needed highways and other public works in the postwar periods. Long-range planning provided the kind of guidance essential in a state that has been characterized by rapid population growth. However, such farsightedness plus his emphasis upon co-operation with organized labor and sponsorship of New Deal-like measures such as state compulsory health insurance earned him the enmity of many elements within his own party.

Warren's final term as governor was marked by the elimination of much of the unsavory influence of lobbying in Sacramento. Arthur H. Samish, "king of the lobbyists," whose career dated back to the 1920s, was once the most powerful man in the state and virtually dictated the legislation demanded by his clients. Efforts of the Democrats to curb him in 1939 were unsuccessful but when he boasted of his influence in California in an interview with a writer for a national magazine in 1949 his power began to wane. Samish finally went to federal prison for income tax evasion and his role as "the third branch of California government" came to an end.

When Warren went to the Supreme Court, his lieutenant governor,

Goodwin J. Knight, succeeded him. Long active in state politics, possessed of more political charm than the more taciturn Warren, "Goodie" Knight endeared himself to the conservatives within his party by actively opposing many of the more liberal portions of Warren's program. However, as governor, Knight soon realized that to be successful—and thus to be elected on his own—he had to have the support of Democrats and especially organized labor. He learned that to be an effective governor of California he had to be bipartisan.

Easily re-elected in 1954, Knight would probably have continued in the gubernatorial chair if California Republicans had not decided to commit political hara-kiri. In 1958 Senator William F. Knowland, of the Oakland publishing family, apparently decided that the governor's office was a better launching platform for the presidency than the United States Senate. Well known for his strong conservative views and his support of the "China lobby," Knowland forced Knight to run for the Senate while he contested Democrat Pat Brown for the governorship. Such internecine warfare is a luxury which California political parties cannot afford. If it takes place in the primaries it is normally fatal in the general election. The election of 1958 cast the GOP into the political wilderness. The once mighty Republican party was overwhelmed as it lost control of the legislature and all but one of the constitutional offices. Republicans licked their wounds after the debacle and rued the day when they earned the united wrath of organized labor by championing "Right to Work" legislation.

While Warren and Knight were leading California from the state-house, Richard Milhous Nixon was emerging on the national political scene. Born in Yorba Linda, educated at Whittier College and the law school at Duke University, Nixon defeated the popular liberal Jerry Voorhis for Congress in 1946. Catapulted into political prominence by the Hiss-Chambers affair, he was elected to the United States Senate in 1950. When Dwight David Eisenhower was seeking a running mate in 1952 in his successful bid for the presidency, Nixon received the nod. This remarkable rise to the second highest office in the land from obscurity within six years was greatly aided by the nation's preoccupation with subversion on the home front. Nixon's supporters claim that he had performed a great public service by revealing those who were "soft on Communism" and helped protect America from its home-grown Reds. Nixon's detractors claim that he used the spurious issue of loyalty to blacken unjustly the reputation of innocent men. Democratic spokesmen never forgave him for his vehement statements which made the party responsible for "twenty years of crime, corruption and Communism." Regardless of who was right he narrowly missed winning the presidency in the contest with John F. Kennedy in 1960. Bouncing back from this setback and his defeat for the governorship of California in 1962 he went on to win the presidency in 1968 by a narrow margin. He was the first native-born Californian to win the presidency.

Edmund G. "Pat" Brown, who won the governorship in a contest with a leading Republican, Senator William F. Knowland, and retained it in a battle with a presidential aspirant, Richard M. Nixon, is a native of San Francisco. An experienced veteran of the Bay City's district attorney's office, he was elected attorney general in 1950 and retained that office until he was elevated to the gubernatorial chair. Brown profited from Republican divisiveness but he had definite political talents, building a political following during the years of Republican ascendancy. He sometimes appeared inept and bungling, but he championed a program of social reform. Because he was elected with the help of organized labor, who had found Knowland's sponsorhip of the Right to Work proposal anathema, labor was politically rewarded with a series of measures expanding existing social welfare benefits. Cross-filing in elections was ended, numerous consumer protection devices were enacted, and a statewide agency to co-ordinate long-range planning was created. Aid to highways and schools were increased and a master plan for higher education set up. Of all of Brown's programs, which included many measures to end racial discrimination, none was more important than the California Water Plan. In spite of vigorous opposition from the northern part of the state, where much of his political support lay, Brown pushed this project, which takes water from the north where it is sometimes too abundant to the south where it has almost always been in short supply. A giant dam at Oroville 735 feet high, tallest in the nation, harnessed the Feather River. An extensive network of aqueducts supplemented by reservoirs transported the water southward. Although some felt that future desalinization of ocean water made such a costly project unnecessary, it has effectively guaranteed the future growth of the state.

Elected with the support of a broad coalition, Brown was unable to satisfy most members of it. As a result he came in for increasing attacks by members of his own party, especially members of the CDC. Then too, there were not enough political plums for all of the party faithful and intense rivalry for the succession to the governorship caused Democrats to fight among themselves in much the same way as the Republicans. In 1964 this cost them a United States Senate seat when a bitter primary fight between the popular controller Alan Cranston and Pierre Salinger led to a victory for the latter. He, in turn, was upset by the Republican actor, George Murphy in the general election.

What nationally prominent Republicans could not do, that is, defeat Brown for the governorship, was accomplished by a political neophyte, Ronald Reagan, in 1966. An actor whose roles were usually confined to B-grade movies, Reagan was long a Democrat. Converted to conservatism late in life, he attained national prominence with a fund-raising speech for the GOP standard-bearer, Barry Goldwater, in 1964. Reagan was the public relations man's dream of what a candidate should be: he was handsome, projected a good television image, and was superbly able to appear to be all things to all people. Although he had flirted with extremist groups, his public relations firm made him into a candidate of the center. On the other hand, Brown suffered from dissatisfaction within his own party, which was revealed by a surprisingly strong showing by Mayor Sam Yorty in the primary contest. Disturbances on the Berkeley campus of the University of California were also blamed on the Brown administration. But the most significant factor in the Democratic debacle was Brown's support of measures that would have legally eliminated racial discrimination in the sale and renting of housing. Many interpreted that measure as an attack against the rights of homeowners. The disastrous Watts riots of 1965 further heightened "white backlash" and lessened the prestige of the administration. As a result Brown was defeated for re-election in 1966 by a margin of more than a million votes. The Democrats lost all other state elective offices except that of attorney general, although they retained a narrow superiority in both houses of the legislature.

One of Governor Reagan's most frequently delivered speeches, prior to his election, stressed that economies in government could be effected by simply cutting all budget requests by 20 per cent. He tried this approach in Sacramento but limited it to a 10 per cent slash. Boasting that his administration was business-oriented, he promised to "squeeze, cut, and trim" while accusing the Democrats of having "looted and drained [the state] of its financial resources in a manner unique in our history." When he discovered that some 70 per cent of the budget was already earmarked he made most of his cuts in mental health and higher education. Ignoring the fact that the training provided by the state universities and colleges had made available a trained manpower pool which in turn had attracted new industry to California, he attacked higher education at every opportunity. With all of the much heralded "economy" the first Reagan budget was still the highest in history, and new taxes were necessary to meet it. After many charges that Democrats had bankrupted California, it was finally revealed that the state's finances were reasonably sound.

In many respects the Reagan administration is unique. He introduced partisanship into state government in a way that had not been seen for many years. In his vigorous attacks on higher education, he followed the example set by Governor Friend W. Richardson, but in the hoopla and promotion with which he tackled the duties of the governorship he was more like "Sonny Jim" Rolph. Many Californians were concerned that showmanship would conceal the fact that Reagan was negative in outlook with his sights firmly fixed backward, and was lacking in the long-range viewpoint which had characterized the tenures of Warren, Knight, and Brown. Eric Hoffer, the famous San Francisco longshoreman turned philosopher, spoke for many when he said in a television interview: "Reagan is a B-picture hero. He has a mortal hatred against A pictures. He wants to turn California into a B picture to be run on a B-picture budget but this state will remain in the A category in spite of Reagan."

A curious facet of California politics in the 1960s was the rise to prominence of political extremism of the right typified by the John Birch Society. This secret organization was built on the premise that the Communists had infiltrated most important positions in the national government. Named as part of this bizarre conspiracy were such Americans as Dwight David Eisenhower, his brother Milton, Secretary of State John Foster Dulles, and Chief Justice Earl Warren. Billboards flourished along the highways with the demand: "Impeach Earl Warren." John Rousselot and Edgar Hiestand, two California Republican congressmen, were avowed members. In 1970 John Schmitz, a Republican state senator from rigidly conservative Orange County and prominent Birch society member, was elected to Congress.

While most GOP office seekers agreed with Richard M. Nixon that the society was "the monkey on the elephant's back," and were quick to disassociate themselves from it, Governor Reagan was not. When Senator Thomas H. Kuchel, a liberal Republican from Anaheim, denounced the society in vigorous language he aroused much antipathy. In 1968 ultraconservative school superintendent Max Rafferty defeated Kuchel in the GOP primary in one of the more significant campaigns in the state's history. The bitterness resulted in a division within Republican ranks which helped Democrat Alan Cranston to make a political comeback and be elected United States Senator.

In the opening year of the seventies, California was still dominated by the political personalities of the sixties. Jesse Unruh, long-time speaker of the assembly, challenged Governor Reagan. Despite a distinguished record in the legislature, Unruh was handicapped by a divided Democratic party and a shortage of campaign funds and was defeated by Reagan by 501,057 votes. However, the Democrats elected John Tunney to the United States Senate and regained control of both the assembly and the senate in the 1970 election. This made it more difficult for Governor Reagan to accomplish the major goals on which he campaigned successfully in 1966 and again in 1970—such things as tax reform, overhaul of the welfare program, and a general reform of the public school system. Although the Democrats lacked the votes to override the governor's veto, Reagan had to compromise with them to pass his program. The opposition party was also in a strong position to reapportion to their advantage. Unfortunately, California could ill afford such partisan bickering as the economic downturn which began in 1968 continued into the seventies and caused unemployment, an increase in welfare rolls, and a state financial crisis.

CHAPTER XXI

The Clash of Cultures

California did not provide the "good life" for all who came, for the Golden State has had a long history of racial discrimination practiced against those not of northern European extraction. The Anglos who came during the gold rush were openly hostile to their Hispanic counterparts. They were even hostile to the native-born Californios. Solicitude for the welfare of the Indian has never been characteristic of frontiersmen but treatment of these native Americans of California was more harsh than elsewhere. Discrimination against black Americans in early California was less because they were relatively few in numbers. On the other hand there were many Chinese, and they were, during the first three quarters of a century of statehood, the target of much prejudice.

The Chinese, with their pigtails, strange dress, and stranger habits (from the viewpoint of Anglo miners), were discriminated against from the time they first arrived in large numbers in 1852. A basic reason for prejudice was economic. They were unwelcome because it was widely believed that their presence depressed the prevailing wage scale. The fact that agitation against the Chinese was most pronounced during downturns in the economy substantiates the belief that economic competition was a real cause of racial discrimination. A popular ditty expressed the feelings of Californians:

> Dust the pagans, far and near,
> From your fields and homes so dear,
> Falter not, your duty's clear;
> They or you must go.

Governor John Bigler, the first of many politicians to use the tactic, attempted to use the miners' resentment toward coolie labor as a vote-getting technique in 1852, and there were numerous efforts to drive out the Chinese in the 1850s and 1860s. Perhaps the worst attack occurred in Los Angeles in 1871. Kearneyism in the 1870s led to the denial of the Orientals' right to vote in the California constitution of 1879, and in 1882 federal legislation excluded further Chinese immigration.

The curtailment of immigration did not eliminate racial prejudice against the Chinese. Most Chinese were confined to ghettos contemptuously labeled "Chinatowns," the largest located in San Francisco. Of course, many Chinese preferred to live with their countrymen, while others considered their residence in America only temporary, and planned to return to their homeland as soon as they made their "fortune." Chinese labor continued to be popular with employers, especially farmers. As a result hoodlums attacked the Chinese at every opportunity: Chinese restaurants were pillaged, freshly ironed laundry was spattered with mud, dogs were unleashed upon innocent people, and pigtail hunting was a popular sport. In the courts they did not have "a Chinaman's chance." Attacks of this nature and continued racial discrimination caused many Chinese to return home. By 1928 the Chinese population dropped to only 28,812.

A number of factors combined to alter the position of Chinese in California. As their numbers declined, fear of the "yellow peril" also diminished. In 1884 the Chinese threat was considered very real when they made up 10 per cent of the total population, but with the state's phenomenal increase in population since the 1880s, the percentage of Chinese declined until it was less than 1 per cent in 1960. Dread by Caucasian laborers of their oriental competitors was lessened by the Chinese exodus to other western states and their entrance into small businesses such as hand laundries, specialty restaurants, and curio shops, economic endeavors with limited appeal. Only in San Francisco was there continued fear of the cheap labor of the Chinese.

Acculturation also took place with the passage of years. Some men returned home to stay and others maintained families in China while working in the United States. A fortunate few brought wives from China illegally, usually via Canada. The Chinese in the United States gradually shed their distinctive oriental dress for that of the occidental world, learned English, and, in general, became Americanized. Children from these homes attended American schools and their learning helped bridge the once great gap between the two cultures.

American foreign policy also played a role in helping the Chinese gain acceptance in California. The Hay Open Door Policy in 1899 marked the beginning of the United States role as the protector of China. This policy was made official by pacts growing out of the Washington Naval Conference of 1922 and was strengthened in the 1930s. As fear of Japanese aggression in the Orient grew, antagonism toward Japanese-Americans in California increased, and as sympathy with China's struggle against military attack expanded, popular acceptance of Chinese-Americans became almost universal. One example was changing movie roles in the late 1930s: Japanese replaced Chinese as oriental villains while the latter were portrayed as "good guys." In 1943 the federal government finally repealed the exclusion laws against Chinese, apparently with the approval of the general public.

Improved stature in the public eye helped reduce economic discrimination. The shortage of labor at the beginning of World War II opened doors in employment areas which had been barred. Some found jobs in aircraft plants or shipyards. Federal regulations which forbade discrimination extended opportunities. The years since 1945 have seen discriminatory practices gradually lessened. Such changes have been made easier by a Chinese educational level which is higher than that of Caucasians. Several Chinese-Americans have been Nobel prize winners in the abstract sciences. One indicator of their talent in this area is the fact that in 1971 the number enrolled at the prestigious California Institute of Technology was twelve times their fraction of the total American population.

Unfortunately, not all Chinese-Americans have been successful. The problems of San Francisco's Chinatown are similar to those of other ghettos in America. Some 42,000 people crowd into twenty square blocks. The median income in 1970 was $4500 a year, the educational level was approximately fifth-grade, unemployment was double the city average, and many of those working in the area's garment shops barely earned a living. There has been a steady exodus to the suburbs by the affluent third- and fourth-generation families. An influx of immigrants, mainly from Taiwan and Hong Kong, have taken their place. Members of families which had been separated for years were permitted to enter the United States and large numbers of Chinese women came in after 1946. Since the elimination of the old quota system, with the passage of the Immigration Act of 1965, an estimated 2500 to 3000 per year have entered San Francisco. Their numbers have brought problems of education, language training, health services, employment, and housing.

FROM "THE RISING SUN"

The Japanese, who began arriving in California in numbers after the Chinese exclusion in the 1880s, were at first welcomed. They brought their families with them (or sent home for "picture brides" at the first opportunity) and their habits and customs were more acceptable than those of the Chinese. Farmers welcomed them for since they came in family units there was more cheap labor available for work in the fields. Like their fellow Orientals, the Japanese were excellent workers and were used to a lower standard of living. Consequently they provided an efficient and quiescent work force. However, when their thriftiness enabled them to purchase land and compete with their former employers, they became as objectionable as the Chinese.

This effort of the Japanese to improve themselves was interpreted by a San Francisco *Chronicle* editorial in 1910 as the source of Caucasian resentment: "Had the Japanese laborer throttled his ambition to progress along the lines of American citizenship and industrial development, he probably would have attracted small attention of the public mind. Japanese ambition is to progress beyond mere servility to the plane of the better class of American workman and to own a home with him. The moment that this position is exercised, the Japanese ceases to be an ideal laborer."

Despite being initially limited to marginal land, Japanese farmers who worked their own farms as tenants or owners were usually successful. The ability to pool capital with fellow nationals, past experience in intensive farming, cheap labor (frequently within the immediate family), and willingness to do the kind of stoop labor often shunned by other farmers were all factors helping to make their efforts profitable.

By 1921 Japanese farmers produced 12.3 per cent of California's total farm produce. A slow decline began after this peak year but by 1941 Japanese still raised 41 per cent of California's truck crops. Specializing in truck garden produce they sometimes virtually monopolized the growing and marketing of certain crops such as celery, strawberries, carrots, onions, lettuce, and tomatoes.

Success brought retribution. In 1913 the California Alien Land Law, the Webb-Heney bill, was passed. This measure barred land ownership to Japanese aliens and limited leasing to three years. Attorney General Webb described the law's objective in 1913: "It seeks to limit their [Japanese] presence here, for they will not come in large numbers and long abide with us if they may not acquire land." Initially, the law was easily circumvented by placing land titles in the name of Japanese children (who were American citizens by birth) or Caucasian friends. The need for agricultural labor and produce during World War I also blunted the effects of the law, but in 1921 an amendment was passed outlawing the practices used to circumvent the Alien Land Law. This measure discouraged Japanese farmers and caused many to move to the city. In 1952 the State Supreme Court stamped it unconstitutional.

Next to agriculture the major economic activity of Japanese was in small shops and businesses such as stores, eating places, laundries, dry cleaning establishments, plant nurseries and barbershops. Such enterprises depended in large measure for their success on the cohesiveness of the Japanese community. Patronage by Caucasians fluctuated in concert with the anti-Japanese campaigns in the press—such campigns usually took place during periods of economic strife or elections.

Contract gardening was also an important occupation of the Japanese. In the 1920s the number of estates in California grew and the effective care of lawns, flowers, hedges, and trees became an absolute necessity. Because of the existing stereotype of the Japanese they found it easy to obtain employment as gardeners. By 1940 there were 1650 Japanese gardeners listed in a Southern California business directory, and there were hundreds more employed on private estates.

Unlike many European immigrants, the Japanese who came to America had four years of compulsory schooling, and usually an additional four years of optional schooling. Thus, the Issei (first-generation Japanese migrants) had an understanding and familiarity with education that were passed on to their children, the Nisei. To Japanese children the school was an opportunity to excel and studies have shown that they were equal to Caucasians in IQ and achievement, despite the obvious language handicap. But efforts to use American schools as a means of advancement met with resistance from Caucasians.

In 1906 the San Francisco school board passed a resolution requiring Japanese school children (ninety-three were involved) to attend a segregated oriental school in Chinatown. The action was mainly unnoticed by the press in California and the rest of the United States but was sensationally reported in Japan. One reputable journal demanded: "Stand up, Japanese nation! Our countrymen have been HUMILIATED on the other side of the Pacific. Our poor boys and girls have been expelled from the public schools by the rascals of the United States . . . Why do we not insist on sending war ships?"

The vigor of Japanese protest to what was interpreted as a racial insult alarmed authorities in Washington but federal officials had no authority over the public schools of San Francisco. President Theodore Roosevelt sent a special investigator to the scene and privately complained: "I am being horribly bothered about the Japanese business. The infernal fools in California . . . insult the Japanese recklessly and in the event of war it will be the Nation as a whole which will pay the consequences."

Unable to pressure local school officials, the President invited them to a meeting at the White House where a compromise was reached wherein San Francisco permitted Japanese school children of proper age and preparation to attend school with Caucasians. This face-saving concession pacified the Japanese government, which in turn consented to the Gentlemen's Agreement of 1907-8. This arrangement promised that no more passports would be issued to Japanese desiring to come to the United States. In 1924 migration from Japan was virtually banned by federal legislation in violation of the agreement.

The continuing discrimination against the Japanese in California poisoned relations between the United States and Japan in the twentieth century. After 1906 when Japan humbled Russia in war, their leaders were not inclined to overlook racial slights. Their more outspoken nationalists looked at the San Francisco school episode, the Webb-Heney bill, the Gentlemen's Agreement limiting immigration, and its repudiation by the Exclusion Act of 1924 as affronts to national honor. The degree to which such things strengthened the hands of the militarists of Japan and contributed to the coming of war with the United States is somewhat uncertain. However, there can be no doubt that discrimination against the Japanese in California worsened United States-Japanese relations in a most critical time.

The San Francisco school action was the most sensational effort to discriminate against Japanese school children but similar steps were taken throughout California. However, despite segregation in substandard schools, Japanese children were consistently praised by Caucasian teachers and administrators as ideal students. In some schools the granting of academic awards was discontinued because Japanese children won most of them.

But all former discrimination against the Japanese faded in comparison to that practiced during World War II. The removal of native-born Americans from their homes and their imprisonment in concentration camps could only be justified as a means of protecting them from maltreatment by "patriotic" white Californians. Those who returned to California after the war continued to climb both socially and economically despite the setback they received in the forced sale of their lands, businesses, and personal possessions at great sacrifice during the war. The Japanese continued to be healthier, wealthier, and wiser (if their greater education is any criterion) than their non-Japanese counterparts. A sense of guilt for their maltreatment during the war years, appreciation of the military contributions of the Nisei, recognition of the virtues of the Japanese people, and a growing maturity when it comes to racial matters have combined to lessen discrimination since 1945.

Filipinos succeeded the Japanese in the 1920s as the preferred oriental laborers on California's farms. Only 2674 in number in the state in 1920, they increased to 30,470 by 1930. Arriving at the rate of more than 4000 a year from Hawaii or the Philippine Islands, they constituted a labor force of more than 25,000 single men in 1930, mainly in the Salinas and San Joaquin valleys. In 1960 their numbers had only grown to 65,459. They have remained predominantly agricultural workers with relatively low incomes and a low level of education.

In many respects, the position of Filipinos in California's race history has been unique. They have suffered the same kind of discrimination as Chinese and Japanese although their numbers have always been small. Numerous riots against Filipinos involving loss of life, many injuries, and much property damage have occurred. Yet they were not aliens and were considered as wards of the federal government. Culturally they had more in common with Mexican-Americans in terms of religion and language than they had with their fellow Orientals. There were twice as many men as women in the Filipino segment of the population. Common cultural elements and the scarcity of Filipino women led to much intermarriage between Filipino men and Mexican women.

NORTH FROM MEXICO

It has been traditional for Californians to exalt their Hispanic heritage; this has been reflected in the emphasis upon Spanish architecture, the glorification of the missions, the observance of numerous fiestas, and the deification of the figures of the colonial period such as Father Junípero Serra. Unfortunately, these favorable attitudes have not been extended to California's Mexican citizenry, who have been exploited and who have been the recipients of much racial discrimination.

Originally small in numbers, California's Mexican population increased sharply to 368,013 by 1930. The Mexican Revolution which began in 1910 and the subsequent turmoil were principally responsible. By 1960 this number had grown to 1,426,538, with an 88 per cent increase taking place in the decade of the 1950s. Such growth came partially from Mexican immigration, but much of it has also been from the states of the Southwest. Like others the Mexican-American was attracted by the affluence of California and the lack of overt discrimination. The movement of people from the interior of Mexico and the rural areas of Texas or New Mexico reinforced the existing stereotype of the Mexican-American. To Anglos he was uneducated, lacked initiative, and was best suited for stoop labor in the fields. Such attitudes strengthened antagonism.

Although educators, predominantly Anglo, did little to encourage learning for those envisioned as laborers in the fields, Mexicans, unlike Orientals, did little themselves to close the cultural gap. The problem was measured in 1960 when a study revealed that Californians with Spanish surnames had completed only 8.6 years of schooling while non-whites had completed 10.6 years and Anglos 12.2 years. Language difficulties were partially responsible. But the fact that a similar pattern prevails in Mexico suggests other reasons as well. First of all, Hispanic culture does not value schooling as highly as does the Anglo or the Oriental. The failure of the Roman Catholic Church to stress learning for the masses is one explanation. Then too, people of a rural background who struggle for the merest essentials of life cannot see the future value of learning. Imperative, immediate needs preclude attention to long-range goals. The Mexican-Americans lack the acquisitive instinct of the Anglo: no Puritan ethic drives him. In other words, he is more apt to be satisfied with his existing station in life and he is unwilling to work to improve it. At one time the educated Mexican-American met such discrimination in the job market that he and his countrymen questioned the value of education. But perhaps the best reason why the Mexican in California has not accepted Anglo culture is that he is suffering from cultural indigestion. Unlike other American immigrants whose second and third generations have adopted the ways of the new nation, the Mexican has had to absorb succeeding waves of Spanish-speaking migrants. He has his "own" world in California which is distinct and separate from that of the Anglo complete with businesses, newspapers, television, and radio stations. A person could live out his life in the ghettos of East Los Angeles without close contact with the English-speaking world. He neither absorbs nor emulates the culture of the Anglo.

Although some contend that the Anglo and Mexican are destined to live apart permanently like the English and French in Canada, there is evidence of change. The number of Mexicans who have

occupancy by blacks or members of other specified minorities were used until the Supreme Court outlawed them in 1948. Thereafter, gentlemen's agreements by realtors and lending agencies were used to prevent the renting or sale of property in white neighborhoods to blacks. In 1959 the Democratic-dominated legislature passed the Unruh Civil Rights Act, which forbade such discriminatory practices by realtors. The 1963 legislature passed the Rumford Act, which banned discrimination in the rental or sale of residential property of more than four units and provided stiff penalties for violation. A strong reaction came within a year when the California Real Estate Association sponsored a proposition which in effect outlawed all legislation seeking to regulate the sale or rental of property on racial grounds. The voters passed the measure by a margin of two to one and told black Californians that they were destined to remain in their ghettos indefinitely. The courts ultimately nullified this blatant racist measure but the blow to human dignity could not be completely undone.

Antagonism over housing, unemployment, inadequate public transportation and welfare programs, and long-standing resentment against the police combined to provoke the holocaust of Watts, which began on August 11, 1965. Television also played a role in triggering the event. Through television, black Californians escaped the ghetto. The images which came to him through the tube of affluent America made it possible for him to see the limitations of his own life in sharp contrast. The television set also established a level of consumerism in black viewers as well as white. When widespread resentment boiled over as a result of a police arrest consumerism and widespread antagonism combined to make for widespread looting. More often than not, the loot consisted of the items which a thousand TV commercials had extolled as the symbols of affluent society. Television stations covered the event as though it were a spectacular and brought its vivid scenes into the living rooms of thousands of viewers. In striking contrast were the scenes of an international beauty contest which an enterprising station broadcast. Before order was restored, 34 persons, mostly black, were killed, 1032 injured, with property damage estimated to have been in excess of $40,000,000. The poverty of the residents of the "palm tree ghetto" of Watts was intensified. More significantly, the long years of trying to teach whites and blacks to live in harmony were of no avail. California obviously still had a long way to go before attaining racial harmony.

AMERICAN INDIANS

The American Indian is another "native" minority that has not participated in the affluence of California. In fact, the first Californians are on the lowest rung of the economic and social ladder. Their life expectancy is forty-four years, as compared to seventy-one for white Americans, and their average income is the lowest of any of the state's minorities. The average years of schooling, 7.6 for men, is well below that of blacks and Mexican-Americans. Their housing, on reservations or in the cities, is generally inadequate, typical of the ghettos of Watts or East Los Angeles.

The number of first Californians resident in the state in 1960 was difficult to determine. The original estimate of 133,000 when the Spanish first arrived in 1769 had shrunk to only 15,000 in 1900. Since that date their numbers have slowly grown. In 1950 the official census recorded 19,947 and in 1960, 39,014, which represented the highest percentage increase of any ethnic group. However, authoritative sources claim that there were approximately 75,000 American Indians in California in 1960. This may be true, for census takers did not identify many Indians of this generation. The Indians of today are concealed often by Anglo and Hispanic surnames, and live behind the façade of modern culture in the form of TV sets, deepfreezes, and telephones. Approximately one half of this total were recent migrants from Arizona, New Mexico, and Oklahoma.

The American Indian is no longer confined to a reservation. Only 7400 (19 per cent) of the 39,014 counted by the Census Bureau lived on or adjacent to reservations in 1960. Officially 53 per cent were listed as urban in 1960, with 8839 of this total living in the Los Angeles area. However, a national newsmagazine claimed in 1970 that there were 60,000 Indians in Los Angeles and 20,000 in San Francisco. If these figures were correct it indicated that there has been a great increase in urbanization during the decade.

There are eighty-two Indian reservations and rancherias (group homesites) widely scattered throughout California. Only eighteen of these sites had more than 100 Indians resident in 1960, and only three had more than 500. They are Hoopa Valley in the northwest corner of the state along the Trinity and Klamath rivers with 992 Hoopa Indians; Fort Yuma Reservation in the extreme southeastern corner with 965 Yuma Indians; Bishop Reservation in Inyo County with 570 Paiute Indians.

Interest in the status of California's Indians was heightened by the seizure of Alcatraz Island on November 20, 1969, and its continued occupation. Leaders of the Indian group demanded that the island be devoted to an institute of native American studies, an Indian medical center, an ecological research center, and an Indian museum.

Perhaps Californians, along with other Americans, have discovered that the American Indian does not belong only to the past. He still lives, but, like members of other minority groups, not too well. At their annual conference in 1961 the National Congress of American Indians issued the following declaration: "What we ask of America is not charity. We ask only that the nature of our situation be recognized and made the basis of policy and action. In short, the Indians ask for assistance, technical and financial, for the time needed, to regain in the America of the space age some measure of the adjustment they enjoyed as the original possessors of their native land."

CHAPTER XXII

Things Cultural

The history of culture in the Golden State is as difficult to evaluate as other aspects of California's development. Some would deny that there has been anything significant or different about the state's cultural development while others describe the cultural scene contemptuously as "a putty culture, not yet hardened into shape." Still others would claim that the lack of restraint has led an uncritical populace to accept anything dubbed "artistic." A contemporary observer contends "We are producing with staggering velocity and astonishing self-assurance, the most mechanical, regimented, sterile, uncultured, inhuman urban environment in the history of the world."

There is some evidence that California is the center of the modern mass culture. Dr. Abbott Kaplan claims that the "upsurge of interest in the arts is apparent throughout the country; but nowhere more so than in California." The sale of books, attendance at the opera and the theater, art exhibits, and the general interest in cultural activities are evidence that the state is not an intellectual desert. If there are distinct traits of amateurishness in the commitment of the state's citizenry to the arts, they are only following the traditional patterns of Americans everywhere. For if California is "the window to the future" that some claim, it is also "the window to the past" and reflects typical national values in things cultural.

The culture which has emerged in California is a product of its unique history. The state entered the Union without territorial status; in population, the growth was almost instantaneous; and in the economic realm, the transformation was equally rapid. Those who were attracted by the gold rush were a cross section of the United States' population. Politicians, lawyers, physicians, journalists, merchants, farmers, and laborers came for the opportunities they saw in this new land of El Dorado. They were from New England, New

York City, the South, and the midwestern frontier, but worldwide interest in the gold also brought people from the far corners of the globe. Thus, California became a real melting pot, a land of many peoples. So the culture, truly representative of the cosmopolitan society which spawned it, was as rich and diverse as the peoples who comprised the population of California.

In its emphasis upon things practical, California's culture was very similar to that of the colonial frontier from its inception until its move westward. Men concerned with wresting a living from nature were much more interested with what will work rather than the purely aesthetic. In this frontier environment, where established artists were few and artistic standards non-existent, artists were those who felt inspired. Without the critics and authorities of an established community, they created. That the result would be dominated by the amateur and the primitive is self-evident. Much of what they did promptly sank into oblivion but some of the work of these early artists and writers has become part of California's cultural heritage.

The cultural heritage of California was different from that of the rest of the nation, for it grew out of the "instant" society that was created as a result of the gold rush. Frontiersmen in New England, for example, struggled for generations with an inhospitable environment. In the effort to provide the necessities of life little time remained to be concerned with things of the spirit. In California, on the other hand, ample wealth was available to support all forms of cultural expression from 1850 on. Western mines produced more than $50,000,000 a year in gold and when this began to decline, silver from Nevada took up the slack. Just as wealth was the key to the cultural flowering of Italy in the Renaissance so gold was the basis of the sophistication of the arts in the Golden State. Had the mines alone provided the basis of the state's wealth, California would have been soon deserted by miners eager to return home. By the 1850s there were vulgar displays by the nouveaux riches in San Francisco but schools were also built, opera and the theater were patronized, and the newspapers and magazines made their appearance.

The early sophistication which appeared continued to be an important ingredient of the cultural scene and in some areas the state led the Atlantic community in the arts. But if this sophistication has continued so also has a certain primitiveness that has continued into the second half of the twentieth century. This has resulted from California's inability to settle down like other frontiers. Franklin Walker suggests that "San Francisco became the mother of a score of daughter frontiers." Others have pointed to the continuing "frontiering" of California as each successive wave of population has renewed the frontier.

LITERATURE OF THE FRONTIER

The literature of the California frontier was steeped in pragmatism. It was the work of men who had little formal training and who were concerned with their immediate environment. They wrote what they saw, heard, felt, smelled, tasted, and experienced. Newspapers and magazines made an early appearance but fiction did not prosper. As every day was filled with the unusual and sometimes the bizarre, the truthful record of events was frequently much stranger than fiction.

No one was better able to write of life on the mining frontier than Louise Clappe. Her twenty-three letters to her sister, published as *The Shirley Letters,* ably display feminine sensibility when it comes to accurately describing the detail of everyday life. Accompanying her physician husband to the mines, she described life in a place where there were "no newspapers, no churches, lectures, concerts or theaters; no fresh books, no shopping, calling nor gossiping little tea-drinkings; no parties, no balls, no picnics, no tableaux, no charades, no latest fashions, no daily mail, (we have an express once a month), no promenades, no rides nor drives; no vegetables but potatoes and onions, no milk, no eggs, no *nothing?*" A sensitive New Englander, she wrote of the physical hardship and the brutalizing effects of the frontier, especially in the maltreatment of the Mexican, and in the administration of vigilante justice. Although the letters were never intended for publication, they have remained among the finest descriptions of mining life ever penned.

Alonzo Delano, writing as "Old Block," effectively captured the true spirit of the miner's life. Instead of concentrating on the rich strikes of the lucky ones, he related the heartbreak of those who gambled all they had to come to the mines and after years of back-breaking labor, illness, and physical deprivation failed to strike it rich. In spite of much personal tragedy he never lost his sense of humor. (A Cyrano de Bergerac nose encouraged him to be amiable.) His articles originally appeared in newspapers and magazines but were published in 1853 as *Chips from the Old Block*. His popularity stemmed from his ability to describe "the greenhorn, the miner, the trader, the gambler, and other Western types with just the right combination of realism, homely philosophy, pathos, and humor."

George H. Derby, writing as John Phoenix, was even more of a humorist than Old Block, although a career in the United States Army is not normally a spawning ground for a comedian. Derby once sent a recommendation to the War Department that the regulation uniform add a three-inch ring so the infantry sergeant could hook the soldier with a pole if he attempted retreat. It could also enable cavalrymen to hook themselves into the saddle. Another story discussed the hazards of building a military road through the wild life of San Francisco. One of his reports related the plight of the deceased soldier from Yuma who telegraphed from hell for his blankets. No phase of California life escaped Derby's satire, but unfortunately many of his stories were unprintable in his day. Like Mark Twain, whom he influenced, Derby's humor reflected the coarseness of the American frontier.

John Rollin Ridge (Yellow Bird), who was one-half Cherokee, wrote perhaps the greatest hoax in the history of California letters. His *Life and Adventures of Joaquin Murieta, the Celebrated California Bandit* created a western folk tale that is still accepted as accurate by many. Repelled by the maltreatment of the native Californios by the Anglos, Ridge depicted Joaquin as a pure-blooded Spaniard (the age would not have accepted a Mexican hero) who was driven into outlawry through no fault of his own. Although a highwayman, he was portrayed as a gallant Robin Hood who robbed the rich to give to the poor and defended his people against the hated gringo.

Numerous newspapers and magazines made their appearance during the gold rush, indicating a high percentage of literacy among the new arrivals. Their pages, filled with articles on the California scene of the 1850s, have considerable value to the historian. These newspapers and magazines provided the apprenticeship for later writers, two of whom, Francis Bret Harte and Samuel Clemens, enjoy national reputations. Bret Harte edited the *Overland Monthly*, perhaps the best of these magazines, which first published his tales and poems of the West.

It was not until Harte discovered the California scene that he emerged as a writer. His real-life characters of the mining camp shocked many in that genteel age but his depiction of death, gunplay, and romance provided a formula for western drama that is still common on the television screen. Although he believed himself to be a literary realist, and to some extent he was, Harte introduced the tendency to romanticize California's mining frontier—even before that frontier was tamed!

Samuel Clemens' career as a river pilot was ended by the Civil War, when his position as a Missourian forced him to fight former friends no matter which side he chose and prompted him to seek refuge in the West. He settled in Nevada with his brother, where he tried silver mining before turning to journalism. His path inevitably brought him to San Francisco and to ultimate fame as the greatest writer of frontier California.

Like Bret Harte, Mark Twain left the California frontier when he attained literary prominence but it never left him. He remained a product of this turbulent era: Mark Twain's coarse, exaggerated humor reflected the frontier. Although he was to use the locale of his native state for much of his writing, the gold rush era left its stamp upon him. Mark Twain had the frontiersman's ability to see through cant and hypocrisy, to find real human beings instead of the pompous stuffed shirts of the more civilized world, and also to view established and even revered institutions with the jaundiced eye of an iconoclast.

Joaquin Miller, another of California's literary frontier figures, attained his greatest fame in England. Capitalizing on the Londoners' love of the "noble savage," Miller played the part of the uncouth frontiersman to the hilt. He attended fashionable dinners in typical miner's garb and on occasion he emitted war whoops upon entering a stately drawing room. His reputation as an eccentric helped sell his poetry and partially masked his literary shortcomings. Miller's *Songs of the Sierras*, his only worthwhile contribution to California literature, captures the grandeur of the state's scenery.

Fiction writers were not the only ones to discover that Californians wanted to romanticize their frontier even before it had disappeared. The new West did not have a history and it therefore embarked on the task of creating one. Hubert Howe Bancroft had been a successful businessman and invested his fortune in the writing of a history of western America from Alaska to Central America. His lack of formal education did not deter him, for, like Henry Ford, he realized that with money one could always hire brains. But he was also following a California tradition of attacking difficult tasks regardless of his amateur status. The application of commercial methods to do the writing of history enabled him to produce thirty-nine volumes which are still of value. His extensive bibliographies continue to aid scholars. Bancroft also gathered a tremendous quantity of source material which might otherwise have been lost to posterity. His personal library, built systematically over a half century, became the largest and richest collection of printed and manuscript materials of western Americana in the United States. It was acquired by the University of California, Berkeley, in 1913. Though the gold miner turned historian attempted to produce only factual works his enthusiasm for the project he had undertaken caused him to romanticize and overstate.

A MATURE LITERARY WORLD

By the 1870s the frontier era in California literature was over. Bret Harte had left the editorship of *Overland Monthly* for the East Coast and England, leaving "his creative ability and popularity behind." Even he recognized what had happened to his artistic talents when he lamented: "I grind out the old tunes on the old organ, and gather up the coppers." Mark Twain and Joaquin Miller soon followed Harte; Miller returned to California, but Twain's departure was permanent. The new generation of writers which followed took up different themes and introduced new literary forms.

Ambrose Bierce arrived in San Francisco in the late 1860s and soon became the "literary dictator" of the Pacific coast. He decided to "purify journalism in this town by instructing such writers as it is worthwhile to instruct, and assassinating those that it is not." It was probably only in the West that a man like Bierce could flourish. Described as "the bitterest American that ever lived" who wrote with a pen "thrice dipped in gall," his use of invective and personal attack as well as biting satire has seldom been equaled. A brief residence in England had made him an Anglophile who looked with distaste upon life in California. Nothing was immune from the attack of his caustic pen. Women and the clergy were special objects of his ridicule. In searching for a clergyman to wed him, it was difficult to find a minister who would perform the ceremony and be acceptable to Bierce. Bierce was as obsessed with the macabre as Edgar Allan Poe and his newspaper columns were filled with commentaries on violent accidents, homicides, suicides, and assorted acts of mayhem. He disappeared in Mexico in 1913 under mysterious circumstances. His most enduring book was *The Devil's Dictionary* but his influence upon other writers of the age was perhaps of more lasting significance than his own production.

Frank Norris, the son of well-to-do Chicagoans, came to California in 1884 when only fourteen. He studied art in Paris and attended Harvard and the University of California and was a newspaper correspondent in the Boer War. Apparently influenced by Emile Zola, the French proponent of the problem novel, Norris espoused in his writings the sociological doctrine of survival of the fittest. Norris planned to tell the epic story of California wheat but death left the task incomplete. His most famous book, *The Octopus*, describes the wheat boom in the San Joaquin Valley in the 1870s and shows the manner in which the Southern Pacific Railroad ensnared the farmers in its tentacles. *The Pit*, the second volume in Norris' planned trilogy, was concerned with the unsavory machinations of the wheat market in Chicago before it was subject to regulation. Death at the early age of thirty-two cut down Norris, one of California's most promising novelists.

Jack London, born in San Francisco in 1876, was a true product of California, perhaps even of some of the more unsavory features of it. Like Topsy he just growed to manhood on the Oakland waterfront while sampling at an early age the many forms of debauchery available. His experiences brought him into contact with, as he put it, "the pit, the abyss, the human cesspool, the shambles, and the charnel house of our civilization." After a career as a hobo and working at odd jobs, he attended the University of California briefly, only to be repelled by the intellectually stultifying effects of the classroom. His education was really obtained from the streets, from his activities in the Alaskan gold rush, and as a working journalist.

A superb storyteller, London's *The Sea Wolf* and *The Call of the Wild* won him world acclaim. His writings reveal a Darwinian glorification of brute force. He was a Nietzschean who was interested in power and its manipulation. More significantly, he was a social critic of the first order and all of his work reflected this role. Disillusionment with the shortcomings of American society in the early twentieth century drove him into the Socialist party but he was too much of an individualist to accept the regimentation of Marxism. He was a restless and tumultuous soul, and death, hastened by alcoholism, removed Jack London from the California scene in 1916 at the age of forty.

Upton Sinclair was a social critic like Jack London, but there the similarity ends. Robert Glass Cleland described Sinclair as a "faddist, passionate social reformer, source of an endless flow of tracts, plays, and novels, producer of best sellers or near-best sellers with almost monotonous regularity, [he] is probably the most widely read California author of this or any other generation." Born in 1878, he published his first novel in 1901, attained national prominence with *The Jungle* in 1906, and continued to produce almost a hundred novels and plays before his death in 1968.

A resident of California since 1915, Sinclair used his pen to stress his Socialist belief that American capitalism was the root of all evil. His rich characters were invariably evil and useless while the poor were virtuous. He directly influenced much reform legislation and won a Pulitzer prize in 1942. He was a propagandist as much as a literary figure. He was instrumental in organizing the American Civil Liberties Union, ran for Congress several times as well as for governor of California. Upton Sinclair was truly a remarkable figure on the Californian scene regardless of how future generations of literary critics evaluate his writings.

Robinson Jeffers, California's greatest poet, was more than a social critic. He was a nihilist who had lost all confidence in man. Like

F. Scott Fitzgerald he came out of a generation "grown up to find all Gods dead, all wars fought, all faiths in man shaken." Son of a classical scholar and theologian from Pennsylvania, Jeffers' training in Greek and the Bible is evident throughout his writings. They are also permeated with melancholy that has prompted comparison with Eugene O'Neill. After graduation from Occidental College he studied medicine, forestry, and law before an independent income enabled him to settle at Carmel-by-the-Sea on the Monterey peninsula. His poems have given the "feel" of the Carmel coast to readers throughout the world. In the post-World War II period there was a revival of interest in his work. A society that had itself lost confidence in its ability to find solutions for the problems of the atomic age turned to this poet who found landscapes and seascapes of far more significance than human beings.

What Robinson Jeffers was to California poetry, John Steinbeck was to the California novel. Jeffers used the granite and redwood coast for the locale of most of his poems while Steinbeck used his native Salinas Valley as a setting for many of his novels. Both writers depicted the world as cruel and impersonal which twists and snuffs out the lives of helpless individuals with reckless abandon, but there the similarity ends. While Jeffers does not lament at what he sees happening to what he considers contemptible human beings, Steinbeck has compassion for suffering man. Like Upton Sinclair he was confident that man can solve his problems.

Born in Salinas in 1902, Steinbeck grew up in a ranching community, but also came to know the fruit orchards and the fish canneries from personal experience. In his early writings he displayed an understanding and an empathy for the neglected citizens of Mexican heritage. A superb reporter, he knew intimately the people about whom he wrote. His stark realism shocked many readers. His greatest novel, *The Grapes of Wrath,* so harshly depicted the plight of the Okies in California fields that Kern County authorities banned the book from its libraries and burned the copies available.

Steinbeck was most concerned with the loss of human dignity entailed in the plight of the migrant workers. He asked questions about a society which will feed its horses when they are not working but denies bread to unemployed human beings. The book was an indictment of the society of that day.

STEINBECK AND THE DEPRESSION

The works of the roots of the vines, of the trees, must be destroyed to keep up the price, and this is the saddest bitterest thing of all. Carloads of oranges dumped on the ground. The people came for miles to take the fruit, but this could not be. How would they buy oranges at 20¢ a dozen if they could drive out and pick them up? And men with hoses squirt kerosene on the oranges, and they are angry at the crime, angry at the people who have come to take the fruit . . .

Burn corn to keep warm, it makes a hot fire. Dump potatoes in the river and place guards along the banks to keep the hungry people from fishing them out. Slaughter the pigs and bury them, and let the putrescence drip down into the earth . . .

There is a crime here that goes beyond denunciation. There is a sorrow that weeping cannot symbolize. There is a failure here that topples all our success . . . And children dying of pellagra must die because a profit cannot be taken from an orange. And coroners must fill in the certificates —died of malnutrition—because the food must rot, must be forced to rot.

The people with nets come to fish for potatoes in the river, and the guards hold them back; they come in rattling cars to get the dumped oranges, but the kerosene is sprayed. And they stand still and watch the potatoes float by, listen to the screaming pigs being killed in a ditch and covered with quicklime, watch the mountains of oranges slop down to a putrefying ooze; and in the eyes of the people there is a failure; and in the eyes of the hungry there is a growing wrath. In the souls of the people the grapes of wrath are filling and growing heavy, growing heavy for the vintage.

John Steinbeck, *The Grapes of Wrath,*
pp. 476–77.

Continuing to write into the 1960s, California's greatest novelist produced best sellers but confounded literary critics. Often dealing in abstract ideas and symbols, he was difficult to understand. Perhaps the greatest obstacle to his continued acceptance has been Steinbeck's optimistic belief that men and women can somehow solve their problems in an age of pessimism. The Nobel prize for literature awarded him in 1962 was a fitting climax to a distinguished literary career and a life which ended in 1968.

California has produced scores of lesser literary figures. William Saroyan has written effectively of the agricultural region around Fresno utilizing his Armenian background. Walter van Tilburg Clark's *The Ox-Bow Incident* is one of the better presentations of the brutalizing effect of vigilante frontier justice. Many authors have used satire to voice their displeasure with aspects of California life. Nathanael West's *The Day of the Locust* is a biting satire of the effect upon recent migrants and the retired life in Southern California. Budd Schulberg's *What Makes Sammy Run* attacks the artificiality of Hollywood. The English Aldous Huxley's *After Many a Summer Dies the Swan* and Evelyn Waugh's *The Loved One* satirize the California way of death.

PAINTING

Among those drawn to the gold fields were trained artists. Those with ability—and even some without—discovered that there was more gold to be mined with the paintbrush than with a pick and shovel. Once the prospect of "striking it rich" as a miner no longer existed, the gold-based economy of California continued to lure painters from the far corners of the world. In the last half of the nineteenth century it is estimated that some twelve hundred men of varying degrees of training and artistic talent found their way to San Francisco.

The nouveaux riches of the state, like their counterparts of Renaissance Italy, wanted paintings to decorate their gaudy mansions and portraits to preserve their likenesses for posterity. Thus wealth, that essential ingredient of cultural expression through the ages, provided the cornerstone of early California painting. In addition to portraits, the early artist found numerous themes in the state: the historical scenes at the mines (in this respect he was the photographer of his day), the grandeur of the mountains and the seashore, the uniqueness of the flora of California. Like artists everywhere of that day they also drew upon mythology as subjects and themes.

Long before the gold rush the first Californians, the Indians, used rock paintings to depict the world in which they lived. As noted previously, the outstanding example of their artistic expression was their basketwork. Indian neophytes, under the tutelage of the Spanish padres, covered the mission walls with murals of religious themes. Although many paintings of this nature have been lost, enough remain to suggest the talent possessed by these nameless artists. In addition to directing the abilities of their charges, the Spanish padres also brought paintings and sculptures from Mexico to decorate the missions. That a greater flowering of typical Mexican-Spanish art did not take place can be attributed to the great distance from Mexico, the poverty of California, and the turmoil existing in the latter years of Spanish and Mexican rule.

Among the first of the gold rush artists was William Smith Jewett, who painted a large oil in 1850 depicting an immigrant family on a mountain crest. He was the first to popularize the distinctiveness of the California landscape and a grateful legislature commissioned him to do a portrait of John A. Sutter for the state capitol at a fee of $5000.

The best of the early painters was the German-born Charles C. Nahl (1818–75). Educated in Europe with his half-brother, Hugo William Arthur Nahl, also a California artist, this formal training was always reflected in his paintings. Charles designed the bear on the California state flag, and Hugo the state seal. Charles also prepared the sketches for two popular books by Alonzo Delano, but his real claim to fame rests on his talent as an interpreter of the gold rush. His paintings are reproductions of actual mining scenes and his "Saturday Evening in the Mines" and "Sunday Morning in the Mines" are huge canvases which recapture the rowdy spirit of the age. Art critics denigrate Nahl's Teutonic thoroughness which prompted him to crowd his paintings with minutiae but his wealth of accurate detail is a boon to the student of the gold rush. In spite of the fact that his paintings earned him great wealth, Nahl was little known outside of California.

Of far greater national renown was Albert Bierstadt (1830–1902). Like Nahl, he was born and educated in Germany, and by the 1870s he was the most widely known active American painter. Famed for his landscapes, he roamed and painted much of the West before discovering California and the Yosemite Valley. Bierstadt's paintings were intended to impress the viewer with the grandeur of the western wilderness. He became identified with the flamboyant nationalism of the post-Civil War era by painting romanticized panoramas of his adopted country.

Among the large number of landscapists to use California scenery was Thomas A. Ayres (ca 1816–58), who was the first to paint Yosemite. His "High Falls" is his most famed work. Thomas Hill (1829–1908) was similar to Bierstadt in that he stressed enormous panoramic views of mountains. "Yosemite Valley" is probably his most successful painting but he is more widely known for his "Driving the Last Spike," a hugh canvas which depicts the completion of the transcontinental railroad. The tendency to overstate in this panorama is seen in his inclusion of railroad officials who had not been present, some having been dead for years. Like Hill, Thomas Moran (1837–1926) was also born and educated in England. Moran also painted panoramic enormities, but was considered more talented by some critics than many of his contemporaries. He attempted to capture on his canvases not only all outdoors itself, but the lofty spiritual and moral elevations that came with viewing landscape at its grandest. Most famed for his paintings of the Yellowstone region, Moran stressed Yosemite and coastal scenes in his California work. William Keith (1838–1911) was a different type of landscapist. He avoided the grandiose panorama. His canvases of live oaks and the golden grass fields had a touch of the mystical induced by the use of shade and light. Instead of bombast, his quiet meadows and placid streams spoke of the serenity of California. Self-trained, he remains the best-known and most widely honored painter which California has produced. He influenced many young painters. Most notable of these was Gutzon Borglum, who emphasized the romantic and dramatic in art and western themes. Although Borglum's greatest fame was earned as a sculptor of Mount Rushmore, he began his career as a painter of western landscapes, and his residence in California in the 1890s unquestionably left its mark on his later work.

Charles Dorman Robinson (1847–1933) was another artist who concentrated on the Yosemite Valley. Before his brush was stilled, he produced some hundred paintings on the subject. In the midst of the San Francisco fire he worked day and night to sketch the disaster. From these labors came "The Fire" a canvas 12 by 30 feet. In 1911 he painted another unique picture of a sea-air battle of the future.

Thaddeus Welch (1844–1919), a naturalistic artist who became known as the "painter of Marin," produced paintings depicting nature's beauties and colors. Henry Joseph Brener (1860–1932) effectively used light and shadow to induce emotional response to his works on California scenery. An art editor, he also promoted the cause of his profession. Will Sparks (1862–1937) painted the missions as well as landscapes. Charles J. Dickman (1863–1943) found his primary inspiration in the Monterey area although his mural landscapes included mountains and Death Valley. Xavier Martinez (1893–1943) was born in Mexico and studied under Whistler. His work exhibits an unusual sense of color and his handling of Indians suggests the force and vigor of Diego Rivera. Toby Edward Rosenthal (1848–1916) was trained in Germany and his works always reflected scrupulous craftsmanship. Sometimes he spent three years on a single work. After "The Trial of Constance Beverly," unveiled in 1884, he was hailed as one of America's greatest artists.

The San Francisco fire of 1906 destroyed much California art but it also provided patrons who needed replacements. The early twentieth century also saw the gradual eclipse of the distinctive character of California art. More and more art critics decreed that the standards of New York and Paris must be those of the Golden State. Yet the past of California was the subject of murals in the Mark Hopkins Hotel by Frank Van Sloun (1879–1938) and Maynard Dixon (1875–1946). Other buildings, both public and private, have a variety of frescoes depicting the history of the state, some of them by painters of national fame.

Lacking the wealth, and hence the patrons, art in Southern California lagged far behind that of the bay area. However, a number of artists were attracted to the region. The great attraction to landscape painters in the southland was, as one artist put it, "the mocking brilliancy of the sky." In the pre-smog era at the onset of the present century, artists from the East had to unlearn most of what they had previously been taught about light and color if they were to do justice to the sun-drenched landscape. Some succeeded, but most early landscapists of the area were unsuccessful in their efforts to capture the dazzling brilliance of Southern California light.

Many of the early artists were brought in by the Santa Fe and Southern Pacific railroads, who were more interested in calendar art as a lure for tourists than in "art for art's sake." The most talented included William Wendt (1865–1946), who came to Los Angeles in 1908 and soon became the leading painter of Southern California, with "Land of Heart's Desire" his best-known work. Elmer Wachtel (1864–1929) soon surpassed him as the best-selling landscapist but both had a host of imitators. Although as previously mentioned, Gutzon Borglum was influenced by William Keith and his residence in the Sierras, he first emerged as a painter in Southern California. While ranching with his brother near Santa Ana, he maintained a studio in Los Angeles where he painted pastoral scenes featuring sheep. His later canvases display influence from his residence in the southern part of the state.

The San Francisco Exposition of 1915 provided an opportunity for California artists to exhibit but it also led to a stress on French moderns. The professional art schools also stressed impressionism, accelerating change in California art. Today there are so many different artists resident in the state that virtually every approach to painting is represented. Scores of art "centers" exist and numerous galleries or sidewalk exhibits endeavor to sell the burgeoning production of canvases. How many of these artists are likely to find lasting fame is another question, however.

Since the turn of the century important museums and galleries have multiplied throughout the state. No longer is the San Francisco area the sole art center of the state. The Henry E. Huntington Art Gallery at San Marino and the Los Angeles County Museum of Art are among the best of those found outside the bay area. More importantly, the state now has enough wealthy art collectors to gather in a fair share of the art treasures of the world.

SCULPTURE

California's first eminent sculptor was Douglas Tilden (1860–1935). Doubly handicapped, a deaf-mute from the age of five, this native won world renown as a sculptor of sports figures. Among the best-known works are "The Baseball Player," "The Football Players," "The Tired Boxer," and "The Mechanics' Fountain." Robert I. Aitken (1878–   ), another native son, was one of Tilden's many pupils to win fame in his own right. An impressionist in his work,

Aitken did the four heroic figures representing Fire, Air, Water, and Earth at the San Francisco Pan-Pacific Exposition in 1915. His statue of the Scotch poet Robert Burns, located in the Library of Congress, is probably his best-known work.

Arthur Putnam (1873–1930) became the nation's most celebrated wild animal sculptor. In addition to numerous statues of mountain lions, bears, coyotes, and pumas he did reliefs and ornamental sculpture for buildings and mansions in San Francisco. Melvin Earl Cummings (1876–1936), a Mormon from Utah, originally carved in wood. His bust of Douglas Tilden earned him the patronage of Mrs. Phoebe Hearst. He worked with Putnam on the Sloat Memorial but is best remembered for his ornamental work on the Sather Gate on the Berkeley campus of the University of California. Ralph Stackpole (1885–   ) also collaborated with Putnam and did work for the Pan-Pacific Exposition. His best works are the Coleman Fountain and Swanston Fountain in Sacramento and his statue of John Wesley Powell in the Department of the Interior building in Washington, D.C.

ARCHITECTURE

Architecture in California is the product of a number of influences. It reflected a people's desire to retain the known, to surround themselves in their new environment with homes and buildings they had been familiar with since childhood or which were popular in the style-setting eastern portion of the country. This tendency led the settlers of the 1850s to build homes with steep-pitched roofs to prevent snow from accumulating in areas which had never seen a snowfall, to build three-story homes with basements on ranches where the price of land was no problem, and to build homes with numerous bay windows so as to better catch the sun in a land where the problem was to minimize sunshine. This effort to reproduce familiar styles in the building of homes prompted one observer to comment that in a California gold town one could see "a New England farmhouse sandwiched between a prim Cotswold cottage and an elegant French chateau, while a bit farther down the street one comes on a Swiss chalet and, atop a neighboring hill, a white colonial manor house, complete with colonnaded façade, that might have been transported bodily from the Virginia countryside."

A comparable slavishness to styles established in other parts of the country existed in the construction of public buildings. One eastern architect, in designing a San Francisco skyscraper, even incorporated provision for steam pipes in the cornices of the building so as to prevent the formation of icicles! Even when a more innovative than average architect used structural steel in his design, he was forced by the weight of tradition to mask what might otherwise have been a tall graceful building in heavy stone so as to give it the proper Gothic appearance then in vogue.

Despite the ability to attract numerous qualified architects from the rest of the nation, California's commercial and public buildings have been singularly lacking in innovation. This has resulted from a typical California emphasis on the practical rather than the aesthetic. Evidence of this is seen in the fate of Daniel H. Burnham's "Grand Design" for San Francisco. The earthquake and fire of 1906 provided a marvelous opportunity to put it into practice as the city rebuilt, but, as one observer commented, "The need to rebuild quickly argued against the desire to rebuild differently. The grand scheme was fought over, modified, cut down, fought over—and finally 'the damndest finest ruins' were more or less re-erected. The Burnham Plan was big enough, but the Almighty Quick Buck was bigger." Only the idea of a civic center survived. Willis Polk, who assisted Burnham in the drafting of his master plan, became known as "the man who rebuilt San Francisco." Although most of Polk's structures lacked distinction he did produce the Hallidie building in 1918. It was a unique creation. On every side, great expanses of glass and line led the eye skyward. It became known as the world's first "glass skyscraper."

More innovative in a different way than the Hallidie building in San Francisco was the Bradbury building completed in 1893 in Los Angeles. It was designed by George Herbert Wyman, who had no formal training in design or construction. Just why Lewis Bradbury, who made a fortune in Mexican mining, should have selected a complete novice for so important a project remains a mystery. Wyman, who came to Los Angeles for his health, received inspiration for his task from Edward Bellamy's utopian novel, *Looking Backward*. One passage in it described the typical business structure as "a vast hall full of light received not alone from the windows on all sides but from the dome, the point of which was a hundred feet above." In the Bradbury building, a large skylight produces the desired effect and the building's spaciousness is enhanced by having the offices of each floor open on a series of balconies which surround an interior court. The use of "clerestory windows, the seemingly endless use of wrought iron and oak, the columns, arcades and staircases" combine to make this structure one of lasting beauty.

Efforts to adapt Franciscan mission architecture for a style distinctly "Californian" failed because it was a building form ill-suited to the commercial world of the late nineteenth and twentieth centuries. The mission revival of the 1890s saw the erection of the so-called mission railroad stations of the Southern Pacific. However, the search for a style adaptable to "the Mediterrean blue of our skies and sea, to the mellow brown of our rolling hills in autumn" ended in the copying of the New Mexico pueblo.

The full realization of a peculiarly Spanish colonial architecture came with the work of Bertram Goodhue, who designed most of the structures at the Panama Pacific Exposition in San Diego in 1915. Virtually ignoring the mission style, he borrowed heavily from Churrigueresque as well as Moorish and Italian styles. The eclectic result established the pattern followed in the building of Hearst's San Simeon castle and to a lesser extent in the rebuilding of Santa Barbara after the earthquake of 1925 and the building of San Clemente in the 1920s. To some it represented the flowering of an architecture peculiarly Californian, while others considered the combination of so many diverse styles an affront to good taste.

Virtually every conceivable style of house has been built in California, as its citizens have not been afraid to be innovative in this respect. But most of them have been copied from the particular preference popular at the time elsewhere in the nation. Most of the construction, of necessity, has been in wood and stucco. The mission style was at least original. It had its beginnings at the turn of the century, was given an additional impetus by the Panama Pacific Exposition at San Diego in 1915, and continued into the twenties. It was so popular that architects dubbed it a "mission craze" and one individual announced, "Give me neither Romanesque nor Gothic;

much less Italian Renaissance, and least of all English Colonial—this is California—give me Mission." Its distinguishing architectural features were thick walls, tile roofs, arched windows and doorways, and wide, hollow columns. Intended to emulate Mexican adobe, the buildings were usually of wood frame finished with stucco.

The mission-style home was soon dated but many of its features were incorporated into the bungalow or California ranch house. In spite of efforts to claim that the bungalow was indigenous to California it was probably an importation which was modified before being passed on to the nation. The designation "bungalow" is an Anglicized corruption of the word "Bengali," used to refer to the thatched houses which evolved from the service tents used by the British in India. The exact date of the bungalow's arrival in California has not been settled but it may have been as early as 1888. In any event the bungalow has remained as the California ranch house. Its popularity arises from the fact that it is attuned to the climate of the state and to the way of life of its inhabitants. Size and cost may vary but there is usually a patio in the rear, sometimes protected by one wing of the house, thus allowing for the outdoor living so much a part of the California scene. This emphasis upon privacy with the living room facing the patio may symbolize the desire of the California family to shut out as much of the world as possible.

In the 1960s the high price of land caused more multiple-style dwelling units to be constructed than single-family residences. Perhaps this marks the beginning of the end of the California dream that every family could have its own private home. Instead many will have to be content with rental units, co-operatively owned apartments or condominiums. But it is difficult to predict the future of home construction in California. The only sure thing is its impermanence. Buildings and homes are torn down to make way for new structures instead of being remodeled as they are in a more stable part of the nation. But the people are also on the move, changing residences on an average of every four years. The novelist Myron Brinig in *The Flutter of an Eyelid* complained that "Neither was there any permanence here, any roots. Houses were literally builded on sand, and if not sand, their foundations were insecurely laid in clay."

EDUCATION

There was little formal education during the Spanish and Mexican eras in California. Some governors encouraged the establishment of schools but met with little success. There was a chronic lack of financial resources, and little interest on the part of a populace more concerned with ranching than scholarship. There were few qualified teachers available and efforts to use retired or invalid soldiers in this capacity failed as few were academically qualified or interested in the difficult task of communicating with children in the classroom. Fifty-five schools were started in the Spanish and Mexican periods but few kept their doors open longer than a few weeks. All were elementary schools except the effort of W. E. P. Hartnell. His Seminario de San Jose had an enrollment of fourteen boys when it opened on January 1, 1834, but it lasted only a year and a half. In the closing years of the Mexican period some affluent parents sent their boys to the Hawaiian Islands or even Paris for their schooling.

United States acquisition followed by the gold rush and the Yankee invasion brought the American system of education. Gold fever was an important magnet drawing lawyers, doctors, teachers, professors, preachers, and businessmen to California. This unique society had a greater interest in education than usual on the frontier. The constitution established a system of public instruction headed by a superintendent of public instruction. This commitment, spelled out in the constitution, was neglected in the first few years of state government. There were more pressing matters in the embryo period of the gold rush and Governor Burnett failed to mention education in his first message and the first legislature neglected to appropriate funds for education.

Most of the early American schools were the efforts of Protestant clerics who usually operated a school as a part of their church. In 1851 the legislature authorized local communities to tax in support of schools and a year later gave modest state support. Elementary schools emerged in most communities and by the end of the decade some 64 per cent of school-age children attended classes. The importance of education to California was stressed by John Swett, a New Englander who became superintendent of public instruction in 1862, when he declared "Her [California's] population is drawn from all nations. The next generation will be a composite one, made up of the heterogeneous atoms of all nationalities. Nothing can Americanize these chaotic elements and breathe into them the spirit of our institutions but the public schools."

Swett was largely responsible for success in the fight to make California's elementary schools free and open to all. The superintendent of public instruction was also credited for legislative adoption of the Revised School Law in 1866 which fixed state and county school taxes at adequate levels. This law also established district school libraries, county teachers' institutes, and city boards of examination. Not until 1874 was a compulsory school attendance law passed. In 1884 California became the first state to use a uniform series of elementary textbooks printed in the state printing office. Initially sold to students, they were distributed free after 1912.

The first public high school was established in San Francisco in 1856 and by 1879 there were sixteen in the state. There were also a large number of private academies. Local taxes were the support of high schools until the amendment of the state school law in 1903. Since that date the number of secondary schools has grown rapidly.

As the wealthiest state in the West, California traditionally spent more on educating her students than other states, usually being surpassed only by New York in the country as a whole. This was accomplished in spite of a phenomenal increase in enrollment in the public schools. Total enrollment doubled from 1914 to 1940, reaching the 1,000,000 mark in the latter year. From 1940 it only took thirteen years to reach 2,000,000, seven years later it was 3,000,000, five years later it was 4,000,000, and by 1968 it was 4,440,924. Such rapid growth has taxed school administrators to find adequate financing to build classrooms and employ qualified teachers. In general, they have been successful in meeting these difficult challenges.

However, during the decade of the 1960s the state's public schools increasingly came under attack. Failure adequately to educate children of ethnic minorities, especially those of Negro or Hispanic background, became an issue. The existence of de facto segregation based upon residential patterns brought a suit in federal court in 1970 against Pasadena schools and prompted numerous other school boards to review their own situations. A report in 1966 showing that first- and second-grade California children were behind the national average in reading ability alarmed many parents. Rightist groups were convinced that schools were corrupting traditional American values and pressured administrators and school boards to adopt practices reflecting their views. In the Magnolia school district in Anaheim, members of the John Birch Society seized control of the school board, forced many principals and teachers to leave, altered the school curriculum, and precipitated much turmoil before a bipartisan middle-of-the-road faction ousted them from the school board in a recall election in 1964.

Many taxpayers became convinced that schools were not performing their function and throughout the state, school revenue measures were defeated at the polls. As a result of such questioning of the role of the schools, Dr. Max Rafferty was elected superintendent of public instruction in 1962 and re-elected in 1966 on a platform calling for a return to the three R's. However, there was little indication that his tenure in office brought significant changes.

California pioneered in the introduction of and emphasis upon community colleges. In 1907 the legislature authorized high schools to offer postgraduate courses of study. These "upward extensions of high school" grew slowly at first but by 1970 there were eighty-five California campuses, the largest number of any state. Most of the operating costs of such schools are defrayed by local taxes with the state contributing approximately one third. Community colleges provide three types of programs: standard collegiate courses on the freshman and sophomore level; vocational and technical programs leading to employment; and general non-credit or adult education work, usually in an extended day program.

By 1970 community colleges were a significant part of the state's system of higher education with a total enrollment in excess of 600,000. Popularly known as "city colleges," campuses are found throughout the state and vary in size from a few hundred students to more than fifteen thousand. They also vary in quality with the best having highly qualified faculties offering an instructional program equal to that of the best four-year institutions in the nation.

These institutions have helped many students obtain an education by enabling them to attend classes while living at home and have allowed others to go to college part time while working full time.

The first state constitution called for the establishment of a state university to promote "literature, the arts, and sciences." No move was made to implement this provision and what later became the University of California originated in 1853 as a private academy quartered in an Oakland dance hall. The school did not prosper and its sponsors turned the "College of California" over to the state in 1868 along with an excellent tract of land in the hills north of Oakland. In 1873 the first class of twelve was graduated and the fall term began on the Berkeley campus. In 1870 it took the then radical step of admitting women. In 1874 there was a bitter controversy over whether the university should place primary emphasis on "agriculture and mechanic arts." President Daniel Coit Gilman won the fight for a diversified course of instruction.

The university grew slowly at first but by 1923 was the largest in the world with an enrollment of 14,061. Other campuses have been established but Berkeley remains the most prestigious. In 1919 university regents absorbed the state normal school in Los Angeles and in 1927 created a new campus at Westwood which became the University of California at Los Angeles in 1931. Santa Barbara State College joined the university system in 1944 and became a general campus in 1959. The university farm at Davis, established in 1905, and the citrus experiment station at Riverside, established in 1907, were both converted to general campuses in 1959.

The Scripps Institution of Biological Research at La Jolla opened in 1912, added a School of Science and Engineering in 1959 and became a general campus in 1964 known as the University of California at San Diego. Additional new campuses were opened at Irvine in 1964 and at Santa Cruz in 1965. In theory the nine campuses are equal, but in 1968 more than one half of the 98,780 students of the university were enrolled at Berkeley or UCLA. Since 1961 only students in the top 12.5 per cent of their high school class are eligible to attend as freshmen at the university.

The burgeoning state college system was an outgrowth of the normal school. The first state normal school was established in San Francisco in 1862 and moved to San Jose in 1870. Other normal schools were established in Los Angeles (1882), Chico (1889), San Diego (1897), San Francisco (1899), Santa Barbara (1908), Fresno (1911), and Humboldt (1913). Until 1900 the normal school provided only a two-year teacher-training program but this was lengthened to three years, and then four. California Polytechnic College at San Luis Obispo had a different origin than the other state colleges. It opened in 1901 as a vocational high school but developed into an agricultural and engineering college by 1940. A campus was begun on the Voorhis site in 1938 with the Kellogg ranch being acquired in 1949. The Kellogg-Voorhis or Pomona campus became a separate institution in 1966, also known as California Polytechnic State College.

The normal schools were named teachers colleges in 1921 and state colleges in 1935. Since the end of World War II, new campuses have been created at Sacramento, Los Angeles, Long Beach, Northridge, Fullerton, Hayward, Stanislaus, Sonoma, Dominguez Hills, Bakersfield, and San Bernardino. Many of these institutions have impressive plants, learned faculties, enrollments of more than twenty thousand, and are actually multipurpose universities.

Under the Master Plan for Higher Education adopted in 1960 the state colleges are under a central administration headed by a chancellor with policy being set by a board of trustees. Actually much of the control of the system remains in the legislature, as that body has been reluctant to grant the state colleges the autonomy enjoyed by the university. The primary function of the state colleges is instruction for undergraduates and graduates through the master's degree. State college faculty are encouraged to do research only if it is directly related to their teaching. Only high school graduates in the top one third of their class are eligible for admission as freshmen to state colleges.

Private colleges were established in California almost as early as the first public schools. Santa Clara College (now the University of Santa Clara) and California Wesleyan College (now the University of the Pacific at Stockton) both opened their doors in Stockton in 1851. St. Vincent's College (now Loyola University) was opened in Los Angeles in 1865. By 1870 Catholics had also established St. Ignatius (now the University of San Francisco), College of the Holy Name, and St. Mary's. In 1887 Presbyterians chartered what developed into Occidental College and Congregationalists founded Pomona College. Whittier College, President Richard M. Nixon's alma mater, was begun by the Quakers in the nineties, and in 1909 the Baptists opened a college at Redlands. Throop College of Technology was a unique institution. Founded in 1890, it evolved into the California Institute of Technology and has become one of the world's leading centers of scientific research and education. A number of denominations have established colleges in recent years. Among these are George Pepperdine, Los Angeles; United States International University, San Diego; California Lutheran, Thousand Oaks; the University of San Diego; Chapman College, Orange; and Biola College, La Mirada.

Only two of the state's private institutions have developed into multipurpose universities. The University of Southern California was established in 1879 in Los Angeles on land donated by "a Jew, a Catholic, and a Protestant." After the boom of the eighties had spent itself the institution had a difficult task surviving. Not until the 1920s did the university experience rapid growth. In recent years it has been eclipsed by UCLA, although its professional schools are highly respected. For decades they produced the bulk of the area's doctors, dentists, lawyers, and school administrators.

In 1887 Leland Stanford started a university in the memory of his son on his farm at Palo Alto. Although the institution was the most richly endowed in the world at the time, skeptics doubted that it could attract a competent faculty or an adequate student body. David Starr Jordan, one of the nation's leading educators, headed Stanford in its earlier years and helped ensure its success. Known as the Harvard of the West, its faculty and student body in recent years have been those of a distinguished academic institution. A distinguished alumnus, Herbert C. Hoover, initiated the establishment of the Library on War, Peace, and Revolution. It has become a unique depository of materials of these phenomena in the troubled twentieth century. Stanford and the University of Southern California accounted for some one third of the total enrollment in 1970 in California's private institutions.

By 1970 higher education in California, like the public schools, was under attack from many sides. The University of California had been a center of controversy from 1949–52 over loyalty oaths required of the faculty, but this conflict was insignificant compared to the furor created by the free speech movement in 1964. The dissension created continued and became a major political issue in 1966. Many observers contend that Ronald Reagan's promise to clean up "the mess in Berkeley" was a major factor in his successful bid for the governorship. Disorders have also occurred on the campuses at San Francisco State, Los Angeles State, and San Fernando Valley State in recent years. They were caused by disagreements over ethnic studies programs, administrative blunders, and discontent with existing academic policy. Unrest on campuses reflected unrest in society. The draft, the Vietnam conflict, civil rights issues all contributed. Student activists mobilized sympathizers on campus and went forth to battle for their favored cause. University officials disapproved and the consequence was conflict.

The Reagan administration's hostility toward public higher education was apparent in the prompt dismissal of university president Clark Kerr in January 1967, and in efforts to reduce budgets of the state colleges and university drastically and impose tuition. These actions have helped generate more turmoil and unrest on the campuses. If continued they will also end the day that an education was available to all who are qualified, as enrollments have declined in proportion to the school-age population. Needed buildings were not started. Essential building construction has been curtailed, programs have been cut back or eliminated, and austerity is the watchword. Many fear for the future of California's system of higher education and some flatly predict it will be transformed into a system of mediocrity. The growing state financial crisis has been used to justify budgetary stringency and encouraged further cuts in higher education funding.

CHAPTER XXIII

A New Society?

POLLUTED AIR, LAND, AND WATER

There are more than twenty million residents of California, as of this writing, approximately one tenth of the population of the United States. More are on the way. They came during the sixties at the rate of two thousand a day, but since a thousand residents left daily for other climes and places, the net gain was a thousand. It was commonly assumed that this was a recent phenomenon, but in fact, this pattern of growth is more than a century old. For the past hundred years, the average rate of population increase has been 3.8 per cent annually. Some experts believe the rate will fall as the century comes to a close and some believe the population will total but forty million at the dawn of the twenty-first century—a mere 100 per cent increase over the present population. Twenty-five million will be living in Southern California in a collection of cities which will sprawl over an area that reaches from the Mexican border to San Luis Obispo. The growth will also push northward along the coast to San Francisco and eastward through much of the great inland valley.

The problems which accompany this growth are enough to boggle the mind of the most sanguine planner and policy maker, although until recently few people showed real concern. As the decade of the seventies opened, however, public and private citizens were speaking out in increasing numbers. The seventies may be a decade in which the politics of pollution dominate as pension politics once dominated the political arena. Politicians have discovered the ecology issue. Some scientists are encouraged, but many continue to air pessimistic forecasts of an impending "environmental disaster." Typical of this viewpoint is Professor Paul Ehrlich of Stanford University's Department of Biological Sciences, who flatly declared in 1970, "We are playing environmental roulette, overbreeding, putting crud in the atmosphere, poisoning our water, killing our fish, sloshing pesticides which kill the insects that kill the pests (sheer idiocy), heading straight into the worst crisis mankind has ever seen."

Pollution takes many forms. Polluted air is one of the more obvious, for it can be seen, smelled, and even tasted. The faculty of a medical school in Los Angeles where the problem of "smog" is most obvious issued a joint statement declaring that the polluted environment posed hazards to health that dictated moving to another area. Air pollution has forced farmers to abandon or drastically curtail the growth of ten crops in Los Angeles County which included celery, spinach, lettuce, and beets. Air pollution is killing the big trees of the Southern California mountains at a fearful rate. In the San Bernardino National Forest, 1,300,000 trees have been affected, and 15 per cent are already dead. The time may come when the great pine trees of the San Gabriels will be seen only in the form of plastic-encased specimens in museums. And for that matter, an enterprising plastic company may one day find a market for plastic replicas of the trees to be implanted in the hillsides, substitutes which will be impervious to smog. Recently the Los Angeles County Medical Association advised school authorities to eliminate physical activities during smoggy days to avoid damage to young respiratory systems. A number of school districts immediately implemented the proposal and on such days, typical physical education classes become sedentary.

Smog is but one of the problems of pollution which confront California. Pollution is a matter of water as well as of air and evidences of the pollution which man has done can be seen or measured in California's rivers, bays, lakes, and oceans. Clear Lake in northern California may already be polluted beyond recall and the "azure gem" of the Sierras, Lake Tahoe, is following the same route. Inadequate supplies of water to support the population in the life-style of affluent America is another. Growing urban slums which expand unnoticed until blight has become nearly irreversible is a third. A spreading "slurbia" which is swallowing up agricultural land at the rate of more than 100 acres a day, a perennial locus of unemployment, a crime rate which continues to spiral upward, overcrowded parks, beaches, camps, an urban transportation problem of growing magnitude and complexity, the pressures on a system of assessment and taxation in the midst of a continuing inflationary spiral, and the need to build physical facilities to accommodate a growing population—all are problems that California faces. And the list is by no means complete. Many of these problems are found in other states, but some of them are either unique or have added dimensions and complexity in California.

Many of California's problems reflect the disharmony between man and his environment which is found in many places in the modern world. Technology has enabled man to do many things which had been impossible. Everywhere he has tinkered with and altered his environment. The emphasis is usually on the domination of nature by man as he attempts to occupy, control, and exploit the environment. As man has done these things, without much concern for tomorrow, he has upset ecological balances, altered the basic characteristics which nature evolved over perhaps aeons of time, and he has introduced new factors which further threaten the complex chain of interactions between living things and the physical environment. What man has done along these lines can be seen or detected in most parts of the world; what he has done is often readily apparent in California.

In California most of the damage is a reflection of man's technology. Here factories, plants, and automobiles pour out fumes and pollutants. Freeways dump motorists into massive traffic jams. The offal of an affluent society pours out in the form of rubbish and garbage in the amount of a ton per person per year. All threaten to overwhelm the environment.

That which man has done in California is more visible because of the sharp contrast between what was and what is and because of the brief time span which encompasses the two. Substantial portions of what was once a near Eden have been transformed and the result is dismaying. What was done was done with great speed. Many Californians can recall the golden time when the air was bright and clear and vistas of orange trees against a background of snow-covered mountain ranges in December were common. The fish, big and small, once teemed in the clear and sparkling coastal waters, and as recently as 1929 Los Angeles landed half again as much tonnage as

Boston. Overfishing, technological "efficiencies," and pollution of various kinds have sharply changed the picture. Species of fish have been eliminated and others are threatened with extinction.

Marine pollution of a massive scale came in late January 1969 when an offshore well some 5 miles from Santa Barbara blew out. A jet of gas and drilling mud rose through the sea and 100 feet into the air. It took months to control the runaway well. In the interim, oil polluted the sea although at a much smaller rate than the estimated five thousand barrels a day at the beginning of the spill. The huge slick created, despite the frantic efforts of oilmen, spread over the ocean and was carried by wind and current to widespread sections of the coast until 45 miles of mainland beaches were blackened. The damage done to the environment is not accurately known and may be more menacing in appearance than in fact, but to the people on the scene, the disaster is graphic evidence of the need to curb the activities which pollute the environment.

The well was being drilled in an area leased by the Interior Department and state and local authorities have no jurisdiction over it. A citizen's group, GOO for Get Oil Out, is passionately devoted to stopping the operation of this well and others like it, but they have not found much support in the courts, which generally find the activities of the companies protected by contract law. Such legal defeats seem to embolden the conservationists, who predict future disasters if the drilling continues and if we fail to adhere to a new commandment, "Thou shalt not pollute the earth." The companies, however, which profit from the established contractual rights, are apparently not ready to forgo such advantages for the sake of high-minded ideals.

The coastal waters themselves are polluted on a vast scale by hundreds of millions of gallons of sewage which is dumped daily. A billion gallons a day is dumped into Southern California coastal waters. In Santa Monica Bay, so massive is the outpouring of warm sewage water that new convection currents have been created in the bay which change its ecology. The time may not be distant, in fact it has arrived in several places, where the properly equipped surfer or beachgoer will need not only the usual equipment but a combination of shots to protect himself from the contamination in the water. The pollution is not only the organic wastes of civilization but a number of inorganic substances, industrial chemicals of various kinds, pesticides, insecticides, herbicides, and petroleum products.

The chemical pollutants are not always detectable without sensitive instruments, but the damage they do is immense. In the San Joaquin Valley, the richest large agricultural center in the world, 20 per cent of the total DDT manufactured in the United States is sprayed by crop-dusting planes. The mechanisms of application, e.g., a crop-dusting plane, are highly visible, but the damage done to life and environment by DDT is insidious and invisible. Scientists have discovered that the prevailing eastward winds of the valley distribute DDT over widespread areas and as high as the 12,000-foot level of the Sierras. There it can be found in the tissues of the fauna, an insidious toxic agent whose effects on life forms are imprecisely known. In the late sixties, three fourths of the city of Delano's water wells were found to have dangerous concentrations of the chemicals used in abundance in fertilizers in the surrounding area of fields and vineyards. The nitrates in question are almost as lethal to man as they are beneficial to plants. Similar conditions have been found elsewhere. DDT and other agricultural chemicals are also picked up in the watersheds of the Great Valley and dumped into San Francisco Bay. A long-life chemical which is absorbed by various life forms which come into contact with it, DDT has been found in the far corners of the world, in the depths of the oceans, in the Arctic and Antarctic. And everywhere it has gone, DDT has had deleterious effects. It is widely suspected as a toxic agent which threatens the decimation of various fowl and even the extinction of some forms of bird life. The near extinction of the brown pelican seems clearly linked to DDT and there may be many other examples of a similar sort. Belated steps are being taken in the early seventies to curtail the use and abuse of not only DDT but organic phosphates and other lethal chemicals.

Steps are also being taken to curtail other kinds of pollutants and activities which damage the environment. Los Angeles was the first of the major cities to take steps to eliminate and curtail aerial pollutant producers and it partially cleared its skies of pollution from stationary sources by taking more than forty thousand offenders to court and levying fines of more than $1,000,000. But while this was taking place, the real problem was worsening. Los Angeles County, the world's largest smog factory, with 4083 square miles has millions of pollutant producers. They take the form of automobiles, 3,900,-000 which burn 8,000,000 gallons of gasoline daily; 14,500 diesel engines which consume 150,000 gallons of diesel fuel a day; 1505 jet-powered aircraft flights which burn 700,000 gallons of kerosene; 11,000 piston-driven aircraft flights and 700 helicopter flights which consume 150,000 gallons of gasoline daily.

The pollutants produced by this legion of fossil-fuel engines are trapped in the area by an "inversion" or layer of warm air and walls in the form of mountains to east and north and the Pacific Ocean to the west and south. When conditions are right, the smog factory works efficiently, visibility is reduced, eyes water, plants are affected, and men, women, children, and animals find breathing impaired. What was once beautiful and which ever bloomed has been transformed into something far different.

The experts who concern themselves with these problems are often confounded by their inability to do much about air pollution. When smog devices are introduced to curtail the emission of some kinds of pollutants, a growing number of cars offsets such a development. And bigger cars and engines, which produce emissions which are not touched by the smog devices, aggravate the problem. Los Angeles County, which has more automobiles than any foreign country, is finding the problem of curtailing the automobile, responsible for 90 per cent of the smog, very difficult. While some forms of pollutants have been diminished, the tonnage of pollutants poured out has been cut from 1800 tons daily in 1966 to 1459 daily in 1969, but this has been offset by a sharp rise in the amounts of toxic nitrogen oxides which internal-combustion engines emit. The problem resists solution. In 1970, despite a comprehensive program, on 241 days the pollution in the Los Angeles Basin exceeded limits for satisfactory air set by the state Air Resources Board. The head of the California Institute of Technology Environmental Quality Laboratory, Lester Lees, expressed his concern about the unwillingness of the authorities to undertake the multifaceted attack which was essential to solving the problem.

As the smog-control men look into the future they see a time when all of the earth will have an atmosphere like that of Los Angeles on a smoggy day if a way is not found to stop pollution of the atmosphere. Its coming is hastened by the consumption of fossil fuels, produced at the rate of two billion barrels a day, the destruction of plant life, the changing of the atmosphere by using up oxygen and overproducing carbon monoxide and carbon dioxide as well as other chemicals. Scientists have a window to the future and their work in California's polluted skies may help them avert the calamity which is portended in the skies of Los Angeles almost daily.

THE AFFLUENT ECONOMY

As the sixties came to a close, California was the most prosperous state in the most prosperous nation in the world in its time of greatest prosperity. Everywhere the signs of affluence were visible. One startling statistic highlighted the magnitude of the prosperity: considered as an entity, California's economic output exceeded that of all but five of the nations of the world. The construction industry, which suffered setbacks in the middle sixties, was up almost 87 per cent from the levels reached ten years before, unemployment reached a ten-year low of a little more than 4 per cent of the labor force, and as 1969 came to a close, the farmers of the state were reaping a record harvest of cash and anticipating a further rise in income in the future. Farm receipts hit $4,110,000,000, which meant an average net income of more than $15,000, an increase of almost 15 per cent in a single year.

As the decade of the seventies opened, California's highly diversified and sophisticated economy produced a total product of $108,-800,000,000 and predictions of a $150,000,000,000 economy by 1975 were being made. Manufacturing, construction, agriculture, and mining were responsible for $34,800,000,000; distribution of commodities (trade and utilities) contributed $28,200,000,000; service industries' share was $29,600,000,000; and government services amounted to $16,200,000,000. Personal income of California's citizenry rose more than 10 per cent in the final year of the sixties to a total of $87,100,000,000. Outside of the United States, Britain, West Germany, Japan, France, and the U.S.S.R., California's economy was the largest in the world in terms of total output of goods and services. About eight million workers were employed. This was the glowing picture before the Nixon administration adopted deliberate policies designed to restrain the burgeoning economy of the United States. In the first months of the new decade of the seventies, the pinch was felt in California as well as the nation.

The general prosperity is due to a considerable degree to the aerospace and defense industries, which account for approximately 10 per cent of civilian jobs, 40 per cent of manufacturing jobs, a third of all industrial output, and from a 33.3 to 50 per cent of total personal income. In 1969 a list of the top twenty concerns in the United States concerned with such work was liberally sprinkled with well-known California companies like McDonnell Douglas, General Dynamics, North American Rockwell Corporation, Kaiser Industries Corporation, Thompson, Ramo, Woolridge, Northrop, Aerojet-General, Standard Oil of California, Litton Industries, and was headed by Lockheed Aircraft. In 1969 about $3,000,000,000 in prime contract awards, amounting to almost 20 per cent, were awarded California firms by the Defense Department. This was almost 50 per cent more than was awarded New York, the second-ranked state.

Built primarily on a foundation of government expenditures and contracts for research and development as well as production, the present as well as the future of these concerns are determined by decisions made by government figures and other factors often beyond the control of management. The result is a general insecurity which reaches into all levels of the industry. A cancellation of a single contract may result in widespread unemployment. This may be the first link in a chain of adversity which may reach into every aspect of the economy of a city or region. A drop in employment may trigger a drop in real estate values, a rise in mortgage fore-closures, and a wave of bankruptcies of small businesses.

A decline in the total spending of the Defense Department or NASA, a change in technology which outmodes a weapons system, a rapprochement between the United States and its adversaries, a political decision to award a contract to a non-California concern all can have tremendous impact. Such things produce insecurity for the community involved in aerospace and defense which ofttimes affects the citizenry in subtle ways. Sometimes the citizenry becomes advocates of policies which will lead to decisions to support their community and sometimes insecurity and naked self-interest combine to overwhelm reason and logic. When government contracts are endangered, Californians may be as wary and dangerous as lionesses guarding their cubs.

Thus, in the latter part of 1969 when the Nixon administration adopted deliberate policies designed to restrain the burgeoning economy of the United States, there was an immediate impact in California. Distortions in the economy, probably the result of the Vietnam conflict, invited harsh measures. They came in the form of cutbacks, cancellations, stretch-outs in aerospace and military contracts. The closing of military bases, the postponement of a number of public works projects, the changeover in weapons systems from land-based to submarine-based missiles, the completion of moon probe projects, and high interest rates which discouraged home building combined to curtail employment. In aerospace the loss amounted to about two thousand jobs a month. Employment which had hit a peak of 615,400 in December 1967 dropped to 455,300 at the close of 1969, and continued to drop. Since the bulk of this industry was concentrated in Southern California, it was severely affected.

Industry policy makers have been looking for ways to broaden their base into fields which are not subject to these uncertainties. Commercial aviation was expected to provide some relief. Lockheed and McDonnell Douglas anticipated a sharp rise in commercial aviation sales in the form of the giant passenger jetliners. Some put the potential increase in sales at almost 300 per cent in the seventies from $4,000,000,000 to $11,000,000,000 at the end of the decade. Other concerns looked to foreign sales and activities to sustain them. Kaiser Steel, for instance, was expanding not only its domestic operations but its activities in Australia and Canada. By the end of 1971 nearly half of Kaiser's operations in basic steel and raw materials and minerals were to be overseas.

While some parts of the housing industry were off their record pace of the late sixties, prospects for the future were still bright. The influx of out-of-state money to sustain the California mortgage market brought a record total of $14,900,000,000 in 1969, up by $2,500,000,000 over the previous year. Despite tight money and high interest rates, perhaps because of such things, national investment in California real estate continued until it covered some 800,000 loans. While the influx of population promised a continuation of the demand for housing in California and a perpetuation of the mortgage market, there was some concern about the ramifications of the long-range outflow of money which would be necessary in the amortization of these loans. The Department of Employment predicted a sharp increase in the number of jobs in professional, clerical, and service fields. Continued growth makes for more jobs and vice versa.

There are some voices who are calling for an end to growth. As they look about the landscape of Southern California, as well as other areas of rapid growth and development, they are repelled. A new organization called Lesser California was launched in 1969, dedicated to the proposition that the one thing which California does not need is more people. Devoted to bringing this about, its members encourage people to go elsewhere and encourage others not to come. They quote with effect a statement that nearly half a million people come to California each year and by so doing "tend to destroy what they came to find." And some predict that as Californians increase and multiply, they will ultimately transform the area into a repulsive region which will attract few newcomers and drive many of its residents into exile. When the vistas of oranges and roses in December, magnificent views of coastline, mountain ranges, and forests are replaced by a panorama of concrete and steel structures over which hangs an enormous pall of yellowish-tan, stinking, smarting air, the pattern of movement into and out of the state will change.

Some Californians are not willing to await the time when the state's ugly vistas will bring an end to in-migration. Typical of this new approach is the Porter-Cologne Water Quality Control Act, a tough new law which prescribes fines for polluters of water of as much as $6000 per day. More significantly perhaps is a section which labels as a violator anyone who destroys another's right to the aesthetic enjoyment of any of California's water resources.

THE FREEWAY SYSTEM

Not only are there more people living in this most urban of the states, they are the most mobile in the world. The population is not only relatively young but it is getting younger by the infusion of immigrants below forty. It is also a mobile population which has more cars, buses, trucks, motorcycles, airplanes, power cruisers, helicopters, and the like than any similar group in the world. Californians travel literally billions of miles each month on these varied vehicles and their scurrying about from home to shop and back again and on a thousand other trips and errands has created a massive industry based upon the production and servicing of these transportation vehicles and facilities.

A good part of the traveling involves a system of freeways and highways which are superior in quality and extent to any other system in the world. Today, in addition to thousands of miles of superior highways, there are 3000 miles of freeways in operation. The entire system, when completed in 1980, will consist of 12,000 miles and every community in the state of more than five thousand residents will have a freeway connection to the network.

The first segment of the system was built shortly before World War II. Some 6 miles in length, this revolutionary new highway, devoid of traffic signals and intersections, provided a speedy and convenient route for motorists traveling between downtown Los Angeles and Pasadena. World War II delayed construction but shortly after hostilities in the Pacific ended, work was resumed on the network. Thereafter, it went steadily forward as huge earth-moving machines rumbled night and day, and concrete-processing machines which could lay a ribbon of concrete 12 feet wide a mile long in a day worked sometimes around the clock. By now billions of dollars have been expended, thousands of tons of steel, concrete, and building materials have been consumed.

The changes which come in the wake of the freeways are enormous. The metropolitan area of Los Angeles now has nearly 500 miles in use and an additional 1000 miles are on the planning boards. They provide a means whereby millions of Angelenos utilize their millions of cars and trucks to live in one part of the extended metropolitan area and work in another. Access to recreation areas has been improved dramatically. Cities are nearer—by two hours' driving time in the case of Los Angeles and San Francisco—and within cities travel on the freeways is not only swifter but much safer than on surface streets. Moreover, in addition to the savings in terms of lives, the savings in terms of time, gas, oil, and maintenance amount to hundreds of millions of dollars annually.

The fact that these benefits are being achieved while the system as a whole is on a "no toll" and "pay as you go" basis is remarkable. Unlike other states, California has financed the system through taxes, half from a state gasoline tax, another portion from vehicle registration fees, and a third portion from a contribution by the federal government. Uncle Sam contributes 90 per cent of the cost of the 2177 miles of the network which is part of the federal interstate system.

While few would deny some of the obvious values of the freeway system, its creation has brought a number of problems. A number of rather sharp criticisms have been leveled at the system and its proponents. The Division of Highways, which is responsible for the program, is criticized as a vast bureaucracy of seventeen thousand employees which spends more than $700,000,000 a year. It is described as engineer-dominated, insensitive to aesthetic, social, and cultural ramifications of the freeway system. The critics say its planners look upon the highways they design as a means to get somewhere. They are cost-conscious, slide rule dominated engineers who think in terms of "the most miles for the dollar." The insensitivity engendered has led to the needless destruction of parklands, farmlands, and established neighborhoods.

The critics' indictment stipulates that the freeway planners seldom consider the aesthetics of their creations—consequently most freeways are sterile and unattractive ribbons of concrete which may be admirable, but only to engineers. Since they are built to accommodate the largest of the trucks which rumble although they represent less than 1 per cent of the vehicles which use them, they are perhaps four times as costly to build as necessary. And since the bulk of the revenue which supports the department comes from gasoline tax dollars which are earmarked rather than from appropriations, the Highway Department is described as less responsive to the legislature than other state agencies. Highway traffic is stimulated by the construction of freeways, thereby producing an increase in gasoline tax dollars which makes it possible to build more freeways which means more traffic which means more tax dollars which . . . Someday the irrational circle will be broken and the planners will think in terms of an integrated program of multimode transportation facilities which will cover the state. That the need is great is revealed in the fact that two thirds of the surface of downtown Los Angeles is devoted to the automobile in the form of streets, parking lots, or freeways. In 1969 there was some talk of diverting some of the gasoline tax dollars from traditional uses to research in smog and rapid transit feasibility studies.

San Francisco was one of the early battlegrounds of the freeway enthusiasts and their opponents. Despite considerable opposition, the Embarcadero Freeway was completed across a broad segment of the city. When it was finished it dominated not only the landscape but the thinking of a great many of the city's residents as far as freeways were concerned. After contemplating the damage done to the city's appearance, enough public indignation was aroused to block additions to it. As a result, the programmed network stands half completed and periodically threatened with dismantling by vociferous enemies of the State Division of Highways and all its works.

San Francisco was also the scene of an attempt to solve transportation problems of the modern urban era by constructing a rapid transit system. As its title indicates, the Bay Area Rapid Transit District or BART is intended to cover the bay area with a system of subways and surface railways which will move large numbers of people over its 75 miles of track at high speed, at low cost, and in comfort. Originally estimated to cost more than $1,000,000,000, its construction was threatened by escalating costs until supplementary financing by a sales tax was made available.

Meanwhile, other forms of transportation continue to grow. California's trucking industry is one of the nation's largest, involving literally thousands of trucks and trailers and a broad range of occupational specialists to keep them rolling. About 30 per cent of all operating trucks are directly involved in agriculture; another substantial segment serves manufacturing industry either by carrying raw materials to the scene of production or carrying away the finished product. The state has a million and a half trucks, approximately 12 per cent of vehicle registrations. They provide a vital service to the economy, for at one time or another, practically everything grown or made is shipped on a truck.

The trucking industry is not only large but innovative. Some of the first piggyback operations in the United States began in California as truckers drove rigs to railroad yards where trailers were placed on flatcars for subsequent delivery to rail centers hundreds of miles away. There they were hitched again to rigs and driven to destinations. Sharp gains in efficiency arose out of such operations and the practice has become national in scope.

California's major harbors have also been the scene of experimentation and innovations. Under a pact negotiated by union longshoremen and shippers which provides safeguards for maritime workers displaced by technological developments, a number of changes have come to the waterfront. New cargo-handling techniques which cut costs and promote efficiency have been adopted. One of the most promising developments has been the widespread use of containers under which cargo is loaded into standard-size containers at the point of origin and then shipped intact to its destination. In Los Angeles a giant crane which can lift two 20-ton containers at once at the rate of forty per hour has been constructed. It makes it possible for a ship to be loaded and unloaded within twenty-four hours, whereas the same operation might previously have taken as many days. The system may also be co-ordinated with highways and railroads so that containers may be placed directly on freight cars or trucks and sped on their way. The result may be a savings of two weeks in shipments from Japan to Chicago. Some planners are looking to such traffic joining Europe and Asia, the United States serving as a giant land bridge between the two oceans involved.

The major ports of the coast reflect such technological improvements, the general prosperity, the conflict in Vietnam, and the growth and development of California's economy. The ports of Los Angeles and Long Beach, presently separated by a political line which divides the two cities, handles a combined tonnage of 42,000,000, and were second only to New York City in United States customs collections. Both ports plan major building programs which will almost double the present number of 125 berths. Present tonnage handled, 26,000,-000 for Los Angeles and 16,000,000 for Long Beach, is expected to double. Long Beach has the largest man-made pier in the world, a massive grain terminal which can store more than 1,000,000,000 bushels and move it at the rate of 43,000 bushels an hour. It has a bulk oil terminal which can handle the supertankers which are being built in increasing numbers and bulk loaders for dry cargo which rival any like facilities in the world. In effect, the builders and planners of the harbors have laid the basis for a great superharbor of the future.

CALIFORNIA NOW

"California is a window to the future" and "California is what the rest of the United States will be" are two formulations which are widely quoted. A review of recent California history points out the manner in which these generalizations are validated by the California experience. It was in California that the first great black ghetto explosion took place in 1965. Watts was a portent of things to come to San Francisco's Hunters Point and to Detroit, Cleveland, Akron, New York, Boston, Chicago, and Washington, D.C. It was also in California that the first big campus uprising took place in the form of the free speech movement in Berkeley in 1964.

The Golden State spawned a hippie and pop-drug culture and made a household word of Haight-Ashbury, a San Francisco neighborhood. The currents which bring into being new life-styles gather force in California. The contrast between what is and what should be produced rising resentment among black and brown minorities, and the anxiety and resentment of those who had arrived toward those who were still trying to become part of the affluent society gave strength to a conservative political trend. In the sixties, California sent John Birch Society members to the state legislature and to Congress. A crime rate moves inexorably upward; in 1969 almost 5 per cent of California's twenty million residents were arrested. The suicide rate continued to climb until it became one of the leading causes of death; alcoholism became epidemic in some of the major cities, where it cut across all segments of the population; drugs, hard and soft, were in more widespread use than in any other state and the number of heroin addicts in California was exceeded only in New York. In the state of sunshine and flowers, one of every two weddings ends in divorce and the rate is climbing. A new "family law act" designed to bring rationality to the process of ending marriages "in which irreconcilable differences have caused the irremediable breakdown of the marriage" took effect in January 1970 and experts await anxiously its results. The roll of human problems in California is legion and there is good reason for men of good will and common sense to despair.

On the other hand there are some hopeful signs to be seen in the California scene. If smog, urban blight, pollution, and social conflict are prominent, so are organized and rational attempts to deal with these problems. If California's skies are the color of burnished brass because of pollution, they also look down on the most advanced research centers of air pollution in the country. The University of California, long considered the most prestigious public institution of learning in the world, has ongoing research programs into the causes and cures of air pollution, which set the pace for other states as well as the federal government. UC researchers dominate this area, and UC research grants amount to almost 20 per cent of the funds expended in this field.

The program utilizes the resources of one of the largest scientific populations in the country. About eleven thousand civilian scientists work in the Southern California area and the world's leading authority on air pollution, Dr. A. J. Haagen-Smit of the faculty of the California Institute of Technology, has access to them. Dr. Haagen-Smit believes that a pre-smog atmosphere can be brought to Los Angeles by a systems approach to the problem. Not only must the emissions from the automobiles be controlled, but fossil-fuel power plants must be eliminated from the Southern California basin and lead-free fuels must become standard for cars.

THE CAMPUS SCENE

California universities and colleges have contributed a great deal to the state's growth and prosperity but in recent years that contribution has been overlooked by large parts of the citizenry who sharply recoiled against the free speech movement of Mario Savio and college demonstrations against the draft and the Vietnam conflict. For generations the university's scientists have tackled the problems of California growers and produced a wide variety of solutions to problems and technological innovations which made it possible for California farmers to (for example) produce rice which could compete on the home market in Japan. A university scientist, Dr. Karl F. Meyer, developed the basic technology which underlies the modern American canning industry.

California's farmers are the most productive in the world in part because of their acceptance and application of new ideas discovered in University of California laboratories, tested in the university's field stations, and spread throughout the state by the university's Agricultural Extension Service. The impact of the university is not confined to the agricultural hinterland. In fact, scarcely any aspect of the daily life of Californians has gone unaffected by the pervasive influence of university research. The university has also attracted the scientists, more Nobel laureates (fourteen in 1969) than any other institution, who made discoveries and literally shaped the modern world. Its faculties have trained a large share of the professionals, technicians, management specialists, and artisans who staff the most modern industrial system in the world. The most unique contribution of the university to the modern age was the development of the scientific know-how which produced the first atomic bombs in 1945. From that time to this, atomic energy has loomed over the university until funds derived from the Atomic Energy Commission were responsible for about a fourth of the annual billion-dollar budget. Hundreds of employees and faculty members work in a complex of installations which are located in three states. Fully half of the funds expended are in weapons research.

In the process the university became a multiversity, an expensive, complex apparatus which attracted great numbers of the brightest students in America. As its campus population in Berkeley reached thirty thousand, it became an increasingly impersonal place where its faculty members were primarily concerned with the weighty projects of their own research and career. And when the administration of this megauniversity, insensitive to the social issues which troubled its student body, attempted to impose restrictions on its students the resulting confrontation known round the world as the free speech movement began. The free speech movement initiated a great period of turmoil on the campus at Berkeley. Almost as soon as one crisis was passed another began and in each, rhetoric and violence escalated. The demands for an ethnic studies school in 1969, followed almost immediately by the People's Park controversy, produced such in-

ditional grading policies, addition of student members to faculty committees, ombudsmen, faculty evaluation handbooks, elimination of hidebound courses, grade appeals systems are but a few of the changes that have come to California college campuses in recent years. Many of these changes are quite superficial, however, and many people point to the inflexible and enduring nature of most of the institutions. The university attempted to avoid some of the problems of the megauniversity by innovations in the structuring, governance, and operation of some of its new campuses. Observers came from all over the world to see and admire Santa Cruz, San Diego, and Irvine, but budgetary cuts threaten these promising developments as well.

California's educational system was shaken on a different front recently by two court decisions. A superior court judge, Alfred Gitelson, declared in effect that de facto as well as de jure segregation of pupils in the public schools of Los Angeles was unconstitutional. He ordered a prompt restructuring of the Los Angeles school system so that the schools within the district would be racially and ethnically balanced. The decision brought anguished outcries from the administrators of the system, who declared it would only impoverish the district by expensive bussing of students. The decision will be appealed and perhaps overturned on the appellate level. That a substantial portion of the electorate disapproved of Judge Gitelson's decision was manifested in his defeat for re-election the next time he faced the voters at the polls. Some observers found it ironic that in the City of the Angels, the schools were still segregated some fifteen years after the Supreme Court of the United States declared the practice in violation of the Constitution. A federal judge, Manuel Real, also decreed in 1970 the integration of the Pasadena school system, where residential neighborhood patterns facilitated de facto segregation. The governing board declined to appeal the decision and made plans for compliance.

THE AGRIBUSINESS SCENE

In the farms and fields of California there was also turmoil, change, and controversy. California farms and ranches, always big, were larger than ever in the first year of the seventies. The average-size farm had grown to about 650 acres, although only thirty years before the average size was 250 acres. Increased size was accompanied by increases in most other things associated with farming. Capital costs were up considerably, the amount of equipment had sharply increased, production of crops had increased, the use of fertilizers, insecticides, and herbicides was also up. Farmers tended to be more efficient, more scientific, and practiced the latest management techniques. The economic decline of the family farm in California continued through the sixties and into the seventies. In 1960 there were 108,000 farms in the state which averaged 359 acres. By 1970 there were only 56,000 farms, averaging 654 acres. According to official statistics of the Department of Agriculture, forty-five corporations controlled 61 per cent of California's prime agricultural land.

Vertical integration was an important trend as ranchers invested in allied enterprises. Producers who owned bagging and boxing plants and a piece of a farm supply service became more common. The use of a computer to help guide every aspect of farm operation was next on the agenda. When that development takes place corn growers will aim for 450 to 600 bushels an acre as compared to the present average yield of 200 bushels. Present success is taken to be a portent of the future. The San Joaquin Valley, the richest farming region in the world produced more than $2,000,000,000 in farm products in 1969. Three counties, Fresno, Tulare, and Kern, were the three top counties in the United States in terms of agricultural output.

California's farms are a continuing scene of conflict. The weapons and tactics have changed sharply since the 1920s when the IWW and primitive trade unions sought to organize farm laborers but the adversaries remain the same. Once criminal syndicalism statutes and vigilantes combined to make the life of the farm labor organizer hazardous and his work ineffectual. Today the law is a dead letter and vigilantism is generally conspicuous in its absence from the fields of farm labor strife, where a leader in the form of a charismatic Chicano, Cesar Chavez, has built an effective union. Financed in part by established labor unions, the National Farm Workers Association is headquartered in Delano. On the national scene sympathizers and fellow trade unionists have made boycott an effective weapon. A number of tough, recalcitrant growers have already come to terms and while others hold out, the NFWA appears to be on the verge of creating an effective labor union in California's fields where some 288,000 workers are employed.

The end of the *bracero* program, technically in 1964 actually in the summer of 1968, strengthened the efforts to organize farm workers, for growers no longer had a docile, efficient, and ample labor force of *braceros* to draw upon. However, the fact that thousands of illegal as well as legal Mexican nationals find their way into the fields today makes Cesar Chavez's work more difficult. Drawn by wage rates which are five times those of Mexico over a border which is easy to cross, they come by the thousands, acquire Social Security cards, and merge into the local labor force. Thousands of local farm workers are displaced thereby, millions of dollars in taxes and million of dollars in wages are lost. The net result is that agriculture receives a labor subsidy and the federal government's policy of moving people off welfare rolls and onto payrolls is undermined.

Meanwhile, there are forces at work which dictate an eventual resolution of the problems and the conflicts. As farm workers push toward higher wages and better conditions, growers move toward better management and greater utilization of farm machines which will eliminate much of the farm work force. Some of the machines are in use, others are on the drawing board. The time of their coming and the almost complete mechanization of farm operations is imminent.

California farmers and growers had a new problem to deal with as the sixties came to a close, as the California Water Plan ran into unexpected difficulties. Acclaimed by former Governor Pat Brown as one of the two crowning achievements of his administration, the Water Plan had been hailed as the most important legislative enactment of this century. Under it, facilities were to be built to impound water in the north and subsequently distribute it to the parched land of Southern California. The benefits would be multiple. Not only would the natural maldistribution of water in California where the area inhabited by 80 per cent of the people gets 20 per cent of the natural precipitation be dealt with, but flood control, power generation, and recreation will be enhanced.

The complex of facilities, which included the giant Oroville Dam, which rises some 700 feet into the air, and a series of canals (which will be one of two man-made features of the world visible from the moon) were enormously expensive. The state shouldered the burden, however, with the expectation that the project when completed would be an unmitigated boon, not only to the landowners whose fertile fields lay fallow without it, but also to the growing megalopolis of Southern California. The first deliveries were expected in 1972, just about the time when current supplies would be stretched to the limit.

Quite unexpectedly, a roadblock in the form of high interest rates and a constitutional provision appeared in the late sixties. The constitution forbade an interest rate in excess of 5 per cent on state bonds and since current interest rates were at the 8 per cent level on similar bonds, the California water bonds could not be sold. As the money on hand was expended, the project was faced with the possibility of shutting down. Inflation and high interest rates plus the constitutional restriction were threatening to be more formidable barriers than any the builders had encountered.

Various solutions were proposed. One took the form of an initiative to change the constitution and remove the 5 per cent ceiling on bonds. Governor Reagan supported that initiative. Another proposal was to levy a special assessment on property which would sharply increase in value as a result of the project. The constitution restriction was removed in the 1970 election but high interest rates remain a problem. Construction remained on schedule and the first deliveries were made in early 1972.

Even if the problem of money were resolved, there is still another problem which confronts the project in the form of conservationists. Their attack on the project has been gathering momenteum in recent years as ecological concerns have become more prominent. The charges they make are manifold. First, they claim that the removal of large amounts of water from northern California will damage the region seriously. The removal of large amounts of fresh water from the watershed of the San Joaquin-Sacramento system will alter the mix of seawater and fresh water and damage the ecology of the bay and lower delta region. The new opponents of the plan also point out that the completion of the system will permit a continuation of the spiraling growth of the population of Southern California. While Southern California boosters and developers find it difficult to believe that anyone would be opposed to this unplanned urbanization, there are substantial numbers of people in Southern California who believe that the one thing that Southern California does not need is more people. The conservationists also attack another aspect of the program which would dump into San Francisco Bay by means of a north-south canal the waste water from the irrigated farming in the San Joaquin Valley. Loaded with pesticides, fertilizers, insecticides, herbicides, and various salts leached from the soils, this waste water could further damage the ecology of San Francisco Bay. Where all this will end is difficult to say as of this writing.

THE KINGDOM OF HIPPIEDOM

Few aspects of the kaleidoscope of modern California are more intriguing than the hippie youth subculture in all of its colorful glory. The alienation of the young in California, misunderstood and misinterpreted by even the well informed and well meaning of the older generation, is a phenomenon found almost everywhere. One finds representatives of the "unhitched" generation throughout the state, gamboling in the meadows of Yosemite National Park and sitting stony-eyed in the front row center seats of a Hollywood theater. Long-haired, garbed in freaked-out clothing of varied and brilliant hues, they look upon themselves as portents of a brighter tomorrow and in word and deed they stand aloof from the present world.

To those who identify with the present and find its comfort and affluence alluring and reassuring of the validity of their own lives, the disaffected young are regarded with mixed anxiety, astonishment, and antagonism. And when the representatives of the two groups come cheek by jowl in living room, or in public, the young are likely to be indifferent or patronizing to their elders and their elders tend to respond in anger or sorrow.

The generation gap is very much in evidence in California. For a relatively brief span of time, the collection of the more bizarre types in Haight-Ashbury captured the attention of the world news media. Sunset Strip became a similar mecca in Southern California and long outlived the northern California center of hippiedom. The great dispersal of dissident youth continues; some wind up in Berkeley, others settle in Big Sur, Venice, or along the Russian River, still others settle in forest settings, where they commune with nature and each other. The constellation of drugs which were an indispensable part of their life-style a short time ago has changed. LSD is no longer regarded as the key to a great experience, but positively avoided by those experienced in the way that it has acted to "distort" rather than expand consciousness. Marijuana is more widely used than ever, but hard drugs are looked upon with much less favor than formerly.

To the older generation of the present, possibly the most prolific pill-consuming generation in the history of man, there is no understanding of these hippie rebels. To the adults who survived the Depression and World War II, and who have learned to live with atomic and hydrogen bombs, intercontinental ballistic missiles, and twenty-five years in which an Armageddon between the Soviet Union and the United States impended, the present is quite tolerable. A material abundance of unprecendented dimensions makes life in the Golden State soft, pleasant, and enjoyable. Color TV sets, two cars and sometimes three, houses filled with expensive furniture and every labor-saving device known to man—these are the things which make for the good life, and they find it difficult to believe that their offspring will reject such things and the life they represent.

But this seems to be a fundamental need of the young hippie. His long hair sets him apart from the carefully groomed representative of "straight" society; his dress of psychedelic hues, fabrics, and designs or cast-off clothing from a salvage store or a combination of the two does the same thing. In perfectly obvious traits of behavior and styles of living, he is not only "doing his thing" but stating that he does not want to do the straight thing. While some hippies were apolitical in thought and deed, dissidents of a similar life-style were in the forefront of anti-Vietnam, anti-military, and anti-draft activities. They incurred the wrath of the establishment and the antagonism of large segments of the general population. The view of the dissidents of their world was to be seen in the underground press. The Los Angeles *Free Press* in Southern California and the *Berkeley Barb* in the bay area were the principal newspapers but there were many others of limited circulation. There were enough outlets in California to justify a news service, and enough circulation to provide young hippie street vendors of the paper with survival "bread." Moreover, the underground press was moving to the college and high school campus.

The hostility between young and old in California is frequently reinforced as a result of campus dissent. To the adults of California, who finance a great system of higher education, the college campus is the key to a bright future. When their offspring reject that assumption, refuse to program themselves through undergraduate training toward a place in the straight world, and even make it difficult for others to take advantage of the educational opportunities of the campus, adults are astonished, resentful, and angry. The antagonism engendered has political ramifications. Great blocs of voters, antagonized by the activities of the hippie-radical-activist, vote enthusiastically for the politico who identifies himself with the stable forces of the society.

A similar political phenomenon grows out of the other process of change and dissent. The defeat of Senator Pierre Salinger in 1964 was influenced by his opposition to an initiative which would have tended to perpetuate segregation in housing. More recently a mayoralty race in Los Angeles turned on the fact that a black councilman, Thomas Bradley, faced a white incumbent, Samuel Yorty. The occurrence of the People's Park controversy which dominated the TV screens shortly before the election probably reinforced an incipient antagonism to Bradley.

California's political history has had its share of ugly episodes but none matched in malignity the assassination of Senator Robert F. Kennedy in 1968. Taking place only days after an Oregon primary defeat at the hands of Senator Eugene McCarthy, Kennedy's last campaign in California was an all-out carefully planned and orchestrated effort. All the finesse of a seasoned campaign organization went into the final battle and produced the victory which was imperative if the second Kennedy was to go on to 1600 Pennsylvania Avenue. But madness intervened, despoiled democracy, and struck down the young politico from New York whose national constituency ran across all cultural and ethnic lines. Ironically, his last public words, perhaps overheard by his assassin, focused on the violence in America and his heartfelt belief that it might be eliminated from the land.

In the closing years of the decade of the sixties, a resurgence of conservatism brought a triumvirate of Rafferty, Reagan, and Murphy to three of the major posts of political power. Two were eliminated in the 1970 election, but the governor remains. The Democratic party was in disarray after the 1968 convention and campaign, which left great segments of the party alienated, dispirited, or disillusioned. The slow process of rebuilding was under way as the seventies opened, but it was obvious to many observers that the circumstances which had provided Governor Reagan with a million-vote victory in 1966 were still in evidence. A long-time Kennedy associate and the closest thing to a professional in this land where amateur politics loomed large in the political arena, Jesse Unruh was apparently not convinced that the incumbent was invulnerable. And the governor himself inadvertently indicated his vulnerability by attempting to change in the late sixties to the garb of a political moderate. The swing vote in California was still the approximate one million nominally Democratic but unpredictable center whose support generally decided major elections. Unruh supporters were cheered by polls which indicated that a small margin separated the two candidates, but realists who were aware of the impact of television on modern campaigning noted that the governor was as skillful in its use as the Democratic aspirant was inexperienced. The realists proved right election eve when Reagan emerged with a half-million-vote victory.

Californians who looked back through the rearview mirror of history and reflected on the sixties as a new decade opened saw a number of things which might help them to look into the future. For the most part, the problems of the past decade were still unresolved. The problems of growth, the despoilment of the environment, the strife of class and ethnic groups still troubled the land. The endless war in Vietnam, the draft, and the role of the military in American society troubled the young. The middle-aged were entrapped in the affluence of a consumer society. As members of a society which was beset with economic problems like ongoing inflation which amounted to 6 per cent of the consumer food dollar in 1969, they had good reason to be insecure. Uncertainty arose as well out of the vagaries of military procurement which might bring overnight diasaster to a company, or an industry or its employees. In the cities of this thoroughly urbanized state where 90 per cent of the population lived in cities, there was disquiet. Unemployment grew generally until it exceeded 7 per cent of the work force in mid-1971. Unemployment rates in the ghettos climbed in part because of national deflationary policies but at the same time national projects to train hard-core unemployed were continued. The police, who frequently found themselves in the uncomfortable middle between those who demanded change now and those who were as determined to stand by the status quo, broke into the news from time to time.

In short, California was in the opening year of the seventies, a divided and troubled state in a divided and troubled nation. There were those who preferred not to examine the reality of the present too carefully, but reluctance to look problems in the eye leads to few solutions. If the citizenry of California were confronted with great problems, they were also faced with great opportunities to devise solutions to problems that vexed not alone the state but the nation. And the citizenry of California had as well technological resources which put a man on the moon and had unmatched potential. How they would be used in the seventies will be revealed.

Bibliography

I. THE STAGE

Austin, Mary, *The Land of Little Rain* (1903)
Durrenberger, R. W., W. B. Byron, and J. C. Kimura, *Patterns on the Land* (1957)
Federal Writers' Project, *California, A Guide to the Golden State* (1939)
Felton, Ernest L., *California's Many Climates* (1965)
Griffin, Paul F., and Robert N. Young, *California, the New Empire State: A Regional Geography* (1957)
Gudde, Erwin G., *California Place Names* (1960)
Hoover, Mildred Brooke, *Historic Spots in California* (1937)
Lantis, David W., Rodney Steiner, and Arthur E. Karinen, *California: Land of Contrast* (1963, 1971).
Meigs, Peveril 3rd, *Climates of California* (1938)
Muir, John, *The Mountains of California* (1894)
———, *The Yosemite* (1912)
Peattie, Roderick, *The Pacific Coast Ranges* (1946)
Zierer, Clifford M., ed., *California and the Southwest* (1956)

II. THE FIRST CALIFORNIANS

Bancroft, Hubert Howe, *The Native Races*, 5 vols. (1874–75)
Caughey, John W., *The Indians of Southern California in 1852* (1952)
Heizer, Robert F., and Mary Ann Whipple, eds., *The California Indians, A Source Book* (1951)
Hodge, F. W., ed., *Handbook of the American Indians North of Mexico*, 2 vols. (1907–10)
Kroeber, Alfred L., *Handbook of the Indians of California* (1925)
Kroeber, Theodora, *The Inland Whale* (1959)
———, *Ishi in Two Worlds: A Biography of the Last Wild Indian in North America* (1961)
Merriam, C. Hart, *Studies of California Indians* (1955)

III. THE AGE OF EXPLORATION

Bolton, H. E., *Padre on Horseback* (1932)
——, *Rim of Christendom* (1936)
——, *Spanish Exploration in the Southwest, 1542–1706* (1916)
Chapman, Charles E., *History of California: The Spanish Period* (1921)
Dunne, Peter M., *Pioneer Black Robes on the West Coast* (1940)
Mathes, W. Michael, *Vizcaino and Spanish Explorations in the Pacific Ocean* (1968)
Powell, Philip W., *Soldiers, Indians and Silver: The Northward Advance of New Spain, 1550–1600* (1952)
Richman, Irving Berdine, *California Under Spain and Mexico, 1535–1847* (1911)
Schurz, William, *The Manila Galleon* (1939)
Wagner, Henry R., *Cartography of the Northwest Coast of America to the Year 1800* (1937)
——, *Juan Rodriguez Cabrillo, Discoverer of the Coast of California* (1941)
——, *Spanish Voyages to the Northwest Coast of America in the Sixteenth Century* (1929)

IV. THE SPANISH ERA

Bancroft, Hubert Howe, *History of California*, 7 vols. (1890)
Bolton, Herbert E., *Anza's California Expeditions*, 5 vols. (1930)
——, *Fray Juan Crespi, Missionary Explorer* (1927)
——, *The Spanish Borderlands* (1921)
Chapman, Charles E., *History of California: The Spanish Period* (1921)
Cutler, Donald C., *Malaspina in California* (1960)
Dunne, Peter M., *Pioneer Jesuits in Northern Mexico* (1944)
Englebert, Omer, *The Last of the Conquistadores: Junipero Serra, 1713–1784* (1956)
Geiger, Maynard J., *The Life and Times of Fray Junipero Serra*, 2 vols. (1959)
Golder, Frank A., *Russian Expansion on the Pacific, 1641–1848* (1914)
Priestley, Herbert I., *Franciscan Explorations in California* (1946)
——, *A Historical, Political, and Natural Description of California by Pedro Fages* (1937)
——, *Jose de Galvez, Visitador—General of New Spain* (1916)
Sanchez, Nellie Van de Grift, *Spanish Arcadia* (1929)

V. THE MEXICAN ERA

Arnaz, Jose, "Memoirs of a Merchant," tr. & ed. by Nellie Van de Grift Sanchez, *Touring Topics* (September, October, 1928)
Bancroft, Hubert Howe, *California Pastoral* (1888)

Chapman, Charles E., *History of California: The Spanish Period* (1921)
Cleland, Robert G., *The Cattle on a Thousand Hills* (1951)
Dakin, Susanna, *The Lives of William Hartnell* (1949)
——, *A Scotch Paisano; Hugo Reid's Life in California, 1832–1853* (1939)
Dana, Richard Henry, *Two Years Before the Mast* (1840)
Davis, William Heath, *Seventy-five Years in California* (1929)
Geary, Gerald J., *The Secularization of the California Missions* (1934)
Hutchinson, C. Alan, *Frontier Settlement in Mexican California* (1969)
Robinson, Alfred H., *Life in California*
Rolle, Andrew F., *An American in California: The Biography of William Heath Davis, 1822–1909* (1956)
Sanchez, Nellie Van de Grift, *Spanish Arcadia* (1929)
Servin, Manuel P., "The Secularization of the California Missions; a Reappraisal," *Southern California Quarterly*, XLVII (June 1965)
Tays, George, "Mariano Guadalupe Vallejo and Sonoma—A Biography and a History," *CHSQ*, XVI–XVII, 161–205 (1932)

VI. THE INTRUDERS

Anderson, Vern, *Surveyor of the Sea, The Life and Voyages of Captain George Vancouver* (1960)
Atherton, Gertrude, *Rezanov* (1906)
Bancroft, Hubert Howe, *California Pastoral* (1888)
Bidwell, John, *A Journey to California, 1841*, Francis P. Farquhar, ed. (1964)
Billington, Ray, *The Far Western Frontier* (1956)
Bynum, Lindley, ed., *Journal of a Voyage Between China and the North-Western Coast of America Made in 1804 by William Shaler* (1935)
Cleland, Robert G., *This Reckless Breed of Men: The Trappers and Fur Traders of the Southwest* (1952)
Cooke, Philip St. George, *The Conquest of New Mexico and California* (1878)
Cutler, Donald C., *Malaspina in California* (1960)
Dakin, Susanna, *Scotch Paisano, Hugo Reid's Life in California* (1939)
Dana, Richard Henry, *Two Years Before the Mast* (1840)
De Voto, Bernard, *The Year of Decision* (1942)
Ewers, John C., ed., *The Adventures of Zenas Leonard* (1959)
Frémont, John C., *Memoirs of My Life* (1887)
Graebner, Norman, *Empire on the Pacific* (1955)
Hawgood, John, "The Pattern of Yankee Infiltration in Mexican Alta California 1821–1846," *Pacific Historical Review*, XXVII, 27–38 (February 1958)
Ledyard, John, *A Journal of Captain Cook's Last Voyage to the Pacific Ocean* (1783)
Lyman, George D., *John Marsh, Pioneer* (1930)
Marti, Werner H., *Messenger of Destiny: The California Adventures, 1846–1847, of Archibald H. Gillespie* (1960)
Morgan, Dale, *Jedediah Smith and the Opening of the West* (1953)

Nevins, Allan, *Frémont, Pathmaker of the West* (1939)
Nunis, Doyce B., ed., *The California Diary of Faxon Dean Atherton 1836–1839* (1964)
Ogden, Adele, *The California Sea Otter Trade, 1784–1848* (1941)
Okun, S. B., *The Russian-American Company* (1951)
Pattie, James O., *The Personal Narrative of James Ohio Pattie* (1831)
Preuss, Charles, *Exploring with Frémont* (1958)
Robinson, Alfred, *Life in California* (1846)
Rolle, Andrew, *An American in California: The Biography of William Heath Davis* (1956)
Royce, Josiah, *California, from the Conquest in 1846 to the Second Vigilance Committee* (1886)
Sellers, Charles, *James K. Polk, Continentalist* (1966)
Stewart, George R., *The California Trail* (1962)
——, *Ordeal by Hunger* (1936)
Stone, Irving, *Men to Match My Mountains: The Opening of the Far West 1840–1900* (1956)
Sullivan, Maurice S., *The Travels of Jedediah Smith* (1934)
Tikhmenev, P., *Historical Survey of the Formation of the Russian-American Fur Company*, 2 vols. (1861–63)
Vancouver, George, *A Voyage of Discovery to the North Pacific Ocean and Round the World*, 3 vols. (1798)
Wilbur, Marguerite Eyer, ed., *Vancouver in California, 1792–1794* (1953)
Woodward, Arthur, *Lances at San Pascual* (1948)
Zollinger, James P., *Sutter the Man and His Empire* (1939)

VII. THE GOLDEN FLEECE

Bailey, Paul, *Sam Brannan and the California Mormons* (1959)
Bancroft, Hubert Howe, *California, Inter Pocula* (1888)
Borthwick, J. D., *Three Years in California* (1857)
Bruff, J. Goldsborough, *Gold Rush* (1944)
Bryant, Frank, *What I Saw in California* (1848)
Buffum, E. Gould, *Six Months in the Gold Mines* (1850)
Caughey, John W., *Gold Is the Cornerstone* (1948)
Clappe, Louise M., *The Shirley Letters from California Mines in 1851–52*, Thomas C. Russell, ed. (1922)
Colton, Walter, *Three Years in California* (1850)
Delano, Alonzo, *Life on the Plains and in the Diggings* (1854)
Gudde, Edwin G., *Sutter's Own Story* (1936)
Kemble, John H., *The Panama Route, 1848–69* (1943)
Lewis, Oscar, *Sea Routes to the Gold Fields* (1949)
Marryat, Frank, *Mountains and Molehills* (1855)
Monaghan, Jay, *Australians and the Gold Rush*
Paul, Rodman, *California Gold* (1947)
——, *Mining Frontiers of the Far West, 1848–1880* (1963)
Royce, Josiah, *California* (1886)

Shinn, Charles H., *Mining Camps* (1885)
Soule, Gihon and Nisbet, *Annals of San Francisco* (1855)
Stewart, George R., *The California Trail* (1962)
Taylor, Bayard, *Eldorado*, 2 vols. (1850)
Wilson, Iris H., *William Wolfskill, 1798–1866* (1965)
Zollinger, James Peter, *Sutter, The Man and His Empire* (1939)

VIII. THE AMERICANIZATION OF CALIFORNIA

Barker, Charles, ed., *Memoirs of Elisha Oscar Crosby* (1945)
Bell, Horace, *Reminiscences of a Ranger or Early Times in Southern California*
    (1927)
Browne, F. Ross, *Report of the Debates in the Convention of California on
    the Formation of the State Constitution* (1850)
Colton, Rev. Walter, *Three Years in California* (1850)
Cowan, Robert G., *The Admission of the Thirty-First State by the Thirty-
    First Congress* (1962)
Davis, Winfield J., *History of Political Conventions in California 1849–1892*
    (1893)
Ellison, William H., *A Self-Governing Dominion, California 1849–1860* (1950)
Goodwin, Cardinal, *The Establishment of State Government in California,
    1846–1850* (1914)
Grivas, Theodore, *Military Governments in California, 1846–1850* (1963)
Hansen, Woodrow J., *This Search for Authority in California* (1960)
Hurt, Peyton, "The Rise and Fall of the Know Nothings in California,"
    California Historical Society Quarterly, IX, 16–49, 99–128 (March and
    June 1930)
Hutchinson, C. Alan, *Frontier Settlement in Mexican California* (1969)
Nichols, Roy F., *Disruption of American Democracy* (1948)
O'Meara, James, *Broderick and Gwin* (1881)
Royce, Josiah, *California from the Conquest in 1846 to the Second Vigilance
    Committee in San Francisco* (1886)
Scherer, James, *Thirty-First Star* (1942)
Shutes, Milton H., *Lincoln and California* (1943)
Thomas, Lately, *Between Two Empires, The Life Story of William M. Gwin*
    (1969)
Williams, David A., *David C. Broderick, A Political Portrait* (1969)

IX. VIGILANTES, FILIBUSTERS, AND DUELISTS

Bancroft, Hubert Howe, *Popular Tribunals*, 2 vols. (1887)
Bell, Major Horace, *On the Old West Coast* (1930)
Buchanan, A. Russell, *David S. Terry of California, Dueling Judge* (1956)
Carr, Albert Z., *The World and William Walker* (1963)
Caughey, John Walton, *Their Majesties, the Mob* (1960)
Coblentz, Stanton A., *Villains and Vigilantes* (1936)

Ellison, William H., *A Self-Governing Dominion* (1950)

O'Meara, James, *The Vigilance Committee of 1856, by a Pioneer Journalist* (1887)

Rolle, Andrew F., "California Filibustering and the Hawaiian Kingdom," *Pacific Historical Review*, XIX, 251–64 (August 1950)

Royce, Josiah, *California from the Conquest in 1846 to the Second Vigilance Committee in San Francisco* (1886)

Scherer, James A. B., *The Lion of the Vigilantes, William T. Coleman* (1939)

Scruggs, William O., *Filibusters and Financiers* (1916)

Sherman, William T., *Memoirs*, 2 vols. (1875)

Shinn, Charles H., *Mining Camps* (1885)

Stewart, George R., *Committee of Vigilance, Revolution in San Francisco, 1851* (1964)

Walker, William, *The War in Nicaragua* (1860)

Williams, David A., *David C. Broderick, A Political Portrait* (1969)

Williams, Mary Floyd, *History of the San Francisco Committee of Vigilance of 1851* (1921)

Wistar, Isaac J., *Autobiography*, 2 vols. (1914)

Wyllys, Rufus K., *The French in Sonora, 1850–1854* (1932)

X. TRANSPORTATION

Banning, William and George H., *Six Horses* (1930)

Berthold, Victor M., *The Pioneer Steamer "California" 1848–1849* (1932)

Bloss, Roy S., *Pony Express—The Great Gamble* (1959)

Bradley, Glenn D., *The Story of the Pony Express* (1913)

Clark, A. H., *The Clipper Ship Era, 1843–1869* (1910)

Clark, George R., *Leland Stanford* (1931)

Conkling, Roscoe P. and Margaret B., *The Butterfield Overland Mail, 1857–1869*, 3 vols. (1947)

George, Henry, "What the Railroad Will Bring Us," *Overland*, I, 297–304 (1868)

Griswold, Wesley S., *A Work of Giants: Building the First Transcontinental Railroad* (1963)

Hafen, Leroy R., *The Overland Mail, 1849–1860* (1926)

Howard, Robert West, *The Great Iron Trail: The Story of the First Transcontinental Railroad* (1963)

Hungerford, Edward, *Wells Fargo: Advancing the American Frontier* (1949)

Judah, Theodore D., *A Practical Plan for Building the Pacific Railroad* (1857)

Kemble, John H., *The Panama Route, 1828–1869* (1943)

Lang, Walter B., ed., *The First Overland Mail*, 2 vols. (1940, 1945)

Lewis, Oscar, *The Big Four: The Story of Huntington, Stanford, Hopkins and Crocker, and of the Building of the Central Pacific* (1938)

Lucia, Ellis, *The Saga of Ben Holladay: Giant of the Old West* (1959)

McNairn, Jack, and Jerry MacMullen, *Ships of the Redwood Coast* (1945)

Riesenberg, Felix, Jr., *Golden Gate, The Story of San Francisco Harbor* (1940)

Settle, Raymond W. and Mary L., *Saddles and Spurs, The Pony Express Saga* (1955)
——, *War Drums and Wagon Wheels: The Story of Russell, Majors, and Waddell* (1966)
Smith, Waddell, *The Story of the Pony Express* (1966)
Tallack, William B., *The California Overland Express; The Longest Stage Ride in the World* (1935)
Twain, Mark, *Roughing It* (1872)
Wheat, Carl I., "A Sketch of the Life of Theodore D. Judah," *California Historical Society Quarterly*, IV, 219–71 (September 1925)
Winther, Oscar O., *Express and Stagecoach Days in California* (1936)

XI. THE INDIAN CONFRONTATION

Bonsal, Stephen, *Edward Fitzgerald Beale, A Pioneer in the Path of Empire* (1912)
Brandon, William, *The American Heritage Book of Indians* (1961)
Browne, J. Ross, *The Indians of California* (1864; 1944)
——, "The Indian Reservations in California," *Harper's* (August 1861)
Caughey, John W., ed., Benjamin D. Wilson's report in *The Indians of Southern California in 1852* (1952)
Cook, Sherbourne F., *The Conflict between the California Indian and White Civilization*, Part III, *The American Invasions, 1848–1870* (1943)
Dale, Edward E., *The Indians of the Southwest* (1949)
Ellison, Joseph, *California and the Nation* (1927)
Ellison, William H., "The Federal Indian Policy in California, 1846–1860," *Mississippi Valley Historical Review*, IX, 37–67 (1922)
——, *A Self-governing Dominion* (1950)
Fernandez, Ferdinand F., "Except a California Indian: A Study in Legal Discrimination," *Historical Society of Southern California Quarterly*, L, 161–75 (1968)
Grover, LaFayette, *Modoc War* (1874)
Hoopes, Alban W., *Indian Affairs and Their Administration, with Special Reference to the Far West, 1849–1860* (1932)
Jackson, Helen Hunt, *Century of Dishonor* (1881)
Kenny, Robert W., *History and Proposed Settlement of Claims of California Indians* (1944)
Kroeber, Theodora, *Ishi in Two Worlds* (1961)
Leonard, Charles B., "Federal Indian Policy in the San Joaquin Valley: Its Application and Results," Ph.D. Dissertation, University of California, Berkeley (1928)
Meacham, *Wigwam and War-Paint, or the Royal Chief in Chains* (1875)
Murray, Keith A., *The Modocs and Their War* (1959)
Sutton, Imre, "Land Tenure and Changing Occupancy on Indian Reservations in Southern California," Ph.D. Dissertation, UCLA (1964)
Thomas, Richard, "The Mission Indians: A Study of Leadership and Cultural Contact," Ph.D. Dissertation, UCLA (1963)

XII. THE SEETHING SEVENTIES

Baker, Charles, *Henry George* (1955)

Barth, Gunther, *Bitter Strength, A History of the Chinese in the United States, 1850–1870* (1964)

Brown, James L., *The Mussel Slough Tragedy* (1958)

Coolidge, Mary R., *Chinese Immigration* (1909)

Cross, Ira B., *Frank B. Roney: Irish Rebel and California Labor Leader* (1931)

——, *A History of the Labor Movement in California* (1935)

Daggett, Stuart, *Chapters on the History of the Southern Pacific* (1922)

Daniels, Roger, and Harry H. Kitano, *American Racism: Exploration of the Nature of Prejudice* (1970)

Davis, Winfield J., *History of Political Conventions in California 1849–1892* (1893)

Eaves, Lucille, *A History of California Labor Legislation* (1910)

Gates, Paul Wallace, "California's Agricultural College Lands," *Pacific Historical Review,* XXX (May 1961)

——, "The Homestead Law in an Incongruous Land System," *American Historical Review,* XLI (July 1936)

Heizer, Robert F., and Alan F. Almquist, *The Other Californians* (1971)

Howard, Robert W., *The Great Iron Trail: The Story of the First Transcontinental Railroad* (1963)

Kelley, Robert L., *Gold vs. Grain, The Hydraulic Mining Controversy in California's Sacramento Valley* (1959)

Lavender, David, *The Great Persuader, Collis P. Huntington* (1970)

Lewis, Oscar, *The Big Four* (1938)

Lyman, George D., *Ralston's Ring, California Plunders the Comstock Lode* (1937)

McWilliams, Carey, *California, the Great Exception* (1949)

Norris, Frank, *The Octopus* (1901)

Ping Chiu, *Chinese Labor in California, 1850–1880: An Economic Study* (1963)

Sandmeyer, Elmer C., *The Anti-Chinese Movement in California* (1939)

Stedman, J. C., and R. A. Leonard, *The Workingmen's Party of California* (1878)

Swisher, Carl B., *Motivation and Political Technique in the California Constitutional Convention, 1878–1879* (1931)

Treadwell, Edward F., *The Cattle King* (1931)

Tutorow, Norman E., *Leland Stanford, Man of Many Careers* (1971)

XIII. TOWARD AN AMERICAN ECONOMY

Becker, Robert H., *Diseños of California Ranchos* (1964)

Carosso, Vincent P., *The California Wine Industry, 1830–1859* (1951)

Cleland, Robert G., *Cattle on a Thousand Hills* (1951)

Gates, Paul W., *California Ranchos and Farms 1846–1862* (1967)

Hoffman, Ogden, *Report of Land Cases Determined in the United States District Court for the Northern District of California* (1862)

Hutchison, Claude B., *California Agriculture* (1946)

Jones, William Carey, *Report on the Subject of Land Titles in California* (1850)

Melville, John, *The Story of Wines in California* (1962)

Newmark, Harris, *Sixty Years in Southern California, 1853–1913* (1916)

Pitt, Leonard, *The Decline of the Californios: A Social History of the Spanish Speaking Californians, 1846–1890* (1966)

Robinson, W. W., *Land in California* (1948)

Taylor, Frank J., and Earl M. Welty, *Black Bonanza* (1950)

Wentworth, Edward N., *America's Sheep Trails: History, Personalities* (1948)

White, Gerald T., *Formative Years in the Far West, A History of Standard Oil Company of California and Predecessors Through 1919* (1962)

XIV. BOOM!

Alexander, J. A., *The Life of George Chaffey* (1925)

Austin, Mary, *The Land of Little Rain* (1903)

Cooper, Erwin, *Aqueduct Empire: A Guide to Water in California, Its Turbulent History and Its Management Today* (1968)

Cumberland, William W., *Cooperative Marketing, Its Advantages as Exemplified in the California Fruit Growers Exchange* (1917)

Dumke, Glenn S., *The Boom of the Eighties in Southern California* (1944)

Gardner, Kelsey B., and A. W. McKay, *The California Fruit Growers Exchange System* (1950)

Matson, Charles H., *The Story of Los Angeles Harbor* (1925)

Mayo, Morrow, *Los Angeles* (1933)

Nadeau, Remi A., *City-makers, The Men Who Transformed Los Angeles from Village to Metropolis . . . , 1868–1876* (1948)

——, *The Water Seekers* (1950)

Nordhoff, Charles, *California for Health, Pleasure, and Residence* (1872)

Teague, Charles C., *Fifty Years a Rancher* (1944)

Van Dyke, T. S., *Millionaires of a Day* (1890)

——, *Southern California* (1886)

Wilbur, Ray, and Elwood Mead, *Construction of Hoover Dam* (1935)

XV. THE PROGRESSIVE ERA

Bean, Walton, *Boss Ruef's San Francisco* (1952)

Brown, J. L., *The Mussel Slough Tragedy* (1958)

Daggett, Stuart, *Chapters on the History of the Southern Pacific* (1922)

Davis, Winfield J., *History of Political Conventions in California, 1849–1892* (1893)

Dobie, Edith, *The Political Career of Stephen Mallory White* (1927)

Haymond, Creed, *The Central Pacific Railroad and the United States* (1887–89)

Hichborn, Franklin, *The System* (1915)

Hutchinson, William H., *Oil, Land and Politics*, 2 vols. (1965)

Kennedy, John C., *The Great Earthquake and Fire, San Francisco, 1906* (1963)

Lavender, David, *The Great Persuader, Collis P. Huntington* (1971)

Lewis, Oscar, *The Big Four* (1938)

Ludwig, Ella A., *History of the Harbor District of Los Angeles* (1928)

Matson, Clarence H., *Building a World Gateway, The Story of Los Angeles Harbor* (1945)

Mowry, George E., *The California Progressives* (1951)

Older, Fremont, *My Own Story* (1919)

Olin, Spencer C., *California's Prodigal Sons: Hiram Johnson and the Progressives* (1968)

Putnam, Jackson K., "The Persistence of Progressivism in the 1920s: The Case of California," *Pacific Historical Review*, XXXV, 395–411 (Nov. 1966)

Steffens, Lincoln, *The Autobiography of Lincoln Steffens*, 2 vols. (1931)

Thomas, Gordon, and Max Morgan Witts, *The San Francisco Earthquake* (1971)

Thomas, Lately, *A Debonair Scoundrel* (1962)

Walters, Donald E., "Populism in California, 1889–1900," Ph.D. Dissertation, University of California, Berkeley (1952)

Wells, Evelyn, *Fremont Older* (1916)

Willard, Charles D., *The Free Harbor Contest at Los Angeles* (1899)

XVI. THE LABOR STORY

Adamic, Louis, *Dynamite: The Story of Class Violence in America* (1935)

Adams, Graham, *The Age of Industrial Violence, 1910–1915* (1966)

Bernstein, Irving, *The Lean Years: A History of the American Worker 1920–1933* (1960)

Brissenden, Paul F., *The I.W.W.: A Study of American Syndicalism* (1920)

Camp, William M., *San Francisco: Port of Gold* (1947)

Cronin, Bernard C., *Father Yorke and the Labor Movement in San Francisco, 1900–1910* (1943)

Cross, Ira B., *Frank B. Roney, Irish Rebel and California Labor Leader* (1931)

——, *A History of the Labor Movement in California* (1935)

Darrow, Clarence, *The Story of My Life* (1932)

Dowell, Eldredge F., *Criminal Syndicalism Legislation in the United States* (1939)

Dubofsky, Martin, *We Shall Be All: A History of the Industrial Workers of the World* (1969)

Eaves, Lucille, *A History of California Labor Legislation with an Introductory Sketch of the San Francisco Labor Movement* (1910)

Fogelson, Robert M., *The Fragmented Metropolis, Los Angeles, 1850–1930* (1966)

Frost, Richard H., *The Mooney Case* (1968)

Gentry, Curt, *Frame-Up: The Incredible Case of Tom Mooney and Warren Billings* (1967)

Haywood, William D., *Bill Haywood's Book* (1929)

Hichborn, Franklin, *The Case of Charlotte Anita Whitney* (1920)

McKight, Robert E., *Industrial Relations in the San Francisco Bay Area, 1900–1918* (1960)

McWilliams, Carey, *California, the Great Exception* (1949)

——, *Factories in the Field: The Story of the Migratory Farm Labor in California* (1939)

——, *North from Mexico* (1949)

Murray, Robert K., *Red Scare, A Study in National Hysteria, 1919–1920* (1955)

Parker, Cornelia S., *An American Idyll, Carleton H. Parker* (1919)

Perry, Louis and Richard S., *A History of the Los Angeles Labor Movement, 1911–1941* (1963)

Renshaw, Patrick, *The Wobblies* (1967)

Steffens, Lincoln, *The Autobiography of Lincoln Steffens* (1931)

Stimson, Grace L., *Rise of the Labor Movement in Los Angeles* (1955)

Taylor, Paul S., *The Sailors' Union of the Pacific* (1923)

——, *Mexican Labor in the United States* (1929)

Weintraub, Hyman G., *Andrew Furseth, Emancipator of the Seamen* (1959)

Yellen, Samuel, *American Labor Struggles* (1956)

XVII. THE AGE OF PROSPERITY

Daniels, Roger, *The Politics of Prejudice* (1968)

Dohrman, H. T., *California Cult* (1958)

Fulton, H. R., *Motion Pictures* (1960)

Greenwalt, Emmett A., *The Point Loma Community in California, 1897–1942* (1955)

Hine, Robert V., *California's Utopian Colonies* (1953)

Jacobs, Lewis, *The Rise of the American Film* (1939)

Knight, Arthur, *The Liveliest Art* (1957)

McWilliams, Carey, *Southern California Country: An Island on the Land* (1946)

Mavity, Nancy Barr, *Sister Aimee* (1931)

Putnam, Jackson K., "The Persistence of Progressivism in the 1920's: The Case of California, *Pacific Historical Review*, XXXV, 395–411 (November 1966)

Rae, John B., *Climb to Greatness: The American Aircraft Industry, 1920–1960* (1968)

Thomas, Lately, *Storming Heaven* (1970)

XVIII. THE DEPRESSION DECADE

Burke, Robert E., *Olson's New Deal for California* (1953)

California Emergency Relief Administration, *Economic Trends in California 1929–1934* (1935)

Chambers, Clärke A., *California Farm Organizations . . . 1929–1941* (1952)

Delmatier, Royce D., "The Rebirth of the Democratic Party in California, 1928–1938," Ph.D. Dissertation, University of California, Berkeley (1955)

Eliel, Paul, *The Waterfront and General Strikes* (1934)

Farrelly, David, and Ivan Hinderaker, eds., *The Politics of California* (1951)

Fuller, Varden, "The Supply of Agricultural Labor as a Factor in the Evolution of Farm Organization in California," Ph.D. Dissertation, University of California, Berkeley (1939)

Goldbeck, Herman G., "The Political Career of James Rolph, Jr.," M.A. Thesis, University of California, Berkeley (1936)

Goldschmidt, Walter, *As You Sow* (1947)

Holtzman, Abraham, *The Townsend Movement: A Political Study* (1963)

Lange, Dorothea, and Paul S. Taylor, *An American Exodus: A Record of Human Erosion* (1939)

Larsen, Charles E., "The Epic Campaign of 1934," *Pacific Historical Review*, XXVII, 127–48 (May 1958)

Melendy, H. Brett, and Benjamin F. Gilbart, *The Governors of California* (1965)

Putnam, Jackson K., "The Influence of the Older Age Groups on California Politics, 1920–1940," Ph.D. Dissertation, Stanford (1964)

——, *Old Age Politics in California* (1970)

Schlesinger, Arthur M., Jr., *The Politics of Upheaval* (1960)

Servin, Manuel P., "The Pre-World War II Mexican American: An Interpretation," *California Historical Society Quarterly*, XLIV, 325–32 (1966)

Sinclair, Upton, *The Autobiography of Upton Sinclair* (1962)

——, *I, Candidate for Governor, and How I Got Licked* (1934)

——, *I, Governor of California, and How I Ended Poverty* (1933)

Slobodek, Mitchell, *A Selective Bibliography of California Labor History* (1964)

Steinbeck, John, *Grapes of Wrath* (1939)

Townsend, Francis E., *New Horizons: An Autobiography* (1943)

Whiteman, Luther, and Samuel L. Lewis, *Glory Roads; the Psychological State of California* (1936)

Woolf, Paul N., *Economic Trends in California, 1929–1934* (1935)

XIX. ARSENAL OF DEMOCRACY

Arnold, H. H., *Global Mission* (1949)

Barnhart, Edward N., "The Individual Exclusions of Japanese Americans in World War II," *Pacific Historical Review*, XXIX, 111–130 (May 1960)

Bloom, Leonard, and Ruth Riemar, *Removal and Return* . . . (1949)

Bosworth, Allan R., *America's Concentration Camps* (1967)

Bureau of Labor Statistics Bulletin 824, *Wartime Employment, Production, and Conditions of Work in Shipyards* (1945)

Cunningham, William G., *The Aircraft Industry, A Study in Industrial Location* (1951)

Girdner, Audrie, and Anne Loftis, *The Great Betrayal* (1969)

Grether, Ewald T., *The Steel Using Industries of California* (1946)

Grodzins, Morton, *Americans Betrayed: Politics and the Japanese Evacuation* (1949)

Johnson, Kenneth M., *Aerial California: An Account of Early Flight in Northern and Southern California, 1849 to World War 1* (1961)

Levenson, Leonard G., "Wartime Development of the Aircraft Industry," *Monthly Labor Review,* LIX, 909–10 (November 1944)

McDonald, Bernard A., *Air Transportation in the Immediate Post-War Period* (1944)

McWilliams, Carey, *California, The Great Exception* (1949)

———, *Prejudice: Japanese-Americans, Symbol of Racial Intolerance* (1944)

Manard, Crosby, ed., *Flight Plan for Tomorrow, The Douglas Story* (1966)

National Resources Planning Board, Pacific Southwest Region, *Industrial Development* (1942)

Okubo, Mine, *Citizen 13660* (1946)

Taylor, Frank J., and Lawton, Wright, *Democracy's Air Arsenal* (1947)

Thomas, Dorothy S., and Richard S. Nishimoto, *The Spoilage* (1946)

XX. THE NEW AGE OF TECHNOLOGY

Baer, Markell C., *Story of the California Republican Assembly* (1955)

Brown, Edmund G., *Reagan and Reality* (1970)

Cannon, Lou, *Ronnie and Jessie* (1969)

Carney, Francis, *Rise of the Democratic Clubs in California* (1958)

Chambers, Clarke H., *California Farm Organizations* (1952)

Cleland, Robert Glass, *California in Our Time 1900–1940* (1947)

Craig, Richard B., *The Bracero Program* (1971)

Cunningham, William G., *The Aircraft Industry, A Study in Industrial Location* (1951)

Dalmatier, Royce D., Clarence McIntosh, and Earl G. Waters, *The Rumble of California Politics* (1970)

de Roos, Robert, *The Thirsty-Land: The Story of the Central Valley Project* (1948)

Gardner, David P., *The California Oath Controversy* (1967)

Hill, Gladwin, *Dancing Bear* (1968)

Katcher, Leo, *Earl Warren: A Political Biography* (1968)

Lamott, Kenneth, *Anti-California: Report from our First Parafascist State* (1963, 1971)

Mazo, Earl, *Richard Nixon: A Political and Personal Portrait* (1959, 1960)

Phillips, Herbert L., *Big Wayward Girl: An Informal Political History* (1968)

Rand, Christopher, *Los Angeles, The Ultimate City* (1967)

Reagan, Ronald, *Where's the Rest of Me?* (1965)

Rogin, Michael P., and John L. Shover, *Political Change in California: Critical Elections and Social Movements, 1890–1966* (1970)

Samish, Artie, *Secret Boss of California* (1971)

Steiner, Stan, *LaRaza: The Mexican Americans* (1969)

Thompson, Warren S., *Growth and Changes in California's Population* (1955)

Velie, Lester, "The Secret Boss of California," *Collier's*, CXXIV, 11–13, 71–72 (August 13, 1949), and 12–13, 60, 62–63 (August 20, 1949)

XXI. THE CLASH OF CULTURES

California, Department of Industrial Relations, Division of Fair Employment Practices, *American Indians in California: Population, Education, Employment, Income* (1965)

——, *Californians of Japanese, Chinese, and Filipino Ancestry* (1965)

Chiu, Ping, *Chinese Labor in California, 1850–1880: An Economic Study* (1963)

Cohen, Jerry, and William S. Murphy, *Burn, Baby, Burn! The Los Angeles Race Riot, August 1965* (1966)

Conot, Robert, *Rivers of Blood, Years of Darkness* (1967)

Daniels, Roger, *The Politics of Prejudice: The Anti-Japanese Movement in California and the Struggle for Japanese Exclusion* (1962)

Fisher, Lloyd S., *The Harvest Labor Market in California* (1953)

Frakes, George E., and Curtis B. Solbery, eds., *Minorities in California History* (1971)

Galarza, Ernesto, *Merchants of Labor: The Mexican Bracero Story* (1964)

Gilmore, N. Ray, and Gladys W. Gilmore, "The Bracero in California," *Pacific Historical Review*, XXXII (August 1963)

Grebler, Leo, Joan W. Moore and Ralph C. Guzman, *The Mexican-American* (1970)

Heizer, Robert F., and Alan F. Almquist, *The Other Californians* (1971)

Hosokawa, Bill, *Nisei: The Quiet Americans*, 1969.

Kung, Shien Woo, *Chinese in American Life; Some Aspects of Their History, Status, Problems, and Contribution* (1962)

Lee, Rose Hum, *The Chinese in the United States of America* (1960)

McCone, John A., *Violence in the City—an End or a Beginning? A Report of the Governor's Commission on the Los Angeles Riots* (1965)

McWilliams, Carey, *Factories in the Field: The Story of the Migratory Farm Labor in California* (1939)

——, *Ill Fares the Land; Migratory Labor in the United States* (1942)

——, *North from Mexico* (1949)

——, *Prejudice: Japanese-Americans, Symbol of Racial Intolerance* (1944)

Moore, Truman E., *The Slaves We Rent* (1965)

XXII. THINGS CULTURAL

Bingham, Edwin, *Charles F. Lummis, Editor of the Southwest* (1955)

Brinig, Myron, *The Flutter of an Eyelid*, 1933.

Bruce, John, *Gaudy Century: The Story of San Francisco's Hundred Years of Robust Journalism* (1948)

Carpenter, Frederic I., *Robinson Jeffers* (1962)

Carr, William G., *John Swett, The Biography of an Educational Pioneer* (1933)

Clappe, Louise M., *The Shirley Letters from California Mines in 1851–52*, Thomas C. Russell, ed. (1922)

Cleland, Robert Glass, *California in Our Time 1900–1940* (1947)

Cornelius, Brother, *Keith, Old Master of California* (1942)

Doyle, Helen M., *Mary Austin: Woman of Genius* (1939)

Fatout, Paul, *Ambrose Bierce: The Devil's Lexicographer* (1951)

Fernier, William W., *Ninety Years of Education in California* (1930)

French, Warren, *John Steinbeck* (1961)

Harris, Frank, ed., *A Guide to Contemporary Architecture in Southern California* (1951)

Honnold, Douglas, *Southern California Architecture, 1769–1956* (1956)

Kerr, Clark, *The Uses of the University* (1963)

Lewis, Oscar, *Here Lived the Californians* (1957)

Odell, Ruth, *Helen Hunt Jackson* (1939)

Peterson, Martin S., *Joaquin Miller: Literary Frontiersman* (1937)

Powell, Lawrence Clark, *Robinson Jeffers; the Man and His Work* (1932, new editions 1934 and 1940)

——, *California Classics: The Creative Literature of the Golden State* (1971)

Rice, William B., *The Los Angeles Star, 1851–1864* (1947)

Steinbeck, John, *The Grapes of Wrath*, 1939.

Stewart, George R., Jr., *Bret Harte, Argonaut and Exile* (1931)

——, *John Phoenix, Esq., the Veritable Squibob* (1937)

Swanberg, W. A., *Citizen Hearst: A Biography of William Randolph Hearst* (1961)

Walker, Franklin, *Frank Norris* (1932)

——, *A Literary History of Southern California* (1950)

——, *San Francisco's Literary Frontier* (1939)

XXIII. A NEW SOCIETY?

Bartley, Ernest R., *The Tidelands Oil Controversy* (1953)

Bronson, William, *How to Kill a Golden State* (1968)

"California, The Nation Within a Nation," a special issue of the *Saturday Review*, L (September 23, 1967)

California, University of, *Natural Resources: Air, Land, Water* (1964)

Carson, Rachel, *Silent Spring* (1962)

Conot, Robert, *Rivers of Blood, Years of Darkness* (1967)

Coons, Arthur G., *Crises in California Education* (1968)

Daniels, Roger, and Harry H. T. Kitano, *American Racism: Exploration of the Nature of Prejudice* (1970)

Dasmann, Raymond F., *The Destruction of California* (1965)

Dunne, John Gregory, *Delano: The Anatomy of the Great California Grapeworkers' Strike* (1967)

Ehrlich, Paul R., *The Population Bomb* (1968)

Hale, Denis, and Jonathon Eisen, *The California Dream* (1968)

Galarza, Ernesto, *Merchants of Labor: The Mexican Bracero Story* (1964)

Governor's Commission on the Los Angeles Riots, *Violence in the City—An End or a Beginning?* (1965)

Hyde, Philip, and François Lezdet, *The Last Redwoods* (1963)

Lewis, Joseph, *What Makes Reagan Run?: A Political Profile* (1968)

Lillard, Richard, *Eden in Jeopardy, Man's Prodigal Meddling with His Environment: The Southern California Experience* (1966)

Lipset, Seymour M., and Sheldon S. Wolin, *The Berkeley Student Revolt* (1965)

McWilliams, Carey, ed., *California Revolution* (1968)

Nadeau, Remi, *California, The New Society* (1963)

Ostrom, Vincent, *Water and Politics: A Study of Water Policies and Administration in the Development of Los Angeles* (1953)

Rand, Chistopher, *The Ultimate City* (1966)

Wood, Samuel E., *California, Going, Going . . .* (1962)

Wood, Samuel E., and Alfred E. Heller, *The Phantom Cities of California* (1963)

INDEX